The IDG Books Bible Advantage

The *Excel for Windows 95 Bible* is part of the Bible series brought to you by IDG Books Worldwide. We designed Bibles to meet your growing need for quick access to the most complete and accurate computer information available.

Bibles work the way you do: They focus on accomplishing specific tasks — not learning random functions. These books are not long-winded manuals or dry reference tomes. In Bibles, expert authors tell you exactly what you can do with your software and how to do it. Easy to follow, step-by-step sections; comprehensive coverage; and convenient access in language and design — it's all here.

The authors of Bibles are uniquely qualified to give you expert advice as well as insightful tips and techniques not found anywhere else. Our authors maintain close contact with end users through feedback from articles, training sessions, e-mail exchanges, user group participation, and consulting work. Because our authors know the realities of daily computer use and are directly tied to the reader, our Bibles have a strategic advantage.

Bible authors have the experience to approach a topic in the most efficient manner, and we know that you, the reader, will benefit from a "one-on-one" relationship with the author. Our research shows that readers make computer book purchases because they want expert advice on a product. Readers want to benefit from the author's experience, so the author's voice is always present in a Bible series book.

In addition, the author is free to include or recommend useful software in a Bible. The software that accompanies a Bible is not intended to be casual filler but is linked to the content, theme, or procedures of the book. We know that you will benefit from the included software.

You will find what you need in this book whether you read it from cover to cover, section by section, or simply one topic at a time. As a computer user, you deserve a comprehensive resource of answers. We at IDG Books Worldwide are proud to deliver that resource with the *Excel for Windows 95 Bible*.

Karen Bluestein

Karen A. Bluestein
Publisher
Internet: kbluestein@idgbooks.com

Excel for Windows 95® Bible

Excel for Windows 95® Bible

by John Walkenbach

IDG Books Worldwide, Inc.
An International Data Group Company

Foster City, CA ✦ Chicago, IL ✦ Indianapolis, IN ✦ Braintree, MA ✦ Dallas, TX

Excel for Windows 95® Bible

Published by
IDG Books Worldwide, Inc.
An International Data Group Company
919 E. Hillsdale Blvd.
Suite 400
Foster City, CA 94404

Library of Congress Catalog Card No.: 95-78773

ISBN: 1-56884-495-6

Printed in the United States of America

10 9 8 7 6 5 4 3 2 1

1B/RV/QZ/ZV

Distributed in the United States by IDG Books Worldwide, Inc.

Distributed by Macmillan Canada for Canada; by Computer and Technical Books for the Caribbean Basin; by Contemporea de Ediciones for Venezuela; by Distribuidora Cuspide for Argentina; by CITFC for Brazil; by Ediciones ZETA S.C.R. Ltda. for Peru; by Editorial Limusa SA for Mexico; by Transworld Publishers Limited in the United Kingdom and Europe; by AlMaiman Publishers & Distributors for Saudi Arabia; by Simron Pty. Ltd. for South Africa; by IDG Communications (HK) Ltd. for Hong Kong; by Toppan Company Ltd. for Japan; by Addison Wesley Publishing Company for Korea; by Longman Singapore Publishers Ltd. for Singapore, Malaysia, Thailand, and Indonesia; by Unalis Corporation for Taiwan; by WS Computer Publishing Company, Inc. for the Philippines; by WoodsLane Pty. Ltd. for Australia; by WoodsLane Enterprises Ltd. for New Zealand.

For general information on IDG Books Worldwide's books in the U.S., please call our Consumer Customer Service department at 800-762-2974. For reseller information, including discounts and premium sales, please call our Reseller Customer Service department at 800-434-3422.

For information on where to purchase IDG Books Worldwide's books outside the U.S., contact IDG Books Worldwide at 415-655-3021 or fax 415-655-3295.

For information on translations, contact Marc Jeffrey Mikulich, Director, Foreign and Subsidiary Rights, at IDG Books Worldwide, 415-655-3018 or fax 415-655-3295.

For sales inquiries and special prices for bulk quantities, write to the address above or call IDG Books Worldwide at 415-655-3200.

For information on using IDG Books Worldwide's books in the classroom, or for ordering examination copies, contact Jim Kelly at 800-434-2086.

For authorization to photocopy items for corporate, personal, or eductional use, please contact Copyright Clearance Cneter, 222 Rosewood Drive, Danvers, MA 01923, or fax 508-750-4470

About the Author

John Walkenbach is one of the country's leading authorities on spreadsheet software. He holds a Ph.D. from the University of Montana and has worked as an instructor, programmer, and market research manager. He finally found a job he's good at: principal of JWalk and Associates Inc., a one-person, San Diego-based consulting firm that specializes in spreadsheet application development. John is also a shareware developer, and his most popular product is the Power Utility Pak add-in for Excel, which is used by thousands of people throughout the world.

John started writing about spreadsheets in 1984 and has since written more than 250 articles and reviews for publications such as *PC World*, *InfoWorld*, *Windows*, and *PC/Computing*. In addition, he's the author of a dozen other spreadsheet books, including *PC World Excel 5 For Windows Power Programming Techniques* and *Excel For Windows For Dummies Quick Reference* (both from IDG Books Worldwide).

In his spare time, John enjoys composing and playing music in a variety of styles, including blues, bluegrass, and New Age. Currently, his toys include a multisynthesizer MIDI system, a growing collection of acoustic and electric guitars, and a made-in-Montana Flatiron mandolin.

You can reach John on the Internet at 70363.3014@compuserve.com or look for his postings on his favorite Internet hangout, comp.apps.spreadsheets.

ABOUT IDG BOOKS WORLDWIDE

VIII

WINNER
*Eighth Annual
Computer Press
Awards 1992*

IX

WINNER
*Ninth Annual
Computer Press
Awards 1993*

IDG BOOKS WORLDWIDE

Welcome to the world of IDG Books Worldwide.

IDG Books Worldwide, Inc., is a subsidiary of International Data Group, the world's largest publisher of computer-related information and the leading global provider of information services on information technology. IDG was founded more than 25 years ago and now employs more than 7,500 people worldwide. IDG publishes more than 235 computer publications in 67 countries (see listing below). More than 60 million people read one or more IDG publications each month.

Launched in 1990, IDG Books Worldwide is today the #1 publisher of best-selling computer books in the United States. We are proud to have received 8 awards from the Computer Press Association in recognition of editorial excellence, and our best-selling ...*For Dummies*™ series has more than 17 million copies in print with translations in 25 languages. IDG Books Worldwide, through a recent joint venture with IDG's Hi-Tech Beijing, became the first U.S. publisher to publish a computer book in the People's Republic of China. In record time, IDG Books Worldwide has become the first choice for millions of readers around the world who want to learn how to better manage their businesses.

Our mission is simple: Every one of our books is designed to bring extra value and skill-building instructions to the reader. Our books are written by experts who understand and care about our readers. The knowledge base of our editorial staff comes from years of experience in publishing, education, and journalism — experience which we use to produce books for the '90s. In short, we care about books, so we attract the best people. We devote special attention to details such as audience, interior design, use of icons, and illustrations. And because we use an efficient process of authoring, editing, and desktop publishing our books electronically, we can spend more time ensuring superior content and spend less time on the technicalities of making books.

You can count on our commitment to deliver high-quality books at competitive prices on topics consumers want to read about. At IDG Books Worldwide, we value quality, and we have been delivering quality for more than 25 years. You'll find no better book on a subject than an IDG book.

John J. Kilcullen

John Kilcullen
President and CEO
IDG Books Worldwide, Inc.

IDG Books Worldwide, Inc., is a subsidiary of International Data Group, the world's largest publisher of computer-related information and the leading global provider of information services on information technology. International Data Group publishes over 235 computer publications in 67 countries. More than sixty million people read one or more International Data Group publications each month. The officers are Patrick J. McGovern, Founder and Board Chairman; Kelly Conlin, President; Jim Casella, Chief Operating Officer. International Data Group's publications include: **ARGENTINA'S** Computerworld Argentina, Infoworld Argentina; **AUSTRALIA'S** Computerworld Australia, Computer Living, Australian PC World, Australian Macworld, Network World, Mobile Business Australia, Publish!, Reseller, IDG Sources; **AUSTRIA'S** Computerwelt Oesterreich, PC Test; **BELGIUM'S** Data News (CW); **BOLIVIA'S** Computerworld; **BRAZIL'S** Computerworld, Connections, Game Power, Mundo Unix, PC World, Publish, Super Game; **BULGARIA'S** Computerworld Bulgaria, PC & Mac World Bulgaria, Network World Bulgaria; **CANADA'S** CIO Canada, Computerworld Canada, InfoCanada, Network World Canada, Reseller; **CHILE'S** Computerworld Chile, Informatica; **COLOMBIA'S** Computerworld Colombia, PC World; **COSTA RICA'S** PC World; **CZECH REPUBLIC'S** Computerworld, Elektronika, PC World; **DENMARK'S** Communications World, Computerworld Denmark, Computerworld Focus, Macintosh Produktkatalog, Macworld Danmark, PC World Danmark, PC Produktguide, Tech World, Windows World; **ECUADOR'S** PC World Ecuador; **EGYPT'S** Computerworld (CW) Middle East, PC World Middle East; **FINLAND'S** MikroPC, Tietoviikko, Tietoverkko; **FRANCE'S** Distributique, GOLDEN MAC, InfoPC, Le Guide du Monde Informatique, Le Monde Informatique, Telecoms & Reseaux; **GERMANY'S** Computerwoche, Computerwoche Focus, Computerwoche Extra, Electronic Entertainment, Gamepro, Information Management, Macwelt, Netzwelt, PC Welt, Publish, Publish; **GREECE'S** Publish & Macworld; **HONG KONG'S** Computerworld Hong Kong, PC World Hong Kong; **HUNGARY'S** Computerworld SZT, PC World; **INDIA'S** Computers & Communications; **INDONESIA'S** Info Komputer; **IRELAND'S** ComputerScope; **ISRAEL'S** Beyond Windows, Computerworld Israel, Multimedia, PC World Israel; **ITALY'S** Computerworld Italia, Lotus Magazine, Macworld Italia, Networking Italia, PC Shopping Italy, PC World Italia; **JAPAN'S** Computerworld Today, Information Systems World, Macworld Japan, Nikkei Personal Computing, SunWorld Japan, Windows World; **KENYA'S** East African Computer News; **KOREA'S** Computerworld Korea, Macworld Korea, PC World Korea; **LATIN AMERICA'S** GamePro; **MALAYSIA'S** Computerworld Malaysia, PC World Malaysia; **MEXICO'S** Compu Edicion, Compu Manufactura, Computacion/Punto de Venta, Computerworld Mexico, MacWorld, Mundo Unix, PC World, Windows; **THE NETHERLANDS'** Computer! Totaal, Computable (CW), LAN Magazine, Lotus Magazine, MacWorld; **NEW ZEALAND'S** Computer Buyer, Computerworld New Zealand, Network World, New Zealand PC World; **NIGERIA'S** PC World Africa; **NORWAY'S** Computerworld Norge, Lotusworld Norge, Macworld Norge, Maxi Data, Networld, PC World Ekspress, PC World Nettverk, PC World Norge, PC World's Produktguide, Publish& Multimedia World, Student Data, Unix World, Windowsworld; **PAKISTAN'S** PC World Pakistan; **PANAMA'S** PC World Panama; **PERU'S** Computerworld Peru, PC World; **PEOPLE'S REPUBLIC OF CHINA'S** China Computerworld, China PC Info Magazine, Computer Fan, PC World China, Electronics International, Electronics Today/Multimedia World, Electronic Product World, China Network World, Software World Magazine, Telecom Product World; **PHILIPPINES'** Computerworld Philippines, PC Digest (PCW); **POLAND'S** Computerworld Poland, Computerworld Special Report, Networld, PC World/Komputer, Sunworld; **PORTUGAL'S** Cerebro/PC World, Correio Informatico/Computerworld, MacIn; **ROMANIA'S** Computerworld, PC World, Telecom Romania; **RUSSIA'S** Computerworld-Moscow, Mir - PK (PCW), Sety (Networks); **SINGAPORE'S** Computerworld Southeast Asia, PC World Singapore; **SLOVENIA'S** Monitor Magazine; **SOUTH AFRICA'S** Computer Mail (CIO), Computing S.A., Network World S.A., Software World; **SPAIN'S** Advanced Systems, Amiga World, Computerworld Espana, Communicaciones World, Macworld Espana, NeXTWORLD, Super Juegos Magazine (GamePro), PC World Espana, Publish; **SWEDEN'S** Attack, ComputerSweden, Corporate Computing, Macworld, Mikrodatorn, Natverk & Kommunikation, PC World, CAP & Design, Datalngenjoren, Maxi Data,Windows World; **SWITZERLAND'S** Computerworld Schweiz, Macworld Schweiz, PC Tip; **TAIWAN'S** Computerworld Taiwan, PC World Taiwan; **THAILAND'S** Thai Computerworld; **TURKEY'S** Computerworld Monitor, Macworld Turkiye, PC World Turkiye; **UKRAINE'S** Computerworld, Computers+Software Magazine; **UNITED KINGDOM'S** Computing/Computerworld, Connexion/Network World, Lotus Magazine, Macworld, Open Computing/Sunworld; **UNITED STATES'** Advanced Systems, AmigaWorld, Cable in the Classroom, CD Review, CIO, Computerworld, Computerworld Client/Server Journal, Digital Video, DOS World, Electronic Entertainment Magazine (E2), Federal Computer Week, Game Hits, GamePro, IDG Books Worldwide, Infoworld, Laser Event, Macworld, Maximize, Multimedia World, Network World, PC Letter, PC World, Publish, SWATPro, Video Event; **URUGUAY'S** PC World Uruguay; **VENEZUELA'S** Computerworld Venezuela, PC World; **VIETNAM'S** PC World Vietnam.
08/15/95

Dedication

For my Mom.

Credits

Publisher
Karen A. Bluestein

Acquisitions Manager
Gregory Croy

Acquisitions Editor
Ellen L. Camm

Brand Manager
Melisa M. Duffy

Editorial Director
Andy Cummings

Editorial Assistant
Nate Holdread

Production Director
Beth Jenkins

Supervisor of Project Coordination
Cindy L. Phipps

Supervisor of Page Layout
Kathie S. Schnorr

Pre-Press Coordinator
Steve Peake

Associate Pre-Press Coordinator
Tony Augsburger

Media/Archive Coordinator
Paul Belcastro

Project Editor
Susan Pines

Editors
Susan Christopherson
Kerrie Klein
Regina Snyder
Becky Whitney

Technical Reviewer
Michael Drips

Associate Project Coordinator
J. Tyler Connor

Production Staff
Gina Scott
Carla C. Radzikinas
Patricia R. Reynolds
Melissa D. Buddendeck
Dwight Ramsey
Robert Springer
Theresa Sánchez-Baker
Leslie Popplewell
Cameron Booker
Megan Briscoe
Drew R. Moore
Mark Owens
Laura Puranen

Proofreader
Kathleen Prata

Indexer
Anne Leach

Book Design
Drew R. Moore

Cover Design
three 8 creative group

Acknowledgments

This is the 13th book that I've written for IDG Books. I was fortunate enough to be associated with this publisher in its early days, and I've been around to watch it grow to the phenomenon that it is today. Thanks to everyone at IDG Books who played a part in getting this book into your hands. Special thanks to Sue Pines, my project editor. Her ongoing support and words of encouragement helped make this a very rewarding project. I look forward to our next project together.

I must also acknowledge Microsoft for supplying me with a seemingly endless stream of beta versions of Windows 95 and Office 95. During the early stages of writing this book, I had the opportunity to meet with some members of the Excel development team in Redmond. I'm convinced that the typical computer user has absolutely no idea of the amount of effort that goes into a product such as Excel. I was impressed.

Much of the inspiration for this book came from two sources: the comp.apps.spreadsheets Usenet newsgroup and the Excel Forum on CompuServe. Thanks to all participants in these groups whose problems and questions gave me ideas for topics in the book. I'm also indebted to those who contributed files to the companion CD-ROM. I think it's the best collection of software in any spreadsheet book.

A word of thanks to my friend and client Jay Hardymon for leaving me in peace during the late stages of writing (and I'm still waiting for that shipment of okra). Thanks also to my good friend VaRene for helping me make it through the long hours at the keyboard.

Finally, thanks to all of the people throughout the world who have taken the time to let me know that my books have made an impact. My goal is to write books that go well beyond the material found in competing books. Based on the feedback that I've received, I think I'm succeeding. Writing software books may not be the most glamorous job, but I can't think of anything else that I'd rather be doing.

John Walkenbach
La Jolla, California

(The publisher would like to give special thanks to Patrick J. McGovern, without whom this book would not have been possible.)

Production Notes

I wrote this book over a period of 90 days using two computers (one for each hand). My main system was a 486/66, with 16MB of RAM running Windows for Workgroups 3.11. I used Word for Windows 6.0 to write the text, using a template provided by IDG Books. I made heavy use of Word's outlining feature, and each chapter was stored as a separate document. I bought a new computer (a 486/100, with 16MB of RAM) solely for the purpose of running the Windows 95 and Microsoft Office 95 betas.

I used this dual-CPU arrangement just in case the betas caused problems. In retrospect, the Windows 95 betas proved to be more stable than Windows 3.11 — but that's another story. The computers were connected using SneakerNet (one of these days, I'll install a *real* network). I used HiJaak for Windows to capture the screens in PCX format.

The Word files were transferred to my editor via CompuServe. In a futile attempt to keep my monthly CompuServe bill out of the three-digit range, I used snail mail to submit the screen shots. All of the files were subjected to thorough copyediting and technical editing and were returned to me for corrections and final approval.

The finalized files were imported into PageMaker on the Macintosh. After a professional proofreader and the IDG Books staff reviewed the page proofs, the book was sent electronically to the printer. The index was compiled manually by a professional indexer.

In the final weeks of the project, I contracted a local production firm, Bob Hoffman Video Productions, to produce my CD-ROM's video introduction and convert it to an AVI file. They also produced the CD-ROM master, eliminating the need to transport the huge AVI file to another vendor. I wrote the `Autorun.exe` program (which starts when the CD-ROM is inserted) in Visual Basic 3.0. I used the Windows 95 Backup program to generate a series of floppy disks, which were combined with the AVI file on the CD master. I reviewed and approved the master, and it was sent to the IDG Books manufacturing department.

If all goes well, the next time that I read this, it will be in the form of a real live book — complete with a CD-ROM and a suggested retail price. Isn't technology grand?

—JW

Contents at a Glance

Table of Contents

Introduction

Thanks for purchasing the *Excel for Windows 95 Bible* — your complete guide to a powerful and easy-to-use spreadsheet product.

I think that Excel for Windows 95 is the best spreadsheet program on the market (trust me, I've used them all). Excel has been around in various incarnations for almost a decade, and each subsequent release pushes the spreadsheet envelope a bit further — in some cases, a *lot* further. My goal in writing this book is to share with you some of what I know about Excel, and in the process make you more efficient on the job.

The book contains everything you need to know to learn the basics of Excel and then move on to more advanced topics at your own pace. You'll find many useful examples as well as some of the tips and slick techniques that I've accumulated over the years. The book is an excellent alternative to the printed material that's included with Excel (which is skimpier than ever), and is *much* more comprehensive. And, with all due respect to Microsoft's documentation department, I think that you'll find this book a lot more interesting than the manuals.

Is This Book for You?

The Bible series from IDG Books Worldwide is designed for beginning, intermediate, and advanced users. This book covers all the essential components of Excel and provides clear and practical examples that you can adapt to your own needs.

Excel can be used at many levels — from the simple to the extremely complex. I think I've drawn a good balance here, focusing on the topics that are most useful to most users. The following can help you decide whether this book is for you.

Yes — If you have no spreadsheet experience

If you're new to the world of spreadsheets, welcome to the fold. This book has everything that you need to get started with Excel and then advance to other topics as the need arises.

Yes — If you've used previous versions of Excel

If you've used Excel 5, you'll feel right at home with Excel for Windows 95. There aren't all that many major new features. If you're moving up from Excel 3 or Excel 4, you'll have lots to learn because Microsoft has made many improvements in the past few years. In any case, this book will get you up to speed quickly. By the way, check out Appendix C for a quick preview of what's new in Excel for Windows 95.

Yes — If you've used Excel for the Macintosh

The Macintosh version of Excel is very similar to the Windows 95 version. If you're moving over from the Mac platform, you'll find some good background information as well as specific details to make your transition as smooth as possible.

Yes — If you've used DOS versions of 1-2-3 or Quattro Pro

If you're abandoning a text-based spreadsheet such as 1-2-3 or Novell's Quattro Pro in favor of a more modern graphical product, this book will serve you well. You'll have a head start because you already know what spreadsheets are all about, and you'll discover some great new ways of doing things.

Yes — If you've used Windows versions of 1-2-3 or Quattro Pro

If you've tried the others and are convinced that Excel is the way to go, this book quickly teaches you what Excel is all about and why it has such a great reputation. Because you're already familiar with Windows *and* spreadsheets, you'll be able to breeze through many introductory topics.

No — If you're an Excel expert who wants to learn some powerful customization techniques using the Visual Basic for Applications (VBA) programming language

I had to draw the line somewhere. Although I cover VBA programming in this book (and provide examples on the companion CD-ROM), I don't go into the depth that very advanced users may require. Rather, I refer you to my *Excel for Windows 95 Power Programming Techniques, 2nd Edition*, scheduled for publication by IDG Books Worldwide in early 1996.

No — If you want to learn all about Windows 95

Although I tell you enough about Windows 95 to get by, this book is not intended to be a Windows 95 manual. Try Brian Livingston's *Windows 95 Secrets* (IDG Books Worldwide, 1995), Alan Simpson's *Windows 95 Uncut* (IDG Books Worldwide, 1995), or *Windows 95 For Dummies* (IDG Books Worldwide, 1995) by Andy Rathbone.

Maybe — If you want just enough to get by

This book certainly tells you just enough to get by, but if that's all you want, it's probably overkill. Check out Greg Harvey's *Excel For Windows 95 For Dummies* (IDG Books Worldwide, 1995). It's cheaper and has fewer pages. Even if you don't consider yourself a dummy, you might enjoy the way he presents the material — very light-hearted, with a definite de-emphasis on technical matters.

Software Versions

This book was written for Excel for Windows 95 (also known as Excel 7), but most of the information also applies to Excel 5. If you use any version of Excel prior to Version 5, this book won't do you much good because the earlier versions are drastically different from Excel for Windows 95.

You should know which version of Excel you have, as well as which version of Windows you're using. Refer to the table that follows and identify the versions of Excel and Windows that you have.

	Windows 95	*Windows NT*	*Windows 3.1 or Windows for Workgroups 3.1*
Excel for Windows 95	Perfect. This is the ideal combination — the versions I used to prepare this book	This will work, but the screens in the figures will look different	This will not work. Excel for Windows 95 requires a 32-bit operating system
Excel 5	This will work, but some of the features discussed are not available in Excel 5	This will work, but the screens in the figures will look different. Some of the features discussed are not available in Excel 5	This will work, but the screens in the figures will look different. Some of the features discussed are not available in Excel 5

If your particular software versions don't place you in the upper-left corner of the preceding table, I highly recommend that you do whatever it takes to get there. Upgrading is relatively inexpensive, and you'll see significant performance improvements.

Conventions in This Book

Take a minute to scan through this section to learn some of the typographical conventions used in this book.

Excel commands

In Excel, as in all Windows programs, you select commands from the pull-down menu system. In this book, such commands appear in normal typeface but are distinguishable because the commands have a single letter underlined, just as they appear in the menus. The underlined letter represents the *hot key letter*. For example, if I mention the File⇨Save command, note that *F* and *S* are underlined. These correspond to the single letter keys that you can use to access the commands from the keyboard. In this example, you would press Alt+F and then S to issue the File⇨Save command.

Filenames, named ranges, and your input

Input that you make from the keyboard appears in **bold**. Filenames and named ranges may appear in a different font. Lengthy input usually appears on a separate line. For instance, I may instruct you to enter a formula such as the following:

```
="Part Name: " &VLOOKUP(PartNumber,PartList,2)
```

Key names

Names of the keys on your keyboard appear in normal type. When two keys should be pressed simultaneously, they are connected with a plus sign, like this: Press Alt+E to select the Edit menu. Here are the key names as I refer to them throughout the book:

Alt	down arrow	Num Lock	right arrow
Backspace	End	Pause	Scroll Lock
Caps Lock	Home	PgDn	Shift
Ctrl	Insert	PgUp	Tab
Delete	left arrow	Print Screen	up arrow

Functions

Excel's built-in worksheet functions appear in uppercase, like this: Enter a SUM formula in cell C20.

Mouse conventions

I assume that you're using a mouse or some other pointing device. You'll come across some of the following mouse-related terms:

Mouse pointer: The small graphic figure that moves on-screen when you move your mouse. The mouse pointer is usually an arrow, but it changes shape when you move to certain areas of the screen or when you're performing some actions.

Point: Move the mouse so that the mouse pointer is on a specific item. For example, "Point to the Save button on the toolbar."

Press: Press the left mouse button and keep it pressed. Normally, this is used when dragging.

Click: Press the left mouse button once and release it immediately.

Right-click: Press the right mouse button once and release it immediately. The right mouse button is used in Excel to pop up shortcut menus appropriate for whatever is currently selected.

Double-click: Press the left mouse button twice in rapid succession. If your double-clicking doesn't seem to be working, you can adjust the double-click sensitivity using the Windows Control Panel program.

Drag: Press the left mouse button and keep it pressed while you move the mouse. Dragging is often used to select a range of cells or to change the size of an object.

What the Icons Mean

Throughout the book, you'll notice special graphic symbols, or *icons,* in the left margin. These call your attention to points that are particularly important or relevant to a specific group of readers. The icons in this book are as follows:

New! This symbol denotes features that are new to Excel for Windows 95. If you've upgraded from Excel 5, this cues you in on features new to Excel for Windows 95. If you're still using Excel 5, this icon warns you of features that aren't available in your version.

Note This signals the fact that something is important or worth noting. This may alert you to a concept that helps you master the task at hand, or it may denote something that is fundamental to understanding subsequent material.

Tip A tip icon marks a more efficient way of doing something that may not be obvious.

Cross-Reference This symbol indicates that a related topic is discussed elsewhere in this book.

This indicates that the material uses an example file on the companion CD-ROM.

Caution I use this symbol when there is a possibility that the operation I'm describing could cause problems if you're not careful.

How This Book Is Organized

Notice that the book is divided into seven main parts.

Part I: "Getting Started" — This part consists of three chapters, which provide background about Excel and Windows 95. Chapter 3 is a hands-on guided tour of Excel, which gives new users an opportunity to get their feet wet immediately.

Part II: "Introductory Concepts" — The chapters in Part II cover the basic concepts with which all Excel users should be familiar.

Part III: "Advanced Features" — This part consists of six chapters dealing with topics that are sometimes considered advanced. Many beginning and intermediate users will find this information useful as well.

Part IV: "Analyzing Data" — The broad topic of data analysis is the focus of the chapters in Part IV. Users of all levels will find some of these chapters of interest.

Part V: "Other Topics" — This part consists of three chapters that didn't quite fit into any other part. The chapters deal with using Excel with other applications, auditing and proofing your work, and exploring the fun side of Excel (yes, Excel *does* have a fun side).

Part VI: "Customizing Excel" — Part VI is for those who want to customize Excel for their own use or who are designing workbooks or add-ins that will be used by others. I briefly discuss the XLM macro system, but I focus primarily on Visual Basic for Applications.

Part VII: "Appendixes" — The appendixes consist of supplemental and reference material that may be useful to you.

How to Use This Book

This book is not intended to be read cover-to-cover. Rather, it's a reference book that you can consult when

✦ You're stuck while trying to do something.

✦ You need to do something that you've never done before.

✦ You have some time on your hands, and you're interested in learning something new.

You'll find that the index is quite comprehensive and that each chapter typically focuses on a single broad topic. If you're just starting out with Excel, I recommend that you read the first three chapters to gain a basic understanding of the product and then do some experimenting on your own. After you've become familiar with Excel's environment, you can refer to the chapters that interest you most. Some users, however, will prefer to follow the chapters in order. Part II was designed with these users in mind.

Don't be discouraged if some of the material is over your head. Most users get by just fine using only a small subset of Excel's total capabilities. In fact, the 80/20 rule applies here: 80 percent of Excel users use only 20 percent of its features. As you'll see, using only 20 percent of Excel's features still gives you *lots* of power at your fingertips.

About the Companion CD-ROM

The inside back cover of this book contains a CD-ROM with dozens of useful examples from the book (plus lots of other bonus files). As you'll see, my writing style emphasizes examples. I know that I learn more from a well-thought-out example than from reading a dozen pages. I've found that this is true for many other people. Consequently, I spent a lot of time developing the examples on the companion CD-ROM. So, don't overlook them. Appendix F further describes the material on the CD-ROM.

When you see this icon, you can open the example file and try out the example for yourself.

Power Utility Pak Coupon

Toward the back of the book you'll find a coupon that you can redeem for a copy of my Power Utility Pak software — a collection of 21 useful Excel utilities, plus 23 new worksheet functions. This product normally sells for $39.95, but I'm making it available to readers of this book for only $9.95, plus shipping and handling. I developed this package using VBA exclusively, and the complete source files also are available for those who want to learn slick VBA techniques.

I think that you'll find the Power Utility Pak useful in your day-to-day work with Excel, and I urge you to take advantage of this offer. The CD-ROM contains the shareware version of the Power Utility Pak, so you can try it out before ordering the complete version.

Contacting the Author

I'm always happy to hear from readers of my books. The best way to contact me is by e-mail at the following Internet address:

70363.3014@compuserve.com

If you don't have access to electronic mail, you can send snail mail to me in care of the publisher.

Getting Started

The three chapters in this part fill you in on background about Excel and Windows 95. They also give new users a chance to sample some of Excel's features.

P A R T

◆ ◆ ◆ ◆

In This Part

Chapter 1
A Bit of Background

Chapter 2
Basic Windows 95
Knowledge

Chapter 3
Getting Acquainted
with Excel

◆ ◆ ◆ ◆

A Bit of Background

CHAPTER 1

Every book has to start somewhere. This chapter starts from square one and introduces you to the concept of a spreadsheet. I include lots of interesting background information on Excel and Windows.

What Is Excel?

Excel is a software product that falls into the general category known as *spreadsheets*. Excel is one of several spreadsheet products that you can run on your PC. Others include 1-2-3 and Quattro Pro.

A spreadsheet (including Excel) is a highly interactive computer program that consists of a collection of rows and columns that are displayed on-screen in a scrollable window. The intersection of each row and column is called a *cell,* and a cell can hold a number, a text string, or a formula that performs a calculation using one or more other cells. It's easy to copy cells, move cells, and modify any formulas you create. A spreadsheet can be saved in a file for later use or discarded after it has served its intended purpose. The cells in a spreadsheet can be formatted in any number of ways and printed for hard-copy reference. In addition, groups of numerical cells can be used to generate charts and maps.

The most significant advantage of an electronic spreadsheet is that the formulas recalculate their results if you change any of the cells they use. As a result, once you get your spreadsheet set up by defining formulas, you can use this "model" to explore different possibilities with little additional effort on your part. Excel is currently the best-selling Windows spreadsheet — and I hope to explain why in the pages of this book.

Windows Makes It Happen

Excel runs under Microsoft Windows. If you're new to the fold, this section provides a quick overview of what makes Windows so appealing.

Although Windows is now installed on virtually all new PCs and is considered the standard operating environment, it wasn't always that way. In the early days of personal computing, all software was text-based (no graphics), and you could run only one program at a time. Even worse, just about every program you used had an entirely different look and feel. For example, depending on which program you were running, pressing the F1 function key might bring up a help display, save your file, erase characters, or give you a quick exit from the program. Back in the old days, you had to be on your toes.

Microsoft Windows evolved gradually and the early versions were much different from today's Windows 95. (Figure 1-1 shows what Windows 95 looks like on a computer screen.) The big turning point in the story of Windows occurred in May 1990. This is when Microsoft released Windows 3.0 — the first version that really made it feasible to use Windows. In the summer of 1995 (after many delays) Microsoft released Windows 95. This is a major upgrade — actually, a new product — that is a complete operating system.

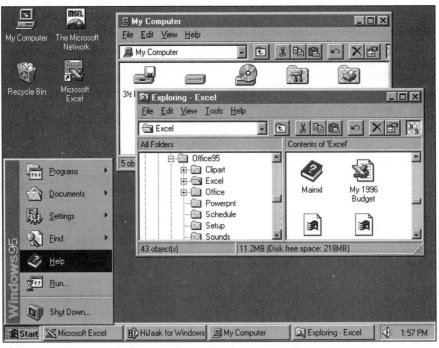

Figure 1-1: Windows 95 is a complete operating system.

Today, almost all PC software is developed for Windows. So, what makes Windows so special? I think that five aspects of Windows are responsible for its success.

Common user interface

By *user interface,* I'm referring to the methods by which the user (you) interacts with the software. A user interface consists of a number of components, including menus, toolbars, and shortcut keys. You've probably noticed that all the programs you run under Windows tend to look pretty much the same. For example, they all have a menu along the top, most of them use toolbars, and they almost always use the same shortcut keys for basic operations such as copying and pasting. This consistency is important because it enhances overall productivity. In short, if you learn to use one Windows program, you have a head start on learning others.

Multitasking

As the term implies, *multitasking* is the capability to perform more than one task at a time. In this case, a *task* is a program. You probably already know that you can run more than one program at a time when you use Windows and that you can easily switch among programs. For example, you may be running Excel and remember that you need to whip off a quick memo to your staff. There's no need to close down Excel; you can just open your word processor in another window.

Say that you're downloading a humongous file from the Internet that will take 20 minutes. Rather than sit and stare at the bytes-transferred message, you can jump to another program and do something more productive. It gets even better. Some programs (but not many, yet) also support *multithreading.* This means that the program can be working on one thing while you're doing another thing in the same program. The current version of Excel doesn't support such multithreading, but I expect that a future version will.

Shared resources

In the pre-Windows days, every program had to provide its own separate support for things such as printers and video drivers. In other words, every time you installed a program, you had to go through a tedious process of choosing the proper printer and video-display driver. In many cases, your printer wasn't actually supported, so you had to figure out which one to "emulate." If you acquired a new printer, you had to go through another tedious process of changing the printer setting for all your software.

Windows eliminates this by handling all this information centrally. For example, Windows keeps track of which printer(s) you have, so every Windows software program simply calls on Windows to do the actual printing.

WYSIWYG

WYSIWYG, as nearly everyone on the planet knows, stands for What You See Is What You Get. This term aptly describes most Windows programs. The formatting that you apply appears on-screen and also prints looking exactly the same. You may take this for granted, but we old-timers wasted far too much paper trying to get our printouts to look right.

The fun factor

Finally, most people agree that Windows is fun to use. The capability to personalize your system with wallpaper and sounds and to play with slick screen savers helps make Windows popular.

The Evolution of Excel

Excel for Windows 95 is actually Excel 7 in disguise. A bit of rational thinking might lead you to think that this is the seventh version of Excel. Think again; Microsoft may be a successful company, but their version-naming techniques can be quite confusing. As you'll see, Excel for Windows 95 is actually the fifth version of Excel.

Excel 2

This was the original version of Excel for Windows, which first appeared in late 1987. It was labeled Version 2 to correspond to the Macintosh version (which was the original Excel). Because Windows wasn't in widespread use at the time, this version included a *run-time* version of Windows — a special version with just enough features to run Excel and nothing else. This version was quite crude by today's standards and was actually quite ugly.

Excel 3

At the end of 1990, Microsoft released Excel 3 for Windows. This was a significant improvement in both appearance and features. It included toolbars, drawing capabilities, worksheet outlining, add-in support, 3-D charts, workgroup editing, and lots more.

Excel 4

Excel 4 hit the streets in the spring of 1992. This version made quite an impact in the marketplace because Windows was becoming more popular. It had lots of new features, many of which made it easier for beginners to get up to speed quickly.

Excel 5

In early 1994, Excel 5 appeared on the scene. This version introduced tons of new features, including multisheet workbooks and the new Visual Basic for Applications (VBA) macro language. Like its predecessor, Excel 5 took top honors in just about every spreadsheet comparison published in the trade magazines.

Excel 7

Technically, this version is called Excel for Windows 95 (there is no Excel 6). It began shipping in the summer of 1995. On the surface, it doesn't seem that much different from Excel 5. There are only a few *major* new features, and most Excel 5 users will have absolutely no problem adapting. But if you could look under the hood (which you can't), you would find that this version uses more advanced 32-bit code, and the calculation algorithms have been fine-tuned for speed. Note that it uses the same file format as Excel 5, so you can share your workbooks with users who haven't yet upgraded.

A major difference, which is actually due to Windows 95, is the fact that Excel can use long filenames — up to 255 characters. This means that you can name a file `Budget Summary for 1996` rather than `BDGSUM96`.

Excel's Role in Microsoft Office 95

Chances are that your copy of Excel came to you as one of several programs bundled together in what's known as Microsoft Office 95 — a "suite" of software that also includes Word (a word processor), PowerPoint (a presentation graphics program), and Schedule Plus (scheduling software). Office 95 Professional (more expensive) also includes the Access database management program.

You'll notice a striking resemblance among these products. The menus are virtually identical, the toolbars are quite similar, and the dialog boxes all have the same look and feel. In fact, these programs all work amazingly well with each other. But for now, just understand that Excel plays a key role in Microsoft's software strategy. It's positioned as the company's number cruncher, and it can even crunch numbers for the other applications. Eventually, all of the applications in Microsoft Office will include the VBA macro language. In Office 95, only Excel and Access support VBA. By the way, if you also have Access installed on your system, you'll find that it works particularly well with Excel for Windows 95.

Cross-
Reference   I discuss issues related to interapplication operability in Chapter 29.

Excel's Competitors

Although Excel is usually considered the best spreadsheet available, it's not without its competitors. Its two main competitors are 1-2-3 for Windows and Quattro Pro for Windows.

The three leading spreadsheets are remarkably similar in their basic capabilities. For example, they all let you work with multiple worksheets in a single file; they all support a wide variety of charts; and they all have macro capabilities to help you automate or customize your work.

Many users, myself included, find that Excel is superior to the other products in terms of both power and ease of use.

What Excel Has to Offer

Excel is a feature-rich product that can be used at many different levels. Chances are that you won't need all of Excel's features, but it's a good idea to at least be familiar with what they can do. For example, you may be tempted to seek out another software product and not even realize that Excel has a feature that can accomplish a particular task. Or, you could be spending lots of time performing a task that Excel can handle automatically.

The following is a quick overview of what Excel can do for you. All of these topics, of course, are discussed in subsequent chapters of this book.

Multisheet files

Excel's files (called *workbooks*) can consist of any number of separate sheets. The sheets can be worksheets, chart sheets, macro sheets, or custom dialog boxes. This feature makes it very easy to organize your work. For example, you can keep all of your budgeting spreadsheets in a single workbook.

Multiple document interface

Excel enables you to work with many files at once; it's not necessary to close down a file even if you need to consult another (see Figure 1-2). This capability makes it easy to transfer information between worksheets in different workbooks.

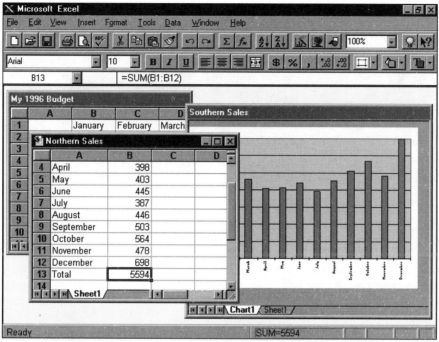

Figure 1-2: Excel lets you work with as many different files as you need.

File compatibility

Excel has its own file format, identifiable by the XLS file extension. In addition, Excel can read files produced by other spreadsheet programs, such as 1-2-3 (DOS and Windows versions), Quattro Pro (DOS and Windows versions) and MultiPlan. It also can read text files and dBASE files.

Context-sensitive help

Computer documentation keeps getting better. In the past, users were lucky if the manual that accompanied a software product accurately covered all the features. Nowadays, the trend is away from written manuals and towards online help. Almost all applications, including Excel, emphasize *online help* — in other words, you can get help on-screen while working in Excel. Excel's online help is excellent and extremely detailed.

New!   The Answer Wizard is new to Excel for Windows 95. This is essentially a new way to get online help by asking English-language questions. Figure 1-3 shows an example of the Answer Wizard in action.

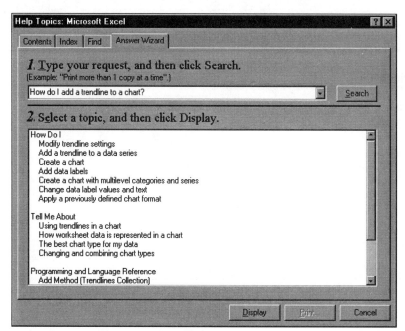

Figure 1-3: The Answer Wizard displays a list of Help topics in response to your question.

TipWizard

One of Excel's most interesting features is the TipWizard. Excel is continually monitoring what you do. If it thinks that you can perform some action in an easier way, it lights up the TipWizard icon. To learn a tip or shortcut, click on the icon. Excel displays a brief tip for you, and you can jump to a detailed help screen to learn more. Of course, if you don't like this feature, you can disable it.

Easy-to-use features

Excel may well be the easiest-to-use spreadsheet available. It includes many features designed specifically to make commonly used tasks straightforward and fast for both beginners and experts. The program walks you step-by-step through several procedures, and basic editing and formatting commands are intuitive and efficient. For example, a single dialog box lets you change any aspect of formatting a cell or range, and right-clicking on anything brings up a context-sensitive shortcut menu.

List management

One of Excel's most significant strengths is how it works with lists stored in a worksheet. This feature makes it very easy to sort, filter, summarize, and manipulate data stored in your worksheet.

Built-in functions

Excel includes an enormous collection of built-in functions that you can use in your formulas. In addition to common functions such as SUM and AVERAGE, you can choose functions that perform sophisticated operations that are difficult or impossible to do otherwise. For example, the CORREL function calculates the correlation coefficient for two sets of data. You also can develop other functions by using the Visual Basic for Applications (VBA) macro language (it's not as difficult as you may think).

Customizable toolbars

Excel's *toolbars* — groups of buttons representing commands — are real time-savers, enabling you to perform common commands without using the menu. You can customize your toolbars by adding buttons for tasks that you do most often. To find out what a button does, drag the mouse over a toolbar button and pause for about a second. Excel pops up a brief description of the button.

Flexible text handling

Although Excel's forte is number crunching, it's not too shabby at handling text. You can format or orient text that you put in cells. You also can insert text boxes (which you can move and resize) anywhere on your worksheet.

Rich text formatting

Excel is the only spreadsheet that enables you to easily format individual characters within a cell. For example, if a cell contains text, you can make one letter bold or a different color.

Great charts

Excel's charting features — among the best available in any spreadsheet — enable you to modify and augment a wide assortment of graph types. You can insert a chart anywhere in a worksheet or place it on a special chart sheet.

Integrated mapping

New! A new feature in Excel for Windows 95 lets you display your data in terms of a geographic map (see Figure 1-4). For example, you can easily create an attractive map that shows your company's sales volume by state.

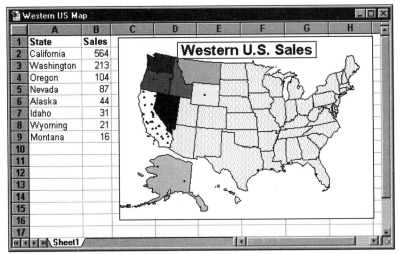

Figure 1-4: This map was generated with only a few mouse clicks.

Drawing tools

Excel includes a set of simple drawing tools that let you create diagrams and basic drawings directly on your worksheet or chart. For example, you can include a simple flow chart along with your numerical analysis.

Worksheet outlining

Spreadsheet outlining, introduced way back in Version 3, is still unique to Excel. This feature enables you to collapse hierarchical information to show any level of detail. People who work with multilevel budgets will find this feature particularly valuable.

Pivot tables

Pivot tables make it easy to change how you view a table of data. It can quickly summarize a list or database, and you can use drag-and-drop techniques to change the layout of the table. If you work with multidimensional data, you should check out this powerful feature.

Advanced analytical tools

Analytical types will get particularly excited about Excel, whose unique *array* feature enables you to do things that are impossible in other spreadsheets. Excel also includes goal seeking, a powerful Solver feature, and the Analysis ToolPak add-in, which provides extensive statistical, financial, engineering, and scientific functions and procedures.

Flexible printing and print preview

When it's time to put your work on paper, you'll be pleased to see how easy it is. Besides normal WYSIWYG formatting, Excel provides the best print previewer I've seen. From the preview window, you can easily make last-minute adjustments, including new column widths and margins.

Worksheet auditing and annotation

No one's perfect, but Excel can help you get closer to that goal. Excel provides a variety of auditing tools to help you track down errors and potential errors in your worksheet formulas.

 A new feature in Excel for Windows 95 automatically displays notes attached to cells when the user drags the mouse over a cell that contains a note. This is an excellent way to remind others (or yourself) what a particular cell represents.

Scenario management

Spreadsheets are often used for *what-if analysis* — change one or more assumptions and observe the effects on dependent formulas. Excel simplifies this process with its scenario manager. You can name scenarios, switch among scenarios (with just a few mouse clicks), and generate reports that summarize the results of your scenarios.

Spell checking and AutoCorrect

An integrated spell checker spots spelling errors in your worksheets and charts. You need not ever again display a chart titled "Bugdet Review" in a crowded boardroom.

Excel for Windows 95 has borrowed a handy feature, AutoCorrect, from Microsoft Word. This corrects many types of input errors as you type. For example, if you enter BUdget into a cell, Excel automatically changes the second letter to a lowercase *u*. You can also use this feature to develop your own shorthand. For example, you can instruct Excel to replace IWC with International Widget Corporation.

Templates

If your work tends to fall into a few specific categories, it may be worth your time to set up custom spreadsheet *templates*, which are preconfigured shells that include text, row, and column headings, formats, column widths, macros, and so on. You can use these templates to help you create similar spreadsheets.

New! Excel for Windows 95 has a new Template Wizard that walks you through the steps required to create a custom template. The latest version of Excel also includes several handy templates that you may find useful. An example of such a template is shown in Figure 1-5.

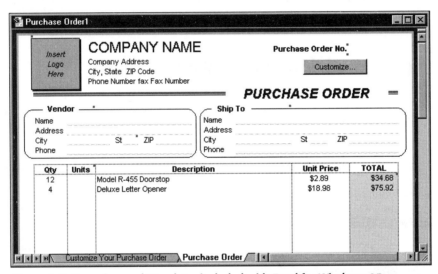

Figure 1-5: One of several templates included with Excel for Windows 95.

Sound

If you have a microphone and a sound card installed for Windows, you can attach sound notes to cells in a worksheet. This lets you provide verbal instructions to someone who will use the worksheet.

Database management

You can work with spreadsheet data as if Excel were a database. Excel not only features all the standard database commands, but it also enables you to work with databases stored in external files.

Excel for Windows 95 includes a feature known as *Data Access Objects*. This is useful for advanced users who want to perform database operations in their macros.

XLM macro compatibility

In previous Excel versions, you could create macros using special macro functions in XLM documents. Although Visual Basic for Applications is a much better macro language, Excel for Windows 95 still supports XLM macros. This means that you can continue to run macros developed for previous versions of Excel.

Visual Basic for Applications (VBA)

VBA is a powerful programming language built right into Excel (as well as several other Microsoft products). After you learn VBA's ropes, you can do magic with your Excel workbooks.

Custom dialog boxes

Excel makes it very easy to create custom dialog boxes. Custom dialogs are usually used in conjunction with VBA macros that you write.

Worksheet controls

Excel lets you insert functional controls (such as buttons, scrollbars, list boxes, and check boxes) directly on your worksheet. You can even link them to cells without using macros. See Figure 1-6 for an example of such controls.

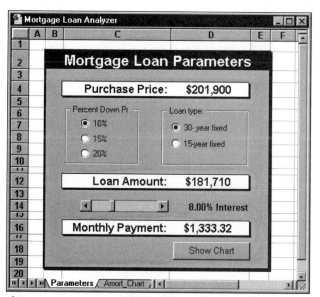

Figure 1-6: You can add dialog box controls directly to your worksheet to make it easier to use.

Protection options

If you need to keep others (or yourself) from modifying your worksheet, you'll find that Excel offers a variety of protection techniques. For example, you can protect cells that contain formulas to eliminate the possibility of accidentally deleting an important formula.

Add-in capability

Although Microsoft didn't originate the concept of spreadsheet add-ins, it has implemented the feature well in Excel. When you load an add-in, you enhance the program's functionality. Excel includes several add-ins, and you can even use VBA to create your own add-ins.

Data exchange

Excel can access all normal Windows features, such as copying and pasting between different applications, as well as the powerful Dynamic Data Exchange (DDE) facility, which creates data links between different applications.

OLE 2 support

Excel supports Microsoft's Object Linking and Embedding (OLE 2) technology, which makes data sharing easier than ever. For example, you can embed a Word for Windows document in a worksheet and then access all WinWord features — right in your worksheet.

Cross-platform consistency

Excel runs on the Macintosh and the PC (in Windows); in fact, the versions are virtually identical across the two platforms. If you learn the Windows version, you can move to a Mac and feel right at home.

Summary

In this chapter, I introduce the concept of a spreadsheet and present a brief history of Excel. I also discuss why Microsoft Windows is important and examine Excel's role in Microsoft Office 95. The bulk of the chapter provides an overview of Excel's key features — all of which will be covered in subsequent chapters.

✦   ✦   ✦

Basic Windows 95 Knowledge

To use Excel, you must have a basic understanding of
Windows 95. In this chapter, I introduce you to some key
Windows 95 concepts that will help you become a more productive Excel user. This is by no means a complete Windows 95
primer. There are lots of other books that cover Windows 95 in
depth — including several published by IDG Books.

What Is Windows 95?

Microsoft Windows is a software product that has been around
for quite a while. The latest version, Windows 95, is arguably the
most ambitious software project ever undertaken. No software
product in history has ever been as eagerly anticipated as
Windows 95. It began shipping in August 1995 — well over a year
late. Based on my early experiences with Windows 95, I think it
was well worth the wait.

Windows 95 is essentially the software that makes your computer work. Without Windows, you could not run Excel (or any
other Windows product). Excel, in turn, relies on Windows for
many of its operations. For example, when you print an Excel
worksheet, the printing is actually done by Windows, not Excel.
Windows 95 also supports *multitasking* — which means that you
can run more than one program at the same time and easily
switch among them.

Cross-
Reference
As you may have concluded from the preceding discussion,
Windows 95 must be installed on your computer before you can
install Excel. If Excel isn't yet installed on your system, refer to
Appendix A.

Strange as it may seem (to me, at least), I've known many Excel
users who didn't have the slightest idea of what Windows is all
about. To them, Windows is just a container for the icon that
they double-click to start up Excel.

These users are typically quite surprised to discover that there is a lot more to Windows lurking behind the scenes. For example, Windows

✦ Gives you several tools that let you manipulate files on your disks.

✦ Is quite customizable, and you can easily personalize your system in several ways.

✦ Has lots of useful utilities, including the capability to play sounds and videos.

✦ Includes several amusing games.

Windows 95 is unlike any previous version of Windows. For the first time, Windows 95 is a complete *operating system*.

Previous versions of Windows required that a version of DOS (Disk Operating System) be installed on the system. No more. Windows 95 can be installed on a system that doesn't have DOS installed. To the average user, this really doesn't mean much. But for computer types (like me), this is a drastic departure.

Unlike DOS, Windows 95 is a 32-bit operating system. Again, this doesn't have a lot of meaning for most users. Suffice it to say that a 32-bit operating system lets you do more things with your computer and do them faster. Yet another improvement is the capability to use long filenames (up to 255 characters). With previous versions of Windows and DOS, filenames were limited to eight characters.

To make a long story short, Windows 95 is a drastic step forward that makes personal computing easier and more powerful than ever.

Just Click on Start

When you turn on your computer, Windows 95 starts up automatically. The appearance of your opening screen (the Windows *desktop*) varies, because Windows 95 is highly customizable.

The Windows taskbar, usually located at the bottom of your screen, has a button labeled Start. When you click the Start button, it expands to display a menu, as shown in Figure 2-1. The items on this menu depend on how your system is set up and which programs you have installed.

Tip   If you have a Microsoft Natural keyboard, you can press the Windows key (situated between Ctrl and Alt) to access the Start menu.

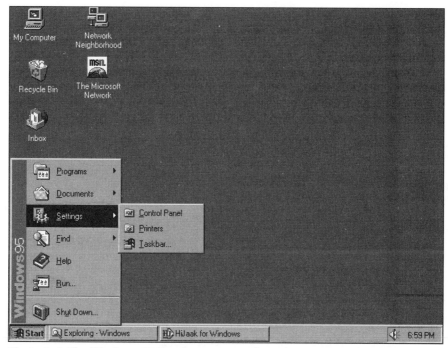

Figure 2-1: The Windows 95 Start button expands to show a menu.

The Start button's menu displays (at least) the following items:

✦ **Programs**. Use this menu to run a program installed on your computer. Clicking this menu item displays another menu, and some of the choices on the next menu may lead to another menu. Just keep traversing the menu until you locate the program that you want to run.

✦ **Documents**. This menu displays the last 15 documents that you worked on. This lets you click a document to make the appropriate program start up and open the document. For example, if you click an Excel workbook file, Excel starts and the selected file opens for you. If Excel already is running, the document opens and Excel is activated.

✦ **Settings**. This menu has at least three choices: Control Panel, Printers, and Taskbar. The Control Panel option lets you change many of the Windows 95 settings. Printers lets you change your printer or adjust its settings. Taskbar lets you change how the taskbar works.

✦ **Find**. This menu lets you locate a file or folder, a computer on your network, or a document on the Microsoft Network. For example, you may have created a file called `Expense Account` but forgotten which folder you put it in. Figure 2-2 shows the dialog box that you get if you search for a file or folder.

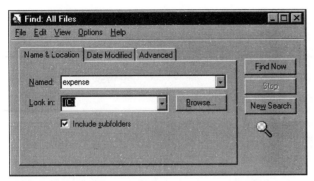

Figure 2-2: Windows 95 makes it easy to locate files and folders on your hard drive.

✦ **Help**. This menu displays the Windows help system. You can search for a keyword and then get a list of items that address the topic in which you're interested.

✦ **Run**. This menu lets you execute a program by typing its filename.

✦ **Shut Down**. Use this menu before you turn off your computer. More about this later.

One of the most frequent operations that you will perform with Windows is to start programs — for example, Excel. Windows 95 gives you several ways to start programs:

✦ Click the Start button in the taskbar. Select the option labeled Programs and keep clicking until you find the program you want to start.

✦ Double-click an icon on the Windows desktop. There may or may not be an Excel icon located there.

✦ Double-click the program's file icon when it's displayed in a window.

✦ Double-click a document file that the program uses. For example, Excel uses XLS files. If you double-click on a file that ends in XLS, Excel starts up and opens the document.

✦ Click the Start button in the taskbar and select the Run option. You can then type the name of the program that you want to start. This isn't the easiest approach, but it's an option.

Adjusting Windows

Everything that you do in Windows occurs in a window. Think of a window as a container that holds a program, a document, or a list of files and folders. For example, when you're running Excel, it runs in a window. When you're viewing a list of files and folders, it appears in a window.

Figure 2-3 shows two windows open. As you can see, windows can overlap. One window, however, is always on "top." This is the active window, and the active window's title bar is a different color. You can activate a different window by clicking it.

Figure 2-3: Two windows. The one in the foreground is the active window.

A window can be in any of three states:

✦ **Maximized:** The window fills the entire screen.

✦ **Minimized:** The window is out of the way, but not closed. It appears as a button on the taskbar.

✦ **Normal:** The window is neither maximized nor minimized. In other words, it's just floating on the desktop.

You can change the state of a window by clicking the appropriate button on the right side of its title bar (the Close button, with the X, closes the window — sometimes without warning — so be careful). For example, if you're finished with a program, you can close it by clicking the Close button. If you'll be using the program again, you may want to minimize it to get it out of the way.

If a window is not maximized or minimized, you can drag it to a new location and change its size by clicking a border and dragging.

Switching among Programs

As I mention earlier, you can run several different programs at the same time. For example, you can run Excel, a word processor, a folder window, and any other programs that you might need. At any given time, however, only one of these programs is the active program — the program that has your attention.

To switch among running programs, you can use any of these techniques:

✦ Click the button in the taskbar that corresponds to the program that you want to activate.

✦ Press Ctrl+Tab to activate the next program.

✦ Press Ctrl+Tab repeatedly. This displays a box with an icon for each running program. Keep pressing Ctrl+Tab until the desired program is highlighted. Then release the keys to activate the program.

Working with Folders and Files

Everything on your computer is stored in files. Files are contained in folders. Folders also can hold other folders, which can hold other folders, and so on. In other words, a particular file might be "nested" in several different folders.

It's to your advantage to understand the concept of folders and files and learn basic file manipulation tasks. In the following sections, I describe some common file manipulations.

Note   In most cases, there are several ways to accomplish a particular action. I don't discuss all possible methods.

Viewing folders

Your desktop has an icon named *My Computer*. When you click this icon, it displays a window that shows your computer's disk drives and system folders. This window has a menu and a toolbar. The toolbar is shown in Figure 2-4, and each toolbar tool is described in the following list, in the order in which the tools appear.

Note You also can use the *Explorer* program to view files and folders. The advantage is that it shows two panes: one with folders and one with the corresponding files.

Figure 2-4: This toolbar appears in the window when you click the My Computer icon or run the Explorer program.

Go to a Different Folder: Lets you select a different folder or a different drive to display in the window. This isn't a button. Rather, it's a list of items.

Up One Level: Displays the folder (or drive) that contains the current folder.

Map Network Drive: Lets you specify a drive letter for a network folder.

Disconnect Net Drive: Lets you disconnect a network drive.

Cut: Deletes the selected files or folders (you can then paste them to another folder).

Copy: Copies the selected files or folders (you can then paste them to another folder).

Paste: Pastes copied or cut files or folders to the current folder.

Undo: Reverses the last file operation that you performed (the name of this button varies, depending on the last file operation).

Delete: Deletes the selected files or folders.

Properties: Displays information about the selected file or folder.

Large Icons: Changes the file and folder display to show large icons.

Small Icons: Changes the file and folder display to show small icons.

List: Changes the file and folder display to show as a list.

Details: Changes the file and folder display to show details.

You can change how the folders and files are displayed by clicking one of the last four icons in the toolbar. Figure 2-5 shows these four different looks. In all cases, you can distinguish a folder from a file by the icon used.

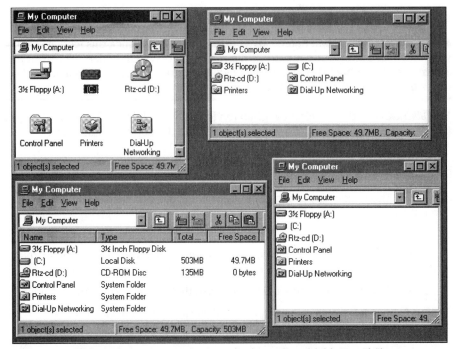

Figure 2-5: Clicking the My Computer icon displays a list of folders and files on your computer. You can choose how to view the files. These views are (clockwise from the upper left): Large Icons, Small Icons, List, and Details.

When you double-click a folder, the folder opens to display its contents, which can be more folders, files, or nothing at all.

The window also includes a menu that you can use to change the view or manipulate the selected file or folder. You also can right-click on a file or folder to display a shortcut menu, which displays a list of operations that you can perform on the file.

Tip   If you have a Microsoft Natural keyboard, you can press the Shortcut key (located below the period key) to display the shortcut menu for the selected item.

Selecting files and folders

Before you can do anything with a file or folder, you must select it. To select an individual file or folder, just click it. The file or folder's name (or icon) appears in reverse video. To select multiple files, press Ctrl while you click each individual file or folder. You also can select one item and hold down Shift while you select another item. This selects all intervening items.

Viewing a file

If you would like to see what's in a file, right-click and select Quick View. This gives you a quick peek at the file without opening the application. Figure 2-6 shows the Quick View window for an Excel file.

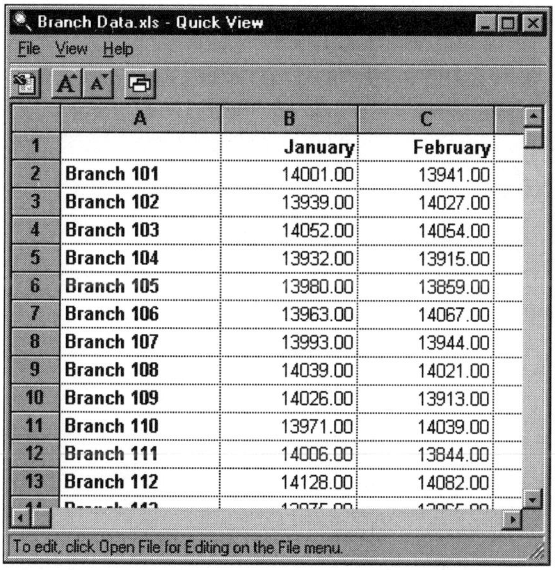

	A	B	C	
1		January	February	
2	Branch 101	14001.00	13941.00	
3	Branch 102	13939.00	14027.00	
4	Branch 103	14052.00	14054.00	
5	Branch 104	13932.00	13915.00	
6	Branch 105	13980.00	13859.00	
7	Branch 106	13963.00	14067.00	
8	Branch 107	13993.00	13944.00	
9	Branch 108	14039.00	14021.00	
10	Branch 109	14026.00	13913.00	
11	Branch 110	13971.00	14039.00	
12	Branch 111	14006.00	13844.00	
13	Branch 112	14128.00	14082.00	

Branch Data.xls - Quick View — File View Help

To edit, click Open File for Editing on the File menu.

Figure 2-6: You can view the contents of a file by using the Quick View option.

Note

Not all files can be viewed with Quick View.

Copying a file or folder

If you need to copy a file, folder, or group of files and/or folders, select the items and click the Copy toolbar button. Then activate the folder where you want to copy them and click the Paste toolbar button.

Tip

You also can copy by pressing Ctrl while you drag the selected icon(s) to another folder.

Tip

To copy to a floppy disk, select the files or folders to copy and then right-click. Select the Send To command from the shortcut menu, and then choose the destination.

Deleting a file or folder

To delete a file or folder, select it and click the Delete button on the toolbar. If you discover that you didn't really want to delete the file, click the Undo button.

Tip   When you delete a file using Windows 95, it's not really deleted. Rather, it is moved to the *Recycle Bin.* You can click the Recycle Bin icon on the desktop to restore a deleted file. Just select the file, right-click, and select Restore from the shortcut menu. The Recycle Bin stores deleted files for an indefinite period of time, depending on how it's set up. To configure your Recycle Bin, right-click the Recycle Bin icon and select Properties from the shortcut menu.

Renaming a file or folder

To rename a file or folder, select it and press F2. Then enter the new name.

Moving a file or folder

If you need to move a file, folder, or group of files and/or folders, select the items and click the Cut toolbar button. Then activate the folder where you want to move them to and click the Paste toolbar button.

Tip

You also can move files or folders by dragging the selected icon(s) to another folder.

Customizing Windows 95

Most users enjoy customizing their systems. Following are some common types of customizations that you can safely make:

- ✦ Change the colors used by Windows.
- ✦ Change the desktop patterns or wallpaper.
- ✦ Change the screen saver used.
- ✦ Change the sounds used by Windows (if you have a sound card).
- ✦ Change the video display resolution.
- ✦ Change how the taskbar works.
- ✦ Adjust your keyboard and mouse settings.

I discuss these in the sections that follow.

Changing the screen colors

Almost everyone I've met likes to change the Windows colors occasionally (it's a great way to keep from working). To do so, right-click the Windows desktop and select Properties from the shortcut menu. This displays a dialog box called Display Properties. This dialog box has several tabs. Click the tab labeled Appearance, and the dialog box will look like Figure 2-7.

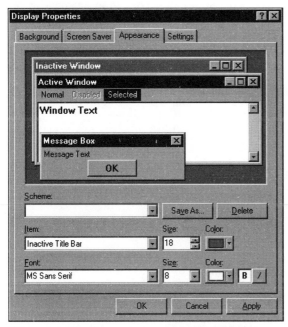

Figure 2-7: The Appearance panel of the Display Properties lets you change the Windows colors.

The top part of the window shows various windows. You can select an item to change by clicking it. For example, if you want to change the color of the active window title bar, click that part of the display (you also can select the item using the Item drop-down list). When an item is selected, you can change its color using the controls at the bottom of the dialog box. You also can change the attributes of the text used in the windows.

Tip

To see how your color change actually will look, click the Apply button.

Windows 95 comes with quite a few "canned" color schemes. You can check these out by using the drop-down list labeled Scheme. Some of these also affect the size of the type used in the windows.

When you're satisfied with your color and type choices, click OK. You also can provide a name for the set of colors by using the Save As button. This adds your custom color set as a new color scheme. This lets you return to that scheme at a later time.

Customizing your desktop

By default, the Windows 95 desktop is pretty much a blank slate. You can, however, customize the desktop by displaying a different pattern or a graphic image as "wallpaper." To do so, right-click anywhere on the desktop and select Properties from the shortcut menu. This displays a dialog box called Display Properties. Click the tab labeled Background, and the dialog box will look like Figure 2-8.

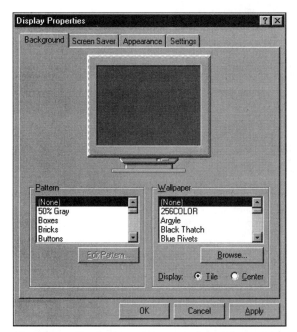

Figure 2-8: The Background panel of the Display Properties dialog box lets you change the desktop's pattern and wallpaper.

Use the two list boxes to make your choices. Click the Apply button to see the effects on your screen. When you're satisfied, click OK.

Changing the screen saver

In the old days, when monochrome monitors were prevalent, screen savers actually had a useful purpose: They prevented a screen image from "burning" the screen elements. Today's monitors don't suffer from this burn-in problem, but screen savers are more popular than ever because they're fun. The Windows 95 screen savers also support a password, which may be useful to you. This requires that a password be entered in order to stop the screen saver display and get back to work.

Windows 95 includes several screen savers that you can use. Right-click anywhere on the desktop and select Properties from the shortcut menu. In the Display Properties dialog box, click the tab labeled Screen Saver, and the dialog box will look like Figure 2-9.

Note If you're working with confidential information, don't rely on the screen saver password to prevent others from accessing your system while you're away. The password can easily be defeated.

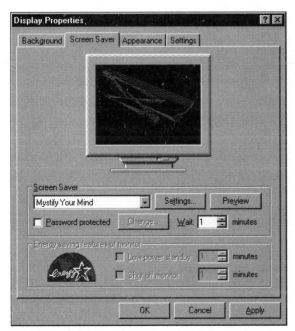

Figure 2-9: The Screen Saver panel of the Display Properties dialog box lets you select a screen saver.

Choose the screen saver that you want from the Screen Saver drop-down list. Click the Preview button to see how it looks. Adjust the other settings and click OK.

Note   If your monitor has a built-in energy-saving feature, you can specify its settings in this dialog box. You can set it so that the monitor is turned off or goes into standby mode after a period of no activity.

Changing your video display

Depending on the monitor and video display card installed in your system, you may be able to choose from several different video resolutions. Right-click anywhere on the desktop and select Properties from the shortcut menu. In the Display Properties dialog box, click the tab labeled Settings, and the dialog box will look like Figure 2-10.

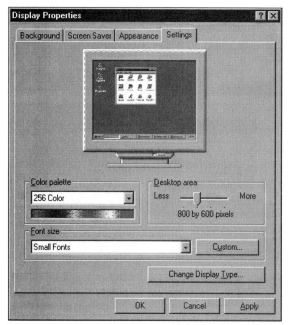

Figure 2-10: The Settings panel of the Display Properties dialog box lets you select a different video resolution.

Use the control in the section labeled Desktop area to specify the video resolution that you want. The choices are as follows:

+ 640 × 480 pixels

+ 800 × 600 pixels

+ 1024 × 768 pixels

+ 1280 × 1024 pixels

Note

Your video card and monitor may not support all four of these options. Only the resolutions that are supported by your equipment will be displayed.

The more pixels there are, the smaller the screen image will be — and the more you can see at once. Generally, you should choose the highest resolution at which you can comfortably read the screen. This depends, in large part, on the quality and size of your monitor. After changing the resolution, click the Apply button to try it out. Windows 95 displays a message asking whether you want to keep that setting.

You also can change the number of colors used, in the Color palette drop-down list. If you change the number of colors, you'll usually have to restart your computer before the change takes effect. You also can choose the font size (large or small) for all resolutions except 640 × 480.

Changing your system sounds

If your system has a sound card installed, you may enjoy having sound effects to accompany your actions. For example, you can have Windows play a particular sound when you start a program. This feature is kind of fun, but it gets old fast.

Click the Start button and select the Settings option, followed by the Control Panel option. Double-click the icon labeled Sounds, and you'll see the dialog box shown in Figure 2-11.

You can select from several preconfigured sound schemes using the Schemes drop-down list (I prefer the Utopia Sound Scheme, with a few customized sounds). Or you can customize the sounds by selecting an event from the Events list and then choosing a WAV file for that event. The Preview button lets you hear the WAV file.

You can save your custom set of sounds as a new sound scheme by clicking the Save As button.

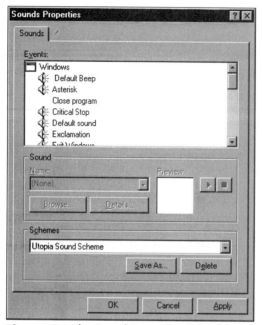

Figure 2-11: The Sound Properties dialog box lets
you set sounds to accompany Windows events.

Changing the taskbar

The taskbar, as I mentioned previously, normally resides at the bottom of the screen.
You can click it and drag it to any of the other three screen sides, however. There
are also some other settings that you can adjust. Right-click the taskbar (but not on a
button) and select Properties from the shortcut menu. You get the dialog box shown
in Figure 2-12.

The options in the Taskbar Options panel are as follows:

   ✦ **Always on top:** This is the default setting. This makes the taskbar visible at all
      times, even when a window is maximized.

   ✦ **Auto hide:** When checked, the taskbar is a thin line. To display the taskbar,
      move the mouse pointer to the line and it reappears.

   ✦ **Show small icons in Start menu:** When checked, the icons in the Start menu are
      smaller in size.

   ✦ **Show Clock:** When checked, the taskbar displays the time of day.

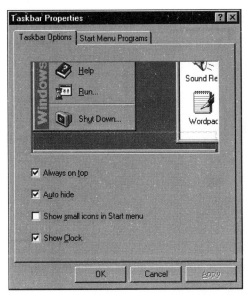

Figure 2-12: The Taskbar Properties dialog box
lets you change settings for the taskbar.

Tip   When the taskbar displays the clock, you can position the mouse pointer over the
clock to see the date and double-click it to adjust the time or date.

Adjusting your keyboard and mouse

You may want to experiment with some different settings for your keyboard and
mouse to see whether they are more comfortable for you. To access these settings,
click the Start button and select the Settings option, followed by the Control Panel
option. Double-click the Mouse icon or the Keyboard icon.

The resulting dialog boxes are tabbed dialog boxes with lots of settings. You can
experiment with these and try out various settings. One that is particularly interesting
is the Pointers panel of the Mouse Properties dialog box (see Figure 2-13).

You can select from a few preconfigured schemes or double-click a pointer and select
a new one from a list of files. Some of the available mouse pointers are animated —
they move, rather than just sit there lifelessly.

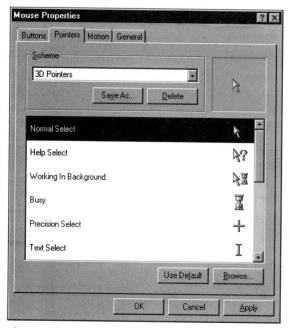

Figure 2-13: Windows 95 lets you select different mouse pointers, including some animated mouse pointers.

Windows Utilities

Windows 95 comes with many utilities that you may find useful. I simply list some of these utilities; if they seem as though they may be of interest, you can check them out for yourself.

Tip
Use the Find command on the Start menu to locate a particular utility, or use the Help command to read more about it.

✦ **Backup:** Lets you backup the files on your hard drive to floppy disks or tape. This is also useful if you need to copy a large file to floppy disks, because it allows a single file to reside on more than one disk.

✦ **Calculator:** A pop-up calculator that can run in standard mode or in scientific mode (see Figure 2-14).

✦ **Calendar:** A simple utility that lets you keep track of appointments.

✦ **Character Map:** Lets you locate special characters in any font. You can copy the characters and paste them into the document that you're working on.

✦ **Disk Defragmenter:** Rewrites the files on your hard drive so that they occupy contiguous sectors. This can speed up file access.

✦ **DriveSpace:** Lets you compress a drive. Don't use this unless you know what you're doing.

✦ **HyperTerminal:** A communications program that you can use to dial other computers or online services.

✦ **Multimedia utilities:** These include a CD-ROM Player, Media Player, Sound Recorder, and Volume Control.

✦ **Paint:** A graphics image editor.

✦ **Phone Dialer:** Dials the phone for you and stores up to eight "speed dial" phone numbers.

✦ **ScanDisk:** Checks your hard drive and reports any problems.

✦ **WordPad:** A functional, albeit somewhat limited, word processing program that supports the Microsoft Word for Windows 6.0 file format.

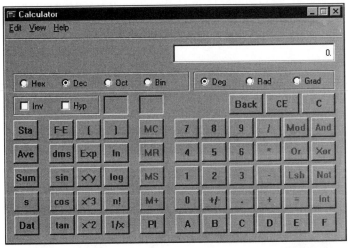

Figure 2-14: The Windows Calculator utility, running in scientific mode.

Windows Games

And what's a discussion of Windows without mentioning the games? Chances are, you've already discovered these. If not, allow me to introduce them.

Note Some system administrators have been known to remove the games from Windows (something about wasting time). If you can't find them on your computer, I guess you're out of luck.

Solitaire

Thousands of Windows users have been caught playing this addictive game when they should be working. I once discovered the CEO of a billion-dollar corporation (that will remain nameless) playing this game when he should have been attending to other matters.

Solitaire is a card game for one (see Figure 2-15). Complete instructions are provided in the online help.

Minesweeper

Minesweeper, shown in Figure 2-16, isn't as popular as Solitaire, but it's a good game nevertheless. Again, consult the online help for the rules of the game.

Note   I wrote a version of this game using Excel's macro language. The game is included with the registered version of my Power Utility Pak shareware (see the coupon in the back of the book).

Hearts

If you're on a network, you can get a group of officemates together and waste some *real* time playing the network version of Hearts (you can also play alone, against your computer). This program is very frequently banned from corporate systems.

Figure 2-15: One of Windows 95's biggest time-wasters.

Figure 2-16: Minesweeper.

Hover

If you've ever played Id Software's Doom, you'll recognize some of the features in Hover — a new game that's on the CD-ROM version of Windows 95. I haven't had much time to explore this game yet, but it looks quite interesting (see Figure 2-17).

Figure 2-17: Hover is a new game that can be found on the Windows 95 CD-ROM.

Quitting Windows

When you're finished with your computer for the day, *do not just turn it off.* Rather, click the Start button on the taskbar and select Shut Down. Windows displays the dialog box shown in Figure 2-18. Make sure that the first item is selected and click Yes. In a few seconds, Windows displays a screen that tells you that you can turn off your computer.

Caution Failure to shut down your computer using the procedure just described can cause all sorts of problems. For example, your disk will be cluttered with unnecessary files, and documents that you are working on will not be closed properly.

Note Some people generally leave their computers on all of the time. If so, there's no need to use this shut down procedure at the end of the day. You may, however, want to turn off your monitor to prolong its life.

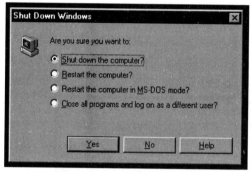

Figure 2-18: This is the proper way to end your computing day.

Summary

This chapter provides a brief overview of Windows 95. I cover some essential topics that all Excel users should know about. These include using the Start button, starting programs, switching among programs that are running, and understanding essential operations that involve files and folders. In addition, I describe how to change some of your system settings, Windows utilities, games, and the proper way to exit Windows 95.

✦   ✦   ✦

Getting Acquainted with Excel

✦   ✦   ✦   ✦

CHAPTER 3

In This Chapter

Identifying the various parts of Excel's window

Identifying the various parts of a workbook window

A hands-on session with Excel

✦   ✦   ✦   ✦

New users are sometimes overwhelmed when they first fire up Excel. It starts with an empty workbook, lots of strange buttons, and unfamiliar commands on the menus. This chapter helps you feel more at home with Excel, explains its main parts, and even gives you a chance to do a few things to get better acquainted.

Starting Excel

Before you can use Excel, it must be installed on your system. And before you can install Excel, Microsoft Windows 95 must be installed on your system. With any luck, Excel is already installed and ready to run. If not, refer to Appendix A for instructions on installing and starting Excel.

Excel's Parts

When Excel starts up, your screen looks something like Figure 3-1. This figure identifies the major parts of Excel's window, which are explained in the following paragraphs.

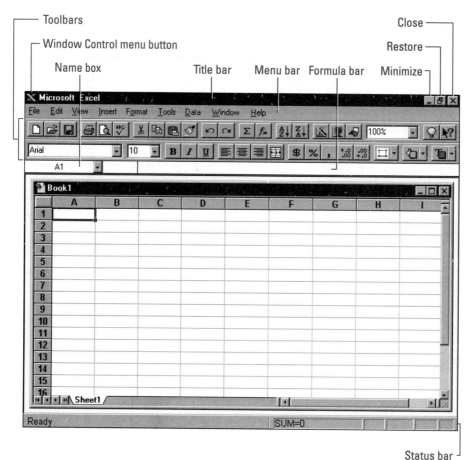

Figure 3-1: Excel runs in a window, which in this case is maximized so it occupies the full screen. The major parts of the window are identified.

Note   This figure shows Excel running in VGA mode (640 × 480 pixels). Your screen may look different if you're running Windows in a different video mode that displays more pixels on-screen.

Title bar

All Windows programs have a title bar. This identifies the name of the program and also holds some control buttons that you can use to modify the window.

Window Control menu button

This button is actually Excel's icon. When you click on it, you get a menu that lets you manipulate Excel's window.

Minimize button

Clicking on this button minimizes Excel's window and displays it in the Windows 95 taskbar.

Restore button

Clicking on this button "unmaximizes" Excel's window so that it no longer fills the entire screen. If Excel isn't maximized, this button is replaced by a Maximize button.

Close button

Clicking on this button closes Excel. If there are any unsaved files, you'll be prompted to save them.

Menu bar

This is Excel's main menu. Clicking on a word on the menu drops down a list of menu items, which is one way for you to issue a command to Excel.

Toolbars

The toolbars hold buttons on which you click to issue commands to Excel.

Formula bar

When you enter information or formulas into Excel, they appear in this line.

Name box

This displays the name of the active cell in the current workbook. When you click on the arrow, the list drops down to display all named cells and named ranges (if any) in the active workbook. You also can use the Name box to quickly give a name to the selected cell or range.

Status bar

This bar displays various messages and the status of the Num Lock, Caps Lock, and Scroll Lock keys on your keyboard.

Parts of a Workbook Window

When you work with Excel, you work with workbooks, each of which appears in a separate window within Excel's workspace.

Figure 3-2 shows a typical workbook window with its major parts identified. These parts are described in the following paragraphs. Notice that a workbook window has many parts in common with Excel's window.

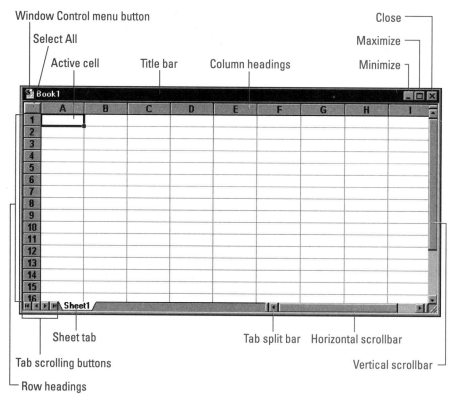

Figure 3-2: An empty Excel workbook, named Book1. The major parts of the workbook window are identified.

Title bar

This identifies the name of the workbook and also holds some control buttons that you can use to modify the window.

Window Control menu button

Clicking on this button (actually an icon) displays a menu that lets you manipulate the workbook window.

Minimize button

Clicking on this button minimizes the workbook window so that only the title bar shows.

Maximize button

Clicking on this button maximizes the workbook window to fill Excel's complete workspace. If the window is already maximized, a Restore button appears in its place.

Close button

Clicking on this button closes the workbook. If the workbook hasn't been saved, you'll be prompted to save it.

Select All button

Clicking on this button selects all cells on the active worksheet of the active window.

Active cell indicator

This dark outline indicates the currently active cell (one of the 4,194,304 cells on each worksheet).

Row headings

Numbers ranging from 1 to 16,384 — one for each row in the worksheet. You can click on a row heading to select an entire row of cells.

Column headings

Letters ranging from A to IV — one for each of the 256 columns in the worksheet. After column Z comes column AA, which is followed by AB, AC, and so on. After column AZ comes BA, BB, and so on until you get to the last column, labeled IV. You can click on a column heading to select an entire column of cells.

Tab scrolling buttons

These buttons let you scroll the sheet tabs to display those that aren't visible.

Sheet tabs

Each of these notebook-like tabs represents a different sheet in the workbook. A workbook can have any number of sheets, and each sheet has its name displayed in a sheet tab.

Tab split bar

This lets you increase or decrease the area devoted to displaying sheet tabs. When you show more sheet tabs, the horizontal scrollbar's size is reduced.

Horizontal scrollbar

Lets you scroll the sheet horizontally.

Vertical scrollbar

Lets you scroll the sheet vertically.

A Hands-On Excel Session

The remainder of this chapter consists of an introductory session with Excel. If you've never used Excel, you may want to follow along on your computer to get a feel for how it works. Don't be alarmed if you don't understand all of the steps — that's what the rest of this book is for. This example assumes that you've been asked to prepare a one-page report that shows your company's quarterly sales broken down by the two sales regions (North and South). This section walks you through the steps required to do the following:

1. Enter a table of data (the sales figures) into a worksheet.

2. Create and copy a formula (to get totals).

3. Format the data so that it looks good.

4. Create a chart from the data.

5. Save the workbook to a file.

6. Print the data and chart (the one-page report).

When you're finished, you'll have a worksheet that looks like the one in Figure 3-3.

On the CD-ROM The workbook that is created in the following exercise is available on the companion CD-ROM. The filename is MYFIRSWK.XLS.

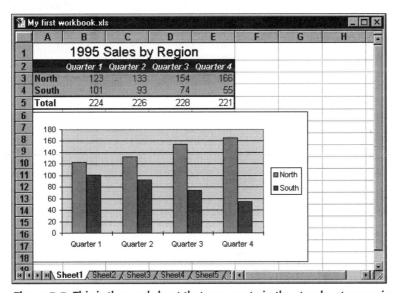

Figure 3-3: This is the worksheet that you create in the step-by-step session.

Note This section is quite detailed and provides every step that you need to reproduce the worksheet shown in Figure 3-3. If you already have experience with a spreadsheet, you may find this a bit *too* detailed. Don't worry. You'll find that the pace picks up in the remainder of the book.

Getting ready

As a first step, you run Excel and maximize its window to fill the entire screen. Then you maximize the blank workbook named Book1.

1. If Excel isn't running, start it. You're greeted with a blank window named Book1. If Excel is already running, click on its Close button to exit Excel. Then restart it so that you see the empty window named Book1.

2. If Excel doesn't fill the entire screen, maximize Excel's window by clicking on the Maximize button in Excel's title bar.

3. Maximize the workbook window so that you can see as much of the workbook as possible. Do this by clicking on the Maximize button in Book1's title bar.

Entering the headings

In this step, you enter the row and column headings into the worksheet named Sheet1 in Book1. When you're finished, the worksheet will look like Figure 3-4.

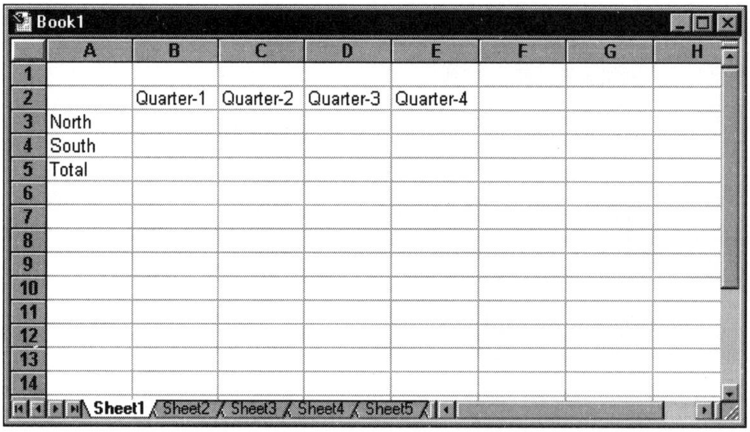

Figure 3-4: The worksheet after entering headings for the data.

1. Move the cell pointer to cell A3 using the direction keys. The Name box displays the cell's address.

2. Enter **North** into cell A3. Just type the text and then press Enter. Depending on your setup, Excel either moves the cell pointer down to cell A4 or the pointer remains in cell A3.

3. Move the cell pointer to cell A4, type **South**, and press Enter.

4. Move the cell pointer to cell A5, type **Total**, and press Enter.

5. Move the cell pointer to cell B2, type **Quarter 1**, and press Enter.

   At this point, you could enter the other three headings manually, but we'll let Excel do the work.

6. Move the cell pointer to cell B2 if it's not already there. Notice the small square at the lower-right corner of the cell pointer. This is called the *fill handle*. When you move the mouse pointer over the fill handle, the mouse pointer changes to a dark cross.

7. Move the mouse pointer to the fill handle until it changes to a cross. Then click and drag to the right until you select the three cells to the right (C2, C3, and C4). Release the mouse button, and you'll see that Excel filled in the three remaining headings for you.

Entering the data

In this step, you simply enter the values for each quarter, for each region.

1. Move the cell pointer to cell B3, type **123**, and press Enter.

2. Move to the remaining cells and enter additional data until your worksheet looks like Figure 3-5.

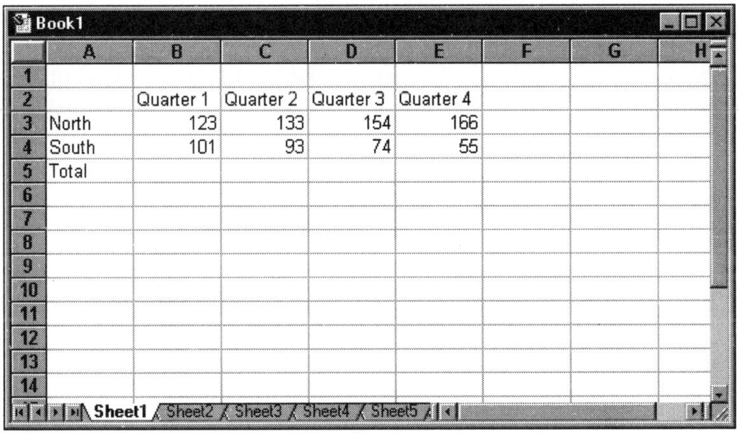

	A	B	C	D	E	F	G	H
1								
2		Quarter 1	Quarter 2	Quarter 3	Quarter 4			
3	North	123	133	154	166			
4	South	101	93	74	55			
5	Total							
6								
7								
8								
9								
10								
11								
12								
13								
14								

Book1

Sheet1 / Sheet2 / Sheet3 / Sheet4 / Sheet5

Figure 3-5: The worksheet after entering the sales data.

Creating a formula

So far, what we've done has been fairly mundane. In fact, you could accomplish the same effect with any word processor. In this step, you take advantage of what a spreadsheet is known for: formulas. You create formulas to calculate the total for each region.

1. Move the cell pointer to cell B5.

2. Locate the *AutoSum button* on the toolbar below the menu and click on it once. The AutoSum button has a Greek sigma on it. The toolbar below the menu is called the Standard toolbar. Notice that Excel inserts the following into the cell:

   ```
   =SUM(B3:B4)
   ```

   This is a formula that calculates the sum of the values in the range B3 through B4.

3. Press Enter to accept the formula. You see that the sum of the two values is displayed in the cell. You could repeat this step for the remaining three quarters, but it's much easier to simply copy the formula to the three cells to the right.

4. Move the cell pointer to cell B5 if it's not already there.

5. Move the mouse pointer to the fill handle. When it changes to a cross, click and drag three cells to the right. Release the mouse button and discover that Excel copied the formula to the cells that you selected.

At this point, your worksheet should look like Figure 3-6. To demonstrate that these are actual "live" formulas, try changing one or two of the values. You'll see that the cells with the formulas change also. In other words, the formulas are recalculating and displaying new results using the modified data.

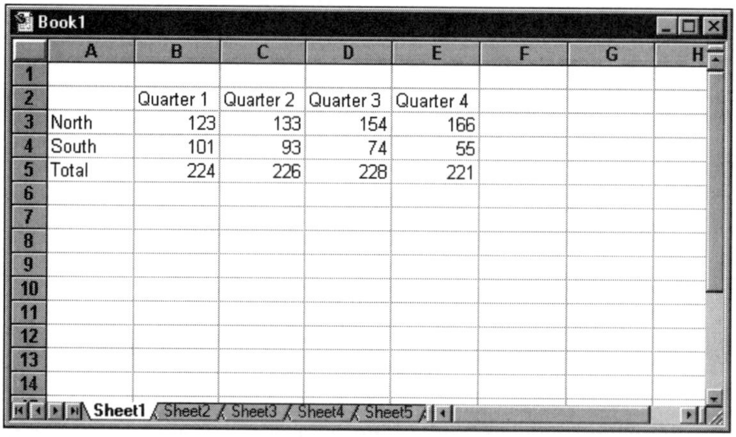

Figure 3-6: The worksheet after inserting a formula and copying it.

Formatting the table

The table looks fine, but it could look even better. In this step, you use Excel's automatic formatting feature to spiff it up a bit.

1. Move the cell pointer to any cell in the table (it doesn't matter which one because Excel will figure it out).

2. Click on the Format menu; it drops down to display its menu items.

3. Select AutoFormat from the list of menu items. Two things happen: Excel determines the table boundaries and highlights the entire table, and it displays the dialog box shown in Figure 3-7.

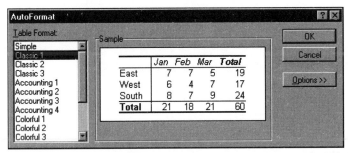

Figure 3-7: Excel's AutoFormat dialog box makes it easy to quickly format a table.

4. The AutoFormat dialog box has 16 "canned" formats from which to choose. Click on the table format named Classic 3. You see an example in the right side of the dialog box.

5. Click on the OK button. Excel applies the formats to your table.

6. The table is still selected, so the colors appear reversed. Click on any cell to remove the highlighting from the table.

Your worksheet should look like Figure 3-8. Note that Excel made the following formatting changes for you automatically:

✦ It changed some of the cell background colors.

✦ It changed some of the cell colors.

✦ It made the column headings italic.

✦ It made the row headings bold.

✦ It added borders.

You could have performed these operations yourself, but it probably would have taken several minutes. Autoformatting can save you lots of time.

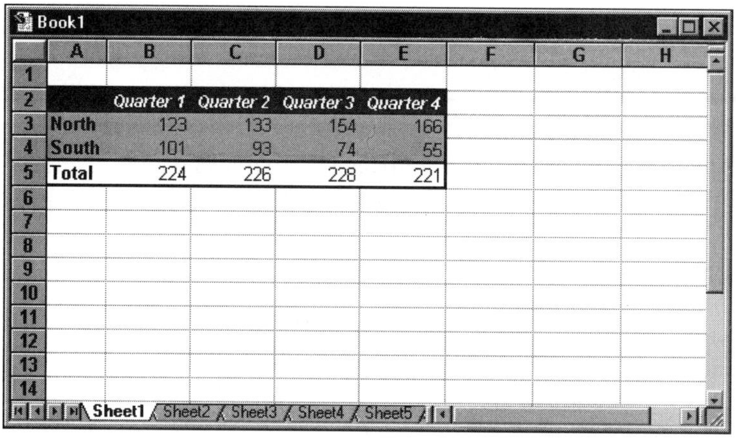

Figure 3-8: Your worksheet after applying automatic formatting.

Adding a title

In this step, you simply add a title to the table, make it bold, and adjust it so that it's centered across the five columns of the table.

1. Move the cell pointer to cell A1.

2. Enter **1995 Sales by Region** and press Enter.

3. Move the cell pointer back to cell A1 if it's not there and click on the Bold button on the Formatting toolbar (the Bold button has a large *B*). This makes the text bold.

4. Click the Font Size arrow (see Figure 3-9) on the Formatting toolbar and select 14 from the list. This makes the text larger.

5. Click in cell A1 and drag to the right until you select A1, B1, C1, D1, and E1 (that is, the range A1:E1).

6. Click on the Center Across Columns button (see Figure 3-9) on the Formatting toolbar. The text in cell A1 is centered across the selected cells.

Your worksheet should look like Figure 3-10.

Figure 3-9: The Font Size arrow (left) and the Center Across Columns button (right) appear on the Formatting toolbar.

	A	B	C	D	E	F	G	H
1		1995 Sales by Region						
2		Quarter 1	Quarter 2	Quarter 3	Quarter 4			
3	North	123	133	154	166			
4	South	101	93	74	55			
5	Total	224	226	228	221			

Book1

Sheet1 / Sheet2 / Sheet3 / Sheet4 / Sheet5

Figure 3-10: Your worksheet after adding a title and formatting it.

Creating a chart

In this step, you create a chart from the data in the table. The chart will be placed on the worksheet directly below the table.

1. Move the cell pointer to cell A2.

2. Click and drag until you've selected all the cells in the rectangle with A2 at the upper left and E4 at the lower right (15 cells in all). Notice that you're not selecting the cells in the row that displays the totals; you don't want the totals to appear in the chart.

3. With the range A2:E4 selected, click on the ChartWizard button on the Standard toolbar. Notice that the mouse pointer changes shape and a message is displayed in the status bar: *Drag in document to create a chart.*

4. Click in the worksheet to create an outline of where the chart will go. Start in cell A6 and drag down to cell G18. When you release the mouse button, Excel displays the dialog box shown in Figure 3-11.

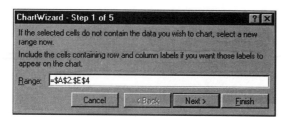

Figure 3-11: The first of five ChartWizard dialog boxes that help you create a chart.

5. In the first step of the ChartWizard, you confirm the range that holds your data. Click on the Next button. The ChartWizard then displays the dialog box shown in Figure 3-12.

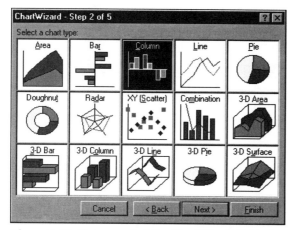

Figure 3-12: The second of five ChartWizard dialog boxes.

6. In the second step, you choose the chart type. The default chart, a Column chart, is highlighted. This is a good choice, so click on Next. The ChartWizard then displays the dialog box shown in Figure 3-13.

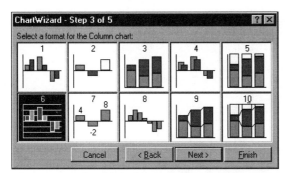

Figure 3-13: The third of five ChartWizard dialog boxes.

7. In this step, you choose the format for the Column chart. Again, the default format is a good choice, so click on Next. The ChartWizard then displays the dialog box shown in Figure 3-14.

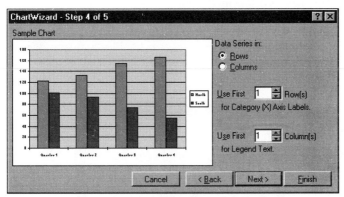

Figure 3-14: The fourth of five ChartWizard dialog boxes.

8. In Step 4 of the ChartWizard, you preview the chart. Everything looks OK, so click on Next. The ChartWizard then displays the dialog box shown in Figure 3-15.

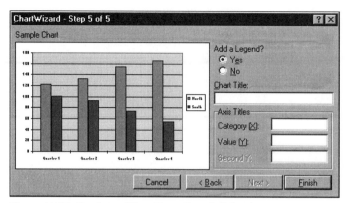

Figure 3-15: The last of five ChartWizard dialog boxes.

9. In the final step of the ChartWizard, you can remove the legend, add a title, and add text for the axes. Because the chart is fine as is, click Finish. Excel then displays the chart where you specified.

Your worksheet should look like Figure 3-16. If you like, you can resize the chart by dragging on any of the eight handles on its borders (the handles appear only when the chart is selected).

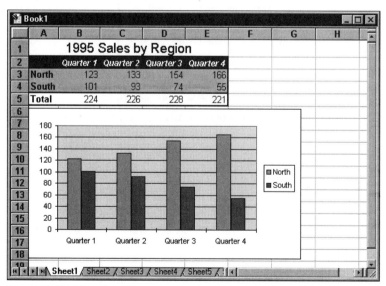

Figure 3-16: The ChartWizard inserts the chart on the worksheet.

Saving the workbook

Up until now, everything that you've done has occurred in your computer's memory. If the power should fail, all would be lost. It's time to save your work to a file. Call this workbook My first workbook.

Excel 95 In Excel 5, the workbook name is limited to eight characters. With Excel for Windows 95, you can use up to 255 characters for a filename.

1. Click on the Save button on the Standard toolbar. The Save button looks like a disk. Excel responds with the dialog box shown in Figure 3-17.

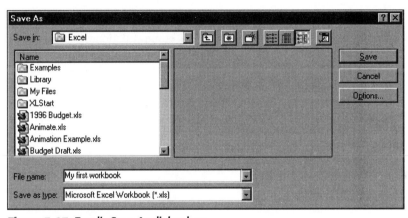

Figure 3-17: Excel's Save As dialog box.

2. In the box labeled File name, enter **My first workbook** and press Enter.

Excel saves the workbook as a file. The workbook remains open so that you can work with it some more.

Printing the report

As the final step, you print this report. I'm assuming that you have a printer attached and that it works properly. To print the worksheet, just click on the Print button on the Standard toolbar (this button has an image of a printer on it). The worksheet (including the chart) is printed using the default settings.

Quitting Excel

As the final step, click on the Close button to exit Excel. Because no changes were made to the workbook since it was last saved, Excel closes down without asking whether you want to save the file.

Summary

If this was your first time using Excel, you probably have lots of questions about what you've just done in the preceding exercise. Those questions will be answered in the next few chapters.

If you're the adventurous type, you may have answered some of your own questions by trying out various buttons or menu items. If so, congratulations. Experimenting is the best way to get to know Excel. Just remember, the worst thing that can happen is that you mess up a workbook file. And if you do your experimentation on unimportant files, you have absolutely nothing to lose.

✦   ✦   ✦

Introductory Concepts

P A R T

The chapters in Part II discuss the basic concepts of Excel — topics with which all Excel users should be familiar.

◆ ◆ ◆

Navigating through Excel

CHAPTER

♦   ♦   ♦   ♦

In This Chapter

All about the windows that Excel uses to hold workbooks

Moving through a worksheet

Using Excel's menus and shortcut menus

Issuing commands using toolbar buttons

Excel's shortcut keys

Techniques for working with dialog boxes

♦   ♦   ♦   ♦

Because you'll spend lots of time working in Excel, it's important that you understand the basics of navigating through workbooks and how to best utilize Excel's user interface. If you worked through Chapter 3, some of this information is already familiar to you, so this is your chance to learn even more.

If you're new to Excel, some of the information in this chapter may not make much sense. It will become clearer as you progress through the other chapters, however.

Working with Excel's Windows

The files that Excel uses are known as *workbooks*. A workbook can hold any number of sheets, and these sheets can be of several different types. The most common type of sheet is a *worksheet;* this is what people usually think of when they think of a spreadsheet. A worksheet has rows and columns, which intersect at a cell.

Figure 4-1 shows Excel with four workbooks open, each in a separate window. One of the windows is minimized and appears at the bottom of the screen (when a workbook is minimized, only its title bar is visible). Note that worksheet windows can overlap, and the title bar of one window is a different color. That's the window that contains the *active workbook*.

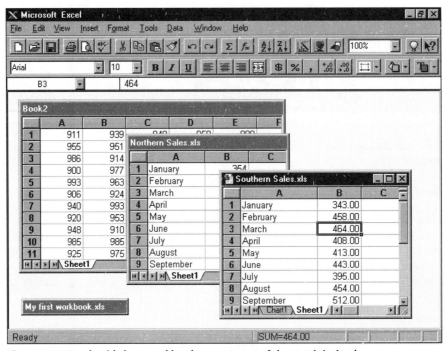

Figure 4-1: Excel, with four workbooks open, one of them minimized.

The workbook windows that Excel uses work much like the windows in any other Windows program. Excel's windows can be one of the following:

✦ Maximized to fill Excel's entire workspace. A maximized window does not have a title bar, and the worksheet's name appears in Excel's title bar. To maximize a window, click on its Maximize button.

✦ Minimized to appear as a small window with only a title bar. To minimize a window, click on its Minimize button.

✦ Restored to a nonmaximized size. To restore a maximized or minimized window, click on its Restore button. Restored windows can be moved and resized to your liking.

If you work with more than one workbook at a time (which is quite common), you have to learn how to move, resize, and switch among the workbook windows.

Note As you're probably aware, Excel itself is contained in a window. Excel's window also can be maximized, minimized, or displayed in a nonmaximized size. When Excel's window is maximized, it fills the entire screen. You can activate other programs by using the Windows taskbar (usually located at the bottom of your screen).

Moving and resizing windows

To move or resize a workbook window, it can't be maximized. You *can* move a minimized window, but doing so will have no effect on its position when it is subsequently restored.

To move a window, click and drag its title bar with your mouse. Note that the windows can extend off-screen in any direction, if you like.

To resize a window, click and drag any of its borders until it's the size you want it to be. When you position the mouse pointer on a window's border, the mouse pointer changes shape to let you know that you can then click and drag. To resize a window horizontally and vertically at the same time, click and drag any of its corners.

If you would like all of your workbook windows to be visible (that is, not obscured by another window), you can fiddle around moving and resizing them manually, or you can let Excel do it for you automatically. The Window⇨Arrange command displays the dialog box shown in Figure 4-2. This dialog box has four window arrangement options. Just select the one you want and click on OK.

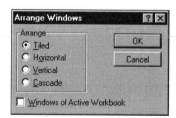

Figure 4-2: The Arrange Windows dialog box makes it easy to arrange the windows of all open workbooks.

Switching among windows

As I mentioned, at any given time, one (and only one) workbook window is the active window. This is the window that accepts your input, and the window on which your commands work. The active window's title bar is a different color, and it's on top of the stack of windows.

There are several ways to make a different window the active workbook:

✦ Click on another window if it's visible. The window you click moves to the top and becomes the active window.

✦ Press Ctrl+Tab to cycle through all open windows until the window that you want to work with appears on top.

✦ Click on the <u>W</u>indow menu and select the desired window from the bottom part of the pull-down menu. The active window has a check mark next to it, as shown in Figure 4-3. This shows up to nine windows. If you have more than nine workbook windows open, choose <u>M</u>ore Windows (which appears below the nine window names).

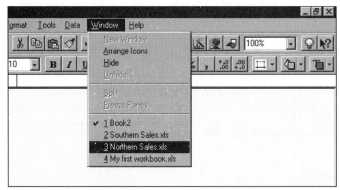

Figure 4-3: You can activate a different window by selecting it from the pull-down <u>W</u>indow menu.

Many users (myself included) prefer to do most of their work with maximized workbook windows. This lets you see more cells and eliminates the distraction of other workbook windows getting in the way. And besides, it's very easy to activate another workbook window when you need to use it.

When you maximize one window, all the other windows are maximized, too (but you can't see them). Therefore, if the active window is maximized and you activate a different window, the new active window also is maximized. If the active workbook window is maximized, you can't select another window by clicking on it (because other windows aren't visible). You must use either Ctrl+Tab or the <u>W</u>indow menu to activate another window.

When would you *not* want to work exclusively with maximized worksheet windows? As you'll see in Chapter 8, Excel has some very handy drag-and-drop features. For example, you can drag a range of cells from one workbook window to another. To do any of this dragging and dropping, both windows must be visible (that is, not maximized).

Note Another point to keep in mind is that a single workbook can be displayed in more than one window. For example, if you have a workbook with two worksheets, you may want to display each worksheet in a separate window. All of the window manipulation procedures described previously still apply.

Closing windows

When you close a workbook window, Excel checks to see whether any changes have been made since the last time the file was saved. If not, the window is closed without a prompt from Excel. If you've made any changes, Excel prompts you to save the file before closing the window. You'll learn more about working with files in the next chapter.

To close a window, simply click on the Close button on the title bar.

Mouseless window manipulation

Although using a mouse to manipulate Excel's windows is usually the most efficient route, you also can perform these techniques using the keyboard. Table 4-1 summarizes the key combinations that manipulate workbook windows.

Table 4-1	
Keystrokes Used to Manipulate Windows	
Key Combination	**Action**
Ctrl+F4	Close a window
Ctrl+F5	Restore a window
Ctrl+F6	Activate the next window
Ctrl+Shift+F6	Activate the previous window
Ctrl+Tab	Activate the next window
Ctrl+Shift+Tab	Activate the previous window
Ctrl+F7	Move a window*
Ctrl+F8	Resize a window*
Ctrl+F9	Minimize a window
Ctrl+F10	Maximize a window
Alt+W[n]	Activate the nth window

* Use the direction keys to make the change, and then press Enter.

Moving around a Worksheet

You'll be spending a lot of time moving through your worksheets, so it pays to learn all the tricks.

Every worksheet consists of rows (numbered 1 through 16384) and columns (labeled A through IV). After column Z comes column AA, after column AZ comes column BA, and so on. The intersection of a row and column is a single cell. At any given time, one cell is the *active cell*. The active cell is indicated by a darker border, as shown in Figure 4-4. Its *address* (that is, its column letter and row number) appears in the Name box. Depending on the technique you use to navigate through a workbook, you may or may not change the active cell.

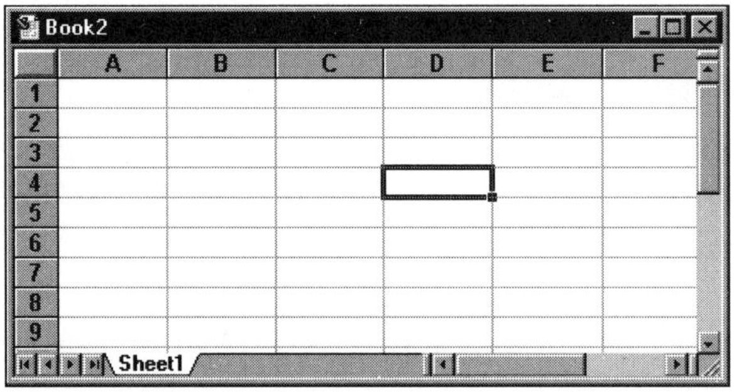

Figure 4-4: The active cell is the cell with the dark border; in this case, cell D4.

How big is a worksheet?

It's interesting to stop and think how big a worksheet really is. There are 256 columns and 16,384 rows. Do the arithmetic and you'll see that this works out to 4,194,304 cells. Remember, this is in just one worksheet. A single workbook can hold more than one worksheet.

If you're using the standard VGA video mode with the default row heights and column widths, you can see 9 columns and 18 rows (or 162 cells) at a time. This works out to less than 0.004 percent of the entire worksheet. Put another way, there are nearly 26,000 screenfuls of information in a single worksheet.

If you started entering a single digit into each cell at a relatively rapid clip of one cell per second, it would take you about 48 days, nonstop, to fill up a worksheet. To print the results of your efforts would require more than 9,000 sheets of paper.

By the way, if you actually *do* fill up a worksheet with values, things will slow down considerably — unless your system has an unusually large amount of memory. Just for fun, I filled all of the cells in a worksheet (I copied them, which took considerably less than 48 days). Windows used disk-based virtual memory to store the huge worksheet, and things slowed down to a crawl (every keystroke resulted in disk swapping). I was curious about the size of such a file. It took more than ten minutes to save the file, which was about 25 megabytes. In summary, I don't recommend filling an entire worksheet.

Using the keyboard

As you probably already know, you can use the standard navigational keys on your keyboard to move around a worksheet. These keys work just as you would expect: down arrow moves the active cell down one row, right arrow moves it one column to the right, and so on. PgUp and PgDn move the active cell up or down one full window (the actual number of rows moved depends on the number of rows displayed in the window).

Tip When Scroll Lock is turned on, you can scroll through the worksheet without changing the active cell. This can be useful if you need to view another area of your worksheet and then quickly return to your original location. Just press Scroll Lock and then use the direction keys to scroll through the worksheet. When you want to return to the original position (the active cell), press Ctrl+Backspace. Then, press Scroll Lock again to turn it off.

Note The Num Lock key on your keyboard controls how the keys on the numeric keypad behave. When Num Lock is on, Excel displays NUM in the status bar at the bottom of its window. When this indicator is on, the keys on your numeric keypad generate numbers. Most keyboards have a separate set of navigational keys located to the left of the numeric keypad. These keys are not affected by the state of the Num Lock key.

Table 4-2 summarizes all of the worksheet movement keys available in Excel.

Table 4-2 Excel's Worksheet Movement Keys	
Key	**Action**
Up arrow	Moves the active cell up one row
Down arrow	Moves the active cell down one row
Left arrow	Moves the active cell one column to the left
Right arrow	Moves the active cell one column to the right
PgUp	Moves the active cell up one screen
PgDn	Moves the active cell down one screen
Alt+PgDn	Moves the active cell right one screen
Alt+PgUp	Moves the active cell left one screen
Ctrl+Backspace	Scrolls to display the active cell
Up arrow*	Scrolls the screen up one row (active cell does not change)
Down arrow*	Scrolls the screen down one row (active cell does not change)
Left arrow*	Scrolls the screen left one column (active cell does not change)
Right arrow*	Scrolls the screen right one column (active cell does not change)

* With Scroll Lock on

Note The actions for some of the keys in the preceding table may be different, depending on the transition options that you've set. Select the Tools⇨Options command and then click the Transition tab in the Options dialog box. If the Transition Navigation Keys option is checked, the navigation keys correspond to those used in 1-2-3. Generally, it's better to use the standard Excel navigation keys than those for 1-2-3.

Tip If you know either the cell address or the name of the cell that you want to activate, you can get there quickly by pressing F5 (the shortcut key for the Edit⇨GoTo command). This command displays a dialog box. Just enter the cell coordinate in the Reference box (or choose a named cell from the list), press Enter, and you're there.

Using a mouse

Navigating through a worksheet with a mouse also works just as you would expect. To change the active cell, just click on a cell and it becomes the active cell. If the cell that you want to activate is not visible in the workbook window, you can use the scrollbars to scroll the window in any direction. To scroll one cell, click on either of the arrows on the scrollbar. To scroll by a complete screen, click on either side of the scrollbar's "thumb." You also can drag the thumb for faster scrolling. Working with the scrollbars is more difficult to describe than to do, so if scrollbars are new to you, I urge you to play around with them for a few minutes. You'll have it figured out in no time.

New! Compared with the previous versions of Excel, the scrollbars work a little differently in Excel for Windows 95. When you drag the scrollbar's thumb, a small yellow box appears that tells you which row or column you will scroll to when you release your finger from the mouse. This is a very useful feature, and I urge you to check it out.

Note Using the scrollbars doesn't change the active cell. It simply scrolls the worksheet. To change the active cell, you must click on a new cell after scrolling.

Notice that only the active workbook window has scrollbars. When you activate a different window, the scrollbars appear.

Giving Commands to Excel

Excel is designed to take orders from you. You give these orders by issuing commands. You can give commands to Excel using the following methods:

✦ Menus

✦ Shortcut menus

✦ Toolbar buttons

✦ Shortcut key combinations

In many cases, you have a choice as to how to issue a particular command. For example, if you want to save your workbook to disk, you can use the menu (the File⇨Save command), a shortcut menu (right-click the workbook's title bar and click Save), a toolbar button (the Save button on the Standard toolbar), or a shortcut key combination (Ctrl+S). The particular method you use is up to you.

The following sections provide an overview of the four methods of issuing commands to Excel.

Using Excel's Menus

Excel, like all other Windows programs, has a menu bar located directly below the title bar (see Figure 4-5). This menu is always available and ready for your command. Excel's menus change, depending on what you're doing. For example, if you're working with a chart, Excel's menus change to give you options that are appropriate for a chart. This all happens automatically, so you don't even have to think about it.

Figure 4-5: Excel's menu bar.

Accessing the menu with a mouse is quite straightforward. Click on the menu that you want and it will drop down to display menu items, as in Figure 4-6. Click on the menu item to issue the command.

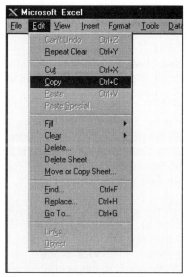

Figure 4-6: Accessing Excel's
Edit menu causes it to display
its menu items.

Some menu items lead to an additional *submenu;* when you click on the menu item, the submenu appears to the right. Menu items that have a submenu display a small triangle. For example, the Edit⇨Clear command has a submenu, shown in Figure 4-7. Excel's designers incorporated submenus primarily to keep the menus from becoming too lengthy and overwhelming to users.

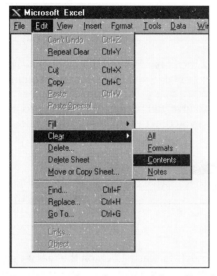

Figure 4-7: The submenu of the Edit⇨Clear command.

Some menu items also have shortcut keys associated with them. If so, they usually display the key combination next to the menu item. For example, the Edit⇨Find command's shortcut key combination is Ctrl+F.

Sometimes, you'll notice that a menu item appears *grayed out.* This simply means that the menu item isn't appropriate for what you're doing. Nothing happens if you select such a menu item.

Note   Menu items that are followed by an ellipsis (three dots) always display a dialog box. Menu commands that don't have an ellipsis are executed immediately. For example, the Insert⇨Cells command results in a dialog box because Excel needs more information about the command. The Insert⇨Rows command doesn't need a dialog box, and this command is issued immediately when you choose the command.

You can issue menu commands using the mouse or the keyboard. Although most users tend to prefer a mouse, others find that accessing the menus with the keyboard is more efficient. This is especially true if you're entering data into a worksheet. Using a mouse means that you have to move your hand, locate the mouse, move it and click it, and then move your hand back to the keyboard. Although this takes only a few seconds, those seconds add up.

To issue a menu command from the keyboard, press Alt and the menu's *hot key* at the same time (the hot key is the underlined letter in the menu). This displays the menu's menu items. Then, press the appropriate hot key for the menu item.

For example, to issue the Data⇨Sort command, press Alt+D, followed by S. You can keep the Alt key pressed while you press S, or not — it doesn't matter.

You also can press Alt alone, or F10. This selects the first menu (the File menu). Then you can use the direction keys to highlight the menu that you want and press Enter. Then use the direction keys to choose the appropriate menu item and press Enter again.

Using Shortcut Menus

Besides the omnipresent menu bar, discussed in the preceding section, Excel features a slew of what are known as *shortcut menus*. A shortcut menu is context sensitive — its contents depend on what you're doing at the time. Shortcut menus don't contain *all* of the relevant commands, just those that are most commonly used for whatever is selected. You can display a shortcut by right-clicking just about anything in Excel.

As an example, examine Figure 4-8, which shows the shortcut menu that appears when you right-click on a cell. The shortcut menu appears at the mouse pointer position, which makes it fast and efficient to select a command.

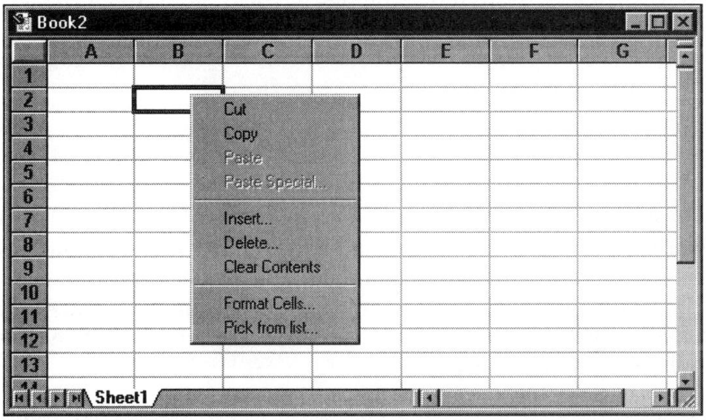

Figure 4-8: Right-clicking on a cell displays this shortcut menu.

Instant help for commands

Excel's menus and toolbars can be a bit daunting at times, especially for newcomers. One approach — the best approach, in my opinion — is to simply try things out and see what happens. If you're not that adventurous, there's an easy way to find what a particular menu command or toolbar button is used for.

When you select a command from the menu, look at the status bar on the bottom of the screen. It displays a description of the command. For the toolbar buttons, drag the mouse pointer over a button (but don't click the button). A small yellow *tooltip* appears that

tells you the name of the button, and the status bar shows a description of what the button does.

For context-sensitive help on a menu command or toolbar button, locate the Help button (shown in the accompanying figure) on the Standard toolbar. Click on this button and the mouse pointer turns into an arrow with a question mark beside it. Now, just select any menu command or tool-bar button, and Excel's help system displays help about the command or button you clicked. Note that the command itself won't be issued.

The shortcut menu that you see depends on what is currently selected. For example, if you're working with a chart, the shortcut menu that appears when you right-click on a chart part contains commands that are pertinent to what is selected. If you took the time to count them all, you would discover that Excel has 25 different shortcut menus.

Tip   Although shortcut menus were invented with mouse users in mind, you also can display a shortcut menu by pressing Shift+F10. Key-activated shortcut menus appear in the upper-left corner of the window.

Excel's Toolbars

Excel, like all leading applications, includes convenient graphical toolbars. Clicking on a button on a toolbar is just another way of issuing commands to Excel. In most cases, toolbar buttons are simply a substitute for a menu command. There are a few toolbar buttons, however, that don't have any menu equivalent. One example is the AutoSum button, which automatically inserts a formula to calculate the sum of a range of cells. This button does not have a menu equivalent.

By default, Excel displays two toolbars (named *Standard* and *Formatting*) directly below the menu bar. All told, Excel has 13 built-in toolbars. You have complete control over which toolbars are displayed and where they are located. In addition, you can even create custom toolbars made up of buttons that you find most useful.

Cross-Reference Learn how to create custom toolbars in Chapter 32.

Table 4-3 lists all of Excel's built-in toolbars.

Table 4-3 Excel's Built-In Toolbars	
Toolbar	**Use**
Standard	Issuing commonly used commands
Formatting	Changing how your worksheet or chart looks
Query and Pivot	Working with external database files and pivot tables
Chart	Manipulating charts
Drawing	Adding drawings and diagrams to a worksheet or chart
TipWizard	Displaying helpful tips
Forms	Creating custom dialog boxes and adding controls to worksheets
Stop Recording	Ending macro recording (one tool only)
Visual Basic	Writing macros in Visual Basic for Applications
Auditing	Identifying errors in your worksheet
Workgroup	Interacting with other users
Microsoft	Quickly launching or switching to another Microsoft application
Full Screen	Switching out of full-screen view (one tool only)

Sometimes, Excel automatically pops up a toolbar to help you with a particular task. For example, if you're working on a chart, Excel displays its Chart toolbar.

Hiding or showing toolbars

To hide or display a particular toolbar, choose the View⇨Toolbars command. Excel displays its Toolbars dialog box, shown in Figure 4-9. This dialog box shows a list of all toolbars that are available — the 13 built-in toolbars plus any custom toolbars. The toolbars that have a check mark next to them are currently visible. To hide a toolbar, click on it to remove the check mark. To display a toolbar, click on it to add a check mark. When you click on the OK button, Excel displays only the toolbars you specified.

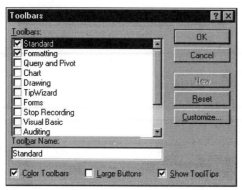

Figure 4-9: Choose which toolbars to display in the Toolbars dialog box.

Tip   The Toolbars dialog box has some other options with which you may want to experiment. If you don't want to see colored toolbar buttons, uncheck the Color Toolbars check box (this is useful if you have a monochrome display, as in a laptop). If you prefer larger buttons, check the Large Buttons check box. And if you find those pop-up tooltips distracting, uncheck the Show ToolTips check box. If you turn the tooltips off, you can still see a description of each button in the status bar at the bottom of the screen.

Moving toolbars

Toolbars can be moved to any of the four sides of Excel's window or be free floating. A free-floating toolbar can be dragged anywhere you want. You also can change its size simply by dragging any of its borders. To hide a free-floating toolbar, click on its Close button.

When a toolbar isn't free floating, it's said to be *docked*. A docked toolbar is stuck to the edge of Excel's window and doesn't have a title bar. Therefore, a docked toolbar can't be resized.

To move a toolbar (docked or free floating), click the mouse anywhere on the background of the toolbar (that is, anywhere except on a button) and drag it. When you drag it toward the window's edge, it automatically docks itself there. When a toolbar is docked, its shape changes to a single row or single column. You'll find, however, that toolbars that contain "nonbutton" buttons can't be docked to the left or right side. An example of a nonbutton is the Zoom control on the Standard toolbar — it's not the size of a normal button. Therefore, the Standard toolbar can't be docked on either the left or right side of the window.

Tip

If a toolbar is docked, you can double-click on its background to undock it. Similarly, you can double-click on the background of a free-floating toolbar to dock it.

Figure 4-10 shows a severe case of toolbar overload. It has a toolbar docked on each of the four edges, plus several floating toolbars.

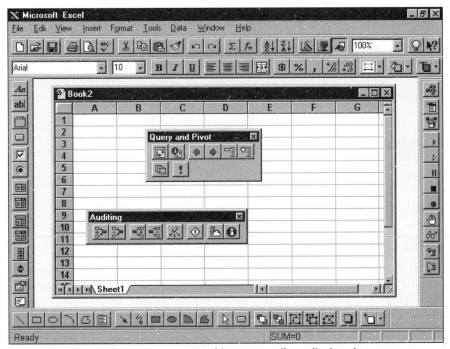

Figure 4-10: Normally, you won't want this many toolbars displayed at once.

Tip

Right-clicking on the background of a toolbar displays a shortcut menu. You can use this shortcut menu to display or hide toolbars. It's faster than using the View➪Toolbars command.

Learning more about toolbars

It would take many pages to describe all of the toolbar buttons available, so I won't even try. I leave it up to you to discover this handy feature on your own. But throughout the rest of the book, I point out toolbar buttons that might be useful in particular situations.

Chapter 32 discusses toolbars in more detail, including how to customize toolbars.

Shortcut Keys

Earlier in this chapter, I mention that some menu commands have equivalent shortcut keys. Usually, the shortcut key combination is displayed next to the menu item — providing a built-in way for you to learn the shortcuts as you select the commands.

Throughout the book, I point out the relevant shortcut keys as I discuss a particular topic.

 Appendix E lists all of the shortcut keys available in Excel.

Working with Dialog Boxes

Earlier in this chapter, you learn that menu items that end with an ellipsis (three dots) will result in a dialog box. All Windows programs use dialog boxes, so you may already be familiar with the concept.

About dialog boxes

You can think of a dialog box as Excel's way of getting more information from you about the command you selected. For example, if you choose the View⇨Zoom command (which changes the magnification of the worksheet), Excel can't carry out the command until it finds out from you what magnification level you want (see Figure 4-11). Dialog boxes can be simple or much more complicated. The Zoom dialog box is one of the simpler dialog boxes found in Excel. Notice that it's made up of several items, known as *controls*.

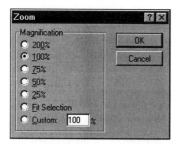

Figure 4-11: Excel's Zoom dialog box appears when you choose the View⇨Zoom command.

When a dialog box appears in response to your command, you make additional choices in the dialog box by manipulating the controls. When you're finished, click the OK button (or press Enter) to continue. If you change your mind, click the Cancel button (or press Escape) and nothing further will happen — it will be as if the dialog box never appeared.

If a dialog box obscures an area of your worksheet that you need to see, you can simply click on the dialog's title bar and drag it to another location. The title bar in a dialog box has two controls: A Help button (Question-mark icon) and a Close button. When you click on the Help button, the mouse pointer displays a question mark. You can click on any part of the dialog box to get a description. Clicking on the Close button is the same as clicking on the Cancel button.

Note   Although a dialog box looks like just another window, it works a little differently. When a dialog box is displayed, you can't do anything in the workbook until the dialog box is closed.

Dialog box controls

Most people find working with dialog boxes to be quite straightforward and natural. The controls usually work just as you would expect, and they can be manipulated with your mouse or directly from the keyboard.

The following sections describe the most common dialog box controls and show some examples.

Navigating dialog boxes using the keyboard

Although dialog boxes were designed with mouse users in mind, some users prefer to use the keyboard at times. With a bit of practice, you'll find that navigating a dialog box directly from the keyboard may be more efficient in some cases.

Every dialog box control has text associated with it, and this text always has one underlined letter (known as a *hot key* or an *accelera-*

tor key). You can access the control from the keyboard by pressing the Alt key along with the underlined letter. You also can use Tab to cycle through all of the controls on a dialog box. Shift+Tab cycles through the controls in reverse order.

When a control is selected, it appears with a darker outline. You can use the spacebar to activate a selected control.

Buttons

A button control is about as simple as it gets. Just click on it, and it does its thing. Every dialog box has at least one button and usually two. The OK button closes the dialog box and executes the command. The Cancel button closes the dialog box with no further action. If the text on a button is followed by an ellipsis, it means that clicking on the button will lead to another dialog box.

Pressing the Alt key along with the button's underlined letter is equivalent to clicking on the button. Pressing Enter is the same as clicking on the OK button, and pressing Esc is the same as clicking on the Cancel button.

Option buttons

Option buttons are sometimes known as radio buttons because they work like the preset station buttons on an old-fashioned car radio. Like these car radios, only one option button at a time can be "pressed." An option button is like choosing a single item on a multiple-choice test. When you click on an option button, the previously selected option button is unselected.

Option buttons are usually enclosed in a group box, and a single dialog box can have several sets of option buttons. Figure 4-12 shows an example of a dialog box with option buttons.

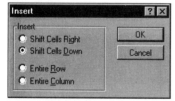

Figure 4-12: This dialog box has four option buttons.

Check boxes

A check box control is used to indicate whether an option is on or off. This is similar to responding to an item on a true-false test. Figure 4-13 shows a dialog box with several check boxes. Unlike option buttons, each check box is independent of the others. Clicking on a check box toggles the check mark on and off.

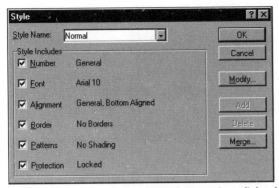

Figure 4-13: An example of check boxes in a dialog box.

Edit boxes

An edit box control accepts text that you type. Some edit boxes also let you specify a worksheet range by dragging in the worksheet. Figure 4-14 shows a dialog box with an edit box control.

Figure 4-14: An edit box control accepts text that you type. Some edit boxes let you specify a worskheet range by dragging in the worksheet.

Spinners

A spinner control makes it easy to specify a number. You can click on the arrows to increment or decrement the displayed value. A spinner is almost always paired with an edit box. You can enter the value directly into the edit box or use the spinner to change it to the desired value. Figure 4-15 shows a dialog box with several spinner controls.

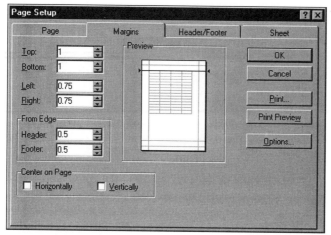

Figure 4-15: This dialog box has several spinner controls.

List boxes

A list box control contains a list of options from which you choose. If the list is longer than will fit in the list box, you can use its vertical scrollbar to scroll through the list. Figure 4-16 shows an example of a list box control.

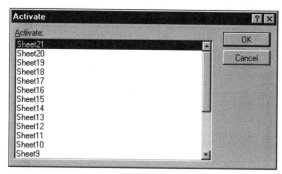

Figure 4-16: An example of a list box control in a dialog box.

Drop-down boxes

Drop-down boxes are similar to list boxes, but they show only a single option at a time. When you click on the arrow on a drop-down box, the list drops down to display additional choices. Figure 4-17 shows an example of a drop-down box control.

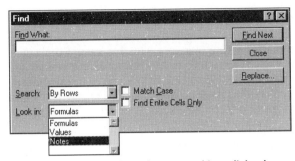

Figure 4-17: A drop-down box control in a dialog box.

Tabbed dialog boxes

Several of Excel's dialog boxes are "tabbed" dialog boxes. A tabbed dialog box includes notebook-like tabs, each of which is associated with a different panel. When you click on a tab, the dialog box changes to display a new panel, which has a new set of controls. The Options dialog box, which appears in response to the Tools⇨Options command, is a good example. This dialog box is shown in Figure 4-18. Notice that it has ten tabs, which makes it functionally equivalent to ten different dialog boxes.

Tabbed dialog boxes are quite convenient because you can make several changes in a single dialog box. When you've made all of your setting changes, click on OK or press Enter.

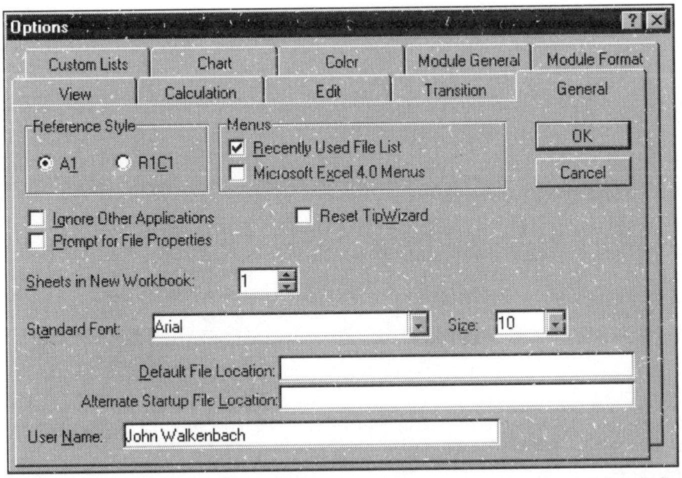

Figure 4-18: The Options dialog box is an example of a tabbed dialog box.

To select a tab using the keyboard, use Ctrl+PgUp or Ctrl+PgDn, or simply press the first letter of the tab that you wish to activate.

Summary

This chapter covers background information that is essential to using Excel efficiently. I discuss methods to manipulate windows (which hold workbooks), as well as several techniques to move around within a worksheet using the mouse or the keyboard. I also discuss the various methods used to issue commands to Excel: menus, shortcut menus, toolbar buttons, and shortcut key combinations. I conclude with a general discussion of dialog boxes — an element common to all Windows programs.

✦   ✦   ✦

Working with Files and Workbooks

♦ ♦ ♦ ♦

In This Chapter

Basic information
about files

Descriptions of the
files used by Excel

Workbook file
operations that you
must know about

Tips on protecting
your files from disaster

♦ ♦ ♦ ♦

Computer users won't get too far without understanding the concept of files. Every computer program uses files. In this chapter, I discuss how Excel uses files and what you need to know about files in order to use Excel.

Some Background on Files

A *file* is an entity that stores information on a disk. A hard disk is usually organized into directories (or folders, in the terminology of Windows 95) to facilitate the organization of files. For example, all of the files that comprise Excel are stored in a separate folder on your computer.

Files can be manipulated in several ways. They can be copied, renamed, deleted, or moved to another disk or folder. These types of file operations are usually performed using the tools in Windows 95 (although you also can perform these operations without leaving Excel).

Computer programs are stored in files, and they also store information that they use in files. Some programs (such as Excel) use files by loading them into memory. Others (such as database programs) access selective parts of a file directly from the disk and don't read the entire file into memory.

New! Windows 95 changes how you work with files. The main difference is that Windows 95 supports long filenames — up to 255 characters in length. Prior to Windows 95, files were limited to eight characters plus a three-character extension that described the type of file. For example, before Windows 95 you had to use a cryptic file name such as `TOPEMP95.XLS` to describe a workbook that listed the top employees for 1995. With Excel for Windows 95, you can call this workbook `Top Employees of 1995`.

Windows 95 also make it easy to access *properties* of files. Properties include information such as file type, size, when it was created, and so on. Excel 95 lets you access some additional custom properties of files that make it easy to locate and categorize your files. For example, you can store information that lets you quickly locate all workbook files that apply to a particular client.

How Excel Uses Files

When you installed Excel on your system, the Setup program copied a number of files to your hard disk and also created several new folders to hold the files. These files consist of the files that are needed to run Excel, plus some sample files and Help files. The Setup program also made (or modified) some entries in the Windows *Registry*. The Registry is a master database of sorts, which keeps track of the software installed on your system and also associates Excel's data files with Excel.

Excel's data files

Excel's primary file type is called a workbook file. When you open a workbook in Excel, the entire file is loaded into memory, and any changes that you make occur only in the copy that's in memory. If your system doesn't have enough memory to hold the file, Windows uses disk-based virtual memory to simulate actual memory. When you save the workbook, Excel saves the copy in memory to your disk, overwriting the previous copy of the file.

Table 5-1 lists the various types of files that Excel supports directly.

Foreign file formats supported

Although Excel's default file format is an XLS workbook file, it also can open and save files generated by several other applications. Table 5-2 contains a list of file formats that Excel can read and write.

Cross-Reference Chapter 22 covers file importing and exporting in detail.

Table 5-1
Data Files Used by Excel

File Type	Description
BAK	Backup file
XLA	Excel add-in file. Several add-ins are supplied with Excel, and you also can create your own add-ins by using the Tools⇨Make Add-In command from a VBA module
XLB	Excel toolbar configuration file
XLC	Excel 4 chart file*
XLL	Excel link library file
XLM	Excel 4 macro file*
XLS	Excel workbook file
XLT	Excel template file
XLW	Excel workspace file

* These files became obsolete beginning with Excel 5. Excel can still read and write these files for compatibility with previous versions, however.

Table 5-2
File Formats Supported by Excel

File Type	Description
WKS	1-2-3 Release 1 spreadsheet format**
WK1	1-2-3 Release 2 spreadsheet format***
WK3	1-2-3 Release 3 spreadsheet format***
WK4	1-2-3 for Windows spreadsheet format
WQ1	Quattro Pro for DOS spreadsheet format
DBF	dBASE database format
SLK	SYLK spreadsheet format
WB1	Quattro Pro for Windows spreadsheet format
CSV	Comma separated value text file format
TXT	Text file format
PRN	Text file format
DIF	Data interchange format

** Excel can open files in this format, but not save them.

*** When you open one of these files, Excel searches for the associated formatting file (either FMT or FM3) and attempts to translate the formatting.

Essential Workbook File Operations

This section describes the operations that you perform with workbook files: opening, saving, closing, deleting, and so on. As you read through this section, keep in mind that you can have any number of workbooks open at any time, and that at any given time only one workbook is the active workbook. The workbook's name is displayed in its title bar (or in Excel's title bar if the workbook is maximized).

Creating a new workbook

When you start Excel, it automatically creates a new (empty) workbook called Book1. This workbook exists only in memory and has not been saved to disk. By default, this workbook consists of 16 worksheets named Sheet1, Sheet2, and so on up to Sheet16. If you're starting a new project from scratch, you can use this blank workbook.

You can always create another new workbook in either of three ways:

> ✦ Use the File⇨New command.
>
> ✦ Click on the New Workbook button on the Standard toolbar (this button has an image of a sheet of paper).
>
> ✦ Press the Ctrl+N shortcut key combination.

You'll be greeted with a dialog box named New (see Figure 5-1). This is a tabbed dialog box that lets you choose a template for the new workbook. If you don't have any custom templates defined, the General tab displays only one option: Workbook. Clicking on this will give you a plain workbook. Templates that are included with Excel are listed in the Spreadsheet Solutions tab. If you choose one of these templates, your new workbook is based on the selected template file.

Cross-Reference I discuss templates later on in this chapter, and Chapter 33 discusses this topic in detail.

Note Clicking on the New button on the Standard toolbar bypasses the New dialog box and creates a new workbook immediately. If you want to create a new workbook based on a template, use either of the other methods.

Tip If you find that you almost always end up closing the default Book1 workbook that appears when you start Excel, you can set things up so that Excel starts without an empty workbook. To do so, you need to edit the command line that you use to start Excel. For example, if you start Excel using a shortcut on your Windows desktop, right-click on the shortcut icon and choose Properties from the menu. Click on the Shortcut tab and add **/e** after the command line listed in the Target field. Here's an example of a command line modified in this manner:

```
C:\MSOFFICE\EXCEL\EXCEL.EXE /e
```

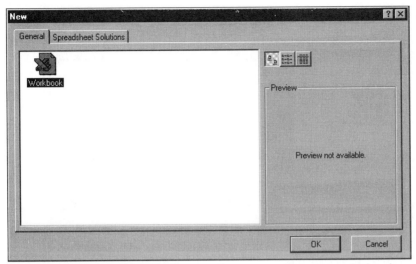

Figure 5-1: The New dialog box lets you choose a template upon which to base the new workbook.

Opening an existing workbook

There are several methods to open a workbook that has been saved on your disk:

✦ Use the File⇨Open command.

✦ Click the Open button on the Standard toolbar (the Open button has an image of a file folder opening up).

✦ Press the Ctrl+O shortcut key combination.

All of these methods result in the Open dialog box, shown in Figure 5-2.

You also can open an Excel workbook by double-clicking on its icon in any folder window. If Excel isn't running, it is started automatically. Or, you can drag a workbook icon into the Excel window to load the workbook.

If you want to open a file that you've used recently, it may be listed at the bottom of the drop-down File menu. This menu lists the last four files that you've worked on. Just click on the filename and the workbook opens for you (bypassing the Open dialog box).

New! The Open dialog box is quite different from previous versions of Excel. In Excel for Windows 95, the Open dialog box combines the features formerly available using the File⇨Find File command, plus many additional features.

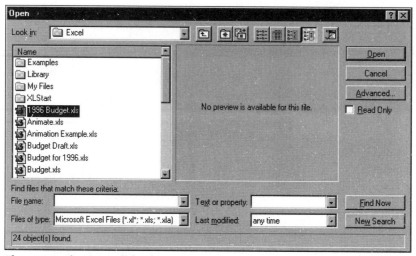

Figure 5-2: The Open dialog box.

To use this dialog box to open a workbook, you must provide two pieces of information: the name of the workbook file (specified in the File name field) and its folder (specified in the Look in field).

There's a lot going on in this dialog box, and it may be a bit overwhelming at first. You can ignore most of it because many of the controls deal with locating files. If you know what folder the file is in, it's simply a matter of specifying the folder and then selecting the filename. Click on OK and the file is opened. You also can just double-click the filename to open it.

> **Tip** You can hold down the Ctrl key and select multiple workbooks. When you click on OK, all of the selected workbook files will open.

> **Tip** Right-clicking on a filename in the Open dialog box displays a shortcut menu with lots of extra choices. For example, you can copy the file, delete it, modify its properties, and so on.

Specifying a folder

The Look in field is actually a drop-down box. Click on the arrow and the box expands to show your system components. You can select a different drive or directory from this list. The Up One Level icon (a file folder with an upward arrow) moves up one level in the folder hierarchy.

Filtering by file type

At the bottom of the Open dialog box, the drop-down list is labeled Files of type. When this dialog box is displayed, it shows Microsoft Excel Files (*.xl*, *.xls, *.xla). This means that the files displayed are filtered, and you see only files that have an extension beginning with the letters XL. In other words, you see only standard Excel files: workbooks, add-ins, and templates.

If you want to open a file of a different type, click on the arrow in the drop-down list and select the file type that you want to open. This will change the filtering and display only the desired files.

Favorite places

Your hard disk probably has dozens of folders, and you can store your Excel workbooks in any folder. If you keep your workbooks in one folder, they will be easy to find. If you have many workbook files, however, you'll probably want to organize them into more folders. For example, you might have a folder for business files and a folder for personal files.

Excel helps you locate workbooks by keeping track of your "favorite places" — folders that you specify to hold your workbook files. Two icons in the Open dialog box are relevant here (see Figure 5-3):

> **Look in Favorites:** This button displays the folders and files that you have designated as favorites.

> **Add to Favorites:** This button lets you add a folder or file to your list of favorites.

This feature can be quite handy, since it eliminates the need to traverse nested folders to find a particular file. If you store your Excel workbooks in more than one folder, it's a good idea to add all of these additional folders to your favorites list. Then, you can just click the Look in Favorites icon to display a list of those folders.

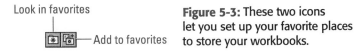

Figure 5-3: These two icons let you set up your favorite places to store your workbooks.

File display preferences

The Open dialog box can display your workbook filenames in four different styles:

✦ **List:** As a list of filenames only, displayed in multiple columns

✦ **Details:** As a list of filenames with details about each file (its size, file type, and when it was last modified)

✦ **Properties:** As a list of filenames with file properties displayed in a separate panel for the selected file

✦ **Preview:** As a list of filenames with a preview screen displayed in a separate panel for the selected file

You control the style by clicking on any of the four icons in the upper part of the Open dialog box (see Figure 5-4). The style that you choose is entirely up to you.

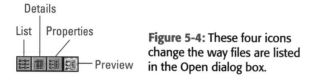

Figure 5-4: These four icons change the way files are listed in the Open dialog box.

Commands and settings

Commands and Settings, the last icon in the Open dialog box, is a bit unusual because clicking on it displays a shortcut menu. Here are the menu items and what they do:

Open Read Only: Opens the selected file in read-only mode. This is equivalent to checking the Read Only check box and opening the file.

Print: Opens the selected file, prints it, and then closes it.

Properties: Displays the Properties dialog box for the selected file. This lets you examine or modify the file's properties without actually opening it.

Sorting: Opens the Sort By dialog box that lets you change the order in which the files are listed. You can sort the file list by name, size, file type, or date.

Search Subfolders: This option displays all matching files in all folders beneath the current folder. If the current folder is your hard drive, selecting this option shows you all matching files on the entire drive.

Group Files by Folder: Shows the files organized by folders. If this option is not checked, the files are displayed without their identifying folder. This is relevant only if the Search Subfolders option is selected.

Map Network Drive: Displays a dialog box that lets you map a network directory to a drive designator.

Saved Searches: Lets you recall a file search that you previously saved.

Searching for files

A common problem among computer users is "losing" a file. You know you saved a file, but you don't remember the folder that you saved it in. Fortunately, Excel makes it fairly easy to locate such lost files using the Open dialog box. This is a rather complex subject, and I address it in detail later in this chapter.

Opening a file as read-only

You may have a workbook that you don't want to modify in any way. If so, you can open the file as read-only to ensure that the original copy is not modified. A read-only file can't be overwritten. You can, however, save the workbook with a different name.

To open a file as read-only, click the Read Only check box in the Open dialog box. Or, as mentioned previously, you can use the shortcut menu that appears when you click the Commands and Settings icon.

Opening workbooks automatically

Many people find that they work on the same workbooks day after day. If this de-scribes you, you'll be happy to know that there's a way to have Excel open specific workbook files automatically whenever you start Excel.

The XLStart folder is located within the Excel folder. Any workbook files (excluding template files) that are stored in this folder open automatically when Excel starts. If one or more files are opened automatically from this folder, Excel won't start up with a blank workbook.

 Note　You can specify an alternate startup folder in addition to the XLStart folder. Choose the Tools⇨Options command and select the General tab. Enter a new folder name in the field labeled Alternate Startup File Location. After doing so, Excel automatically opens all workbook files in both the XLStart folder and the alternate folder that you specified.

Saving workbooks

When you're working on a workbook, it's vulnerable to day-ruining events such as power failures and system crashes. Therefore, you should save your work to disk often. Saving a file takes only a few seconds. But re-creating four hours of lost work takes about four hours.

Excel provides four ways to save your workbook:

✦ Use the File⇨Save command.

✦ Click the Save button on the Standard toolbar.

✦ Press the Ctrl+S shortcut key combination.

✦ Press the Shift+F12 shortcut key combination.

If your workbook has already been saved, it's saved again using the same filename. The original version of the file is overwritten. If you want to save the workbook to a new file, use the File⇨Save As command (or press F12).

If your workbook has never been saved, its title bar displays a name such as Book1 or Book2. Although Excel lets you use these generic workbook names for filenames, it's not recommended. Therefore, the first time that you save a new workbook, Excel displays the Save As dialog box (see Figure 5-5) to let you provide a more meaningful name.

File naming rules

Excel's workbook files are subject to the same rules that apply to other Windows 95 files. A filename can be up to 255 characters, including spaces. This lets you (finally) give meaningful names to your files. You can't, however, use any of the following characters in your filenames:

\ (slash)

? (question mark)

: (colon)

* (asterisk)

" (quote)

< (less than)

> (greater than)

| (vertical bar)

You can use uppercase and lowercase letters in your names to improve readability. The filenames aren't case sensitive, however. If you have a file named My 1995 Budget and try to save another file with the name MY 1995 BUDGET, Excel asks whether you want to overwrite the original file.

If you plan to share your files with others who use a previous version of Excel, you should make sure that the filename is no longer than eight characters with no spaces. Otherwise, the filename will appear rather strange. For example, a file named My 1995 Budget will appear as MY1995~1.XLS. This is because Windows assigns every file an eight-character filename to be compatible with pre-Windows 95 operating systems.

The Save As dialog box is somewhat similar to the Open dialog box. Again, you need to specify two pieces of information: the workbook's name and the folder in which to store it. If you want to save the file to a different folder, select the desired folder in the Save in field. If you want to create a new folder, click on the Create New Folder icon in the Save As dialog box. The new folder is created within the folder that's displayed in the Save in field.

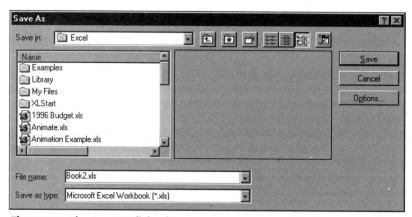

Figure 5-5: The Save As dialog box.

After you've selected the folder, enter the filename in the File name field. There is no need to specify a file extension. Excel adds it automatically, based on the file type specified in the Save as type field.

If a file with the same name already exists in the folder you specified, Excel asks whether you want to overwrite the file with the new file. Be careful with this because there is no way to recover the previous file.

Caution　It's important to remember that saving a file overwrites the previous version of the file on disk. If you open a workbook and then completely mess it up, don't save the file! Instead, close the workbook without saving it, and then open the good copy on disk.

The default file location

When you save a workbook file for the first time, the Save As dialog box proposes a folder in which to save it. Normally, this is the folder where Excel is installed. If you like, you can change the default file location. To do so, choose the Tools⇨Options command and click on the General tab in the Options dialog box. Then enter the folder's path into the field labeled Default File Location. After doing so, the Save As dialog box defaults to this folder.

Saving your work automatically

If you're the type who gets so wrapped up in your work that you forget to save your file, you may be interested in Excel's AutoSave feature. AutoSave automatically saves your workbooks at a prespecified interval. Using this feature requires that you load an add-in file. This add-in is included with Excel, but it's not normally installed. To load the AutoSave add-in, select the Tools⇨Add-Ins command. This displays a dialog box. Click on AutoSave in the list of add-ins and then click on OK. The add-in will be loaded every time you run Excel. If you no longer want to use AutoSave, repeat the process and uncheck the AutoSave add-in.

When AutoSave is loaded, the Tools menu has a new menu item: AutoSave. Selecting the Tools⇨AutoSave command displays the dialog box shown in the accompanying figure.

This dialog box lets you specify the time interval for saving. In general, you should specify a time interval equal to the maximum amount of time that you're willing to lose. For example, if you don't mind losing 15 minutes of work, set the interval for 15 minutes.

Option buttons let you choose between saving all open workbooks or just the active workbook. Another option lets you specify whether you want to be prompted before the save takes place. If you choose to be prompted, you have the opportunity to cancel the save if you're right in the middle of something important.

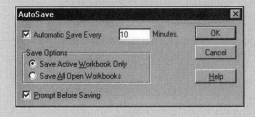

Note, however, that if you override the default folder in the Save As dialog box, the new folder becomes the default. So, if you use the File⇨Save As command to save another workbook, Excel proposes the new default folder.

File save options

The Save As dialog box has a button labeled Options. When you click on this button, Excel displays its Save Options dialog box, shown in Figure 5-6. This dialog box lets you set the following several options.

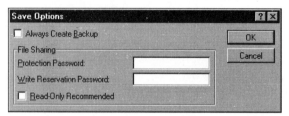

Figure 5-6: The Save Options dialog box.

Always Create Backup: If this option is set, the existing version of the workbook is renamed as a BAK file before the workbook is saved. Doing this makes it possible to go back to the previously saved version of your workbook. Some users like to use this option because it adds another level of safety. Just be aware that your worksheet files will take up about twice as much disk space, so it's a good idea to delete the backup files occasionally.

Protection Password: If you enter a password, the password is required before anyone can open the workbook. You'll be asked to enter the password a second time to confirm it. Passwords can be up to 15 characters long and are case sensitive.

Caution Be careful with this option just described because it is impossible to open the workbook if you forget the password.

Write Reservation Password: This is the password required to save changes to the workbook under the same filename. Use this option if you want to make sure that changes aren't made to the original version of the workbook. In other words, the workbook can be saved with a new name, but a password is required to overwrite the original version.

Read-Only Recommended: If this option is checked, the file can't be saved under its original name. This is another way to ensure that a workbook file isn't overwritten.

Workbook summary information

When you save a file for the first time by closing the Save As dialog box, Excel prompts you for summary information by displaying the Properties dialog box shown in Figure 5-7. This lets you specify lots of descriptive information about the workbook and also displays some details about the file.

Note The Properties dialog box appears by default. If you'd rather not be bothered with this dialog box, just press Enter to dismiss it. Or, you can set things up so that it never appears. To do so, select the Tools⇨Options command, click on the General tab, and remove the check mark from the Prompt for File Properties check box.

The Properties dialog box has five tabs:

General: This panel displays general information about the file — its name, size, location, when it was created, and so on. You can't change any of the information in this panel.

Summary: This panel appears by default when you first save the file. It contains eight fields of information that you can enter and modify. You can use the information in this panel to quickly locate workbooks that meet certain criteria. This is discussed later in the chapter.

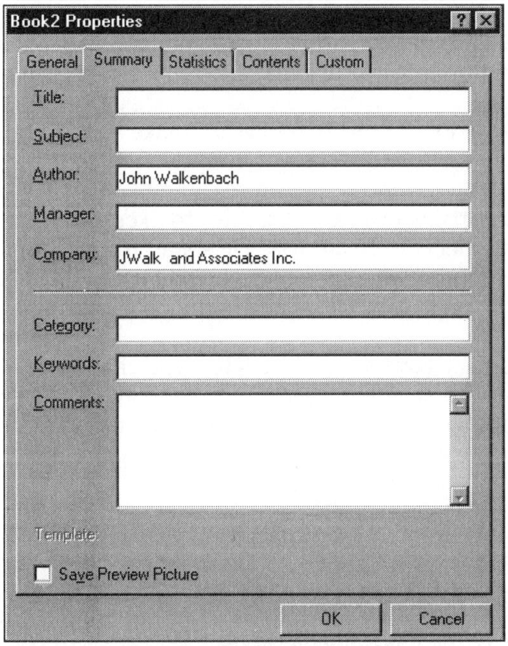

Figure 5-7: You can provide all sorts of information about your workbook in the Properties dialog box.

Statistics: This panel shows additional information about the file, and it can't be changed.

Contents: This panel displays the names of the sheets in the workbook, arranged by sheet type (worksheets, charts, VBA modules, and so on).

Custom: This panel can be quite useful if you use it consistently. Basically, it lets you store a variety of information about the file in sort of a database. For example, if the workbook deals with a client named Smith and Jones Corp., you can keep track of this bit of information and use it to help locate the file later.

> **Note** You also can access the Properties dialog box for the active workbook at any time by selecting the File⇨Properties command from the menu. In addition, you can view the properties of a workbook from the Open dialog box. Right-click on the file in which you're interested and choose Properties from the shortcut menu.

Saving files in older formats

If your colleagues also use Excel, you may find yourself exchanging workbook files. If so, it's important that you know which version of Excel they use. Excel 5 and Excel for Windows 95 can share files with few, if any, problems.

> **Caution** The incompatibilities that may arise involve the VBA macro language. The version of VBA in Excel for Windows 95 contains several new features that will not work in Excel 5.

If you send a workbook to someone who uses an earlier version of Excel (pre-Excel 5), however, you must remember to save the file in a format that the earlier version can read.

> **Note** If the file will be used by someone who doesn't use Windows 95, make sure that you use a file name with eight or fewer characters.

Excel 5 was the first version to use multisheet workbooks. Prior to Excel 5, worksheets, chart sheets, and macro sheets were all stored in separate files. Consequently, if you share a multisheet workbook with someone who still uses one of these older versions, you must save each sheet separately — and in the proper format.

The Save As dialog box has a field labeled Save as type. This lets you choose the format in which to save the file. For example, if you need to send a workbook with three worksheets in it to a colleague who uses Excel 4, you must save it as three separate files, and make sure that you select the Microsoft Excel 4.0 Worksheet option from the Save as type drop-down box (see Figure 5-8).

Closing workbooks

When you're finished with a workbook, you should close it to free the memory it uses. You can close a workbook using any of the following methods:

✦ Use the File⇨Close command.

✦ Click on the Close button in the workbook's title bar.

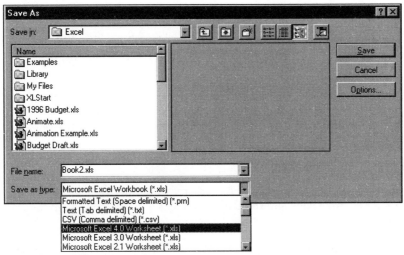

Figure 5-8: You can save an Excel workbook in a format that is readable with previous versions of Excel.

✦ Double-click on the Control icon in the workbook's title bar.

✦ Press the Ctrl+F4 shortcut key.

✦ Press the Ctrl+W shortcut key.

If you've made any changes to your workbook since it was last saved, Excel asks whether you want to save the workbook before closing it.

Tip To close all open workbooks, press the Shift key and choose the File➪Close All command. This command appears only when you hold down the Shift key while you click on the File menu. Excel closes each workbook, prompting you for each unsaved workbook.

Using workspace files

As you know, you can work with any number of workbook files at a time. For example, you might have a project that uses two workbooks, and you like to arrange the windows in a certain way to make it easy to access them both. Fortunately, Excel lets you save your entire workspace to a file. *Workspace,* as used here, means all of the workbooks and their screen positions and window sizes — sort of a snapshot of Excel's current state. Then, you can open the workspace file and Excel is set up exactly as it was when you saved your workspace.

To save your workspace, use the File➪Save Workspace command. Excel proposes the name resume.xlw for the workspace file. You can use this name or enter a different name in the File name field. Click on the Save button, and the workspace will be saved to disk.

Caution It's important to understand that a workspace file doesn't include the workbook files themselves. It includes only the information needed to re-create the workspace. The workbooks in the workspace are saved in standard workbook files. Therefore, if you distribute a workspace file to a coworker, make sure that you also include the workbook files to which the workspace file refers.

Tip If you save your workspace file in the XLStart folder, Excel opens the workspace file automatically when it starts up. This is very handy if you tend to work with the same files everyday, because you can essentially pick up where you left off the previous day.

Deleting a workbook

When you no longer need a workbook file, you may want to delete it from your disk. Doing so will free disk space and reduce the number of files displayed in the Open dialog box.

There are many ways to delete a file using Windows 95, and you can even delete files directly from Excel. You can right-click on a filename in the Open dialog box and choose Delete from the shortcut menu (see Figure 5-9).

Tip If your system is set up to use the Recycle Bin (which is the default setting for Windows 95), you may be able to recover a deleted file later if you discover that it was deleted accidentally.

Finding a workbook

New! One of the best new features in Excel for Windows 95 is its comprehensive tools for cataloging and locating workbook files. That, combined with the capability to use long filenames, should help put an end to the perennial problem of "losing" files.

Using this feature can be a bit confusing at first, but once you get the hang of it you'll discover its advantages. The searching all takes place from the Open dialog box. You can search for files based on

   ✦ The name of the file

   ✦ The type of file

   ✦ Text contained in the file

   ✦ Properties associated with the file

   ✦ When the file was last modified

In the following sections I describe the types of searches that you can perform.

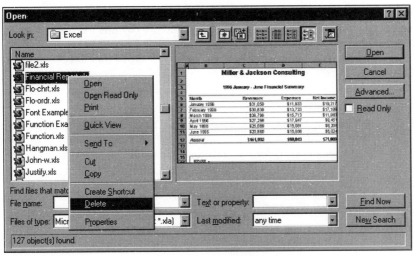

Figure 5-9: You can delete a file without leaving Excel.

Identifying the search scope

Before beginning your search for a file, you must identify the scope of the search. This can be very broad (My Computer) or quite narrow (a single folder). You specify the search scope in the Look in field of the Open dialog box. You can choose My Computer to search all local devices, Network Neighborhood to search network devices, or select a particular folder either locally or on a network.

Most of the time you'll want to search all subfolders also. To specify this, click the Commands and Settings button and select Search Subfolders. If you want the list of found files to be organized by folder, also select the Group files by folder option.

Searching by filename

If you know the filename (or approximate filename), enter it in the File name field. If you aren't sure of the exact filename, you can use wildcard characters to specify an approximate match. Use a question mark (?) as a placeholder for a single character and an asterisk (*) as a placeholder for any number of characters. For example, if you know that the file has the word *Budget* in it, you can enter ***Budget*** to find all file names that contain the word *budget*. To start the search, click the Find Now button.

Note   Some searches may take quite a long time. To stop a search, click the Stop button. The Stop button replaces the Find Now button when a search is in progress.

Searching by file type

The Files of type field lets you specify the type of files to locate. Normally, this will be the default, Microsoft Excel Files. But you can search for other file types by clicking the drop-down arrow and choosing from the list of file types that Excel can open. To start the search, click the Find Now button.

Searching for text in a file

Often, you won't be able to remember the file name, but you will remember a particular piece of information in the file. For example, you may have prepared a report that dealt with company benefits. If your search for a file name that contains *Benefits* fails, you can try a text search for the word *Benefits*. After all, it's quite likely that your worksheet includes this word at least once.

To perform a text search, enter the word or phrase that you're looking for in the field labeled Text or property. Then click the Find Now button to start the search.

Searching by properties

Excel workbooks have a set of properties. Some properties can't be changed, but many can. For example, one of a file's properties is the date and time that it was last accessed. You can't change this property directly — it's automatically updated by the operating system. You can set or examine properties for workbooks using the File⇨Properties command.

To search for files with a particular property, enter the property into the Text or property field and click the Find Now button to begin the search.

Searching by file modification date

You can also search for files based on the date they were last modified. Click the Last modified drop-down arrow, and you'll get a list that represents times: today, last week, this week, and so on. Select the time that matches your needs and click the Find Now button to begin the search.

Combining searches

As you can see, Excel offers some powerful search capabilities. It's even more powerful than you may think, since you can combine these different types of searches. For example, you can search for a file that contains specific text *and* was last modified yesterday. You set up these combined searches by entering criteria into more than one of the fields discussed above.

Note The Open dialog box has another button, labeled Advanced. This button brings up a dialog box called Advanced Find. This box has several additional search features that let you define more specific criteria. Most users will have no need for such sophisticated file searches.

Sharing workbooks with others

Cross-Reference If your system is connected to a network, there are some other issues related to workbook files of which you should be aware. I devote an entire chapter (Chapter 21) to workgroup issues.

Using Template Files

Excel has always had the capability to work with template files, but, oddly, Microsoft never included any template files until Excel for Windows 95. The latest version of Excel comes with ten professional templates developed by Village Software, Inc. You might be able to save yourself a lot of work by using these templates instead of creating a new workbook from scratch.

About templates

A template is basically a worksheet that's all set up with formulas and is ready for you to enter data. The templates distributed with Excel are very nicely formatted and relatively easy to customize. When you open a new workbook based on the template, you save the workbook to a new file. In other words, you don't overwrite the template.

Here is a list of the templates that are included with Excel 95. These templates are located in the Spreadsheet Solutions folder.

Business Planner: Helps you create an income statement, balance sheet, and cash flow summary.

Car Lease Manager: Helps you decide how to negotiate a car lease.

Change Request: Helps you track problems and request fixes to products or processes.

Expense Statement: Helps you create expense report forms and a log to track them.

Invoice: Helps you create invoices.

Loan Manager: Helps you understand the cost of borrowing money and how to save money doing it.

Personal Budgeter: Helps you create a personal budget to track spending and plan savings.

Purchase Order: Helps you create purchase orders to send to vendors.

Sales Quote: Helps you create sales quotes for prospective customers.

Timecard: Helps you create a schedule for managing hourly employees.

Note The Spreadsheet Solutions templates are handy, but be aware that they include a lot of overhead — several worksheets, dialog sheets, a (hidden) macro sheet, and a custom toolbar. Consequently, the workbooks that you generate using these templates might be larger than you would expect. On the positive side, studying how these templates are designed can provide advanced users with some great tips.

Example of using a template

To demonstrate how to make use of the templates, I provide a quick demonstration using the `Invoice` template.

1. Select the File⇨New command (or press Ctrl+N). Excel responds by displaying the New dialog box.

2. Click on the Spreadsheet Solutions tab in the New dialog box. This displays a list of all templates available in that directory.

3. Select the template named `Invoice` and click OK. Excel opens the `Invoice` template, and the workbook's temporary name is `Invoice1` (see Figure 5-10). In addition, the custom toolbar for this template also is displayed.

4. Because you've never used this template before, it's a good idea to read the help file that describes it. Click on the Template Help button on the Invoice toolbar (it has a question mark), and you get brief instructions on how to proceed.

5. The first step is to customize the template. Click on the Customize button, which is located directly on the worksheet. This activates a different worksheet (named Customize Your Invoice). You can simply fill in the blanks with information about your company. The information you enter is transferred to the Invoice worksheet.

6. When you've filled in all of the information on the Customize Your Invoice sheet, click the sheet tab labeled Invoice to reactivate the Invoice worksheet. You see that the invoice now contains the customized information you entered.

7. Fill out the invoice with customer information and product information. Formulas perform the calculations and display the total at the bottom. Notice that some cells have a red dot. These cells contain tips that you can read by moving the mouse over the cell (don't click). These tips provide additional information about what's expected in the cells.

8. You may want to assign a number to the invoice. You can enter one manually, or you can click on the Assign a Number button on the Invoice toolbar to automatically assign a unique number.

9. At this point, you may want to take advantage of a very useful feature that captures the data you entered into a database. To do so, click on the toolbar button labeled Capture Data in a Database. This saves the information in a different workbook file, along with other invoices that you generate from the template.

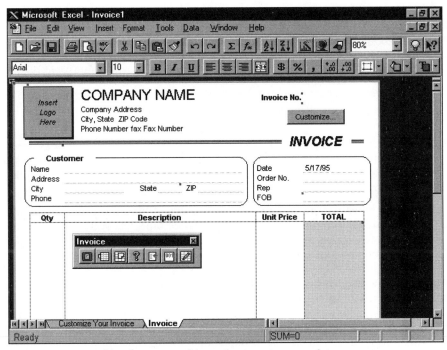

Figure 5-10: A workbook generated from the `Invoice` template.

If any of these templates appear to be useful, I urge you to check them out and work with them a while. They may seem a bit overwhelming at first, but they can save you many hours of work.

Cross-Reference Chapter 33 discusses templates in more detail and describes how to create your own template files.

Protecting Your Work

The final topic in this chapter offers a few words on backing up your work to protect yourself from disaster — or at least save yourself the inconvenience of repeating your work. Earlier in the chapter, you learn how to make Excel create a backup copy of your workbook when you saved the file. That's a good idea, but it certainly isn't the only backup protection you should use.

If you've been around computers for a while, you probably know that hard disks aren't perfect. I've seen many hard disks fail for no apparent reason and with absolutely no advance warning. In addition, files can get corrupted — which usually makes them unreadable and essentially worthless. If a file is truly important, you need to take extra steps to ensure its safety. There are several backup options for ensuring the safety of individual files:

Keep a backup copy of the file on the same drive. This is essentially what happens when you select the Always Create A Backup option when you save a workbook file. Although this offers some protection if you create a mess from the worksheet, it won't do you any good if the entire hard drive crashes.

Keep a backup copy on a different hard drive. This assumes, of course, that your system has more than one hard drive. This offers more protection than the preceding method because it's quite unlikely that both hard drives would fail. If the entire system is destroyed or stolen, however, you're out of luck.

Keep a backup copy on a network server. This assumes that your system is connected to a server on which you can write files. This method is fairly safe. If the network server is located in the same building, however, you're at risk if the entire building burns down or is otherwise destroyed.

Keep a backup copy on a removable medium. This is the safest method. Using a removable medium, such as a floppy disk or tape, lets you physically take the backup to another location. So, if your system (or the entire building) is damaged, your backup copy remains intact.

Most people with good backup habits acquired them because they've been burned in the past (myself included).

Note   Windows 95 comes with software that you can use to back up your entire system. Consult your Windows 95 manual or online help for details.

Summary

This chapter covers the rather broad topic of files. I start with an overview of how computers use files and narrow the scope to cover how Excel uses files. The chapter includes a discussion of the essential file operations you perform from Excel, including creating new workbook files, opening existing files, saving files, and closing files. I also discuss Excel's handy file-searching features that let you locate files quickly, no matter where they are stored. I conclude with an introduction to template files and demonstrate how to use one of the ten business templates that come with Excel.

✦   ✦   ✦

Entering and Editing Worksheet Data

Spreadsheets are used to store data and perform calculations. This Schapter discusses the various types of data that you can enter into Excel.

Types of Worksheet Data

As you know, an Excel workbook can hold any number of worksheets, and each worksheet is made up of cells. A cell can hold any of three types of data:

◆ A value

◆ Text

◆ A formula

Note An Excel worksheet also can hold charts, drawings, diagrams, pictures, buttons, and other objects. These objects actually reside on the worksheet's *draw layer,* which is an invisible layer on top of each worksheet. I discuss the draw layer in Chapter 14. This chapter is concerned only with data you enter into worksheet cells.

Values

Values, also known as numbers, represent a quantity of some type: sales, number of employees, atomic weights, test scores, and so on. Values that you enter into cells can be used in formulas or provide the basis for charts. Values also can be dates (such as 6/9/95) or times (such as 3:24 a.m.), and you'll see that you can manipulate these types of values quite efficiently.

Figure 6-1 shows a worksheet with some values entered in it.

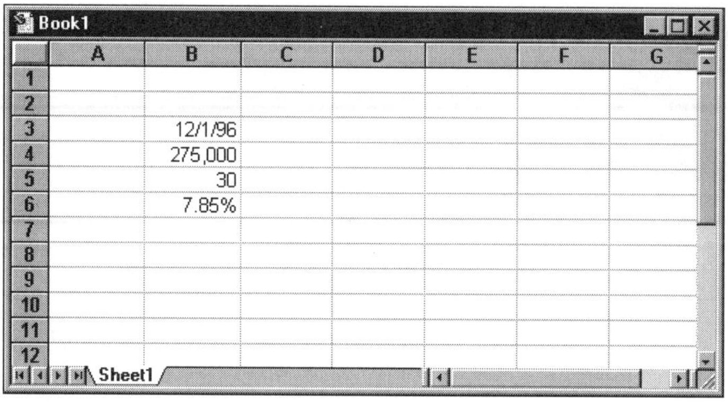

Figure 6-1: Values entered in a worksheet.

Text

Most worksheets also include plain text in some of their cells. You can insert text to serve as labels for values, headings for columns, or to provide instructions about the worksheet. Text that begins with a number is still considered text. For example, if you enter an address such as **1425 Main St.** into a cell, Excel considers this to be text rather than a value.

Figure 6-2 shows a worksheet with text in some of the cells. In this case, the text is used to clarify what the values mean.

Excel's numerical limitations

New users often are curious about the types of values that Excel can deal with. In other words, how large can numbers be? And how accurate are large numbers?

Excel's numbers are precise up to 15 digits. For example, if you enter a large value such as 123,123,123,123,123,123 (18 digits), Excel actually stores it with only 15 digits of precision: 123,123,123,123,123,000. This may seem quite limiting, but in practice it rarely causes any problems.

Here are some of Excel's other numerical limits:

Largest positive number: 9.9E+307

Smallest negative number: −9.9E+307

Smallest positive number: 1E−307

Largest negative number: −1E−307

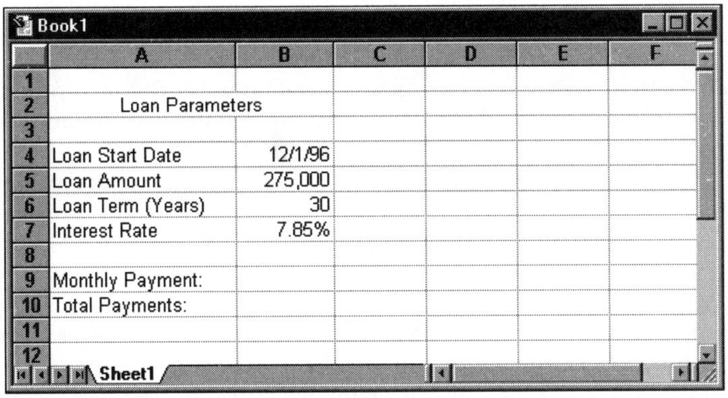

Figure 6-2: This worksheet consists of text and values.

Formulas

Formulas are what make a spreadsheet a spreadsheet — otherwise, you'd just have a strange word processor that was very good working with tables. Excel lets you enter powerful formulas that use the values (or text) in cells to calculate a result. When you enter a formula into a cell, the formula's result appears in the cell. If you change any of the values used by a formula, the formula recalculates and shows the new result. Figure 6-3 shows a worksheet with values, text, and formulas.

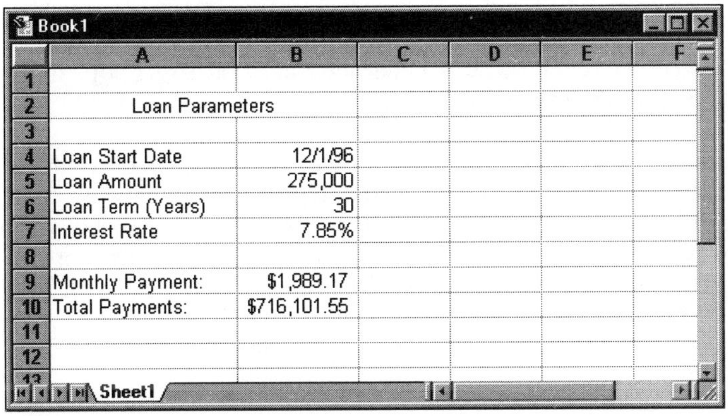

Figure 6-3: The cells in the last row of this worksheet contain formulas to calculate the sum of the values.

Cross-Reference Chapter 9 discusses formulas in detail.

Entering Values

Entering values into a cell is quite easy. Just move the cell pointer to the appropriate cell (this makes it the active cell), enter the value, and press Enter. The value is displayed in the cell, and it also appears in Excel's formula bar. The formula bar displays the contents of the active cell. You can, of course, include decimal points when entering values and dollar signs; plus signs, minus signs, and commas also are allowed. If you precede a value with a minus sign or enclose it in parentheses, Excel considers it to be a negative number.

Note   Sometimes, the value that you enter won't be displayed exactly as you enter it. More specifically, if you enter a very large number, it may be converted to scientific notation. For example, if you enter **123456789**, it is displayed as **1.23E+08**. This represents "1.23 times 10 to the eighth power." Notice, however, that the formula bar displays the value that you entered originally. Excel simply reformatted the value so that it would fit into the cell. If you make the column wider, the number displays as you entered it.

Later in this chapter I discuss the various ways to format values so that they appear differently.

Entering Text

Entering text into a cell is just as easy as entering a value: Activate the cell, type the text, and press Enter. A cell can contain a maximum of 255 characters. If you type an exceptionally long text entry into a cell, the characters appear to wrap around when they reach the right edge of the window, and the formula bar expands so that the text wraps around. When you've typed the 255th character in a cell, Excel pops up a message that tells you that the text is too long.

What happens when you enter a label that's longer than its column's current width? If the cells to the immediate right are blank, Excel displays the text in its entirety, spilling the entry into adjacent cells. If an adjacent cell is not blank, Excel displays as much of the text as possible (the full text is contained in the cell; it's just not displayed). If you need to display a long text entry that's adjacent to a cell with an entry, you can edit your text to make it shorter, increase the width of the column, or wrap the text within the cell so that it occupies more than one line.

Dates and Times

Often, you need to enter dates and times into your worksheet. To Excel, a date or a time is simply treated as a value — but it's formatted to appear as a date or a time.

If you work with dates, you need to understand Excel's system for working with dates. Excel handles dates using a serial number system. The earliest date that Excel can understand is January 1, 1900. This date has a serial number of 1. January 2, 1900, has a serial number of 2, and so on. This system makes it easy to deal with dates in formulas. For example, you can enter a formula to calculate the number of days between two dates.

Most of the time, you don't have to be concerned with Excel's serial number date system. You can simply enter a date in a familiar format, and Excel takes care of the details behind the scenes.

Here is a sampling of the date formats that Excel recognizes. After entering a date, you can format it to display in a different date format (I discuss such formatting later in the chapter).

Entered into a Cell	Excel's Interpretation
6-1-95	June 1, 1995
6-1-1995	June 1, 1995
6/1/95	June 1, 1995
6/1/1995	June 1, 1995
6-1/95	June 1, 1995
June 1, 1995	June 1, 1995
Jun 1	June 1 of the current year
June 1	June 1 of the current year
6/1	June 1 of the current year
6-1	June 1 of the current year

Caution   As you can see, Excel is rather smart when it comes to recognizing dates that you enter into a cell. It's not perfect, however. For example, Excel does *not* recognize any of the following entries as dates: June 1 1995, Jun-1 1995, and Jun-1/1995. Rather, it interprets these entries as text. If you plan to use dates in formulas, make sure that the date you enter is actually recognized as a date; otherwise, your formulas will produce incorrect results.

When working with times, you simply extend Excel's date serial number system to include decimals. In other words, Excel works with times by using fractional days. For example, the date serial number for June 1, 1995, is 34851. Noon (halfway through the day) is represented internally as 34851.5.

Again, you normally don't have to be concerned with these serial numbers (or fractional serial numbers for times). Just enter the time into a cell in a recognized format.

Here are some examples of time formats that Excel recognizes.

Entered into a Cell	Excel's Interpretation
11:30:00 am	11:30 a.m.
11:30:00 AM	11:30 a.m.
11:30 pm	11:30 p.m.
11:30	11:30 a.m.

The preceding samples don't have a day associated with them. You also can combine dates and times, however, as follows:

Entered into a Cell	Excel's Interpretation
6/1/95 11:30	11:30 a.m. on June 1, 1995

Changing or Erasing Values and Text

It should come as no surprise that you can change the contents of a cell after the fact. After you enter a value or text into a cell, you can modify it in a number of ways:

✦ Erase the cell's contents.

✦ Replace the cell's contents with something else.

✦ Edit the cell's contents.

Erasing the contents of a cell

To erase the value, text, or formula in a cell, just activate the cell and press Delete. To erase more than one cell, select all of the cells that you want to erase, and then press Delete. Pressing the Delete key removes the cell's contents but doesn't remove any formatting (such as bold, italic, or a different number format) that you may have applied to the cell.

For more control over what gets deleted, you can use the Edit⇨Clear command. This menu item leads to a submenu with four additional choices (see Figure 6-4). These choices are described as follows:

All: Clears everything from the cell

Formats: Clears only the formatting and leaves the value, text, or formula

Contents: Clears only the cell's contents and leaves the formatting

Notes: Clears the note (if one exists) attached to the cell

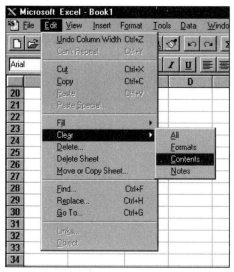

Figure 6-4: Excel provides several options for clearing cells.

Replacing the contents of a cell

To replace the contents of a cell with something else, just activate the cell and make your new entry. It replaces the previous contents. Any formatting that you applied to the cell remains.

Editing the contents of a cell

If the cell contains only a few characters, it's often easier to simply replace it by typing in new data. But if the cell contains lengthy text or a complex formula and you need to make a slight modification, you'll probably want to edit the cell rather than reenter information.

When you want to edit the contents of a cell, you can use one of three ways to get into cell edit mode:

- ✦ Double-click the cell. This lets you edit the cell contents directly in the cell.

- ✦ Press F2. This lets you edit the cell contents directly in the cell.

- ✦ Activate the cell that you want to edit, and then click in the formula bar. This lets you edit the cell contents in the formula bar.

You can use whichever method you prefer. Some people find it easier to edit directly in the cell; others prefer to use the formula bar. All of these methods cause the formula bar to display three new mouse icons, as shown in Figure 6-5. The X icon cancels editing, and the cell's contents aren't changed (Esc has the same effect). The Check Mark icon completes the editing and enters the modified contents into the cell (Enter has the same effect). The third icon brings up Excel's Function Wizard, which is explained in Chapter 10.

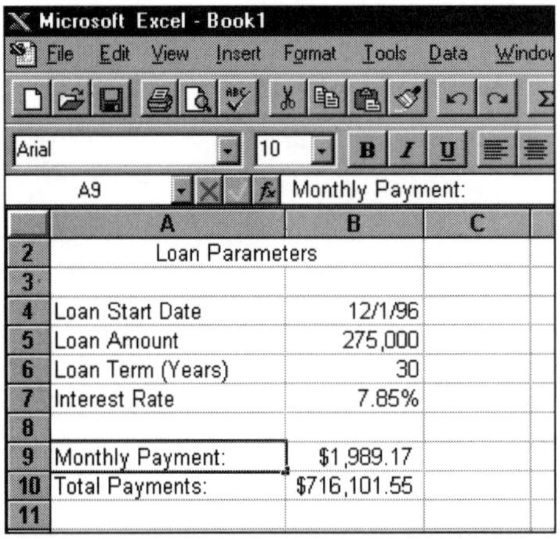

Figure 6-5: The formula bar displays three new icons when you begin editing a cell.

Editing a cell's contents works pretty much as you might expect. The cursor changes to a vertical bar, and you can move the vertical bar by using the direction keys. You can add new characters at the cursor location. Once you're in edit mode, you can use any of the following keys to perform your edits:

Left/right arrow: The left- and right-arrow keys move the cursor left and right one character, respectively, without deleting any characters.

Ctrl+left/right arrow: Moves the cursor to one group of characters to the left and right, respectively.

Shift+left/right arrow: Selects characters to the left or right of the cursor.

Backspace: Erases the character to the immediate left of the cursor.

Delete: Erases the character to the right of the cursor, or all selected characters.

Insert: When you're editing, pressing the Insert key places Excel in OVR (Overwrite) mode. Rather than add characters to the cell, you *overwrite*, or replace, existing characters with new ones, depending on the position of the cursor. If the cursor is above a character and you type in OVR mode, Excel replaces the old character with the character you type.

Home: Moves the cursor to the beginning of the cell entry.

End: Moves the cursor to the end of the cell entry.

Enter: Accepts the edited data.

If you change your mind after editing a cell, you can select Edit⇨Undo (or press Ctrl+Z) to restore the previous cell's contents. You must do this immediately, however — before entering any other data or using any other commands.

Tip
You also can use the mouse to select characters while you're editing a cell. Just click and drag the mouse pointer over the characters that you want to select.

Formatting Values

Values that you enter are normally unformatted. In other words, they simply consist of a string of numerals. In many cases, you'll want to format the numbers so that they are easier to read or are more consistent in terms of the number of decimal places shown.

Figure 6-6 shows two columns of values. The first column consists of unformatted values. The cells in the second column have been formatted to make the values easier to read. If you move the cell pointer to a cell that has a formatted value, you find that the formula bar displays the value in its unformatted state. This is because the formatting affects only how the value is displayed in the cell.

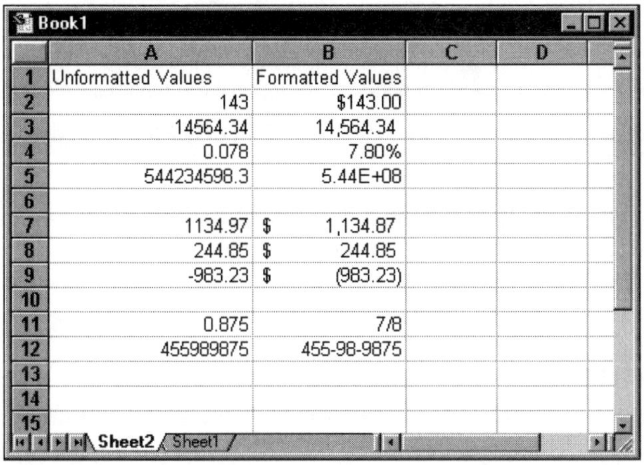

Figure 6-6: Unformatted values (left column) and the same values formatted.

Automatic number formatting

Excel is smart enough to perform some formatting for you automatically. For example, if you enter **12.2%** into a cell, Excel knows that you want to use a percentage format and applies it for you automatically. Similarly, if you use commas to separate thousands (such as **123,456**) Excel applies comma formatting for you.

Formatting numbers using the toolbar

The Formatting toolbar, which is displayed by default, contains several buttons that let you quickly apply common number formats. When you click on one of these buttons, the active cell takes on the specified number format. You also can select a range of cells (or even an entire row or column) before clicking on these buttons. If more than one cell is selected, the number format is applied to all of the selected cells. Table 6-1 summarizes the formats that these Formatting toolbar buttons perform.

<table>
<tr><th colspan="2">Table 6-1
Number-Formatting Buttons on the Formatting Toolbar</th></tr>
<tr><td>*Button Name*</td><td>*Formatting Applied*</td></tr>
<tr><td>Currency Style</td><td>Adds a dollar sign to the left, separates thousands with a comma, and displays the value with two digits to the right of the decimal point</td></tr>
<tr><td>Percent Style</td><td>Displays the value as a percentage with no decimal places</td></tr>
<tr><td>Comma Style</td><td>Separates thousands with a comma and displays the value with two digits to the right of the decimal place</td></tr>
<tr><td>Increase Decimal</td><td>Increases the number of digits to the right of the decimal point by one</td></tr>
<tr><td>Decrease Decimal</td><td>Decreases the number of digits to the right of the decimal point by one</td></tr>
</table>

 Cross-Reference These five toolbar buttons actually apply predefined "styles" to the selected cells. These styles are similar to those used in word processing programs. Chapter 11 describes how to modify existing styles and create new styles.

Other number formats

In some cases, the number formats accessible from the Formatting toolbar are just fine. More often, however, you want more control over how your values appear. Excel offers a great deal of control over number formats.

Figure 6-7 shows Excel's Format Cells dialog box. This is a tabbed dialog box. For formatting numbers, you need to use the tab labeled Number.

When numbers appear to add up incorrectly

It's important to understand that applying a number format to a cell doesn't change the value in any way — formatting changes only how the value looks. For example, if a cell contains .874543, you might format it to appear as 87%. If that cell is used in a formula, the formula uses the full value (.87453), not the displayed value (.87).

In some situations, formatting may cause Excel to display calculation results that appear incorrect, such as when totaling numbers with decimal places (see the accompanying figure). In this example, the values are formatted to display two decimal places. This formatting displays the values rounded. But because Excel uses the full precision in its formula, the sum of these two values appears to be incorrect (10.00 + 10.10 = 20.11). The actual values that are summed are 10.004 and 10.103.

There are several solutions to this problem. You could format the cells to display more decimal places. Or, you can use the ROUND function on individual numbers and specify number of decimal places Excel should round to. I discusses this and other built-in functions in Chapter 10.

Another solution is to instruct Excel to change the worksheet values to match their displayed format. To do this, use the Tools⇨Options command, select the Calculation tab, and check the Precision as Displayed check box. Excel warns you that the underlying numbers will be permanently changed to match their appearance on-screen. If you want to select this option, it's a good idea to backup the worksheet on disk first in case you change your mind.

	A	B	C	D	E	F
1						
2		10.00				
3		10.10				
4		20.11	Total			
5						
6						
7						
8						
9						
10						

There are several ways to bring up the Format Cells dialog box. Start by selecting the cell or cells that you want to format, and then

✦ Select the Format⇨Cells command.

✦ Right-click and choose Format Cells from the shortcut menu.

✦ Press the Ctrl+1 shortcut key.

The Number tab of the Format Cells dialog box displays 12 categories of number formats from which to choose. When you select a category from the list box, the right side of the panel changes to display appropriate options. For example, Figure 6-8 shows how the dialog box looks when you click on the Number category.

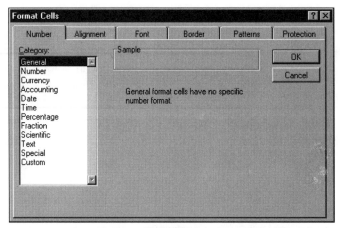

Figure 6-7: The Number tab of the Format Cells dialog box lets you format numbers in just about any way imaginable.

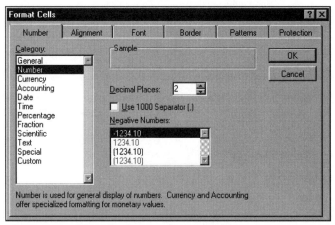

Figure 6-8: Options for the Number category.

The Number category has three options that you can control: the number of decimal places displayed, whether to use a comma for the thousand separator, and how you want negative numbers displayed. Notice that the Negative Numbers list box has four choices (two of which display negative values in red), and the choices change depending on the number of decimal places and your choice for a comma. Also, notice that the top of the panel displays a sample of how the active cell will appear with the selected number format. After you've made your choices, click on OK to apply the number format to all of the selected cells.

Here is a list of the number format categories, along with some general comments.

General: The General number format is the default format. It displays numbers as integers, decimals, or in scientific notation if the value is too wide to fit in the cell.

Number: This format lets you specify the number of decimal places, whether to use a comma to separate thousands, and how to display negative numbers (with a minus sign, in red, in parentheses, or red and in parentheses).

Currency: This format lets you specify the number of decimal places, whether to use a dollar sign, and how to display negative numbers (with a minus sign, in red, in parentheses, or red and in parentheses). This format always uses a comma to separate thousands.

Accounting: This format differs from the Currency format in that the dollar signs always line up vertically.

Date: This category lets you choose from 11 date formats.

Time: This category lets you choose from 6 time formats.

Percentage: This category lets you choose the number of decimal places and always displays a percent sign.

Fraction: This category lets you choose from among 9 fraction formats.

Scientific: This format always displays with an E. You can choose the number of decimal places to display.

Text: Applying the Text number format to a value causes Excel to treat the value as text (even if it looks like a value). This feature is useful for items such as part numbers.

Special: This category contains 4 additional number formats (Zip Code, Zip Code +4, Phone Number, and Social Security Number).

Custom: This category lets you define custom number formats that aren't included in any of the other categories. I describe custom number formats in the next section.

Figure 6-9 shows an example from each category.

The best way to learn about number formats is to experiment. Enter some values on a worksheet and practice applying number formats.

Note   If the cell displays a series of pound signs (such as #########) it means that the column is not wide enough to display the value using the number format that you selected. The solution is to make the column wider or change the number format.

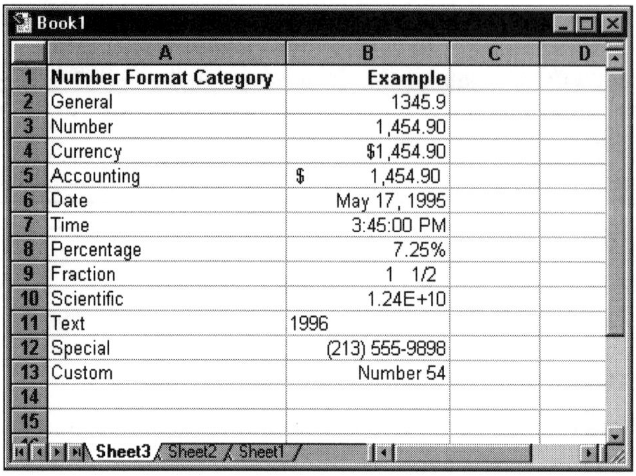

	A	B	C	D
1	Number Format Category	Example		
2	General	1345.9		
3	Number	1,454.90		
4	Currency	$1,454.90		
5	Accounting	$ 1,454.90		
6	Date	May 17, 1995		
7	Time	3:45:00 PM		
8	Percentage	7.25%		
9	Fraction	1 1/2		
10	Scientific	1.24E+10		
11	Text	1996		
12	Special	(213) 555-9898		
13	Custom	Number 54		
14				
15				

Figure 6-9: Examples of values with various number formats.

Tip   Most of the time, you'll apply number formats to cells that already contain values. You also can preformat cells with a specific number format. Then, when you enter a value, it takes on the format that you specified. You can preformat specific cells, entire rows or columns, or even the entire worksheet. Rather than preformat an entire worksheet, however, it's a better idea to change the number format for the Normal style (unless you specify otherwise, all cells use the Normal style). You can change the Normal style by selecting the Format➪Style command. In the Style dialog box, click on the Modify button and then choose the new number format for the Normal style. Refer to Chapter 11 for more information about styles.

Custom number formats

As previously mentioned, the Custom number format category lets you create number formats that aren't included in any of the other categories. Excel gives you a great deal of flexibility in creating custom number formats, but it can be rather tricky. Basically, you construct a number format by specifying a series of codes. You enter this code sequence in the Type field when the Custom category is selected in the Number panel of the Format Cells dialog box. Here's an example of a simple number format code:

```
0.000
```

This code consists of placeholders and a decimal point. The code tells Excel to display the value with three digits to the right of the decimal place.

Here's another example:

```
00000
```

This custom number format has five placeholders and displays the value with five digits (no decimal point). This is a good format to use when the cell will hold a zip code (in fact, this is the code actually used by the Zip Code format in the Special category). When you format the cell with this number format and then enter a zip code such as 06604 (Bridgeport, CT), the value is displayed with the leading zero. If you enter this number into a cell with the General number format, it displays as 6604 (no leading zero).

If you scroll through the list of number formats in the Custom category in the Format Cells dialog box, you see many more examples. Most of the time, you'll be able to use one of these codes as a starting point, and only slight customization will be needed.

Excel also makes it possible to specify different format codes for positive numbers, negative numbers, zero values, and text. You do so by separating the codes with a semicolon. The codes are arranged in the following structure:

```
Positive format; Negative format; Zero format; Text format
```

Here's an example of a custom number format that specifies a different format for each of these types:

```
[Green]General;[Red]General;[Black]General;[Blue]General
```

This example takes advantage of the fact that there are special codes for colors. A cell formatted with this custom number format displays its contents in a different color, depending on the value. In this case, positive numbers are green, negative numbers are red, zero is black, and text is blue.

The number format that follows (three semicolons) consists of no format codes for each part of the format structure — essentially hiding the contents of the cell:

```
;;;
```

Table 6-2 lists the formatting codes available for custom formats, along with a brief description. These codes are further described in Excel's online help.

Table 6-2
Codes Used in Creating Custom Number Formats

Code	Comments
General	Displays the number in General format
#	Digit placeholder
0 (zero)	Digit placeholder
?	Digit placeholder
.	Decimal point
%	Percentage
,	Thousands separator
E- E+ e- e+	Scientific notation
$ – + / ( ) : space	Displays this character
\	Displays the next character in the format
*	Repeats the next character to fill the column width
_	Skips the width of the next character
"text"	Displays the text inside the double quotation marks
@	Text placeholder
[color]	Displays the characters in the color specified
[COLOR n]	Displays the corresponding color in the color palette, where n is a number from 0 to 56
[condition value]	Lets you set your own criteria for each section of a number format

Table 6-3 lists the codes used in creating custom formats for dates and times.

Note Custom number formats are stored with the worksheet. To make the custom format available in a different workbook, you must copy a cell that uses the custom format to the other workbook.

On the CD-ROM Figure 6-10 shows several examples of custom number formats, and the workbook is included on the CD that accompanies this book. The workbook is named CSTMNUMF.XLS Studying these examples will help you understand the concept and may give you some ideas for your own custom number formats.

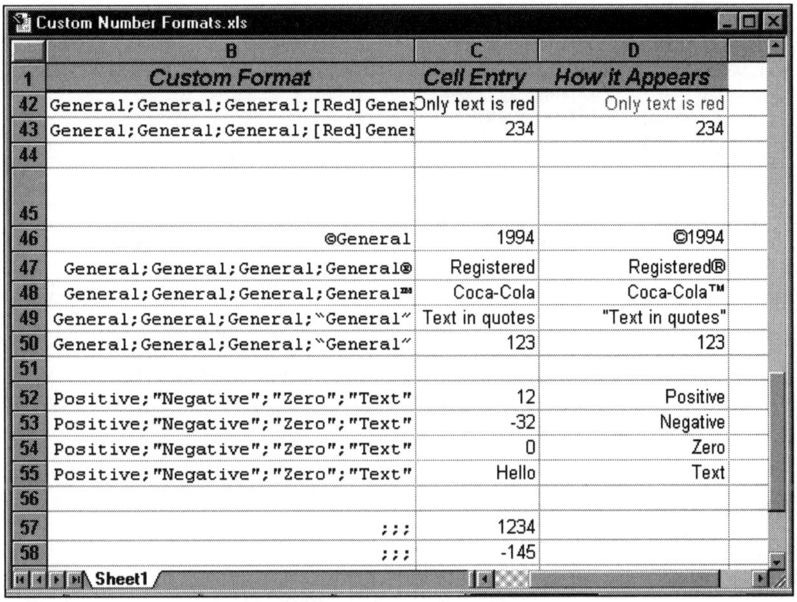

	B	C	D
	Custom Format	*Cell Entry*	*How it Appears*
42	General;General;General;[Red]General	Only text is red	Only text is red
43	General;General;General;[Red]General	234	234
44			
45			
46	©General	1994	©1994
47	General;General;General;General®	Registered	Registered®
48	General;General;General;General™	Coca-Cola	Coca-Cola™
49	General;General;General;"General"	Text in quotes	"Text in quotes"
50	General;General;General;"General"	123	123
51			
52	Positive;"Negative";"Zero";"Text"	12	Positive
53	Positive;"Negative";"Zero";"Text"	-32	Negative
54	Positive;"Negative";"Zero";"Text"	0	Zero
55	Positive;"Negative";"Zero";"Text"	Hello	Text
56			
57	;;;	1234	
58	;;;	-145	

Figure 6-10: Examples of custom number formats.

Basic Cell Formatting

The preceding section discussed number formatting. This section discusses some of the basic *stylistic* formatting options available to you. These formatting techniques apply to values, text, and formulas. The options discussed here are those that are available from the Formatting toolbar. Complete formatting options are available in the Format Cells dialog box, which appears when you choose the Format⇨Cells command (or press Ctrl+).

Cross-Reference The concept of worksheet stylistic formatting is discussed in detail in Chapter 11.

It's important to remember that the formatting you apply works with the selected cell or cells. Therefore, you need to select the cell (or range of cells) before applying the formatting.

Alignment

When you enter text in a cell, it's normally left-justified in the cell. Values, on the other hand, are displayed right-aligned in the cell.

Table 6-3
Codes Used in Creating Custom Formats for Dates and Times

Code	Comments
m	Displays the month as a number without leading zeros (1–12)
mm	Displays the month as a number with leading zeros (01–12)
mmm	Displays the month as an abbreviation (Jan–Dec)
mmmm	Displays the month as a full name (January–December)
d	Displays the day as a number without leading zeros (1–31)
dd	Displays the day as a number with leading zeros (01–31)
ddd	Displays the day as an abbreviation (Sun–Sat)
dddd	Displays the day as a full name (Sunday–Saturday)
yy or yyyy	Displays the year as a two-digit number (00–99), or as a four-digit number (1900–2078)
h or hh	Displays the hour as a number without leading zeros (0–23), or as a number with leading zeros (00–23)
m or mm	Displays the minute as a number without leading zeros (0–59), or as a number with leading zeros (00–59)
s or ss	Displays the second as a number without leading zeros (0–59), or as a number with leading zeros (00–59)
[]	Displays hours greater than 24, or minutes or seconds greater than 60
AM/am/A/a/PM/pm/P/p	Displays the hour using a 12-hour clock; if no AM/PM indicator is used, the hour uses a 24-hour clock

You easily can change the alignment of a cell's contents by selecting the cell and then clicking on the appropriate button on the Formatting toolbar. The relevant buttons are as follows:

Align Left: Aligns the text to the left side of the cell. If the text is wider than the cell, it spills over to the cell to the right. If the cell to the right is not empty, the text is truncated and not completely visible.

Center: Centers the text in the cell. If the text is wider than the cell, it spills over to cells on either side if they are empty. If the adjacent cells aren't empty, the text is truncated and not completely visible.

Align Right: Aligns the text to the right side of the cell. If the text is wider than the cell, it spills over to the cell to the left. If the cell to the left is not empty, the text is truncated and not completely visible.

Center Across Columns: Centers the text over the selected columns. This is useful for precisely centering a heading over a number of columns.

Font and text size

You easily can change the font and the size of the text by using the Font and Font Size tools on the Formatting toolbar. These tools are drop-down lists rather than buttons. Click the arrow on the tool to display a list of fonts or font sizes (see Figure 6-11). Then choose the font or size that you want.

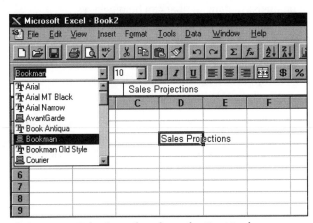

Figure 6-11: Selecting a font from the Font tool.

Attributes

The Formatting toolbar also has buttons that let you make the selected cells bold, italic, or underlined. As you might expect, clicking the appropriate tool makes the change. These buttons actually are toggles. So, if the cell is already bold, clicking on the Bold button takes the bold off.

Borders

Another type of formatting is borders — lines drawn around all or part of selected cells or ranges. The Borders button on the Formatting toolbar is an unusual tool. It displays 12 miniature icons rather than a drop-down list, and the entire palette of icons can be dragged to any location (see Figure 6-12).

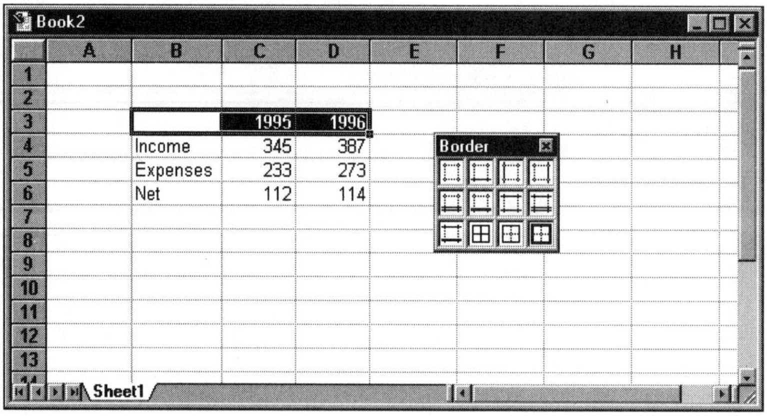

Figure 6-12: The Borders tool on the Formatting toolbar can be dragged anywhere on-screen.

To add a border to the selected cell or cells, just click on the icon that corresponds to the type of border you want. The upper-left icon removes all borders from the selected cells.

Note   Normally, Excel displays gridlines in the worksheet to delineate cells. If you add border formatting, you'll probably want to turn off the gridline display. To do so, choose the Tools⇨Options command, click on the View tab, and uncheck the Gridlines check box. This will make it easier to see the effects of borders.

Colors

The Color tool lets you quickly change the background color of the cell, and the Font Color tool lets you change the text color. These tools are similar to the Borders tool and also can be moved to a different location.

Data Entry Tips

I wrap up this chapter with some useful tips and techniques that can make your data entry more efficient.

Move the cell pointer after entering data?

Depending on how Excel is configured, pressing the Enter key after entering data into a cell may automatically move the cell pointer to another cell. Some users find this annoying; others like it. To change this setting, choose the Tools⇨Options command and click on the Edit tab. The check box that controls this behavior is labeled Move Selection after Enter.

A new feature in Excel for Windows 95 lets you specify the direction in which the cell pointer moves (down, left, up, or right). This also is controlled in the Edit panel of the Options dialog box.

Use arrows instead of Enter

Throughout this chapter, I've mentioned several times that you use the Enter key when you're finished making a cell entry. Well, that's only part of the story. You can use any of the direction keys instead of Enter. And, not surprisingly, these direction keys send you in the direction that you indicate. For example, if you're entering data in a row, press the right-arrow key rather than Enter. The other arrow keys work as expected, and you can even use PgUp and PgDn (although I don't know why you would want to).

Selecting cells before entering data

Here's a tip that most Excel users don't know about. If you preselect a range of cells, Excel automatically moves the cell pointer to the next cell when you press Enter. If the selection consists of multiple rows, Excel moves down the column; when it reaches the end of the column, it moves to the top of the next column. To skip a cell, just press Enter without entering anything. To go backward, use Shift+Enter. If you prefer to enter the data by rows rather than by columns, use Tab rather than Enter.

If you have lots of data to enter, this technique can save you a few keystrokes — and also ensure that the data you enter winds up in the proper place.

Use Ctrl+Enter for repeated information

If you need to enter the same data into multiple cells, your first inclination may be to enter it once and then copy it to the remaining cells. Here's a better way: Select all the cells that you want to contain the data, enter the value, text, or formula, and then press Ctrl+Enter. The single entry will be inserted into each cell in the selection.

Automatic decimal points

If you're entering lots of numbers with a fixed number of decimal places, you may be interested in this tip that makes Excel work like some adding machines. Select the Tools⇨Options command and click on the Edit tab. Check the check box labeled Fixed Decimal and make sure that it's set for two decimal places. When the Fixed Decimal option is set, Excel supplies the decimal points for you automatically. For example, if you enter **12345** into a cell, Excel interprets it as 123.45 (it adds the decimal point). To restore things back to normal, just uncheck the Fixed Decimal check box in the Options dialog box.

Note

Changing this setting doesn't affect any values that you have already entered.

Using AutoFill

Excel's AutoFill feature makes it very easy to insert a series of values or text items in a range of cells. It uses the AutoFill handle (the small box at the lower left of the active cell). You can drag the AutoFill handle to copy the cell or automatically complete a series.

Cross-Reference   Chapter 7 discusses AutoFill in detail.

Using AutoComplete

New!   AutoComplete, new to Excel 95, lets you type the first few letters of a text entry into a cell, and Excel automatically completes the entry based on other entries that you've already made in the column. If your data entry task involves repetitious text, this feature is for you.

Here's how it works. Say that you're entering product information in a column. One of your products is named *Widgets*. The first time that you enter *Widgets* into a cell, Excel remembers it. Later, when you start typing *Widgets* in that same column, Excel recognizes it by the first few letters and finishes typing it for you. Just press Enter and you're done. It also changes the case of letters for you automatically. If you start entering *widget* (with a lowercase *w*), Excel will make the *w* uppercase to be consistent with the previous entry in the column.

Besides reducing typing, this feature also ensures that your entries are spelled correctly and are consistent.

Tip   You also can access this feature by right-clicking on the cell and selecting Pick from List from the shortcut menu. With this method, Excel displays a drop-down box with all of the entries in the current column. Just click on the one that you want, and it's entered automatically.

If you find this feature distracting, you can turn it off in the Edit panel of the Options dialog box. Just remove the check mark from the check box labeled Enable AutoComplete for Cell Values.

Entering the current date or time into a cell

Sometimes, you need to date-stamp or time-stamp your worksheet. Excel provides two shortcut keys that do this for you:

> **Current date:** Ctrl+; (semicolon)
>
> **Current time:** Ctrl+Shift+; (semicolon)

Forcing a new line in a cell

If you have lengthy text in a cell, you can force Excel to display it in multiple lines within the cell. Use Alt+Enter to start a new line in a cell. Figure 6-13 shows an example of text in a cell that is displayed in multiple lines. When you add a line break, Excel automatically changes the cell's format to Wrap Text. More about the Wrap Text formatting feature in Chapter 11.

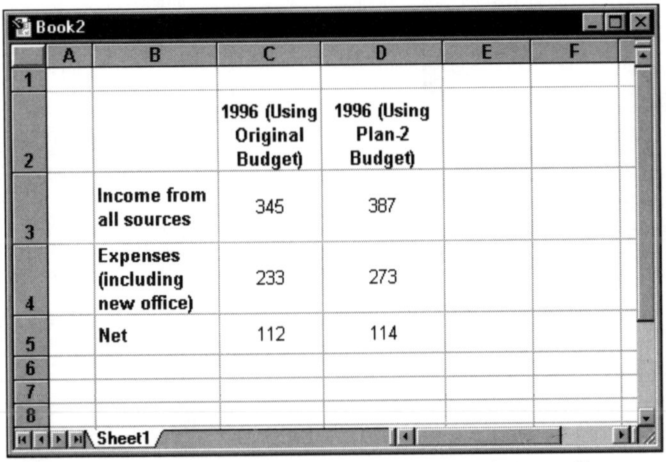

		1996 (Using Original Budget)	1996 (Using Plan-2 Budget)		
	Income from all sources	345	387		
	Expenses (including new office)	233	273		
	Net	112	114		

Figure 6-13: Alt+Enter lets you force a line break in a cell.

Entering fractions

If you would like Excel to enter a fraction into a cell, leave a space between the whole number part and the fractional part. For example, to enter the decimal equivalent of 6 $^7/_8$, enter **6 7/8** and press Enter. Excel enters 6.875 into the cell and automatically formats the cell as a fraction. If there is no whole number part (for example, $^1/_8$), you must enter a zero first, like this: **0 1/8**.

Using a data entry form

If you're entering data that is arranged in rows, you might find it easier to use Excel's built-in data form for data entry. Figure 6-14 shows an example of this.

Start by defining headings for the columns in the first row of your data entry range. You can always erase these entries later if you don't need them. Excel needs headings for this command to work, however. Select any cell in the header row and choose the Data⇨Form command. Excel asks whether you want to use that row for headers (answer Yes). It then displays a dialog box with edit boxes and several buttons. You

Figure 6-14: Excel's built-in data form can simplify many data entry tasks.

can use Tab to move between the edit boxes. When you complete the data for a row, click on the New button. Excel dumps the data into the worksheet and clears the dialog box for the next row.

Cross-Reference This data form feature has lots of other useful buttons; I discuss it further in Chapter 23.

Macro options

As you'll see in later chapters, you also can create macros to simplify data entry tasks. For example, you can define a simple macro that automatically types your company name when you press a specific key combination or click a button.

Summary

A worksheet cell can contain a value, text, or a formula. This chapter focuses on the task of entering values and formulas. I explain Excel's method of dealing with dates and times and also introduce the concept of number formatting — which makes numbers appear differently but doesn't affect their actual value. I also discuss common editing techniques and basic stylistic formatting. I conclude with a series of general data entry tips.

✦   ✦   ✦

Essential Spreadsheet Operations

◆   ◆   ◆   ◆

In This Chapter

Key operations that
involve worksheets

Methods to make
working with
worksheets easier

Techniques for
working with entire
rows and columns

◆   ◆   ◆   ◆

This chapter discusses the common spreadsheet operations
that you need to know. A thorough knowledge of these
procedures will make you work more efficiently.

Working with Worksheets

When you open a new workbook in Excel, the workbook has
some number of worksheets in it. The exact number is determined by the Sheets in New Workbook setting in the General tab
of the Options dialog box.

By default, this number of worksheets is 16. There's absolutely
no reason, however, why a new workbook should have 16
worksheets in it. In all of my years of working with spreadsheets,
I have never needed this many. Besides, it's very easy to add a
new worksheet when you need one. Although empty worksheets
really don't use much additional memory or disk storage space,
they just get in the way. I strongly recommend that you change
the default value to one worksheet. To do so, issue the
Tools⇨Options command, select the General tab, and change
the Sheets in New Workbook setting to 1. After doing this, all
new workbooks will have only a single worksheet.

It may be helpful to think of a workbook as a notebook and
worksheets as pages in the notebook. As with a notebook, you
can activate a particular sheet, add new sheets, remove sheets,
copy sheets, and so on. The remainder of this section discusses
the operations that you perform with worksheets.

Activating worksheets

At any given time, one workbook is the active workbook, and one sheet in the active workbook is the active sheet. To activate a different sheet, just click on its sheet tab located at the bottom of the workbook window. You also can use the following shortcut keys to activate a different sheet:

Ctrl+PgUp: Activates the previous sheet if there is one

Ctrl+PgDn: Activates the next sheet, if there is one

If your workbook has several sheets, all tabs may not be visible. You can use the tab scrolling buttons (see Figure 7-1) to scroll the sheet tabs.

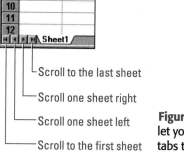

Scroll to the last sheet

Scroll one sheet right

Scroll one sheet left

Scroll to the first sheet

Figure 7-1: The tab scrolling buttons let you scroll the sheet tabs to display tabs that are not visible.

The sheet tabs share space with the worksheet's horizontal scrollbar. You also can drag the tab split box (see Figure 7-2) to display more or fewer tabs. Dragging the tab split box simultaneously changes the number of tabs and the size of the horizontal scrollbar.

Tab split box

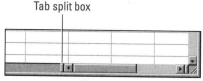

Figure 7-2: Dragging the tab split box lets you see more (or fewer) sheet tabs.

Tip   Right-clicking on any of the tab-scrolling buttons displays a list of sheets in the workbook. You can quickly activate a sheet by selecting it from the list.

Adding a new worksheet

There are three ways to add a new worksheet to a workbook:

✦ Select the Insert⇨Worksheet command.

✦ Right-click on a sheet tab, choose the Insert command from the shortcut menu, and then select Worksheet from the Insert dialog box.

✦ Press Shift+F11.

Any of these methods cause Excel to insert a new worksheet before the active worksheet, and the new worksheet becomes the active worksheet. The new worksheet, of course, has a sheet tab that displays its name.

Tip   To add additional worksheets after inserting a worksheet, press F4 (the shortcut for the Edit⇨Repeat command) once for each additional sheet that you want to add.

Cross- Chapter 33 discusses how to create and use worksheet templates. This feature allows
Reference you to add specially formatted or customized worksheets to an existing workbook.

Deleting a worksheet

If you no longer need a worksheet, or if you want to get rid of an empty worksheet in a workbook, you can delete it. There are two ways to do this:

✦ Select the Edit⇨Delete Sheet command.

✦ Right-click on the sheet tab and choose the Delete command from the shortcut menu. Excel asks you to confirm the fact that you want to delete the sheet.

Tip   You can delete multiple sheets with a single command by selecting the sheets that you want to delete. To do so, press Ctrl while you click on the sheet tabs that you want to delete. Then, use either of the preceding methods. To select a group of contiguous sheets, click on the first sheet tab, press Shift, and then click the last sheet tab.

Caution When you delete a worksheet, it's gone for good. This is one of the few operations in Excel that can't be undone.

Changing a worksheet's name

Worksheets, by default, are named Sheet1, Sheet2, and so on. It's usually a good idea to provide more meaningful names to your worksheets. To change a sheet's name, use any of the following methods:

✦ Choose the Format⇨Sheet⇨Rename command.

✦ Double-click on the sheet tab.

✦ Right-click on the sheet tab and choose the Rename command from the shortcut menu.

In any of these cases, Excel displays the Rename Sheet dialog box (see Figure 7-3). Enter the new name and click on OK. The sheet tab displays the new name.

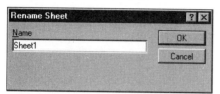

Figure 7-3: It's a good idea to give worksheets more meaningful names.

Sheet names can be up to 31 characters, and spaces are allowed. You can't use the following characters in sheet names:

[]	square brackets
:	colon
/	slash
\	backslash
?	question mark
*	asterisk

Keep in mind that the name you give will be displayed on the tab and that a longer name results in wider tabs. Therefore, if you use lengthy sheet names, you'll be able to see fewer sheet tabs without scrolling.

Moving a worksheet

Sometimes, you want to rearrange the order of worksheets in a workbook. If you have a separate worksheet for each sales region, for example, it might be helpful to arrange the worksheets in alphabetical order or by total sales. You also might want to move a worksheet from one workbook to another.

If you want to move a worksheet to a different workbook, both workbooks must be open. There are two ways to move a worksheet to a different location in the workbook or to a different workbook:

✦ Select the Edit➪Move or Copy Sheet command.

✦ Click on the sheet tab and drag it to its desired location (either in the same workbook or in a different workbook). When you drag, the mouse pointer changes to a small sheet and a small arrow guides you.

Dragging is usually the easiest method, but if the workbook has many sheets, you may prefer to use the menu command. This command displays the dialog box shown in Figure 7-4. This dialog box lets you select the workbook and the new location.

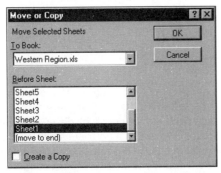

Figure 7-4: The Move or Copy dialog box.

Note

If you move a worksheet to a workbook that already has a sheet with the same name, Excel changes the name to make it unique. For example, Sheet1 becomes Sheet1 (2).

Tip

You also can move multiple sheets at once by selecting them: Press Ctrl while you click on the sheet tabs that you want to move.

Copying a worksheet

You can make an exact copy of a worksheet — either in its original workbook or in a different workbook. The procedures are similar to those for moving a workbook:

✦ Select the Edit⇨Move or Copy Sheet command. Select the location for the copy and make sure that the check box labeled Create a Copy is checked.

✦ Click on the sheet tab, press Ctrl, and drag it to its desired location (either in the same workbook or in a different workbook). When you drag, the mouse pointer changes to a small sheet with a plus sign on it.

Note

If necessary, Excel changes the name of the copied sheet to make it unique within the workbook.

Hiding and unhiding a worksheet

In some cases, you may want to hide a worksheet. Hiding a worksheet is useful if you don't want others to see it, or if you just want to get it out of the way. When a sheet is hidden, its sheet tab is hidden also.

To hide a worksheet, choose the Format⇨Sheet⇨Hide command. The active worksheet (or selected worksheets) will be hidden from view. Every workbook must have at least one visible sheet, so Excel won't allow you to hide all sheets in a workbook.

To unhide a hidden worksheet, choose the Format⇨Sheet⇨Unhide command. Excel pops up a dialog box that lists all hidden sheets. Chose the sheet that you want to unhide and click on OK.

Zooming worksheets

Excel lets you scale the size of your worksheets. Normally, everything you see is at 100 percent. You can change the "zoom percentage" from 10 percent (very tiny) to 400 percent (huge). Using a small zoom percentage can help you get a bird's-eye view of your worksheet to see how it's laid out. Zooming in is useful if your eyesight isn't quite what it used to be and you have trouble deciphering those 8-point sales figures. Figure 7-5 shows a window zoomed to 10 percent and a window zoomed to 400 percent.

The easiest way to change the zoom factor of the active worksheet is to use the Zoom Control on the Standard toolbar. Just click on the arrow and select the desired zoom factor. Your screen transforms immediately. The Selection option on the pull-down list zooms the worksheet to display only the selected cells. This option is useful if you want to view only a particular range. Zooming only affects the active worksheet; other worksheets in the workbook are not affected.

For finer control over the zoom factor, use the View⇨Zoom command. This command displays the dialog box shown in Figure 7-6. You can enter a value between 10 and 400 into the edit box next to the Custom option.

 Note   The zoom factor affects only how the worksheet is displayed on-screen. It has no effect on how it is printed. There are separate options for changing the size of your printed output (use the File⇨Page Setup command). See Chapter 12 for details.

Views, Split Sheets, and Frozen Panes

This section discusses a few additional options at your disposal.

Multiple views

Sometimes, you might like to view two different parts of a worksheet at once. Or, you might want to examine more than one sheet in the same workbook. You can accomplish either of these actions by opening a new view to the workbook. You do this by displaying your workbook in one or more additional windows.

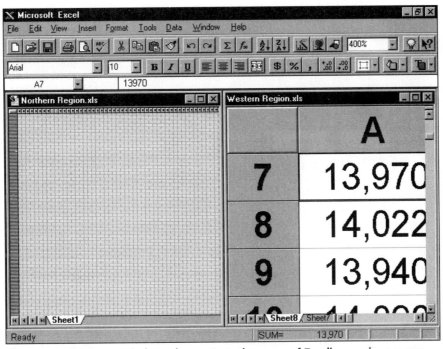

Figure 7-5: These two windows demonstrate the range of Excel's zooming powers.

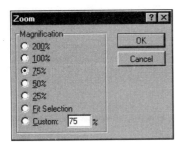

Figure 7-6: The Zoom dialog box.

To create a new view of the active workbook, choose the Window➪New Window command. Excel displays a new window with the active workbook. Figure 7-7 shows an example of this. Notice the text in the windows' title bars: *Budget.xls:1* and *Budget.xls:2*.

To help you keep track of the windows, Excel appends a colon and a number to each window.

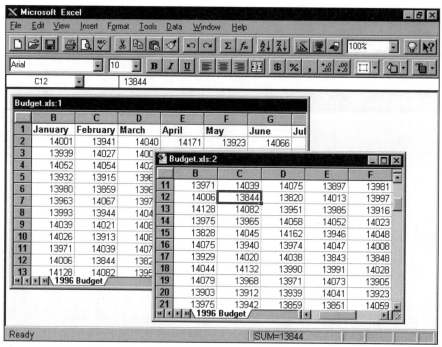

Figure 7-7: Two views of the same workbook.

A single workbook can have as many views (that is, separate windows) as you like. Each window is independent of the others. In other words, scrolling to a new location in one window doesn't cause scrolling in the other window(s). This also lets you display a different worksheet in a separate window. Figure 7-8 shows three views in the same workbook. Each view is displaying a different worksheet.

You can close these additional windows using the standard methods. For example, clicking on the Close button on the title bar closes the active window but doesn't close the other windows.

> **Cross-Reference**
> As you'll see in Chapter 8, displaying multiple windows for a workbook also makes it easier to copy information from one worksheet to another. You can use Excel's drag-and-drop procedures to do this.

Splitting panes

If you prefer not to clutter your screen with additional windows, Excel provides another option for viewing multiple parts of the same worksheet. The Window⇨Split command splits the active worksheet into two or four separate panes. The split occurs at the location of the cell pointer. You can use the mouse to drag the pane and make it the size you desire.

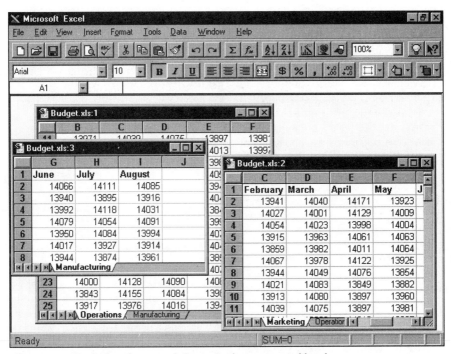

Figure 7-8: Displaying three worksheets in the same workbook.

Figure 7-9 shows a worksheet split into four panes. Notice that row numbers and column letters aren't continuous. In other words, splitting panes lets you display widely separated areas of a worksheet in a single window. The two top-to-bottom stacked panes always have the same column headings, and the two side-by-side panes always have the same row headings. To remove the split panes, choose the Window➪Remove Split command.

Tip   Another way to split and unsplit panes is to drag either the vertical or horizontal split bar. Figure 7-10 shows where these split bars are located. To remove split panes using the mouse, drag the pane separator all the way to the edge of the window, or just double-click on it.

Freezing panes

Many worksheets, such as the one shown in Figure 7-11, are set up with row and column headings.

When you scroll through such a worksheet, it's very easy to get lost when the row and column headings scroll out of view, as you can see in Figure 7-12. Excel provides a handy solution to this problem: freezing panes.

Naming views

Some users may be interested in a feature called *named views*. This feature lets you give names to various views of your worksheet and to switch quickly among these named views. A view includes settings for window size and position, frozen panes or titles, outlining, zoom factor, the active cell, print area, and many of the settings in the Options dialog box. Optionally, a view can include hidden print settings and hidden rows and columns. If you find that you're constantly fiddling with these settings and then changing them back, using named views can save you lots of effort.

The named views feature is an add-in that must be loaded. If the View⇨View Manager command isn't available, open the add-in by selecting the Tools⇨Add-Ins command and then selecting the View Manager add-in from the list displayed in the Add-Ins dialog box. When View Manager is loaded, you have

access to a new command: View⇨View Manager. When you select this command, you get the dialog box shown in the accompanying figure.

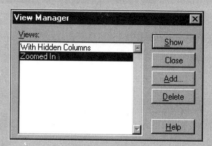

The View Manager dialog box displays a list of all named views. To select a particular view, just select it from the list and click on the Show button. To add a view, click on the Add button and provide a name. To delete a named view from the list, click on the Delete button.

	B	C	D	G	H	I	J	K
11	13971	14039	14075	14027	13969	13918		
12	14006	13844	13820	13951	14014	13852		
13	14128	14082	13951	14041	13980	13918		
14	13975	13965	14058	13960	14073	14066		
15	13828	14045	14162	14036	14111	13940		
16	14075	13940	13974	14056	13904	13972		
55	13942	14123	14064	13934	13850	13915		
56	13940	13954	13881	13859	13856	13963		
57	13960	14015	13833	13976	13911	14123		
58	13990	14148	14033	13907	13932	13895		
59	14099	14008	13964	14027	14024	14014		
60	13962	13972	13973	14160	13949	13935		
61	14098	14032	13952	14106	13855	14064		
62	13979	13823	14141	14017	14098	13949		
63	14023	13877	13946	14033	13910	13977		

Budget.xls — Operations

Figure 7-9: This worksheet is split into four panes.

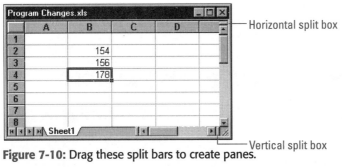

Horizontal split box

Vertical split box

Figure 7-10: Drag these split bars to create panes.

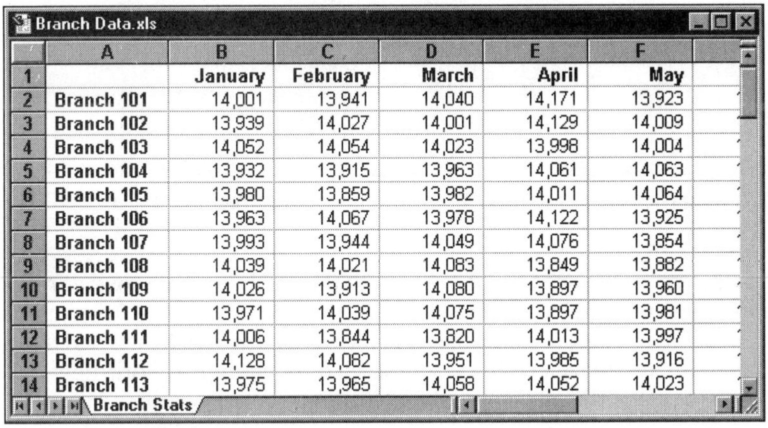

	A	B	C	D	
		January	February	March	April	May
1		**January**	**February**	**March**	**April**	**May**
2	Branch 101	14,001	13,941	14,040	14,171	13,923
3	Branch 102	13,939	14,027	14,001	14,129	14,009
4	Branch 103	14,052	14,054	14,023	13,998	14,004
5	Branch 104	13,932	13,915	13,963	14,061	14,063
6	Branch 105	13,980	13,859	13,982	14,011	14,064
7	Branch 106	13,963	14,067	13,978	14,122	13,925
8	Branch 107	13,993	13,944	14,049	14,076	13,854
9	Branch 108	14,039	14,021	14,083	13,849	13,882
10	Branch 109	14,026	13,913	14,080	13,897	13,960
11	Branch 110	13,971	14,039	14,075	13,897	13,981
12	Branch 111	14,006	13,844	13,820	14,013	13,997
13	Branch 112	14,128	14,082	13,951	13,985	13,916
14	Branch 113	13,975	13,965	14,058	14,052	14,023

Branch Stats

Figure 7-11: A worksheet with row and column headings.

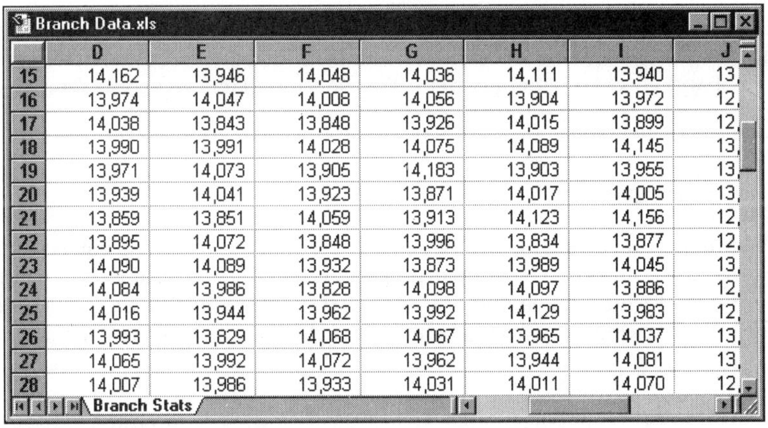

	D	E	F	G	H	I	J
15	14,162	13,946	14,048	14,036	14,111	13,940	13,
16	13,974	14,047	14,008	14,056	13,904	13,972	12,
17	14,038	13,843	13,848	13,926	14,015	13,899	12,
18	13,990	13,991	14,028	14,075	14,089	14,145	13,
19	13,971	14,073	13,905	14,183	13,903	13,955	13,
20	13,939	14,041	13,923	13,871	14,017	14,005	13,
21	13,859	13,851	14,059	13,913	14,123	14,156	12,
22	13,895	14,072	13,848	13,996	13,834	13,877	12,
23	14,090	14,089	13,932	13,873	13,989	14,045	13,
24	14,084	13,986	13,828	14,098	14,097	13,886	12,
25	14,016	13,944	13,962	13,992	14,129	13,983	12,
26	13,993	13,829	14,068	14,067	13,965	14,037	13,
27	14,065	13,992	14,072	13,962	13,944	14,081	13,
28	14,007	13,986	13,933	14,031	14,011	14,070	12,

Branch Stats

Figure 7-12: It's easy to lose your bearings when the row and column headers scroll out of view.

Figure 7-13 shows the worksheet from the previous figure, but with frozen panes. In this case, row 1 and column A are frozen in place. This keeps the headings visible while scrolling through the worksheet.

	A	H	I	J	K	L	Dece
1		July	August	September	October	November	
54	Branch 153	14,058	14,131	12,949	13,037	12,990	
55	Branch 154	13,850	13,915	12,977	13,054	13,007	
56	Branch 155	13,856	13,963	13,046	12,979	13,032	
57	Branch 156	13,911	14,123	12,971	12,915	12,966	
58	Branch 157	13,932	13,895	13,042	12,997	12,990	
59	Branch 158	14,024	14,014	12,987	12,956	13,019	
60	Branch 159	13,949	13,935	12,996	13,060	13,045	
61	Branch 160	13,855	14,064	12,996	13,009	13,021	
62	Branch 161	14,098	13,949	13,043	12,960	12,971	
63	Branch 162	13,910	13,977	13,004	12,949	13,030	
64	Branch 163	13,952	13,878	12,981	13,049	12,975	
65	Branch 164	14,011	14,044	13,031	12,949	13,011	
66	Branch 165	13,949	14,059	12,963	13,024	13,032	

Figure 7-13: A worksheet with the row and column headings frozen in place.

To freeze panes, start by moving the cell pointer to the cell below the row to freeze and to the right of the column to freeze. Then select the Window⇨Freeze Panes command. Excel inserts dark lines to indicate the frozen rows and columns. You'll find that these frozen rows and column remain visible as you scroll throughout the worksheet. To remove the frozen panes, select the Window⇨Unfreeze Panes command.

Working with Rows and Columns

Every worksheet has exactly 16,384 rows and 256 columns. Although it would be nice to be able to specify the number of rows and columns for each worksheet, these values are fixed and you can't change them. This section discusses some worksheet operations that involve rows and columns.

Inserting rows and columns

Although the number of rows and columns in a worksheet is fixed, you can still insert and delete rows and columns. These operations don't change the number of rows or columns. For example, inserting a new row moves the other rows down to accommodate it. The last row is simply removed from the worksheet (as long as it's empty; see the note that follows).

To insert a new row or rows, you can use any of the following techniques:

✦ Select an entire row or multiple rows by clicking on the row numbers in the worksheet border. Select the Insert⇨Rows command.

✦ Select an entire row or multiple rows by clicking on the row numbers in the worksheet border. Right-click and choose Insert from the shortcut menu.

✦ Move the cell pointer to the row that you want to insert and select the Insert⇨Rows command. If you select multiple cells in the column, Excel inserts additional rows that correspond to the number of cells selected in the column.

The procedure for inserting a new column or columns is the same (but you use the Insert⇨Column command).

Note If the last column (column IV) contains information, Excel won't let you insert a new column. Similarly, if the last row (row 16384) contains information, you can't insert a new row. You can use this to your advantage. For example, if you want to ensure that no one adds new rows or columns to your worksheet, simply enter something (anything) into cell IV16384. Attempting to add a row or column displays the dialog box shown in Figure 7-14.

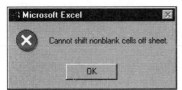

Figure 7-14: Excel's way of telling you that you can't add a new row or column.

You also can insert cells rather than just rows or columns. Select the range into which you want to add new cells and select the Insert⇨Cells command. To insert cells, the other cells must be shifted to the right or shifted down. Therefore, Excel displays the dialog box shown in Figure 7-15 to find out the direction that you want to shift the cells.

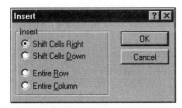

Figure 7-15: When you insert cells, Excel needs to know the direction to shift the cells to make room.

Caution Shifting cells around could cause problems in other places in your worksheet, so use caution with the Insert⇨Cells command. Better yet, avoid it if you can and insert entire rows or columns. In fact, I've *never* used this command.

Deleting rows and columns

To delete a row or rows, use any of the following methods:

✦ Select an entire row or multiple rows by clicking on the row numbers in the worksheet border; then select the Edit⇨Delete command.

✦ Select an entire row or multiple rows by clicking on the row numbers in the worksheet border. Right-click and choose Delete from the shortcut menu.

✦ Move the cell pointer to the row that you want to insert and select the Edit⇨Delete command. In the dialog box that appears, choose the Entire Row option. If you select multiple cells in the column, Excel deletes all selected rows.

Deleting columns works the same way. If you discover that you accidentally deleted a row or column, select the Edit⇨Undo command (or Ctrl+Z) to undo the action.

Changing column widths and row heights

Excel lets you change the widths of columns and the height of rows.

Changing column widths

Column width is measured in terms of the number of characters that will fit into the cell's width. By default, each column's width is 8.43. This is actually a rather meaningless measure because in most fonts the width of individual characters varies — the letter *i* is much narrower than the letter *W*.

There are a number of ways to change the width of a column or columns. Before changing the width, you can select multiple columns so that the width will be the same for all selected columns. To select multiple columns, click and drag in the column border, or press Ctrl while you select individual columns. To select all columns, click on the Select All button in the upper-left corner of the worksheet border (or press Ctrl+spacebar).

✦ Drag the right column border with the mouse until the column is the desired width.

✦ Choose the Format⇨Column⇨Width command and enter a value in the Column Width dialog box.

✦ Choose the Format⇨Column⇨AutoFit Selection command. This adjusts the width of the selected column so that the widest entry in the column fits.

✦ Double-click on the right border of a column to automatically set the column width to the widest entry in the column.

Tip   To change the default width of all columns, use the Format⇨Column⇨Standard Width command. This displays a dialog box into which you enter the new default column width. All columns that haven't been previously adjusted take on the new column width.

Changing row heights

Row height is measured in points (a standard unit of measurement in the printing trade). The default row height depends on the font defined in the Normal style. Excel adjusts row heights automatically to accommodate the tallest font in the row. So, if you change the font size of a cell to, say, 20 points, Excel makes the column taller so that the entire text is visible.

You can set the row height manually, however, using any of several techniques. As with columns, you can select multiple rows.

✦ Drag the lower row border with the mouse until the row is the desired height.

✦ Choose the Format⇨Row⇨Height command and enter a value (in points) in the Row Height dialog box.

✦ Double-click on the bottom border of a row to automatically set the row height to the tallest entry in the row. You also can use the Format⇨Row⇨AutoFit command for this.

Changing the row height is useful for spacing out rows and is preferable to inserting empty rows between lines of data. Figure 7-16 shows a simple report that uses taller rows to produce a double-spaced effect.

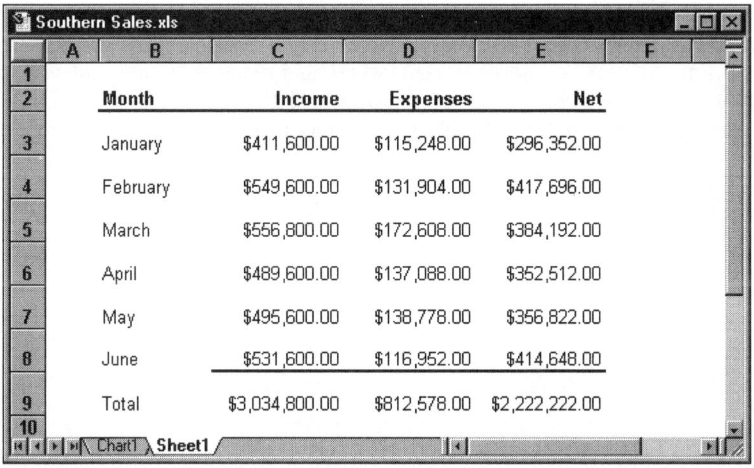

Month	Income	Expenses	Net
January	$411,600.00	$115,248.00	$296,352.00
February	$549,600.00	$131,904.00	$417,696.00
March	$556,800.00	$172,608.00	$384,192.00
April	$489,600.00	$137,088.00	$352,512.00
May	$495,600.00	$138,778.00	$356,822.00
June	$531,600.00	$116,952.00	$414,648.00
Total	$3,034,800.00	$812,578.00	$2,222,222.00

Figure 7-16: Changing row heights is the best way to space out the rows in a report.

Hiding rows and columns

Excel lets you hide rows and columns. This might be useful if you don't want users to see particular information. To hide a row or rows, select the row or rows and choose the Format⇨Row⇨Hide command. To hide a column or columns, select the column or columns and choose the Format⇨Column⇨Hide command.

You also can drag the row or column's border to hide it. To hide a row, drag the bottom border upward. To hide a column, drag the column's right border to the left.

Note A hidden row is actually a row with its height set to 0. Similarly, a hidden column has a column width of 0. When you use the arrow keys to move the cell pointer, cells in hidden rows or columns are skipped. In other words, you can't use the arrow keys to move to a cell in a hidden row or column.

Unhiding a hidden row or column can be a bit tricky because it's difficult to select a row or column that's hidden. The solution is to select the columns or rows that are adjacent to the hidden column or row (select at least one column or row on either side). Then, select the Format⇨Row⇨Unhide or the Format⇨Column⇨Unhide command. Another method is to use the Edit⇨Go To command (or its F5 equivalent) to activate a cell in a hidden row or column. For example, if column A is hidden, you can press F5 and specify cell A1 (or any other cell in column A). This moves the cell pointer to the hidden column. Then you can use the appropriate command to unhide the column.

Summary

This chapter delves into some important operations that all Excel users should know about. I cover topics dealing with adding and removing worksheets, renaming worksheets, and moving and copying worksheets. I also discuss topics that help you control the view of your worksheet: freezing panes and splitting panes. I conclude with a discussion of operations that involve entire rows or columns.

✦　　✦　　✦

Working with Cells and Ranges

CHAPTER

8

✦   ✦   ✦   ✦

In This Chapter

Essential operations
that involve cells and
ranges: selecting,
copying, moving, and
so on

Naming cells and
ranges (and why this
is a good idea)

Deleting and
redefining names

✦   ✦   ✦   ✦

This chapter discusses some techniques that you use to work with cells and ranges.

Cells and Ranges

As you know, a cell is a single addressable element in a worksheet that can hold a value, text, or a formula. A cell is identified by an *address,* which is made up of its column letter and row number. For example, cell D12 is the cell in the fourth column and the twelfth row.

A group of cells is called a *range.* You designate a range address by specifying its upper-left cell address and its lower-right cell address, separated by a colon.

Here are some examples of range addresses:

A1:B1	Two cells that occupy one row and two columns
C24	A range that consists of a single cell
A1:A100	100 cells in column A
A1:D4	16 cells (four rows by four columns)
C1:C16384	An entire column of cells; this range also can be expressed as C:C
A6:IV6	An entire row of cells; this range also can be expressed as 6:6
A1:IV16386	All cells in a worksheet

Note When you're simply navigating through a worksheet or formatting cells, it's not all that important that you know the range address with which you're working. Understanding cell addresses is most important when creating formulas, as you'll see in the next chapter.

Alternate cell addresses

In the normal course of "spreadsheeting," you reference cells by their column letter and row number (cell D16 for the cell at the intersection of the fourth column and sixteenth row, for example). You may not know it, but Excel gives you a choice in this matter. You can select the Tools⇨Options command (General tab) and then choose the R1C1 option. After selecting this option, the column borders in your worksheets are displayed as numbers rather than as letters. Furthermore, all cell references in your formulas use this different notation.

If you find RC notation confusing, you're not alone. RC notation isn't too bad when you're dealing with absolute references. But, when relative references are involved, the brackets can drive you batty.

The numbers in the brackets refer to the relative position of the reference. For example, R[-5]C[-3] specifies the cell that's five rows above and three columns to the left. On the other hand, R[5]C[3] references the cell that's five rows *below* and three columns to the *right*. If the brackets are omitted, it specifies the same row or column: R[5]C refers to the cell five rows below in the same column.

Virtually every Excel user that I know uses the standard letter-number notation, although one well-known spreadsheet book author swears by RC notation and, in one of his books, he makes a good case for using it. But he didn't convert me. I use standard notation throughout the book.

See the table for examples of how normal formulas would translate to RC notation.

Formulas Using Column Letters and Row Numbers	Formulas Using RC Notation
=$A$1	=R1C1
=A1+A2+A3	=R[-3]C+R[-2]C+R[-1]C
=(A1+A2)/$A$3	=(R[-3]C+R[-2]C)/R3C1

Selecting ranges

To perform an operation on a range of cells in a worksheet, you must select the range of cells. For example, if you want to make the text bold for a range of cells, you must select the range and then click the Bold button on the Formatting toolbar.

When you select a range, the cells appear in reverse video. The exception is the active cell, which remains its normal color. Figure 8-1 shows an example of a selected range in a worksheet.

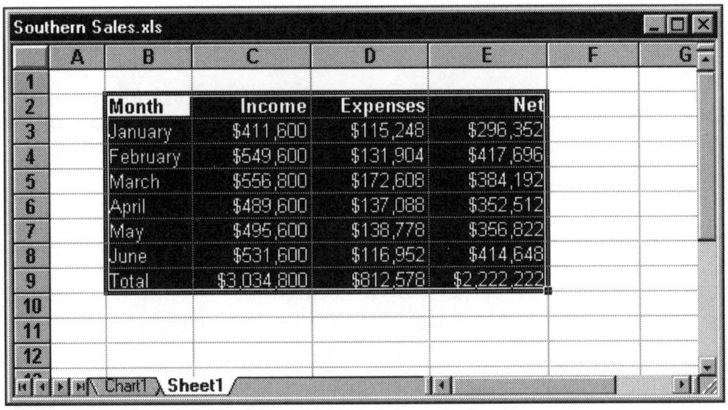

Southern Sales.xls						
	Month	Income	Expenses	Net		
	January	$411,600	$115,248	$296,352		
	February	$549,600	$131,904	$417,696		
	March	$556,800	$172,608	$384,192		
	April	$489,600	$137,088	$352,512		
	May	$495,600	$138,778	$356,822		
	June	$531,600	$116,952	$414,648		
	Total	$3,034,800	$812,578	$2,222,222		

Figure 8-1: When you select a range, it appears highlighted. The active cell within the range is not highlighted.

You can select a range in several ways:

✦ Click the mouse and drag to highlight the range. If you drag to the end of the screen, the worksheet will scroll.

✦ Press F8 and then move the cell pointer with the direction keys to highlight the range. Press F8 again to return the direction keys to normal movement. Another way to select a range using the keyboard is to press the Shift key while you use the direction keys to select a range.

✦ Use the Edit⇨Go To command (or press F5) and enter a range's address manually into the Go To dialog box. When you click on OK, Excel selects the cells in the range that you specified.

Selecting complete rows and columns

You can select entire rows and columns much as you select ranges. There are several ways to do this:

✦ Click on the row or column border to select a single row or column.

✦ To select multiple adjacent rows or columns, simply click on a row or column border and drag to highlight additional rows or columns.

✦ To select multiple (nonadjacent) rows or columns, press Ctrl while you click on the rows or columns that you want.

✦ Press Ctrl+spacebar to select a column. The column of the active cell will be highlighted.

✦ Press Shift+spacebar to select a row. The row of the active cell will be high-lighted.

✦ Click on the Select All button (or Ctrl+Shift+spacebar) to select all rows. Selecting all rows is the same as selecting all columns, which is the same as selecting all cells.

Selecting noncontiguous ranges

Most of the time, the ranges that you select will be *contiguous* — a single rectangle of cells. Excel also lets you work with noncontiguous ranges. A *noncontiguous range* consists of two or more ranges (or single cells), not necessarily next to each other. This is also known as a *multiple selection*. If you want to apply the same formatting to cells in different areas of your worksheet, one approach is to make a multiple selection. When the appropriate cells or ranges are selected, the formatting that you select is applied to them all. Figure 8-2 shows a noncontiguous range selected in a worksheet.

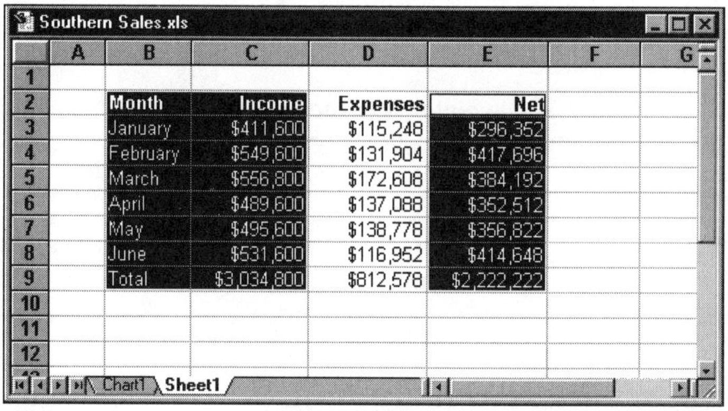

Figure 8-2: Excel lets you select noncontiguous ranges, as shown here.

You can select a noncontiguous range in several ways:

✦ Hold down Ctrl while you click the mouse and drag to highlight the individual cells or ranges.

✦ From the keyboard, select a range as described previously (using F8 or the Shift key). Then press Shift+F8 to select another range without canceling the previous range selections.

✦ Use the Edit⇨Go To command and enter a range's address manually into the Go To dialog box. Separate the different ranges with a comma. When you click on OK, Excel selects the cells in the ranges that you specified (see Figure 8-3).

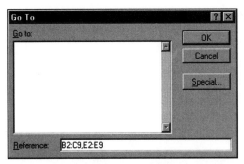

Figure 8-3: Enter a noncontiguous range by separating the ranges with a comma. This example will select a noncontiguous range made up of two ranges: B2:C9 and E2:E9.

Selecting multisheet ranges

So far, this discussion has focused on ranges on a single worksheet. As you know, an Excel workbook can contain more than one worksheet. And, as you might expect, ranges can extend across multiple worksheets. You can think of these as three-dimensional ranges.

Say that you have a workbook set up to track expenses by department. A common approach is to use a separate worksheet for each department. This approach makes it easy to organize the data, and you can click on a sheet tab to view the information for a particular department.

On the CD-ROM The CD-ROM included with this book contains a workbook file named DEPBUDG.XLS, shown in Figure 8-4. You can use this workbook to practice selecting multisheet ranges, and I refer to it in the example that follows. The workbook has four sheets named Total, Marketing, Operations, and Manufacturing. The sheets are laid out identically. The only difference is the values. The Total sheet contains formulas that compute the sum of the corresponding items in the three departmental worksheets.

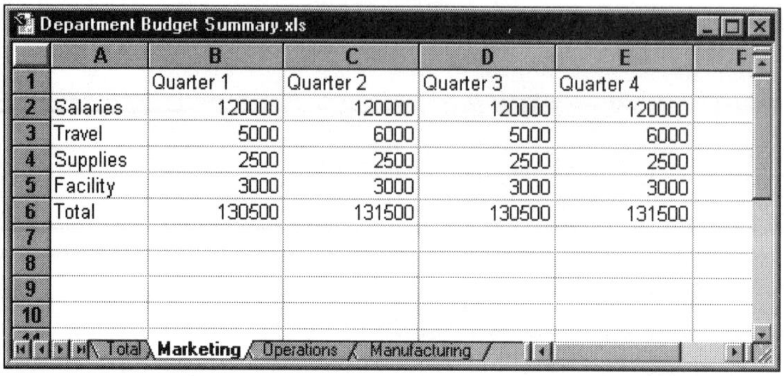

Figure 8-4: A sample workbook that uses multiple worksheets.

The worksheets in the Department Budget Summary workbook aren't formatted in any way. If you want to apply number formats, for example, one (not so efficient) approach is to simply format the values in each worksheet separately. A better technique is to select a multisheet range and format the cells in all of the sheets at once. Here's a step-by-step example of multisheet formatting using the Department Budget Summary workbook.

1. Open the Department Budget Summary workbook and activate the Total worksheet.

2. Select the range that contains values: B2:E6.

3. Press Shift and click on the sheet tab labeled Manufacturing. This selects all worksheets between the active worksheet (Totals) and the sheet tab that you clicked — in essence, a three-dimensional range of cells (see Figure 8-5). Notice that the title bar displays *[Group]*. This is a reminder that you've selected a group of sheets and that you're in Group edit mode.

4. Click the Comma Style button on the Formatting toolbar. This applies comma formatting to the selected cells.

5. Click one of the other sheet tabs. This selects the sheet and also cancels Group mode; *[Group]* will no longer be displayed in the title bar.

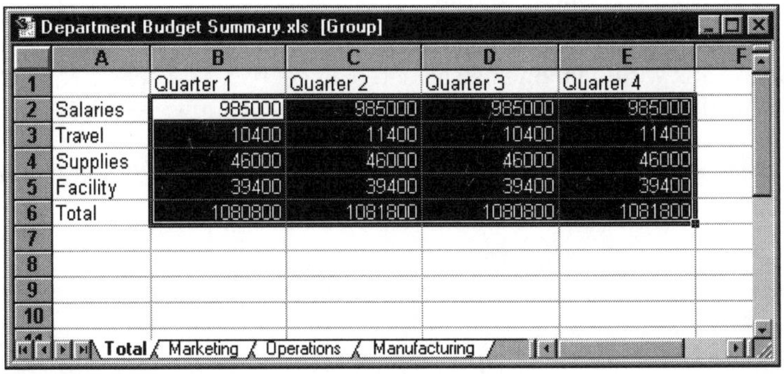

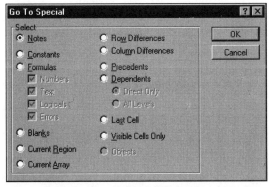

Figure 8-5: Excel in Group mode. A three-dimensional range of cells is selected.

If you examine the sheets, you'll notice that the comma formatting was applied to all of the values in the selected sheets.

In general, selecting a multisheet range is a simple two-step process: Select the range on one sheet and then select the worksheets to include in the range. You can press Shift to select a group of contiguous worksheets or hold down Ctrl to select individual worksheets. If all of the worksheets in a workbook aren't laid out the same, you can skip the sheets that you don't want to format. In either case, the selected sheet tabs appear in reverse video, and Excel displays *[Group]* in the title bar.

Special selections

Earlier, I mentioned the Edit⇨Go To command (or F5) as a way to select (or go to) a cell or range. Excel also provides a way to select only "special" cells in the workbook or in a selected range. You do this by choosing the Edit⇨Go To command, which brings up the Go To dialog box. Clicking the Special button displays the Go To Special dialog box shown in Figure 8-6.

Figure 8-6: The Go To Special dialog box lets you select specific types of cells.

After making your choice in the dialog box, Excel selects the qualifying subset of cells in the current selection. Usually, this results in a multiple selection. If you bring up the Go To Special dialog box with only one cell selected, Excel bases its selection on the active area of the worksheet. If no cells qualify, Excel lets you know.

Table 8-1 offers a description of the options available in this dialog box. Some of the options can be quite useful.

Table 8-1
Select Special Options

Option	What It Does
Notes	Selects only the cells that contain cell notes (see the next section). Ctrl+Shift+? is the shortcut for this.
Constants	Selects all nonempty cells that don't contain formulas. This option is useful if you have a model set up, and you want to clear out all input cells and enter new values. The formulas will remain intact.
Formulas	Selects cells that contain formulas. You can further qualify this by selecting the type of result: numbers, text, logical values (true or false), or errors. These terms are described in the next chapter.
Blanks	Selects all empty cells.
Current Region	Selects a rectangular range of cells around the active cell. This range is determined by surrounding blank rows and columns. Ctrl+* is the shortcut key for this.
Current Array	Selects the entire array. I discuss arrays in Chapter 20.
Row Differences	Analyzes the selection and selects cells that are different from other cells in each row. Ctrl+\ is the shortcut for this.
Column Differences	Analyzes the selection and selects the cells that are different from other cells in each column. Ctrl+Shift+| is the shortcut for this.
Precedents	Selects cells that are referred to in the formulas in the active cell or selection. You can select either direct precedents or precedents at any level.
Dependents	Selects cells with formulas that refer to the active cell or selection. You can select either direct dependents or dependents at any level.
Last Cell	Selects the bottom-right cell in the worksheet that contains data or formatting. Ctrl+End is the shortcut for this.
Visible Cells Only	Selects only visible cells in the selection. This option is useful when dealing with outlines or an autofiltered list.
Objects	Selects all graphic objects on the worksheet.

Annotating a Cell

Excel's cell note feature lets you attach a note to a cell. This feature is useful when you need to document a particular value. It's also useful to help you remember what a formula does. To add a note to a cell, select the cell and choose the Insert⇨Note command (or Shift+F2). Excel displays the Cell Note dialog box, which is shown in Figure 8-7.

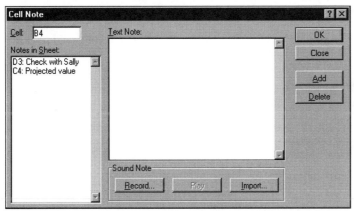

Figure 8-7: The Cell Note dialog box lets you add a descriptive note to a cell.

Enter the text for the cell note into the Text Note box and click on OK. This dialog box lists all notes in the workbook, and you can add notes to multiple cells without closing the dialog box. Use the Add button to add a note, and then select the next cell using the Cell edit box. When you're finished adding cell notes, click on OK.

Cells that have a note attached display a small red dot in the upper-right corner. When you move the mouse pointer over a cell that contains a note, Excel displays the note in a pop-up box (similar to the tooltips for toolbar buttons). This is a new feature in Excel 95. In previous versions, the only way to view a cell note was to use the Insert⇨Note command.

If your computer is equipped with a sound card and microphone, you also can add an audio note to the cell (or import a sound file). Click on the Record button to record an audio note, or click on the Import button to import a sound file, which must be in the WAV format.

Be careful with sound notes because they take up lots of memory and storage space. Using audio notes can make the size of your workbook increase significantly.

Deleting Cell Contents

To erase the contents of a cell or range, select the cell or range and press Delete. Or you can use the Edit⇨Clear command.

Tip   To erase cells using only the mouse, select the cell or range to be deleted. Then click the fill handle — the small square at the lower left of the selection indicator (see Figure 8-8). When you move the mouse pointer over the fill handle, the pointer changes to a cross. As you drag up and/or to the left, Excel grays out the selection. Release the mouse button to erase the grayed selection.

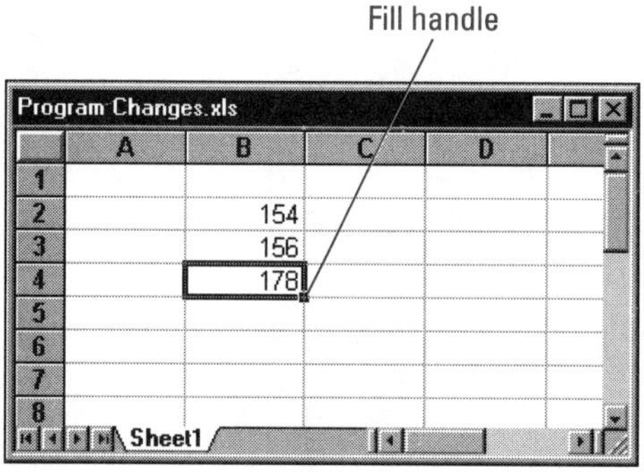

Fill handle

Figure 8-8: Use the fill handle to erase cell contents using the mouse.

Copying a Range

Often, you'll want to copy the contents of a cell to another cell or range. Copying is a very common spreadsheet operation, and there are several types of copying allowed. You can do any of the following:

✦ Copy a cell to another cell.

✦ Copy a cell to a range of cells. The source cell is copied to every cell in the destination range.

✦ Copy a range to another range. Both ranges have to be the same size.

Note   Copying a cell normally copies the cell contents and any formatting that was applied to the original cell. When you copy a cell that contains a formula, the cell references in the copied formulas are changed automatically to be relative to their new destination. More on this in the next chapter.

Copying consists of two steps (although there are shortcut methods, as you'll see later):

1. Select the cell or range to copy (the source range) and copy it to the Windows Clipboard.

2. Move the cell pointer to the range that will hold the copy (the destination range) and paste the Clipboard contents.

Caution When you paste information, Excel overwrites — without warning — any cells that get in the way. If you find that some essential cells were overwritten by pasting, execute the Edit⇨Undo command (or press Ctrl+Z) immediately.

Because copying is used so often, Excel gives you many different methods. I discuss each method in the following sections.

About the Windows Clipboard

In several places throughout this chapter, I mention the Windows Clipboard. The Clipboard is an area of memory that stores information that has been cut or copied from a Windows program. The Clipboard can store data in a variety of formats. Because it is managed by Windows, information on the Clipboard can be pasted to other Windows applications, regardless of where it originated from (I discuss the topic of interapplication copying and pasting in Chapter 29). Normally, you can't see information stored on the Clipboard (nor would you want to).

You can, however, run the Clipboard Viewer program, which comes with Windows, to view the Clipboard contents. The accompanying figure shows an example of this program running.

I copied a range of cells from Excel, and the figure shows how it appears in the Clipboard Viewer. You can use the Clipboard Viewer's Display menu to view the data in different formats. You also can save the Clipboard contents in a file, which you can then open at a later time.

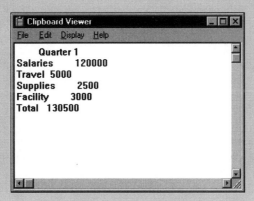

Copying by using toolbar buttons

The Standard toolbar has two buttons that are relevant here: the Copy button and the Paste button. Clicking on the Copy button transfers a copy of the selected cell or range to the Clipboard. After performing the copy part of this operation, activate the cell that will hold the copy and click on the Paste button.

If you're copying a range, you don't need to select an entire range before clicking on the Paste button. You need only activate the upper-left cell in the destination range.

Copying by using menu commands

If you prefer, you can use the following menu commands for copying and pasting:

Edit⇨Copy: Copies the selected cells to the Clipboard

Edit⇨Paste: Pastes the Clipboard contents to the selected cell or range

Copying by using shortcut menus

You also can use the Copy and Paste commands on the shortcut menu, as shown in Figure 8-9. Select the cell or range to copy, right-click, and choose Copy from the shortcut menu. Then, activate the cell to copy to, right-click, and choose Paste from the shortcut menu.

	A	B	C	D	E
1		Quarter 1	Quarter 2	Quarter 3	Quarter 4
2	Salaries	120000	120000	120000	120000
3	Travel	5000	6000	5000	6000
4	Supplies	2500	2500	2500	2500
5	Facility	3000	3000	3000	3000
6	Total	130500			

Cut
Copy
Paste
Paste Special...

Insert...
Delete...
Clear Contents

Format Cells...
Pick from list...

Total \ **Marketing** \ Operations \ Manufacturing

Figure 8-9: Right-clicking displays a shortcut menu, which contains Copy and Paste commands.

Copying by using shortcut keys

The copy and paste operations also have shortcut keys associated with them:

Ctrl+C: Copies the selected cells to the Clipboard

Ctrl+V: Pastes the Clipboard contents to the selected cell or range

Note These shortcut keys also are used by most other Windows applications.

Copying by using drag and drop

Excel also lets you copy a cell or range by dragging. Select the cell or range that you want to copy and then move the mouse pointer to one of its four borders. When the mouse pointer turns into an arrow, press Ctrl; the mouse pointer will be augmented with a small plus sign. Then, simply drag the selection to its new location, keeping the Ctrl key pressed. The original selection remains behind, and Excel makes a new copy when you release the mouse button.

Note If the mouse pointer doesn't turn into an arrow when you point to the border of a cell or range, you need to make a change to your settings. Select the Tools➪Options command, click the Edit tab, and place a check mark on the option labeled Allow Cell Drag and Drop.

Copying to adjacent cells

Often, you'll find that you need to copy a cell to an adjacent cell or range. This need is quite common when working with formulas. For example, if you're working on a budget, you might create a formula to add up the values in column B. You can use the same formula to add up the values in the other columns. Rather than reenter the formula, you'll want to copy it to the adjacent cells.

Excel provides some additional options on its Edit menu for copying to adjacent cells. To use these commands, select the cell that you're copying plus the cells that you are copying to (see Figure 8-10). Then, issue the appropriate command for one-step copying.

Edit➪Fill➪Down (or Ctrl+D): Copies the cell to the selected range below

Edit➪Fill➪Right (or Ctrl+R): Copies the cell to the selected range to the right

Edit➪Fill➪Up: Copies the cell to the selected range above

Edit➪Fill➪Left: Copies the cell to the selected range to the left

Dragging scraps to the desktop

Excel for Windows 95 has a new feature that lets you drag a selected range to the Windows desktop. The official name for this copied range is a *scrap.* The accompanying figure shows a scrap that was dragged to the desktop. The scrap, which is in the lower right corner of the screen, appears as an icon.

Dragging a range from a worksheet to the Windows desktop creates a copy of the selec-

tion that you can use at a later time. For example, you can drag it to another worksheet or to another application. When you drag a scrap to another worksheet, it creates an embedded OLE object (see Chapter 29 for more details). After a scrap has served its intended purpose, you can right-click it and choose Delete to remove it from the desktop.

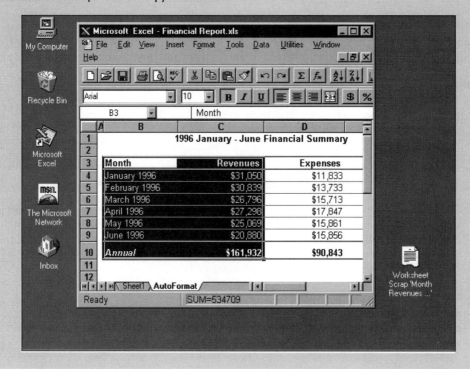

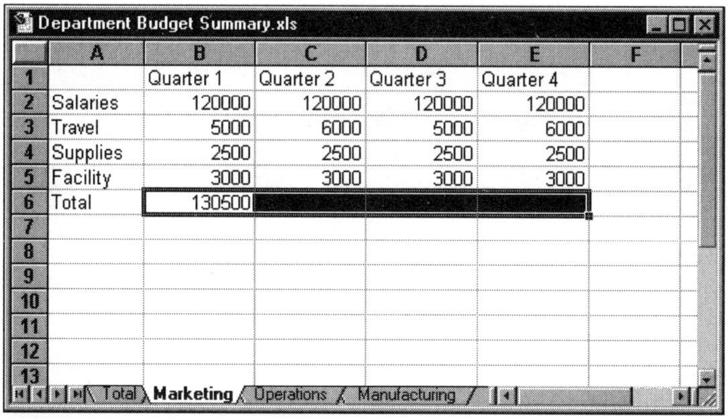

Figure 8-10: To copy to adjacent cells, start by selecting the cell to copy plus the cells that you want to copy to.

Tip Yet another way to copy to adjacent cells is to drag the selection's fill handle. Excel copies the original selection to the cells that you highlight while dragging. This is an example of AutoFill. I discuss more uses for this feature in Chapter 9.

Copying a Range to Other Sheets

The copy procedures described previously also work as expected when you want to copy a cell or range to another worksheet, even if the worksheet is in a different workbook. The only difference is that you must activate the other worksheet before you select the location to copy to. You also can copy a cell or range to a *group* of worksheets with a single command.

On the CD-ROM The CD-ROM included with this book contains a workbook file named DEPBUDG.XLS. You can use this workbook to practice copying a range to multiple sheets, and I refer to it in the example that follows. Assume that you add text to cell A8 in the Totals worksheet. The text is *Preliminary budget, not approved* (see Figure 8-11). After adding the text, you realize that it should appear in all department sheets as well. Following is a step-by-step summary of how to copy the contents of cell A8 on the Totals worksheet to the other sheets in the workbook.

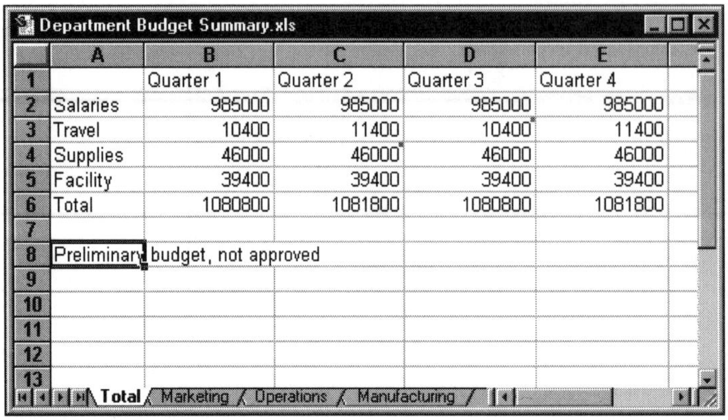

	A	B	C	D	E
1		Quarter 1	Quarter 2	Quarter 3	Quarter 4
2	Salaries	985000	985000	985000	985000
3	Travel	10400	11400	10400	11400
4	Supplies	46000	46000	46000	46000
5	Facility	39400	39400	39400	39400
6	Total	1080800	1081800	1080800	1081800
7					
8	Preliminary budget, not approved				

Figure 8-11: You easily can copy the text in cell A8 to all other sheets in the workbook.

1. Open the workbook and activate the Total worksheet.
2. Enter **Preliminary budget, not approved** into cell A8.
3. With cell A8 selected, click on the Copy button on the Standard toolbar (or use any of the other methods described previously).
4. Enter Group edit mode: Click on the Marketing sheet tab, press Shift, and then click the Manufacturing sheet tab. Select cell A8.
5. Click on the Paste button to paste the Clipboard contents to the selected cell in the selected sheets.

You can verify that the copy operation was successful by clicking on the various department sheets.

Tip

An even faster way to perform this operation is to select all of the sheets (which puts you in Group edit mode) and then activate cell A8 in the Totals worksheet. Press F2 (as if to edit the cell), and then press Enter. The "edited" cell contents will appear in cell A8 of all selected cells. This method produces the same results as described previously but avoids the copy and paste steps.

Moving a Cell or Range

Copying a cell or range doesn't modify the cell or range that was copied. If you want to relocate a cell or range to another location, you'll find that Excel is quite accommodating.

Recall that the Edit⇨Copy command makes a copy of the selected cell or range and puts the copy on the Clipboard. The Edit⇨Cut command also places the selection on the Clipboard, but it removes it from its original location as well. To move a cell or range, therefore, requires two steps:

1. Select the cell or range to copy (the source range) and copy it to the Windows Clipboard.

2. Activate the cell that will hold the moved cell or range (the destination range) and paste the Clipboard contents. The destination range can be on the same worksheet or in a different worksheet — or in a different workbook.

Tip   You also can move a cell or range by dragging it. Select the cell or range to be copied and then move the mouse pointer to either of its four borders. When you do so, the mouse pointer turns into an arrow. Drag the selection to its new location and release the mouse button. This option is similar to copying a cell, except that you don't press Ctrl while dragging.

Other Cell and Range Operations

As you know, the Edit⇨Paste command simply transfers the Clipboard contents to the selected location in your worksheet. You may be interested to know about a much more versatile version of this command: Edit⇨Paste Special. In order for this command to be available, you need to copy a cell or range to the Clipboard (using Edit⇨Cut won't work). Then select the cell where you want to paste. You'll get the dialog box shown in Figure 8-12. This dialog box has several options, which I explain in the following sections.

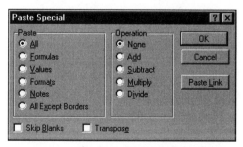

Figure 8-12: The Paste Special dialog box.

Pasting formulas as values

Normally, when you copy a range that contains formulas, the formulas get copied, and Excel automatically adjusts the cell references. The Values option in the Paste Special dialog box lets you copy the *results* of formulas. The destination for the copy can be a new range or the original range. In the latter case, the original formulas will be replaced by their current values.

Pasting cell formats only

If you've applied formatting to a cell or range, you can copy only the formatting and paste it to another cell or range. Use the Formats option in the Paste Special dialog box. This can save a great deal of time if you've applied lots of formatting to a cell and want to duplicate the formatting elsewhere.

Pasting cell notes

If you want to copy only the cell notes from a cell or range, use the Notes option in the Paste Special dialog box. This option doesn't copy cell contents or formatting.

Skipping blanks when pasting

The Skip Blanks option in the Paste Special dialog box prevents Excel from overwriting cell contents in your paste area with blank cells from the copied range. This option is useful if you're copying a range to another area, but you don't want the blank cells in the copied range to overwrite existing data.

Transposing a range

The Transpose option in the Paste Special dialog box changes the orientation of the copied range. Rows become columns and columns become rows. Any formulas in the copied range are adjusted so that they work properly when transposed. Note that this check box can be used with the other options in the Paste Special dialog box. Figure 8-13 shows an example of a horizontal range that was transposed to a vertical range.

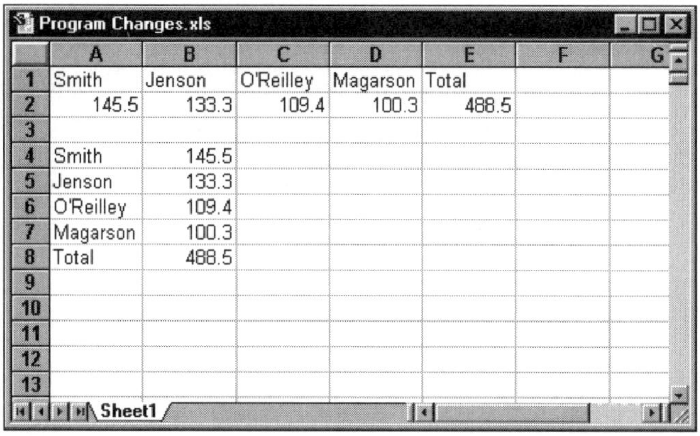

	A	B	C	D	E	F
1	Smith	Jenson	O'Reilley	Magarson	Total	
2	145.5	133.3	109.4	100.3	488.5	
3						
4	Smith	145.5				
5	Jenson	133.3				
6	O'Reilley	109.4				
7	Magarson	100.3				
8	Total	488.5				

Figure 8-13: The range in A1:E2 was transposed to A4:B8.

Performing mathematical operations without formulas

The option buttons in the Operation section of the Paste Special dialog box let you perform an arithmetic operation. For example, you can copy a range to another range and select the Multiply operation. Excel will multiply the corresponding values in the source range and the destination range and replace the destination range with the new values.

Figure 8-14 shows another example of using a mathematical operation with the Paste Special dialog box. The objective is to increase the values in B4:B10 by ten percent. I copied the contents of cell B1 to the Clipboard. I then selected B4:B10 and issued the Edit⇨Paste Special command. Choosing the Multiply operation will cause each cell in B4:B10 to be multiplied by the value on the Clipboard, effectively increasing the cell values by ten percent.

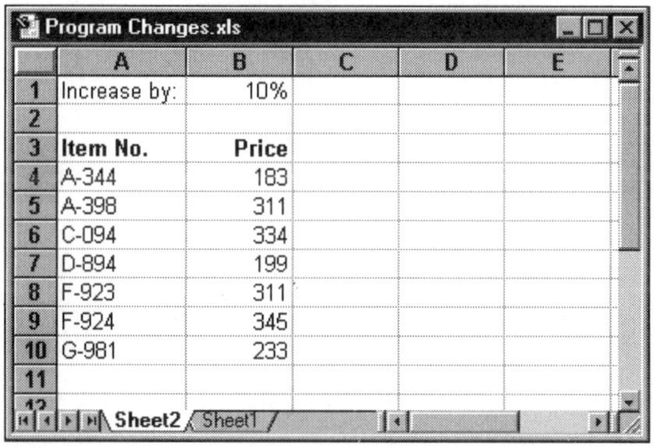

	A	B
1	Increase by:	10%
2		
3	**Item No.**	**Price**
4	A-344	183
5	A-398	311
6	C-094	334
7	D-894	199
8	F-923	311
9	F-924	345
10	G-981	233

Figure 8-14: Using the Paste Special command to increase the values in a range by ten percent.

Naming Cells and Ranges: The Basics

By now, you've probably noticed that dealing with cryptic cell and range addresses can sometimes be confusing (this will become even more apparent when you deal with formulas, which are covered in the next chapter). Fortunately, Excel lets you assign descriptive names to cells and ranges. For example, you can name a cell Interest_Rate and you can name a range JulySales.

Advantages of using names

Using names offers the following advantages:

♦ A meaningful range name (such as Total_Income) is much easier to remember than a cell address (such as AC21).

♦ You can quickly move to areas of your worksheet by using the Name box, located at the left side of the formula bar (click on the arrow to drop down a list of defined names), or by choosing the Edit⇨Go To command (or F5) and specifying the range name.

♦ When you select a named cell or range, the name appears in the Name box.

♦ Creating formulas is easier. You can paste a cell or range name into a formula by using the Insert⇨Name⇨Paste command, or by selecting a name from the Name box.

♦ Names make your formulas more understandable and easier to use. =Income–Taxes is more intuitive than =D20–D40.

♦ Macros are easier to create and maintain when you use range names rather than cell addresses.

♦ You can give a name to a value or formula — even when the value or formula doesn't exist on the worksheet. For example, you can create the name Interest_Rate for a value of .075. Then you can use this name in your formulas (more about this in the next chapter).

Valid names

Although Excel is quite flexible about the names that you can define, it does have some rules:

♦ Names can't contain any spaces. You might want to use an underscore or a period character to simulate a space (such as Annual_Total or Annual.Total).

♦ You can use any combination of letters and numbers, but the name must not begin with a number (such as 3rdQuarter), or look like a cell reference (such as Q3).

✦ Symbols, except for underscore and period, aren't allowed. Although it's not documented, I've found that Excel also allows a backslash (\) and question mark (?).

✦ Names are limited to 255 characters. Trust me, using a name anywhere near this length is not a good idea.

✦ You can use single letters (except for R or C), but this is generally not recommended because it defeats the purpose of using meaningful names.

Caution Excel also uses a few names internally for its own use. Although you can create names that override Excel's internal names, it's best to avoid doing so. To be on the safe side, avoid using the following for names: `Print_Area`, `Print_Titles`, `Consolidate_Area`, and `Sheet_Title`.

Creating names manually

There are several ways to create names. This section discusses two methods to create names manually.

Using the Define Name dialog box

To create a range name, start by selecting the cell or range that you want to name. Then, select the Insert⇨Name⇨Define command (or press Ctrl+F3). Excel displays the Define Name dialog box, shown in Figure 8-15.

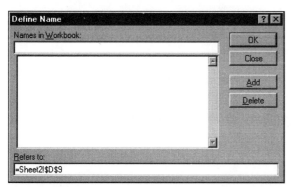

Figure 8-15: Create names for cells or ranges by using the Define Name dialog box.

Type a name in the edit box labeled Names in Workbook (or use the name that Excel proposes, if any). The active or selected cell or range address appears in the Refers to text box. Verify that the address listed is correct, then click on OK to add the name to your worksheet and close the dialog box. Or, you can click on the Add button to continue adding names to your worksheet. If you do this, you must specify the Refers to range by typing an address (make sure to begin with an equal sign) or by pointing to it in the worksheet. Each name appears in the list box.

Using the Name box

A slightly faster way to create a name is to use the Name box. Select the cell or range to name, then click on the Name box and enter the name. Press Enter to create the name. If a name already exists, you can't use the Name box to change the reference that the name refers to. Attempting to do so will simply select the name that you enter.

Note When you enter a name in the Name box, you *must* press Enter to actually register the name. If you type a name and then click in the worksheet, Excel will not create the name.

The Name box is a drop-down list, and it shows all names in the workbook (see Figure 8-16). When you select a named cell or range, its name appears in the name box. To select a named cell or range, click on the Name box and select the name. Excel selects the named cell or range. Oddly enough, there is no way to access the Name box from the keyboard; a mouse is required. Once you click on the Name box, however, you can use the direction keys and Enter to select a name.

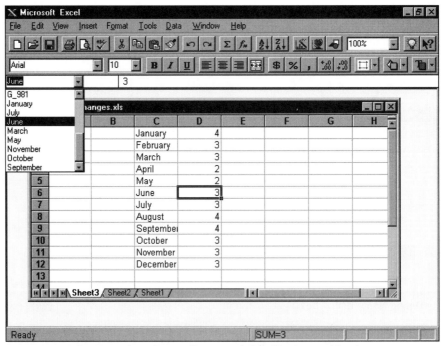

Figure 8-16: The Name box shows all names defined in the workbook.

Creating names automatically

Often, you may have a worksheet that contains text that you want to use for names for adjacent cells or ranges. Figure 8-17 shows an example of such a worksheet. In this case, you might want to use the text in column A to create names for the corresponding values in column B. Excel makes this very easy to do.

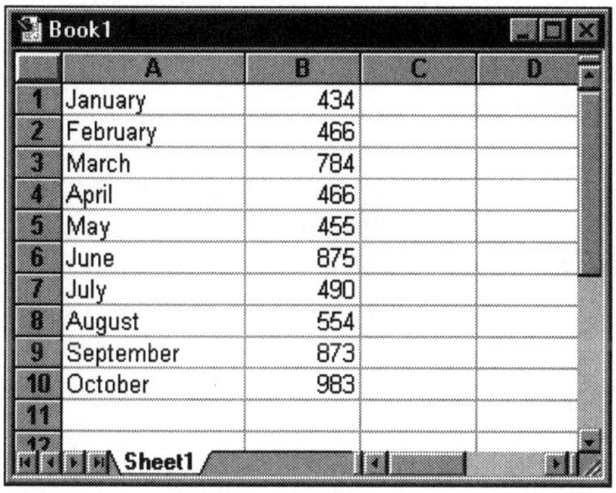

	A	B	C	D
1	January	434		
2	February	466		
3	March	784		
4	April	466		
5	May	455		
6	June	875		
7	July	490		
8	August	554		
9	September	873		
10	October	983		
11				

Book1 · Sheet1

Figure 8-17: Excel makes it easy to create names by using text in adjacent cells.

To create names using adjacent text, start by selecting the name text and the cells that you want to name (these can be individual cells or ranges of cells). The names must be adjacent to the cells you're naming (a multiple selection is not allowed here). Then choose the Insert⇨Name⇨Create command (or Ctrl+Shift+F3). Excel displays the Create Names dialog box, shown in Figure 8-18. The check marks in this dialog box are based on Excel's analysis of the selected range. For example, if it finds text in the first row of the selection, it proposes that you create names based on the top row. If Excel didn't guess correctly, you can change the check boxes. Click on OK and the names are created in a jiffy.

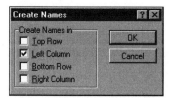

Create Names

Create Names in
☐ Top Row
☑ Left Column
☐ Bottom Row
☐ Right Column

OK
Cancel

Figure 8-18: The Create Name dialog box.

Note If the text contained in a cell results in an invalid name, Excel modifies the name to make it valid. For example, if a cell contains the text *Net Income* (which is invalid for a name because it contains a space), Excel converts the space to an underscore character. If Excel encounters a value or a formula where text should be, however, it doesn't convert it to a valid name. It simply doesn't create a name.

Caution It's a good idea to double-check the names that Excel creates. Sometimes the Insert⇨Name⇨Create command works counterintuitively. Figure 8-19 shows a small table of text and values. If you select the entire table, choose the Insert⇨ Name⇨Create command, and accept Excel's suggestions (Top Row and Left Column options), you'll find that the name `Products` doesn't refer to A2:A5 as you would expect. Rather, it refers to B2:C5. If the upper-left cell of the selection contains text and you choose the Top Row and Left Column options, Excel uses that text for the name of the entire data — excluding the top row and left column. So, before you accept the names that Excel creates, take a minute to make sure that they refer to the correct ranges.

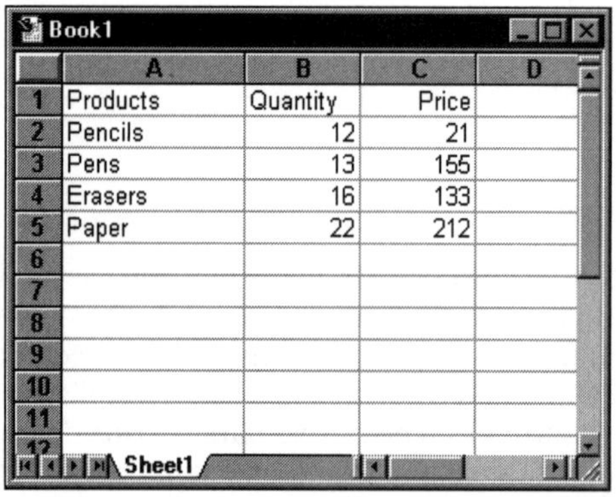

	A	B	C	D
1	Products	Quantity	Price	
2	Pencils	12	21	
3	Pens	13	155	
4	Erasers	16	133	
5	Paper	22	212	

Figure 8-19: Creating names from the data in this table may produce unexpected results.

Creating a table of names

You may want to create a list of all names in the workbook. This might be useful for tracking down errors or as a way to document your work. To create a table of names, first move the cell pointer to an empty area of your worksheet — the table will be created at the active cell position. Use the Insert⇨Name⇨Paste command (or F3). Excel displays the Paste Name dialog box shown in Figure 8-20. This dialog box lists all of the defined names. To paste a list of names, click the Past List button.

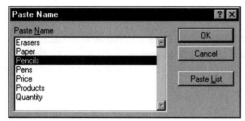

Figure 8-20: The Paste Name dialog box.

Caution The list that Excel pastes will overwrite any cells that get in the way, so make sure that the active cell is located in an empty portion of the worksheet.

Deleting names

If you no longer need a defined name, you can delete it. Choose the Insert⇨Name⇨ Define command to display the Define Name dialog box. Choose the name that you want to delete from the list and click on the Delete button.

Caution Be extra careful when deleting names. If the name is used in a formula, deleting the name causes the formula to become invalid (it will display #NAME?). Even worse, deleting a name can't be undone. It's a good practice to save your workbook before you delete any names.

If you delete the rows or columns that contain named cells or ranges, the names contain an invalid reference. For example, if cell A1 on Sheet1 is named Interest and you delete row 1 or column A, Interest then refers to =Sheet1!#REF! (that is, an erroneous reference). If you use Interest in a formula, the formula will display #REF.

Redefining names

After you've defined a name, you may want to change the cell or range to which it refers. You can use the Define Name dialog box to do this. Select the Insert⇨Name⇨ Define command, click on the name that you want to change, and edit the cell or range address in the Refers to edit box. If you like, you can click on the edit box and select a new cell or range by pointing in the worksheet.

Note Excel automatically adjusts the cells to which your names refer. For example, assume that cell A10 is named Summary. If you delete a row above row 10, Summary will then refer to cell A9. This is just what you would expect to happen, so you don't need to be concerned about it.

Changing names

Excel doesn't have a simple way to change a name once the name is created. If you create a name and then realize that it's not the name you wanted — or, perhaps, that you spelled it incorrectly — you must create the new name and then delete the old name.

Learning more about names

Cross-Reference Excel offers some additional features when it comes to using names — features unmatched in any of its competitors. These advanced naming features are most useful when working with formulas. I discuss these features in Chapter 9.

Summary

In this chapter I discuss the basic worksheet operations that involve cells and ranges. These operations include selecting, copying, moving, deleting, and working with ranges that extend across multiple worksheets in a workbook. I also introduce the topic of names. This is an important concept that can make your worksheets more readable and easier to maintain.

✦   ✦   ✦

Creating and Using Formulas

◆ ◆ ◆ ◆

In This Chapter

An overview of how
Excel uses formulas

How to enter and edit
formulas

When to use absolute
cell referencing

Identifying errors in
your formulas

Controlling how Excel
calculates formulas

Handling circular
references

Useful naming
techniques

◆ ◆ ◆ ◆

Formulas are what make a spreadsheet so useful. Without formulas, a spreadsheet would be nothing more than a word processor with a very powerful table feature (and not much else). A worksheet without formulas is essentially dead. Using formulas adds life and lets you calculate results from the data stored in the worksheet. This chapter introduces formulas and helps you get up to speed with this important element.

Introducing Formulas

To add a formula to a worksheet, you enter it into a cell. You can delete, move, and copy formulas just like any other item of data. Formulas use arithmetic operators to work with values, text, worksheet functions, and other formulas to calculate a value in the cell. Values and text can be located in other cells, which makes changing data easy and gives worksheets their dynamic nature. For example, Excel recalculates formulas if an assumption (represented by data) changes. In essence, you can see multiple scenarios quickly by changing the data in a worksheet and letting formulas do the work.

A formula entered into a cell can consist of any of the following elements:

✦ Operators such as + (for addition) and * (for multiplication)

✦ Cell references (including named cells and ranges)

✦ Values

✦ Worksheet functions (such as SUM)

A formula can consist of up to 1,024 characters. When you enter a formula into a cell, the cell displays the result of the formula.

The formula itself appears in the formula bar when the cell is activated, however.

Here are a few examples of formulas:

=150*.05	Multiplies 150 times .05. This formula uses only values and isn't all that useful.
=A1+A2	Adds the values in cells A1 and A2.
=Income–Expenses	Subtracts the cell named Expenses from the cell named Income.
=SUM(A1:A12)	Adds the values in the range A1:A12.
=A1=C12	Compares cell A1 with cell C12. If they are identical, the formula returns TRUE, otherwise it returns FALSE.

Note   Notice that formulas always begin with an equal sign. This is how Excel distinguishes formulas from text.

Operators used in formulas

Excel lets you use a variety of operators in your formulas. Table 9-1 lists the operators that Excel recognizes. In addition to these, Excel has many built-in functions that let you perform more operations. These functions are discussed in detail in Chapter 10.

<table>
<tr><th colspan="2">Table 9-1
Operators Used in Formulas</th></tr>
<tr><th>Operator</th><th>Name</th></tr>
<tr><td>+</td><td>Addition</td></tr>
<tr><td>-</td><td>Subtraction</td></tr>
<tr><td>*</td><td>Multiplication</td></tr>
<tr><td>/</td><td>Division</td></tr>
<tr><td>^</td><td>Exponentiation</td></tr>
<tr><td>&</td><td>Concatenation</td></tr>
<tr><td>=</td><td>Logical comparison</td></tr>
<tr><td>></td><td>Logical comparison</td></tr>
<tr><td><</td><td>Logical comparison</td></tr>
</table>

You can, of course, use as many operators as you need (formulas can be quite complex). Figure 9-1 shows a worksheet with a formula in cell B5. The formula is as follows:

```
=(B2-B3)*B4
```

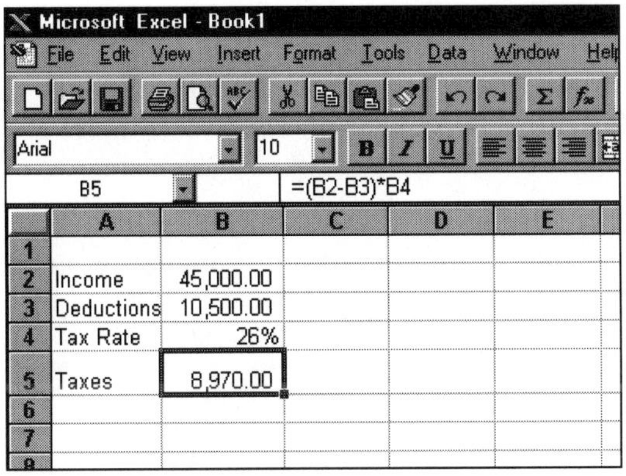

Figure 9-1: A formula that uses two operators.

In this example, the formula subtracts the value in B3 from the value in B2 and then multiplies the result by the value in B4. If the worksheet had names defined for these cells, the formula would be a lot more readable. Here's the same formula after naming the cells:

```
=(Income-Expense)*TaxRate
```

Now are you beginning to understand why using names is such an important concept? Following are some additional examples of formulas that use various operators.

="Part-"&"23A"	Joins *(concatenates)* the two text strings to produce *Part-23A*.
=A1&A2	Concatenates the contents of cell A1 with cell A2. Concatenation works with values as well as text. If cell A1 contains 123 and cell A2 contains 456, this formula would return the value 123456.
=6^3	Raises 6 to the third power (216).
=216^(1/3)	Returns the cube root of 216 (6).
=A1<A2	Returns TRUE if the value in cell A1 is less than the value in cell A2. Otherwise, it returns FALSE. Logical comparison operators also work with text. If A1 contained *Bill* and A2 contained *Julia,* the formula would return TRUE because Bill comes before Julia in alphabetical order.

| =A1<=A2 | Returns TRUE if the value in cell A1 is less than or equal to the value in cell A2. Otherwise, it returns FALSE. |
| =A1<>A2 | Returns TRUE if the value in cell A1 isn't equal to the value in cell A2. Otherwise, it returns FALSE. |

Operator precedence

In an earlier example, I used parentheses in the formula to control the order in which the calculations occur. The formula without parentheses would look like this:

```
=Income-Expense*TaxRate
```

If you enter the formula without the parentheses, you'll discover that Excel computes the wrong answer. To understand why this is so, you need to understand a concept called *operator precedence*. This is basically the set of rules that Excel uses to perform its calculation. Table 9-2 lists Excel's operator precedence. This table shows that exponentiation has the highest precedence (that is, it's performed first) and logical comparisons have the lowest precedence.

Table 9-2
Operator Precedence in Excel Formulas

Symbol	Operator	Precedence
^	Exponentiation	1
*	Multiplication	2
/	Division	2
+	Addition	3
-	Subtraction	3
&	Concatenation	4
=	Equal to	5
<	Less than	5
>	Greater than	5

You use parentheses to override Excel's built-in order of precedence. Returning to the previous example, the formula that follows doesn't use parentheses and is therefore evaluated using Excel's standard operator precedence. Because multiplication has a higher precedence, the `Expense` cell is multiplied by the `TaxRate` cell. Then this result is subtracted from `Income`. This isn't what was intended.

```
=Income-Expense*TaxRate
```

The correct formula, which follows, uses parentheses to control the order of operations. Expressions within parentheses are always evaluated first. In this case, Expense is subtracted from Income and the result is multiplied by TaxRate.

```
=(Income-Expense)*TaxRate
```

You can also *nest* parentheses in formulas. Nesting means putting parentheses inside of parentheses. If you do so, Excel evaluates the most deeply nested expressions first and works its way out. Figure 9-2 shows an example of a formula that uses nested parentheses.

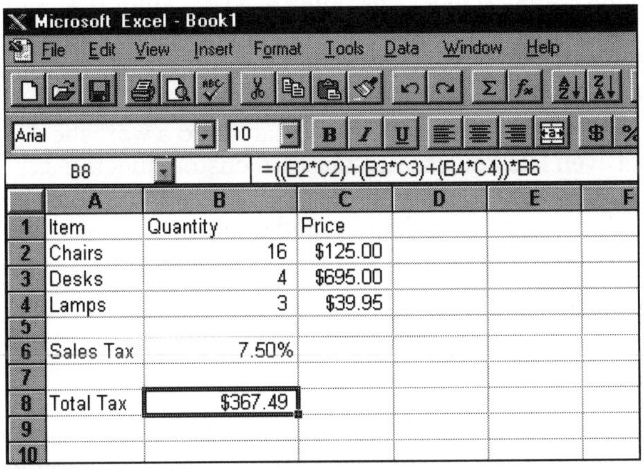

Figure 9-2: A formula with nested parentheses.

```
=((B2*C2)+(B3*C3)+(B4*C4))*B6
```

This formula has four sets of parentheses — three sets are nested inside of the fourth set. Excel evaluates each nested set of parentheses and then adds up the three results. This sum is then multiplied by the value in B6.

Tip   It's a good idea to make liberal use of parentheses in your formulas. I often use parentheses even when they aren't necessary to clarify the order of operations and make the formula easier to read. For example, if you want to add 1 to the product of two cells, the following formula will do it:

```
=1+A1*A2
```

I find it much clearer, however, to use the following formula (with superfluous parentheses):

```
=1+(A1*A2)
```

Tip   Every left parenthesis, of course, must have a matching right parenthesis. If you have
many levels of nested parentheses, it can get confusing. If the parentheses don't
match, Excel pops up a message telling you so and won't let you enter the formula.
Fortunately, Excel lends a hand in helping you match parentheses. When you're
entering or editing a formula that has parentheses, pay attention to the text. When the
cursor moves over a parenthesis, Excel momentarily makes it and its matching
parenthesis bold. This lasts for less than a second, so be alert.

Excel's built-in functions

Excel provides a bewildering number of built-in worksheet functions that you can use
in your formulas. These include common functions (such as SUM, AVERAGE, and
SQRT) as well as functions designed for special purposes such as statistics or engineering. Functions can greatly enhance the power of your formulas. They can simplify
your formulas and make them easier to read, and in many cases they let you perform
calculations that would not be possible otherwise. If you can't find a worksheet
function that you need, Excel even lets you create your own custom functions.

Cross-
Reference   I discuss Excel's built-in functions in the next chapter, and Chapter 35 covers the
basics of creating custom functions using VBA.

Entering Formulas

As I mentioned earlier, a formula must begin with an equal sign to let Excel know that
the cell contains a formula rather than text. There are basically two ways to enter a
formula into a cell: enter it manually or enter it by pointing to cell references. I discuss
each of these methods in the following sections.

Entering formulas manually

Entering a formula manually involves, well, entering a formula manually. You simply
type an equal sign (=) followed by the formula. As you type, the characters appear in
the cell as well as in the formula bar. You can, of course, use all of the normal editing
keys when entering a formula.

Entering formulas by pointing

The other method of entering a formula still involves some manual typing, but you can
simply point to the cell references instead of entering them manually. For example, to
enter the formula =A1+A2 into cell A3, follow these steps:

1. Move the cell pointer to cell A3.

2. Type an equal sign (=) to begin the formula. Notice that Excel displays *Enter* in
the status bar.

3. Press the up arrow twice. As you press this key, notice that Excel displays a faint moving border around the cell and that the cell reference appears in cell A3 and in the formula bar. Also notice that Excel displays *Point* in the status bar.

4. Type a plus sign (+). The faint border disappears and *Enter* reappears in the status bar.

5. Press the up arrow one more time. A2 is added to the formula.

6. Press Enter to end the formula.

Pointing to cell addresses rather than entering them manually is usually more accurate and less tedious.

Note If you're a hard-core mouse fanatic, you may be interested in the fact that Excel provides a set of toolbar tools that insert various characters into a formula for you. These include tools to insert all of the operators, plus tools to insert parentheses, colon, comma, percent sign, and dollar sign. These tools aren't contained on any of the prebuilt toolbars, so you must create a custom toolbar to use them (or you can add them to an existing toolbar). See Chapter 32 for details on customizing toolbars.

Tip When you create a formula that refers to other cells, the cell that contains the formula has the same number format as the first cell it refers to.

Pasting names

If your formula uses named cells or ranges, you can type the name in place of the address or choose the name from a list and have Excel insert the name for you automatically. There are three ways to do this:

✦ Select the Insert⇨Name⇨Paste command. Excel displays its Paste Name dialog box with all of the names listed (see Figure 9-3). Select the name and click on OK. Or, you can double-click on the name, which inserts the name and closes the dialog box.

✦ Press F3. This also displays the Paste Name dialog box.

✦ Click on the Name box and select a name from the list.

Caution The Name box displays only the first 100 names in the workbook, in alphabetical order. So, don't be alarmed if you have more than 100 names and a name doesn't appear in the Name box.

Referencing Cells Outside the Worksheet

Formulas can refer to cells on other worksheets — and the worksheets don't even have to be in the same workbook. Excel uses a special type of notation to handle these types of references.

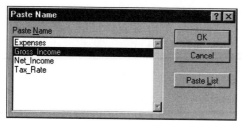

Figure 9-3: The Paste Name dialog box lets you insert a name into a formula.

Cells in other worksheets

To use a reference to a cell in another worksheet in the same workbook, use the following format:

```
SheetName!CellAddress
```

In other words, precede the cell address with the worksheet name, followed by an exclamation point. Here's an example of a formula that uses a cell on the Sheet2 worksheet:

```
+A1*Sheet2!A1
```

This formula multiplies the value in cell A1 on the current worksheet by the value in cell A1 on Sheet 2.

Note   If the worksheet name in the reference includes one or more spaces, you must enclose it in single quotation marks. For example, here's a formula that refers to a cell on a sheet named All Depts:

```
+A1*'All Depts'!A1
```

Cells in other workbooks

To refer to a cell in a different workbook, use this format:

```
=[WorkbookName]SheetName!CellAddress
```

In this case, the cell address is preceded by the workbook name (in brackets), the worksheet name, and an exclamation point. Here's an example of a formula that uses a cell reference in the Sheet1 worksheet in a workbook named Budget:

```
=[Budget.xls]Sheet1!A1
```

Note If the workbook name in the reference includes one or more spaces, you must enclose it (and the sheet name) in single quotation marks. For example, here's a formula that refers to a cell on Sheet1 in a workbook named `Budget For 1996`:

```
+A1*'[Budget For 1996]Sheet1'!A1
```

When a formula refers to cells in a different workbook, the other workbook doesn't need to be open. If the workbook is closed, you must add the complete path to the reference. Here's an example:

```
+A1*'C:\ Office95\Excel\[Budget For 1996]Sheet1'!A1
```

 Cross-Reference I discuss this topic of file linking in detail in Chapter 19.

Entering references to cells outside the worksheet

The easiest way to create formulas that refer to cells not in the current worksheet is to use the pointing technique described earlier. Excel takes care of the details involving the workbook and worksheet references. The workbook that you're using in your formula must be open to use the pointing method.

 Note If you point to a different worksheet or workbook when creating a formula, you'll notice that Excel always inserts absolute cell references. Therefore, if you plan to copy the formula to other cells, make sure that you change the cell references to relative. This concept of absolute versus relative cell references is discussed in the following section.

Absolute versus Relative References

It's important to distinguish between *relative* and *absolute cell references.* By default, Excel creates relative cell references in formulas. The distinction becomes apparent when you copy a formula to another cell.

Relative references

Figure 9-4 shows a worksheet with a formula in cell D2. The formula, which uses the default relative references, is as follows:

```
=B2*C2
```

When you copy this formula to the two cells below it, Excel doesn't produce an exact copy of the formula; rather, it generates these formulas:

Cell D3:   `=B3*C3`

Cell D4:   `=B4*C4`

In other words, Excel adjusted the cell references to refer to the cells that are relative to the new formula. Think of it like this: The original formula contained instructions to multiply the value two cells to the left by the value one cell to the left. When you copy the cell, these instructions get copied, which results in the new formulas. Usually, this is exactly what you want. You certainly don't want to copy the formula verbatim; if you did, the new formulas would produce the same value as the original formula.

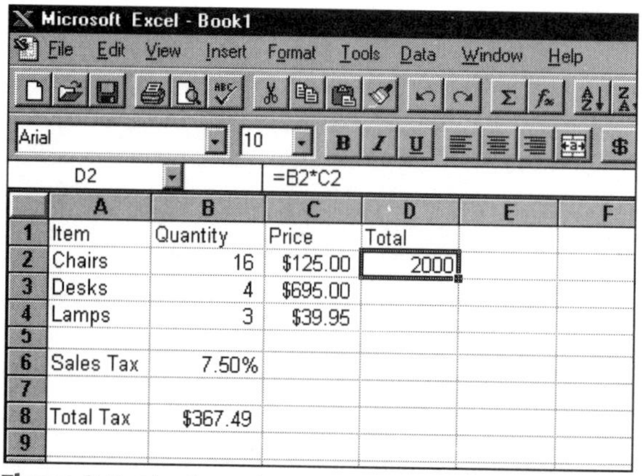

Figure 9-4: The formula will be copied to the cell below.

Note When you cut and paste a formula (move it to another location), the cell references in the formula aren't adjusted. Again, this is what you normally want to happen. When you move a formula, you generally want it to continue to refer to the original cells.

Absolute references

There are times, however, when you *do* want a cell reference to be copied verbatim. Figure 9-5 shows an example of this.

In this example, cell B7 contains a sales tax rate. The formula in cell D2 is as follows:

```
=(B2*C2)*$B$7
```

Notice that the reference to cell B7 has dollar signs before the column part and before the row part. These dollar signs make it an absolute cell reference. When you copy this formula to the two cells below, Excel generates the following formulas:

Cell D3:   `=(B3*C3)*$B$7`

Cell D4:   `=(B4*C4)*$B$7`

In this case, the relative cell references were changed but the reference to cell B7 wasn't changed because it's an absolute reference.

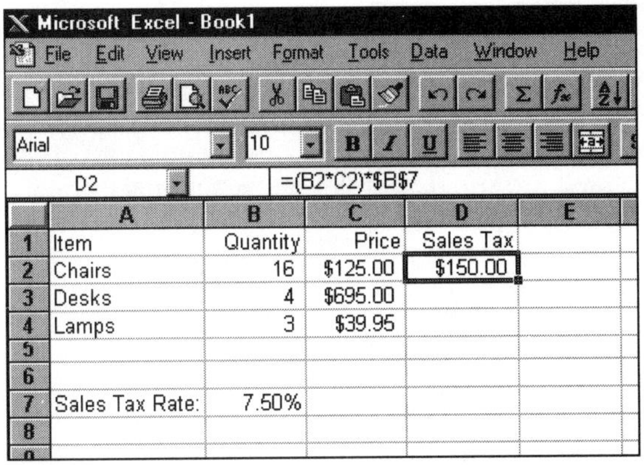

Figure 9-5: A formula that uses an absolute cell reference.

Mixed references

An absolute reference uses two dollar signs in its address: one for the column part and one for the row part. Excel also allows mixed references in which only one of the address parts is absolute. Table 9-3 summarizes all of the possible types of cell references.

When would you use a mixed reference? Figure 9-6 shows an example of a situation in which a mixed reference is appropriate. This worksheet will contain a table of values in which each cell will consist of the value in column A multiplied by the value in row 1. The formula in cell B2 is as follows:

```
=B$1*$A2
```

Table 9-3 Types of Cell References	
Example	*Type*
A1	Relative reference
$A$1	Absolute reference
$A1	Mixed reference (column part is absolute)
A$1	Mixed reference (row part is absolute)

Figure 9-6: This formula uses a mixed reference.

This formula contains two mixed cell references. In the B$1 reference, the row part is absolute, but the column part is relative. In the $A2 reference, the row part is relative, but the column part is absolute. You can copy this formula to the range B2:E5 and each cell will contain the correct formula. For example, the formula in cell E5 would be as follows:

```
=E$1*$A5
```

Entering nonrelative references

You can enter nonrelative references (absolute or mixed) manually by inserting dollar signs in the appropriate positions. Or, you can use a handy shortcut: the F4 key. When you're entering a cell reference — either manually or by pointing — you can press F4 repeatedly to have Excel cycle through all four reference types.

For example, if you enter **=A1** to start a formula, pressing F4 converts the cell reference to +$A$1. Pressing F4 again converts it to +A$1. Pressing it again displays +$A1. Pressing it one more time returns to the original +A1. Keep pressing F4 until Excel displays the type of reference you want.

Note   When you name a cell or range, Excel (by default) uses an absolute reference for the name. For example, if you give the name SalesForecast to A1:A12, the Refers to box in the Define Name dialog box lists the reference as $A$1:$A$12. This is almost always what you want. If you copy a cell that has a named reference in its formula, the copied formula contains a reference to the original name.

When a Formula Returns an Error

Sometimes when you enter a formula, Excel displays a value that begins with a pound sign (#). This is a signal that the formula is returning an error value. You'll have to correct the formula (or correct a cell that is referenced by the formula) to get rid of the error display.

Note If the entire cell is filled with pound cells, this means that the column isn't wide enough to display the value. You can either widen the value or change the number format of the cell.

Table 9-4 lists the types of error values that may appear in a cell that has a formula.

Note Formulas may return an error value if a cell that they refer to has an error value. This is known as the ripple effect — a single error value can make its way to lots of other cells that contain formulas that depend on the cell.

Editing Formulas

You can edit your formulas just like you can edit any other cell. You might need to edit a formula if you make some changes to your worksheet and you need to adjust the formula to accommodate the changes. Or, the formula may return one of the error values described in the previous section.

Table 9-4
Excel Error Values

Error Value	Explanation
#DIV/0!	The formula is trying to divide by zero (an operation that's not allowed on this planet). This also occurs when the formula attempts to divide by a cell that is empty.
#NAME?	The formula uses a name that Excel doesn't recognize. This can happen if you delete a name that's used in the formula or if you have unmatched quotes when using text.
#N/A	The formula is referring (directly or indirectly) to a cell that uses the NA functions to signal the fact that data is not available.
#NULL!	The formula uses an intersection of two ranges that don't intersect (this concept is described later in the chapter).
#NUM!	There is a problem with a value; for example, you specified a negative number where a positive number is expected.
#REF!	The formula refers to a cell that isn't valid. This can happen if the cell has been deleted from the worksheet.
#VALUE!	The formula includes an argument or operand of the wrong type. An operand is a value or cell reference that a formula uses to calculate a result.

As I discuss in Chapter 6, there are three ways to get into cell edit mode:

✦ Double-click on the cell. This lets you edit the cell contents directly in the cell.

✦ Press F2. This lets you edit the cell contents directly in the cell.

✦ Activate the cell that you want to edit, and then click in the formula bar. This lets you edit the cell contents in the formula bar.

Tip While you're editing a formula, you can select multiple characters by dragging the mouse over them or by holding down Shift while you use the direction keys.

Tip You might have a lengthy formula that you can't seem to edit correctly — and Excel won't let you enter it because of the error. In this case, you can convert the formula to text and tackle it again later. To convert a formula to text, just insert a space character before the initial equal sign. When you're ready to try again, remove the initial space to convert it back to a formula.

Changing When Formulas Are Calculated

You've probably noticed that the formulas in your worksheet get calculated immediately. If you change any cells that the formula uses, the formula displays a new result with no effort on your part. This is what happens when Excel's Calculation mode is set to Automatic. In this mode (which is the default mode) Excel follows these rules when calculating your worksheet:

✦ When you make a change — enter or edit data or formulas, for example — Excel calculates immediately those formulas that depend on new or edited data.

✦ If it's in the middle of a lengthy calculation, Excel temporarily suspends calculation when you need to perform other worksheet tasks; it resumes when you're finished.

✦ Formulas are evaluated in a natural sequence. In other words, if a formula in cell D12 depends on the result of a formula in cell D11, cell D11 is calculated before D12.

Sometimes, however, you may want to control when Excel calculates formulas. For example, if you create a worksheet with thousands of complex formulas, you'll find that things can slow to a snail's pace while Excel does its thing. In such a case, you would want to set Excel's Calculation mode to Manual. You can do this in the Calculation panel of the Options dialog box (see Figure 9-7).

To select Manual Calculation mode, click on the Manual option button. When you switch to Manual Calculation mode, the Recalculate Before Save check box is automatically turned on. You can turn this off if you want to speed up file saving operations.

If your worksheet uses any data tables (described in Chapter 26), you may want to select the Automatic Except Tables option. Data tables can be notoriously slow to calculate.

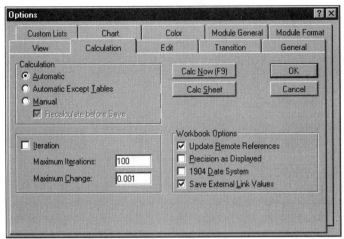

Figure 9-7: The Options dialog box lets you control when Excel calculates formulas.

When you're working in Manual Calculation mode, Excel displays CALC in the status bar when you have any uncalculated formulas. You can use the following shortcut keys to recalculate the formulas:

F9: Calculates the formulas in all open workbooks

Shift+F9: Calculates only the formulas in the active worksheet. Other worksheets in the same workbook won't be calculated.

Note

Excel's Calculation mode isn't specific to a particular worksheet. When you change Excel's Calculation mode, it affects all open workbooks, not just the active workbook.

Handling Circular References

When you're entering formulas, you may occasionally see a message from Excel like the one shown in Figure 9-8. This indicates that the formula you just entered will result in a *circular reference*. A circular reference occurs when a formula refers to its own value — either directly or indirectly. For example, if you enter **=A1+A2+A3** into cell A3, this is a circular reference because the formula in cell A3 refers to cell A3. Every time the formula in A3 is calculated, it must be calculated again because A3 has changed. The calculation would go on forever — in other words, the answer will never be resolved.

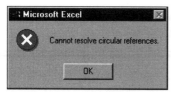

Figure 9-8: Excel's way of telling you that your formula contains a circular reference.

When you get the circular reference message after entering a formula, Excel lets you enter the formula and displays a message in the status bar to remind you that a circular reference exists. In this case, the message would read *Circular: A3*. If you activate a different workbook, the message would simply display *Circular* (without the cell reference).

Note   Excel won't tell you about a circular reference if the Iteration setting is on. You can check this in the Options dialog box (in the Calculation panel). If Iteration is on, Excel performs the circular calculation the number of times specified in the Maximum Iterations field (or until the value changes by less than .001 — or whatever value is in the Maximum Change field). There are a few situations in which you would use a circular reference intentionally (see a following section). In these cases, the Iteration setting must be on. It's best, however, to keep the Iteration setting off so that you'll be warned of circular references. Most of the time, a circular reference indicates an error that must be corrected.

Indirect circular references

In the preceding example, the error is quite obvious and is easy to correct. Sometimes, however, circular references are indirect. In other words, a formula may refer to a formula that refers to a formula that refers back to the original formula. In some cases, it may require a bit of detective work to get to the problem.

Cross-Reference   You may be able to get some assistance identifying a formula's dependents and precedents by using Excel's auditing tools, which I discuss in Chapter 30.

Intentional circular references

On the CD-ROM   As I mentioned previously, you can use a circular reference to your advantage in some situations. Figure 9-9 shows a simple example. This workbook is included on the companion CD-ROM and is named CIRCREF.XLS

In this example, a company has a policy of contributing five percent of its net profit to charity. The contribution itself, however, is considered an expense and is therefore subtracted from the net profit figure. This produces a circular reference — but this circular reference can be resolved if the Excel's Iteration setting is turned on.

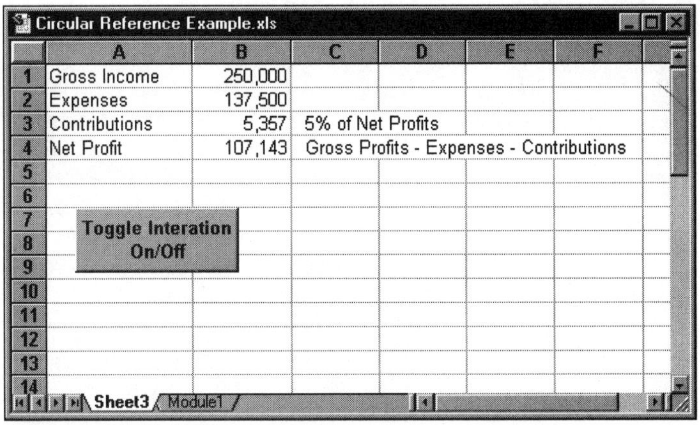

Figure 9-9: An example of an intentional circular reference.

The `Contributions` cell contains the following formula:

```
=5%*Net_Profit
```

The `Net Profit` cell contains the following formula:

```
=Gross_Income-Expenses-Contributions
```

These formulas produce a resolvable circular reference (the mathematically minded might see some similarities between this type of circular reference and a simultaneous equation). Excel keeps calculating until the formula results don't change anymore. To get a feel for how this works, open the workbook and substitute various values for `Gross Income` and `Expenses`. If the Iteration setting is off, Excel displays its Circular Reference message and won't display the correct result. If the Iteration setting is on, Excel keeps calculating until the `Contributions` value is, indeed, five percent of `Net Profit`. In other words, the result gets increasingly accurate until it converges on the final solution.

For your convenience, I include a button on the worksheet that toggles the Iteration setting on and off by using a macro.

Note Depending on your application, you may need to adjust the settings in the Maximum Iterations field or the Maximum Change field in the Options dialog box. For example, to increase accuracy, you can make the Maximum Change field smaller. If the result doesn't converge after 100 iterations, you can increase the Maximum Iterations field.

Using AutoFill rather than formulas

In Chapter 8, I discuss AutoFill as a quick way to copy a cell to adjacent cells. AutoFill also has some other uses, which may even substitute for formulas in some cases. I'm surprised to find that many experienced Excel users don't take advantage of the AutoFill feature — which can be a real time-saver.

Besides being a shortcut way to copy cells, AutoFill can quickly create a series of incremental values. For example, if you need a list of values from 1 to 100 to appear in A1:A100, you could do it with formulas. You would enter **1** in cell A1, the formula **=A1+1** into cell A2, and then copy the formula to the 98 cells below.

You also could use AutoFill to create the series for you without using a formula. To do so, enter **1** into cell A1 and **2** into cell A2. Select A1:A2 and drag the fill handle down to cell A100.

When you use AutoFill in this manner, Excel analyzes the selected cells and uses this information to complete the series. If cell A1 contained 1 and cell A2 contained 3, Excel would recognize this pattern and fill in 5, 7, 9, and so on. This also works with decreasing series (10, 9, 8, and so on) and dates. If there is no discernible pattern in the selected cells, Excel performs a linear regression and fills in values on the calculated trend line.

Excel also recognizes common series names such as months and days of the week. If you enter Monday into a cell and then drag its fill handle, Excel fills in the successive days of the week. You also can create custom AutoFill lists using the Custom Lists panel of the Options dialog box. Finally, if you drag the fill handle with the right mouse button, Excel displays a shortcut menu to let you select an AutoFill option.

Advanced Naming Techniques

As promised in the preceding chapter, this section describes some additional techniques that involve names.

Sheet level names

Normally, a name that you create can be used anywhere within the workbook. In other words, names, by default, are "book level" names rather than "sheet level" names. But what if you have several worksheets in a workbook and you want to use the same name (such as Dept_Total) on each sheet? This is an example of when you would need to create sheet level names.

To define the name Dept_Total in more than one worksheet, activate the worksheet where you want to define the name, choose Insert➪Name➪Define and precede the name with the worksheet name and an exclamation point in the Names in Workbook box. For example, to define the name Dept_Total on Sheet2, activate Sheet2 and enter the following in the Define Name dialog box:

```
Sheet2!Dept_Total
```

If the worksheet name contains at least one space, enclose it in single quotation marks, like this:

```
'Adv Dept'!Dept_Total
```

You also can create a sheet level name by using the Name box. Select the cell or range, activate the Name box, and enter the name, preceded by the sheet's name and an exclamation point (as shown previously).

When you write a formula that uses a sheet level name on the sheet where it's defined, you don't need to include the worksheet name in the range name (the Name box won't display the worksheet name either). If you use the name in a formula on a different worksheet, however, you must use the entire name (sheet name, exclamation point, and name).

Note Only the sheet level names on the current sheet appear in the Name box. Similarly, only sheet level names in the current sheet appear in the list when you access the Paste Name or Define Name dialog boxes.

Using sheet level names can become complicated if you have an identical book level name and sheet level name (yes, Excel does allow this). In such a case, the sheet level name takes precedence over the book level name — but only in the worksheet in which the sheet level name is defined. For example, a cell might have a book level name of Total defined on Sheet1. You also can define a sheet level name of Total (in, say Sheet2). When Sheet1 is active, Total refers to the sheet level name. When any other sheet is active, Total refers to the book level name. You can refer to a sheet level name in a different worksheet, however, by preceding the name with the worksheet name and an exclamation point (such as Sheet1!Total). To make your life easier, just avoid using the same name at the book level and sheet level.

Using multisheet names

Names even can extend into the third dimension; that is, they can extend across multiple worksheets in a workbook. You can't simply select the multisheet range and enter a name in the Name box, however. Excel makes you do a little additional work to define a multisheet name.

You must use the Insert Name dialog box to create a multisheet name, and you must enter the reference in the Refers to box manually. The format for a multisheet reference is as follows:

```
FirstSheet:LastSheet!RangeReference
```

In Figure 9-10, a multisheet name is being defined for A1:C12 that extends across Sheet1, Sheet2, and Sheet3.

Once the name is defined, you can use it in formulas. This name won't appear in the Name box, however, or in the Go To dialog box. In other words, Excel lets you define the name but it doesn't give you a way to automatically select the cells to which the name refers.

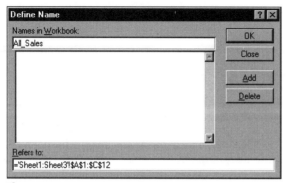

Figure 9-10: Creating a multisheet name.

Naming constants

Even many advanced Excel users don't realize that you can give a name to an item that doesn't even appear in a cell. For example, if formulas in your worksheet use a sales tax rate, you would probably insert the tax rate value into a cell and use this cell reference in your formulas. To make things easier, you would probably also give this cell a name such as `SalesTax`.

Here's another way to do it: Choose the Insert⇨Name⇨Define command (or press Ctrl+F3) to bring up the Define Name dialog box. Enter the name (in this case, `SalesTax`) into the Names in Workbook field. Then click on the Refers to box and delete its contents and replace it with a value such as .075 (see Figure 9-11). Don't precede the constant with an equal sign. Click on OK to close the dialog box.

You've just created a name that refers to a constant rather than a cell or range. If you type **=SalesTax** into a cell, you'll see that this simple formula returns .075 — the constant that you defined. You also can use this constant in a formula such as =A1*SalesTax.

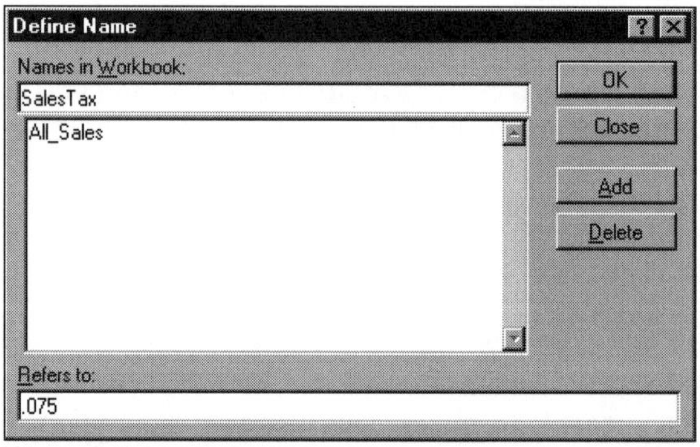

Figure 9-11: Defining a name that refers to a constant.

As with all names, named constants are stored with the workbook. They can be used on any worksheet in the workbook.

In the preceding example, the constant was a value. A constant also can be text, however. For example, you can define a constant for your company's name. If you work for Microsoft, you can define the name MS for Microsoft Corporation.

Note Named constants don't appear in the Name box or in the Go To dialog box — which makes sense, because these constants don't reside anywhere tangible. They do appear in the Paste Names dialog box, however, which *does* make sense because you'll be using these names in formulas.

As you might expect, you can change the value of the constant by accessing the Define Name dialog box and simply changing the value in the Refers to box. When you close the dialog box, the formulas that use this name are recalculated using the new value.

Although this technique is useful in many situations, the main drawback is that the value is rather difficult to change. Having a constant located in a cell makes it much easier to modify. If the value is truly a "constant," however, you won't need to change it.

Naming formulas

This section takes the preceding section to the next logical level: naming formulas. Figure 9-12 shows an example of this. In this case, the name MonthlyRate refers to the following formula:

```
=Sheet1!$B$1/12
```

When you use the name MonthlyRate in a formula, it uses the value in B1 divided by 12. Notice that the cell reference is an absolute reference.

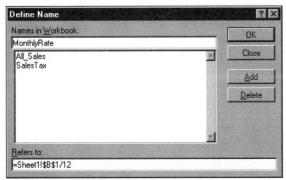

Figure 9-12: Excel lets you give a name to a formula that doesn't exist in the worksheet.

Naming formulas gets more interesting when you use relative references rather than absolute references. When you use the pointing technique to create a formula in the Refers to box, Excel always uses absolute cell references, which is unlike its behavior when you create a formula in a cell.

Figure 9-13 shows a name, Power, being created for the following formula:

```
=Sheet1!A1^Sheet1!B1
```

Notice that cell C1 is the active cell. This is very important. When you use this named formula in a worksheet, the cell references are always relative to the cell that contains the name. For example, if you enter **=POWER** into cell D12, cell D12 displays the result of B12 raised to the power of the value contained in cell C12.

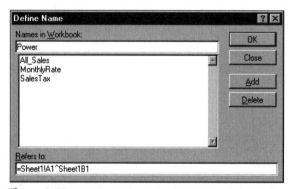

Figure 9-13: Naming a formula that uses relative cell references.

On the CD-ROM The NMDFORM.XLS workbook on the companion CD-ROM contains additional examples of this technique.

Range intersections

This section describes an interesting concept that is unique to Excel: *range intersections*. Excel uses an intersection operator — a space — to determine the overlapping references in two ranges. Figure 9-14 shows a simple example. The formula in cell G5 is as follows:

```
=B1:B7 A4:E4
```

and returns 4, the value in cell B4 — that is, the value at the intersection of the two ranges.

Note The intersection operator is one of three *reference* operators for ranges. Table 9-5 lists these operators.

Table 9-5 **Reference Operators for Ranges**	
Operator	**What It Does**
: (colon)	Specifies a range
, (comma)	Specifies the union of two ranges
(space)	Specifies the intersection of two ranges

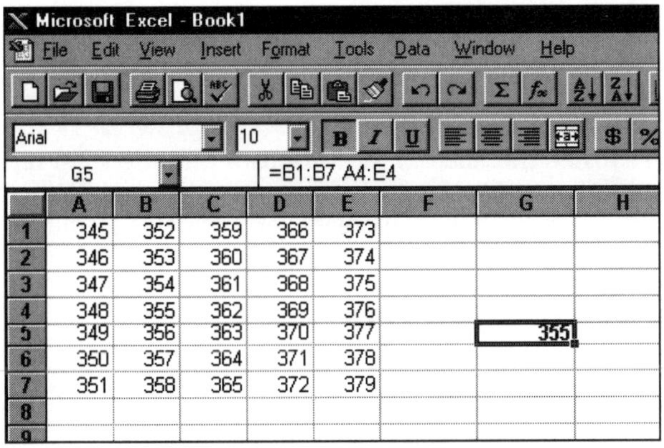

Figure 9-14: An example of an intersecting range.

The real value of knowing about range intersections is apparent when you use names. Examine Figure 9-15, which shows a table of values. I selected the entire table and then used the Insert➪Name➪Create command to create names automatically. Excel created the following names:

North	=Sheet1!$B$2:$E$2	Qtr1	=Sheet1!$B$2:$B$5
South	=Sheet1!$B$3:$E$3	Qtr2	=Sheet1!$C$2:$C$5
West	=Sheet1!$B$4:$E$4	Qtr3	=Sheet1!$D$2:$D$5
East	=Sheet1!$B$5:$E$5	Qtr4	=Sheet1!$E$2:$E$5

With these names defined, you'll find that you can create formulas that are very easy to read. For example, to calculate the total for quarter 4, just use this formula:

    =SUM(Qtr4)

But it really gets interesting when you use the intersection operator. Move to any blank cell and enter the following formula:

    =Qtr1 West

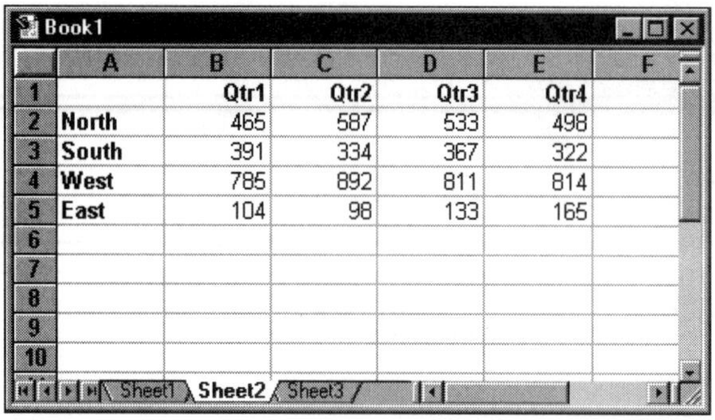

	A	B	C	D	E	F
1		Qtr1	Qtr2	Qtr3	Qtr4	
2	North	465	587	533	498	
3	South	391	334	367	322	
4	West	785	892	811	814	
5	East	104	98	133	165	

Figure 9-15: This table demonstrates how to use range intersections.

You'll find that this formula returned the value for the first quarter for the West region. In other words, it returned the value where the `Qtr1` range intersects with the `West` range. Naming ranges in this manner can help you create very readable formulas.

Applying names to existing references

When you create a new name for a cell or a range, Excel doesn't automatically use the name in place of existing references in your formulas. For example, assume that you have the following formula in cell F10: =A1–A2.

If you define a name `Income` for A1 and `Expenses` for A2, Excel won't automatically change your formula to =Income–Expenses. It's fairly easy to replace cell or range references with their corresponding names, however.

To apply names to cell references in formulas after the fact, start by selecting the range that you want to modify. Then, choose the Insert⇨Name⇨Apply command. Excel displays the Apply Names dialog box, shown in Figure 9-16. Select the names that you want to apply by clicking on them, and click on OK. Excel replaces the range references with the names in the selected cells.

The Apply Names dialog box has some options. If you click on the Options button, the dialog box expands to display even more options. Most of the time, the defaults will work just fine. For more control over the names that you apply, however, you may want to use one or more of its options. These are described in Excel's online Help.

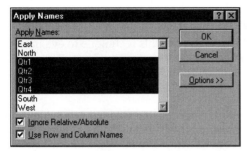

Figure 9-16: The Apply Names dialog box lets you replace cell or range references with names.

Tips for Working with Formulas

I conclude this chapter with a few additional tips and pointers relevant to formulas.

Don't hard code values

When you create a formula, think twice before using a value. For example, if your formula calculates sales tax (which is 6.5 percent), you may be tempted to enter a formula such as:

```
+A1*.065
```

A better approach is to insert the sales tax rate in a cell and use the cell reference. Or, you can define it as named constant using the technique I presented earlier in this chapter. Doing so makes it easier to modify and maintain your worksheet. For example, if the sales tax range changed to 6.75 percent, you would have to modify every formula that uses the old value. If the tax rate is stored in a cell, you simply change one cell and all of the formulas are updated.

Using the formula bar as a calculator

If you simply need to perform a calculation, you can use the formula bar as a calculator. For example, enter the following formula — but don't press Enter:

```
=(145*1.05)/12
```

If you press Enter, Excel enters the formula into the cell. But because this formula will always return the same result, you might prefer to store the formula's result rather than the formula. To do so, press F9 followed by Enter. Excel stores the formula's result (12.6875) rather than the formula. This also works if the formula uses cell references.

This is most useful when you use worksheet functions. For example, to enter the square root of 221 into a cell, enter **=SQRT(221)**, press F9, and press Enter. Excel enters the result: 14.8660687473185. You also can use this technique to evaluate just part of a formula. Consider this formula:

```
=(145*1.05)/A1
```

If you want to convert just the part in the parentheses to a value, get into edit mode and drag the mouse over the part that you want to evaluate (that is, select 145*1.05). Then, press F9 followed by Enter. Excel converts the formula to the following:

```
=152.25/A1
```

Making an exact copy of a formula

As you know, when you copy a formula, Excel adjusts its cell references when you paste it to a different location. Sometimes you may want to make an exact copy of the formula. One way to do this is to convert the cell references to absolute values, but this isn't always desirable. A better approach is to select the formula while you're in edit mode and then copy it to the Clipboard as text. There are several ways to do this. Here's a step-by-step example of how to make an exact copy of the formula in A1 and copy it to A2:

1. Double-click on A1 to get into edit mode.

2. Drag the mouse to select the entire formula. You can drag from left to right or from right to left (see Figure 9-17).

3. Click on the Copy button on the Standard toolbar. This copies the selected text to the Clipboard.

4. Press Enter to end edit mode.

5. Activate cell A2.

6. Click on the Paste button to paste the text into cell A2.

You also can use this technique to copy just *part* of a formula to use in another formula. Just select the part of the formula that you want to copy by dragging the mouse; then use any of the available techniques to copy the selection to the Clipboard. You can then paste the text to another cell.

Note   Formulas (or parts of formulas) copied in this manner won't have their cell references adjusted when they are pasted to a new cell. This is because the formulas are being copied as text, not as actual formulas.

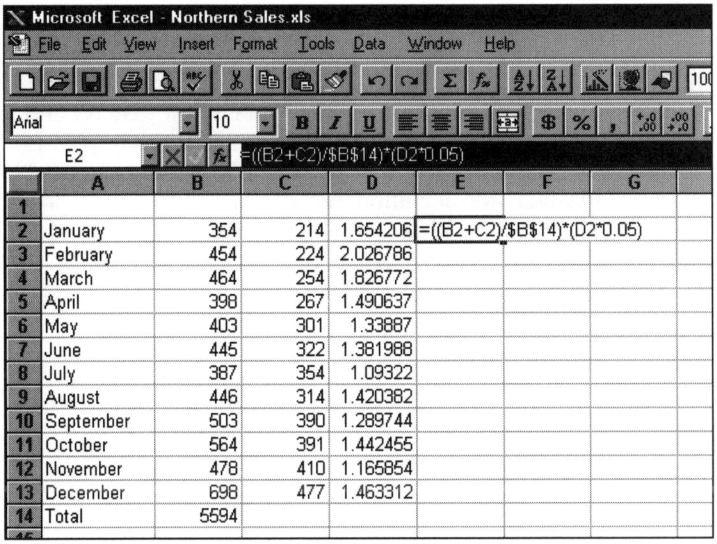

Figure 9-17: Selecting a formula before copying it as text.

Converting formulas to values

If you have a range of formulas that will always produce the same result (that is, dead formulas), you may want to convert them to values. As I discuss in the previous chapter, you can use the Edit⇨Paste Special command to do this. Assume that range A1:A20 contains formulas that have calculated a result and that they will never change. To convert these formulas to values:

1. Select A1:A20.

2. Click on the Copy button.

3. Select the Edit⇨Paste Special command. Excel displays its Paste Special dialog box.

4. Click on the Values option button and then click on OK.

5. Press Enter or Esc to cancel paste mode.

Array formulas

Excel supports another type of formula called an *array formula*. Array formulas can be extremely powerful because they let you work with complete ranges of cells rather than individual cells. You'll find that you can perform some amazing feats using array formulas. This is a rather advanced concept, which I cover in Chapter 20.

Summary

In this chapter I introduce the concept of formulas. Formulas are entered into cells and use values found in other cells to return a result. I explain how to enter and edit formulas, when to use absolute cell references, how to identify errors in your formulas, and how to handle circular references (either accidental or intentional). I also explain how to set Excel to Manual Recalculation mode — and why you would need to do so. I also discuss some additional naming techniques that can make your formulas even more powerful. I conclude with a series of tips that can help you get the most out of formulas.

✦   ✦   ✦

Using Worksheet Functions

In the preceding chapter, I discuss formulas. This chapter continues with coverage of Excel's built-in worksheet functions.

What Is a Function?

Functions, in essence, are built-in tools that are used in formulas. They can make your formulas perform powerful feats and save you a great deal of time. Functions can do the following:

 ◆ Simplify your formulas

 ◆ Allow formulas to perform calculations that are otherwise impossible

 ◆ Speed up some editing tasks

 ◆ Allow "conditional" execution of formulas — giving them rudimentary decision-making capability

Function examples

Here's an example of how a built-in function can simplify a formula. To calculate the average of the values in ten cells (A1:A10), you need to construct a formula like this:

```
=(A1+A2+A3+A4+A5+A6+A7+A8+A9+A10)/10
```

Not very pretty, is it? Even worse, this formula would have to be changed if you added another cell to the range. You can replace this formula with a much simpler one that uses one of Excel's built-in worksheet functions:

```
=AVERAGE(A1:A10)
```

Next, I show an example of how using a function can let you perform calculations that would not be possible otherwise. What if you need to determine the largest value in a range? There's no way a formula could tell you the answer without using a function. Here's a simple formula that returns the largest value in the range A1:D100:

```
=MAX(A1:D100)
```

Functions can sometimes eliminate manual editing. Assume that you have a worksheet with 1,000 names, all in uppercase. Your boss sees the listing and informs you that the names will be mail merged with a form letter and that uppercase is not acceptable: JOHN F. SMITH must appear as John F. Smith. You *could* spend the next several hours reentering the list — or you could use a formula like this, which uses a function to convert the text in cell A1 to proper case:

```
=PROPER(A1)
```

Enter this formula once, and copy it down to the next 999 rows. Then use the Edit⇨Paste Special command (with the Values option) to convert the formulas to values. Delete the original column, and you've just accomplished several hours of work in less than a minute.

One last example should convince you of the power of functions. Suppose that you have a worksheet that calculates sales commissions. If the salesperson sold more than $100,000 of product, the commission rate is 7.5 percent; otherwise, the commission rate is 5.0 percent. Without using a function, you would have to create two different formulas and make sure that the correct formula is used for each sales amount. Here's a formula that uses the IF function to ensure that the correct commission is calculated, regardless of the sales amount:

```
=IF(A1<100000,A1*0.05,A1*0.075)
```

More about functions

All told, Excel comes with more than 300 functions. And if that's not enough, you can purchase additional, specialized, functions from third-party suppliers and even create your own custom functions (using VBA), if you're so inclined.

It's easy to be overwhelmed by the sheer number of functions, but you'll probably find that you use only a dozen or so functions on a regular basis. And as you'll see, Excel's Function Wizard (described later in this chapter) makes it easy to locate and insert a function, even if it's not one you're familiar with.

Cross-Reference   Appendix D contains a complete listing of Excel's worksheet functions, with a brief description of each.

Function Arguments

In the preceding examples, you may have noticed that all the functions used parentheses. The information inside the parentheses is called an *argument*. Functions vary in how they use arguments. Depending on the function, a function may use:

✦ No arguments

✦ One argument

✦ A fixed number of arguments

✦ An indeterminate number of arguments

✦ Optional arguments

An example of a function that doesn't use an argument is RAND, which returns a random number between 0 and 1. Even if a function doesn't use an argument, however, you must still provide a set of empty parentheses, like this:

```
=RAND( )
```

If a function uses more than one argument, each argument is separated by a comma. The examples at the beginning of the chapter used cell references for arguments. Excel is quite flexible when it comes to function arguments, however. Rather than consisting of a cell reference, the argument can consist of literal values or text strings, or expressions.

Accommodating former 1-2-3 users

If you've ever used any of the 1-2-3 spreadsheets (or any versions of Quattro Pro), you'll recall that these products require that functions be preceded with an "at" sign (@). Excel is smart enough to distinguish functions without having to flag them with a symbol.

Because old habits die hard, however, Excel accepts @ symbols when you enter functions in your formulas — but it removes them as soon as the formula is entered.

These competing products also use two dots (..) as a range operator — for example,

A1..A10. Excel also lets you use this notation when you enter formulas, but it replaces it with its own range operator, a colon (:).

This accommodation goes only so far, however. Excel still insists that you use the standard Excel function names and doesn't recognize or translate those used in other spreadsheets. For example, if you enter the 1-2-3 @AVG function, Excel flags it as an error (Excel's name for this function is AVERAGE).

Using names as arguments

As you've seen, functions can use cell or range references for their arguments. When Excel calculates the formula, it simply uses the current contents of the cell or range to perform its calculations. The SUM function returns the sum of its argument(s). To calculate the sum of the values in A1:D20, you can use:

```
=SUM(A1:A20)
```

And, not surprisingly, if you've defined a name for A1:A20 (such as Sales), you can use the name in place of the reference:

```
=SUM(Sales)
```

Tip   In some cases, you may find it useful to use an entire column or row as an argument. For example, the formula that follows sums all values in column B:

```
=SUM(B:B)
```

This technique is particularly useful if the range that you're summing changes (if you're continually adding new sales figures, for instance). If you do use an entire row or column, just make sure that the row or column doesn't contain extraneous information that you don't want included in the sum. You might think that using such a large range (a column is 16,384 cells) might slow down calculation time — this isn't true. Excel's recalculation engine is quite efficient.

Literal arguments

A *literal argument* is basically a value or text string that you enter into a function. For example, the SQRT function takes one argument. Here's an example of a formula that uses a literal value for the function's argument:

```
=SQRT(225)
```

Using a literal argument with a simple function like this defeats the purpose of using a formula. This formula always returns the same value, so it could just as easily be replaced with the value 15. Using literal arguments makes more sense with formulas that use more than one argument. For example, the LEFT function (which takes two arguments) returns characters from the beginning of its first argument; the second argument specifies the number of characters. If cell A1 contains the text *Budget*, the following formula returns the first letter, or *B*:

```
=LEFT(A1,1)
```

Expressions as arguments

Excel also lets you use *expressions* as arguments. Think of an expression as a formula within a formula. When Excel encounters an expression as a function's argument, it evaluates the expression and then uses the result as the argument's value. Here's an example:

```
=SQRT((A1^2)+(A2^2))
```

This formula uses the SQRT function, and its single argument is an expression. When Excel evaluates the formula, it starts by evaluating the expression in the argument and then computes the square root of the result.

Other functions as arguments

Because Excel can evaluate expressions as arguments, it should not be surprising that these expressions can include other functions. Writing formulas that have functions within functions is sometimes known as *nesting* functions. Excel starts by evaluating the most deeply nested expression and works its way out. Here's an example of a nested function:

```
=SIN(RADIANS(B9))
```

The RADIANS function converts degrees to radians — which is the unit used by all of Excel's trigonometric functions. If cell B9 contains an angle in degrees, the RADIANS function converts it to radians, and then the SIN function computes the sine of the angle.

You can nest functions as deeply as you need, as long as you don't exceed the 1,024-character limit for a formula.

Changeable range references

Many functions contain a range reference as an argument. For example, the function that follows uses the range A10:A20.

```
=SUM(A10:A20)
```

If you add a new row between rows 10 and 20, Excel expands the range reference for you. If you add a new row between rows 12 and 13, the formula changes to the following:

```
=SUM(A10:A21)
```

In most cases this is exactly what you want to happen. If you insert a new row at row 10, however, Excel does *not* include the new row in the range reference. If you insert a new row at the end of the range, this new row is not added to the function's reference either. This type of behavior often confuses new users, who think that Excel should be able to read their minds and change their formulas accordingly.

(continued)

(continued)

If you need to work with expandable ranges in your functions, there are a number of things you can do:

✦ Use a complete column or row as a reference. The following formula always returns the sum of every value in column A:

```
=SUM(A:A)
```

✦ Use an additional row in your range reference. If you have data in A1:A10 and you may need to expand the range by adding new rows, change the reference to A1:A11 (and make sure that cell A11 is blank). Then you can insert a new row at row 11 and the range reference will include the new row.

Ways to Enter a Function

There are two ways to enter a function into a formula: manually or by using Excel's Function Wizard.

Entering a function manually

If you're familiar with the function — you know how many arguments it takes and the types of arguments — you may choose to simply type the function and its arguments into your formula. Often this method is the most efficient.

Tip   When you enter a function, Excel always converts it to uppercase. It's a good idea to use lowercase when entering functions. If Excel doesn't convert it to uppercase, it means that it doesn't recognize your entry as a function — you spelled it incorrectly.

Tip   If you omit the closing parenthesis, Excel adds it for you automatically. For example, if you enter **=SUM(A1:C12** and press Enter, Excel corrects the formula by adding the right parenthesis.

Using the Function Wizard

Excel's *Function Wizard* provides a way to enter a function and its arguments in a semiautomated manner. Using the Function Wizard ensures that the function is spelled correctly and has the proper number of arguments in the correct order.

Displaying the Function Wizard

The Function Wizard consists of two dialog boxes that assist you step-by-step in entering functions. You can invoke the Function Wizard by using any of the following methods:

✦ Choose the Insert⇨Function command from the menu.

✦ Click on the Function Wizard button on the Standard toolbar.

✦ Press Shift+F3.

✦ Click on the Function Wizard box on the Formula bar (available only when you're entering or editing a formula).

Any of these options displays the first of two Function Wizard dialog boxes, shown in Figure 10-1.

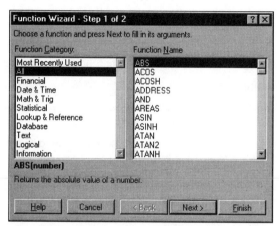

Figure 10-1: The first of two Function Wizard dialog boxes.

The dialog box shows the 11 function categories in the Function Category list box (it may show more function categories if custom functions are available). When you select a category, the Function Name list box displays the functions in the selected category.

The Most Recently Used category lists the functions you've used most recently. The All category lists all the functions available across all categories. Use this if you know a function's name but aren't sure of its category.

When you select a function in the Function Name list box, notice that the function (and its argument names) is displayed in the dialog box, along with a brief description of what the function does.

Using the Function Wizard: An example

In this section, I present a step-by-step example that explains how to use the Function Wizard to insert a function into a formula. The formula uses the AVERAGE function to compute the average of a range of cells.

1. Open a new workbook and enter values into A1:A6 (any values will do).

2. Activate cell A7. This cell will contain the formula.

3. Click on the Function Wizard button on the Standard toolbar. Excel displays the first of two dialog boxes. You can watch the function being built in the formula bar.

4. Because the AVERAGE function is in the Statistical category, click on Statistical in the Function Category list box. The Function Name list box displays the statistical functions.

5. Click on AVERAGE in the Function Name list box. The dialog box shows the function and its list of arguments. It also displays a brief description of the function.

6. Click on the Next button. Excel displays the second Function Wizard dialog box, shown in Figure 10-2. This dialog box prompts you for the function's arguments.

7. Activate the edit box labeled number1.

8. Select the range A1:A6 in the worksheet. This range appears in the edit box, and the dialog box also shows the result in the box labeled Value.

9. Because you're finding the example of only one range, there's no need to enter any additional arguments. Click on the Finish button.

Cell A7 now contains the following formula, which returns the average of the values in A1:A6:

```
=AVERAGE(A1:A6)
```

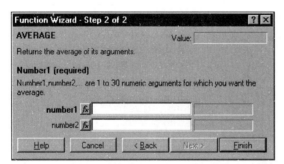

Figure 10-2: The second Function Wizard dialog box.

More about the Function Wizard

The best way to become familiar with the Function Wizard is to use it. Following are some additional tips to keep in mind when using the Function Wizard:

✦ Click on the Help button at any time to get help about the function you selected.

✦ If you're starting a new formula, the Function Wizard automatically provides the initial equal sign for you.

✦ If the active cell is not empty when you invoke the Function Wizard, the contents are overwritten.

✦ You can use the Function Wizard to insert a function into an existing formula. Just edit the formula and move the cursor to the location where you want to insert the function. Then invoke the Function Wizard and make your choices.

✦ In the second Function Wizard dialog box, clicking on the Back button goes back to the first dialog box, where you can select a different function.

✦ If you change your mind about entering a function, you can click on the Cancel button in either dialog box to cancel the Function Wizard.

✦ The number of edit boxes displayed in the second dialog box is determined by the number of arguments used by the function you selected. If a function uses no arguments, there are no edit boxes. If the function uses a variable number of arguments (such as the AVERAGE function), Excel adds a new edit box every time you enter an optional argument.

✦ The box to the right of each argument edit box displays the current value for each argument.

✦ A few functions have more than one form (INDEX is an example). If you select such a function, Excel displays another dialog box that lets you choose which form you want to use (this dialog box is labeled Step 1a).

✦ If you click on the Finish button without specifying the arguments, Excel inserts the function with placeholders for the arguments. You'll need to replace these placeholders with actual arguments. You also can enter the function manually and then press Ctrl+Shift+A; Excel inserts argument placeholders in the formula (and avoids the Function Wizard altogether). Figure 10-3 shows what the argument placeholders look like.

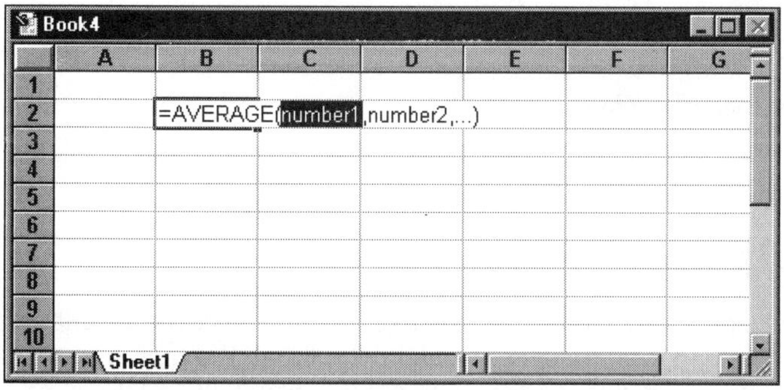

Figure 10-3: Excel inserts argument placeholders to tell you the number of arguments and their names.

✦ If you only need help remembering a function's arguments, type an equal sign and the function's name, and then press Ctrl+A. This step immediately displays the second Function Wizard dialog box.

✦ To quickly locate a function in the Function Name list, activate the list box, press the first letter of the function name, and then scroll to the desired function. For example, if the All category is selected and you want to insert the SIN function, click on the Function Name list box and press S. This selects the first function that begins with S — very close to SIN.

✦ If you want to use a function for an argument (a nested function), click on the button to the left of the edit box when prompted for arguments in the second dialog box. Excel displays the first Function Wizard dialog box and lets you choose another function. The dialog box displays *[Nested]* in its title bar, however, to remind you that you're creating a nested function. You can use as many as seven levels of nested functions — which gets *very* confusing, I assure you.

✦ If the active cell contains a formula that uses one or more functions, the Function Wizard lets you edit each function. It displays a separate dialog box for each function in the formula, as shown in Figure 10-4. Notice that the text in the title bar tells you which function you're editing and how many functions are in the formula.

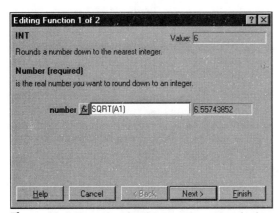

Figure 10-4: If you invoke the Function Wizard when the active cell contains a formula with one or more functions, you can edit each of the functions.

Function Examples

This section presents examples of formulas that use functions. I cover all categories listed in the Function Wizard, but not every available function. For more information about a particular function, consult the online help. For a list of all functions by category, use the Function Wizard (or see Appendix D).

Note In some cases, the category to which a function is assigned seems arbitrary. For example, COUNT is in the Statistical category, but COUNTIF is in the Math & Trig category. Functions that return logical values (such as ISERROR and ISNUMBER) are in the Information category rather than in the Logical category (which would be more logical).

Mathematical and trigonometric functions

Excel provides 52 functions in this category, more than enough to do some serious number crunching. The category includes common functions such as SUM and INT as well as plenty of esoteric functions — one of which may be just what you need.

COUNTIF

The COUNTIF function is useful if you want to count the number of times a specific value occurs in a range. This function takes two arguments: the range that contains the value to count and a criteria used to determine what to count. Figure 10-5 shows a worksheet set up with student grades. I used the COUNTIF function in the formulas in column E. For example, the formula in E2 is as follows:

```
=COUNTIF(B:B,D2)
```

Notice that the first argument consists of a range reference for the entire column B. This makes it easy to insert new names without having to change the formulas.

	A	B	C	D	E	F	G
	Student	**Grade**		**Grade**	**Count**		
2	Bowe	C		A	4		
3	Daily	C		B	5		
4	Ferguson	B		C	6		
5	Gibbons	C		D	1		
6	Hanks	C		F	1		
7	Jinno	C					
8	Johnson	A					
9	Kramer	B					
10	Ling	C					
11	Mills	A					
12	Peterson	F					
13	Smith	B					
14	Spence	A					
15	Spencer	B					

Function Examples.xls

SUMIF / Sheet2 \ COUNTIF

Figure 10-5: Using the COUNTIF function to create a distribution of grades.

Cross-Reference You also can use the Analysis ToolPak add-in to create frequency distributions. See Chapter 28 for details.

INT

The INT function returns the integer (nondecimal) portion of a number by truncating all digits after the decimal point. The example that follows returns 412:

```
=INT(412.98)
```

RAND

The RAND function, which takes no arguments, returns a uniform random number that is greater than or equal to 0 and less than 1. Uniform means that all numbers have an equal chance of being generated. This function is often used in worksheets to simulate events that aren't completely predictable — such as winning lottery numbers or fourth-quarter sales. This function returns a new result whenever the worksheet is calculated.

In the example that follows, the formula returns a random number between 0 and 12 (but 12 will never be generated):

```
=RAND()*12
```

The following formula generates a random integer between two values. The cell named Lower contains the lower bound, and the cell named Upper contains the upper bound:

```
=INT((Upper-Lower+1)*RAND()+Lower)
```

Volatile functions

Some Excel functions belong to a special class of functions called *volatile*. No, these aren't functions that cause your worksheet to explode. Rather, a volatile function is recalculated whenever calculation occurs in the workbook — even if the formula that contains the function is not involved in the recalculation.

The RAND function is an example of a volatile function. This function generates a new random number every time the worksheet is calculated. Other volatile functions are as follows:

AREAS   INDEX   OFFSET

CELL   INDIRECT   ROWS

COLUMNS   NOW   TODAY

A side effect of using these volatile functions is that Excel always prompts you to save the workbook — even if no changes were made. For example, if you open a workbook that contains any of these volatile functions, scroll around a bit (but don't change anything), and then close the file, Excel asks whether you want to save the workbook.

You can circumvent this behavior by using Manual Recalculation mode, with the Recalculate before Save option turned off.

ROMAN

The ROMAN function converts a value to its Roman numeral equivalent (hey, I never said *all* the functions were useful). Unfortunately for old-movie buffs, there is no function to convert in the opposite direction. The function that follows returns MCMXCVI:

    =ROMAN(1996)

ROUND

The ROUND function rounds a value to a specified digit to the left or right of the decimal point. This function is often used to control the precision of your calculation. ROUND takes two arguments: the first is the value to be rounded; the second is the digit. If the second argument is negative, the rounding occurs to the left of the decimal point. Table 10-1 demonstrates, with some examples, how this works.

Table 10-1
Examples of Using the ROUND Function

Function	Result
=ROUND(123.457,2)	123.46
=ROUND(123.457,1)	123.50
=ROUND(123.457,0)	123.00
=ROUND(123.457,-1)	120.00
=ROUND(123.457,-2)	100.00
=ROUND(123.457,-3)	0.00

Caution   Don't confuse rounding a value with number formatting applied to a value. When a formula references a cell that has been rounded with the ROUND function, the formula uses the rounded value. If a number has been formatted to *appear* rounded, formulas that refer to that cell use the actual value stored.

Note   If your work involves rounding, also check out the ROUNDUP and ROUNDDOWN functions. In addition, the FLOOR and CEILING functions let you round to a specific multiple — for example, you can use FLOOR to round a value down to the nearest multiple of 10 (124.5 would be rounded to 130).

PI

The PI function returns the value of π significant to 14 decimal places. It doesn't take any arguments and is simply a shortcut for the value 3.14159265358979. In the example that follows, the formula calculates the area of a circle (the radius is stored in a cell named Radius):

    =PI()*(Radius^2)

SIN

The SIN function returns the sine of an angle. The *sine* is defined as the ratio between the opposite side and the hypotenuse of a triangle. SIN takes one argument — the angle expressed in radians. To convert degrees to radians, use the RADIANS function (there's also a DEGREES function to do the opposite conversion). For example, if cell F21 contains an angle expressed in degrees, the formula that follows returns the sine:

```
=SIN(RADIANS(F21))
```

Note

Excel contains the full complement of trigonometric functions. Use the Function Wizard to find out more or consult the online help.

On the CD-ROM

The companion CD-ROM contains a workbook named RTTRIANG.XLS. The Right Triangle worksheet solves right triangles by determining the length of the third side, given two sides. It also displays a graphic triangle showing the proportions of the triangle (see Figure 10-6).

Figure 10-6: This worksheet solves right triangles.

SQRT

The SQRT function returns the square root of its argument. If the argument is negative, this function returns an error. The example that follows returns 32:

```
=SQRT(1024)
```

Tip

To compute a cube root, raise the value to the $1/3$ power. The example that follows returns the cube root of 32768 — which is 32. Other roots can be calculated in a similar manner.

```
=32768^(1/3)
```

SUM

If you analyzed a random sample of workbooks, it's a safe bet that you would discover that the SUM is the most widely used function. It's also among the simplest. It takes from one to 30 arguments. To calculate the sum of three ranges (A1:A10, C1:10, and E1:E10), you would use three arguments, like this:

```
=SUM(A1:A10,C1:10,E1:E10)
```

The arguments don't have to be all the same type. For example, you can mix and match single cell references, range references, and literals, as follows:

```
=SUM(A1,C1:10,125)
```

Tip Because the SUM function is so popular, the Excel designers made it very accessible — automatic, in fact. To insert a formula that uses the SUM function, just click on the AutoSum button on the Standard toolbar. Excel analyzes the context and suggests a range for an argument. If it suggested correctly (which it usually does), press Enter or click on the button again. If it's not correct, just drag the mouse and make the selection yourself. To insert a series of SUM formulas — to add up several columns of numbers, for example — select the entire range and then click on AutoSum. In this case, Excel knows exactly what you want, so it doesn't to ask you to confirm it.

SUMIF

The SUMIF function is similar to the COUNTIF function (described earlier), but SUMIF returns the sum of the qualifying cells instead of counting them. Figure 10-7 displays a worksheet with a table that shows sales by month and by region. I used the SUMIF function in the formulas in column F. For example, the formula in F2 is as follows:

```
=SUMIF(B:B,E2,C:C)
```

	A	B	C	D	E	F	G	H
1	Month	Region	Sales		Regional Summary			
2	Jan	North	2,062		North	13,121		
3	Jan	South	8,257		South	35,258		
4	Jan	West	6,004		West	17,960		
5	Jan	East	828		East	21,933		
6	Feb	North	5,136					
7	Feb	South	10,769					
8	Feb	West	4,514					
9	Feb	East	8,135					
10	Mar	North	1,881					
11	Mar	South	8,093					
12	Mar	West	1,638					
13	Mar	East	6,612					
14	Apr	North	4,042					
15	Apr	South	8,139					

Figure 10-7: The SUMIF function returns the sum of values if the values meet specified criteria.

SUMIF takes three arguments. The first argument is the range you're using in the selection criteria — in this case, the entire column B. The second argument is the selection criteria, a region name in the example. The third argument is the range of values to sum if the criteria is met. In this example, the formula in F2 adds the values in column C only if the corresponding text in column B matches the region in column E.

Cross-Reference You also can use Excel's pivot table feature to perform these operations. I cover pivot tables in Chapter 25.

Text functions

Although Excel is primarily known for its numerical prowess, it has 23 built-in functions that are designed to manipulate text. I demonstrate a few of them in this section.

CHAR

The CHAR function returns a single character that corresponds to the ANSI code specified in its argument (these codes range from 1 to 255). The CODE function performs the opposite conversion. The formula that follows returns the letter *A*:

```
=CHAR(65)
```

This function is most useful for returning symbols that are difficult or impossible to enter from the keyboard. For example, the formula that follows returns the copyright symbol (©):

```
=CHAR(169)
```

Figure 10-8 shows the characters returned by the CHAR function for arguments from 1 to 255 (using the Arial font).

Note Not all codes produce printable characters, and the characters may vary depending on the font used.

LEFT

The LEFT function returns a string of characters of a specified length from another string, beginning at the leftmost position. This function uses two arguments. The first argument is the string and the second argument (optional) is the number of characters. If the second argument is omitted, Excel extracts the first character from the text. In the example that follows, the formula returns the letter *B:*

```
=LEFT("B.B. King")
```

The formula that follows returns the string *Albert*:

```
=LEFT("Albert King",5)
```

Character Set Using CHAR.xls

#	Ch	#	Ch	#	Ch	#	Ch	#	Ch	#	Ch	#	Ch	#	Ch	#	Ch	#	Ch	#	Ch
1	□	26	□	51	3	76	L	101	e	126	~	151	—	176	°	201	É	226	â	251	û
2	□	27	□	52	4	77	M	102	f	127	□	152	˜	177	±	202	Ê	227	ã	252	ü
3	□	28	□	53	5	78	N	103	g	128	□	153	™	178	²	203	Ë	228	ä	253	ý
4	□	29	□	54	6	79	O	104	h	129	□	154	š	179	³	204	Ì	229	å	254	þ
5	□	30	□	55	7	80	P	105	i	130	,	155	›	180	´	205	Í	230	æ	255	ÿ
6	□	31	□	56	8	81	Q	106	j	131	ƒ	156	œ	181	µ	206	Î	231	ç		
7	□	32		57	9	82	R	107	k	132	„	157	□	182	¶	207	Ï	232	è		
8	□	33	!	58	:	83	S	108	l	133	…	158	□	183	·	208	Ð	233	é		
9	□	34	"	59	;	84	T	109	m	134	†	159	Ÿ	184	¸	209	Ñ	234	ê		
10	□	35	#	60	<	85	U	110	n	135	‡	160		185	¹	210	Ò	235	ë		
11	□	36	$	61	=	86	V	111	o	136	ˆ	161	¡	186	º	211	Ó	236	ì		
12	□	37	%	62	>	87	W	112	p	137	‰	162	¢	187	»	212	Ô	237	í		
13	□	38	&	63	?	88	X	113	q	138	Š	163	£	188	¼	213	Õ	238	î		
14	⌐	39	'	64	@	89	Y	114	r	139	‹	164	¤	189	½	214	Ö	239	ï		
15	□	40	(	65	A	90	Z	115	s	140	Œ	165	¥	190	¾	215	×	240	ð		
16	□	41	)	66	B	91	[	116	t	141	□	166	¦	191	¿	216	Ø	241	ñ		
17	□	42	*	67	C	92	\	117	u	142	□	167	§	192	À	217	Ù	242	ò		
18	□	43	+	68	D	93	]	118	v	143	□	168	¨	193	Á	218	Ú	243	ó		
19	□	44	,	69	E	94	^	119	w	144	□	169	©	194	Â	219	Û	244	ô		
20	□	45	-	70	F	95	_	120	x	145	'	170	ª	195	Ã	220	Ü	245	õ		
21	□	46	.	71	G	96	`	121	y	146	'	171	«	196	Ä	221	Ý	246	ö		
22	□	47	/	72	H	97	a	122	z	147	"	172	¬	197	Å	222	Þ	247	÷		
23	□	48	0	73	I	98	b	123	{	148	"	173	-	198	Æ	223	ß	248	ø		
24	□	49	1	74	J	99	c	124			149	•	174	®	199	Ç	224	à	249	ù		
25	□	50	2	75	K	100	d	125	}	150	–	175	¯	200	È	225	á	250	ú		

Figure 10-8: Characters returned by the CHAR function.

Note Excel also has a RIGHT function that extracts characters from the right of a string of characters and a MID function (described after the next section) that extracts characters from any position.

LEN

The LEN function returns the number of characters in a string of text. For example, the following formula returns 12:

```
=LEN("Stratocaster")
```

If you don't want to count leading or trailing spaces, use the LEN function with a nested TRIM function. For example, if you want to know the number of characters in the text in cell A1 (without any extraneous spaces), use this formula:

```
=LEN(TRIM(A1))
```

MID

The MID function returns characters from a text string. It takes three arguments. The first argument is the text string. The second argument is the position where you want to begin extracting. The third argument is the number of characters you want to extract. If cell A1 contains the text *Joe Louis Walker*, the formula that follows returns *Louis*:

```
=MID(A1,5,5)
```

REPLACE

The REPLACE function replaces characters with other characters. The first argument is the text containing the string you're replacing. The second argument is the character position where you want to start replacing. The third argument is the number of characters to replace. The fourth argument is the new text that will replace the existing text. In the example that follows, the formula returns *Albert Collins:*

```
=REPLACE("Albert King",8,4,"Collins")
```

SEARCH

The SEARCH function lets you identify the position in a string of text in which another string occurs. It takes three arguments. The first argument is the text you're looking for. The second argument is the string you're searching in. The third argument (optional) is the position to start looking at. If it's omitted, Excel starts searching from the beginning of the text.

In the example that follows, assume that cell A1 contains the text *John Lee Hooker.* The formula returns 5 because the first space character was found at the fifth character position.

```
=SEARCH(" ",A1,1)
```

To find the second space in the text, use a nested SEARCH function that uses the result of the first search (incremented by one character) as its third argument. Here it is:

```
=SEARCH(" ",A1,SEARCH(" ",A1,1)+1)
```

The following formula uses the LEFT function to return the characters to the left of the first space in the text in cell A1. For example, if A1 contains *Jimmy Dawkins,* the formula would return the first name *Jimmy.*

```
=LEFT(A1,SEARCH(" ",A1))
```

The preceding formula has a slight flaw: If the text in cell A1 contains no spaces, the formula results in an error. Here's an improved version that returns the entire string in A1 if it doesn't contains a space:

```
=IF(ISERROR(SEARCH(" ",A1)),A1,LEFT(A1,SEARCH(" ",A1)))
```

UPPER

The UPPER function converts characters to uppercase. If cell A1 contains the text *Lucille*, the formula that follows returns *LUCILLE*.

```
=UPPER(A1)
```

Note Excel also has a LOWER function (to convert to lowercase) and a PROPER function (to convert to proper case). In proper case, the first letter of each word is capitalized.

Logical functions

The Logical category contains only six functions (although several other functions could, arguably, be placed in this category). In this section, I discuss three of these functions.

IF

The IF function is one of the most important of all functions. This function can give your formulas decision-making capability.

The IF function takes three arguments. The first argument is a logical test that must be either TRUE or FALSE. The second argument is the formula's result if the first argument is TRUE. The third argument is the formula's result if the first argument is FALSE.

In the example that follows, the formula returns *Positive* if the value in cell A1 is greater than zero, and returns *Negative* otherwise:

```
=IF(A1>0,"Positive","Negative")
```

Notice that the first argument (A1>0) evaluates to logical TRUE or FALSE. This formula has a problem in that it returns the text *Negative* if the cell is blank or contains 0. The solution is to use a nested IF function to perform another logical test. The revised formula is as follows :

```
=IF(A1>0,"Positive",IF(A1<0,"Negative","Zero"))
```

The formula looks complicated, but when you break it down, you see that it's rather simple. Here's how the logic works. If A1 is greater than 0, the formula displays *Positive* and nothing else is evaluated. If A1 is not greater than zero, however, the second argument is evaluated. The second argument is as follows:

```
IF(A1<0,"Negative","Zero")
```

This is simply another IF statement that performs the test on A1 again. If it's less than 0, the formula returns *Negative*. Otherwise, it returns *Zero*. You can nest IF statements as deeply as you need to — although it can get very confusing after three or four levels.

Using nested IF functions is quite common, so it's in your best interest to understand how this concept works. Mastering it will definitely help you create more powerful formulas.

Figure 10-9 shows an example of using the IF function to calculate sales commissions. In this example, the normal commission rate is 5.5 percent of sales. If the sales rep exceeds the sales goal, the commission rate is 6.25 percent. The formula in cell C6, shown as follows, uses the IF function to make a decision regarding which commission rate to use based on the sales amount:

```
=IF(B6>=SalesGoal,B6*BonusRate,B6*CommissionRate)
```

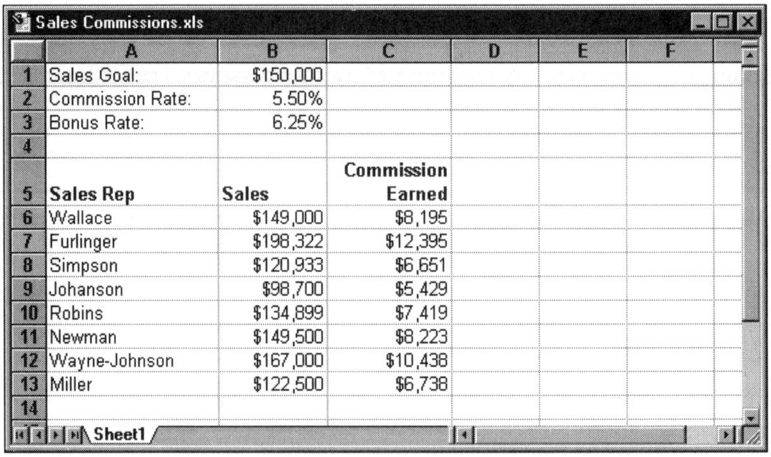

Sales Commissions.xls

	A	B	C	D	E	F
1	Sales Goal:	$150,000				
2	Commission Rate:	5.50%				
3	Bonus Rate:	6.25%				
4						
5	**Sales Rep**	**Sales**	**Commission Earned**			
6	Wallace	$149,000	$8,195			
7	Furlinger	$198,322	$12,395			
8	Simpson	$120,933	$6,651			
9	Johanson	$98,700	$5,429			
10	Robins	$134,899	$7,419			
11	Newman	$149,500	$8,223			
12	Wayne-Johnson	$167,000	$10,438			
13	Miller	$122,500	$6,738			
14						

Sheet1

Figure 10-9: Using the IF statement to calculate sales commissions.

AND

The AND function returns a logical value (TRUE or FALSE) depending on the logical value of its arguments. If all its arguments return TRUE, then the AND function returns TRUE. If at least one of its arguments returns FALSE, then AND returns FALSE.

In the example that follows, the formula returns TRUE if the values in cells A1:A3 are all negative:

```
=AND(A1<0,A2<0,A3<0)
```

The formula that follows uses the AND function as the first argument for an IF function. If all three cells in A1:A3 are negative, this formula displays *All Negative*. If at least one is not negative, the formula returns *Not All Negative:*

```
=IF(AND(A1<0,A2<0,A3<0),"All Negative","Not All Negative")
```

OR

The OR function is similar to the AND function, but it returns TRUE if at least one of its arguments is TRUE; otherwise, it returns FALSE. In the example that follows, the formula is TRUE if either A1, A2, or A3 is TRUE:

```
=OR(A1<0,A2<0,A3<0)
```

Information functions

Excel's 15 functions in the Information category return a variety of information about cells. Many of these return logical TRUE or FALSE.

CELL

The CELL function returns information about a particular cell. It takes two arguments. The first argument is a code for the type of information to display. The second argument is the reference to the cell in which you're interested.

The example that follows uses the "type" code, which returns information about the type of data in the cell. It returns *b* if the cell is blank, *l* if it contains text (a label), or *v* if the cell contains a value or formula. For example, if cell A1 contains text, the following formula returns *l*.

```
=CELL("type",A1)
```

If the second argument contains a range reference, Excel uses the upper left cell in the range.

Note   Excel contains other functions that let you determine the type of data in a cell. The following functions may be more useful: ISBLANK, ISERR, ISERROR, ISLOGICAL, ISNA, ISNONTEXT, ISNUMBER, ISREF, ISTEXT, and TYPE.

Table 10-2 lists the possible values for the first argument of the CELL function. Make sure that you enclose the first argument in quotation marks.

Table 10-2	
Codes for the CELL function Info_Type Argument	
Type	**What It Returns**
address	The cell's address
col	Column number of the cell
color	*1* if the cell is formatted in color for negative values — otherwise, *0*
contents	The contents of the cell
filename	Name and path of the file that contains the cell (returns empty text if the workbook has not been saved)
format	Text value corresponding to the number format of the cell
prefix	Text value corresponding to the label prefix of the cell; this is provided for 1-2-3 compatibility
protect	*0* if the cell is not locked; *1* if the cell is locked
row	Row number of the cell
type	Text value corresponding to the type of data in the cell
width	Column width of the cell rounded off to an integer

INFO

The INFO function takes one argument — a code for information about the operating environment. In the example that follows, the formula returns the path of the current folder (that is, the folder that Excel displays when you choose the File⇨Open command.)

```
=INFO("directory")
```

Table 10-3 lists the valid codes for the INFO function. The codes must be enclosed in quotation marks.

Table 10-3
Codes for the INFO Function

Code	What It Returns
directory	Path of the current folder
memavail	Amount of memory available, in bytes
memused	Amount of memory being used, in bytes
numfile	Number of worksheets in all open workbooks (including hidden workbooks and add-ins)
origin	Returns the cell reference of the top- and leftmost cell visible in the window based on the current scrolling position
osversion	Current operating system version, as text
recalc	Current recalculation mode — Automatic or Manual
release	Version of Excel
system	Name of the operating environment — mac (for Macintosh) or pcdos (for Windows)
totmem	Total memory available on the system, in bytes

ISERROR

The ISERROR function returns TRUE if its argument returns an error value. Otherwise, it returns FALSE. This function is useful for controlling the display of errors in a worksheet.

Figure 10-10 shows a worksheet set up to track monthly sales. Each month, the worksheet is updated with two figures: the number of sales reps and the total sales. Formulas in columns E and F calculate the percentage of the sales goal (Actual Sales divided by Sales Goal) and the average sales per sales rep. Notice that the formulas in column F display an error when the data is missing. Cell F2 contains a simple formula:

```
=D2/C2
```

To avoid displaying an error for missing data, change the formula to the following and copy it to the cells that follow. If the division results in an error, the formula displays nothing. Otherwise, it displays the result.

```
=IF(ISERROR(D2/C2),"",D2/C2)
```

Monthly Sales Tracking.xls							
	A	B	C	D	E	F	G
1	Month	Sales Goal	Sales Reps	Actual Sales	Pct. of Goal.	Avg per Rep	
2	January	500,000	12	487,903	97.6%	40,659	
3	February	500,000	14	512,098	102.4%	36,578	
4	March	525,000	14	518,733	98.8%	37,052	
5	April	525,000	13	508,933	96.9%	39,149	
6	May	550,000	15	558,973	101.6%	37,265	
7	June	575,000			0.0%	#DIV/0!	
8	July	575,000			0.0%	#DIV/0!	
9	August	575,000			0.0%	#DIV/0!	
10	September	575,000			0.0%	#DIV/0!	
11	October	600,000			0.0%	#DIV/0!	
12	November	600,000			0.0%	#DIV/0!	
13	December	600,000			0.0%	#DIV/0!	

Figure 10-10: This worksheet is displaying an error for formulas that refer to missing data.

Note Excel offers several other functions that let you trap error values: ERROR.TYPE, ISERR, and ISNA. Also, note that the preceding formula could have used the ISBLANK function to test for missing data.

Date and time functions

If you use dates or times in your worksheets, you owe it to yourself to check out Excel's 14 functions that work with these types of values. In this section I demonstrate a few of these functions.

Cross-Reference To work with dates and times, you should be familiar with Excel's serial number date-and-time system. See Chapter 6.

TODAY

The TODAY function takes no argument. It returns a date that corresponds to the current date — that is, the date set in the system. If you enter the following formula into a cell on June 16, 1996, the formula returns 6/16/96:

```
=TODAY()
```

Excel also has a NOW function that returns the current system date and the current system time.

DATE

The DATE function displays a date based on its three arguments: year, month, and day. This function is useful if you want to create a date based on information in your worksheet. For example, if cell A1 contains 1996, cell B1 contains 12, and cell C1 contains 25, the following formula returns the date for December 25, 1996:

```
=DATE(A1,B1,C1)
```

DAY

The DAY function returns the day of the month for a date. If cell A1 contains the date 12/25/96, the following formula returns 25:

```
=DAY(A1)
```

Note Excel also includes the YEAR and MONTH functions that extract from a date the year part and month part, respectively.

WEEKDAY

The WEEKDAY function returns the day of the week for a date. It takes two arguments: the date and a code that specifies the type of result (the second argument is optional). The codes are listed in Table 10-4 .

	Table 10-4 **Codes for the WEEKDAY Function**	
Code	*What It Returns*
1 or omitted	Numbers 1-7, corresponding to Sunday through Saturday
2	Numbers 1-7, corresponding to Monday through Sunday
3	Numbers 0-6, corresponding to Monday through Sunday

If cell A1 contains 12/25/96, the formula that follows returns 4 — which indicates that this date is a Wednesday:

```
=WEEKDAY(A1)
```

Tip You also can format cells that contain dates to display the day of the week as part of the format. Use a custom format code of ddd (for abbreviated days of the week) or dddd (for fully spelled days of the week).

TIME

The TIME function displays a time based on its three arguments: hour, minute, and second. This function is useful if you want to create a time based on information in your worksheet. For example, if cell A1 contains 8, cell B1 contains 15, and cell C1 contains 0, the following formula returns 8:15:00 AM: =TIME(A1,B1,C1)

HOUR

The HOUR function returns the hour for a time. If cell A1 contains the time 8:15:00 AM, the following formula returns 8:

```
=HOUR(A1)
```

Note Excel also includes the MINUTE and SECOND functions, which extract the minute part and second part, respectively, from a time.

Financial functions

The Financial function category includes 15 functions designed to perform calculations that involve money.

Depreciation functions

Excel offers five functions to calculate depreciation of an asset over time. The function you choose depends on the type of depreciation you use. Figure 10-11 shows a chart that depicts how an asset is depreciated over time, using each of the five depreciation functions.

On the CD-ROM The worksheet that generated the chart is available on the CD-ROM that accompanies this book. It is called DEPRECIA.XLS.

Table 10-5 summarizes the depreciation functions and the arguments used by each. For complete details, consult the online help system.

Table 10-5		
Excel's Depreciation Functions		
Function	*Depreciation Method*	*Arguments**
SLN	Straight-line	Cost, Salvage, Life
DB	Declining balance	Cost, Salvage, Life, Period, [Month]
DDB	Double-declining balance	Cost, Salvage, Life, Period, Month,[Factor]
SYD	Sum-of-the year's digits	Cost, Salvage, Life, Period
VDB	Variable-declining balance	Cost, Salvage, Life, Start Period, End Period, [Factor], [No Switch]

* Arguments in brackets are optional

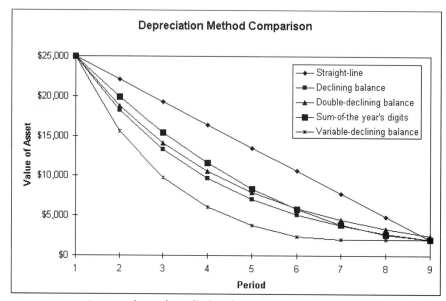

Figure 10-11: A comparison of Excel's five depreciation functions.

The arguments for the depreciation functions are described as follows:

Cost: Original cost of the asset

Salvage: Salvage cost of the asset after it has been fully depreciated

Life: Number of periods over which the asset will be depreciated

Period: Period in the Life for which the calculation is being made

Month: Number of months in the first year; if omitted, Excel uses 12

Factor: Rate at which the balance declines; if omitted, it is assumed to be 2 (that is, double-declining)

Loan and annuity functions

Table 10-6 lists the functions that can help you perform calculations related to loans and annuities.

Notice that these functions all use pretty much the same arguments — although the exact arguments used depend on the function. To use these functions successfully, you must understand how to specify the arguments correctly. The following list explains these arguments:

Rate: Interest rate per period. If payments are made monthly, for example, you must divide the annual interest rate by 12.

Table 10-6
Loan and Annuity Functions

Function	Calculation	Arguments*
FV	Future Value	Rate, Nper, Pmt, [PV], [Type]
PV	Present Value	Rate, Nper, Pmt, [PV], [Type]
PMT	Payment	Rate, Nper, PV, [FV], [Type]
PPMT	Principal Payment	Rate, Per, Nper, PV, [FV], [Type]
IPMT	Interest Payment	Rate, Per, Nper, PV, [FV], [Type]
RATE	Interest Rate per Period	Nper, Pmt, PV, [FV], [Type], [Guess]
NPER	Number of Periods	Rate, Pmt, PV, [FV], [Type]

* Arguments in brackets are optional

Nper: Total number of payment periods. For a 30-year mortgage loan with monthly payments, Nper would be 360.

Pmt: Fixed payment made each period for an annuity or a loan. This usually includes principal and interest (but not fees or taxes).

FV: Future value (or a cash balance) after the last payment is made. The future value for a loan is 0. If FV is omitted, Excel uses 0.

Type: Either 0 or 1, and indicates when payments are due. Use 0 if the payments are due at the end of the period and 1 if they are due at the beginning of the period.

Guess: Used only for the RATE function. It's your best guess of the internal rate of return. The closer your guess, the faster Excel can calculate the exact result.

On the CD-ROM
The workbook named AMORTSCH.XLS on the accompanying CD-ROM demonstrates the use of the PMT, PPMT, and IPMT functions to calculate a fixed-interest amortization schedule.

Lookup and Reference functions

The 15 functions in the Lookup and Reference category are used to perform table lookups and obtain other types of information. I demonstrate some of these functions in this section.

VLOOKUP

The VLOOKUP function can be quite useful when you need to use a value from a table, such as a table of tax rates. This function retrieves text or a value from a table, based on a specific key in the first column of the table. The retrieved result is at a specified horizontal offset from the first row of the table.

Figure 10-12 shows an example of a lookup table (named PartsList) in range D2:F9. The worksheet is designed so that a user can enter a part number into cell B2 (which is named Part), and formulas in cells B4 and B5 return the appropriate information for the part by using the lookup table. The formulas are as follows:

Cell B4: =VLOOKUP(Part,PartsList,2,FALSE)

Cell B5: =VLOOKUP(Part,PartsList,3,FALSE)

The formula in B4 looks up the value in the cell named Part in the first column of the table named PartsList. It returns the value in the column that corresponds to its third argument (column 2). The fourth argument tells Excel that it must find an exact match. If the fourth argument is TRUE (or omitted), Excel returns the next largest value that is less than the lookup value (the values in the first column must be in ascending order). Using an inexact match is useful for income-tax tables in which an income may fall into a range of values. In other words, there won't be a line in the table for every possible income.

If you enter a value that is not found in the table, the formula returns #N/A. You can change the formula to produce a more user-friendly error message by using the ISNA function. The revised formula is as follows:

    =IF(ISNA(VLOOKUP(Part,PartsList,2,FALSE)),"NotFound",VLOOKUP(Part,PartsList,2,FALSE))

If you enter a part that is not in the list, this formula returns *Not Found* rather than #N/A.

	A	B	C	D	E	F
1						
2	Enter Part No. -->	319		Part Number	Name	Unit Cost
3				145	Mesh Rod	$5.95
4	Name	Piano Nail		155	Puddle Joint	$12.95
5	Unit Cost	$0.99		187	Penguin Bolt	$1.29
6				205	Finger Nut	$0.98
7				225	Toe Bolt	$0.49
8				319	Piano Nail	$0.99
9				377	Mule Pipe	$9.95

Figure 10-12: A vertical lookup table.

Note The HLOOKUP function works exactly like VLOOKUP except that it looks up the value horizontally in the table's first row.

MATCH

The MATCH function searches a range for a value or text and returns the relative row or column in which the item was found. Figure 10-13 shows a simple example. The worksheet contains the month names in A1:A12. Cell C3 contains the following formula:

```
=MATCH(C1,A1:A12,0)
```

It returns 7 because cell C1 contains July, and July is the seventh element in the range A1:A12.

The third argument for the MATCH function specifies the type of match you want (0 means an exact match). Values of 1 and –1 are used when you'll accept an inexact match.

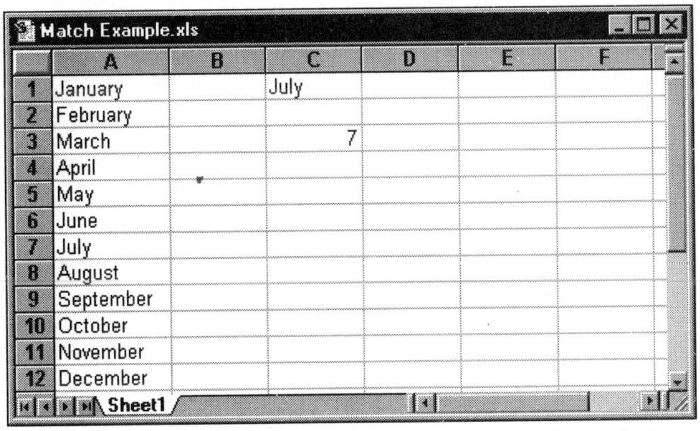

Figure 10-13: Using the MATCH function to return a relative position in a range.

INDEX

The INDEX function returns a value from a range using a row index (for a vertical range), column index (for a horizontal range), or both (for a two-dimensional range). The formula that follows returns the value in A1:J10 that is in its fifth row and third column:

```
=INDEX(A1:J10,5,3)
```

On the CD-ROM The CD-ROM that accompanies this book contains a workbook that demonstrates the INDEX function and the MATCH function. The workbook, shown in Figure 10-14, displays the mileage between selected U.S. cities. The workbook is named MILEAGE.XLS.

Note The OFFSET function performs a similar function.

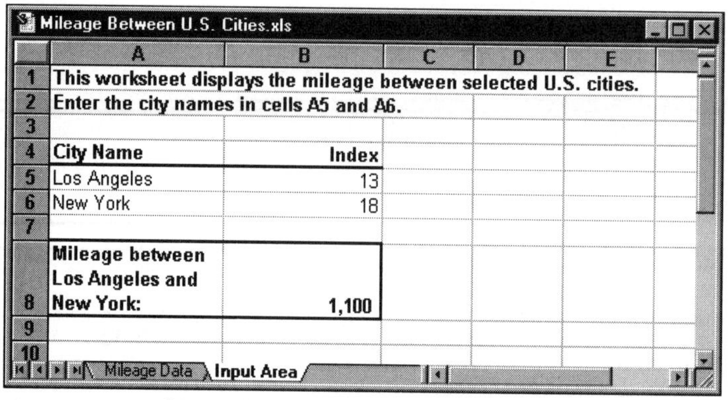

Figure 10-14: This workbook uses the INDEX and MATCH functions to look up the mileage between selected U.S. cities.

INDIRECT

The INDIRECT function returns the value in a cell specified by its text argument. For example, the following formula returns the value (or text) in cell A1:

```
=INDIRECT("A1")
```

This function is most useful when it uses a reference as its argument (not a literal, as shown previously). For example, if cell C9 contains the text *Sales*, the following formula returns the value in the cell named `Sales`:

```
=INDIRECT(C9)
```

This concept can be a bit difficult to grasp but, after you master it, you can put it to good use. Figure 10-15 shows a multisheet workbook with formulas that use the INDIRECT function to summarize the information on the other worksheets in the workbook. Cell B2 contains the following formula, which was copied to the other cells:

```
=INDIRECT("'"&$A2&"'"&"!"&B$1)
```

This formula builds a cell reference by using text in row 1 and column A. The argument is evaluated as follows:

```
'Denver'!Sales
```

The Denver sheet has a range named `Sales`. Therefore, the indirect function returns the value in the cell named `Sales` on the Denver worksheet.

On the CD-ROM This file, named INDIREF.XLS, is available on the CD-ROM included with this book.

Figure 10-15: These formulas use the INDIRECT function to summarize values contained in the other workbooks.

Statistical functions

The Statistical category contains a whopping 71 functions that perform various calculations. Many of these are quite specialized, but several are useful for nonstatisticians.

AVERAGE

The AVERAGE function returns the average (arithmetic mean) of a range of values. This is equivalent to the sum of the range divided by the number of values in the range. The formula that follows returns the average of the values in the range A1:A100:

```
=AVERAGE(A1:A100)
```

If the range argument contains blanks or text, these cells aren't included in the average calculation. As with the SUM formula, you can supply any number of arguments.

Note   Excel also provides the MEDIAN function (which returns the middle-most value in a range) and the MODE function (which returns the value that appears most frequently in a range).

MAX and MIN

Use the MAX function to return the largest value in a range and the MIN function to return the smallest value in a range. The following formula displays the largest and smallest values in a range named Data; using the concatenation operator causes the result to appear in a single cell:

```
="Smallest: "&MIN(Data)&" Largest: "&MAX(Data)
```

For example, if the values in Data range from 12 to 156, this formula returns *Smallest: 12 Largest: 156.*

LARGE and SMALL

The LARGE function returns the *n*th-largest value in a range. For example, to display the second-largest value in a range named Data, use the following formula:

```
=LARGE(Data,2)
```

The SMALL function works just as you would expect: It returns the *n*th-smallest value in a range.

COUNT and COUNTA

The COUNT function returns the number of values in a range. The COUNTA function returns the number of nonblank cells in a range. For example, the following formula returns the number of nonempty cells in column A:

```
=COUNTA("A:A")
```

Database functions

Excel's Database function category consists of a dozen functions that are used when working with database tables (also known as lists) stored in a worksheet. These functions all begin with the letter *D*, and they all have nondatabase equivalents. For example, the DSUM function is a special version of the SUM function that returns the sum of values in a database that meet a specified criteria. A database table is a rectangular range with field names in the top row. Each subsequent row is considered a record in the database.

Cross-Reference: To use a database function, you must specify a special criteria range in the worksheet. This type of criteria range is the same one that is used with Excel's Data⇨Filter⇨Advanced Filter command. I discuss this topic in Chapter 23.

Figure 10-16 shows a database table with a criteria range set up above it in A1:C2. The criteria range can be located anywhere in the workbook.

The DSUM function calculates the sum of the values in a specified field, filtered by the criteria table. For example, to calculate the expenses for Johnson, enter **Johnson** under the Name field in the criteria field. Then enter the following formula into any cell (this assumes that the database table is named Data and that the criteria range is named Criteria):

```
=DSUM(Data,"Amount",Criteria)
```

The formula returns the sum of the Amount field, but only for the records that meet the criteria in the range named Criteria. You can change the criteria, and the formula displays the new result. For example, to calculate the expenses in January, enter **January** under the Month field in the Criteria range (and delete any other entries).

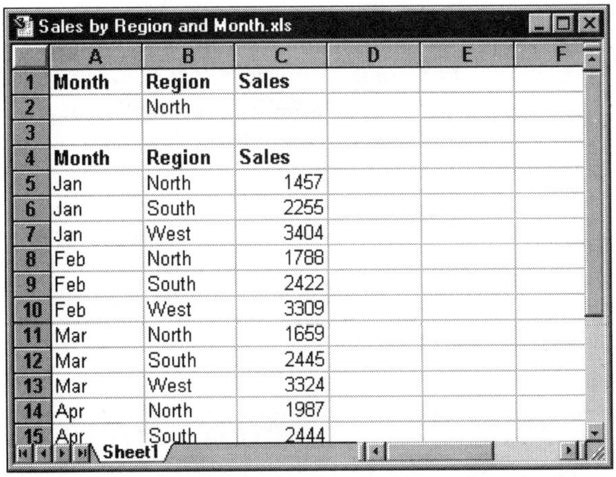

Sales by Region and Month.xls

	A	B	C	D	E	F
1	**Month**	**Region**	**Sales**			
2		North				
3						
4	**Month**	**Region**	**Sales**			
5	Jan	North	1457			
6	Jan	South	2255			
7	Jan	West	3404			
8	Feb	North	1788			
9	Feb	South	2422			
10	Feb	West	3309			
11	Mar	North	1659			
12	Mar	South	2445			
13	Mar	West	3324			
14	Apr	North	1987			
15	Apr	South	2444			

Sheet1

Figure 10-16: A simple database table and a criteria range above it.

On the CD-ROM

If you want to use several DSUM formulas, you can have each of them refer to a different criteria range (you can use as many criteria ranges as you like). The CD-ROM included with this book has an example of such usage. The workbook is named SUM_DATA.XLS. The other database functions work exactly like the DSUM function.

Analysis ToolPak functions

When you begin to feel familiar with Excel's worksheet functions, you can explore those that are available when the Analysis ToolPak is loaded. This add-in provides you with dozens of additional worksheet functions.

When this add-in is loaded, the Function Wizard displays a new category, Engineering. It also adds new functions to the following function categories: Financial, Date & Time, Math & Trig, and Information.

Cross-Reference

I discuss the Analysis ToolPak in Chapter 28. See Appendix D for a summary of the Analysis ToolPak function.

Creating Megaformulas

Often, spreadsheets require intermediate formulas to produce a desired result. After you get the formulas working correctly, it's often possible to eliminate the intermediate formulas and use a single *megaformula* instead (this term is my own — there is no official name for such a formula). The advantages? You use fewer cells (less clutter) and recalculation takes less time. Besides, people in the know will be impressed with your formula-building abilities. The disadvantage? The formula may be impossible to decipher or modify.

Here's an example: Imagine a worksheet with a column of people's names. And suppose that you've been asked to remove all middle names and middle initials from the names — but not all names have a middle name or initial. Editing the cells manually would take hours, so you opt for a formula-based solution. Although this task is not a difficult one, it normally involves several intermediate formulas. Also assume that you want to use as few cells as possible in the solution.

Figure 10-17 shows the solution, which requires six intermediate formulas. The names are in column A; the end result goes in column H. Columns B through G hold the intermediate formulas. Table 10-7 shows the formulas used in this worksheet, along with a brief description of each.

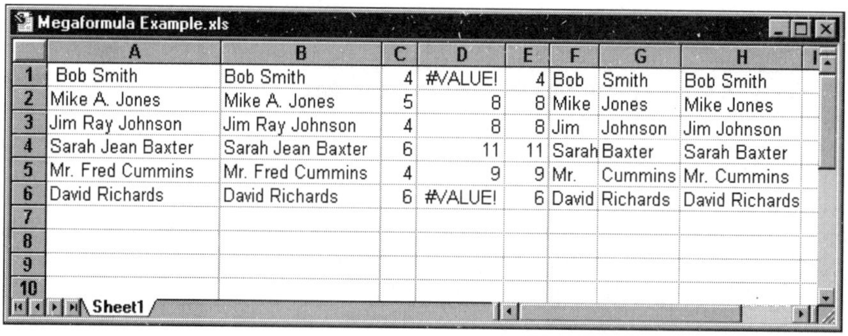

	A	B	C	D	E	F	G	H	
1	Bob Smith	Bob Smith	4	#VALUE!	4	Bob	Smith	Bob Smith	
2	Mike A. Jones	Mike A. Jones	5	8	8	Mike	Jones	Mike Jones	
3	Jim Ray Johnson	Jim Ray Johnson	4	8	8	Jim	Johnson	Jim Johnson	
4	Sarah Jean Baxter	Sarah Jean Baxter	6	11	11	Sarah	Baxter	Sarah Baxter	
5	Mr. Fred Cummins	Mr. Fred Cummins	4	9	9	Mr.	Cummins	Mr. Cummins	
6	David Richards	David Richards	6	#VALUE!	6	David	Richards	David Richards	
7									
8									
9									
10									

Megaformula Example.xls — Sheet1

Figure 10-17: Removing the middle names and initials requires six intermediate formulas.

Table 10-7
Intermediate Formulas

Cell	Intermediate Formula	What It Does
B1	=TRIM(A1)	Removes excess spaces
C1	=FIND(" ",B1,1)	Locates first space
D1	=FIND(" ",B1,C1+1)	Locates second space (returns an error if there is no second space)
E1	=IF(ISERROR(D1),C1,D1)	Uses the first space if no second space
F1	=LEFT(B1,C1)	Extracts the first name
G1	=RIGHT(B1,LEN(B1)-E1)	Extracts the last name
H1	=F1&G1	Concatenates the two names

You can eliminate all the intermediate formulas by creating what I call a huge formula (a megaformula). You do so by starting with the end result and then replacing each cell reference with a copy of the formula in the cell referred to (but don't copy the equal sign). Fortunately, you can use the Clipboard to copy and paste. Keep repeating this process until cell H1 contains nothing but references to cell A1. You end up with the following megaformula in one cell:

```
=LEFT(TRIM(A1),FIND("",TRIM(A1),1))&RIGHT(TRIM(A1),LEN(TRIM(A1))-
IF(ISERROR(FIND(" ",TRIM(A1),FIND(" ",TRIM(A1),1)+1)),FIND("
",TRIM(A1),1),FIND(" ",TRIM(A1),FIND(" ",TRIM(A1),1)+1)))
```

When you're satisfied that the megaformula is working, you can delete the columns that hold the intermediate formulas because they are no longer used.

The megaformula performs exactly the same task as all the intermediate formulas — although it's virtually impossible for anyone (even the original author) to figure out. If you decide to use megaformulas, make sure that the intermediate formulas are performing correctly before you start building a megaformula. Even better, keep a copy of the intermediate formulas somewhere in case you discover an error or need to make a change.

On the CD-ROM

This workbook, named MEGAFORM.XLS, is on the companion CD-ROM.

Note

Your only limitation is that Excel's formulas can be no more than 1,024 characters. Because a megaformula is so complex, you may think that using one would slow down recalculation. Actually, the opposite is true. As a test, I created a worksheet that used a megaformula 16,384 times. Then I created another worksheet that used six intermediate formulas. As you can see in Table 10-8, the megaformula recalculated faster and also resulted in a much smaller file.

Table 10-8 Intermediate Formulas versus Megaformula		
Method	*Recalc Time (seconds)*	*File Size*
Intermediate formulas	35	5.73 MB
Megaformula	21	2.06MB

Creating Custom Functions

Although Excel offers more functions than you'll ever need, it's likely that you'll eventually search for a function you need and not be able to find. The solution is to create your own. Excel is the only spreadsheet that lets you create custom worksheet functions without using a programming language such as C.

If you don't have the skills to create your own functions, you may be able to purchase custom Excel functions from a third-party provider that specializes in your industry. Or you can hire a consultant to develop functions that meet your needs.

To create a custom function, you must be well-versed in Visual Basic for Applications (VBA) or Excel's XLM macro language. When you create a custom function, you can use it in your worksheet, just like the built-in functions.

Cross-Reference   I cover custom worksheet functions in Chapter 35.

Learning More about Functions

This chapter has just barely skimmed the surface. Excel has hundreds of functions I haven't mentioned. To learn more about the functions available to you, I suggest that you browse through them by using the Function Wizard and click on the Help button when you see something that looks useful. The functions are thoroughly described in Excel's online help system. Figure 10-18 shows an example of the help available for a function.

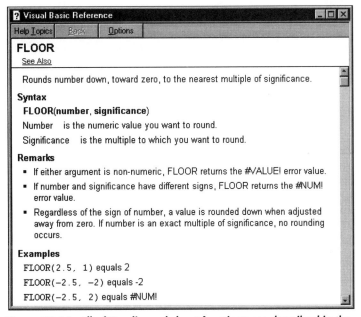

Figure 10-18: All of Excel's worksheet functions are described in the online help system.

Summary

This chapter discusses the built-in worksheet functions available in Excel. These functions are arranged by category, and you can enter them into your formulas manually (by typing them) or by using the Function Wizard. I present many examples of functions across the various categories.

✦   ✦   ✦

Worksheet Formatting

In Chapter 6, I discuss number formatting, which lets you change the way that values are displayed in their cells. This chapter covers what I refer to as *stylistic* formatting, which is purely cosmetic.

Overview of Stylistic Formatting

Stylistic formatting you apply to worksheet cells doesn't affect the actual content of the cells. Rather, the goal of such formatting is to make your work easier to read or more attractive. The types of formatting I discuss in this chapter consist of the following:

✦ Using different type fonts, sizes, and attributes

✦ Changing the way cells contents are aligned within cells

✦ Using colors in the background or foreground in cells

✦ Using patterns for cell background

✦ Using borders around cells

✦ Using a graphic background for your worksheet

On the CD-ROM The companion CD-ROM contains a file named FORMATS.XLS, which demonstrates some techniques used in this chapter.

Why bother with formatting?

Some users — especially those who cut their eyeteeth using a spreadsheet that had no stylistic formatting options — tend to shy away from formatting. After all, these formats don't do anything to make the worksheet more accurate, and formatting just takes valuable time.

I'll be the first to admit that stylistic formatting isn't essential for every workbook you develop. If no one except you will ever see it, you may not want to bother. If anyone else will use your workbook, however, I strongly suggest that you spend some time applying simple formatting. Figure 11-1 shows an example of how even simple formatting can significantly improve a worksheet's readability.

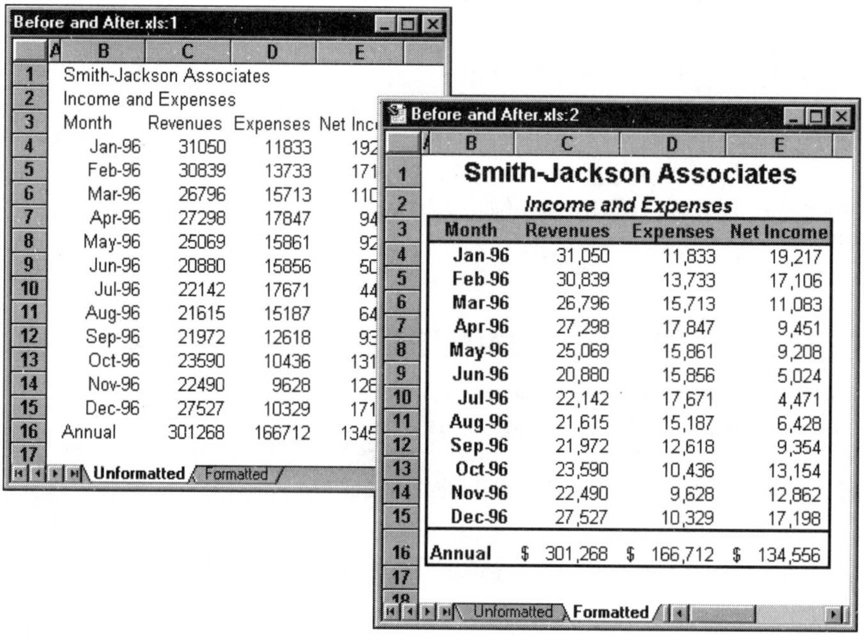

Figure 11-1: Before and after applying simple stylistic formatting.

On the other hand, some users go overboard with formatting. I've downloaded many Excel worksheets from online services such as CompuServe and America Online. Some of these worksheets are hideous and don't convey a professional image. The main problems are too many different fonts and sizes and overuse of color and borders.

Eventually you'll strike a happy medium with your stylistic formatting: not too much, but enough to clarify what you're trying to accomplish.

When to format

When you're developing a worksheet, you can apply stylistic formatting at any time. Some people prefer to format their work as they go along (I'm in this group). Others wait until the workbook is set up and then apply the formatting as the final step (the icing on the cake). The choice is yours.

The Formatting toolbar

In Chapter 6, I introduce the Formatting toolbar, which is a quick way to apply simple stylistic formatting. Figure 11-2 shows this toolbar.

Figure 11-2: The Formatting toolbar contains many tools to apply formats.

In many cases, this toolbar may contain all the formatting tools you need. But some types of formatting require using the Format Cells dialog box. This chapter covers the finer points of stylistic formatting, including options not available on the Formatting toolbar.

The Format Cells dialog box

Throughout this chapter, I refer to the Format Cells dialog box. This is a tabbed dialog box from which you can apply nearly any type of stylistic formatting (as well as number formatting). The formats selected in the Format Cells dialog box apply to the current selection of cells.

After selecting the cell or range to format, you can bring up the Format Cells dialog box by using any of the following methods:

✦ Choose the Format⇨Cells command.

✦ Press Ctrl+1.

✦ Right-click on the selected cell or range and choose Format Cells from the shortcut menu.

Figure 11-3 shows the Format Cells dialog box. When you first access this dialog box, the Number panel is displayed. You can choose another panel by clicking on any of the six tabs. When you display this dialog box again, Excel displays it with the panel you were last using.

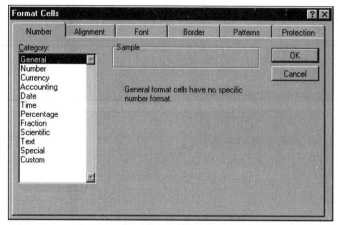

Figure 11-3: The Format Cells dialog box contains six tabs, each of which controls a different aspect of formatting.

Working with Fonts

One of the elements that distinguishes a graphical user interface (GUI) such as Windows 95 from a character-based interface (such as plain old DOS) is fonts. A GUI can display different fonts in different sizes and with different attributes (bold, italic, underline). A character-based display typically shows one font of the same size and may be able to handle different font attributes.

You can use different fonts, sizes, or attributes in your worksheets to make various parts stand out — as in the headers for a table. You also can adjust the font size to make more information appear on a single page.

Tip Reducing the font size so that your report fits on a certain number of pages isn't always necessary. Excel has a handy option that automatically scales your printed output to fit on a specified number of pages. I discuss this option in Chapter 12.

About fonts

When you select a font, Excel displays only the fonts that are installed on your system. Windows 95 includes several fonts, and you can acquire additional fonts from a variety of sources. For best results, you should use TrueType fonts. These fonts can be displayed and printed in any size, without the "jaggies" that characterize nonscalable fonts.

If you plan to distribute a workbook to other users, you should stick with the fonts that are included with Windows. If you open a workbook and your system doesn't have the font with which the workbook was created, Windows attempts to use a similar font. Sometimes this works, and sometimes it doesn't. To be on the safe side, use only the fonts that follow if you plan to share your workbook with others:

✦ Arial

✦ Courier New

✦ Symbol

✦ Times New Roman

✦ Wingdings

The default font

By default, the information you enter into Excel uses the 10-point Arial font. A font is described by its typeface (Arial, Times New Roman, Courier New, and so on) as well as by its size, measured in points (there are 72 points in one inch). Excel's row height is, by default, 12.75 points. Therefore, 10-point type entered into 12.75-point rows leaves a nice distance between the characters in adjacent rows.

Note If you have not manually changed a row's height, Excel automatically adjusts the row height based on the tallest text you enter into the row. It even adjusts for bold text (which makes the text slightly higher). You can, of course, override this adjustment and change the row height to any size you like. Excel's row height must be in 0.25-point increments. For example, if you enter a row height of 15.35, Excel makes the row 15.5 points high (it always rounds up).

The default font is the font specified by the Normal style. All cells have the Normal style unless you specifically apply a different style. If you want to change the font for all cells that have the Normal style, you simply change the font used in the Normal style. Here's how to do it:

1. Choose the Format⇨Style command. Excels displays the Style dialog box.

2. Make sure that Normal appears in the drop-down box labeled Style, and click on the Modify button. Excel displays the Format Cells dialog box.

3. Choose the font and size you want as the default, and click on OK to return to the Style dialog box.

4. Click on OK again to close the Style dialog box.

The font for all cells that use the Normal style changes to the font you specified. Changing the font for the Normal style can be done at any time. I discuss Excel's style feature later in this chapter.

Tip   If you want to change the default font permanently, create a template that uses a different font for the Normal style. I discuss templates in Chapter 33.

Changing fonts

The easiest way to change the font or size for selected cells is to use the Font and Font Size tools on the Formatting toolbar. Just select the cells, click on the appropriate tool, and choose the font or size from the drop-down list.

You also can use the Font panel in the Format Cells dialog box, as shown in Figure 11-4. This panel lets you control several other properties of the font from a single dialog box. Notice that you also can change the font style (bold, italic), underlining, color, and effects (strikethrough, superscript, or subscript). If you click on the check box labeled Normal Font, Excel displays the selections for the font defined for the Normal style.

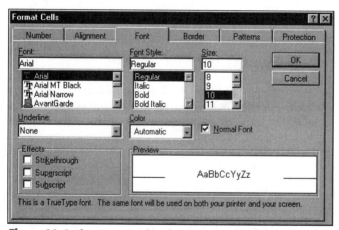

Figure 11-4: The Font panel in the Format Cells dialog box.

Note   Notice that Excel provides four different underlining styles. For the two accounting underline styles, dollar signs and percent signs aren't underlined. In the two nonaccounting underline styles, the entire cell contents are always underlined.

Selecting fonts and attributes with shortcut keys

If you prefer to keep your hands on the keyboard, you can use the following shortcut keys to quickly format a selected range:

Ctrl+5	Strikethrough
Ctrl+Shift+F	Font Tool

Ctrl+B	Bold
Ctrl+I	Italic
Ctrl+U	Underline

These shortcut keys (except for Ctrl+Shift+F) act as a toggle. For example, you can turn bold on and off by repeatedly pressing Ctrl+B.

Figure 11-5 shows examples of font formatting.

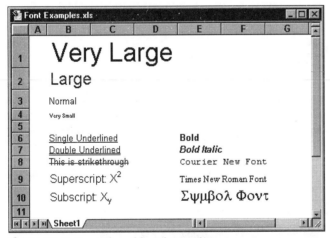

Figure 11-5: Examples of font formatting.

Using multiple fonts in one cell

If a cell contains text, Excel also lets you format individual characters in the cell. To do so, get into edit mode and then select the characters you want to format. You can select characters by dragging the mouse over them or by holding down the Shift key as you press the left- or right-arrow key. Then use any of the standard formatting techniques. The changes apply to only the selected characters in the cell. This technique doesn't work with cells that contain values or formulas.

Figure 11-6 shows a few examples of using different fonts, sizes, and attributes in a cell.

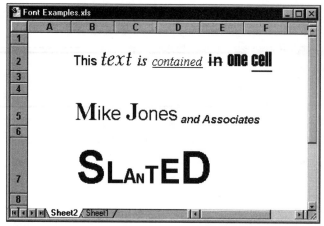

Figure 11-6: You can use different fonts, sizes, or attributes for selected characters in text.

Changing Cell Alignment

Cell alignment refers to how a cell's contents are situated in the cell. The contents of a cell can be aligned both vertically and horizontally in the cell. The effect you see depends on the cell's height and width. For example, if the row uses standard height, you may not be able to notice any changes in the cell's vertical alignment (but if you increase the row's height, these effects are apparent).

Figure 11-7 shows some examples of cells formatted with the various horizontal and vertical alignment options.

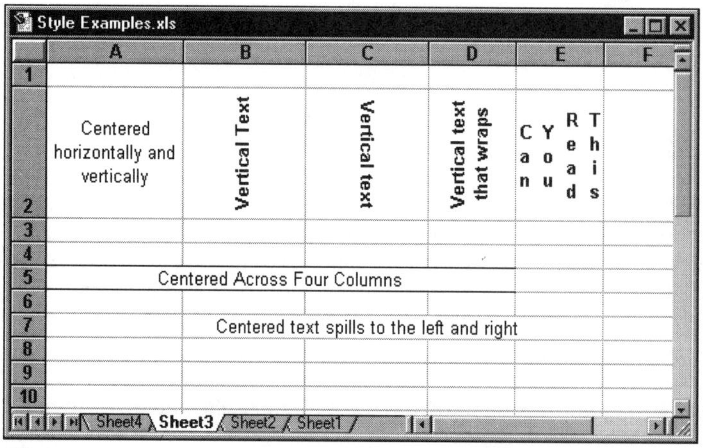

Figure 11-7: Examples of Excel's alignment options.

Horizontal alignment options

You can apply most of the horizontal alignment options by using the tools on the Formatting toolbar. Or you can use the Alignment panel in the Format Cells dialog box, as shown in Figure 11-8.

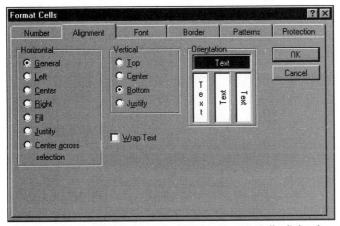

Figure 11-8: The Alignment panel in the Format Cells dialog box.

The horizontal alignment options are as follows:

✦ **General:** Aligns numbers to the right and text to the left and centers logical and error values. This option is the default alignment.

✦ **Left:** Aligns the cell contents to the left side of the cell. If the text is wider than the cell, it spills over to the cell to the right. If the cell to the right is not empty, the text is truncated and not completely visible.

✦ **Center:** Centers the cell contents in the cell. If the text is wider than the cell, it spills over to cells on either side if they are empty. If the adjacent cells aren't empty, the text is truncated and not completely visible.

✦ **Right:** Aligns the cell contents to the right side of the cell. If the text is wider than the cell, it spills over to the cell to the left. If the cell to the left isn't empty, the text is truncated and not completely visible.

✦ **Fill:** Repeats the contents of the cell until the cell's width is filled. If cells to the right also are formatted with Fill alignment, they also are filled.

✦ **Justify:** Justifies the text to the left and right of the cell. This option is applicable only if the cell is formatted as wrapped text and uses more than one line.

✦ **Centered across selection:** Centers the text over the selected columns. This option is useful for precisely centering a heading over a number of columns.

Vertical alignment options

To change the vertical alignment, you must use the Format Cells dialog box (these options are not available on the Formatting toolbar). The vertical alignment options are as follows:

✦ **Top:** Aligns the cell contents to the top of the cell.

✦ **Center:** Centers the cell contents vertically in the cell.

✦ **Bottom:** Aligns the cell contents to the bottom of the cell.

✦ **Justify:** Justifies the text vertically in the cell; this option is applicable only if the cell is formatted as wrapped text and uses more than one line.

Figure 11-9 shows examples of vertical alignment.

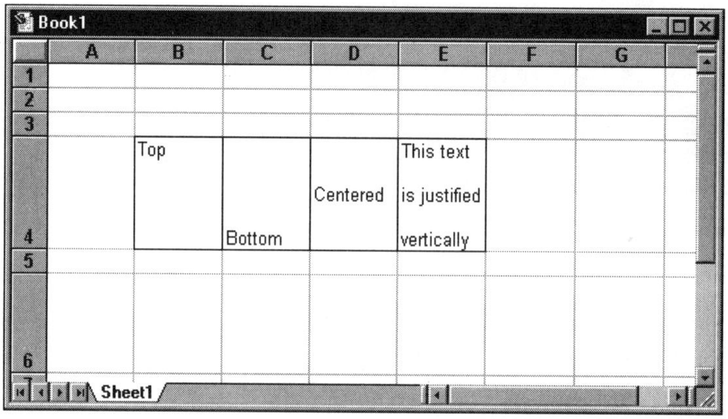

Figure 11-9: Examples of vertical alignment.

Other alignment options

The Alignment tab has two other options you can set. These options are independent of the vertical and horizontal alignment options, so you can enable these options with other formatting options:

✦ **Wrap text:** Displays the text on multiple lines in the cell, if necessary. This option is useful for column headings because it enables you to display lengthy headings without having to make the column too wide.

✦ **Orientation:** Displays the text vertically, rotated left, or rotated right.

Another type of justification

Excel provides another way to justify text, using its Edit⇨Fill⇨Justify command. This command has nothing to do with the alignment options discussed in this chapter. The Edit⇨Fill⇨Justify command is useful for re-arranging text in cells so that it fits in a specified range. For example, you may import a text file that has very long lines of text.

You easily can justify this text so that it's displayed in narrower lines. The accompanying figures show a range of text before and after I used this command.

This command works with text in a single column. It essentially redistributes the text in the cells so that it fits into a specified range.

You can make the text either wider (so that it uses fewer rows) or narrower (so that it uses more rows).

Select the cells to be justified (all in one column) and then extend the selection to the right so that the selection is as wide as you want the end result to be. Choose the Edit⇨Fill⇨Justify command, and Excel redistributes the text.

Blank rows serve as paragraph markers. If the range you select isn't large enough to hold all the text, Excel warns you and allows you to continue or abort. Be careful, because justified text overwrites anything that gets in its way.

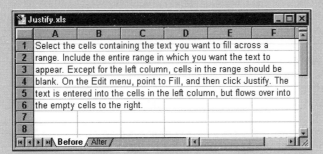

Tip The problem with using different orientation options is that the row height must be increased to display the text. Sometimes a preferable option is to use a text box to hold vertically oriented text. The advantage is that a text box is free floating, and you don't have to increase the row height. I discuss text boxes (and other drawing tools) in Chapter 15.

Colors and Shading

In the early days of personal computers, color monitors were an expensive luxury. Nowadays most people use color monitors. The main exception is laptop users — although color laptop systems are becoming more reasonably priced.

Tip I've known people who avoid using color in worksheets because they are uncertain of how the colors will translate when printed on a black-and-white printer. With Excel, that's not a valid reason. You can instruct Excel to ignore the colors when you print. You do this by checking the Black and White check box in the Sheet panel of the Page Setup dialog box (choose the File⇨Page Setup command to display this dialog box).

You control the color of the cell's text in the Font panel of the Format Cells dialog box, and you control the cell's background color in the Patterns panel. Tools on the Formatting toolbar (Font Color and Color) change the color of both these items.

A cell's background can be solid (one color) or consist of a pattern that uses two colors. To select a pattern, click on the Pattern drop-down list in the Format Cells dialog box. It expands as shown in Figure 11-10. Choose a pattern from the top part of the box and a second color from the bottom part. The first pattern in the list is "None" — use this option if you want a solid background. The Sample box to the right shows how the colors and pattern will look. If you plan to print the worksheet, you need to experiment to see how the color patterns translate to your printer.

Entering text in a cell with a patterned background usually looks terrible and makes the text difficult (or impossible) to read. Most of the time you'll use a background pattern for cells that don't contain any text. For example, you can use patterns to create a thick border around a range. Make the bordering columns and rows relatively narrow and the same thickness. You also can use patterns to create an interesting drop shadow effect. Figure 11-11 shows examples of this feature.

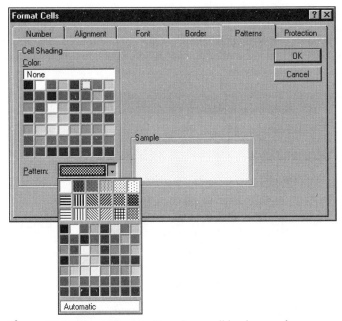

Figure 11-10: Choosing a pattern for a cell background.

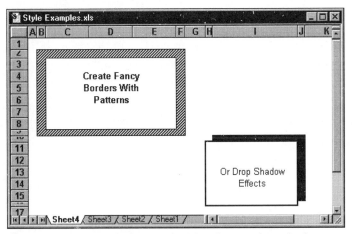

Figure 11-11: You can create a thick border or a drop-shadow effect by using background colors and patterns.

Another use for background colors is to make a large table of data easier to read. If you have a background in data processing, you're undoubtedly familiar with computer printer paper that has alternating green-and-white horizontal shading. You can use background colors to simulate this effect in Excel. See Figure 11-12 for an example.

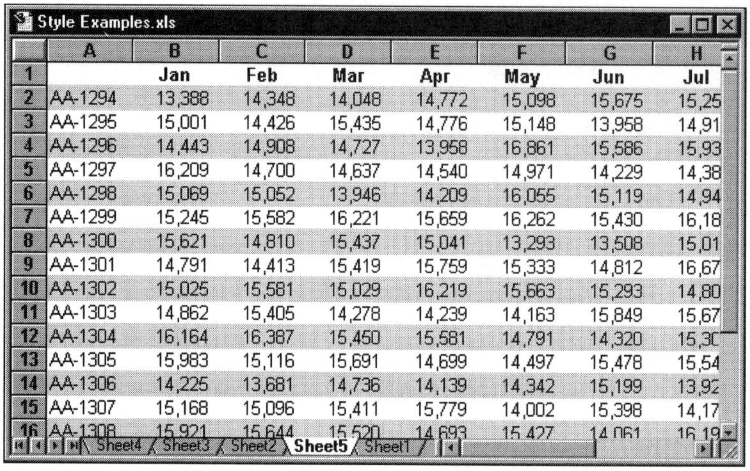

	A	B	C	D	E	F	G	H
1		Jan	Feb	Mar	Apr	May	Jun	Jul
2	AA-1294	13,388	14,348	14,048	14,772	15,098	15,675	15,25
3	AA-1295	15,001	14,426	15,435	14,776	15,148	13,958	14,91
4	AA-1296	14,443	14,908	14,727	13,958	16,861	15,586	15,93
5	AA-1297	16,209	14,700	14,637	14,540	14,971	14,229	14,38
6	AA-1298	15,069	15,052	13,946	14,209	16,055	15,119	14,94
7	AA-1299	15,245	15,582	16,221	15,659	16,262	15,430	16,18
8	AA-1300	15,621	14,810	15,437	15,041	13,293	13,508	15,01
9	AA-1301	14,791	14,413	15,419	15,759	15,333	14,812	16,67
10	AA-1302	15,025	15,581	15,029	16,219	15,663	15,293	14,80
11	AA-1303	14,862	15,405	14,278	14,239	14,163	15,849	15,67
12	AA-1304	16,164	16,387	15,450	15,581	14,791	14,320	15,30
13	AA-1305	15,983	15,116	15,691	14,699	14,497	15,478	15,54
14	AA-1306	14,225	13,681	14,736	14,139	14,342	15,199	13,92
15	AA-1307	15,168	15,096	15,411	15,779	14,002	15,398	14,17
16	AA-1308	15,921	15,644	15,520	14,693	15,427	14,061	16,19

Figure 11-12: Shading alternate lines can make a lengthy table easier to read.

Tip Here's a quick way to apply shading to every other row. This technique assumes that you want to shade every odd-numbered row in the range A1:F100. Start by shading A1:F1 with the color you want. Then select A1:F2 and copy it to the Clipboard. Next select A3:F100 and choose Edit⇨Paste Special (with the Formats option).

Tip To quickly hide the contents of a cell, make the background color the same as the font color. The cell contents are still visible in the formula bar when the cell is selected, however.

About the color palette

Excel gives you 56 colors from which to choose. These colors are known as the *palette*. You can examine the colors in the palette by clicking on the Color or Font Color tool on the Formatting toolbar. You may notice that these colors aren't necessarily unique (some are repeated).

Chances are, you're running Windows in a video mode that supports at least 256 colors. So why can you use only 56 colors in Excel? Good question. That's just the way Excel was designed.

You're not limited to the 56 colors that some unknown techie in Redmond came up with, however. You can change the colors in the palette to whatever you like. To do so, access the Options dialog box and click on the Color tab, as shown in the accompanying figure.

You'll see that there seems to be some rationale for the colors in the palette. For example, the first 16 are designated standard colors.

These are followed by 8 chart fill colors, 8 chart line colors, and 24 "other" colors.

If you want to change a color, double-click on it. Excel responds with a dialog box named Color Picker. Click on and drag the mouse until you see a color you like. Then click on OK, and the color you selected replaces the previous color.

If your worksheet uses the replaced color, the new color takes over. If your system is using a video driver that supports only 16 colors, some of the colors will be made by blending two colors (*dithering*). Dithered colors can be used for cell backgrounds, but text and lines are displayed using the nearest solid color. If you want to revert back to Excel's standard colors, click on the Reset button.

Each workbook stores its own copy of the color palette, and you even can copy color palettes from another workbook (which must be open). Use the Options dialog box's drop-down box labeled Copy Colors From.

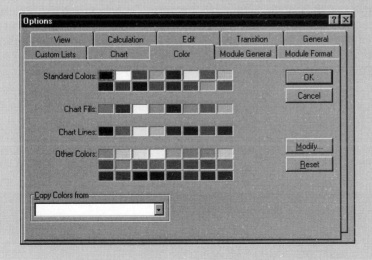

Borders and Lines

Borders often are used to group a range of similar cells or simply to delineate rows or columns. Excel offers eight different styles of borders, as you can see in the Border panel in the Format Cells dialog box (see Figure 11-13). This dialog box works with the selected cell or range and lets you specify which border style to use for each border of the selection.

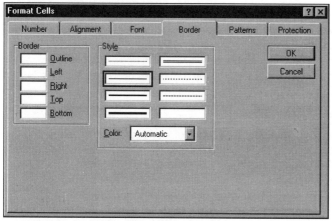

Figure 11-13: The Border panel of the Format Cells dialog box.

Before you invoke this dialog box, select the cell or range to which you want to add borders. First choose a line style and then choose the border position for the line style. If you want to put an outline around the selection, choose the Outline option. Excel displays the selected border style in the dialog box. You can choose different styles for different border positions. You also can choose a color for the border. Using this dialog box may require some trial and error, but you'll get the hang of it. Figure 11-14 shows examples of borders in a worksheet.

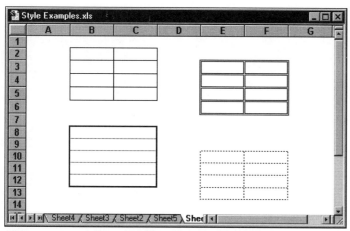

Figure 11-14: Examples of using borders in a worksheet.

Tip
If you use border formatting in your worksheet, you might want to turn off the grid display to make the borders more pronounced. Use the View panel of the Options dialog box to do this.

Applying a border to the bottom of a cell is not the same as applying the underline attribute to the font. These two operations result in quite different effects, as you see in Figure 11-15.

Style Examples.xls					
	A	B	C	D	E	F
1		Border		Underlining		
2		132.43		132.43		
3		129.36		129.36		
4		144.93		144.93		
5		406.72		406.72		
6						
7						
8						

Figure 11-15: Underlined text versus a bottom border.

Producing 3-D effects

You can use a combination of borders and background shading to produce attractive 3-D effects on your worksheet. These 3-D effects resemble raised or depressed panels, as shown in the accompanying figure.

For best results, use a light gray background color. To produce a raised effect, apply a white border to the top and left side of the range and a dark gray border on the bottom and right side.

To produce a sunken effect, use a dargray border on the top and left side and a white border on the bottom and right side. You can vary the line thickness to produce different effects.

The 3D Shading utility, which is part of the Power Utility Pak, makes it easy to produce these effects. The shareware version of the Power Utility Pak is available on the companion CD-ROM.

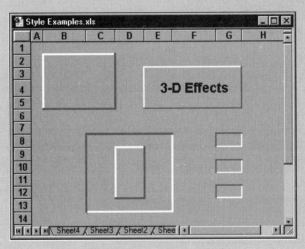

Adding a Worksheet Background

A new feature in Excel 95 is *sheet backgrounds*. This feature lets you choose a graphics file to serve as a background for a worksheet — similar to the wallpaper you may display on your Windows desktop. The graphic you choose is repeated so that it tiles the entire worksheet.

To add a background to a worksheet, choose the Format⇨Sheet⇨Background command. Excel displays a dialog box that lets you choose a graphics file. When you locate a file, click on OK. Excel tiles your worksheet with the graphic. Most graphics make it difficult to view text, so you generally have to use a background color for cells that contain text (see Figure 11-16). You'll also want to turn off the gridline display because the gridlines show through the graphic.

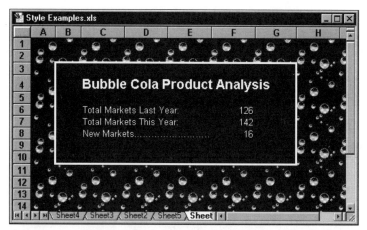

Figure 11-16: This worksheet has a graphic background. Cells that contain text use a colored background with white text, which overrides the graphic.

Note The graphic background is for display only — it doesn't get printed when you print the worksheet.

Copying formats by painting

If you want to copy the formats from a cell to another cell or range, you can use the Edit⇨Paste Special command and click on the Formats option. Another option is to use the Format Painter button on the Standard toolbar (it's the button with the paintbrush image).

Start by selecting the cell or range that has the formatting attributes you want to copy. Then click on the Format Painter button. Notice that the mouse pointer appears as a paintbrush. Next, click on and drag (paint) the cells to which you want to apply the formats. Release the mouse button, and the painting is finished (and you don't have to clean the brush).

Double-clicking on the Format Painter button causes the mouse pointer to remain a paintbrush after you release the mouse button.

This lets you paint other areas of the worksheet with the same formats. To get out of paint mode, click on the Format Painter button again (or press Esc).

AutoFormatting

So far, this chapter has described the individual formatting commands and tools at your disposal. Excel also has a feature known as *AutoFormatting* that can automatically perform many types of formatting for you. Figure 11-17 shows an unformatted table in worksheet and the same table that was formatted using one of Excel's AutoFormats.

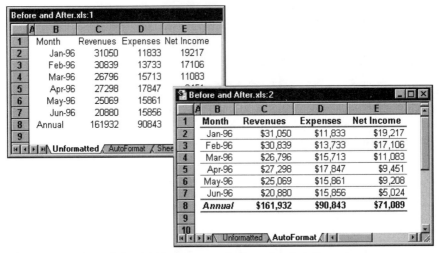

Figure 11-17: A worksheet table before and after using AutoFormat.

Using AutoFormats

To apply an AutoFormat, move the cell pointer anywhere within a table you want to format (Excel determines the table's boundaries automatically). Then choose the Format⇨AutoFormat command. Excel responds with the dialog box shown in Figure 11-18. Choose one of the 17 AutoFormats from the list and click on OK. Excel formats the table for you.

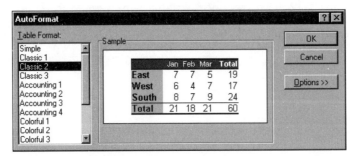

Figure 11-18: The AutoFormat dialog box.

Excel's AutoFormatting is smarter than it may appear on the surface. For example, it analyzes the data contained in the table and formats the table to handle items such as subtotals. Figure 11-19 shows an example of a table that contains a subtotal line for each department. When I applied an AutoFormat, the formatting took these subtotals into account and produced an attractive table in about one second.

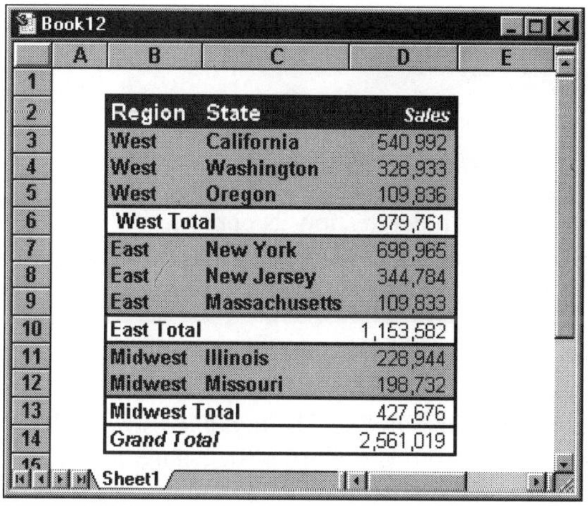

Region	State	Sales
West	California	540,992
West	Washington	328,933
West	Oregon	109,836
West Total		979,761
East	New York	698,965
East	New Jersey	344,784
East	Massachusetts	109,833
East Total		1,153,582
Midwest	Illinois	228,944
Midwest	Missouri	198,732
Midwest Total		427,676
Grand Total		2,561,019

Figure 11-19: AutoFormatting even accommodates subtotals in a table.

Controlling AutoFormats

I would have wagered good money that Excel 95 would allow user-defined AutoFormats (after all, the latest version of Quattro Pro for Windows has that feature). But I would have lost the bet. Although you can't define your own AutoFormats, you can control the type of formatting that is applied. When you click on the Options button in the AutoFormat dialog box, the dialog box expands to show six options (see Figure 11-20).

Initially, the six check boxes are all checked — which means that Excel will apply formatting from all six categories. If you want it to skip one or more categories, just uncheck the appropriate box before you click on OK. For example, when I use AutoFormats, I hardly ever want Excel to change the column widths, so I turn off the Width/Height option. If you've already formatted the numbers, you may want to turn off the Number option.

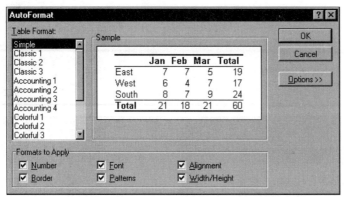

Figure 11-20: The AutoFormat dialog box expanded to show its options.

Using Named Styles

Perhaps one of the most underutilized features in Excel is its *named style* feature — something that was borrowed from the word processing genre. As a side note, named styles may also be the most underutilized feature in word processors.

If you find yourself continually applying the same combination of fonts, lines, and shading in your worksheets, it's to your advantage to create and use named styles. Named styles save time and reduce formatting errors by applying formats you specify in a single step. This feature also is useful for helping you to apply consistent formats across your worksheets.

The real advantage of styles, however, is that you can change a component of a style and then all the cells using that named style automatically incorporate the change. Suppose that you apply a particular style to a dozen cells scattered throughout your worksheet. Later you realize that these cells should have a font size of 14 points rather than 12 points. Rather than change each one, simply edit the style. All cells with that particular style change automatically. This can be a significant time-saver.

A style can consist of settings for six different attributes, although a style doesn't have to use all the attributes. You may recognize these attributes; they correspond to the six panels in the Format Cells dialog box. The attributes that make up a style are as follows:

✦ Number format

✦ Font (type, size, and color)

✦ Alignment (vertical and horizontal)

✦ Borders

✦ Pattern

✦ Protection (locked and hidden)

By default, all cells have the Normal style. In addition, Excel provides five other built-in styles — all of which control only the cell's number format. The styles available in every workbook are listed in Table 11-1.

Table 11-1		
Excel's Built-In Styles		
Style Name	*Description*	*Number Format Example*
Normal	Excel's default style	1234
Comma*	Comma with two decimal places	1,234.00
Comma[0]	Comma with no decimal places	1,234
Currency*	Left-aligned dollar sign with two decimal places	$ 1,234.00
Currency[0]	Left-aligned dollar sign with no decimal places	$ 1,234
Percent*	Percent with no decimal places	12%

* This style can be applied by clicking a button on the Standard toolbar.

If these styles don't meet your needs (and they probably don't), you can easily create new styles.

Applying styles

This section discusses the methods you can use to apply existing styles to cells or ranges.

Toolbar buttons

As mentioned in the preceding section, three buttons on the Standard toolbar are used to attach a particular style to a cell or range. It's important to understand that when you use these buttons to format a value, you're really changing the cell's style. Consequently, if you later want to change the Normal style, those cells won't be affected by the change.

Using the Style tool

If you plan to work with named styles, you might want to make an addition to one of your toolbars. In fact, I strongly suggest that you do so. Excel has a handy Style tool available. But (oddly) it's not on any of the built-in toolbars — maybe this is why the named style feature is underutilized. To add the Style tool to a toolbar (the Formatting toolbar is a good choice), follow these steps:

1. Right-click on any toolbar and choose Customize from the shortcut menu. Excel displays its Customize dialog box.

2. In the Categories list box, click on Formatting. The Buttons box displays all available tools in the Formatting category.

3. Click on the Style tool (it's labeled *Style*) and drag it to your Formatting toolbar. If you drag it in the middle, the other tools scoot over to make room for it.

4. If the formatting toolbar is too wide to show all the tools, you can make two of them (the Zoom tool and the new Style tool) narrower by clicking on and dragging their right border. You also can get rid of any tools you never use by simply dragging them away (don't worry, you can always reset the toolbar to its original state).

5. When the toolbar looks the way you want it, click on the Close button in the Customize dialog box.

The new Style tool displays the style of the selected cell and also lets you quickly apply a style — or even create a new style. To apply a style by using the Style tool, just select the cell or range, click on the Style tool, and choose the style you want to apply.

Using the Format⇨Style command

You also can apply a style by using the Format⇨Style command. Excel will display its Style dialog box. Just choose the style you want to apply from the Style Name drop-down list. Using the Style tool is a much quicker way to apply a style.

On the CD-ROM The accompanying CD-ROM contains a workbook in which I've defined several styles. You may want to open this workbook and experiment with them. The workbook is named STYLES.XLS.

Creating new styles

There are two ways to create a new style: using the Format⇨Style command or using the Style tool. To create a new style, first select a cell and apply all the formatting that will be included in the new style. You can use any of the formatting available in the Format Cells dialog box.

When the cell is formatted to your liking, choose the Format⇨Style command. Excel displays its Style dialog box, shown in Figure 11-21. The name displayed in the Style Name drop-down list is the current style of the cell (probably Normal). This box is highlighted, so you can simply enter a new style name by typing it. When you do so, Excel displays the words *By Example* to indicate that it's basing the style on the current cell.

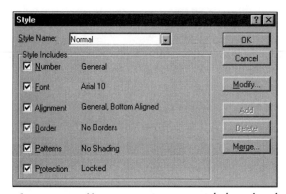

Figure 11-21: You can create a new style by using the Style dialog box.

The check boxes display the current formats for the cell. By default, all check boxes are checked. If you don't want the style to include one or more format categories, uncheck the appropriate box(es). Click on OK to create the style.

Note You also can create a style from scratch in the Style dialog box. Just enter a style name and then click on the Modify button to select the formatting.

Tip   If you followed my advice and added the Style tool to one of your toolbars, you can create a new style without using the Style dialog box. Just format a cell, activate the Style tool, and type the name. The only disadvantage to this method is that you can't specify which format categories to omit from the style. But as you'll see next, it's easy to modify an existing style.

Overriding a style

After you apply a style to a cell, you can apply additional formatting to it by using any formatting method discussed in this chapter. Formatting modifications you make to the cell don't affect other cells that use the same style.

Modifying a style

To change an existing file, call up the Style dialog box. Choose from the drop-down box the style you want to modify. You can make changes to the check boxes to include or exclude any of the format categories. Or you can click on the Modify button. Excel displays the familiar Format Cells dialog box. Make the changes you want and click on OK. Click on OK again to close the Style dialog box. All the cells with the selected style are modified with the new formatting.

Tip   You also can change a style by modifying the formatting of a cell that uses the style. After doing so, activate the Style tool and reselect the style name. Excel asks whether you want to redefine the style based on the selection. Respond in the affirmative to change the style — and all of the cells that use the style.

Deleting a style

If you no longer need a style, you can delete it. To do so, activate the Style dialog box, choose the style from the list, and click on Delete. All the cells that had the style revert back to the Normal style.

Note   If you applied additional formatting to a cell that had a style applied to it and then you delete the style, the cell retains all its additional formatting.

Merging styles from other workbooks

You may create one or more styles you use frequently. Although you could go through the motions and create these styles for every new workbook, a better approach is to merge the styles from a workbook that already has them created.

To merge styles from another workbook, the workbook that contains the styles to be merged must be open. Choose the Format⇨Style command and click on the Merge button. Excel displays a list of all open workbooks, as shown in Figure 11-22. Select the workbook and click on OK. The active workbook then contains all styles from the other workbook.

Figure 11-22: Merging styles from another workbook is a good way to make your workbooks look consistent.

Caution When you're merging styles, colors are based on the palette stored with the workbook. If the workbook from which you're merging has a different color palette, the colors used in the merged styles may not look the same.

Controlling Styles with Templates

When you start Excel, it loads with a number of default settings, including the settings for stylistic formatting. If you find that you spend a great deal of time changing the default elements, you should know about templates.

Here's an example. You may prefer to use 12-point Arial rather than 10-point Arial as the default font. And maybe you prefer that Wrap Text be the default setting for alignment. Changing defaults is easy to do when you know about templates.

The trick is to create a workbook with the Normal style modified to the way you want it. Then save the workbook as a template in your XLStart folder. After doing so, selecting the File⇨New command displays a dialog box from which you can choose the template for the new workbook. Template files also can store other named styles. This is an excellent way to give your workbooks a consistent look.

Cross-Reference Chapter 33 discusses templates in detail.

Summary

This chapter explores all topics related to stylistic formatting: different fonts and size, alignment options, applying colors and shading, and using borders and lines. I discuss Excel's AutoFormat feature, which can format a table of data automatically. The chapter concludes with a discussion of named styles, an important concept that can save you time and also make your worksheets look more consistent.

✦   ✦   ✦

Printing
Your Work

Many worksheets that you develop with Excel are designed to serve as printed reports. You'll find that printing from Excel is quite easy, and you can generate attractive, well-formatted reports with minimal effort. But, as you'll see, Excel has plenty of printing options, which are explained in this chapter.

One-Step Printing

The Print button on the Standard toolbar is a quick way to print the current worksheet using the default settings. Just click on the button, and Excel sends the worksheet to the printer. If you've changed any of the default print settings, Excel uses the new settings; otherwise, it uses the following default settings:

+ Prints the active worksheet (or all selected worksheets), including any embedded charts or drawing objects

+ Prints one copy

+ Prints the entire worksheet

+ Prints in portrait mode

+ Doesn't scale the printed output

+ Uses 1-inch margins for the top and bottom and .75-inch margins for the left and right

+ Prints the sheet name as a header on each page and puts page numbers in the footer of each page

+ For wide worksheets that span multiple pages, it prints down and then across

As you might suspect, you can change any of these default print settings.

When you print a worksheet, Excel prints only the *active area* of the worksheet. In other words, it won't print all four million cells — just those that have data in them. If the worksheet contains any embedded charts or drawing objects, they also are printed (unless you have modified the Print Object property of the object).

Note   If you create a workbook based on a template, the template may contain different default settings. I discuss templates in Chapter 33.

Adjusting Your Print Settings

The sections that follow discuss the various print settings that you can modify. You adjust these settings in two different dialog boxes:

✦ The Print dialog box (accessed with the File➪Print command or Ctrl+P).

✦ The Page Setup dialog box (accessed with the File➪Page Setup command). This is a tabbed dialog box with four panels.

Both of these dialog boxes have a Print Preview button that previews the printed output on-screen.

Settings in the Print Dialog Box

The following sections discuss the options available in the Print dialog box. The Print dialog box is where you actually start the printing (unless you used the Print button on the Standard toolbar). After you've selected your print settings, click on OK from the Print dialog box to print your work.

Selecting a printer

Before printing, make sure that the correct printer is selected (applicable only if you have access to more than one printer). You do this in the Print dialog box, shown in Figure 12-1. You can select the printer from the drop-down list labeled Printer. This dialog box also lists information about the selected printer, such as its status and where it's connected.

Clicking on the Properties button displays a property box for the selected printer. The exact dialog box that you see depends on the printer. This dialog box lets you adjust printer-specific settings. In most cases, you won't have to change any of these settings, but it's a good idea to be familiar with the settings that you can change.

If you check the Print to file check box, the output will be sent to a file. Excel will prompt you for a filename before it begins printing. The resulting file will *not* be a standard text file. Rather, it will include all of the printer codes required to print your worksheet. Printing to a file is useful if you don't have immediate access to a printer. You can save the output to a file and then send this file to your printer at a later time.

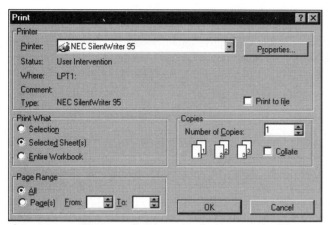

Figure 12-1: The Print dialog box.

Tip To save your worksheet as a text file, use the File⇨Save As command, and select the desired text file format from the drop-down list labeled Save as type.

Specifying what to print

The Print What section of the Print dialog box lets you specify what to print. You have three options:

✦ **Selection:** Prints only the range the you selected before issuing the File⇨Print command.

✦ **Selected Sheet(s):** Prints the active sheet or all sheets that you selected. You can select multiple sheets by pressing Ctrl and clicking on the sheet tabs. If multiple sheets are selected, each sheet begins printing on a new page.

✦ **Entire Workbook:** Prints the entire workbook, including chart sheets, dialog sheets, and VBA modules.

Sending a fax from Excel

If you have a fax board installed in your system, you can fax a worksheet to someone. The process works just like printing — but you have to select the fax as your printer in the Print dialog box. Then, print your worksheet as usual (all settings discussed in this chapter apply to faxing as well as printing). Instead of going to the printer, the worksheet will be faxed to the recipient whom you specify. The procedure for specifying the fax's recipient vary depending on your fax software.

Excel remembers the last "printer" you selected, so when you want to print normally, make sure that you select a printer.

Note If you choose the Selected Sheet(s) option, Excel prints the entire sheet — or just the range named `Print_Area`. Each worksheet can have a range named `Print_Area`. You can set the print area by selecting it and then choosing the File⇨Print Area⇨Set Print Area command. This is a standard named range, so you can edit the range's reference manually if you like. `Print_Area` also can consist of noncontiguous ranges (a multiple selection).

 In Excel 5, Microsoft removed the command to set the print area. This resulted in thousands of calls to its technical support line. Consequently, this command is now back in Excel for Windows 95.

After you print a worksheet, Excel displays dashed lines to indicate where the page breaks will occur. This is a very useful feature because the display adjusts dynamically. For example, if you find that your printed output is too wide to fit on a single page, you can adjust the column widths (keeping an eye on the page break display) until they are narrow enough to print on one page.

Tip If you don't want to see the page breaks displayed in your worksheet, access the Options dialog box, click on the View tab, and remove the check mark from the Automatic Page Breaks check box.

Printing multiple copies

The Print dialog box also lets you select how many copies to print. The upper limit is 32,767 copies — not that anyone would ever need that many copies. You also can specify that you want the copies collated. If you choose this option, Excel prints the pages in order for each set of output. If you're printing only one page, the Collate setting is ignored.

Printing selected pages

If your printed output uses multiple pages, you can select which pages to print in the Print dialog box. In the Page Range section, indicate the number of the first and last pages to print. You can use the spinner controls or type the page numbers in the edit boxes.

Settings in the Page Setup Dialog Box

The following sections discuss the options available in the Page Setup dialog box.

Controlling page settings

Figure 12-2 shows the Page panel of the Page Setup dialog box. This panel lets you control the following settings:

✦ **Orientation:** This is either Portrait (tall pages) or Landscape (wide pages). Landscape orientation might be useful if you have a wide range that doesn't fit on a vertically oriented page.

✦ **Scaling:** You can set a scaling factor manually or let Excel scale the output automatically to fit on the desired number of pages. Scaling can range from 10 percent to 400 percent of normal size. If you want to return to normal scaling, enter 100 in the box labeled % Normal Size.

✦ **Paper Size:** This setting lets you select the paper size that you're using. Click on the box and see the choices.

✦ **Print Quality:** If the installed printer supports it, you can change the printer's resolution — which is expressed in dots per inch (dpi). The higher the number, the better the quality. Higher resolutions take longer to print.

✦ **First Page Number:** You can specify a page number for the first page. This is useful if the pages you're printing will be part of a larger document and you want the page numbering to be consecutive. Use Auto if you want the beginning page number to be 1 — or to correspond to the pages that you selected in the Print dialog box. If you're not printing page numbers in your header or footer, this setting is irrelevant.

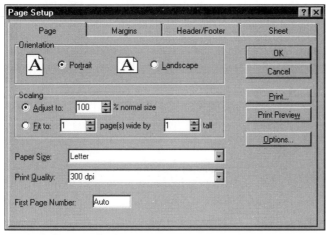

Figure 12-2: You control page settings in the Page panel of the Page Setup dialog box.

Adjusting margins

A margin is the blank space on the side of the page. The wider the margins, the less space that is available for printing. You can control all four page margins from Excel. Figure 12-3 shows the Margins tab of the Page Setup dialog box.

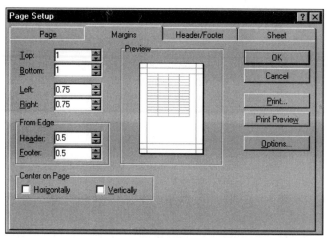

Figure 12-3: The Margins tab of the Page Setup dialog box.

To change a margin, click on the appropriate spinner (or you can enter a value directly).

Note The Preview box is a bit deceiving because it doesn't really show you how your changes look in relation to the page. Rather, it simply displays a darker line to let you know which margin you're adjusting.

In addition to the page margins, you can adjust the distance of the header from the page's top and the distance of the footer from the page's bottom. These settings should be less than the corresponding margin; otherwise, the header or footer may overlap with the printed output.

Normally, Excel prints a page at the top and left margins. If you would like the output to be centered vertically or horizontally, check the appropriate check box.

Tip You also can change the margins while you're previewing your output — ideal for last-minute adjustments before printing. I discuss print previewing later in the chapter.

Changing the header or footer

A header is a line of information that appears at the top of each printed page. A footer, on the other hand, is a line of information that appears at the bottom of each printed page. Headers and footers each have three sections: left, center, and right. For example, you can specify a header that consists of your name left justified, the worksheet name centered, and the page number right justified.

The Header/Footer tab of the Print Options dialog box is shown in Figure 12-4. This dialog box displays the current header and footer and gives you other header and footer options in the drop-down lists labeled Header and Footer.

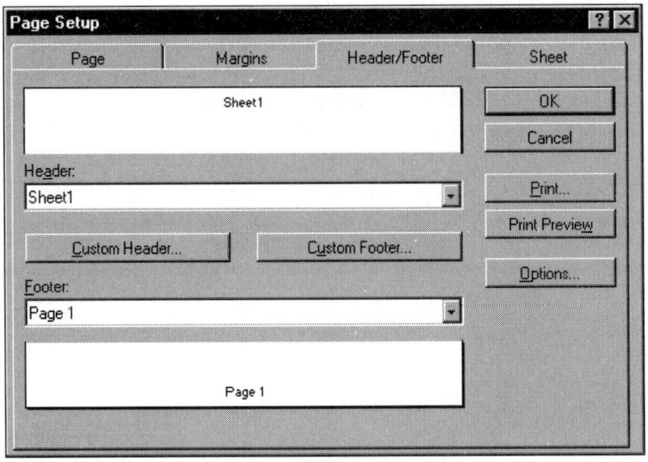

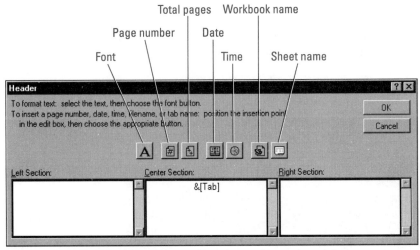

Figure 12-4: The Header/Footer tab of the Page Setup dialog box.

When you click on the Header (or Footer) drop-down, Excel displays a list of pre-defined headers. If you see one that you like, select it. You'll then be able to see how it looks in context — which part is left justified, centered, or right justified. If you don't want a header or footer, choose the option labeled (*none*).

If none of the predefined headers or footers is exactly what you want, you can define a custom header or footer. Start by selecting a header or footer that's similar to the one you want to create (you'll use the selected header or footer as the basis for the customized one). Click on the Custom Header or Custom Footer button, and Excel displays a dialog box like the one shown in Figure 12-5.

Figure 12-5: If none of the predefined headers or footers is satisfactory, you can define a custom header or custom footer.

This dialog box lets you enter text or codes in each of the three sections. To enter text, just activate the section and enter the text. To enter variable information, such as the current date or the page number, you can click on one of the buttons. Clicking on the button inserts a special code. The buttons and their functions are listed in Table 12-1.

Table 12-1 Custom Header/Footer Buttons and Their Functions		
Button	**Code**	**Function**
Font	Not applicable	Lets you choose a font for the selected text
Page Number	&[Page]	Inserts the page number
Total Pages	&[Pages]	Inserts the total number of pages to be printed
Date	&[Date]	Inserts the current date
Time	&[Time]	Inserts the current time
File	&[File]	Inserts the workbook name
Sheet	&[Tab]	Inserts the sheet's name

You can combine text and codes, and insert as many codes as you like into each section. If the text you enter uses an ampersand (&), you must enter the ampersand twice (because an ampersand is used by Excel to signal a code). For example, to enter the text *Research & Development* into a section of a header or footer, enter **Research && Development.**

You also can use different fonts and sizes in your headers and footers. Just select the text that you want to change and click on the Font button. Excel displays its Fonts dialog box so that you can make your choice. If you don't change the font, Excel uses the font defined for the Normal style.

Tip   You can use as many lines as you like. Use Alt+Enter to force a line break for multiline headers or footers.

After you define a custom header or footer, it appears at the bottom of the appropriate drop-down list in the Header/Footer panel of the Page Setup dialog box. You can have only one custom header and one custom footer in a workbook. So, if you edit a custom header, for example, it replaces the existing custom header in the drop-down list.

Note   Unfortunately, there is no way to print the contents of a specific cell in a header or footer. For example, you might want Excel to use the contents of cell A1 as part of a header. The only way to do this is to manually enter the cell's contents.

Controlling sheet options

The Sheet tab of the Page Setup dialog box (shown in Figure 12-6) contains several additional options.

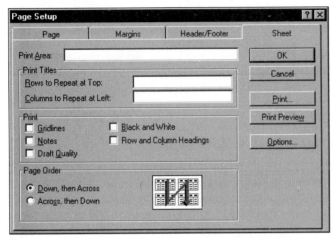

Figure 12-6: The Sheet tab of the Page Setup dialog box.

Print Area

The Print Area box lists the range defined as the print area. If you select a range of cells and choose the Selection option in the Print dialog box, the selected range address appears in this box. Excel also defines this as the reference for the `Print_Area` name.

If the Print Area box is blank, it means that Excel will print the entire worksheet. You can activate this box and select a range (Excel will modify its definition of `Print_Area`), or you can enter a previously defined range name into the box.

Print Titles

Many worksheets are set up with titles in the first row and descriptive names in the first column. If such a worksheet requires more than one page, you may find it difficult to read subsequent pages because the text in the first row and first column won't be printed. Excel offers a simple solution: *print titles*.

Note Don't confuse print titles with headers; these are two different concepts. Headers appear at the top of each page and contain information such as the worksheet name, date, or page number. Print titles describe the data being printed, such as field names in a database table or list.

You can specify rows to repeat at the top of every printed page, or columns to repeat at the left of every printed page. To do so, just activate the appropriate box and select the rows or columns in the worksheet. Or, you can enter these references manually. For example, to specify rows 1 and 2 as repeating rows, enter **1:2**.

Note   In the old days, users often were surprised to discover that print titles appeared twice on the first page of their printouts. That's because they defined a print area that included the print titles. Excel now handles this automatically, however, and doesn't print titles twice if they are part of the print area.

Tip   You can specify different print titles for each worksheet in the workbook. Excel remembers print titles by creating sheet-level names (Print_Titles).

Print

The section labeled Print contains five check boxes:

✦ **Gridlines:** If checked, Excel prints the gridlines to delineate cells. If you turned off the gridline display in the worksheet (in the View panel of the Options dialog box), Excel unchecks this box for you automatically. In other words, the default setting for this option is determined by the gridline display in your worksheet.

✦ **Notes:** If checked, Excel prints cell notes. If the worksheet has no cell notes, this option is grayed out. Cell notes are printed beginning on a separate page. Unfortunately, Excel doesn't print the cell reference to which each note refers.

✦ **Draft Quality:** If checked, the printing is done in draft mode. In draft mode, Excel doesn't print embedded charts or drawing objects, cell gridlines, or borders. This usually reduces the printing time.

✦ **Black and White:** If checked, Excel ignores any colors in the worksheet and prints everything in black and white. This lets you format your worksheet for screen viewing yet still get readable print output.

✦ **Row and Column Headings:** If checked, Excel prints the row and column headings on the printout. This makes it easy to identify specific cells from a printout.

Page Order

The final section of the Sheet tab lets you specify the order in which the pages are generated from the worksheet. For large printouts, you may prefer that the pages be printed (and numbered) in a particular way.

Printer-specific options

You may have noticed that the Print dialog box has a button labeled Properties. Clicking on this button displays another dialog box that lets you adjust properties specific to the selected printer. See Figure 12-7 for an example. You can also access this dialog box from the Page Setup dialog box (click the Options button).

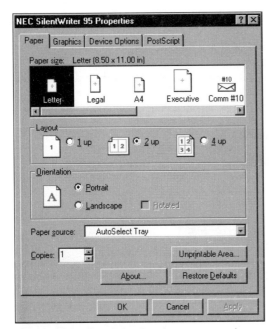

Figure 12-7: This dialog box lets you set printer-specific options.

Some of the printer settings can be set directly from Excel. Other settings may not be accessible from Excel, and you can change them here. For example, if your printer uses multiple paper trays, you can select which tray to use.

Using Print Preview

Excel's print preview feature displays an image of the printed output on your screen. This is a very handy feature that lets you see the result of the options that you set before you actually send the job to the printer. It'll save you lots of time — not to mention printing supplies.

Accessing print preview

There are several ways to access the print preview feature:

   ✦ Select the File⇨Print Preview command.

   ✦ Click on the Print Preview button on the Standard toolbar. Or, you can press Shift and click on the Print button on the Standard toolbar (the Print button serves a dual purpose).

✦ Click the Preview button in the Print dialog box.

✦ Click the Print Preview button in the Page Setup dialog box.

Any of these methods changes Excel's window to a preview window, as shown in Figure 12-8.

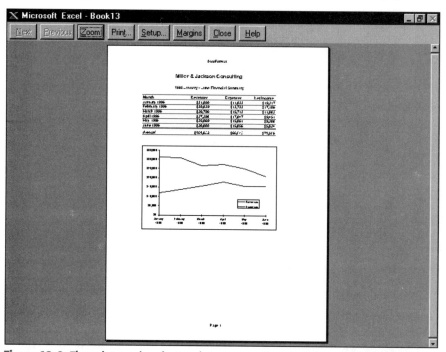

Figure 12-8: The print preview feature lets you see the printed output before you send it to the printer.

The preview window has several buttons along the top:

✦ **Next:** Displays an image of the next page.

✦ **Previous:** Displays an image of the previous page.

✦ **Zoom:** Zooms the display in or out. There are two levels of zooming, and this button toggles between them. You also can just click on the preview image to toggle between zoom modes.

✦ **Print:** Sends the job to the printer.

✦ **Setup:** Displays the Page Setup dialog box so that you can adjust some settings. When you close the dialog box, you return to the preview screen so that you can see the effects of your changes.

✦ **Margins:** Displays adjustable columns and margins. This useful feature is described shortly.

✦ **Close:** Closes the preview window.

✦ **Help:** Displays help for the preview window.

Making changes while previewing

When you click on the Margins button in the preview window, Excel adds markers to the preview that indicate column borders and margins (see Figure 12-9). You can drag the column or margin markers to make changes that appear on-screen.

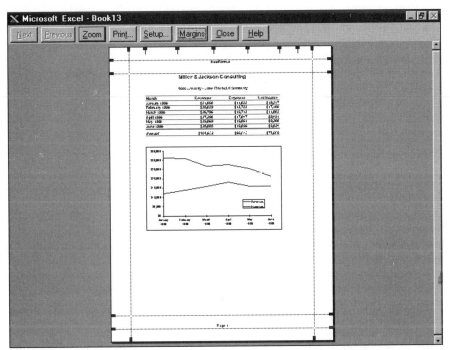

Figure 12-9: You can adjust column widths or margins directly from the print preview window.

For example, if you print a worksheet and discover that the last column is being printed on a second page, you can adjust the column widths or margins in the preview window to force the last column to print on a single page. After you drag one of these markers, Excel updates the display so that you can see what effect it had.

When you make changes to the column widths in the preview window, these changes also are made to your worksheet. Similarly, changing the margins in the preview window changes the settings that appear in the Margins panel of the Page Setup dialog box.

Using the View Manager Add-In

It's not uncommon to create a workbook that is used to store a variety of information. It's quite likely that you would want to print several different reports from the workbook. If this sounds familiar, you need to know about Excel's View Manager.

The View Manager add-in enables you to give names to various views of your worksheet, and you can quickly switch among these named views. A view includes settings for the following:

✦ Print settings as specified in the Page Setup dialog box (optional)

✦ Hidden rows and columns (optional)

✦ Display settings as specified in the Options Display dialog box

✦ Selected cells and ranges

✦ The active cell

✦ Window sizes and positions

✦ Frozen panes

For example, you might define a view that hides a few columns of numbers, another view with a print range defined as a summary range only, another view with the page setup set to landscape, and so on.

Note   The View Manager is an add-in. In other words, it's not really part of Excel per se. Rather, it can be installed if needed. If you did a complete installation of Excel, the View Manager add-in should be installed and ready to go. You can verify that it is installed by selecting the Tools⇨Add-Ins command. View Manager should be listed in the list of add-ins (and it should have a check mark next to it to indicate that it's installed). If it's not in the list, you'll need to reinstall Excel to use this feature. Reinstalling just this add-in takes only a few minutes.

To use View Manager, first set up your worksheet with the view that you want to name. This can include any of the settings listed previously. For example, you might create a view that has a specific range of cells defined as the print range. Then, select the View⇨View Manager command. Excel displays a dialog box that lists all named views. Initially, this list will be empty, but you can click on the Add button to add a view in the Add View dialog box, shown in Figure 12-10.

Figure 12-10: The Add View dialog box lets you add a named view.

Enter a name for the view and make any adjustments to the check boxes. Click on OK and the view is saved. You can add as many views as you like and easily switch among them.

On the CD-ROM The companion CD-ROM contains a workbook with several views defined, so you can see how this feature works. The workbook is named VIEW_MAN.XLS.

Using the Report Manager Add-In

Most people find that the View Manager suits their needs just fine. But for even more power, you might want to check out the Report Manager. Report Manager enables you to set up a sequence of sheets, views (created with the View Manager, as described in the preceding section), and scenarios (defined with the Scenario Manager). You then can print these as a single report. In other words, the Report Manager can automate what would otherwise be a tedious manual task.

Like View Manager, the Report Manager is an add-in. Report Manager works in conjunction with the View Manager add-in.

Note If you did a complete installation of Excel, Report Manager should be installed and ready for action. You can verify that it is installed by selecting the Tools⇨Add-Ins command. Report Manager should appear in the list of add-ins (and it should have a check mark to indicate that it's installed). If it's not in the list, you'll need to reinstall Excel to use Report Manager.

To start, choose the File⇨Print Report command. Excel displays the Print Report dialog box. Initially, this dialog box won't list any reports because none is defined. This dialog box lets you print reports, add reports, edit report definitions, and delete reports that you no longer need. To define a report, click on the Add button. Excel displays the Add Report dialog box, shown in Figure 12-11.

This dialog box lets you enter a name for the report and add views (which you must have defined previously using the View Manager). You also can add scenarios. As you add sections, they appear in the list at the bottom of the dialog box. You can define as many of these reports as you need.

Figure 12-11: The Add Report dialog box.

On the CD-ROM The companion CD-ROM contains a workbook (named REP_MAN.XLS) with several reports defined.

More about Printing

This section provides some additional information regarding printing.

Using manual page breaks

As you may have discovered, Excel handles page breaks automatically. After you print or preview your worksheet, it even displays dashed lines to indicate where page breaks will occur. Sometimes, however, you'll want to force a page break — either a vertical or a horizontal one. For example, if your worksheet consists of several distinct areas, you may want to print each area on a separate sheet of paper.

Inserting a page break

To insert a vertical manual page break, move the cell pointer to the cell that will begin the new page, but make sure that the pointer's in column A; otherwise, you'll insert a vertical page break and a horizontal page break. For example, if you want row 14 to be the first row of a new page, activate cell A14. Then, choose the Insert➪Page Break command. Excel displays a dashed line to indicate the page break. The dashed line for manual page breaks is slightly thinner than those for natural page breaks.

To insert a horizontal page break, move the cell pointer to the cell that will begin the new page, but in this case, make sure that it's in row 1. Select the Insert⇨Page Break command to create the page break.

Tip   When manipulating page breaks, it's often helpful to zoom out with the zoom feature. This gives you a bird's-eye view of the worksheet, and you can see more pages at once. Figure 12-12 demonstrates zooming out.

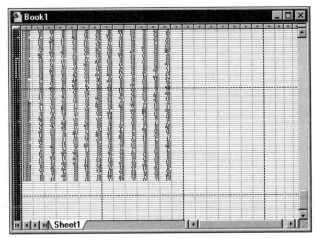

Figure 12-12: Zooming out can give you a better idea of where page breaks (indicated by dashed lines) occur.

Removing a page break

To remove a vertical manual page break, move the cell pointer anywhere in the first row beneath the manual page break and select the Insert⇨Remove Page Break command (this command appears only when the cell pointer is in the first row following a manual page break).

To remove a horizontal manual page break, perform the same procedure, but position the cell pointer anywhere in the first column following a horizontal page break.

Tip   To remove all manual page breaks in the worksheet, click on the Select All button (or press Ctrl+A); then choose the Insert⇨Remove Page Break command.

Problems with fonts (when WYS isn't WYG)

Sometimes, you may find that the printed output doesn't match what you see on-screen. This is almost always due to a problem with the fonts that you use. If your printer doesn't have a font that you use to display your worksheet, Windows attempts to match it as best as it can. Often, it's not good enough.

This problem can almost always be solved simply by using TrueType fonts; these scalable fonts are designed for both screen viewing and printing.

Printing noncontiguous ranges on a single page

You may have discovered that Excel lets you specify a print area that consists of noncontiguous ranges (a multiple selection). For example, if you need to print, say, A1:C50, D20:F24, and M11:P16, you can press Ctrl while you select these ranges, and then issue the File⇨Print command and choose the Selection option. Better yet, give this multiple selection a range name so that you can quickly activate the same ranges the next time.

Printing multiple ranges is a handy feature, but you may not like the fact that Excel prints each range on a new sheet of paper — and there is no way to change this behavior.

One solution to this problem is to create live *snapshots* of the three ranges and paste these snapshots to an empty area of the worksheet. Then you can print this new area that consists of the snapshots, and Excel won't skip to a new page for each range.

To create a live snapshot of a range, select the range and copy it to the Clipboard. Then activate the cell where you want to paste the snapshot (an empty worksheet is a good choice) and choose the Edit⇨Paste Picture Link command to paste a live link (see the Note that follows). Repeat this procedure for the other ranges. After you've pasted them, you can rearrange the snapshots any way you like. You'll notice that these are truly live links: change a cell in the original range and the change appears in the linked picture. Figure 12-13 shows an example of snapshots made from several ranges.

Note The Edit⇨Paste Picture Link command is available only if you press Shift while you click on the Edit menu. You also can use the Camera tool to paste a linked picture, but you'll have to add this tool to a toolbar because it doesn't appear on any of the built-in toolbars (you can find it in the Utility category in the Customize dialog box). Apparently, Microsoft is trying to keep this useful technique to itself.

Hiding cells before printing

You may have a worksheet that contains confidential information. You may want to print the worksheet, but not the confidential parts. Several techniques prevent certain parts of a worksheet from printing.

✦ When you hide rows or columns, the hidden rows won't be printed.

✦ You can effectively hide cells or ranges by making the text color the same color as the background color.

✦ You also can hide cells by using a custom number format that consists of three semicolons (;;;).

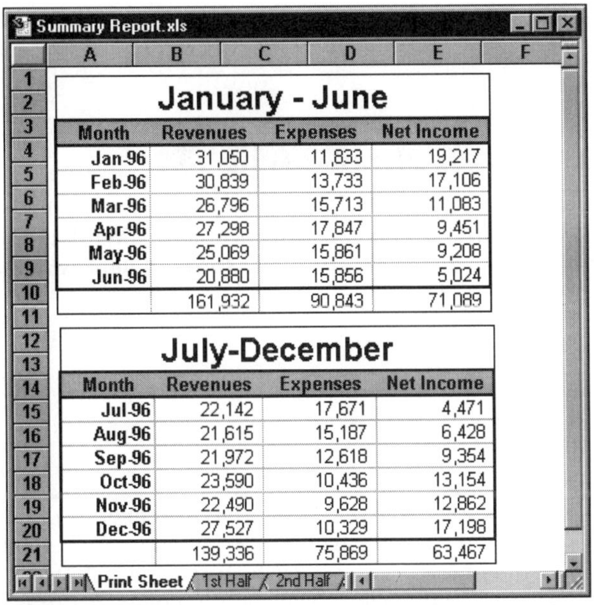

Summary Report.xls

January - June			
Month	Revenues	Expenses	Net Income
Jan-96	31,050	11,833	19,217
Feb-96	30,839	13,733	17,106
Mar-96	26,796	15,713	11,083
Apr-96	27,298	17,847	9,451
May-96	25,069	15,861	9,208
Jun-96	20,880	15,856	5,024
	161,932	90,843	71,089

July-December			
Month	Revenues	Expenses	Net Income
Jul-96	22,142	17,671	4,471
Aug-96	21,615	15,187	6,428
Sep-96	21,972	12,618	9,354
Oct-96	23,590	10,436	13,154
Nov-96	22,490	9,628	12,862
Dec-96	27,527	10,329	17,198
	139,336	75,869	63,467

Figure 12-13: These objects are linked pictures of ranges elsewhere in the workbook. This makes it possible to print nonadjacent ranges on a single sheet.

- ✦ You can mask off a confidential area of a worksheet by covering it with a rectangle object. Click on the Rectangle tool on the Drawing toolbar and drag the rectangle to the proper size. For best results, you can make the rectangle white with no border.
- ✦ You can use a text box object, available using the Text Box tool on the Formatting toolbar, to mask off a range. The advantage to using a text box is that you can add text to it with information about the concealed data (see Figure 12-14).

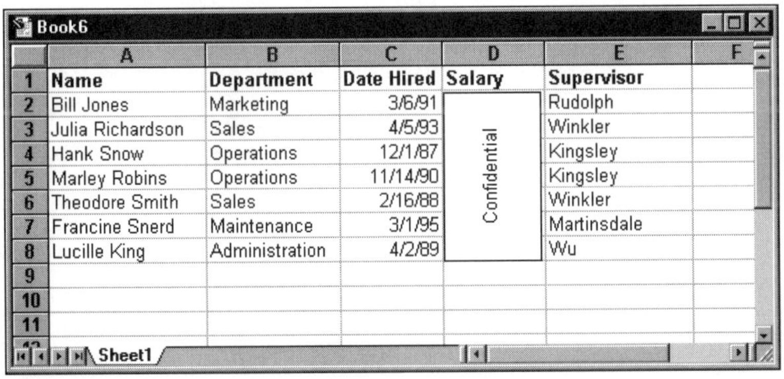

Book6

Name	Department	Date Hired	Salary	Supervisor
Bill Jones	Marketing	3/6/91	Confidential	Rudolph
Julia Richardson	Sales	4/5/93		Winkler
Hank Snow	Operations	12/1/87		Kingsley
Marley Robins	Operations	11/14/90		Kingsley
Theodore Smith	Sales	2/16/88		Winkler
Francine Snerd	Maintenance	3/1/95		Martinsdale
Lucille King	Administration	4/2/89		Wu

Figure 12-14: You can use a text box to hide confidential data so that it won't print.

Tip   If you find that you must regularly hide data before you print certain reports, consider using the View Manager add-in to create a named view that doesn't show the confidential information.

Using a template to change printing defaults

If you find that you're never satisfied with Excel's default print settings, you may want to create a template with the print settings that you use most often. After doing so, you can create a new workbook based on the template, and the workbook will have your own print settings for defaults.

Cross-
Reference   I discuss template files in Chapter 33.

Summary

This chapter presents the basics and some fine points of printing in Excel. You learn how to use the Print dialog box and the Page Setup dialog box to control what gets printed, and how. You also learn about the print preview feature, which shows how the printed output will look before it hits the paper. The chapter covers features such as manual page breaks, the View Manager and Report Manager add-ins, tips on printing noncontiguous ranges on a single sheet, and hiding cells that contain confidential information.

✦   ✦   ✦

Chart-Making Basics

C harts — also known as graphs — have been an integral
part of spreadsheets since the early days of Lotus 1-2-3.
Charting features have improved significantly over the years,
and you'll find that Excel provides you with the tools to create a
wide variety of highly customizable charts. In fact, there's so
much capability here that I present the information in two
chapters. This chapter presents the basic information you'll
need to know to create charts and make simple modifications to
them. Chapter 16 continues with a discussion of advanced
options and a slew of chart-making tricks and techniques.

Overview of Charts

Basically, a chart is a way to present a table of numbers visually.
Displaying data in a well-conceived chart can make it more
understandable, and often you can make your point more
quickly. Charts are particularly useful for getting a visual picture
of a lengthy series of numbers and their relationships. Making a
quick chart helps you spot trends and patterns that would be
nearly impossible to identify in a range of numbers.

Charts are based on numbers that appear in a worksheet. Before
you can create a chart, you have to enter some numbers.
Normally, the data used by a chart resides in a single worksheet,
in one file — but that's not a strict requirement. A single chart
can use data from any number of worksheets or even from
different workbooks.

When you create a chart in Excel, you have two options for
placing the chart:

♦ Insert the chart directly into a worksheet as an object (this
is known as an *embedded* chart). See Figure 13-1 for an
example.

✦ Create the chart as a new chart sheet in your workbook (see Figure 13-2). A chart sheet differs from a worksheet in that it can hold a single chart and doesn't have cells. When a chart sheet is activated, Excel's menus change to those appropriate for working with a chart.

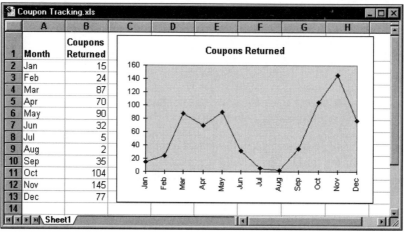

Figure 13-1: An embedded chart is inserted directly on a worksheet.

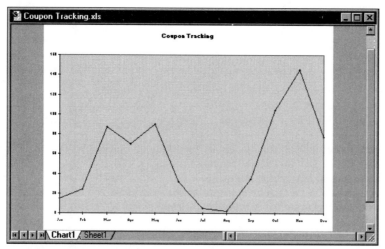

Figure 13-2: This chart is on a separate chart sheet.

Each method has its advantages, as you'll see later in this chapter. Regardless of which chart-making option you choose, you have complete control over the chart's appearance. You can change the colors, move the legend, format the numbers on the scales, add gridlines, and so on.

Converting a range of numbers into a chart is quite easy, and many people find this aspect of Excel to be rather fun. You can experiment with different chart types to determine the best way to make your case. If that isn't enough, you can make a variety of adjustments to your charts, such as adding annotations, clip art, and other bells and whistles. The real beauty of Excel's charts, however, is that they are linked to worksheet data. So if your numbers change, the charts reflect those changes instantly.

Chart types

You're probably aware that there are many chart types: bar charts, line charts, pie charts, and so on. Excel lets you create all the basic chart types and even some esoteric chart types such as radar charts and doughnut charts. Table 13-1 lists Excel's chart types and the number of AutoFormats associated with each. An AutoFormat is basically a variation on a basic chart type.

Table 13-1 Excel's Chart Types			
Chart Type	*AutoFormats*	*Chart Type*	*AutoFormats*
Area	5	XY (Scatter)	6
Bar	10	3-D Area	7
Column	10	3-D Bar	5
Combination	6	3-D Column	8
Line	10	3-D Line	4
Pie	7	3-D Pie	7
Doughnut	7	3-D Surface	4
Radar	6		

Cross-Reference See "Reference: Excel's Chart Types" in this chapter for a complete listing of Excel's chart AutoFormats.

Which chart type to use?

A common question asked by beginning chart makers is how to determine the most appropriate chart type for the data. The answer is that there is no answer. I'm not aware of any hard-and-fast rules for determining which chart type is best for your data. The best rule of thumb is to use the chart type that gets your message across in the simplest way.

Figures 13-3, 13-4, and 13-5 show the same data plotted using three chart different types. Although all three charts represent the same information, they look quite different.

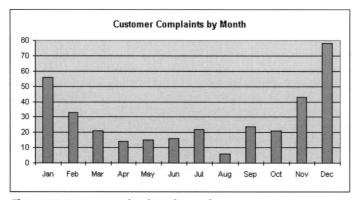

Figure 13-3: An example of a column chart.

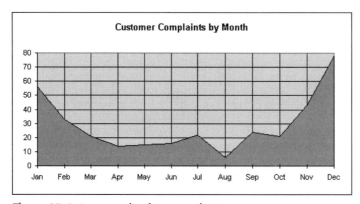

Figure 13-4: An example of an area chart.

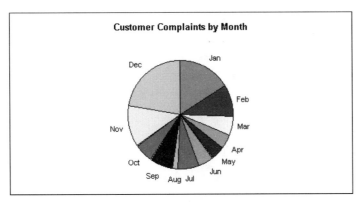

Figure 13-5: An example of a pie chart.

The column chart is probably the best choice for this particular set of data because it clearly shows the information for each month in discrete units. The area chart may not be appropriate because it seems to imply that the data series is continuous; that is, that there are points in between the 12 actual data points (this same argument could be made against using a line chart). The pie chart is simply too confusing. Pie charts are most appropriate for a data series in which you want to emphasize propor- tions. Too many data points makes a pie chart impossible to interpret.

Fortunately, Excel makes it very easy to change a chart's type after the fact. My suggestion is to experiment with various chart types until you find the one that represents your data accurately and clearly — and as simply as possible.

The ChartWizard

The easiest way to create a chart is to use the ChartWizard. The ChartWizard consists of a series of interactive dialog boxes that guide you through the process of creating the exact chart you need. Figure 13-6 shows one of the ChartWizard dialog boxes.

Cross-Reference In Chapter 3, I present a step-by-step introductory example that creates a simple chart using the ChartWizard. If you're new to chart making, you may want to work through that example. I explain the ChartWizard in detail later in this chapter.

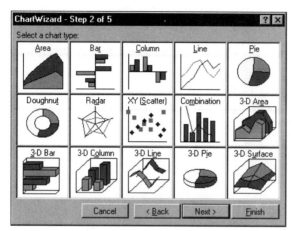

Figure 13-6: One of several dialog boxes displayed by the ChartWizard.

Creating a chart with one keystroke

For a quick demonstration of how easy it is to create a chart, follow these instructions. This example bypasses the ChartWizard and creates a chart on a separate chart sheet.

1. Enter data to be charted into a worksheet. Figure 13-7 shows an example of data that's appropriate for a chart.

2. Select the range of data you entered in Step 1.

3. Press F11. Excel inserts a new chart sheet (named Chart1) and displays the chart based on the selected data. Figure 13-8 shows the result.

	A	B	C	D
1		Region 1	Region 2	
2	January	46	98	
3	February	48	85	
4	March	55	76	
5				
6				
7				

1st Quarter by Region.xls — Sheet1

Figure 13-7: This range would make a good chart.

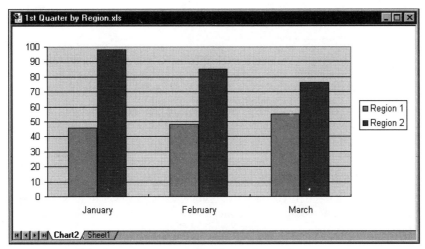

Figure 13-8: This chart was generated with one keystroke.

In this simple example, Excel created its default chart type (which is a two-dimensional column chart) by using the default settings. For more control over the chart-making process, you'll want to use the ChartWizard.

Note   In some cases, Excel can't determine how to chart the selected data — for example, if the range doesn't include any text, Excel can't determine whether the chart should plot rows or columns. In such a case, Excel fires up the ChartWizard so that you can clarify your intentions.

How Excel Handles Charts

A chart is essentially an object that Excel creates. This object is made up of one or more data series, and these data series are displayed graphically (how they are displayed depends on the selected chart type). For example, if you create a line chart that uses two data series, it contains two lines — each representing one data series. The lines are distinguishable from each other by thickness, color, or data markers used. The data series in the chart are linked to cells in the worksheet.

Most charts can have any number of data series. The exception is a pie chart, which can display only one data series. If your chart uses more than one data series, you may want to use a legend to distinguish each series. Excel *does* place a limit on the number of categories (or data points) in a data series: 4,000. Most users never run up against this limit.

One way to distinguish charts is by the number of axes they use:

✦ Common charts, such as column, line, and area charts, have a category axis and a value axis. The category axis is normally the horizontal axis, and the value axis is normally the vertical axis (this is reversed for bar charts, in which the bars extend from the left of the chart rather than from the bottom).

✦ Pie charts and doughnut charts have no axes (but they do have calories). A pie chart can display only one data series. A doughnut chart can display multiple data series.

✦ A radar chart is a special chart that has one axis for each point in the data series. The axes extend from the center of the chart.

✦ True 3-D charts have three axes: a category, value, and series axis that extends into the third dimension. Refer to the sidebar, "3-D or not 3-D? That is the question," for a discussion about Excel's 3-D charts.

After a chart is created, it's not stagnant. You can always change its type, add custom formatting, add new data series to it, or change an existing data series so that it uses data in a different range.

Before you create a chart, you need to determine whether you want it to be an embedded chart or a chart that resides on a chart sheet. I discuss this topic in the sections that follow.

Embedded charts

An embedded chart basically floats on top of a worksheet on the worksheet's draw layer. As with other drawing objects (such as a text box or a rectangle), you can move a chart, resize it, change its proportions, adjust its borders, and perform other operations.

Cross-
Reference   I discuss Excel's drawing objects and the draw layer in Chapter 14.

To make any changes to the actual chart in an embedded chart object, you must double-click on it. This activates the chart, and Excel's menus now include commands appropriate for working with charts. The main advantage to using embedded charts is that you can print the chart next to the data it uses. Figure 13-9 shows an example of a report that includes an embedded chart.

3-D or not 3-D? That is the question

Some of Excel's charts are referred to as 3-D charts. This terminology can be a bit confusing, because some of these so-called 3-D charts aren't technically 3-D charts. Rather, they are 2-D charts with a perspective look to them; that is, they appear to have some depth. The accompanying figure shows two "3-D" charts.

The chart on the left isn't a true 3-D chart, although Excel classifies it as such. It's simply a 2-D chart that uses perspective to add depth to the columns. The chart on the right is a true 3-D chart because the data series extend into the third dimension.

A true 3-D chart has three axes: a value axis (the height dimension), a category axis (the width dimension), and a series axis (the depth dimension).

If I had designed Excel, I would have created three general categories of charts:

◆ 1-dimensional charts: Include pie charts, doughnut charts, and radar charts. Pie charts can have depth as an option.

◆ 2-dimensional charts: Include line charts, column charts, bar charts, area charts, and XY (Scatter) charts. All these except XY charts can have depth as an option.

◆ 3-dimensional charts: Include line charts, column charts, bar charts, area charts, and surface charts. All 3-D charts use depth (it's not an option).

Throughout this book, however, I continue to use Excel's (technically incorrect) terminology to avoid confusion.

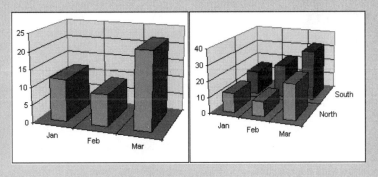

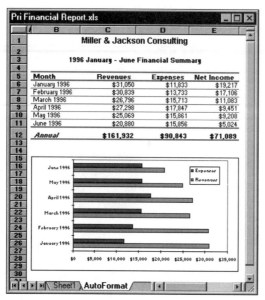

Figure 13-9: This report includes an embedded chart.

Chart sheets

When you create a chart on a chart sheet, it occupies the entire sheet. If you plan to print a chart on a page by itself, using a chart sheet is your best choice. If you have many charts to create, you may want to create each one on a separate chart sheet to avoid cluttering your worksheet. This technique also makes it easier to locate a particular chart, because you can change the names of the chart sheets' tabs.

When a chart sheet is active, Excel's menus change. For example, the Data menu disappears, and other menus include commands appropriate for working with charts.

Normally, a chart in a chart sheet is displayed in WYSIWYG mode: the printed chart will look just like the image on the chart sheet. If the chart doesn't fit in the window, you can use the scrollbars to scroll it or adjust the zoom factor.

You also can specify that the chart in a chart sheet is sized according to the window size. Do this with the View⇨Sized with Window command. When this setting is enabled, the chart adjusts itself when you resize the workbook window (it will always fit perfectly in the window). In this mode, the chart you're working on may or may not correspond to how it looks when printed.

Moving and copying charts

If you created a chart directly in a chart sheet, you can still embed it in a worksheet. First, select the entire chart by clicking on an outer border and copy it to the Clipboard. Activate the worksheet in which you want to insert the chart and paste it. The resulting chart will be very large, so you'll probably want to resize it. This procedure leaves you with two copies of the chart, both of which are linked to the original worksheet data. If you no longer need the copy on the chart sheet, delete the sheet.

As far as I can tell, there is no official way to copy or move an embedded chart to a chart sheet. You can accomplish a similar effect, however. First, create an empty chart sheet. Start by selecting an empty cell. Then choose Insert➪Chart➪As New Sheet. When the ChartWizard dialog box appears, click on the Finish button. This creates a chart sheet with nothing in it.

Then you can select an embedded chart, copy it to the Clipboard, and paste it into the empty chart sheet. Actually, you can paste any number of embedded charts into an empty chart window. This can be useful if you want to print several charts on a page by themselves, such as a series of pie charts. Because you can control the zoom factor of the chart sheet, you can see the entire page, which makes it easy to lay out your page on-screen.

It's important to understand that this procedure does *not* create actual chart sheet charts. Rather, they are embedded charts that happen to reside on a chart sheet. What's the difference? When you activate a true chart sheet, you can modify the chart elements directly. When you activate a chart sheet that contains an embedded chart, you must double-click on the embedded chart before you can modify it.

Creating Charts

In this section I discuss the methods you can use to create embedded charts as well as charts on chart sheets. Both types can be created with or without the assistance of the ChartWizard.

Note   Excel always has a default chart type. Normally, this is a column chart (but you can change this type, as you'll see later). If you create a chart without using the ChartWizard, Excel creates the chart by using the default type. If you use the ChartWizard, Excel prompts you for the chart type, so the default chart type becomes irrelevant.

Creating an embedded chart by using the ChartWizard

There are two ways to invoke the ChartWizard to create an embedded chart:

✦ Select the data to be charted (optional), and then choose the Insert➪Chart➪On This Sheet command.

✦ Select the data to be charted (optional) and click on the ChartWizard button on the Standard toolbar. The ChartWizard button also appears on the Chart toolbar, described in the sidebar "The Chart toolbar."

In either case, the mouse pointer changes to a miniature chart and the status bar message reads: *Drag in document to create chart.* I explain the ChartWizard in detail later in this chapter.

Creating an embedded chart directly

To create an embedded chart without using the ChartWizard, do one of the following:

✦ Select the data to be charted and then click on the Default Chart tool on the Chart toolbar. This always creates a chart of the default type.

The Chart toolbar

The Chart toolbar appears whenever you click on an embedded chart or activate a chart sheet. This toolbar, shown in the accompanying figure, includes five tools. You can use these tools to make some common chart changes:

Chart type: This tool expands to display 14 chart types when you click on the arrow. After it's expanded, you can drag this tool to a new location — creating, in effect, a miniature floating toolbar.

Default chart: Converts the selected chart to the default chart type.

ChartWizard: Invokes the ChartWizard. If you click on this tool when a chart is selected, you get an abbreviated version of the ChartWizard that includes only the first and fourth dialog boxes.

Horizontal gridlines: Toggles the display of horizontal gridlines in the selected chart.

Legend: Toggles the legend display in the selected chart.

Excel includes several other chart-related tools that aren't on the Chart toolbar. You can customize the toolbar to include these additional tools. These tools are in the Charting category in the Customize dialog box.

In addition, several tools on the other toolbars also work with charts. Examples include the Color, Font Color, Bold, Italic, and Font.

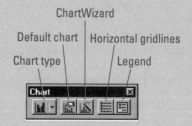

✦ Select the data to be charted and then click on the Chart Type tool on the Chart toolbar.

 Note The Chart Type tool on the Chart toolbar displays an icon for the last selected chart. This tool can be expanded, however, to display all 14 chart types (see Figure 13-10). Just click on the arrow to display the additional chart types. After it's expanded, you can drag this tool to a new location — creating, in effect, a miniature floating toolbar.

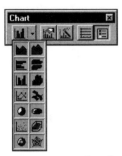

Figure 13-10: The Chart Type tool expands to let you create a chart of the type you want.

After using either technique, the mouse pointer changes to a miniature chart and the status bar message reads: *Drag in document to create chart.* Click on and drag in the worksheet to specify the size and location of the chart. When you release the mouse button, Excel creates the chart.

Creating a chart on a chart sheet by using the ChartWizard

To use the ChartWizard to create a new chart sheet, select the data to be charted (optional) and then select the Insert⇨Chart⇨As New Sheet command. This starts the ChartWizard, which is explained in detail shortly.

Creating a chart on a chart sheet directly

To create a new chart on a chart sheet using the default chart type, select the data to be charted and press the F11 key. This command inserts a new chart sheet. The chart is created from the selected range without accessing the ChartWizard.

Creating a Chart with the ChartWizard

Most Excel users use the ChartWizard for creating charts. The main exception is when you have many charts of the same type to create. In such a case, it's more efficient to change the default type to match the chart type you're using and then create the charts quickly by avoiding the ChartWizard. I discuss how to change the default chart type later in this chapter.

The ChartWizard consists of a series of five dialog boxes that prompt you for various settings for the chart. By the time you reach the last dialog box, the chart is usually just what you need. You may need to perform some modifications — such as changing colors or adding gridlines — but by and large, the ChartWizard is a great help.

Selecting the data

Before you invoke the ChartWizard, select the data that will be included in the chart. This step isn't necessary, but it makes things easier for you. If you don't select the data before invoking the ChartWizard, you can select it in the first ChartWizard dialog box.

When you select the data, include items such as labels and series identifiers. Figure 13-11 shows a worksheet with a range of data set up for a chart. This data consists of monthly sales for two regions. You would select the entire range, including the month names and region names.

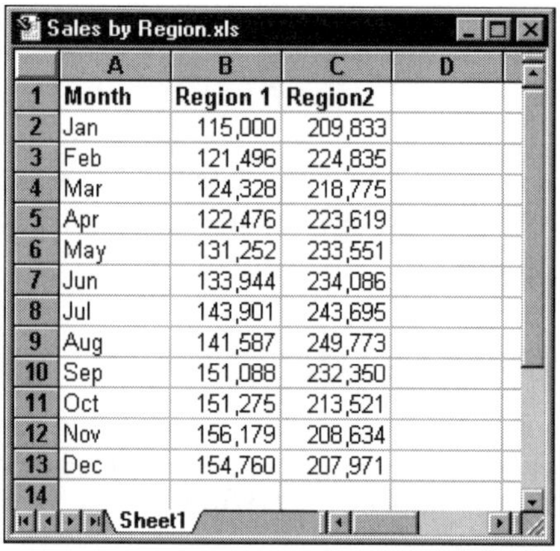

	A	B	C	D
	Month	Region 1	Region2	
1	Jan	115,000	209,833	
2	Feb	121,496	224,835	
3	Mar	124,328	218,775	
4	Apr	122,476	223,619	
5	May	131,252	233,551	
6	Jun	133,944	234,086	
7	Jul	143,901	243,695	
8	Aug	141,587	249,773	
9	Sep	151,088	232,350	
10	Oct	151,275	213,521	
11	Nov	156,179	208,634	
12	Dec	154,760	207,971	

Figure 13-11: Data to be charted.

Tip
The data you're plotting doesn't have to be contiguous. You can press Ctrl and make a multiple selection. Figure 13-12 shows an example of how to select noncontiguous ranges for a chart. In this case, Excel uses only the selected cells for the chart.

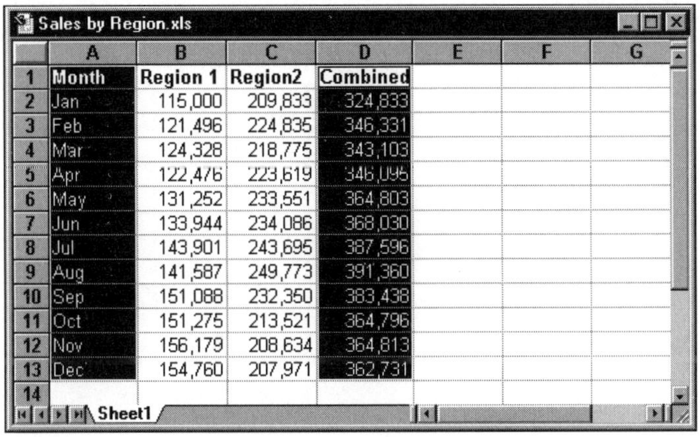

Sales by Region.xls

	A	B	C	D	E	F	G
1	Month	Region 1	Region2	Combined			
2	Jan	115,000	209,833	324,833			
3	Feb	121,496	224,835	346,331			
4	Mar	124,328	218,775	343,103			
5	Apr	122,476	223,619	346,095			
6	May	131,252	233,551	364,803			
7	Jun	133,944	234,086	368,030			
8	Jul	143,901	243,695	387,596			
9	Aug	141,587	249,773	391,360			
10	Sep	151,088	232,350	383,438			
11	Oct	151,275	213,521	364,796			
12	Nov	156,179	208,634	364,813			
13	Dec	154,760	207,971	362,731			
14							

Sheet1

Figure 13-12: Selecting noncontiguous ranges to be charted.

After selecting the data, invoke the ChartWizard (clicking on the ChartWizard button on the Standard toolbar is the most convenient method).

Identifying the area for the chart

When you first invoke the ChartWizard, the mouse pointer changes shape (small cross and a miniature chart). Click and drag in the worksheet to delineate the approximate size and location of the embedded chart. This step isn't too critical because it's easy to change the size and location after you create the chart. As you drag, Excel displays a dark border, as shown in Figure 13-13. You can drag anywhere in the worksheet, even over nonblank cells.

Release the mouse button and Excel displays the first ChartWizard dialog box. The chart isn't created until the ChartWizard finishes.

Tip
If you press Shift while you drag in the worksheet, the chart is a perfect square. If you press Alt when you drag, the chart's borders snap to the nearest cell borders — resulting in a chart that's perfectly aligned with cells.

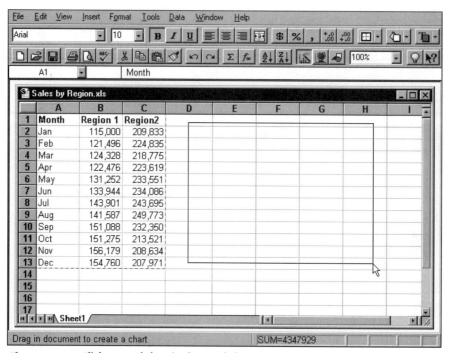

Figure 13-13: Click on and drag in the worksheet to specify the chart's size and location.

ChartWizard Step 1 of 5

Figure 13-14 shows the first ChartWizard dialog box. If you selected a range of cells before invoking the ChartWizard, that range's address appears in the Range box. Otherwise, you have to specify the range that contains the data to be charted. You can enter the range reference manually or point and select it in the worksheet. Again, a multiple selection is allowed.

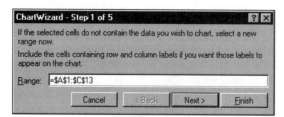

Figure 13-14: The first of five ChartWizard dialog boxes.

When you've selected (or verified) the range reference, click on the Next button to move on to the next step.

ChartWizard Step 2 of 5

In the second step of the ChartWizard (shown in Figure 13-15), you specify the general chart type you want to create. You have 15 choices from which to choose, displayed as icons (these images don't represent your actual data).

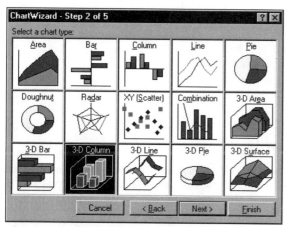

Figure 13-15: In the second ChartWizard dialog box, you specify the general chart type.

Click on the Next button to advance to the next dialog box or double-click on the image of the chart you want.

Note At any time while using the ChartWizard, you can go back to the preceding step by clicking on the Back button. Or you can click on Finish to end the ChartWizard. If you end it early, Excel creates the chart by using the information you provided up to that point.

ChartWizard Step 3 of 5

The third ChartWizard dialog box varies depending on your choice in the preceding dialog box. This step shows all available AutoFormats for the chart type you selected. An AutoFormat is essentially a variation of the basic chart that uses some options. For example, AutoFormat #3 for a column chart stacks the data series on top of each other (a *stacked* column chart). Figure 13-16 shows the eight AutoFormats for a 3-D column chart. Choose the AutoFormat you want and move to the next step.

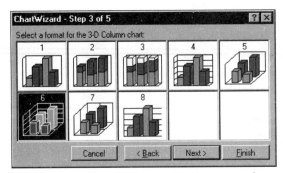

Figure 13-16: After choosing a chart type, you choose an AutoFormat — a variation of the basic chart type.

ChartWizard Step 4 of 5

Step 4 of the ChartWizard displays the chart by using the actual data and also lets you modify (or verify) Excel's choices in creating the chart. The options depend on the chart type you selected. Figure 13-17 shows the dialog box that appears for the 3-D column chart.

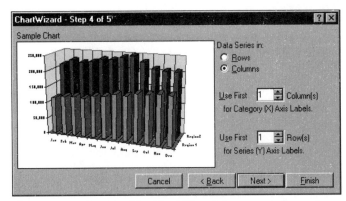

Figure 13-17: Step 4 of the ChartWizard gives you a chance to modify Excel's guesses.

If you change any of these options, the chart displayed in the dialog box is updated so that you can see the effects of your changes.

Note The first option in this dialog box deals with the orientation of the data (arranged in rows or columns). This choice is a critical one that will have a drastic effect on the look of your chart. Most of the time, Excel guesses correctly — but not always. Notice that you can use multiple rows and columns for category labels and legend text. If you specify multiple columns or rows, you must have selected these rows or columns in Step 1. In any case, the chart displayed in the dialog box accurately reflects the choices in effect (so that no guessing is involved).

On the CD-ROM The companion CD-ROM contains an example that illustrates the effect of a chart's orientation. The file is named ORIENTANT.XLS.

ChartWizard Step 5 of 5

The final ChartWizard dialog box, shown in Figure 13-18, lets you add various text elements to the chart: a legend, title, and titles for the axes. Again, the displayed chart is updated so that you can see the changes as you make them.

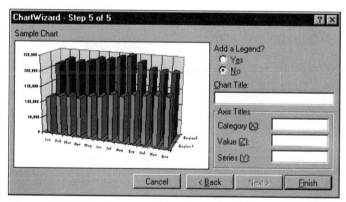

Figure 13-18: The last step of the ChartWizard lets you enter labels.

If you didn't select cells that contained series labels when you started, Excel uses dummy names if you select the legend option. For example, the first series appears as Series 1, the second as Series 2, and so on.

When you're satisfied with the chart that appears in the dialog box, click on Finish. Excel inserts the chart by using the options you specified. You can move or resize the embedded chart by using standard click-and-drag techniques.

When you create a 3-D chart, you may be surprised at how small the actual chart is in relation to the size of the chart object. Unfortunately, there is nothing you can do about it. A 3-D chart is smaller because Excel needs to leave room in case you rotate the chart (a technique I discuss in Chapter 16).

Note Changing the size or proportions of an embedded chart can drastically alter the way it looks and prints. For example, the size of the text within a chart doesn't change proportionally, and the legend may be too large on smaller charts. After you resize an embedded chart, you may have to make some adjustments to make sure that the chart is still legible.

Basic Chart Modifications

After you create a chart, you can modify it at any time. Before you can modify a chart, it must be activated. To activate an embedded chart, double-click on it. To activate a chart on a chart sheet, just click on its sheet tab.

The modifications you can make to a chart are extensive. This section covers some of the more common chart modifications:

   ✦ Changing the chart type

   ✦ Moving chart elements

   ✦ Deleting chart elements

Others type of chart modifications are discussed in Chapter 16.

Changing the chart type

To change the chart type of the active chart, use either of the following methods:

   ✦ Use the Chart Type button on the Chart toolbar. Click on the drop-down arrow, and this button expands to show all 15 basic chart types.

   ✦ Choose the Format⇨AutoFormat command.

The Format⇨AutoFormat command displays the dialog box shown in Figure 13-19. When the Built-In option is selected, the Galleries box displays the names of the 14 chart categories (plus a Combination chart type). Selecting a chart type displays the various AutoFormats for the selected chart type. Just choose an AutoFormat and click on OK. The chart changes to the type you selected.

Caution If you've customized some aspects of your chart, choosing a new AutoFormat may override some or all of the changes you've made. For example, if you've added gridlines to the chart and then select an AutoFormat that doesn't use gridlines, your gridlines disappear. Therefore, it's a good idea to make sure that you're satisfied with the chart before you make too many custom changes to it.

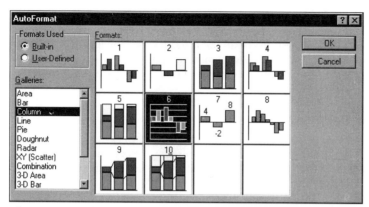

Figure 13-19: The AutoFormat dialog box lets you change the chart's type.

If you click on the User-Defined option, the list box displays the name of any user-defined AutoFormats. If you haven't defined any AutoFormats, this box shows MS Excel 4.0 — this is the default chart type for Excel 4.0. I suppose that Microsoft included this one for nostalgia buffs.

Cross-Reference In Chapter 16, I explain how to create custom AutoFormats.

You also can use the Format⇨Chart Type command to change a chart's type. This command lets you change the type of the entire chart or just a data series. If you want to make one series a column chart and another series a line chart, you can do it in the Chart Type dialog box, shown in Figure 13-20. Select the series you want to change, and then select the Selected Series option.

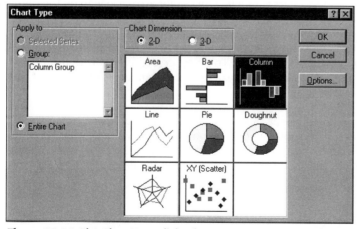

Figure 13-20: The Chart Type dialog box.

Moving and deleting chart elements

Some of the chart parts can be moved (any of the titles and the legend). To move a chart element, simply click on it to select it, and then drag it to the desired location in the chart. To delete a chart element, select it and then press Delete.

Other modifications

When a chart is activated, you can select various parts of the chart to work with. Modifying a chart is similar to everything else you do in Excel: First, you make a selection (in this case, select a chart part). Then you issue a command to do something with the selection.

You can use the Color tool on the Standard toolbar to change colors. For example, if you want to change the color of a series, select the series and choose the color you want from the Color tool. You'll find that many other toolbar tools work with charts. For example, you can select the chart's legend and then click on the Bold tool to make the legend text bold.

When you double-click on a chart element (or press Ctrl+1), its Formatting dialog box appears. The dialog box that appears varies, depending on the item selected. In most cases, the dialog box is of the tabbed variety. Many modifications are self-evident — for example, changing the font used in a title. Others, however, are a bit more tricky. Chapter 16 discusses these chart modifications in detail.

Changing the Default Chart Type

Throughout this chapter, I mention the default chart type many times. Excel's default chart type is a 2-D column chart with a light gray plot area, a legend on the right, and horizontal gridlines.

If you don't like the looks of this chart or if you normally use a different type of chart, you can easily change the default chart. To do so, create a chart with the characteristics you want in your default chart. For example, you can make it a line chart with a white plot area with no legend.

When you're satisfied with the sample chart, make sure that it's activated and then choose the Tools⇨Options command. Click on the Chart tab in the dialog box and then click on the Use the Current Chart button (see Figure 16-21). If you've defined any custom AutoFormats, you can pick one of them from the list.

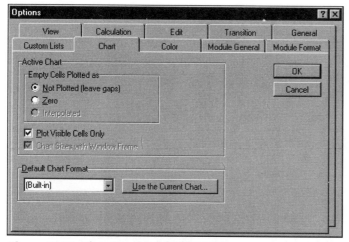

Figure 13-21: Changing the default chart type.

If you have many charts of the same type to create, it's much more efficient to change the default chart format to the chart type with which you're working. Then you can create all your charts without using the ChartWizard — saving quite a bit of time.

Printing Charts

There's nothing special about printing embedded charts; it works just like printing a worksheet (see Chapter 12). As long as the embedded chart is included in the Print_Area, the chart is printed as it appears on-screen.

Note If you print in Draft mode, embedded charts aren't printed. Also, if you don't want a particular embedded chart to appear on your printout, right-click on the chart and choose Format Object from the Shortcut menu. Activate the Properties tab in the Format Object dialog box and remove the check mark from the Print Object check box.

If the chart is on a chart sheet, it prints on a page by itself. If you access Excel's Page Setup dialog box when the chart sheet is active, the Sheet tab is replaced with a tab named Chart. Figure 13-22 shows the Chart panel of the Page Setup dialog box.

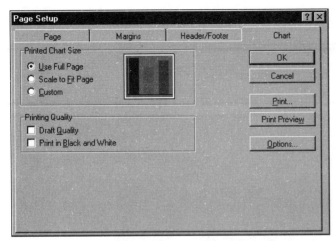

Figure 13-22: The Chart panel of the Page Setup dialog box.

This dialog box has several options:

> **Use Full Page:** The chart is printed to the full width and height of the page margins. This choice is usually not a good one because the chart's relative proportions change and you lose the WYSIWYG advantage.

> **Scale To Fit Page:** Expands the chart proportionally in both dimensions until one dimension fills the space between the margins. This option usually results in the best printout.

> **Custom:** Prints the chart as it appears on your screen. Use the View⇨Sized with Window command to make the chart correspond to the window size and proportions. The chart prints at the current window size and proportions.

Tip   The Printing Quality options work just like those for worksheet pages. If you choose the Draft Quality option for a chart sheet, the chart is printed, but its quality may not be high (the actual effect depends on your printer). Choosing the Print In Black And White option prints the data series with black-and-white patterns rather than colors.

Because charts usually take longer to print than text, it's an especially good idea to use the print preview feature before printing a chart. This feature lets you see what the printed output will look like so that you can avoid surprises.

Reference: Excel's Chart Types

For your reference, I conclude this chapter with a discussion of Excel's chart types and a listing of the AutoFormats for each. This section may help you determine which chart type is best for your data.

On the CD-ROM The companion CD-ROM contains a workbook that has examples of each AutoFormat for every chart type — a total of 103 charts (each chart is on a separate chart sheet). This file is named AUTOFORM.XLS. In addition, I've included a workbook that has the charts shown in the figures in this section. This workbook is named FIG_EXAM.XLS.

Area charts

An *area chart* is similar to a line chart that has been colored in. Area charts that use more than one data series, however, always have the data stacked (unlike a line chart). Figure 13-23 shows an example of an area chart. Stacking the data series lets you clearly see the total plus the contribution by each series.

Table 13-2 lists Excel's five area chart AutoFormats.

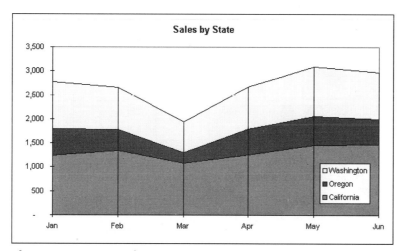

Figure 13-23: An area chart.

Chart Type	AutoFormat	Description
	Table 13-2	
	Area Chart AutoFormats	
Area	1	Standard area chart
Area	2	Area chart, expressed in percentages
Area	3	Area chart with droplines
Area	4	Area chart with horizontal and vertical gridlines
Area	5	Area chart with series names in the chart

Bar charts

A *bar chart* is essentially a column chart that has been rotated 90 degrees to the left. The advantage in using a bar chart is that the category labels may be easier to read (see Figure 13-24 for an example). Bar charts can consist of any number of data series. In addition, the bars can be stacked from left to right, as in AutoFormats 3, 5, 9, and 10. Table 13-3 lists Excel's ten bar chart AutoFormats.

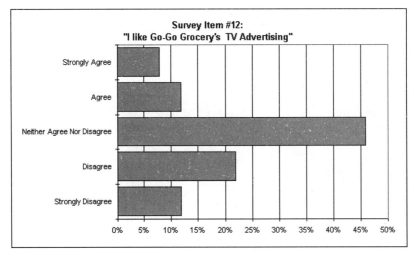

Figure 13-24: If you have lengthy category labels, a bar chart may be a good choice.

	Table 13-3 Bar Chart AutoFormats	
Chart Type	**AutoFormat**	**Description**
Bar	1	Standard bar chart
Bar	2	Bar chart; if only one series, each bar is a different color
Bar	3	Stacked bar chart
Bar	4	Standard bar chart, with overlapping bars
Bar	5	Stacked bar chart, expressed in percentages
Bar	6	Bar chart with vertical gridlines
Bar	7	Bar chart with data labels
Bar	8	Bar chart with no gaps between the bars
Bar	9	Bar chart with series lines
Bar	10	Stacked bar chart with series lines, expressed in percentages

Column charts

Column charts are one of the most common chart types. This type of chart is useful for displaying discrete data (as opposed to continuous data). You can have any number of data series, and the columns can be stacked on top of each other as in AutoFormats 3, 5, 9, and 10. Figure 13-25 shows an example of a column chart. Table 13-4 lists Excel's ten column chart AutoFormats.

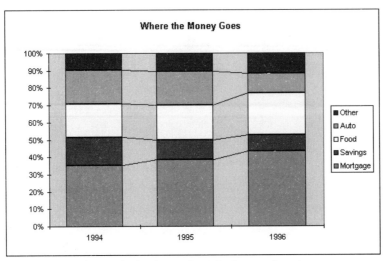

Figure 13-25: This stacked column chart displays each series as a percentage of the total. It may substitute for several pie charts.

Table 13-4
Column Chart AutoFormats

Chart Type	AutoFormat	Description
Column	1	Standard column chart
Column	2	Column chart; if only one series, each column is a different color
Column	3	Stacked column chart
Column	4	Standard column chart, with overlapping columns
Column	5	Stacked column chart, expressed in percentages
Column	6	Column chart with horizontal gridlines
Column	7	Column chart with data labels
Column	8	Column chart with no gaps between the columns
Column	9	Column chart with series lines
Column	10	Stacked column chart with series lines, expressed in percentages

Combination charts

A combination chart can either:

✦ Combine two chart types in one — for example, columns and line.

✦ Use two value axes. In this case, the series can consist of the same type (all lines, for example) or use different types (lines and columns, for example).

Using two value axes is useful when the data series use drastically different scales, as shown in Figure 13-26.

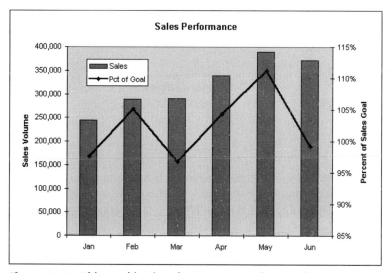

Figure 13-26: This combination chart uses two value axes because the series have drastically different scales.

Combination chart AutoFormats 5 and 6 often are used to plot stock market data. AutoFormat 5 requires four data series, and AutoFormat 6 requires five data series. Table 13-5 lists Excel's six combination chart AutoFormats.

Table 13-5
Combination Chart AutoFormats

Chart Type	AutoFormat	Description
Combination	1	Combination (columns and lines), with one value axis
Combination	2	Combination (columns and lines), with two value axes
Combination	4	Combination (columns and area) with one value axis
Combination	6	Combination (columns and line) with hi-low lines, up-down bars, and two axes; requires five series

Line charts

Line charts are common. They are frequently used to plot data that is continuous rather than discrete. For example, plotting daily sales as a line chart may let you spot trends over time. See Figure 13-27 for an example.

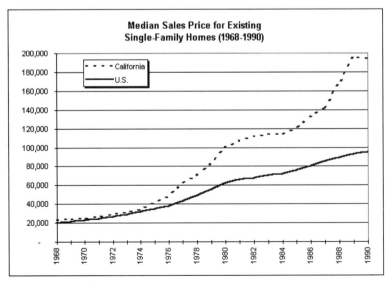

Figure 13-27: A line chart often can help you spot trends in your data.

Three of the line chart AutoFormats (7, 8, and 9) are useful for plotting stock market information. Table 13-6 lists Excel's ten line chart AutoFormats.

	Table 13-6 Line Chart AutoFormats	
Chart Type	**AutoFormat**	**Description**
Line	1	Line chart with markers
Line	2	Line chart without markers
Line	3	Line chart with markers but no lines
Line	4	Line chart with markers and dashed horizontal gridlines
Line	5	Line chart with markers and dashed horizontal and vertical gridlines
Line	6	Line chart with markers and dashed horizontal gridlines; value axis is log scale
Line	7	Line chart with markers, no lines, and hi-low lines
Line	8	Line chart with no markers, no lines, and hi-low lines; requires three series
Line	9	Line chart with no markers, no lines, hi-low lines and upbars; requires four series
Line	10	Line chart with no markers and smoothed lines

Pie charts

A *pie chart* is the only chart type that can display only one data series. This type of chart is useful when you want to show relative proportions or contributions to a whole. Figure 13-28 shows an example of a pie chart. Generally, a pie chart should use no more than five or six data points; otherwise, it's difficult to interpret.

Tip
You can explode a slice of a pie chart. Activate the chart and select the slice you want to explode. Then drag it away from the center. The pie chart AutoFormat 3 has one exploded slice (the first data point) in the series.

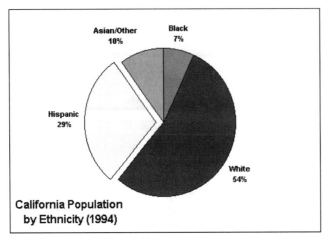

Figure 13-28: A pie chart with one slice exploded.

Note If you create a chart that uses more than one data series and then change it to a pie chart, only the first series is used. Excel remembers the other data series, however, so if you select another chart type, you don't have to add the other series. Table 13-7 lists Excel's seven pie chart AutoFormats.

Table 13-7 **Pie Chart AutoFormats**		
Chart Type	*AutoFormat*	*Description*
Pie	1	Standard pie chart
Pie	2	Black-and-white pie chart, with series names
Pie	3	Pie chart with one exploded slice
Pie	4	Pie chart with all slices exploded
Pie	5	Pie chart with series names
Pie	6	Pie chart with percentage values
Pie	7	Pie chart with series names and percentage values

Doughnut charts

A *doughnut chart* is similar to a pie chart, except that it has a hole in the middle. More important, however, a doughnut chart can display more than one series of data. Figure 13-29 shows an example of a doughnut chart (I added the arrow and series descriptions manually; these items aren't part of a doughnut chart).

Notice that the data series are displayed as concentric rings. As you can see, a doughnut chart with more than one series to chart can be difficult to interpret. Sometimes a better choice is to use a stacked column chart for such comparisons.

Table 13-8 lists Excel's seven doughnut chart AutoFormats.

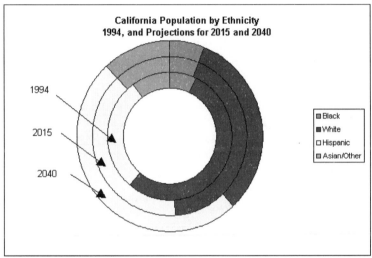

Figure 13-29: A doughnut chart.

Table 13-8 Doughnut Chart AutoFormats		
Chart Type	**AutoFormat**	**Description**
Doughnut	1	Standard doughnut chart
Doughnut	2	Black-and-white doughnut chart with series names
Doughnut	3	Doughnut chart with one exploded slice
Doughnut	4	Doughnut chart with all slices exploded
Doughnut	5	Doughnut chart with series names
Doughnut	6	Doughnut chart with percentage values
Doughnut	7	Doughnut chart with series names and percentage values

Radar charts

You may not be familiar with radar charts. A *radar chart* has a separate axis for each category, and the axes extend out from the center. The value of the data point is plotted on the appropriate axis. If all data points in a series had an identical value, it would produce a perfect circle. See Figure 13-30 for an example of a radar chart. Table 13-9 lists Excel's radar chart AutoFormats.

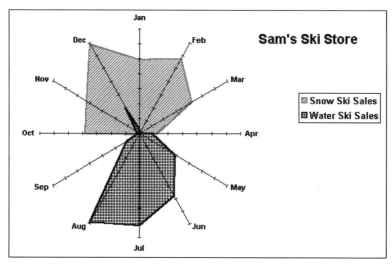

Figure 13-30: A radar chart.

Table 13-9 Radar Chart AutoFormats		
Chart Type	*AutoFormat*	*Description*
Radar	1	Radar chart with lines and markers
Radar	2	Radar chart with lines
Radar	4	Radar chart with major gridlines
Radar	6	Radar chart with no axes and with lines colored in

XY (Scatter) charts

Another common chart type is *XY (Scatter) charts* (also known as *scattergrams*). An XY chart differs from the other chart types in that both axes display values. This type of chart often is used to show the relationship between two variables. Figure 13-31 shows an example of an XY chart that plots the relationship between sales calls and sales. The chart shows that these two variables are positively related: Months in which more calls were made typically had higher sales volumes. Table 13-10 lists Excel's six XY (Scatter) chart AutoFormats.

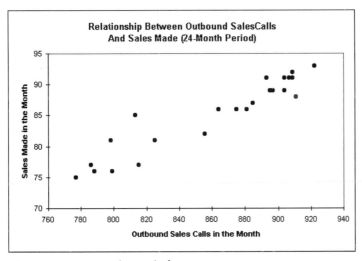

Figure 13-31: An XY (Scatter) chart.

	Table 13-10	
	XY (Scatter) Chart AutoFormats	
Chart Type	**AutoFormat**	**Description**
XY (Scatter)	1	XY chart with markers and no lines
XY (Scatter)	2	XY chart with markers and lines
XY (Scatter)	3	XY chart with markers, no lines, and dashed vertical and horizontal gridlines
XY (Scatter)	4	XY chart with markers, no lines, and horizontal gridlines (log scale on y-axis)
XY (Scatter)	5	XY chart with markers, no lines, and horizontal gridlines (log scale on both axes)
XY (Scatter)	6	XY chart with no markers and smoothed lines

3-D area charts

A *3-D area chart* is similar to a 2-D area chart except that it displays depth. Some of the 3-D area chart AutoFormats are true 3-D charts because they include a third (series) axis. The true 3-D area charts are AutoFormats 5, 6, and 7. Figure 13-32 shows an example of a 3-D area chart that has a series axis. Table 13-11 lists Excel's seven 3-D area chart AutoFormats.

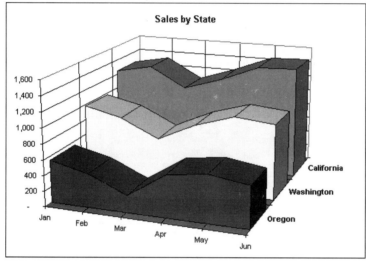

Figure 13-32: A 3-D area chart.

	Table 13-11	
	3-D Area Chart AutoFormats	
Chart Type	**AutoFormat**	**Description**
3-D Area	1	Standard 3-D area chart
3-D Area	2	3-D area chart with series labels
3-D Area	3	3-D area chart with droplines
3-D Area	4	3-D area chart with horizontal gridlines
3-D Area	5	A true 3-D area chart with a series axis
3-D Area	6	A true 3-D area chart with a series axis and horizontal and vertical gridlines
3-D Area	7	3-D area chart with a series axis and vertical gridlines

3-D bar charts

A *3-D bar chart* is similar to a 2-D bar chart, but the bars have depth to them. These 3-D bar charts aren't true 3-D charts because they don't have a series axis. The only advantage in using a 3-D bar chart over a standard bar chart is that you may prefer how they look — they often have a much stronger impact. Figure 13-33 shows an example of a 3-D bar chart. Table 13-12 lists Excel's five 3-D bar chart AutoFormats.

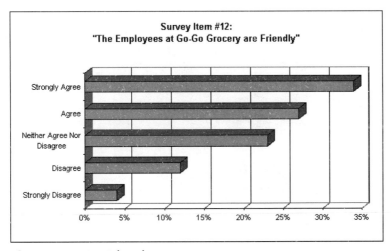

Figure 13-33: A 3-D bar chart.

Table 13-12
3-D Bar Chart AutoFormats

Chart Type	AutoFormat	Description
3-D Bar	1	Standard 3-D bar chart
3-D Bar	2	Stacked 3-D bar chart
3-D Bar	4	3-D bar chart with vertical gridlines

3-D column charts

A *3-D column chart* is similar to a 2-D column chart. Three of the AutoFormats (5, 6, and 7) are true 3-D charts, however, because they have a series axis. Figure 13-34 shows a 3-D column chart. This chart has been rotated so that it's viewed from a different angle (see Chapter 16 for details on rotating 3-D charts). Table 13-13 lists Excel's eight 3-D column chart AutoFormats.

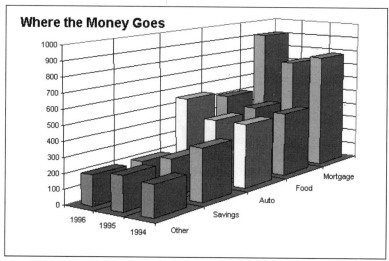

Figure 13-34: This 3-D column chart has been rotated.

	Table 13-13	
	3-D Column Chart AutoFormats	
Chart Type	*AutoFormat*	*Description*
3-D Column	1	Standard 3-D column chart
3-D Column	2	Stacked 3-D column chart
3-D Column	4	3-D column chart with horizontal gridlines
3-D Column	6	A true 3-D column chart with a series axis and horizontal and vertical gridlines
3-D Column	8	3-D column chart with horizontal gridlines and right-angle axes

3-D line charts

All *3-D line charts* are true 3-D charts — the line for each series is displayed in its own plane. Figure 13-35 shows a example of a 3-D line chart. This chart has been rotated so that it's viewed from a higher elevation. Table 13-14 lists Excel's four 3-D line chart AutoFormats.

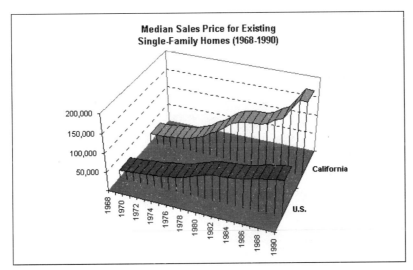

Figure 13-35: A 3-D line chart.

	Table 13-14	
	3-D Line Chart AutoFormats	
Chart Type	**AutoFormat**	**Description**
3-D Line	1	A true 3-D line chart with a series axis
3-D Line	2	A true 3-D line chart with a series axis and horizontal and vertical gridlines
3-D Line	4	A true 3-D line chart with a series axis and horizontal and vertical gridlines (log scale on y-axis)

3-D pie charts

A *3-D pie chart* is identical to a 2-D pie chart except that it is displayed with depth. You can rotate a 3-D chart to get a better view, and you also can explode one or more pie slices. Figure 13-36 shows an example of a 3-D pie chart, rotated and with all slices exploded. Table 13-15 lists Excel's seven 3-D pie chart AutoFormats.

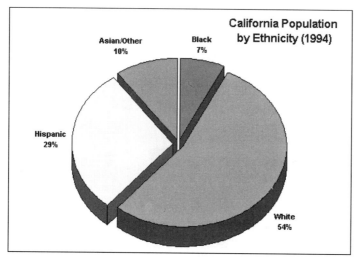

Figure 13-36: A 3-D pie chart

	Table 13-15	
	3-D Pie Chart AutoFormats	
Chart Type	*AutoFormat*	*Description*
3-D Pie	1	Standard 3-D pie chart
3-D Pie	2	Black-and-white 3-D pie chart with series names
3-D Pie	4	3-D pie chart with all slices exploded
3-D Pie	6	3-D pie chart with percentage values

3-D surface charts

Three-D surface charts display two or more data series on a surface. As you can see in Figure 13-37, these charts can be quite interesting. Unlike other charts, Excel uses color to distinguish values, not to distinguish the data series. The only way to change these colors is to modify the workbook's color palette by using the Color panel in the Options dialog box. AutoFormats 3 and 4 are actually two-dimensional charts. These charts are a 3-D surface chart viewed from directly above. Table 13-16 lists Excel's four 3-D surface chart AutoFormats.

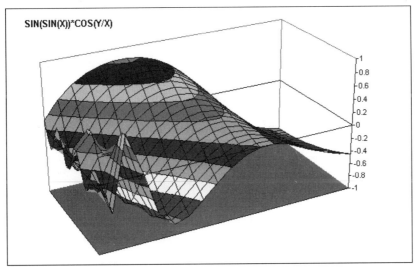

Figure 13-37: A 3-D surface chart.

	Table 13-16	
	3-D Surface Chart AutoFormats	
Chart Type	*AutoFormat*	*Description*
3-D Surface	1	Standard 3-D surface chart
3-D Surface	2	3-D surface chart with no colors
3-D Surface	3	3-D surface chart as viewed from above
3-D Surface	4	3-D surface chart as viewed from above, no color

Summary

In this chapter, I introduce Excel's chart-making feature. Charts can be embedded on a worksheet or created in a separate chart sheet. You can use the ChartWizard to walk you through the chart-making process or create a default chart in a single step. I describe how to change the default chart type.

After a chart is created, you can make many types of modifications. I discuss a few simple modifications, and Chapter 16 presents additional chart information. Printing charts works much like printing worksheets, although you should be familiar with the page setup options when you're printing chart sheets. I conclude the chapter with a complete listing and description of Excel's AutoFormats.

✦   ✦   ✦

Enhancing Your Work with Pictures and Drawings

✦   ✦   ✦   ✦

In This Chapter

Importing graphics
files into a worksheet

Using the Clipboard
to copy graphics

Using Excel's drawing
tools

Using graphics in
worksheets

✦   ✦   ✦   ✦

In Chapter 13 you learned how to create charts from the
numbers in your worksheet. This chapter continues in the
same vein and discusses pictures and drawings. Like charts,
these objects can be placed on a worksheet's draw layer to add
pizzazz to an otherwise boring report.

I discuss three major types of images in this chapter:

✦ Imported bitmap and line-art graphics

✦ Graphic images copied from the Clipboard

✦ Objects created using Excel's drawing tools

Note   Excel 95 also can create another type of graphic image: maps.
But that's the topic for Chapter 17.

Importing Graphics Files

Excel can import a wide variety of graphics files. When you
choose the Insert⇨Picture command, Excel displays the Picture
dialog box, shown in Figure 14-1. This dialog box works just like
the Open dialog box. By default, it displays only the graphic files
Excel can import. As you select files, Excel displays a preview in
the preview window.

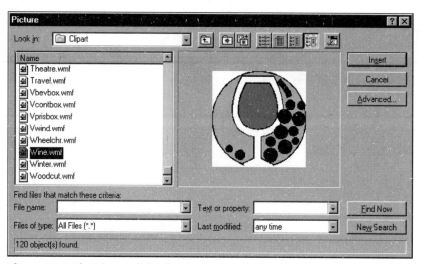

Figure 14-1: The Picture dialog box lets you embed a picture in a worksheet.

An image stored in a computer file is sometimes referred to as clip art. Noncomputerized graphics artists have always had access to books and books of clip art. Clip art is simply a collection of images that can be used freely with no copyright restrictions. Electronic clip art is the computer equivalent of these books. In fact, most word processors, drawing packages, and desktop publishing programs provide a collection of clip art files. If your copy of Excel is part of Microsoft Office, you already have a fair number of clip art files stored in the Clipart folder (which is in the MSOffice folder).

Clip art comes in two main categories: bitmap and vector (picture). Bitmap images are made up of discrete dots. They usually look pretty good at their original size but often lose clarity if you increase or decrease the size. Vector-based images, on the other hand, retain their crispness regardless of their size. Examples of common bitmap file formats include BMP, PCX, DIB, JPG, and GIF. Examples of common vector file formats include CGM, WMF, EPS, and DRW.

Bitmap files vary in the number of colors they use (even black-and-white images use multiple colors because these are usually gray scale images). If you view a 256-color bitmap graphic using a video mode that displays only 16 colors, the image usually doesn't look very good.

You can find thousands of clip art files free for the taking on computer bulletin boards and online services such as CompuServe, America Online, Prodigy, and the Microsoft Network. Figure 14-2 shows an example of a clip art image in a worksheet.

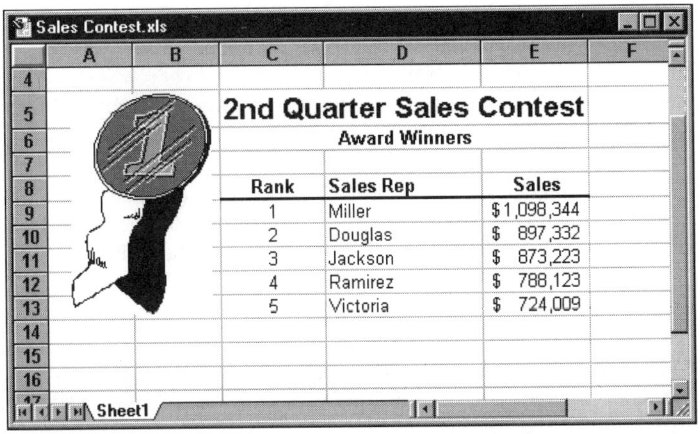

Figure 14-2: An example of a clip art image embedded in a worksheet.

Table 14-1 lists the graphics file types that Excel can import.

Table 14-1	
Graphics File Formats Supported by Excel	
File Type	**Description**
BMP	Windows bitmaps
CDR	Corel Draw graphics
CGM	Computer Graphics Metafiles
DRW	Micrografx Designer/Draw
DXF	AutoCAD format 2-D
EPS	Encapsulated Postscript
HGL	HP Graphics Language
PCT	Macintosh graphics
PCX	Bitmap graphics
TGA	Targa graphics format
TIF	Tagged Interchange Format
WMF	Windows metafile
WPG	WordPerfect graphics

Caution Using bitmap graphics in a worksheet can dramatically increase the size of your workbook, resulting in more memory usage and longer load and save times.

Cross-Reference Excel also supports Object Linking and Embedding (OLE) as another way to insert graphics objects from other applications. OLE is covered in Chapter 29.

Tip If you want to use a bitmap image for a worksheet's background (similar to wallpaper on the Windows desktop), use the Format⇨Sheet⇨Background command and select a graphics file. The selected graphics file will be tiled on the worksheet. It won't be printed, however.

A word about the draw layer

Every worksheet has what's known as a draw layer. This invisible surface is completely independent of the cells on a worksheet (or the chart on a chart sheet). The draw layer can hold graphics images, drawings, embedded charts, OLE objects, and so on. A chart sheet also has a draw layer.

Objects placed on the draw layer can be moved, resized, copied, and deleted — with no effect on any other elements in the work-sheet.

Objects on the draw layer have properties that relate to how they are moved and sized when underlying cells are moved and sized. When you right-click on a graphic object and choose Format Object from the shortcut menu, you get a tabbed dialog box. Click on the Properties tab (see the accompanying figure) to adjust how the object moves or resizes with its underlying cells.

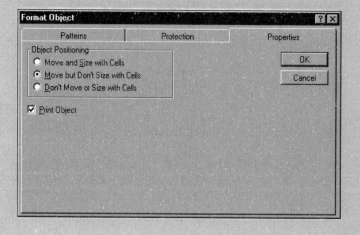

Move and Size with Cells: If this option is selected, the object appears to be attached to the cells beneath it. For example, if you insert rows above the object, the object moves down. If you increase the column width, the object gets wider.

Move but Don't Size with Cells: If this option is checked, the object moves if rows or columns are inserted, but it never changes its size if you change row heights or column widths.

Don't Move or Size with Cells: This option makes the object completely independent of the underlying cells.

The preceding options control how an object is moved or sized with respect to the underlying cells. Excel also lets you "attach" an object to a cell. In the Edit panel of the Options dialog box, place a check mark next to the check box labeled Cut, Copy, and Sort Objects with Cells. After doing so, graphic objects on the draw layer will be attached to the underlying cells.

Because a chart sheet doesn't have cells, objects placed on a chart sheet don't have these options. Such objects do have a property, however, that relates to how the object is sized if the chart size is changed.

Copying Graphics by Using the Clipboard

In some cases, you may want to use a graphic image that is not stored in a separate file or is in a file Excel can't import. For example, you may have a drawing program that uses a file format Excel doesn't support. You may be able to export the file to a supported format, but it may be easier to load the file into the drawing program and copy the image to the Clipboard. Then you can activate Excel and paste the image to the draw layer.

This capability also is useful if you don't want to copy an entire image. For example, a drawing may be made up of several components, and you want to use only one element in Excel. In this case, using the Clipboard is the only route.

Suppose that you see a graphic displayed on-screen but you can't select it — it may be part of a program's logo, for instance. In this case, you can copy the entire screen to the Clipboard and then paste it into Excel. Most of the time, you don't want the entire screen — just a portion of it. The solution is to capture the entire screen, copy it to Windows Paint, and then select the part you want and copy it to Excel. Figure 14-3 demonstrates this technique using Paint.

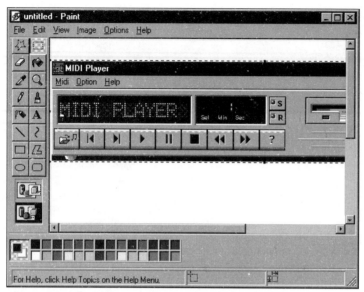

Figure 14-3: The screen was captured and pasted to Paint. You can copy the part you want and paste it to Excel.

Use the following keyboard commands:

PrintScreen: Copies the entire screen to the Clipboard

Alt+PrintScreen: Copies the active window to the Clipboard

Using Excel's Drawing Tools

The discussion so far has focused on using graphics from other sources. If your needs aren't too sophisticated, you can use the drawing tools built into Excel to create a variety of simple (and not so simple) graphics.

The Drawing toolbar

Note   To use Excel's drawing tools, you must display the Drawing toolbar. Drawing objects is one of the few features in Excel that's not available from the menus. Notice that the Standard toolbar has a tool named Drawing. Clicking on this tool toggles the Drawing toolbar on and off.

Figure 14-4 shows the Drawing toolbar. This toolbar has tools to draw simple shapes, a drawing selection tool, tools to control how objects are "stacked," tools to group and ungroup objects, and a tool to change colors and patterns of objects.

Figure 14-4: Using the Drawing toolbar is the only way to create drawings in Excel.

Table 14-2 describes the tools in the Drawing toolbar. The tools are listed in the order in which they appear.

Table 14-2 The Tools on the Drawing Toolbar	
Tool Name	*What the Tool Does*
Line	Inserts a line.
Arrow	Inserts an arrow.
Freehand	Lets you use the mouse to draw free-form lines.
Text Box	Inserts a free-floating box into which you type text.
Create Button	Inserts a clickable button, which is used primarily to execute macros.
Drawing Selection	Selects one or more graphics objects. If you have several objects and you want to select a group of them, use this tool to drag the outline so that it surrounds all the objects. Click on the button again to return to normal selection mode.
Reshape	Reshapes an existing freeform or freehand object.
Rectangle	Inserts a rectangle or a square.
Ellipse	Inserts an oval or a circle.
Arc	Inserts an arc.
Freeform	Inserts connected lines (useful for creating polygons).
Filled Rectangle	Same as the Rectangle tool, but the object is filled with a pattern.
Filled Ellipse	Same as the Ellipse tool, but the object is filled with a pattern.

(continued)

Table 14-2 *(continued)*	
Tool Name	**What the Tool Does**
Filled Arc	Same as the Arc tool, but the object is filled with a pattern.
Filled Freeform	Same as the freeform tool, but the object is filled with a pattern.
Group Objects	After multiple objects are selected, use this tool to combine them into a single object. This tool is useful if you want to resize or move a group of separate items.
Ungroup Objects	After a grouped object has been selected, use this tool to ungroup it.
Bring to Front	If an object is partially obscured by another object, use this tool to bring it to the front of the stack.
Send to Back	If an object is on top of one or more other objects, use this tool to drop it down to the bottom of the stack.
Drop Shadow	Adds a drop shadow effect to a range or object.
Pattern	Changes the pattern and fill colors of an object or range.

Tip   If you like the idea of having the drawing tools available but don't like the idea of giving up valuable screen space for the toolbar, you might want to copy the Shape tool to the Standard or Formatting toolbar (this tool isn't on any of the built-in toolbars). The Shape tool is a "drop-down" tool that contains 14 drawing tools. You can find the Shape tool in the Drawing category of the Customize dialog box.

Drawing objects

Drawing objects with the drawing tools is quite intuitive. Click on a tool and then drag in the worksheet to create the shape (the mouse pointer changes shape, reminding you that you're in draw mode). When you release the mouse button, the object is selected and its name appears in the Name box (see Figure 14-5).

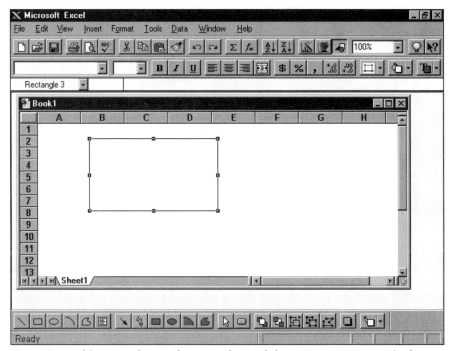

Figure 14-5: This rectangle was drawn on the worksheet. Its name appears in the Name box.

Modifying objects

It should come as no surprise that you can modify drawn objects at any time. First, you must select the object. If the object is filled with a color or pattern, you can click anywhere on the object to select it. If the object is not filled, you must click on the object's border. You can make some modifications using the toolbar buttons — for example, change the fill color. Other modifications require that you use the Format Object dialog box. After selecting one or more objects, you can bring up this dialog box by using any of the following techniques:

   ✦ Choose the Format⇨Object command.

   ✦ Press Ctrl+1.

   ✦ Double-click on the object.

   ✦ Right-click on the object and choose Format Object from the shortcut menu.

The Format Object dialog box has three tabs: Patterns, Protection, and Properties. Figure 14-6 shows the Patterns panel, which works just like the other color selection dialog boxes in Excel.

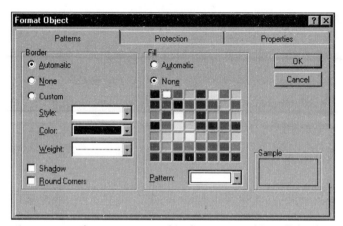

Figure 14-6: The Patterns panel in the Format Object dialog box.

The Protection tab determines whether the object is "locked." Locking has no effect, however, unless the worksheet is protected and the Objects option is in effect. Figure 14-7 shows the Protect Sheet dialog box, which appears when you choose the Tools⇨Protection⇨Protect Sheet command. If the Objects check box is checked, all objects that have their Locked property set can't be modified, moved, or deleted.

The Properties tab of the Format Object dialog box determines how an object is moved and sized with respect to the underlying cells (see the sidebar "A word about the draw layer" earlier in this chapter).

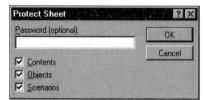

Figure 14-7: The Protect Sheet dialog box has an option that lets you lock all objects that have their Locked property set.

Changing the stack order of drawing objects

As you add drawing objects to the draw layer of a worksheet, you'll find that objects are "stacked" on top of each other in the order in which you add them. New objects are stacked on top of older objects. Figure 14-8 shows an example of drawing objects stacked on top of one another.

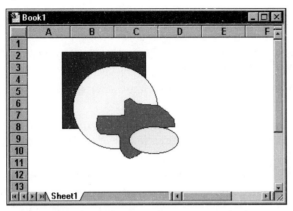

Figure 14-8: These drawing objects are stacked on top of one another.

If you find that an object is obscuring part of another, you can change the order in this stack. Select an object and click on the Bring to Front tool on the Drawing toolbar to move the object to the top of the stack. Click on the Send to Back tool to move the object to the bottom of the stack. You also can use the Format⇨Placement command to do this or the shortcut menu that appears when you right-click on an object.

Grouping objects

Excel lets you combine two or more drawing objects into a single object. This is known as *grouping*. For example, if you create a design that uses four separate drawing objects, you can select them all and click on the Group tool on the Drawing toolbar. Excel combines the objects into a single object. Then you can manipulate this group as a single object (move it, resize it, and so on). Later, if you need to modify one of the objects in the group, you can ungroup them by clicking on the Ungroup tool. This breaks the object into its original components.

You also can group and ungroup objects with the Format⇨Placement command or from the shortcut menu that appears when you right-click on a selection of objects.

Drawing tips

Although drawing objects is quite intuitive, several tips can make this task easier. This section lists some tips and techniques that you should know:

✦ To create a perfect square, press Shift while you draw a rectangle. Similarly, pressing Shift while you draw an ellipse gives you a perfect circle.

✦ To constrain a line or arrow object to angles that are divisible by 45 degrees, press Shift while you draw the object.

✦ To make an object snap to the worksheet row and column gridlines, press the Alt key while you draw the object.

✦ To maintain an object's original proportions when you resize the object, press Shift while dragging any of its borders.

✦ If you press Alt while moving an object, its upper left corner snaps to the row and column gridlines.

✦ You might find it easier to work with drawing objects if you turn off the worksheet gridline. The snap-to-gridline features work even if the gridlines aren't visible.

✦ You can control how objects appear in the View tab of the Options dialog box. Normally, the Show All option is selected. You can hide all objects by choosing Hide All or display objects as placeholders by choosing Show Placeholders (this may speed things up if you have complex objects that take a long time to redraw).

✦ To copy an object with the mouse, click on it once to select it; then press Ctrl while you drag it.

✦ A selected object's name appears in the Name box, but you can't use the Name box to select an object. You can, however, change an object's name by selecting it and then typing the new name in the Name box. Changing the name of graphic objects is most useful when you create macros that manipulate the objects. Otherwise, there's really no need to change the name of an object.

✦ You can rotate the text in a text box by using the Alignment tab on the Format Object dialog box. This tab is handy for adding a vertical title to the rows of a table. Although Excel enables you to rotate text in a cell, it makes the row height as tall as the rotated text — which usually creates an undesirable effect. Using a text box with rotated text is a good alternative.

✦ To select multiple objects, press Ctrl while you click on them. Or use the Drawing Selection tool to select objects by "lassoing" them.

✦ A text box is the only object to which you can add text. It's easy to create the illusion that another object (such as an oval) contains text, however. First, create the oval, and then add a text box on top of it. Enter the text and format the text box with no border and no fill.

✦ To select all objects on a worksheet, use the Edit⇨Go To command (or press F5) and then click on the Special button in the Go To dialog box. Choose the Objects option button and click on OK. All objects will be selected. Use this technique if you want to delete all objects (select them all, and then press Delete).

✦ By default, drawn objects are printed along with the worksheet. If you don't want the objects to print, access the Sheet panel of the Page Setup dialog box and select the Draft option. Or right-click on the object, select Format Object from the shortcut menu, and uncheck the Print Object check box in the Properties panel.

✦ If you want the underlying cell contents to show through a drawn object, access the Patterns tab in the Format Object dialog box and set the Fill to None. Unfortunately, there is no "transparent" setting that enables you to choose a fill color *and* have the cell contents show.

On the CD-ROM
The Power Utility Pak includes several utilities that work with drawing objects. The shareware version of the Power Utility Pak is on the companion CD-ROM in this book. The four utilities that work with drawing objects are as follows:

Reminder Note: This utility creates a nicely formatted reminder note on your worksheet. A single command is all it takes to hide or display all reminder notes on the worksheet.

Perpetual Calendar: This utility inserts an object that displays a calendar for the month of your choice. This calendar can be pasted as a picture object.

Object Properties: This utility lets you adjust the size of any object without using the mouse. It also lets you hide and unhide objects.

Object Align, Size and Space: This handy utility lets you precisely align objects, adjust their size to match a reference object, and evenly space them horizontally or vertically (see Figure 14-9).

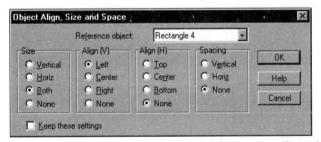

Figure 14-9: This utility, which is part of the Power Utility Pak, makes it easy to align, resize, and space objects evenly.

Drawing Examples

In this section, I provide you with some examples of using Excel's drawing tools. Perhaps these examples will get your own creative juices flowing.

Calling attention to a cell

You can use the Oval object to draw a circle around a particular cell to make it stand out from the others. Or you can create other types of images to do this. Figure 14-10 shows two examples (one subtle, one more flamboyant) of how you could make one cell's value jump out.

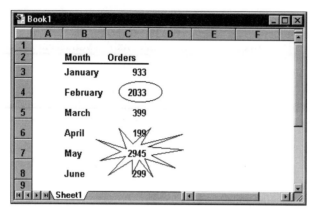

Figure 14-10: Two ways of making a particular cell stand out.

Creating organizational charts

Figure 14-11 shows an organizational chart I created with the drawing tools. This chart consists only of text boxes and lines. To make the box size consistent, I created one and then made copies of it. I also used the Object Align, Size and Space utility (from the Power Utility Pak) to align the text boxes and space them evenly.

On the CD-ROM This workbook, named ORGANIZA.XLS, is available on the companion CD-ROM.

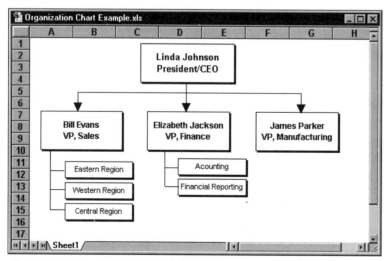

Figure 14-11: This organizational chart was created with Excel's drawing tools.

Creating flow diagrams

You also can create flow diagrams using the drawing tools. This capability often is useful to describe how a process or system works. Figure 14-12 shows an example of a flow diagram made up of shapes, text boxes, and arrows. Because a text box is the only object that can hold text, I placed the text boxes on top of the other objects and removed the border and fill from the text box. After creating the diagram, I selected all the objects and grouped them together so that the diagram could be moved as a single unit.

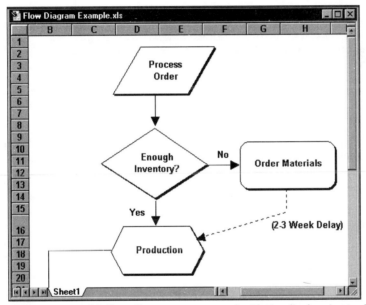

Figure 14-12: This flow diagram was created with Excel's drawing tools.

On the CD-ROM This workbook, named FLOW_DIA.XLS, is available on the companion CD-ROM.

Annotating a worksheet

Using a cell note is one way to annotate your work. The text box object is often a good alternative because you can format the text any way you like (see Figure 14-13). You also can create a simple macro to hide or display the text box by clicking a button.

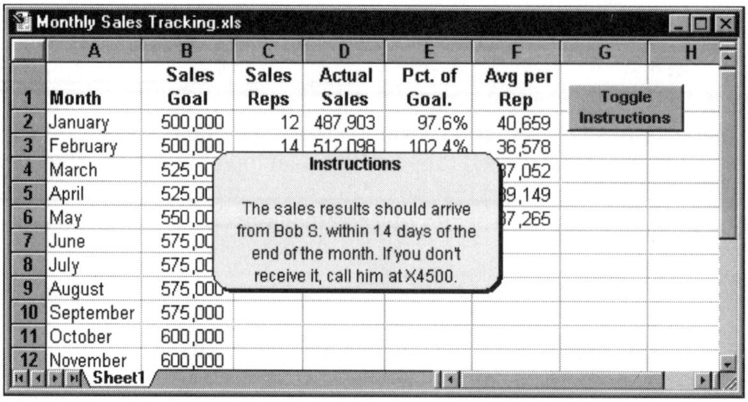

Figure 14-13: You can use a text box to annotate your work or provide instructions for the user.

Creating a vertical title

A text box also is useful for creating vertical titles for a table. In Figure 14-14, the text box was formatted to display the text vertically, and the border was removed. This technique is better than aligning the text vertically in a cell because the row height is not changed.

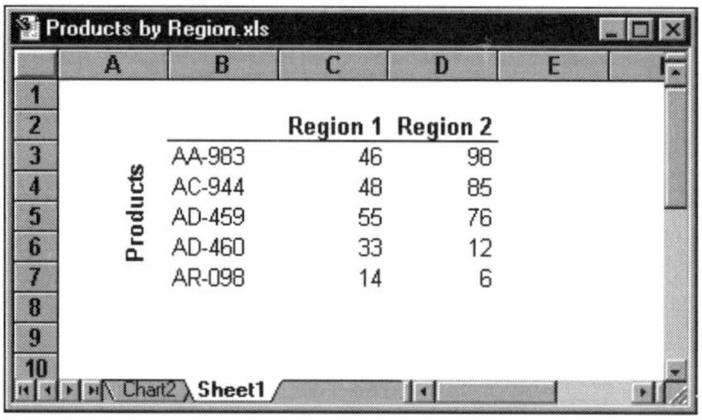

Figure 14-14: Using a text box for a vertical title.

Annotating a chart

One of the most common uses of the drawing tools is to annotate a chart. For example, you can add descriptive text with an arrow to call attention to a certain data point. This technique works for both embedded charts and charts on chart sheets. Figure 14-15 shows an example of an embedded chart that has been annotated.

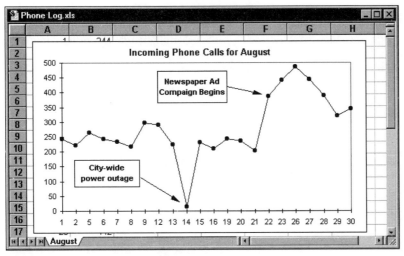

Figure 14-15: Annotating a chart with the drawing tools.

Note If you add drawing objects to an embedded chart, be aware that these objects don't adjust themselves if you resize the chart. Similarly, if you move the chart, the drawing objects you added don't come along. One solution is to select the chart and the drawing objects and then group them into a single object.

Creating a logo

If your company's logo isn't too complicated, you may be able to use the drawing tools to create the logo. Or you can have it scanned and digitized as a graphic file, which you can import into Excel.

Doodling

One of my favorite uses of the drawing tools is for electronic doodling. This is a good way to pass the time when you're put on endless hold while making a phone call. Figure 14-16 shows some of the creations I made while I was on hold for product support (for a company that will remain nameless).

For what it's worth, this file is included on the CD-ROM. It's called DOODLE.XLS.

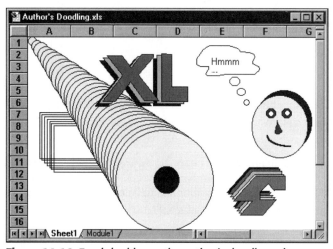

Figure 14-16: Excel doubles as the author's doodle pad.

Using the Camera Tool

One of Excel's best-kept secrets is its Camera tool. This toolbar button is not found on any of the built-in toolbars, so you have to add it to one of the toolbars in order to use it (the Drawing toolbar is a good choice). You can find the Camera tool in the Utility category in the Customize dialog box. It's the button with an image of a camera.

The Camera tool takes a "picture" of a range of cells — including objects on the draw layer. You can then paste that picture object somewhere else on the draw layer. What makes this technique particularly useful is that this picture is linked to the cells. In other words, if you change the contents of a cell that's in a picture, the picture changes. The picture taken by the Camera tool is an exact replica of the original range, including any drawing objects that are over the cells.

Tip You can accomplish the same effect without using the Camera tool. First, select a range and choose Edit⇨Copy. Then press Shift and click on the Edit menu. Choose Paste Picture Link to paste a picture of the selection into your worksheet. If you don't hold down Shift when you select the Edit menu, this command doesn't appear.

Cross-Reference The Camera tool is particularly useful for printing on contiguous ranges. See Chapter 12 for more information.

You also can sever the link that's created when you paste a linked picture object. To do so, select the picture and delete the formula in the formula bar. This is useful for creating pictures of formatted text that uses a font which may not be available on other users' systems.

A related technique involves copying a range as a picture. Select the cell or range to be copied, press Shift, and choose the Edit⇨Copy Picture command. Excel displays a dialog box. Choose the bitmap format. Then, move to another cell and paste the copied picture. In this case, the copied picture is not linked to the source range.

Figure 14-17 shows a picture I captured from cell B3, which was formatted with an unusual font (FZ Jazzy 10 Shadow). The picture accurately reflects the original text even if the workbook is opened on a system that doesn't have the font — which is the case in the figure. Because the system doesn't have this particular font installed, the original cell appears in the closest match (Times New Roman). The picture, however, displays the original font.

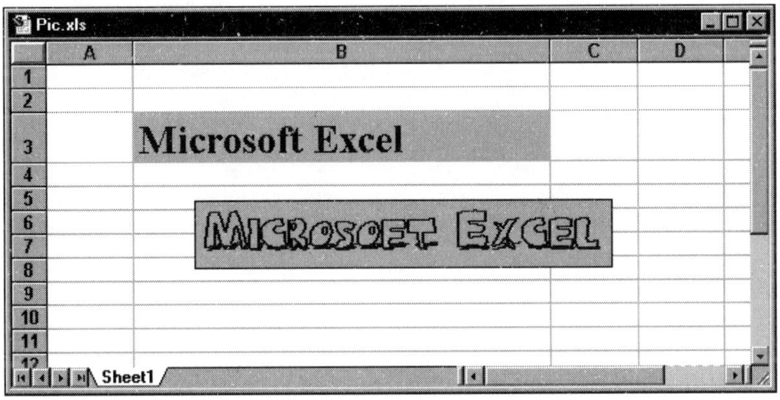

Figure 14-17: Example of a cell copied as a picture.

Creating Simple Animations

You can achieve some interesting and unusual effects by "animating" drawing objects. For example, you can set things up so that your company's logo appears to grow when a workbook is opened. Or, you can make a graphic move around the screen. Performing these types of animation requires writing a macro. It's not difficult to do, but you must understand VBA to write the code (this isn't the type of macro you create by recording your keystrokes).

New! Previous versions of Excel allowed you to create animations, but the result was usually not satisfactory because of excessive screen flashing. This problem has been corrected with Excel 95, however, and animations are very smooth.

On the To see a few examples, open the worksheet called ANIMATED.XLS on the companion
CD-ROM CD-ROM. The first example displays an animated text box, in which the letters are added one at a time, change colors, and appear to flash. The second example shows two balls bouncing around in a rectangle. Both these examples use VBA macros.

Summary

In this chapter, I cover two types of graphic information you can add to a worksheet's draw layer: imported graphic images and objects you draw using Excel's drawing tools. Several examples demonstrate some ways you can use these objects in your workbooks.

✦   ✦   ✦

Putting It All Together

The preceding chapters present basic information about how Excel works. But you probably already realize that simply knowing the commands and shortcuts won't help you create successful workbooks. The point of this chapter is to help you tie it all together and to provide some pointers and examples to help you develop workbooks that do what you want them to do.

The Audience for Spreadsheets

Before we get too far into this, it's useful to pause and think about spreadsheets in general. There are many ways to classify spreadsheets, but it's useful to start out with two broad categories:

+ Spreadsheets that you develop for yourself
+ Spreadsheets that others will be using

As you'll see, the ultimate user of your spreadsheet (you alone, or others) often makes a difference in how you go about developing it and in the amount of effort that you put into it.

Developing spreadsheets for yourself

If you're the only person who will ever use a particular spreadsheet, you don't have to be so concerned with issues such as security, ease of use, and error handling. After all, you developed the spreadsheet, so you know how it was designed. And if an error occurs, you can simply track down the source and correct the problem.

Quick-and-dirty spreadsheets

Chances are, many of the spreadsheets that you develop for your own use are what I call "quick-and-dirty" spreadsheets. Such spreadsheets are fairly small and are developed to quickly solve a problem or answer a question. Here's an example: You're about to buy a new car and you want to figure out your monthly payment for various loan amounts. Another example would be that you need to generate a chart showing your company's sales by month, so you quickly enter 12 values and whip off a chart, which you paste into your word processor.

In this case, you don't really care what the spreadsheet looks like as long as it gives you the correct answer (or in the case of the second example, produces a nice-looking chart). You can probably input the entire model in a few minutes, and you certainly won't take the time to document your work. And in many cases, you won't even bother to save the file.

For-your-eyes-only spreadsheets

As the name implies, no one except you, its creator, will ever see or use the spreadsheets that fall into this category. An example would be a file in which you keep information relevant to your income taxes. You open the file whenever a check comes in the mail, you incur an expense that can be justified as business, you buy tax-deductible Girl Scout cookies, and so on. Another example is a spreadsheet that you use to keep track of your employees' time records (sick leave, vacation, and so on).

Spreadsheets in this category differ from quick-and-dirty spreadsheets in that you use them more than once, you save these spreadsheets to files. But again, they're not worth spending a great deal of time on. You may apply some simple formatting, but that's about it (after all, you don't really need to impress yourself — or do you?). This type of spreadsheet also lacks any type of error detection because you understand how the formulas are set up; you know enough to avoid inputting data that will produce erroneous results. If an error does crop up, you immediately know what caused it.

Spreadsheets in this category sometimes increase in sophistication over time. For example, I have an Excel workbook that I use to track my income by source. This workbook was simple when I first set it up, but I tend to add accoutrements to it nearly every time I use it: more summary formulas, better formatting, and even a chart that displays income by month. My latest modification was to add a trendline to the chart to project income based on past trends.

Developing spreadsheets for others

If others will use a spreadsheet that you develop, you need to pay a lot more attention to minor details. Because of this, such a spreadsheet usually takes longer to create than one that only you will see. The amount of extra effort depends, in large part, on the experience level of the other users. A spreadsheet that will be utilized by an inexperienced computer user is often the most difficult to develop simply because you need to make sure that the spreadsheet is "bulletproof." In other words, you don't want the user to mess things up (erase a formula, for example). In addition, you have to make it perfectly clear how the spreadsheet is to be used. This often means adding more formatting and instructions for the user.

Note As you'll discover in later chapters, you can use Excel as a complete application development environment and develop sophisticated applications that may not even look like a normal spreadsheet. Doing so almost always requires the use of macros and custom interface elements such as buttons, custom toolbars, and custom menus. These topics all are discussed in subsequent chapters.

Characteristics of a Successful Spreadsheet

You create a spreadsheet to accomplish some end result, which could be any of thousands of things. If the spreadsheet is successful, it meets most or all of the following criteria (some of these are appropriate only if the spreadsheet is used by others):

✦ It allows the end user to perform a task that he or she probably would not be able to do otherwise — or a task that would take *much* longer to do manually.

✦ It's the appropriate solution to the problem. Using a spreadsheet isn't always the most suitable approach. For example, you can create an organizational chart with Excel, but if you create org charts for a living, you're better off with a software product designed specifically for that task.

✦ It accomplishes its goal. This may seem like an obvious prerequisite, but I've seen many spreadsheets that fail to meet this test.

✦ It produces accurate results. As you may have discovered by now, it's quite easy to create formulas that produce the wrong results. In most cases, no answer is better than an incorrect answer.

✦ It doesn't allow the user to accidentally (or intentionally) delete or modify important components. Excel has built-in features to help in this area (more on this later).

✦ It's laid out clearly so that the user always knows how to proceed. I've opened far too many spreadsheets and not had a clue as to how to proceed — or even what the purpose was.

✦ Its formulas and macros are well documented so that they can be changed if necessary.

✦ It is designed in such a way that it can be modified in simple ways without making major changes.

You can create spreadsheets at many different levels, ranging from simple fill-in-the-blank templates to extremely complex applications that utilize custom menus and dialog boxes and may not even look like a spreadsheet. The remainder of this chapter focuses on relatively simple spreadsheets — those that can be produced using only the information presented in Parts I and II of this book.

Uses for Spreadsheets

There are millions of spreadsheets in daily use throughout the world. Many of them fit into the quick-and-dirty classification that I described previously. Of the spreadsheets with some lasting value, however, the majority probably fit into one or more of the following very broad categories:

✦ Financial or data analysis models

✦ Reports and presentations

✦ List management

✦ Database access

I discuss each of these briefly in the following sections.

Financial or data analysis models

Before the days of personal computers, large companies relied on mainframe systems to do their financial analysis. Smaller companies used sheets of accounting paper. But things have changed dramatically over the past decade, and now companies of all sizes can perform sophisticated analyses in the blink of an eye.

This category of spreadsheets covers a wide variety of applications, including budgeting, investment analysis, modeling, and statistical data analysis. These applications can range from simple tables of numbers to sophisticated mathematical models designed for "what-if" analyses.

One very common type of spreadsheet is a budget. A budget spreadsheet typically has months along the top and budget categories along the left. Each intersecting cell contains a projected expense — for example, telephone expenses for June. Budgets use SUM formulas to calculate annual totals and totals for each category. Excel's multisheet feature lets you store budgets for different departments or divisions on separate sheets.

Budget categories often are arranged in hierarchy. For example, there could be a category called Personnel expenses, which is made up of subcategories such as salaries, benefits, commissions, bonuses, and so on (see Figure 15-1). In such a case, you can create additional formulas to calculate category totals. Excel's outlining feature is ideal for this, which is the topic of Chapter 18.

Budget Worksheet.xls

	A	B	C	D	E	F	G	
1			January	February	March	April	May	Ju
2	Personnel							
3		Salary	145,050	145,050	145,050	152,000	152,000	
4		Commission	25,000	25,000	25,000	25,000	25,000	
5		Bonus	-	-	-	-	-	
6		**Personnel Total**	**170,050**	**170,050**	**170,050**	**177,000**	**177,000**	
7	Travel							
8		Airfare	2,000	3,000	4,000	4,000	4,000	
9		Lodging	1,200	2,400	3,500	3,500	3,500	
10		Meals	1,000	1,000	1,000	1,000	1,000	
11		Other	1,500	1,500	1,500	1,500	1,500	
12		**Travel Total**	**5,700**	**7,900**	**10,000**	**10,000**	**10,000**	
13	Office							
14		Rent	2,500	2,500	2,500	2,500	2,500	
15		Utilities	900	900	900	900	900	
16		Maintenance	500	500	500	500	500	
17		Cleaning	600	600	600	600	600	
18		Other	1,200	1,200	1,200	1,200	1,200	
19		**Office Total**	**5,700**	**5,700**	**5,700**	**5,700**	**5,700**	

Sheet1

Figure 15-1: This budget worksheet uses formulas to calculate subtotals within each category.

Another type of financial application is a *what-if model.* A what-if model calculates formulas using assumptions specified in a series of input cells. For example, you can create an amortization spreadsheet that calculates details for a loan based on the loan amount, the interest rate, and the term of the loan. This model would have three input cells. Excel's scenario manager is designed to make this type of model easier to handle.

Reports and presentations

Some spreadsheets are designed primarily for their end result: printed output. These spreadsheets take advantage of Excel's formatting and chart-making features to produce attractive, boardroom-quality output.

Of course, any spreadsheet can produce good quality reports, so spreadsheets in this category often fall into another category as well.

List management

Another very common use for spreadsheets is list management. A list is essentially a database table stored in a worksheet. A database table consists of field names (in the top row), with records in the rows below.

Excel has some handy tools that make it very easy to manipulate lists in a variety of ways (see Figure 15-2). List management is the topic of Chapter 23.

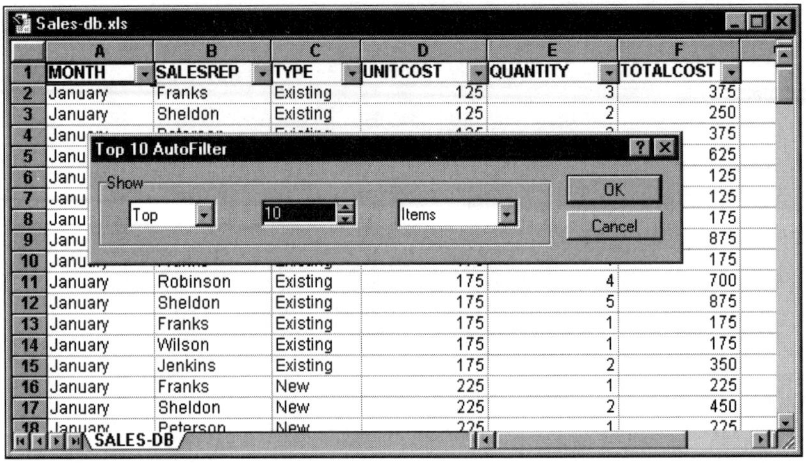

Figure 15-2: Excel makes it easy to work with lists of data.

Database access

Another category of spreadsheets works with data stored in external databases. You can use Excel to query external databases and bring in a subset of the data that meets criteria that you specify. Then you can do what you want with this data, independent of the original database. I discuss this category of spreadsheets in Chapter 24.

Turnkey applications

By a *turnkey application,* I mean a spreadsheet solution that is programmed to work as a stand-alone application. Such an application always requires macros and may involve creating custom menus and custom toolbars.

These applications are large-scale projects designed to be used by a large number of people or over a long period. They often interact with other systems (such as a corporate database) and must be very stable. Although this book touches on some elements of developing such applications, they are actually outside this book's scope.

Steps in Creating a Spreadsheet

This section discusses the basic steps you might follow in creating a spreadsheet. I assume that you're creating a workbook that others may use, so you may skip some of these steps if the spreadsheet is for you only. These steps are for relatively simple spreadsheets — those that don't use macros, custom toolbars, or other advanced features. And, of course, these are only very basic guidelines. Everyone eventually develops his or her style, and you may find a method that works better for you. The basic steps are as follows:

1. Think about what you want to accomplish.
2. Consider the audience.
3. Design the workbook layout.
4. Enter data and formulas.
5. Apply appropriate formatting.
6. Test it.
7. Apply protection as necessary.
8. Document your work.

I discuss each of these steps in the following sections.

Developing a plan

If you're like me, when you set out to create a new spreadsheet, you may have a tendency to jump right in and get to work. Tempting as it may be to create something concrete, try to restrain yourself. The end product is almost always better if you take some time to determine exactly what you're trying to accomplish and come up with a plan of action. The time you spend at this stage usually saves you more time later in the project.

Developing a plan for a spreadsheet may involve collecting information about the following:

◆ How is the problem currently being addressed? And what's wrong with the current solution?
◆ Is a spreadsheet really the best solution to the problem?
◆ How long will the spreadsheet be used?
◆ How many people will be using it?
◆ What type of output, if any, will be required?
◆ Is there existing data that can be imported?
◆ Will the requirements for this project change over time?

The point here is to attempt to learn as much as possible about the project that you're developing. With that information, you can determine a plan of action — which may even mean not using a spreadsheet for the solution.

Consider the audience

If you'll be the only user of the workbook that you're developing, you can skip this step. But if others will be using the result of your efforts, take some time to find out about these people. Knowing the following information often prevents having to make changes later:

✦ **How experienced are the users?** Can they perform basic operations such as copying, inserting rows, and so on? Don't assume that everyone knows as much as you do.

✦ **What software will they be using?** For example, if you develop your spreadsheet using Excel 95, you need to be aware that it can't be loaded into Excel 4 or earlier versions.

✦ **What hardware will they be using?** If your spreadsheet takes three minutes to calculate on your Pentium-based system, it may well take 20 minutes on a slower 386 or 486 system. Also, be aware of different video modes. If you develop your spreadsheet using a 1024×768 video mode, users with an 800×600 or 640×480 display will have a much smaller viewing area.

✦ **Do you want to allow changes?** Often, you want to make sure that your formulas don't get modified. If so, you'll need to perform some basic protection (described later in this chapter).

Designing the workbook layout

One of the important considerations is how you want to lay out the workbook. Before the days of multisheet workbooks, this was a lot more difficult than it is today. When your file has only a single worksheet, you have to plan it carefully to ensure that making a change doesn't affect something else.

Spreadsheets often consist of distinct blocks of information. In the old days, spreadsheet designers often used a layout like the one shown in Figure 15-3. This example is for a spreadsheet that has three main blocks: an input area, a calculation area, and a report area. This *offset block layout* minimizes the possibility of damage. For example, if you delete a column or change its width, it affects only one area. If the areas were laid out vertically, this would not be the case.

Because Excel uses multiple worksheets in a file, however, this type of layout is rarely necessary. It's much easier and more efficient to use a separate worksheet for each block. An added advantage is that you can access the various blocks simply by clicking on the tab (which can be named appropriately).

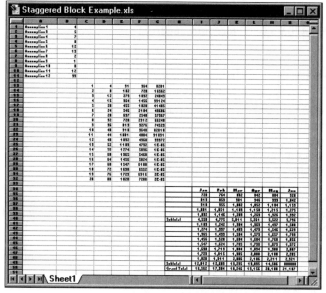

Figure 15-3: This offset block layout is one way to organize a worksheet.

Entering data and formulas

This phase of the spreadsheet development process is often where people begin. But if you've thought through the problem, considered the users, and created an appropriate layout, this phase should go more smoothly than if you jumped right in without the preliminary steps.

The more you know about Excel, the easier this phase is. Formulas are just one part of a spreadsheet. Sometimes you may need to incorporate one or more of the following features (which are all discussed later in the book):

✦ Workbook consolidation

✦ List management

✦ External databases

✦ Outlining

✦ Statistical analysis

✦ Pivot tables

✦ Scenario management

✦ Solver

✦ Mapping

✦ Interaction with other applications

✦ Custom menus or toolbars (which require macros)

Applying appropriate formatting

Many people prefer to format their work as they go along. If that's not your style, this step must be performed. As I mentioned in Chapter 11, almost all worksheets benefit from some stylistic formatting. At the very least, you need to adjust the number formats so that the values appear correctly. If the worksheet will be used by others, make sure that any color combinations you use will be visible for those running on a monochrome system (such as a notebook computer).

Of all of the basic steps in creating a spreadsheet, formatting is the one with the most variety. Although beauty may be in the eye of the beholder, there are some guidelines that you might want to consider:

✦ **Preformat all numeric cells.** Use number formats appropriate for the numbers and make sure that the columns are wide enough to handle the maximum values. For example, if a cell is designed to hold an interest rate, format it with a percent sign. And if you've created an amortization schedule, make sure that the columns are wide enough to handle very large amounts.

✦ **Use only basic fonts**. If others will be using your workbook, stick to the basic TrueType fonts that come with Windows. Otherwise, the fonts may not translate well, and the user may see a string of asterisks rather than a value.

✦ **Don't go overboard with fonts**. As a rule of thumb, never use more than two different typefaces in a single workbook. Usually, one will do just fine (Arial is a good choice). If you use different font sizes, do so sparingly.

✦ **Be careful with color.** Colored text or cell backgrounds can make your workbook much easier to use. For example, if you use a lookup table, you can use color to make it clear where the table's boundaries are. Or, you may want to color-code the cells that will accept user input. Overuse of colors will make your spreadsheet look gaudy and unprofessional, however. Also, make sure that color combinations will work if the workbook is opened on a monochrome notebook computer.

✦ **Consider identifying the active area.** Many spreadsheets are set up using only a few cells — the active area. Inexperienced users often scroll away from the active area and get lost. One technique is to hide all rows and columns that aren't used. Or, you can apply a color background (such as light gray) to all unused cells. This will make the cells in use very clear.

✦ **Remove extraneous elements.** In some cases, you can simplify things significantly by removing elements that might get in the way or cause the screen to appear more confusing than it is. These include items such as automatic page breaks, gridlines, row and column headers, and sheet tabs. These options, which you set in the View panel of the Options dialog box, are saved with the worksheet.

Testing the spreadsheet

Before you actually use your newly created spreadsheet for real work, you'll want to test it thoroughly. This is even more critical if others will be using your spreadsheet. If you've distributed 20 copies of your file and then discover a major error in a formula, you'll have to do a "recall" and send out a corrected copy. Obviously, it's easier to catch the errors before you send out a spreadsheet.

Testing is basically the process of ensuring that the formulas produce correct results under all possible circumstances. There are no rules that I know of for testing a worksheet, so you're pretty much on your own here. I can, however, offer a few guidelines:

- ◆ **Try extreme input values.** If your worksheet is set up to perform calculations using input cells, spend some time and enter very large or very small numbers and observe the effects on the formulas. If the user should enter a percentage, see what happens if you enter a large value. If a positive number is expected, try entering a negative number. This also is a good way to ensure that your columns are wide enough.

- ◆ **Provide data validation.** Although you can't expect your formulas to yield usable results for invalid entries (garbage in, garbage out), you may want to use a formula to verify input so that the user will know why the formulas are producing odd results. For example, if a user enters a value over 1.0, a formula may display the result *ERROR: Enter a percentage.*

- ◆ **Use dummy data.** If you have a budget application, for example, try entering a 1 into each cell. This is a good way to make sure that all of your SUM formulas refer to the correct ranges. An incorrect formula usually stands out from the others.

- ◆ **Get familiar with Excel's auditing tools.** Excel has several quite useful tools that can help you track down erroneous formulas. I discuss these tools in Chapter 30.

Applying appropriate protection

A spreadsheet can be quite fragile. Deleting a single formula often has a ripple effect and causes other formulas to produce an error value or, even worse, incorrect results. I've seen cases in which an inexperienced user deleted a critical formula, panicked, and cemented the mistake by saving the file and reopening it — only to discover, of course, that the original (good) version had been overwritten.

You can circumvent such problems by using the protection features built into Excel. There are two general types of protection:

- ◆ Sheet protection
- ◆ Workbook protection

Protecting sheets

The Tools⇨Protection⇨Protect Sheet command displays the dialog box shown in Figure 15-4.

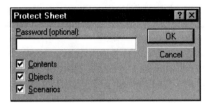

Figure 15-4: The Protect Sheet dialog box.

This dialog box has three check boxes:

✦ **Contents:** Cells that have their Locked property turned on can't be changed.

✦ **Objects:** Drawing objects (including embedded charts) that have their Locked property turned on can't be selected.

✦ **Scenarios:** Defined scenarios that have their Prevent Changes property turned on can't be changed (see Chapter 26 for a discussion of scenario management).

You can provide a password or not in the Protect Sheet dialog box. If you enter a password, the password must be reentered before the sheet can be unprotected. If you don't supply a password, anyone can unprotect the sheet.

By default, all cells have their Locked property turned on. Before protecting a worksheet, you'll normally want to turn the Locked property off for input cells.

You can change the Locked property of a cell or drawing object by accessing its Format dialog box and clicking the Protection tab. Cells have an additional property: Hidden. This is a bit misleading because it doesn't actually hide the cell. Rather, it prevents the cell contents from being displayed in the formula bar. You can use the Hidden property to prevent others from seeing your formulas.

Note   You can't change a cell's Locked property while the sheet is protected. You must unprotect the sheet to make any changes, and then protect it again.

Protection isn't just for worksheets that others will be using. Many people protect worksheets to prevent themselves from accidentally deleting cells.

Protecting workbooks

The second type of protection is workbook protection. The Tools⇨Protection⇨Protect Workbook command displays the dialog box shown in Figure 15-5.

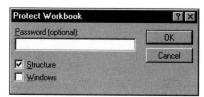

Figure 15-5: The Protect Workbook dialog box.

This dialog box has two check boxes:

✦ **Structure:** Protects the workbook window from being moved or resized.

✦ **Windows:** Prevents any of the following changes to a workbook: adding a sheet, deleting a sheet, moving a sheet, renaming a sheet, hiding a sheet, or unhiding a sheet.

Again, you can supply a password or not, depending on the level of protection you need.

Documenting your work

The final step in the spreadsheet-creation process is documenting your work. It's always a good idea to make some notes about the spreadsheet. After all, you may need to modify the spreadsheet later. The elegant formula that you created last week may be completely meaningless when you need to change it in six months. Here are some general tips on documenting your spreadsheets.

Use the Properties dialog box

The File⇨Properties command displays the Properties dialog box (the Summary panel is shown in Figure 15-6). You may want to take a few minutes to fill in the missing information and enter some comments in the Comments box.

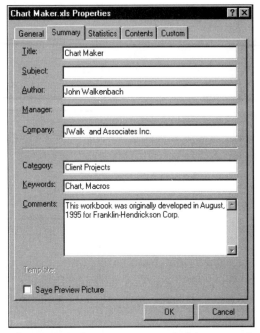

Figure 15-6: The Summary panel of the Properties dialog box.

Use cell notes

As you know, you can document individual cells by using the Insert⇨Note command. The note appears when you move the mouse pointer over the cell. If you don't like the idea of seeing the cell notes appear, turn off the Note Indicator check box in the View tab of the Options dialog box. Unfortunately, this setting applies to all workbooks, so if you turn off the note indicator for one workbook, you turn it off for all of them.

Use a separate worksheet

Perhaps the best way to document a workbook is to insert a new worksheet and store your comments there. Some people also like to keep a running tally of any modifications that they made. You can hide the worksheet so that others can't see it.

Making Your Workbook Easy to Maintain

One of the cardinal rules of spreadsheeting is that things change. You may have a sales-tracking spreadsheet that you've been using for years, and it works perfectly well. But then you're informed that the company has bought out one of your competitors and the sales regions will be restructured. Your sales-tracking workbook suddenly no longer applies.

You can often save yourself lots of time by planning for the inevitable changes. There are a few things that you can do to make your worksheets as modifiable as possible:

✦ **Avoid hard coding values in formulas**. For example, assume that you have formulas that calculate sales commissions using a commission rate of 12.5 percent. Rather than use the value .125 in the formulas, enter it into a cell and use the cell reference. Or, use the technique described in Chapter 9 to create a named constant.

✦ **Use names whenever possible.** Cell and range names make your formulas easier to read and more understandable. When the time comes to modify your formulas, you may be able to modify just the range to which a name refers.

✦ **Use simplified formulas.** Beginning users sometimes create formulas that are more complicated than they need to be. Often, this is because beginners don't know about a particular built-in function. As you gain more experience with Excel, be on the lookout for useful functions that can make your formulas simple and clear. Such formulas are much easier to modify when the time comes.

✦ **Use a flexible layout.** Rather than try to cram everything into a single worksheet, use multiple worksheets. You'll find that this makes expanding much easier, should the need arise.

✦ **Use named styles.** Using named styles makes obtaining consistent formatting much easier if you need to add new data to accommodate a change. I discuss this feature in Chapter 11.

✦ **Keep it clean.** It's also a good idea to keep your workbooks clean and free of extraneous information. For example, if the workbook has empty worksheets, remove them. If you created names that you no longer use, delete them. If there's a range of cells that you used to perform a quick calculation (and you no longer need it), delete the range.

When Things Go Wrong

Many types of errors can occur when you work with Excel (or any spreadsheet, for that matter). These range from inconvenient errors that can be corrected to disastrous errors that can't.

For example, a formula may return an error value when a certain cell that it uses contains a zero. Normally, you can isolate the problem and correct the formula so that the error doesn't appear anymore (this is an example of an easily corrected error). A potentially disastrous error is when you open a worksheet and Excel reports that it can't read the file. Figure 15-7 shows the message you'll get. Unless you made a recent backup, you could be in deep trouble. Unfortunately, this type of error (a corrupted file) occurs more often than you might think.

Figure 15-7: When you see an error message like this, you'd better have a recent backup available.

Good testing helps you avoid problems with your formulas. Making modifications to your work, however, may result in a formula no longer working. For example, you may add a new column to the worksheet and the formulas don't pick up the expanded cell reference. This is an example of when using names could eliminate the need to adjust the formulas.

There will be cases in which you find that a formula just doesn't work as it should. When this happens, try to isolate the problem as simply as possible. I've found that a good way to deal with such formulas is to create a new workbook with a very simplified example of what I'm trying to accomplish. Sometimes, looking at the problem in a different context can shed new light on it.

The only way to prevent disasters — such as a corrupt file — is to develop good backup habits. If a file is important, you should never have only one copy of it. You should get in the habit of making a daily backup on a different storage medium.

Where to Go from Here

This chapter concludes Part II. If you're following the book in chapter number order, you now have enough knowledge to put Excel to good use.

Excel has many more features that may interest you, however. These are covered in the remaining chapters. Even if you're satisfied with what you already know about Excel, I strongly suggest that you at least browse through the remaining chapters. You may see something that can save you hours.

Summary

In this chapter, I distinguish two general categories of spreadsheets: those that you create for yourself only and those that others will use. The approach you take depends on the end user. I also list the characteristics of a successful spreadsheet and discuss basic types of spreadsheets. I discuss the basic steps that you may go through when creating a spreadsheet and cover the features in Excel that let you protect various parts of your work. I conclude with some tips on how to make your spreadsheets easier to maintain and how to handle some common types of errors.

✦   ✦   ✦

Advanced Features

T he chapters in this part cover some advanced topics that help you create more powerful spreadsheets. I discuss additional charting techniques, Excel's new Data Map feature, worksheet outlines, file linking and consolidation, and array formulas. The final chapter provides information related to using Excel in a workgroup.

Advanced Charting

Chapter 13 introduces charting. This chapter takes the topic to the next level. You learn how to customize your charts to the max so that they look exactly as you want. I also share some slick charting tricks that I've picked up over the years.

Chart Customization: An Overview

Often, the basic chart that Excel creates is good enough. If you're using a chart to get a better idea of what your data means, a chart that's based on an AutoFormat usually does just fine. But if you want to create the most effective chart possible, you'll probably want to take advantage of the additional customization techniques available in Excel.

Customizing a chart involves changing its appearance. These changes can be purely cosmetic (such as changing colors or modifying line widths) or quite substantial (such as changing the axis scales or rotating a 3-D chart).

Note Before you can customize a chart, you must activate it. To activate an embedded chart, double-click on it (single-clicking selects the chart but doesn't activate it). To deactivate an embedded chart, just click anywhere in the worksheet. If the embedded chart is larger than the workbook window, it is activated in a separate window. To activate a chart on a chart sheet, click on its sheet tab.

Here's a partial list of the customizations that you can make to a chart:

　　◆ Change any colors, patterns, line widths, marker styles, and fonts.

✦ Change the data ranges that the chart uses, add a new chart series, or delete an existing series.

✦ Choose which gridlines to display.

✦ Determine the size and placement of the legend (or delete it altogether).

✦ Determine where the axes cross.

✦ Adjust the axis scales by specifying a maximum and minimum, change the tick marks and labels, and so on. You also can specify that a scale be represented in logarithmic units.

✦ Add titles for the chart and axes, as well as free-floating text anywhere in the chart.

✦ Add error bars and trend lines to a data series.

✦ Display the data points in reverse order.

✦ Rotate a 3-D chart to get a better view or to add impact.

✦ Replace columns and bars with bitmaps, or replace line chart markers with bitmaps.

Note It's easy to become overwhelmed with all the chart customization options. The more you work with charts, the easier it becomes. Even advanced users tend to experiment a great deal with chart customization, and they rely heavily on trial and error — a technique that I strongly recommend.

Elements of a chart

Before I discuss chart modifications, I need to digress and talk about the various elements of a chart. The parts vary with the type of chart — for example, pie charts don't have axes and only 3-D charts have walls and floors.

When a chart is activated, you can select various parts of the chart with which to work. Modifying a chart is similar to everything else you do in Excel: First you make a selection (in this case, select a chart part), and then you issue a command to do something with the selection. Unlike a worksheet selection, you can select only one chart element at a time. The exception is elements that consist of multiple parts — such as gridlines. Selecting one gridline selects them all.

You can select a chart element by clicking on it. The name of the selected item appears in the Name box. When a chart is activated, you can't access the Name box; it's simply a convenient place for Excel to display the chart element's name. Many of the chart element names include a number that further describes the part. For example, the first axis in a chart is named Axis 1, the second is Axis 2, and so on.

Tip   If you find it difficult to select a specific part of a chart by clicking on it, you also can use the keyboard. Just press the up-arrow or down-arrow key to cycle through all parts in the chart. When a data series is selected, press the right-arrow or left-arrow key to select individual points in the series.

Table 16-1 lists the various elements of a chart (not all of these parts appear in every chart). You might want to create a chart and practice selecting some of these parts. Keep your eye on the Name box to see which chart element is selected.

Table 16-1 Chart Elements	
Part	**Description**
Axis *n*	One of the chart's axes. For example, the value axis is Axis 1.
Chart	The chart's background.
Corners	The corners of 3-D charts (except 3-D pie charts). Select the corners if you want to rotate a 3-D chart using a mouse.
Dropline *n*	A dropline that extends from the data point downward to the axis. For example, the first dropline is Dropline 1.
Floor	The floor of 3-D charts (except 3-D pie charts).
Gridline *n*	A chart can have major and minor gridlines for each axis. For example, the major gridline for the value axis is Gridline 1.
HiLoline *n*	A high-line in a stock market chart. For example, the first HiLoline is HiLoline 1.
Legend	The chart's legend.
Legend Entry *n*	One of the text entries inside of a legend. For example, the first item in the legend is Legend Entry 1.
Legend Key *n*	One of the keys inside of a legend. For example, the key for the first item in the legend is Legend Key 1.
Plot	The chart's plot area — the actual chart, without the legend.
Seriesline *n*	A line that connects a series. For example, the first series line is Seriesline 1.
S*n*	A data series. For example, the first data series is S1.
S*n*E	Error bars for a series. For example, the error bars for the first data series is S1E.
S*n*P*k*	A point in a data series. For example, the second point in the first data series is S1P2.

(continued)

Part	Description
Table 16-1 *(continued)*	
Part	*Description*
S*n*T*k*	A trendline for a data series. For example, the first trendline for the first data series is S1T1.
Text Axis *n*	An axis label. For example, the label for the value axis is Text Axis 1.
Text S*n*	Data labels for a series. For example, Text S1 are data labels for the first series.
Text S*n*P*k*	A data label for a point in a series. For example, the data label for the second point in the first data series is S1P2.
Title	The chart's title.
Upbar *n*	A bar in a stock market chart. For example, the first Upbar is Upbar 1.
Walls	The walls of a 3-D chart only (except 3-D pie charts).

Using the Format dialog box

When a chart element is selected, you can use the menu to work with the selected item. Or, you can right-click and use the shortcut menu. You'll notice that Excel's menus are different when a chart is activated. For example, the Insert menu lets you insert items that are relevant to a chart (titles, a legend, and so on).

Most of the chart formatting that you do occurs in a Format dialog box. Each chart element has a unique Format dialog box. You can access this dialog by using any of the following methods:

✦ Select the Format⇨Selected *Part Name* command (the Format menu displays the actual name of the selected part).

✦ Double-click on a chart part.

✦ Press Ctrl+1.

✦ Right-click on the chart element and choose the Format command from the shortcut menu.

Any of these methods displays a tabbed Format dialog box that lets you make many changes to the selected chart element. For example, Figure 16-1 shows the dialog box that appears when the chart's title is selected.

I discuss the various types of chart modification in detail in the sections that follow.

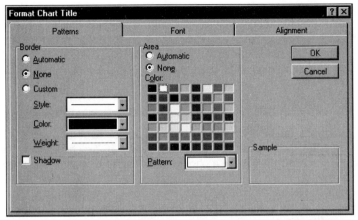

Figure 16-1: The Format dialog box for a chart's title. Each chart part has its own Format dialog box.

Chart Background Elements

As I mention in the preceding section, a chart is made up of many elements. In this section, I discuss two of those elements: the Chart area and the Plot area. These chart items provide a background for other elements in the chart.

The Chart area

The Chart area is an object that contains all other elements in the chart. You can think of it as a chart's master background. You can't change the size of the Chart area. For an embedded chart, it's always the same size as the chart object. For a chart sheet, the Chart area is always the entire sheet.

The Format Chart Area dialog box contains two tabs: Patterns and Font. The Patterns panel lets you change the Chart area's color and patterns and add a border if you like. The Font panel lets you change the properties of *all fonts used in the chart*. Changing the font won't affect fonts that you have previously changed, however. For example, if you make the chart's title 20-point Arial and then change the font to 8-point Arial in the Format Chart Area dialog box, the title's font won't be affected.

The Plot area

The Chart area contains the Plot area, which is the part of the chart that contains the actual chart. Unlike the Chart area, you can resize and reposition the Plot area. The Format Plot area dialog box has only one tab: Patterns. This lets you change the color and pattern of the plot area and also adjust its borders.

Tip   When a chart element is selected, you'll find that many of the toolbar buttons that you normally use for worksheet formatting also work with the selected chart part. For example, if you select the chart's Plot area, you can change its color by using the Color tool on the Formatting toolbar.

Working with Chart Titles

To add titles to a chart, use the Insert⇨Titles command. Excel displays a dialog box that lists the possible titles that a chart can have (see Figure 16-2). The list of titles varies depending on the chart type. Place a check mark next to those that you want to add, and Excel adds dummy titles to the chart. Excel may decrease the size of the plot area to make room for the titles. To edit the text in the titles, select it and enter the new title in the formula bar. Or, you can edit the title in place by selecting the text itself and modifying it directly.

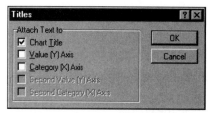

Figure 16-2: The Titles dialog box lets you add titles to a chart.

The titles that Excel adds are placed in the appropriate position, but you can drag them anywhere.

To modify a chart title's properties, access its Format dialog box. This dialog box has tabs for the following:

✦ **Patterns:** For changing the background color and borders

✦ **Font:** For changing the font, size, color, and attributes

✦ **Alignment:** For adjusting the vertical and horizontal alignment and orientation

Tip   Text in a chart is not limited to titles. In fact, you can add free-floating text anywhere you want. To do so, select any part of the chart except a title or data label. Then enter the text in the formula bar. Excel adds a text box in the center of the chart. You can move the text box wherever you want it and format it to your liking.

Working with the Legend

If you created your chart with the ChartWizard, you had an option to include a legend. If you change your mind, you can easily delete the legend or add one if it doesn't exist.

To add a legend to your chart, use the Insert⇨Legend command. If the chart already has a legend, this command has no effect. To remove a legend, select it and press Delete. To move a legend, click on it and drag it to the desired location. Or, you can use the legend's Format dialog box to position the legend (using the Placement panel).

The legend consists of text and keys. A *key* is a small graphic that corresponds to the chart's series. You can select individual text items within a legend and format them separately using the Format Legend Entry dialog (which has only a single panel: Font). For example, you may want to make the text bold to draw attention to a particular data series.

Tip
The Legend tool in the Chart toolbar acts as a toggle. Use this button to add a legend if one doesn't exist and to remove the legend if one exists.

Tip
After you move a legend from its default position, you may want to change the size of the Plot area to fill in the gap left by the legend. Just select the Plot area and drag a border to make it the desired size.

If you didn't include legend text when you originally selected the cells to create the chart, Excel displays *Series 1, Series 2,* and so on in the legend. To add series names, select a chart series and bring up its Format Data Series dialog box. Choose the Name and Values tab. In the Name box, enter a cell reference that contains the label, or enter a label formula directly (for example, **="First Quarter"**).

The Format Legend dialog box has the following tabs:

  ✦ **Patterns:** For changing the background color and border

  ✦ **Font:** For changing the font, size, color, and attributes

  ✦ **Placement:** For specifying where the legend will be positioned in the chart

Changing Gridlines

Gridlines can help you determine what the chart series represent numerically. Gridlines simply extend the tick marks on the axes. Some charts look better with gridlines, whereas others appear more cluttered. It's up to you to decide whether gridlines can enhance your chart. Sometimes, horizontal gridlines alone are enough, although XY charts often benefit from both horizontal and vertical gridlines.

To add or remove gridlines, use the Insert⇨Gridlines command. The Gridlines dialog box is shown in Figure 16-3. Each axis has two sets of gridlines: major and minor. Major units are the ones displaying a label. Minor units are those in between. You can choose which to add or remove by checking or unchecking the appropriate check boxes. If you're working with a true 3-D chart, the dialog box has options for three sets of gridlines.

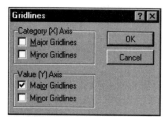

Figure 16-3: The Gridlines dialog box lets you add or remove gridlines from the chart.

Tip
The Horizontal Gridlines tool in the Chart toolbar serves as a gridline toggle. Use this tool to add horizontal gridlines if the chart doesn't have them and to remove the horizontal gridlines if they already exist.

To modify the properties of a set of gridlines, select one gridline in the set and access the Format Gridlines dialog box. This dialog has two tabs:

✦ **Patterns:** For changing the line style, width, and color

✦ **Scale:** For adjusting the scale used on the axis

Cross-
Reference
I discuss scaling in detail in the next section on chart axes.

Modifying the Axes

Charts vary in the number of axes that they use. Pie and doughnut charts have no axes. All 2-D charts have two axes (three if you use a secondary x-axis), and true 3-D charts have three axes. Excel gives you a great deal of control over these axes. To modify any aspect of an axis, access its Format Axis dialog box. The Format Axis dialog box has five tabs:

✦ **Patterns:** For changing the axis line width, tick marks, and placement of tick-mark labels

✦ **Scale:** For adjusting the minimum and maximum axis values, units for major and minor gridlines, and other properties

✦ **Font:** For adjusting the font used for the axis labels

✦ **Number:** For adjusting the number format for the axis labels

✦ **Alignment:** For specifying the orientation for the axis labels

Because the axes' properties can dramatically affect the chart's look, I discuss the Patterns and Scale dialog box tabs separately in the following sections.

Axes patterns

Figure 16-4 shows the Patterns panel of the Format Axis dialog box.

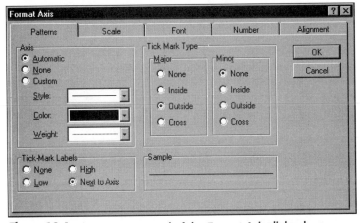

Figure 16-4: The Patterns panel of the Format Axis dialog box.

This panel has three sections:

Axis: This controls the line characteristics of the axis itself (the style, color, and weight of the line).

Tick-Mark Labels: This controls where the axis labels appear. Normally, the labels appear next to the axis. You can, however, specify that the labels appear High (at the top of the chart), Low (at the bottom of the chart), or not at all (None). These options are useful when the axis doesn't appear in its normal position at the edge of the Plot area.

Tick (per screen shot) Mark Type: This controls how the tick marks appear. You can select None (no tick marks), Inside (inside the axis), Outside (outside the axis), or Cross (on both sides of the axis).

Note   Major tick marks are the axis tick marks that normally have labels next to them. Minor
tick marks are in between the major tick marks.

Axes scales

Adjusting the scale of a value axis can have a dramatic affect on the chart's appearance. Manipulating the scale can present a false picture of the data in some cases.
Figure 16-5 shows two charts that use the same data; the only difference is that I've
adjusted the Minimum value on the vertical axis scale. In the first chart, the differences are quite apparent. In the second chart, there appears to be little difference
between the data points.

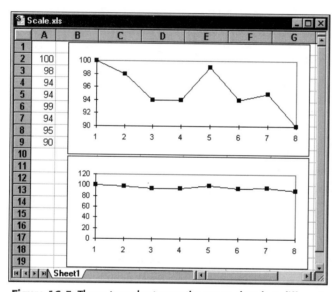

Figure 16-5: These two charts use the same data but different scales.

The actual scale that you use depends on the situation. No hard-and-fast rules exist
about scale, except that you should avoid misrepresenting data by manipulating the
chart to prove a point that doesn't exist.

If you're preparing several charts that use similarly scaled data, keep the scales the
same so that the charts can be compared more easily. The charts in Figure 16-6 show
the distribution of responses for a survey. Because the same scale was not used,
however, comparing the responses across survey items is difficult. All charts in the
series should have the same scale.

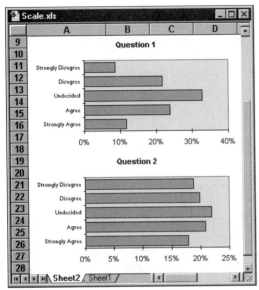

Figure 16-6: These charts use different scales on the value axis, making it difficult to compare the two.

Excel determines the scale for your charts automatically. You can, however, override Excel's choice in the Scale panel of the Format Axis dialog box (see Figure 16-7).

Note

The Scale panel varies slightly depending on which axis is selected.

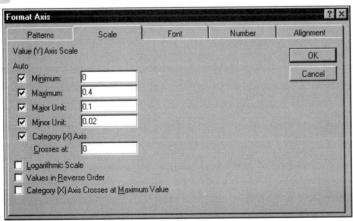

Figure 16-7: The Scale panel of the Format Axis dialog box.

This dialog box offers the following options:

Minimum: For entering a minimum value for the axis. If the check box is checked, Excel determines this value automatically.

Maximum: For entering a maximum value for the axis. If the check box is checked, Excel determines this value automatically.

Major Unit: For entering the number of units between major tick marks. If the check box is checked, Excel determines this value automatically.

Minor Unit: For entering the number of units between minor tick marks. If the check box is checked, Excel determines this value automatically.

***Axis Type* Axis Crosses at:** For positioning the axes at a different location. By default, it's at the edge of the plot area. The exact wording of this option varies, depending on which axis is selected.

Logarithmic Scale: For using a logarithmic scale for the axes. A log scale primarily is useful for scientific applications in which the values to be plotted have an extremely large range. You receive an error message if the scale includes 0 or negative values.

Values in Reverse Order: For making the scale values extend in the opposite direction. For a Value axis, for example, selecting this option displays the smallest scale value at the top and the largest at the bottom (the opposite of how it normally appears).

***Axis Type* Crosses at Maximum Value:** For positioning the axes at the maximum value of the perpendicular axis (normally, the axis is positioned at the minimum value of the perpendicular axis). The exact wording of this option varies, depending on which axis is selected.

Working with Data Series

Every chart is made up of one or more series, which are based on data stored in a worksheet. This data translates into chart columns, lines, pie slices, and so on. This section discusses most of the customizations that you can perform with chart data series.

To work with a data series, you must select it first. Activate the chart and then click on the data series that you want to select. In a column chart, click on a column; in a line chart, click on a line; and so on. When you select a data series, Excel displays the series name in the Name box (for example, S1), and the SERIES formula in the formula bar. A selected data series has a small square on each element of the series.

Many customizations that you perform with a data series use the Format Data Series dialog box, which has up to seven tabs. The number of tabs varies, depending on the type of chart. For example, a pie chart has five tabs, and a 3-D column chart has four tabs. Line and column charts have six tabs, and XY (Scatter) charts have all seven. The possible tabs in the Format Data Series dialog are as follows:

Axis: For specifying which value axis to use for the selected data series. This is applicable only if the chart has two value axes.

Data Labels: For displaying labels next to each data point.

Name and Values: For changing the range used for the Y values and the series name.

Patterns: For changing the color, pattern, and border style for the data series. For line charts, change the color and style of the data marker in this tab.

X Error Bars: For adding or modifying error bars for the Y axis. This is available only for XY charts.

X Values: For changing the range used for the X values (or category labels).

Y Error Bars: For adding of modifying error bars for the Y axis.

I discuss many of these dialog box options in the sections that follow.

Note In addition to the formatting that you can apply using the Format Data Series dialog box, you can perform additional formatting for the chart type group. For example, if you're working with a line chart, you can use the Format⇨Line Group command to apply formats to all lines in the chart. I explain this concept later, in the discussion of combination charts.

Deleting a data series

To delete a data series in a chart, select the data series and press the Delete key. The data series is removed from the chart. The data in the worksheet, of course, remains intact.

Note It's possible to delete all data series from a chart. If so, the chart appears empty. It still retains its settings, however. Therefore, you can add a data series to an empty chart, and it will look like a chart again.

Adding a new data series to a chart

It's common to have to add another data series to an existing chart. You *could* re-create the chart and include the new data series, but it's usually easier to add the data to the existing chart. Excel provides several ways to add a new data series to a chart:

✦ Activate the chart and then click on the ChartWizard tool. You get the first ChartWizard dialog box (the one that displays the range to be plotted). Edit the range reference to include the new data series — or point to the new range in the worksheet. Click on Finish and Excel updates the chart with the new data.

✦ Activate the chart and select the Insert⇨New Data command. Excel displays a dialog box that prompts you for the range of data to add to the chart.

✦ Select the range to be added and copy it to the Clipboard. Then, activate the chart and choose the Edit⇨Paste Special command. Excel responds with the dialog box shown in Figure 16-8. Complete this dialog box to correspond to the data that you selected.

✦ Select the range to be added and drag it into the chart. When you release the mouse button, Excel updates the chart with the data you dragged in. This technique works only if the chart is embedded on the worksheet.

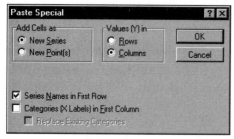

Figure 16-8: Using the Paste Special dialog box is one way to add new data to a chart.

Changing data used by a series

Often, you create a chart that uses a particular range of data, and then you extend the range by adding new data points in the worksheet. For example, the previous month's sales data arrives in your office, and you enter the numbers into your sales-tracking worksheet. On the other hand, you may delete some of the data points in a range that is plotted. For example, you may not need to plot older information. In either case, you'll find that the chart doesn't update itself automatically. When you add new data to a range, it isn't included in the data series. If you delete data from a range, the chart displays the deleted data as zero values.

To update the chart to reflect the new data range, activate the chart, select the data series, and access the Format Data Series dialog box. Select the tab labeled Name and Values (see Figure 16-9). The dialog box shows the chart and lists the formula that specifies the data used (this is in the box labeled Y Values). To change the range, edit this formula so that it refers to the range you want to use in the chart. You also can select the Y Values box and point to the new range in the worksheet. When you close the dialog box, the chart is updated with the new data range.

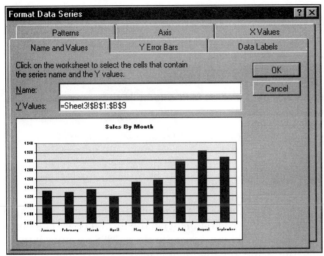

Figure 16-9: You can modify the data series in the Name and Values tab of the Format Data Series dialog box.

Editing the SERIES formula

Every data series in a chart has an associated SERIES formula. This formula appears in the formula bar when you select a data series in a chart (see Figure 16-10). You can edit the range references in the SERIES formula directly. You can even enter a new SERIES formula manually — which adds a new series to the chart (there are, however, easier ways to do this, as I describe previously).

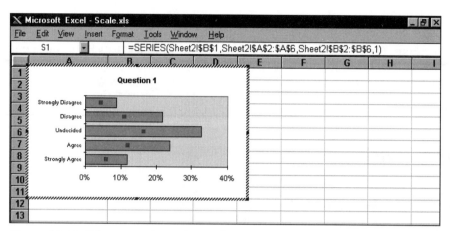

Figure 16-10: When you select a data series, its SERIES formula appears in the formula bar.

A SERIES formula consists of a SERIES function with four arguments. The syntax is as follows:

```
=SERIES(Name_ref,Categories,Values,Plot_order)
```

Excel uses absolute cell references in the SERIES function. To change the data that a series uses, edit the cell references (third argument) in the formula bar. The first and second arguments are optional and may not appear in the SERIES formula. If the series doesn't have a name, the Name_ref argument is missing and Excel uses dummy series names in the legend (Series1, Series2, and so on) . If there are no category names, the Categories argument is missing and Excel uses dummy labels (1, 2, 3, and so on).

Caution   If the data series uses category labels, make sure that you adjust the reference for the category labels also. This is the second argument in the SERIES formula.

Using Names in SERIES formulas

A better way to handle data ranges that change is to use named ranges. Create names for the data ranges that you use in the chart, and then edit the SERIES formula. Replace each range references with the corresponding range name.

After making this change, the chart uses the named ranges. If you change the definition for a name, the chart is updated.

Displaying data labels in a chart

Sometimes, you want your chart to display the actual data values for each point. Or, you may want to display the category label for each data point. Figure 16-11 shows an example of both of these options.

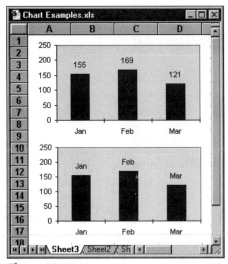

Figure 16-11: One series has data labels for each data point; the other series has category labels for each point.

You specify data labels in the Data Labels panel of the Format Data Series dialog box (see Figure 16-12). This panel has several options. Note that not all options are available for all chart types. If you select the check box labeled Show Legend Key next to Label, each label displays its legend key next to it.

The data labels are linked to the worksheet, so if your data changes, the labels also change. If you would like to override the data label with other text, select the label and enter the new text (or even a cell reference) in the formula bar.

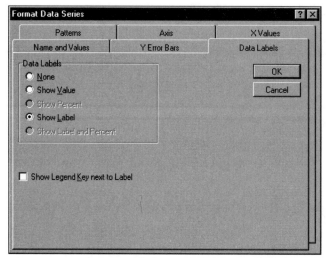

Figure 16-12: The Data Labels panel of the Format Data Series dialog box.

Often, you'll find that the data labels aren't positioned properly — for example, a label may be obscured by another data point. If you select an individual label, you can drag it to a better location.

Tip After adding data labels to a series, format the labels by using the Format Data Labels dialog box.

As you work with data labels, you may discover that Excel's data labels feature leaves a bit to be desired. For example, it would be nice to be able to specify a range of text to be used for the data labels. This would be particularly useful in XY charts in which you want to identify each data point with a particular text item. Unfortunately, this isn't possible. The only way to accomplish this task is to add data labels and then edit each one manually.

Handling missing data

Sometimes, data that you're charting may be missing one or more data points. Excel offers several options on how to handle the missing data. You don't control this in the Format Data Series dialog box (as you might expect). Rather, you must use the Chart panel of the Options dialog box, which is shown in Figure 16-13.

Note The options that you set apply to the entire active chart, and you can't set a different option for different series in the same chart. A chart must be activated when you open the Options dialog box, or the options are grayed out.

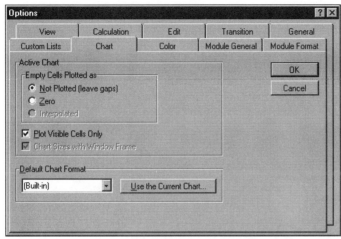

Figure 16-13: The Chart panel of the Options dialog box.

The options in the Chart panel are as follows:

Not Plotted (leave gaps): Missing data is simply ignored, and the data series will have a gap.

Zero: Missing data is treated as zero.

Interpolated: Missing data is calculated using data on either side of the missing point(s).

Controlling a data series by hiding data

Usually, Excel doesn't plot data that is in a hidden row or column. You can sometimes use this to your advantage because it's an easy way to control what data appears in the chart. If you're working with outlines or data filtering (both of which use hidden rows), however, you may not like the idea that hidden data is removed from your chart. To override this, activate the chart, access the Chart Options dialog box, and remove the check mark from the check box labeled Plot Visible Cells Only.

Note The Plot Visible Cells Only option applies only to the active chart. A chart must be activated when you open the Options dialog box. Otherwise, the option is grayed out.

Adding error bars

For certain chart types, you can add error bars to your chart. Error bars often are used to indicate "plus or minus" information that reflects uncertainty in the data. Error bars are appropriate only for area, bar, column, line, and XY charts. Click on the Y Error Bars tab in the Format Data Series dialog box to display the options shown in Figure 16-14.

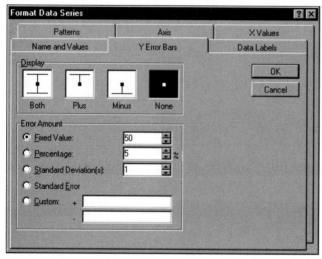

Figure 16-14: The Y Error Bars tab of the Format Data Series dialog box.

Excel enables you to specify several different types of error bars:

Fixed Value: The error bars are fixed by an amount you specify.

Percentage: The error bars are a percentage of each value.

Standard Deviation(s): The error bars are in the number of standard deviation units that you specify (Excel calculates the standard deviation of the data series).

Standard Error: The error bars are one standard error unit (Excel calculates the standard error of the data series).

Custom: You set the error bar units for the upper or lower error bars. You can either enter a value or a range reference that holds the error values you want to plot as error bars.

Figure 16-15 shows a chart with error bars added. After you add error bars, you can access the Format Error Bars dialog box to modify the error bars. For example, you can control the line style and color of the error bars.

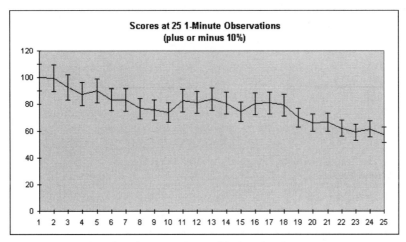

Figure 16-15: This chart has error bars added to the data series.

Note

A data series in an XY chart can have error bars for both the X values and Y values.

Adding a trendline

When you're plotting data over time, you may want to plot a trendline that describes the data. A trendline points out general trends in your data. In some cases, you can forecast future data with trendlines. Excel makes adding a trendline to a chart quite simple. Although you might expect this option to be in the Format Data Series dialog box, it's not. The place to go is the Insert⇨Trendline command. This command is available only when a data series is selected. Figure 16-16 shows the Trendline dialog box.

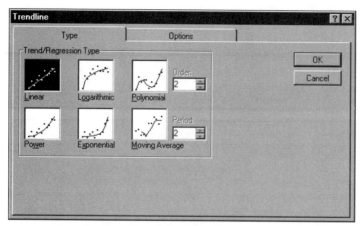

Figure 16-16: The Trendline dialog box offers several different types of automatic trendlines.

The type of trendline that you choose depends on your data. Linear trends are most common, but some data can be described more effectively with another type. One of the options on the Type tab is Moving Average, which is useful for smoothing out "noisy" data. The Moving Average option enables you to specify the number of data points to be included in each average. For example, if you select 5, Excel averages every 5 data points.

When you click on the Options tab in the Trendline dialog box, Excel displays the options shown in Figure 16-17.

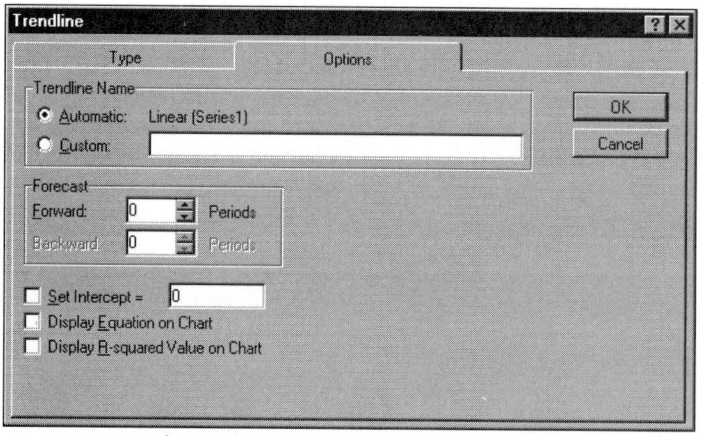

Figure 16-17: The Options tab in the Trendline dialog box enables you to smooth or forecast data.

The Options tab enables you to specify a name to appear in the legend and the number of periods that you want to forecast. Two additional options enable you to specify that the equation used for the trendline appear on the chart and that the R^2 value appear on the chart.

Figure 16-18 shows two charts. The chart on the left depicts scores for 25 observations. The chart on the right is the same chart, but a linear trendline has been added that shows the trend in the data.

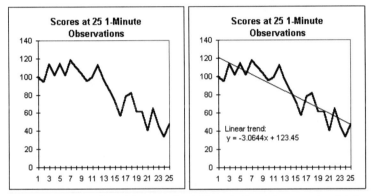

Figure 16-18: Before (chart on the left) and after (chart on the right) adding a linear trendline to a chart.

When Excel inserts a trendline, it may look like a new data series, but it's not. It's a new chart element with a name such as S2T1 (series 2, trendline 1). You can double-click on a trendline to change its formatting.

Creating Combination Charts

A combination chart is a single chart that consists of series that use different chart types. For example, you may have a chart that shows both columns and lines. A combination chart also can use a single type (all columns, for example) but include a second value axis.

The easiest way to create a combination chart is to choose the Combination option in the second step of the ChartWizard. The ChartWizard then presents you with six combination chart subtypes in the next step.

You also can convert an existing chart to a combination chart by changing the chart type for a series. For example, if a chart has two data series (both columns), you can convert one of the series to another type, such as a line. Select the series that you want to change and select the Format⇨Chart Type command (this command is also available from the shortcut menu). Select the chart type for the series and make sure that the Selected Series option is selected. The chart is converted to a combination chart.

Excel offers great flexibility in this area, but you can't combine 2-D and 3-D charts. In addition, not all chart types mix well together. For example, Excel allows you to mix a pie chart and a column chart — but you probably wouldn't want to. As always, if you don't like what you see, choose Edit⇨Undo and try again.

Using secondary axes

If you need to plot data series that have drastically different scales, you probably want to use a secondary scale. For example, assume that you want to create a chart that shows monthly sales along with the average amount sold per customer. These two data series use different scales (the average sales values are much smaller than the total sales). Consequently, the average sales data range will be virtually invisible in the chart. The solution is to use a secondary axis for the second data series. Figure 16-19 shows two charts. The first uses a single value axis, and the second data series is hardly visible. The second chart uses a secondary axis for the second data series — which makes it easy to see.

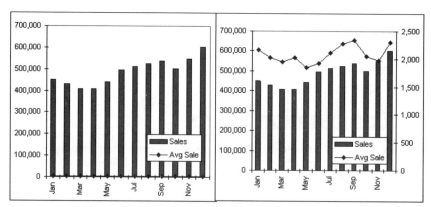

Figure 16-19: These charts show the same data, but the chart on the right uses a secondary axis for the second data series.

Formatting chart type groups

A chart is made up of one or more chart type groups. For example, a plain bar chart has one chart type group (a bar chart type). A combination chart that uses columns and lines has two chart type groups (a column chart type and a line chart type). Excel lets you work with an entire chart type group, which includes all data series for a particular chart type.

When a chart is activated, the Format menu includes a command for each chart type group in the chart. If you're working with a chart that has both columns and lines, the Format menu has a Column Group command and a Line Group command. Choosing one of these commands displays a tabbed dialog box that lets you adjust properties of the chart type group. The dialog box varies with the chart type group. Figure 16-20 shows the Format Column Group dialog box.

Note You can make changes to a chart type group even if your chart isn't a combination chart.

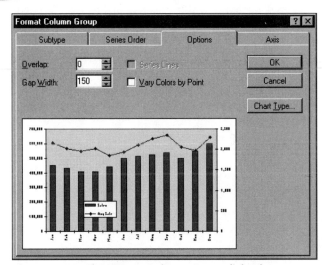

Figure 16-20: The Format Column Group dialog box.

Following are the tabs that you encounter in various Format Group dialog boxes (not all chart type groups have all these tabs):

Subtype: For specifying a different chart subtype. For example, if the chart type group is a column chart, you can change it to a stacked column chart.

Series Order: For adjusting the order in which the series are plotted. This is useful with true 3-D charts.

Options: Presents various options, depending on the chart type group. For example, with a column chart type group, you can adjust the width of the gaps between columns, the degree of overlap of the columns, and other options.

Axes: For specifying which value axis to use for the column group. This is applicable only if the chart has two value axes.

Creating Custom AutoFormats

Excel has more than 100 predefined chart AutoFormats. When you use the ChartWizard to create a chart, you first choose the basic chart type and then select an AutoFormat. Despite the variety of AutoFormats, it's not uncommon to discover that none of the AutoFormats suits the bill. Fortunately, Excel lets you create custom AutoFormats. You can apply a custom AutoFormat to a newly created chart and save a great deal of time.

The first step in designing an AutoFormat is to create a chart that's customized the way you want. For example, you can set any of the colors or line styles, change the scales, modify fonts and type sizes, add gridlines, add a title, and even add free-floating text or graphics images.

When you're satisfied with the chart, choose Format⇨AutoFormat. Alternatively, you can right-click on any chart object; when the shortcut menu appears, choose AutoFormat. In either case, a dialog box appears like the one shown in Figure 16-21.

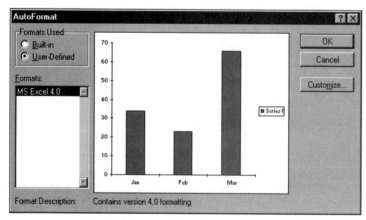

Figure 16-21: The AutoFormat dialog box.

In the Formats Used group box, select the Used-Defined option. The list box beneath it changes to a list of all the custom AutoFormats currently defined. If you haven't defined any AutoFormats, only one is listed: MS Excel 4.0. The MS Excel 4.0 AutoFormat applies the default formatting used in Excel 4's charts.

To create a new AutoFormat based on the current chart, click on the Customize button (which appears when you select the User-Defined option). Another dialog box appears that lists all the defined AutoFormats. Add a new AutoFormat or delete an existing one from this dialog box. To add your new AutoFormat, click on the Add button, which brings up the dialog box shown in Figure 16-22.

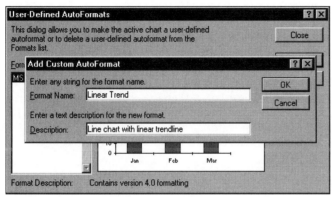

Figure 16-22: The Add Custom AutoFormat dialog box.

Type a name for the AutoFormat in the top text box and a description in the bottom text box. Click on OK to return to the previous step, and then click on the Close button to return to your chart. The AutoFormat name that you supplied now appears whenever you choose the Format⇨AutoFormat command and click on the User-Defined option.

How custom AutoFormats are stored

Custom AutoFormats are stored in a workbook named X15galry, located in the XLStart folder. If you open X15galry you can see that it contains only chart sheets — one for each AutoFormat defined.

Also notice that the series formulas for these charts don't refer to actual worksheet ranges. Rather, the series formulas use arrays entered directly into the series formulas. This makes the charts completely independent of any specific worksheet range.

If you need to make a minor modification to a custom AutoFormat — change a color, for example — you can make the change directly in the X15galry file and then save the file.

If you want your coworkers to have access to your custom AutoFormats, you can copy your X15galry file into their XLstart folder. By copying the file, you enable everyone in your workgroup to produce consistent-looking charts. Be aware, however, that if you replace an existing copy of X15galry with a new one, any custom AutoFormats in the replaced file is lost.

Working with 3-D Charts

One of the more interesting classes of Excel charts is its 3-D charts. Certain situations benefit by the use of 3-D charts because you can depict changes over two different dimensions. Even a simple column chart can command more attention if you present it as a 3-D chart. As I discussed in Chapter 13, not all 3-D charts are true 3-D charts. A true 3-D chart has three axes. Some of Excel's 3-D charts are simply 2-D charts with a perspective look to them.

Modifying 3-D charts

All 3-D charts have a few additional parts that you can customize. For example, most 3-D charts have a *floor* and *walls,* and the true 3-D charts also have an additional axis. You can select these chart elements and format them to your liking. I won't go into the details here because the formatting options are quite straightforward. Generally, 3-D formatting options work just like the other chart elements I discuss.

Rotating 3-D charts

When you start flirting with the third dimension, however, you need to be aware that some data may be completely or partially obscured. Figure 16-23 shows a 3-D bar chart that displays sales data by quarter and by region. Notice, however, that not all columns are visible. Rather than abandon this chart type, it can be salvaged simply by rotating the chart to a more favorable position. You can rotate the chart in one of the following two ways:

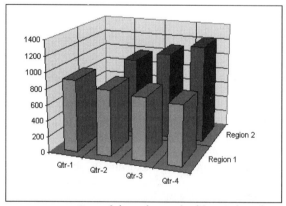

Figure 16-23: One of the columns in this 3-D bar chart is obscured by the columns in front.

✦ Activate the 3-D chart and choose the Format➪3-D View command. The dialog box shown in Figure 16-24 appears. You can make your rotations and perspective changes by clicking the appropriate controls. The sample that you see in the dialog box is *not* your actual chart. The displayed sample just gives you an idea of the types of changes that you're making. Make the adjustments and choose OK to make them permanent (or click on Apply to apply them to your chart without closing the dialog box).

✦ Rotate the chart in real time by dragging corners with the mouse. Click on one of the corners of the chart. Black handles appear and the word *Corners* appears in the Name box. You can drag one of these black handles and rotate the chart's 3-D box to your satisfaction. This method definitely takes some practice. If your chart gets totally messed up, choose Format➪3-D View and then select the Default button to return to the standard 3-D view.

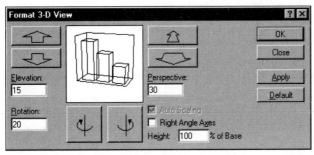

Figure 16-24: The 3-D View dialog box enables you to rotate and change the perspective of a 3-D chart. You also can drag the chart with the mouse.

Tip   When rotating a 3-D chart, hold down the Ctrl key while you drag to see an outline of the entire chart — not just the axes. This technique is helpful because when you drag only the chart's axes, you can easily lose your bearings and end up with a strange-looking chart.

The rotated chart with all bars visible is shown in Figure 16-25.

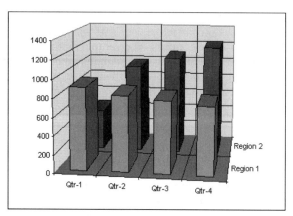

Figure 16-25: The chart from Figure 16-23 after rotating it. Now all columns are visible.

Chart-Making Tricks

In this section, I share chart-making tricks that I've picked up over the years. Some use little-known features, and others are undocumented as far as I can tell. Several tricks let you make charts that you may have considered impossible to create.

Changing a worksheet value by dragging

Excel provides an interesting chart-making feature that also can be somewhat dangerous. This feature lets you change the value in a worksheet by dragging the data markers on two-dimensional line charts, bar charts, column charts, and XY charts.

Here's how it works. Select an individual data point in a chart series (not the entire series) and then drag the black square in the direction in which you want to adjust the value. As you drag the data marker, the corresponding value in the worksheet changes to correspond to the data point's new position on the chart.

If the value of a data point you move is the result of a formula, Excel displays the Goal Seek dialog box (I discuss goal seeking in Chapter 27). Use this dialog box to specify the cell that Excel should adjust in order to make the formula produce the result you pointed out on the chart. This technique is useful if you know what a chart should look like, and you want to determine the values that will produce the chart. Obviously, this feature also can be dangerous because you can inadvertently change values that you shouldn't — so be careful.

Using relative names in SERIES formulas

One of my favorite charting tricks is to use relative names in SERIES formulas. This creates a chart that is based on the data relative to the current cell pointer. I discuss using relative names in Chapter 8, and this is an excellent practical use for the technique.

To demonstrate how it works, I'll create a simple example. The workbook shown in Figure 16-26 contains monthly data for January 1992 through December 1996. The chart plots the entire data series.

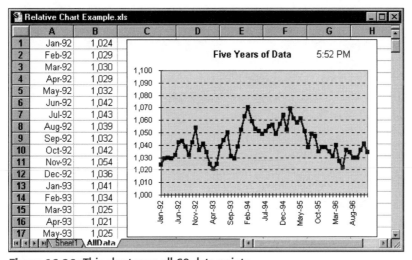

Figure 16-26: This chart uses all 60 data points.

The goal of this exercise is to modify the chart so that it shows only six data points at a time — the data in the row that the cell point is in plus the five rows below it. In other words, the data displayed in the chart will depend on the cell pointer's position.

1. Create a relative name for the months. Select the range A1:A6 and choose the Insert⇨Name⇨Define command. Enter **MonthLabels** for the name and edit the Refers to box so that it reads **=Sheet1!$A1:$A6**.

2. Create a relative name for the data. Select the range B1:B6 and choose the Insert⇨Name⇨Define command. Enter **Data** for the name and edit the Refers to box so that it reads **=Sheet1!$B1:$B6**.

3. Activate the chart and edit the SERIES formula so that it reads:

```
=SERIES(,RELATIVE.XLS!MonthsLabels,RELATIVE.XLS!Data,1)
```

The chart updates to reflect the new range. Notice, however, that it isn't working as planned. If you move the cell pointer to a new row, the chart doesn't update.

4. Here's where the trick comes in. You need to add a volatile function to the worksheet. A volatile function causes the worksheet to recalculate and the range names to be updated. Enter the following into any blank cell: **=NOW()**.

After entering the volatile function, move the cell pointer to any row between row 1 and 55 and press F9 to recalculate. The chart displays the data beginning in the row. Figure 16-27 shows an example.

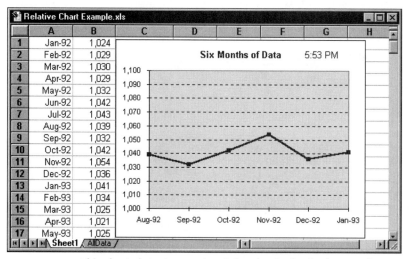

Figure 16-27: This chart plots six months of data beginning in the row that contains the cell pointer.

On the CD-ROM This workbook, named RELATIVE.XLS, is available on the accompanying CD-ROM. You'll also find a more sophisticated example of this technique in the workbook named TIDE.XLS. This example displays a chart of daily tides for La Jolla, California, based on the row that the cell pointer is in.

Unlinking a chart from its data range

A nice thing about charts is that they are linked to data stored in a worksheet. You also can unlink a data series, however, so that it no longer relies on the worksheet data.

To unlink a data series, select it and activate the formula bar. Press F9 and the series formula converts its range references to arrays that hold the values (see Figure 16-28). If you unlink all of the series in the chart, you create a dead graph that uses no data in a worksheet. You can edit the individual values in the arrays if you like, however.

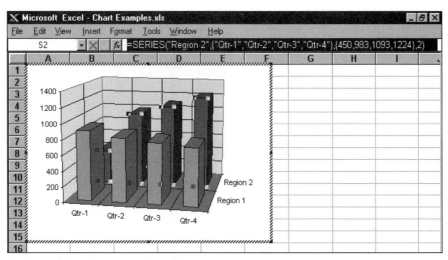

Figure 16-28: This data series no longer uses data in a worksheet.

Creating picture charts

Most users don't realize it, but Excel lets you replace bars, columns, or line chart markers with graphic images. Figures 16-29 and 16-30 show examples of this technique. In the first chart, I replaced columns with pictures of a cow, the topic of the chart. In the second chart, I replaced the line markers with gender symbols. These symbols not only make the chart more interesting but also may eliminate the need for a legend.

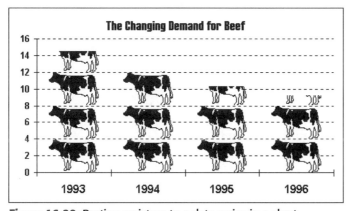

Figure 16-29: Pasting a picture to a data series in a chart.

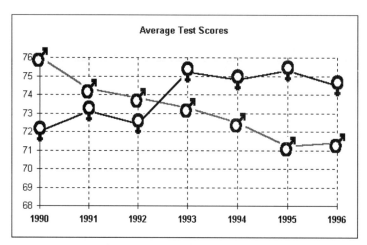

Figure 16-30: Pasting a picture to data markers in a line chart.

This chart technique has limitations. You can only paste pictures into four chart types: columns, bars, lines, and XY (2-D charts only). Adding pictures to your charts, however, is quite simple and uses the standard Windows copy and paste procedures.

The first step is to locate the image that you want and copy it to the Clipboard. Generally, simpler images work better. You may want to paste it into Excel first, where you can adjust the size, remove the borders, and add a background color. When the image is on the Clipboard, activate the chart, select the data series, and choose the Edit⇨Copy command. Your chart is converted. You also can paste the image to a single point in the data series, rather than the entire data series. Just select the point before you paste.

Column and bar charts with pictures pasted in them have a different Patterns panel in their Format Data Series dialog box. The panel gives you options that affect how the image will appear.

Tip   You also can copy data contained in a cell as a picture and then paste this picture to a chart. This is particularly useful with symbol fonts such as Wingdings, which contains many interesting characters. To copy a cell as a picture, first format the cell as desired. You may want to turn off the gridlines because they will be copied, too. Then select the cell, press Shift, and choose the Edit⇨Copy Picture command. This copies the cell as a picture, which you can then paste to a chart data series.

Pasting linked pictures to charts

Another useful charting technique involves pasting linked pictures to a chart. Excel doesn't let you do this directly, but this pasting is possible if you know a few tricks. The technique is useful, for example, if you want your chart to include the data that's used by the chart (see Figure 16-31 for an example). If the data changes, the changes are reflected in the chart as well as in the linked picture.

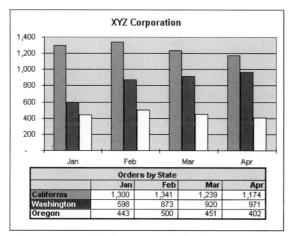

Figure 16-31: This chart uses a linked picture to display the data used in the chart series.

Here are the steps to create the linked picture:

1. Format the data range and create the chart.

2. Select the data range, press Shift, and select the Edit⇨Copy Picture command. Excel displays a dialog box — accept the default options. This copies the range to the Clipboard as a picture.

3. Activate the chart and paste the Clipboard contents. You'll probably have to resize the plot area to accommodate the pasted image.

4. The image that was pasted is a picture, but not a linked picture. To convert the image to a linked picture, select it and then enter the range reference in the formula bar (or simply point it out). For this example, I entered: **=Sheet1!B2:F6**.

The picture is now a linked picture. Changing any of the cells that are used in the chart's SERIES formula is reflected immediately in the linked picture. Other changes, such as formatting changes, won't appear until you activate the chart or change the data used by the chart.

Simple Gantt charts

It's not difficult to create a simple Gantt chart using Excel. *Gantt charts* are used to represent the time required to perform each task in a project. Figure 16-32 shows data that was used to create the Gantt chart in Figure 16-33.

	A	B	C	D	E
		Gantt.xls			
1	Task	Start Date	Duration	End Date	
2	Planning Meeting	2/14/96	1	2/14/96	
3	Develop Questionnaire	2/15/96	5	2/19/96	
4	Print and Mail Questionnaire	2/21/96	4	2/24/96	
5	Receive Responses	2/24/96	14	3/8/96	
6	Data Entry	2/27/96	20	3/17/96	
7	Data Analysis	3/20/96	5	3/24/96	
8	Write Report	3/22/96	9	3/30/96	
9	Distribute Draft Report	4/1/96	1	4/1/96	
10	Solicit Comments	4/2/96	5	4/6/96	
11	Finalize Report	4/7/96	3	4/9/96	
12	Distribute to Board	4/10/96	2	4/11/96	
13	Board Meeting	4/15/96	1	4/15/96	

Figure 16-32: Data used in the Gantt chart.

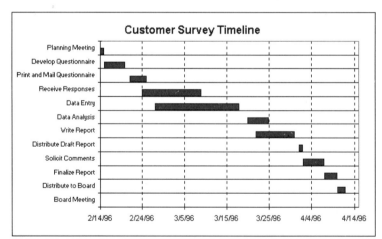

Figure 16-33: You can create a Gantt chart from a bar chart.

Here are the steps to create this chart:

1. Enter the data as shown in Figure 16-32. The formula in cell D2, which was copied to the rows below, is **=B2+C2-1**.

2. Create a stacked bar chart (AutoFormat 3) from the range A2:C13.

3. Adjust the horizontal axis Minimum and Maximum scale values to correspond to the earliest and latest dates in the data (note that you can enter a date into the Minimum or Maximum edit box).

4. Change the fill color of the first data series to None, and remove the borders from the first data series. This essentially makes the data series invisible.

5. Apply other formatting as desired.

Bubble charts

A *bubble chart* lets you display a third range of data in an XY chart. The size of each bubble is proportional to the data. Excel doesn't support bubble charts, but you can create them manually by pasting appropriately sized oval objects to individual markers in an XY chart. This is quite tedious, but it's possible.

On the CD-ROM The companion CD-ROM contains the shareware version of the Power Utility Pak. If you register the product, you get a utility that converts an XY (Scatter) chart into a bubble chart.

Figure 16-34 shows an example of a bubble chart created using the Power Utility Pak.

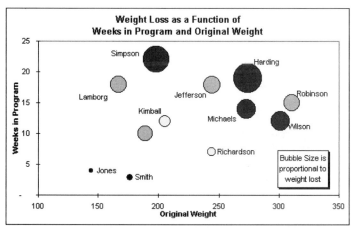

Figure 16-34: The Bubble ChartWizard in the Power Utility Pak converted this XY chart into a bubble chart.

Comparative histograms

With a bit of creativity, you can create charts that you may have considered impossible with Excel. For example, Figure 16-35 shows data that was used to create the comparative histogram chart shown in Figure 16-36. Such charts often display population data.

On the CD-ROM

This workbook, named COMPARAT.XLS, is included on the companion CD-ROM.

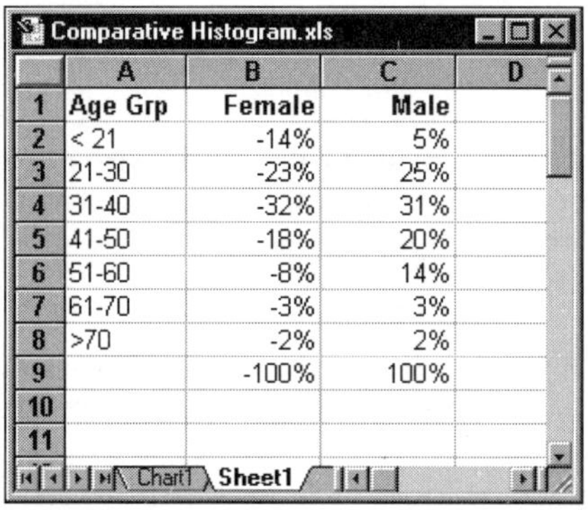

Comparative Histogram.xls

	A	B	C	D
1	Age Grp	Female	Male	
2	< 21	-14%	5%	
3	21-30	-23%	25%	
4	31-40	-32%	31%	
5	41-50	-18%	20%	
6	51-60	-8%	14%	
7	61-70	-3%	3%	
8	>70	-2%	2%	
9		-100%	100%	
10				
11				

Chart1 Sheet1

Figure 16-35: Data used in the comparative histogram chart.

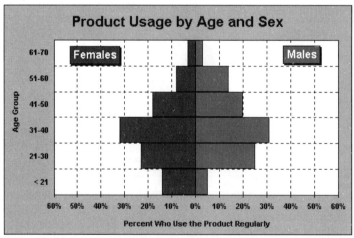

Figure 16-36: Producing this comparative histogram chart required a few tricks.

Here's how to create the chart:

1. Enter the data as shown in Figure 16-35. Notice that the values for females are entered as negative values.

2. Select A1:C8 and create a 2-D bar chart.

3. Apply the following custom number format to the horizontal axis: **0%;0%;0%**. This custom format eliminates the negative signs in the percentages.

4. On the horizontal axis, set the Minimum scale to –.6 and the Maximum scale to +.6. Remember, the negative percent values won't display the negative sign.

5. Select the vertical axis and remove all tick marks. Set the tick-mark labels option to Low. This will keep the axis in the center of the chart but will display the axis labels at the left side.

6. Choose the Format⇨1 Bar Group command and click on the Options panel. Set the Overlap to 100 and the Gap Width to 0.

7. Add two text boxes to the chart (**Females** and **Males**) to substitute for the legend.

8. Apply other formatting as desired.

Animated charts

In some cases, you may find it useful to create an animated chart — one that moves. Animating a chart involves changing the data that one or more chart series is using. The changes are made automatically, so this technique requires macros.

On the
CD-ROM A workbook, named ANIMATED.XLS, is included on the companion CD-ROM.

See-through charts

The Chart area of an embedded chart can be transparent, which exposes the information (and formatting) in the underlying cells. The result can be quite attractive, and you get effects that are otherwise difficult or impossible to create. Figure 16-37 shows an example of such a chart. I used two utilities from the Power Utility Pak to create the 3-D effects: 3-D Cell Shading and Insert 3-D Text.

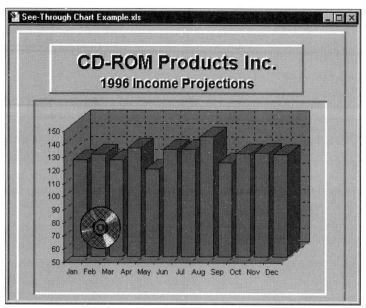

Figure 16-37: The Chart area is set to transparent, so the underlying cells and formatting show through.

This workbook, named SEE_THRU.XLS, is included on the companion CD-ROM.

Summary

This chapter picks up where Chapter 13 left off. I discuss most of the chart customization options in Excel. I demonstrate how to create combination charts and your own custom AutoFormats — which let you apply a series of customizations with a single command. I also discuss 3-D chart and conclude the chapter with many examples that use chart-making tricks.

✦   ✦   ✦

Creating Maps with Data Map

In previous chapters, you saw how you can use a chart to display data in a different — and usually more meaningful — way. This chapter explores the topic of mapping and describes how to present geographic information in the form of a map.

New! Mapping is new in Excel for Windows 95.

Note The mapping feature is not actually part of Excel. Rather, this feature uses an OLE server application named Data Map, which was developed by MapInfo Corporation. Consequently, you'll find that the user interface is quite different from Excel's normal user interface. When a map is active, Excel's menus and toolbars are replaced with the Data Map menus and toolbars.

Caution Since the Data Map feature is new to Excel for Windows 95, be careful when you distribute workbooks that contain maps to users who are running Excel 5. These users can view the maps but cannot make changes or update the maps with different data.

An Overview of Mapping

Mapping, like charting, is a tool that presents data visually. People use maps for a variety of purposes, but the common factor is that maps work with data that has a basis in geography. If you classify information by state, province, or country, chances are that you can represent the data on a map. For example, if your company sells its products throughout the U.S., it may be useful to show the annual sales by state.

An example

Figure 17-1 shows sales data for a company, categorized by state. To understand this information, one has to spend a lot of time examining the data.

On the CD-ROM This workbook, called SALES_ST.XLS, is available on the companion CD-ROM.

	A	B	C	D	E
	State	Product A	Product B	Combined	
1	State	Product A	Product B	Combined	
2	AK	150,800	98,666	249,466	
3	AL	37,700	3,988	41,688	
4	AR	8,700	92,728	101,428	
5	AZ	46,400	33,444	79,844	
6	CA	474,650	653,446	1,128,096	
7	CO	272,600	225,983	498,583	
8	CT	92,800	515,693	608,493	
9	DC	84,100	44,958	129,058	
10	FL	197,200	388,238	585,438	
11	GA	159,500	9,844	169,344	
12	HI	8,700	0	8,700	
13	IA	46,400	3,459	49,859	
14	IL	403,100	196,983	600,083	
15	IN	150,800	196,983	347,783	
16	KS	33,099	63,728	96,827	
17	MA	223,300	156,455	379,755	
18	MD	263,900	254,983	518,883	
19	ME	37,700	33,445	71,145	
20	MI	214,600	388,238	602,838	

Chart1 / Sheet2 \ StateSales /

Figure 17-1: Raw data that shows sales by state.

Figure 17-2 shows the same data displayed in a chart. Although this is an improvement over the raw data table, this type of presentation doesn't really work because of too many data points. In addition, the chart doesn't reveal any information about sales in a particular region.

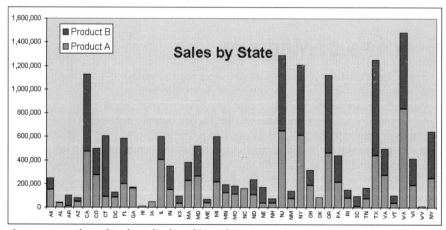

Figure 17-2: The sales data displayed in a chart.

Figure 17-3 shows the sales data presented as a map (it looks even better in color). This presentation uses different colors to represent various sales ranges. Looking at the map, it's clear that this company performs much better in some regions than in others.

Note   The map in Figure 17-3 may be even more revealing if the sales were represented relative to the population of each state — per capita sales. You may not realize it, but this population data is already on your system. When you installed Data Map, a workbook that contains a variety of population statistics was copied to your hard disk. The workbook is named `Mapstats`, and it is located in your Windows\Msapps\ Datamap\Data folder. Figure 17-4 shows the contents sheet for this workbook.

Figure 17-3: The sales data displayed in a map.

Maps available

The Data Map feature supports a good variety of maps and enables you to create maps in several different formats. A single map can display multiple sets of data, each in a different format. For example, your map can show sales by state and indicate the number of sales offices in each state. In addition, your map can display other accouterments such as labels and pin markers.

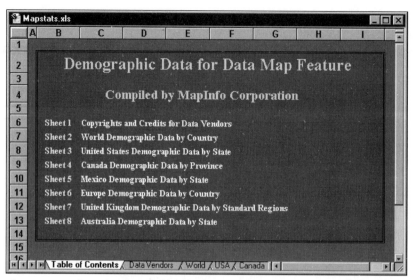

Figure 17-4: The Mapstats workbook contains population statistics that you can use in your maps.

The maps included with Data Map are listed in Table 17-1. As you'll see later, a map can be zoomed to display only a portion. Therefore, you can use the Europe map to zoom in on a particular region or country.

Table 17-1
Maps Included with Data Map

Map	*Description*
Australia	The continent of Australia, by state
Canada	The country of Canada, by province
Europe	The continent of Europe, by country
Mexico	The country of Mexico, by state
North America	The countries of North America (Canada, U.S., Mexico)
U.K. Standard Regions	The countries of the United Kingdom, by region.
U.S. in North America	United States (excluding Alaska and Hawaii insets), by state
U.S. with AK and HI Insets	United States (with Alaska and Hawaii insets), by state
World Countries	The world, by country

Tip   If you would like to order additional maps or data from MapInfo, you can contact the company directly. For information on how to do so, activate a map and click the Help⇨About command.

Creating a Map

Creating a basic map with Data Map is quite simple. In almost all cases, however, you'll want to customize the map. In this section, I discuss the basics of map making.

Setting up your data

The Data Map feature works with data stored in a list format (refer back to Figure 17-1 for an example). The first column should be map region names (such as states or countries). The columns to the right should be data for each area. You can have any number of data columns, because you select which columns to use after the map is created.

Creating the map

To create a map, start by selecting the data. This must be one column of area names and at least one column of data. If the columns have descriptive headers, include these in the selection.

Choose the Insert⇨Map command (or click the Map button on the Standard toolbar). The status bar displays a message: *Drag in document to create map*. Click and drag to specify the location and size of the map. Unlike charts, maps must be embedded on a worksheet (there are no separate map sheets).

Data Map analyzes the area labels and generates the appropriate map. If two or more maps are possible (or if you've developed any custom map templates), you get the dialog box shown in Figure 17-5. Select the desired map from this list.

No Insert⇨Map command?

Excel's mapping feature is performed by an OLE server application. The mapping feature is not an integral part of Excel, and it may not be installed on your system. If the Insert menu doesn't have a Map menu item, this means that the mapping feature is not installed.

To install the mapping feature, you need to rerun Excel's Setup program (or the Microsoft Office Setup program) and specify the mapping feature.

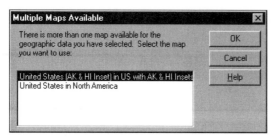

Figure 17-5: If multiple maps are available for your data, you can choose which map to use.

Data Map displays the map using the first column of data. It also displays the Data Map Control dialog box, which I discuss later in the chapter. When the map is created, it is activated. Whenever a map is activated, Excel's menus and toolbars are replaced by Data Map's menus and toolbar. When you click outside of the map, Excel's user interface is restored. You can reactivate a map by double-clicking it.

Setting the map format(s)

When a map first appears, the Data Map Control is visible (see Figure 17-6). This dialog box is used to change the format of the selected map. You can use the Show/ Hide Map Control tool to toggle the display of this dialog box.

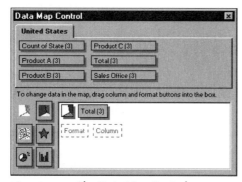

Figure 17-6: The Data Map Control.

By default, maps are created using the Value Shading map format. You can change the format or display two or more formats on a single map. This dialog box works by dragging items. The top of the dialog box displays all available data fields (which correspond to the columns that you selected when you created the map). The bottom part contains the map format information. Six format icons on the left determine the map format (described in the sections that follow). You combine a map format icon with one or more data fields by dragging. For example, you can replace the default map format icon with another one simply by dragging the new icon over the existing one. Some map formats use more than one data field. In such a case, you can drag additional data fields next to the icon.

To change options for a particular map format, double-click the format icon. Or you can use the Map menu and choose the menu item appropriate for the format that you want to change. In either case, you get a dialog box that's appropriate for the map format.

Following are descriptions (and samples) of each map format supported by Data Map.

Value shading

With this map format, each map region is shaded, based on the value of its data. This format is appropriate for data quantitative information such as sales, population, and so on. Figure 17-7 shows an example of a map formatted with value shading (this map is zoomed to show only part of the U.S.). In this example, the sales are broken down into four ranges, and each sales range is associated with a different shading.

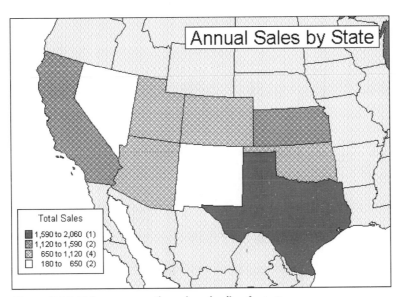

Figure 17-7: This map uses the value shading format.

You can change the interval ranges in the Value Shading Options dialog box, shown in Figure 17-8. You can specify the number of ranges and the method of defining the ranges — an equal number of areas in each range or an equal spread of values in each range. You also can select a color for the shading. The map displays different variations of the single color that you select. You also can choose the summary function used (sum or average). To hide the format from the map, remove the check mark from the Visible check box.

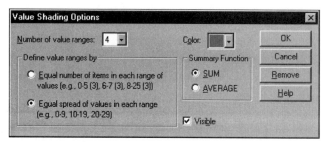

Figure 17-8: The Value Shading Options dialog box.

On the CD-ROM

This workbook, named VALUE.XLS, is available on the companion CD-ROM.

Category shading

With the category shading format, each map region is colored based on a data value. The map legend has one entry (color) for every value of the data range. Therefore, this format is appropriate for data that has a small number of discrete values. For example, you can use the format to identify states that have a sales office, the number of sales reps in a country, and so on. A common use for this format is to identify the states that comprise each sales region. Data need not be numeric. For example, the data can consist of text such as *Yes* and *No*.

Figure 17-9 shows a map that uses category shading to identify states that met the annual sales goal.

Figure 17-9: This map uses the category shading format.

To change the colors in the categories, use the Category Shading Options dialog box.

On the CD-ROM This workbook, named SHADING.XLS, is available on the companion CD-ROM.

Dot density

The dot density map format displays data as a series of dots. Larger values translate into more dots. The dots are placed randomly within a map region. Figure 17-10 shows an example of a map that uses the dot density format. This map depicts population in the U.K. Each dot represents 100,000 people.

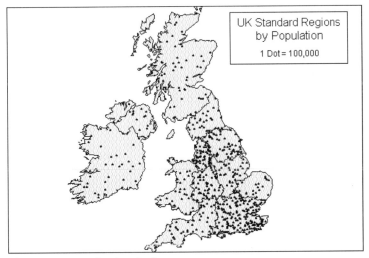

Figure 17-10: A dot density format map.

On the CD-ROM This workbook, named DOT_DEN.XLS, is available on the companion CD-ROM.

To change the number of units for each dot or to change the dot size, access the Dot Density Options dialog box, which is shown in Figure 17-11.

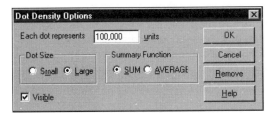

Figure 17-11: The Dot Density Options dialog box.

Graduated symbol

The graduated symbol map format displays a symbol, the size of which is proportional to the area's data value. Figure 17-12 shows an example of this format. I used a Wingdings font character for the symbol. To change the symbol, use the Graduated Symbol Options dialog box. You can select a font, size, and specific character to use.

On the CD-ROM This workbook, named GRADUATE.XLS, is available on the companion CD-ROM.

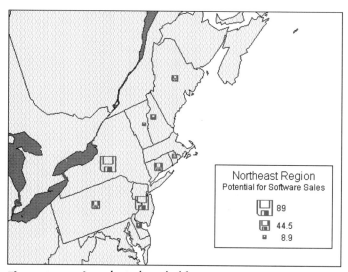

Figure 17-12: A graduated symbol format map.

Pie chart

The pie chart map format requires at least two columns of data. Maps with this format display a pie chart within each map region. Figure 17-13 shows an example. This map shows a pie chart that depicts the relative sales of three products for each state.

On the CD-ROM This workbook, named PIE_CHAR.XLS, is available on the companion CD-ROM.

To change the setting for a pie chart format map, use the Pie Chart Options dialog box, shown in Figure 17-14. This dialog box lets you select a color for each pie slice. If you choose the Graduated option, the size of each pie is proportional to the sum or average of the data. If you don't use the Graduated option, you also can set the diameter of the pies.

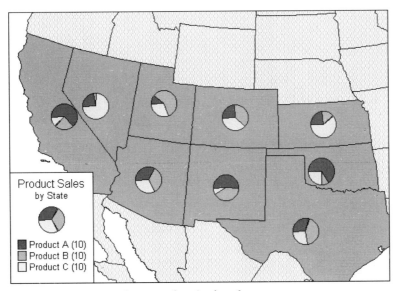

Figure 17-13: A map that uses the pie chart format.

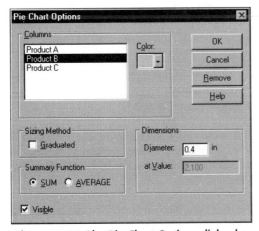

Figure 17-14: The Pie Chart Options dialog box.

Column chart

The column chart map format is similar to the pie chart format — except that it displays a column chart instead of a pie chart. Figure 17-15 shows an example.

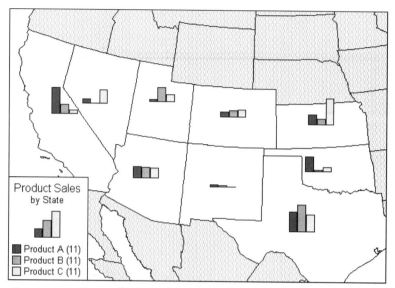

Figure 17-15: A map that uses the column chart format.

On the CD-ROM This workbook, named COLUMN.XLS, is available on the companion CD-ROM.

Combining map formats

As I mentioned, a single map can include multiple formats for different data. You do this by stacking groups of icons and data fields in the Data Map Control dialog box. For example, you can display sales as value shading and number of customers as a dot-density map. Each map format has its own legend.

There are no rules for overlaying multiple map types, so some experimentation usually is necessary. Unless the map is very simple, however, you're generally better off using only one or two map types per map; otherwise, the map gets so complicated that the original goal (making the data clear) is lost.

Figure 17-16 shows an example of a map that uses two formats. The value shading format shows sales broken down into four categories. The graduated symbol format shows the states that have a sales office.

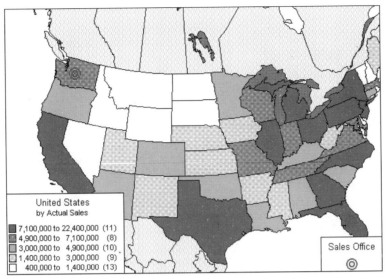

Figure 17-16: An example of a map that uses two map formats.

This workbook, named DUAL_FOR.XLS, is available on the companion CD-ROM.

Customizing Maps

Once a map is created, there are a number of customizations that you can make. I describe these customizations in the following sections.

Using the Data Map toolbar

Whenever a map is activated, the Data Map toolbar appears (see the figure on the next page). Note that this isn't one of Excel's toolbars; rather, this is a special toolbar that appears only when a map is activated. This toolbar is handy for manipulating and customizing the map.

(continued)

(continued)

The tools, from left to right, are as follows:

Selectformat Objects: Turns the mouse pointer into an arrow so you can select objects in the map

Zoom In: Lets you zoom in on a particular area of the map

Zoom Out: Lets you zoom out, making the map smaller

Grabber: Lets you reposition the map within the map window

Map Labels: Lets you add geography labels or data values in the map

Add Text: Lets you add free-floating text to the map

Custom Pin Map: Lets you add pins to the map to indicate specific locations

Display Entire: Displays the entire (unzoomed) map

Redraw Map: Redraws the map

Show/Hide Data Map Control: Toggles the display of the floating Data Map Control dialog box

Zooming in and out

Data Map lets you zoom your map in and out. Zooming in displays less of the map, and zooming out displays more of the map (or makes the entire map smaller). The only way to zoom is to use the Zoom In or Zoom Out tools on the toolbar (no menu commands exist).

To zoom in, click the Zoom In tool and click in the map. The point that you click becomes the center of the zoomed-in map. Or, you can click and drag to zoom in on a particular rectangular area. To zoom out, click the Zoom Out tool and then click in the map. The point that you click becomes the center of the map.

Tip   Holding down the Shift key reverses the effect of either button. For example, if the Zoom In tool is selected, you can press Shift and click in the map to zoom out.

Repositioning a map

You'll find that, after zooming in or out, the map isn't optimally positioned within the map object rectangle. Use the Grabber tool to move the map image within the map object. Just click and drag the map to reposition it.

Adding labels

Usually, a map doesn't have labels to identify areas. You can't add labels to all areas automatically (for example, all states in the U.S.), but you can add individual labels one at a time. You also can insert data values that correspond to a particular map region (such as sales for West Virginia).

Use the Label tool to add labels or data values. Clicking the Label tool displays the dialog box shown in Figure 17-17. The option button labeled Map feature names refers to labels for the various parts of the map (for example, state names in a U.S. map). When you select the Values from option, you can insert data values from a category in the list box. After closing the dialog box, you can drag the mouse pointer over the map. The label or data value appears when the mouse pointer is over a map region. Just click to place the label or data value. Figure 17-18 shows a map with labels and data values added to it.

Tip   If you don't like the fact that a map title always has a border around it (and it can't be removed), delete the title and create your own with the Label tool.

Figure 17-17: The Map Labels dialog box lets you add labels or data values to your map.

Figure 17-18: This map has labels and data values.

To move a label, click and drag it to a new location. You can change the font, size, or color of a label by double-clicking it. Stretching the label (by dragging a border) also makes the font larger or smaller.

Adding text

Besides the labels described in the preceding section, you can add free-floating text to your map using the Text tool. Just click the Text tool, click the area of the map where you want to add text, and enter your text. After text is placed, you can manipulate it like labels.

Adding pins to a map

In some cases, you may want to add one or more identifier icons to your map. This is similar in concept to inserting pins in a wall map to identify various places.

Clicking the Custom Pin Map tool displays a dialog box that asks you to enter a name for a custom pin map (or choose an existing pin map). Enter a descriptive label; you'll be able to bring these same pins into another map (of the same type) later. For example, if you're identifying sales office locations, you can then add the same pins to another map.

When you close the dialog box, the mouse pointer changes to a pushpin. You can place these pins anywhere in your map. When you click the map to place a pin, you also can enter descriptive text. Double-clicking a pin lets you change the symbol used to something other than a pin. Figure 17-19 shows a map with pins added to it.

Figure 17-19: This map has pins to identify specific locations.

Modifying the legend

You have a quite a bit of control over the legend in a map. Note that a map displays a separate legend for each map format that it uses. To modify a legend, double-click it. You get the dialog box shown in Figure 17-20.

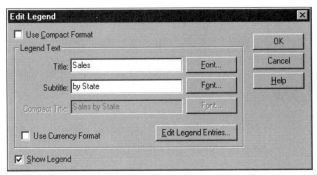

Figure 17-20: The Edit Legend dialog box.

A legend can be displayed in a compact format or its normal format. A compact format takes up less space, but it doesn't give many details. You also can change the legend's title and subtitle (and enter a different title for a compacted legend). Other buttons let you adjust the font (including size and color) and edit the labels used in the legend.

Note   To make other changes to the legend — such as changing the number of data ranges used — select the appropriate menu item on the Map menu. For example, to change the number of ranges used in a value shading map format, select the Map⇨Value Shading Options command.

Adding and removing features

You can add or remove certain features of a map. When you select the Map⇨Features command, you get a dialog box like the one shown in Figure 17-21. This lists all available features for the selected map. To turn a feature on, place a check mark next to it. To turn a feature off, remove the check mark. The features available vary with the map that you're using. If a feature doesn't appear in the list, you can add it by clicking the Add button.

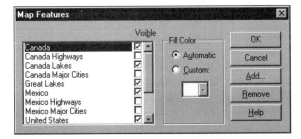

Figure 17-21: The Map Features dialog box.

Figure 17-22 shows a North America map with some features added (major cities, major highways, and world oceans) and some features removed (Canada, Mexico).

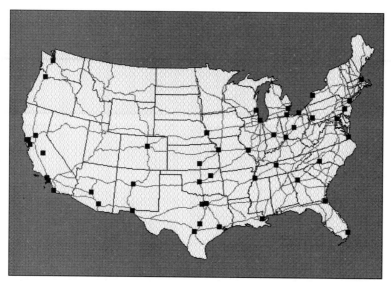

Figure 17-22: This map has features added and removed.

On the
CD-ROM

This workbook, named MAP_FEAT.XLS, is available on the companion CD-ROM.

Table 17-2 lists the features available for each map. You can, however, add features from different maps — add world oceans to a North America map, for instance.

Map	Features
	**Table 17-2** **Map Features Available**

Map	Features
Australia	Airports, Cities, Highways, Major Cities
Canada	Airports, Cities, Forward Sortation Areas, Highways, Lakes, Major Cities
Europe	Airports, Cities, Highways, Major Cities
Mexico	Cities, Highways, Major Cities
U.K.	2-Digit Post Codes, Airports, Cities, Highways, Major Cities, Standard Regions
U.S. in North America	5-Digit Zip Code Centers, Highways, Major Cities, Great Lakes
U.S. (AK & HI Inset)	Airports, Cities, Major Cities
World	Capitals, Countries, Graticule, Oceans

Tip   In some cases, you may want your map to display only specific areas. For example, if your company does business in Missouri, Illinois, Kansas, and Nebraska, you can create a map that shows only these four states. The trick is to create the map and then remove all features from the map using the Map⇨Features command. The map is then limited to those areas that have data. Figure 17-23 shows an example.

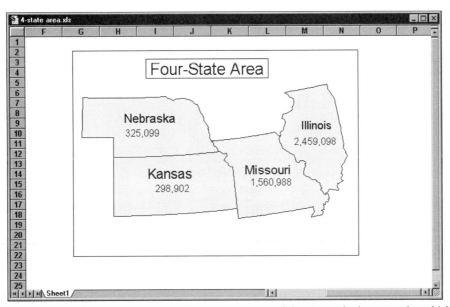

Figure 17-23: This map has all of its features removed, leaving only the states for which data is provided.

Plotting U.S. Zip Codes

Besides recognizing geographic place names, Data Map also recognizes U.S. five-digit zip codes. If the data that you select contains multiple geography information (for example, state names and zip codes), you need to specify which field to use as the geography. Figure 17-24 shows the dialog box that appears to warn you of the existence of multiple geographies.

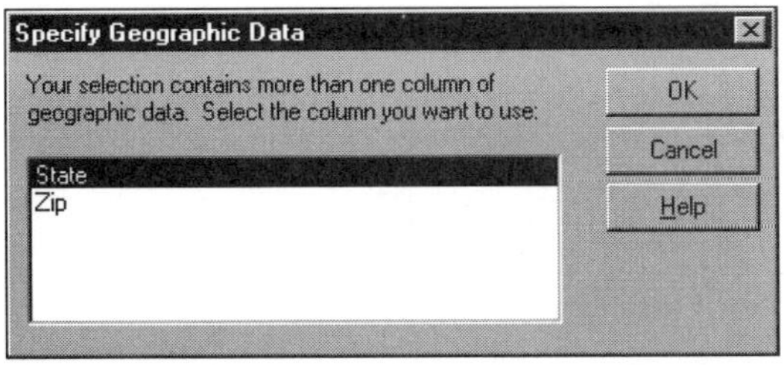

Figure 17-24: This dialog box lets you select the geography to use for your map.

Caution If you want to create a map that uses zip codes, make sure that your zip codes are formatted as values, not as text. Otherwise, they won't be recognized as zip codes.

Because zip codes are continually being added, it's possible that Data Map will not recognize all of your zip codes. If it encounters an unknown zip code, you get the dialog box shown in Figure 17-25. This gives you the opportunity to change the zip code to another one. Or, you can simply discard that item of data by clicking the Discard button.

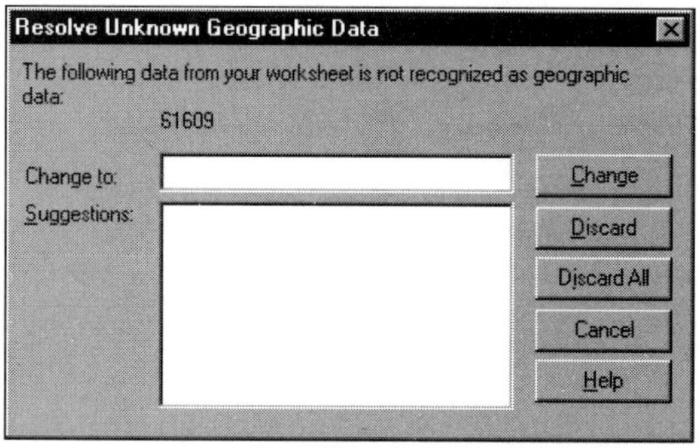

Resolve Unknown Geographic Data

The following data from your worksheet is not recognized as geographic data:

61609

Change to:

Suggestions:

Change
Discard
Discard All
Cancel
Help

Figure 17-25: Data Map displays this dialog box when it doesn't recognize a geographic name.

Figure 17-26 shows a map that depicts customers by zip codes. This is a graduated symbol map (the default format when zip codes are used as the geography). Note that the symbols are placed on the geographic centers of the zip codes and don't shade the entire zip code areas.

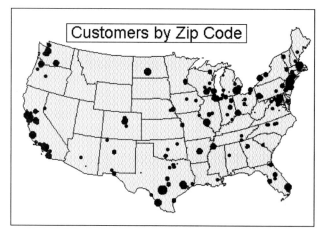

Customers by Zip Code

Figure 17-26: This map shows customers by zip code centers.

Adding More Data to a Map

After you've created a map, you can add additional data to it. Use the Insert⇨Data command to add data from a worksheet range, or use the Insert⇨External Data command to add new data from a database file. Make sure that the data includes geographic labels that match the map to which you're adding data.

Map Templates

As you may have figured out by now, getting a map just right can sometimes take a lot of time. Fortunately, you can save a map template. To do so, create and customize the map and then choose the Map⇨Save Map Template command. You can save a template that includes:

✦ The features that you've added or removed

✦ A particular view (zoomed in or out)

✦ Both of the preceding items

Saved templates then appear in the Multiple Maps Available dialog box that is displayed when you create a map.

Converting a Map to a Picture

You'll find that working with maps can be rather slow — a great deal of work goes on behind the scenes. When you finish with your map, you can convert it to a static picture that is no longer linked to the data. To do so, click the map once to select it (don't double-click it) and choose Edit⇨Copy. Then select the Edit⇨Paste Special command and choose the Picture option. This creates an unlinked picture of the map. Then you can select the original map object and delete it.

Caution

If you convert a map to a picture, there is no way to link data back to the picture. If any of your data changes, or if you want to make any modifications to the map, you have to re-create the map.

Learning More

The Data Map feature is relatively complex, and it definitely takes time to master. The best way to master it is to simply create some maps and perform customizations. As I mention earlier, the user interface is different from Excel's, so you'll have to try some new techniques. Generally, you can find your way around maps by:

✦ Double-clicking objects

✦ Right-clicking objects

✦ Exploring the menus (they change somewhat, depending on the type of map)

✦ Using the Data Map toolbar

Summary

In this chapter, I cover Excel's new Data Map feature — which is actually an OLE server application developed by MapInfo Corporation. I demonstrate how some data is more appropriate for a map than for a chart. I describe the basics of creating and customizing maps and provide an example of each map format.

✦   ✦   ✦

Creating and Using Worksheet Outlines

I f you use a word processor, you may be familiar with the concept of an outline. Most word processors have an outline mode that allows you to view only the headings and subheadings in your document. You can easily expand a heading to show the detail (that is, the text) below it. I used the outline feature in my word processor extensively to write this book.

Excel also is capable of using outlines, and understanding this feature can make working with certain types of worksheets much easier. Worksheet outlining is a feature that's unique to Excel. Surprisingly, this feature hasn't been picked up by the competition.

Introducing Worksheet Outlines

This section introduces you to worksheet outlines and presents an example of how they work. Outlines are most useful for creating summary reports in which you don't want to show all the details. It should go without saying that you can't create an outline from just any worksheet. If your worksheet uses hierarchical data with subtotals, it's probably a good candidate for an outline.

An example

The best way to understand how worksheet outlining works is to look at an example. Figure 18-1 shows a simple budget model without an outline. I inserted subtotals to calculate subtotals by region and subtotals by quarter.

Two-Way Outline Example.xls

	A	B	C	D	E	F	G	H	I
1	**State**	**Jan**	**Feb**	**Mar**	**Q1 Total**	**Apr**	**May**	**Jun**	**Q2 Total**
2	California	1118	1960	1252	**4330**	1271	1557	1679	**4507**
3	Washington	1247	1238	1028	**3513**	1345	1784	1574	**4703**
4	Oregon	1460	1954	1726	**5140**	1461	1764	1144	**4369**
5	Nevada	1345	1375	1075	**3795**	1736	1555	1372	**4663**
6	**West Total**	**5170**	**6527**	**5081**	**16778**	**5813**	**6660**	**5769**	**18242**
7	New York	1429	1316	1993	**4738**	1832	1740	1191	**4763**
8	New Jersey	1735	1406	1224	**4365**	1706	1320	1290	**4316**
9	Massachusetts	1099	1233	1110	**3442**	1637	1512	1006	**4155**
10	Florida	1705	1792	1225	**4722**	1946	1327	1357	**4630**
11	**East Total**	**5968**	**5747**	**5552**	**17267**	**7121**	**5899**	**4844**	**17864**
12	Kentucky	1109	1078	1155	**3342**	1993	1082	1551	**4626**
13	Oklahoma	1309	1045	1641	**3995**	1924	1499	1941	**5364**
14	Missouri	1511	1744	1414	**4669**	1243	1493	1820	**4556**
15	Illinois	1539	1493	1211	**4243**	1165	1013	1445	**3623**

Sheet1

Figure 18-1: A typical budget model with subtotals.

Figure 18-2 shows the same worksheet after I created an outline. Notice that Excel added a new border to the left. This border contains controls that let you determine what level to view. This particular outline has three levels: States, Regions (each region is made up of states), and Grand Total (the sum of each region's subtotal). In the figure, the outline is fully expanded so that all data is visible.

Two-Way Outline Example.xls

	A	B	C	D	E	F	G
1	**State**	**Jan**	**Feb**	**Mar**	**Q1 Total**	**Apr**	**May**
2	California	1118	1960	1252	**4330**	1271	1557
3	Washington	1247	1238	1028	**3513**	1345	1784
4	Oregon	1460	1954	1726	**5140**	1461	1764
5	Nevada	1345	1375	1075	**3795**	1736	1555
6	**West Total**	**5170**	**6527**	**5081**	**16778**	**5813**	**6660**
7	New York	1429	1316	1993	**4738**	1832	1740
8	New Jersey	1735	1406	1224	**4365**	1706	1320
9	Massachusetts	1099	1233	1110	**3442**	1637	1512
10	Florida	1705	1792	1225	**4722**	1946	1327
11	**East Total**	**5968**	**5747**	**5552**	**17267**	**7121**	**5899**
12	Kentucky	1109	1078	1155	**3342**	1993	1082
13	Oklahoma	1309	1045	1641	**3995**	1924	1499
14	Missouri	1511	1744	1414	**4669**	1243	1493
15	Illinois	1539	1493	1211	**4243**	1165	1013
16	Kansas	1973	1560	1243	**4776**	1495	1125
17	**Central Total**	**7441**	**6920**	**6664**	**17683**	**7820**	**6212**
18	**Grand Total**	**18579**	**19194**	**17297**	**51728**	**20754**	**18771**
19							

Sheet1

Figure 18-2: The budget model after creating an outline.

Figure 18-3 depicts the outline displayed at the second level. Now it only shows the totals for the regions (the detail rows are hidden). You can partially expand the outline to show the detail for a particular region. Collapsing the outline to level 1 would show only the headers and the Grand Total row.

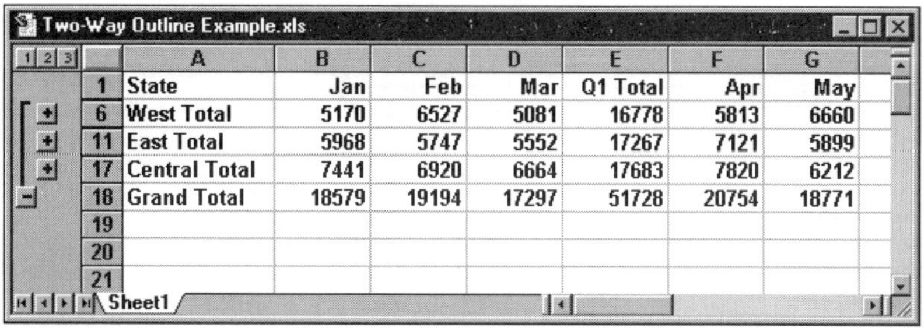

Two-Way Outline Example.xls

	A	B	C	D	E	F	G
1	State	Jan	Feb	Mar	Q1 Total	Apr	May
6	West Total	5170	6527	5081	16778	5813	6660
11	East Total	5968	5747	5552	17267	7121	5899
17	Central Total	7441	6920	6664	17683	7820	6212
18	Grand Total	18579	19194	17297	51728	20754	18771
19							
20							
21							

Sheet1

Figure 18-3: The budget model after collapsing the outline.

Excel can create outlines in both directions. In the preceding examples, the outline was a row outline (vertical). Figure 18-4 shows the same model after I added a column (horizontal) outline. Now, Excel displays another border at the top.

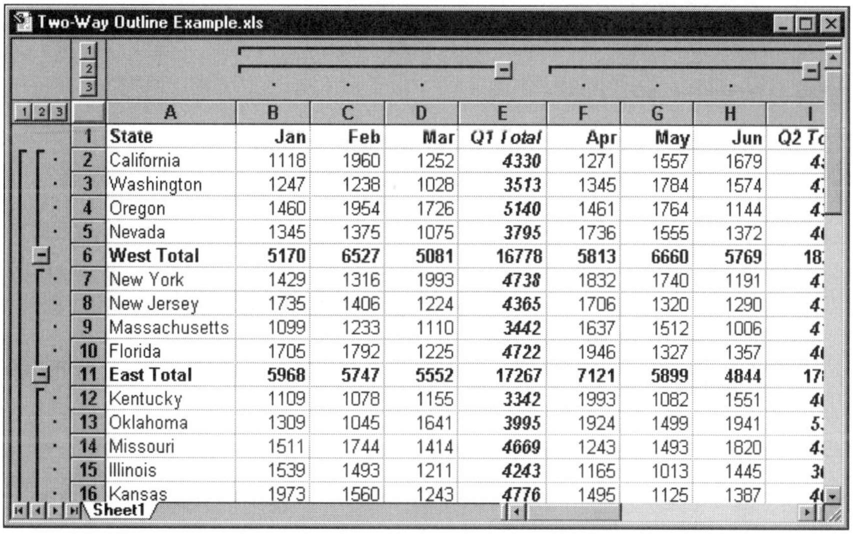

Two-Way Outline Example.xls

	A	B	C	D	E	F	G	H
1	State	Jan	Feb	Mar	Q1 Total	Apr	May	Jun
2	California	1118	1960	1252	4330	1271	1557	1679
3	Washington	1247	1238	1028	3513	1345	1784	1574
4	Oregon	1460	1954	1726	5140	1461	1764	1144
5	Nevada	1345	1375	1075	3795	1736	1555	1372
6	West Total	5170	6527	5081	16778	5813	6660	5769
7	New York	1429	1316	1993	4738	1832	1740	1191
8	New Jersey	1735	1406	1224	4365	1706	1320	1290
9	Massachusetts	1099	1233	1110	3442	1637	1512	1006
10	Florida	1705	1792	1225	4722	1946	1327	1357
11	East Total	5968	5747	5552	17267	7121	5899	4844
12	Kentucky	1109	1078	1155	3342	1993	1082	1551
13	Oklahoma	1309	1045	1641	3995	1924	1499	1941
14	Missouri	1511	1744	1414	4669	1243	1493	1820
15	Illinois	1539	1493	1211	4243	1165	1013	1445
16	Kansas	1973	1560	1243	4776	1495	1125	1387

Sheet1

Figure 18-4: The budget model after adding a column outline.

If a worksheet has both a row and a column outline, you can work with each independently of the other. For example, you can show the row outline at the second level and the column outline at the first level. Figure 18-5 shows the model with both outlines collapsed at the second level. The result is a nice summary table that gives regional totals by quarter.

		A	E	I	M	Q	R	S
	1	State	Q1 Total	Q2 Total	Q3 Total	Q4 Total	Grand Total	
+	6	West Total	16778	18242	18314	19138	72472	
+	11	East Total	17267	17864	17910	18925	71966	
+	17	Central Total	17683	17550	17752	17357	70342	
–	18	Grand Total	51728	53656	53976	55420	214780	
	19							
	20							
	21							
	22							

Figure 18-5: The budget model with both outlines collapsed at the second level.

The workbook shown in the preceding figures is available on the companion CD-ROM. The file is named 2WAY_OUT.XLS.

More about outlines

Following are points to keep in mind about worksheet outlines:

✦ A single worksheet can have only one outline (row, column, or both). If you need to create more than one outline, move the data to a new worksheet.

✦ You can create an outline manually or have Excel do it for you automatically. If you choose the latter option, you may need to do some preparation to get the worksheet in the proper format.

✦ You can create an outline for all data on a worksheet or just a selected data range.

✦ You can remove an outline with a single command.

✦ You can hide the outline symbols (to free screen space) but retain the outline.

✦ You can have up to eight nested levels in an outline.

Cross-
Reference
Worksheet outlines can be quite useful. But if your main objective is to summarize a large amount of data, you might be better off using a pivot table. A pivot table is much more flexible and doesn't require that you create the subtotal formulas; it does the summarizing for you automatically. I discuss pivot tables in Chapter 25.

Creating an Outline

In this section, you learn the two ways to create an outline: automatically and manually. Before getting into the details, I discuss the first step — getting your data ready to be converted to an outline.

Preparing the data

Before you create an outline, you need to ensure that:

✦ The data is appropriate for an outline.

✦ The formulas are set up properly.

Determining appropriate data

What type of data is appropriate for an outline? Generally, the data should be arranged in a hierarchy. An example of hierarchical data is a budget that consists of an arrangement such as the following:

Company

    Division

        Department

            Budget Category

            Budget Item

In this case, each budget item (for example, airfare and hotel expenses) is part of a budget category (for example, travel expenses). Each department has its own budget, and the departments are rolled up into divisions. The divisions make up the company. This type of arrangement is well-suited for a row outline — although most of your outlines probably won't have this many levels.

Once created, you can view the information at any level of detail that you desire. An outline is often useful for creating reports for different levels of management. Upper management may want to see only the Division totals. Division managers may want to see totals by department, and each department manager needs to see the full details for his or her department.

And, as I demonstrated at the beginning of the chapter, time-based information that is rolled up into larger units (such as months and quarters) also is appropriate for a column outline. Column outlines work just like row outlines, however, and the levels need not be time based.

Setting up the formulas

Before creating an outline, you need to make sure that the summary formulas are all entered correctly and consistently. By consistently, I mean in the same relative location. Generally, formulas that compute summary formulas (such as subtotals) are entered below the data to which they refer. In some cases, however, the summary formulas are entered above the referenced cells. Excel can handle either method, but you must be consistent throughout the range that will be outlined. If the summary formulas aren't consistent, automatic outlining won't produce the results you want.

Note   If your summary formulas aren't consistent (that is, some are above and some are below the data), you still can create an outline, but you must do it manually.

Creating an outline automatically

In most cases, the best approach is to let Excel create the outline for you. Excel can do the job in a few seconds, whereas it might take you ten minutes or more.

To have Excel create an outline, move the cell pointer anywhere within the range of data that you're outlining. Then, choose the Data⇨Group and Outline⇨Auto Outline command. Excel analyzes the formulas in the range and creates the outline. Depending on the formulas you have, Excel creates a row outline, a column outline, or both.

If the worksheet already has an outline, you'll be asked whether you want to modify the existing outline. Click on Yes to force Excel to remove the old outline and create a new one.

Note   Excel automatically creates an outline when you use the Data⇨Subtotals command. This command inserts subtotal formulas automatically if your data is set up as a list. I discuss this command in Chapter 23.

Creating an outline manually

Usually, letting Excel create the outline is the best approach. It's much faster and less error prone. If the outline that Excel creates isn't what you had in mind, however, you can create one manually.

When Excel creates a row outline, the summary rows must all be above the data or below the data (they can't be mixed). Similarly, for a column outline, the summary columns must all be to the right of the data or to the left of the data. If your worksheet doesn't meet these requirements, you have two choices:

✦ Rearrange the worksheet so that it does.

✦ Create the outline manually.

Using an outline for text

If you need to present lots of textual information in a workbook — as in user instructions, for example — consider arranging the information in the form of an outline. The accompanying figure shows an example that I developed for one of my shareware products. The user manual is contained on a worksheet, and I created an outline to make locating a specific section easier. I also used a simple macro, attached to a check box, to make it easy for users to expand and collapse the outline.

The workbook shown in the figure is available on the companion CD-ROM. It's named TEXT_OUT.XLS.

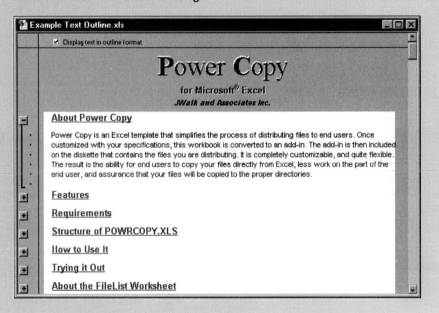

Another reason to create an outline manually is if the range doesn't contain any formulas. You may have imported a file and want to use an outline to display it better. Because Excel uses the formulas to determine how to create the outline, it is not able to make an outline without formulas.

Creating an outline manually consists of creating groups of rows (for row outlines) or groups of columns (for column outlines). To create a group of rows, completely select all the rows that you want included in the group — but do *not* select the row that has the summary formulas. Then choose the Data⇨Group and Outline⇨Group command. Excel displays the outline symbols for the group as it's created. Repeat this for each group that you want to create. When you collapse the outline, rows in the group are hidden. But the summary row, which is not in the group, isn't hidden.

Note If you select a range of cells (rather than entire rows or columns) before creating a group, Excel displays a dialog box asking you what you want to group. It then groups entire rows or columns based on the range that you selected.

You also can select groups of groups. This creates multilevel outlines. When creating multilevel outlines, always start with the innermost groupings and then work your way out. If you group the wrong rows, you can ungroup the group with the Data⇨Group and Outline⇨Ungroup command.

Tip Excel has toolbar buttons that speed up the process of grouping and ungrouping. See the sidebar, "Outling tools." Also, you can use the following keyboard shortcuts:

> **Alt+Shift+right arrow:** Groups selected rows or columns
>
> **Alt+Shift+left arrow:** Ungroups selected rows or columns

Creating outlines manually can be confusing at first. But if you stick with it, you'll become a pro in no time.

Outlining tools

Excel doesn't have a toolbar devoted exclusively to outlining, but it *does* have one that comes close. The Query and Pivot toolbar (see accompanying figure) includes four tools that are handy for working with outlines. There's an additional tool, called Show Outline Symbols, that doesn't appear on any toolbar. This tool toggles the display of the outline symbols on and off. You may want to take a few minutes to add this tool to the Query and Pivot toolbar (see Chapter 32 for details on customizing toolbars). You can find the Show Outline Symbols tool in the Utility category in the Customize dialog box.

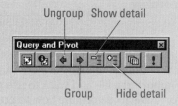

The relevant Query and Pivot toolbar buttons are as follows:

Button Name	What It Does
Ungroup	Ungroups selected rows or columns
Group	Groups selected rows or columns
Show Detail	Shows details of selected summary cell
Hide Detail	Hides details of selected summary cell

Using Outlines

This section discusses the basic operations that you can perform with a worksheet outline.

Displaying levels

To display various outline levels, click on the appropriate outline symbol. These symbols consist of buttons with numbers on them (1, 2, and so on) and buttons with either a plus sign (+) or a minus sign (−).

Clicking on the 1 button collapses the outline as small as it will go. Clicking on the 2 button expands it to show one level, and so on. The number of numbered buttons depends on the number of outline levels. Choosing a level number displays the detail for that level, plus any lower levels. To display all levels, click on the highest level number.

You can expand a particular section by clicking on its + button or collapse a particular section by clicking on its − button. In short, you have complete control over the details that are exposed or hidden in an outline.

If you prefer, you can use the Hide Detail and Show Detail commands on the Data⇨Group and Outline menu to hide and show details. Or you can use toolbar buttons to do the hiding and showing.

Tip   If you find yourself constantly adjusting the outline to show different reports, consider using the View Manager add-in. The View Manager lets you save a particular view and give it a name. Then you can quickly switch among the named views.

Tip   If you want to copy or move rows or columns in an outline, here's a quick way to select the row or column and all of its subordinate rows and columns: Press the Shift key and then click on the group bar (the bar that delineates the grouped rows or columns).

Applying styles to an outline

When you create an outline, you can have Excel apply named styles automatically to the summary rows and columns (see Chapter 11 for a discussion of named styles). It uses styles with names in the following formats (where n corresponds to the outline level):

RowLevel_n

ColLevel_n .

For example, the named style that is applied to the first row level is RowLevel_1.

These styles consist only of formats for the font. This makes distinguishing various parts of the outline a bit easier. You can, of course, modify the styles any way you want. For example, you can use the Format⇨Style command to change the font size or color for the RowLevel_1 style. After doing so, all of the RowLevel_1 cells take on the new formatting. Figure 18-6 shows an outline with the automatic outline styles assigned.

		A	B	C
	1	Dept 1 Income	155	
	2	Dept 1 Expenses	43	
	3	Dept 1 Net	112	
	4	Dept 2 Income	155	
	5	Dept 2 Expenses	43	
	6	Dept 2 Net	112	
	7	*Division A Net*	224	
	8	Dept 1 Income	155	
	9	Dept 1 Expenses	43	
	10	Dept 1 Net	112	
	11	Dept 2 Income	155	
	12	Dept 2 Expenses	43	
	13	Dept 2 Net	112	
	14	*Division B Net*	224	
	15	**Total Company**	**448**	

Figure 18-6: This outline has automatic styles.

You can have Excel apply the styles automatically when it creates an outline, or you can apply them after the fact. You control this in the Outline dialog box, shown in Figure 18-7. This dialog box appears when you select the Data⇨Group and Outline⇨Settings command.

Figure 18-7: The Outline dialog box.

If the Automatic Styles check box is checked when you create the outline, Excel applies the styles automatically. To apply styles to an existing outline, select the outline, choose the Data⇨Group and Outline⇨Settings command, and click on the Apply Styles command. Notice that you also can create an outline using this dialog box.

Tip   You may prefer to use Excel's Format⇨AutoFormat command to format an outline. Many AutoFormats use different formatting for summary cells.

Adding data to an outline

You may need to add additional rows or columns to an outline. In some cases, you may be able to insert new rows or columns without disturbing the outline, and the new rows or columns become part of the outline. In other cases, you'll find that the new row or column is not part of the outline. If you created the outline automatically, just select the Data⇨Group and Outline⇨Auto Outline command again. Excel makes you verify that you want to modify the existing outline. If you created the outline manually, you need to make the adjustments manually.

Removing an outline

If you decide that you no longer need an outline, you can remove it. Select the Data⇨Group and Outline⇨Clear Outline command. The outline is fully expanded (all hidden rows and columns are unhidden), and the outline symbols disappear. The outline styles remain in effect, however.

Caution   Removing an outline can't be undone, so make sure that you really want to remove the outline before selecting this command.

Hiding the outline symbols

The outline symbols displayed when an outline is present take up quite a bit of space (the exact amount depends on the number levels). If you want to see as much as possible on-screen, you can temporarily hide these symbols without removing the outline. There are three ways to do this:

- ✦ Click on the Show Outline Symbols tool. This button is not available on any of the prebuilt toolbars, so you have to add it to one of the others (such as the Query and Pivot toolbar).

- ✦ Access the Options dialog box, select the View panel, and uncheck the Outline Symbols check box.

- ✦ Press Ctrl+8.

Note   When you hide the outline symbols, the outline is still in effect and the worksheet displays the data at the current outline level. That is, some rows or columns may be hidden.

To redisplay the outline symbols, click on the Show Outline Symbols tool again, place a check mark in the Outline Symbols check box in the Options dialog box, or press Ctrl+8.

Tip   If you use the View Manager to save named views of your outline, the status of the outline symbols is also saved as part of the view. This lets you name some views with the outline symbols and other views without them.

Creating charts from outlines

A worksheet outline also is a handy way to create summary charts. If you have a large table of data, creating a chart usually produces a confusing mess. But if you create an outline first, then you can collapse the outline and select the summary data for your chart. Figure 18-8 shows a example of a chart created from a collapsed outline. When you expand an outline that has a chart created from it, the chart shows the additional data.

Note   If your chart shows all of the data in the outline even when it's collapsed, remove the check box from the Plot Visible Cells Only check box in the Chart panel in the Options dialog box.

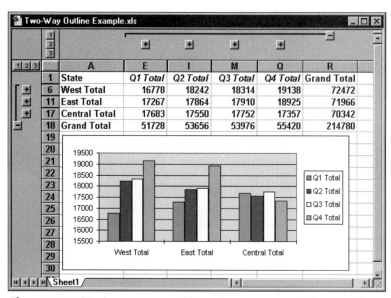

Figure 18-8: This chart was created from the summary cells in an outline.

Summary

This chapter discusses the advantages of creating an outline from worksheet data. It teaches you how to create row outlines and column outlines, either automatically or manually. I also discuss how to use an outline after it is created.

✦   ✦   ✦

Linking and Consolidating Worksheets

◆ ◆ ◆ ◆

In This Chapter

An overview of linking and consolidation and why you might want to use these techniques

Various ways to create links to cells in other workbooks

What to watch out for when you use links

Various ways to consolidate information across worksheets and across different workbooks

◆ ◆ ◆ ◆

This chapter discusses two procedures common in the world of spreadsheets: linking and consolidation. Linking is the process of using references to cells in external workbooks as a way of getting data for use in your worksheet. Consolidation is the process of combining or summarizing information from two or more worksheets (which can be in multiple workbooks).

Linking Workbooks

The term *linking* refers to the process of creating formulas that use values contained in another workbook. In other words, the worksheets are linked together such that one depends on the other. The workbook that contains the link formulas (or external reference formulas) is the *dependent* workbook. The workbook that is the source of the information used in the external reference formula is the *source* workbook. It's important to note that the source workbook doesn't need to be open while the dependent workbook is open.

It's also possible to create links to data in other applications, such as a database program or a word processor. This uses a completely different procedure and is the topic of Chapter 29.

Cross-
Reference

Why link workbooks?

When you start thinking about linking workbooks, you might ask the following question: If Workbook A needs to access data in another workbook (Workbook B), why not just enter the data into Workbook A in the first place? In some cases, you can. But the real value of this procedure is apparent when the source workbook is continually being updated. Creating a link to that workbook means that you'll always have access to the most recent information.

Linking workbooks also can be helpful if you need to consolidate different files. For example, each regional sales manager might store data in a separate workbook. You can create a summary workbook that uses link formulas to retrieve specific data from each workbook and calculate totals across all regions.

Linking also is useful as a way to break up a large model into smaller files. You can create smaller workbook modules that are linked together with a few key external references. Often, this makes your model easier to deal with and uses less memory.

Linking is not without its downside, however. As you'll see later, external reference formulas are somewhat fragile, and it's relatively easy to accidentally sever the links that you create. But you can prevent this from happening if you understand how it works. Later in the chapter I discuss some of the problems that may arise and how to avoid them.

Creating external reference formulas

There are several ways to create an external reference formula:

✦ Type the cell references manually. These references can be lengthy, because they also include workbook and sheet names. The advantage is that the source workbook doesn't have to be open.

✦ Point to the cell references. If the source workbook is open, you can use the standard pointing techniques to create formulas that use external references.

✦ Use the Edit⇨Paste Special command with the Paste Link button. This requires that the source workbook be open.

✦ Use Excel's Data⇨Consolidate command. I discuss this method later in the chapter.

Link formula syntax

I touch on the topic of external reference formula in Chapter 9, and this section takes the concept even further.

The general syntax for an external reference formula is as follows:

```
=[WorkbookName]SheetName!CellAddress
```

The cell address is preceded by the workbook name (in brackets), the worksheet name, and an exclamation point. Here's an example of a formula that uses a cell reference in the Sheet1 worksheet in a workbook named Budget:

```
=[Budget.xls]Sheet1!A1
```

If the workbook name or the sheet name in the reference includes one or more spaces, you must enclose the text in single quotation marks. For example, here's a formula that refers to a cell on Sheet1 in a workbook named Budget For 1996:

```
='[Budget For 1996]Sheet1'!A1
```

When a formula refers to cells in a different workbook, the other workbook doesn't need to be open. If the workbook is closed and it's not in the current folder, you must add the complete path to the reference. Here's an example:

```
='C:\MSOffice\Excel\Budget Files\[Budget For 1996]Sheet1'!A1
```

Creating a link formula by pointing

As I mentioned, you can enter external reference formulas directly, but doing so can be error prone because you must have every bit of information exactly correct. The easier way is to have Excel build the formula for you. Here's how to do it:

1. Open the source workbook.

2. Activate the cell in the dependent workbook that will hold the formula.

3. Begin entering the formula.

4. When you get to the part that requires the external reference, activate the source workbook and select the cell or range.

5. Finish the formula and press Enter.

You'll see that when you point to the cell or range, Excel takes care of the details automatically and creates a syntactically correct external reference. Notice that the cell reference is always an absolute reference (such as $A$1). If you plan to copy the formula to create additional link formulas, you can change the absolute reference to a relative reference by removing the dollar signs.

Note When the source workbook is open, the external reference won't include the path to the workbook. If you close the source workbook, the external reference formulas change to display the full path. If you use the File⇨Save As command to save the source workbook with a different name, Excel changes the external references to use the new filename.

Pasting links

The Paste Special command provides another way to create external reference formulas.

1. Open the source workbook.

2. Select the cell or range that you want to link, and copy it to the Clipboard.

3. Activate the dependent workbook and select the cell where you want the link formula. If you're pasting a range, just select the upper-left cell.

4. Choose the Edit⇨Paste Special command and click on the Paste Link button.

If you copied a single cell, Excel creates the link formula just as if you used the preceding pointing method. If you copied a range, however, Excel creates an array formula that holds the link formula. An array formula is a single formula that is stored in multiple cells. An array formula appears in the formula bar with brackets around it.

Cross-Reference I discuss array formulas in Chapter 20.

Working with external reference formulas

It's important to understand that a single workbook can have links that refer to any number of different source workbooks. This section discusses what you need to know about working with links.

Creating links to unsaved workbooks

Excel lets you create link formulas to unsaved workbooks and even nonexistent workbooks. Assume that you have two workbooks open and neither has been saved (they have names Book1 and Book2). If you create a link formula to Book1 in Book2, and then save Book2, Excel displays the dialog box shown in Figure 19-1. Generally, you should avoid this situation. Simply save the source workbook first.

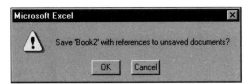

Figure 19-1: This message indicates that the workbook has references to a workbook that hasn't been saved.

You also can create links to documents that don't exist. You might want to do this if you'll be using a source workbook from a colleague, but the file hasn't arrived yet. When you enter an external reference formula that refers to a nonexistent workbook, Excel displays its File Not Found dialog box shown in Figure 19-2. If you click on Cancel, the formula retains the workbook name that you entered, but it returns an error. When the source workbook becomes available, the error goes away and the formula displays its proper value.

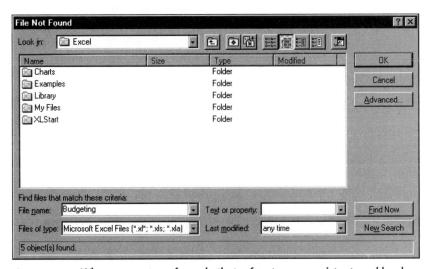

Figure 19-2: When you enter a formula that refers to a nonexistent workbook, Excel displays this dialog box to help you locate the file.

Opening a workbook with external reference formulas

When you open a workbook that contains one or more external reference formulas, Excel retrieves the current values from the source workbooks and calculates the formulas.

If Excel can't locate a source workbook that's referred to in a link formula, it displays its File Not Found dialog and prompts you to supply a workbook to use for the source workbook.

Examining links

If your workbook uses several workbook links, you might want to see a list of source workbooks. To do so, choose the Edit⇨Links command. Excel responds with the Links dialog box shown in Figure 19-3. This dialog box lists all source workbooks plus other types of links to other documents (I explain these other types of links in Chapter 29).

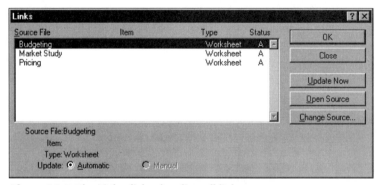

Figure 19-3: The Links dialog box lists all link sources.

Updating links

If you want to ensure that your link formulas have the latest values from their source workbooks, you can force an update. This step might be necessary if you just learned that someone made changes to the source workbook and saved the latest version on your network server.

To update linked formulas with their current value, access the Links dialog box, choose the appropriate source workbook, and click on the Update Now button. Excel updates the link formulas with the latest version of the source workbook.

Note Worksheet links are always set to the Automatic update option in the Links dialog box, and you can't change them to Manual. This only means that the links are updated when the workbook is opened, however. Excel doesn't update links automatically if the source file gets changed.

Changing the link source

There might come a time when you need to change the source workbook for your external references. For example, you might have a worksheet that has links to a workbook named `Preliminary Budget`. Later, you get a finalized version named `Final Budget`.

You *could* change all of the cell links manually, or you could simply change the link source. Do this in the Links dialog box. Select the source workbook that you want to change and click on the Change Source button. Excel displays a dialog box that lets you select a new source file. After you select the file, all external reference formulas are updated.

Severing links

If you have external references in a workbook and then decide that you don't want them, you can convert the external reference formulas to values, thereby severing the links. Follow these steps:

1. Select the range that contains the external reference formulas and copy it to the Clipboard.

2. Choose the Edit⇨Paste Special command. Excel displays the Paste Special dialog box.

3. Select the Values option and click on OK.

4. Press Esc to cancel cut-copy mode.

All formulas in the selected range are converted to their current values.

Potential problems with external reference formulas

Using external reference formulas can be quite useful, but some risk is involved. In other words, the links become severed when you don't want them to. In almost every case, you'll be able to reestablish lost links. If you open the workbook and Excel can't locate the file, you'll be presented with a dialog box to let you specify the workbook and re-create the links. You also can change the source file using the Change Source button in the Links dialog box. The following sections discuss some pointers that you must keep in mind when using external reference formulas.

Renaming or moving a source workbook

If the source document is renamed or moved to a different folder, Excel won't be able to update the links. You need to use the Links dialog box and specify the new source document.

Using the File⇨Save As command

If both the source workbook and the destination workbook are open, Excel doesn't display the full path in the external reference formulas. If you use the File⇨Save As command with the source workbook, Excel modifies the external references to use the new workbook name. In some cases, this may be what you want. But in other cases, it may not be.

Modifying a source workbook

If you open a workbook that is a source workbook for another workbook, be extremely careful if the destination workbook is not open at the same time. For example, if you add a new row to the source workbook, the cells all move down one row. When you open the destination workbook, it continues to use the old cell references — which are now invalid.

To avoid this problem, make sure that the destination workbook is open when you modify the source workbook. If so, Excel adjusts the external references in the destination workbook when you make changes to the source workbook. You also can avoid this problem by using names rather than cell references in your link formula.

Using links to recover data from corrupted files

Sooner or later (with luck, later), it's bound to happen. You attempt to open an Excel workbook, and you get an error telling you that Excel can't access the file. Most of the time this indicates that the file (somehow) got corrupted. If you're lucky, you have a recent backup that you can fall back on. If you're *very* lucky, you haven't made any changes to the file since it was backed up. But let's assume that you fell a bit behind on your backup procedures, and the dead file is the only version you have.

Although I don't know of any method to fully recover a corrupt file, I share with you a method that sometimes lets you recover at least some of the data from worksheets in the file (values, not formulas). Your actual success will depend on how badly the file is corrupted.

This technique involves creating an external reference formula that refers to the corrupt file. You'll need to know the names of the worksheets that you want to recover. For example, assume that you have a workbook named Summary Data that can't be opened.

Further assume that this workbook is stored in a folder named Sheets on the C drive. This workbook has one sheet, named Sheet1. To attempt to recover the data from this worksheet:

1. Open a new workbook.

2. In cell A1, enter the following external reference formula:

   `='C:\Sheets\[Summary Data]Sheet1'!A1`

   If you're lucky, this formula will return the value in cell A1 of Sheet1 in the corrupt file.

3. Copy this formula down and to the right to recover as many valves as you can.

4. Convert the external references formulas to values and save the workbook.

If the corrupt file has additional worksheets, repeat these steps for any other worksheets in the workbook (you'll need to know the exact sheet names).

Intermediary links

Excel doesn't place many limitations on the complexity of your network of external references. For example, Workbook A can have external references that refer to Workbook B, which can be an external reference that refers to Workbook C. In this case, the value in Workbook A ultimately depends on the value in Workbook C. Workbook B is an intermediary link.

I don't recommend these types of links, but if you must use them, be aware that external reference formulas aren't updated if the workbook isn't open. In the preceding example, assume that Workbooks A and C are open. If you change the value in Workbook C, it won't be reflected in Workbook A because Workbook B (the intermediary link) isn't open.

Consolidating Worksheets

I use the term *consolidation* to refer to a number of operations that involve multiple worksheets or multiple workbook files. In some cases, consolidation may involve creating link formulas. Here are two common examples of consolidation:

✦ The budget for each department in your company is stored in a separate worksheet in a single workbook. You need to consolidate the data and create company-wide totals.

✦ Each department head submits his/her budget to you in a separate workbook. Your job is to consolidate these files into a company-wide budget.

Depending on a number of factors, these tasks can be very difficult or quite easy. The main factor is whether the information is laid out exactly the same in each worksheet. If so, the job is relatively simple (as you'll see shortly).

If the worksheets aren't laid out identically, they may be close enough. In the second example, some budget files submitted to you may be missing categories that aren't used by a particular department. In this case, you can use a handy feature in Excel that matches data by using row and column titles. More on this later.

If the worksheets have little or no resemblance to each other, your best bet might be to edit the sheets so that they correspond to each other. In some cases, it may be more efficient to simply reenter the information in a standard format.

You can use any of the following techniques to consolidate information from multiple workbooks:

✦ Use external reference formulas.

✦ Copy the data and use the Paste Special command.

✦ Use Excel's Data⇨Consolidate command.

✦ Use a pivot table. (I discuss this feature in Chapter 25.)

I discuss these methods (except pivot tables) in the sections that follow.

Consolidating worksheets using formulas

Consolidating with formulas simply involves creating formulas that use references to other worksheets or other workbooks. The primary advantages are the following:

✦ Dynamic updating. If the values in the source worksheets change, the formulas are updated automatically.

✦ The source workbooks don't need to be open when you create the consolidation formulas.

If the worksheets that you are consolidating are in the same workbook — and if all of the worksheets are laid out identically — the consolidation task is quite simple. You can just use standard formulas to create the consolidations. For example, to compute the total for cell A1 in worksheets named Sheet2 through Sheet10, enter the following formula:

```
=SUM(Sheet2:Sheet10!A1)
```

You can enter this manually or use the multisheet selection technique that I discuss in Chapter 8. You can then copy this formula to create summary formulas for other cells. Figure 19-4 shows this technique at work.

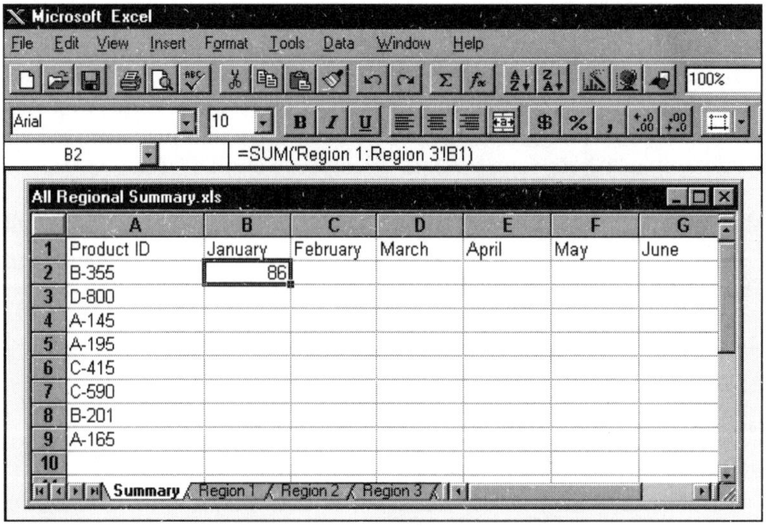

Figure 19-4: Consolidating multiple worksheets by using formulas.

If the consolidation involves other workbooks, you can use external reference formulas to perform your consolidation. For example, if you want to add the values in cell A1 from Sheet1 in two workbooks (named `Region1` and `Region2`), you can use the following formula:

```
=[Region1.xls]Sheet1!A1+[Region2.xls]Sheet1!A1
```

This formula, of course, can include any number of external references up to the 1,024-character limit for a formula. With many external references, such a formula can be quite lengthy and confusing if you need to edit it.

Caution It's important to remember that Excel expands the references to include the full path — which can increase the length of the formula. Therefore, it's possible that this expansion will exceed the limit and create an invalid formula.

If the worksheets that you're consolidating aren't laid out the same, you can still use formulas — but you'll have to ensure that each formula refers to the correct cell.

Consolidating worksheets using Paste Special

Another method of consolidating information is to use the Edit⇨Paste Special command. This method is applicable only when all of the worksheets that you're consolidating are open. The disadvantage — a major disadvantage — is that the consolidation isn't dynamic. In other words, it doesn't generate a formula. So, if any data that was consolidated changes, the consolidation will no longer be accurate.

This technique takes advantage of the fact that the Paste Special command can perform a mathematical operation when it pastes data from the Clipboard. Figure 19-5 shows the Paste Special dialog box.

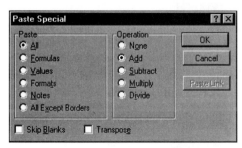

Figure 19-5: The Paste Special dialog box.

To use this method:

1. Copy the data from the first source range.

2. Activate the destination workbook and select the cell where the consolidation will occur.

3. Select the Edit➪Paste Special command, click on the Add option, and click on OK.

Repeat these steps for each source range to be consolidated. As you can see, this can be quite error prone and isn't really a very good method of consolidating data.

Consolidating worksheets using Data➪Consolidate

For the ultimate in data consolidation, use Excel's Data➪Consolidate command. This method is quite flexible, and in some cases it even works if the source worksheets aren't laid out identically. This technique can create consolidations that are *static* (no link formulas) or *dynamic* (with link formulas). The Data➪Consolidate command supports the following methods of consolidation:

✦ **By position:** This method is accurate only if the worksheets are laid out identically.

✦ **By category:** Excel uses row and column labels to match data in the source worksheets. Use this option if the data is laid out differently in the source worksheets or if some source worksheets are missing rows or columns.

Figure 19-6 shows the Consolidate dialog box, which appears when you select the Data➪Consolidate command. Following is a description of the controls in this dialog box.

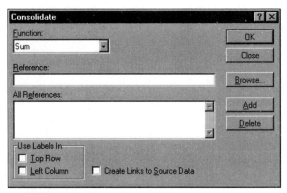

Figure 19-6: The Consolidate dialog box lets you specify ranges to be consolidated.

✦ **Function:** This is where you specify the type of consolidation. Most of the time you'll use Sum, but you also can select from ten other options: Count, Avg, Max, Min, Product, Count Nums, StdDev (standard deviation), StdDevp (population standard deviation), Var (variance), or Varp (population variance).

✦ **Reference:** This text box holds a range from a source file that will be consolidated. You can enter the range reference manually or use any standard pointing technique (if the workbook is open). After the range is entered in this box, click on the Add button to add it to the All References list. If you're consolidating by position, don't include labels in the range. If you're consolidating by category, *do* include labels in the range.

✦ **All References:** This list box contains the list of references that you have added with the Add button.

✦ **Use Labels In:** These check boxes tell Excel to examine the labels in the top row, the left column, or both positions to perform the consolidation. Use these options when you're consolidating by category.

✦ **Create Links to Source Data:** This option, when selected, creates an outline in the destination worksheet that consists of external references to the destination cells. In addition, it includes summary formulas in the outline. If this option isn't selected, the consolidation won't use formulas.

✦ **Browse:** This button displays a dialog box that lets you select a workbook on disk. It inserts the filename in the Reference box, but you have to supply the range reference.

✦ **Add:** This button adds the reference in the Reference box to the All References list.

✦ **Delete:** This button deletes the selected reference from the All Reference list.

An example

To demonstrate the power of the Data⇨Consolidate command, I use a simple example. Figure 19-7 shows three worksheets that will be consolidated. These workbooks report product sales for three months. Notice, however, that they don't all report on the same products. In addition, the products aren't even listed in the same order. In other words, these worksheets aren't laid out identically — which would make it very difficult to create consolidation formulas.

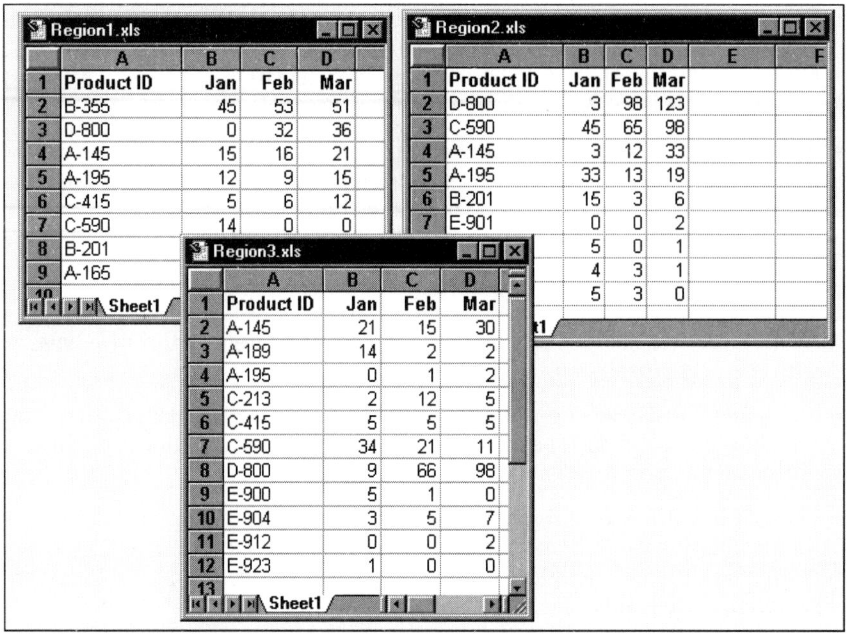

Region1.xls

	A	B	C	D
1	Product ID	Jan	Feb	Mar
2	B-355	45	53	51
3	D-800	0	32	36
4	A-145	15	16	21
5	A-195	12	9	15
6	C-415	5	6	12
7	C-590	14	0	0
8	B-201			
9	A-165			

Region2.xls

	A	B	C	D	E	F
1	Product ID	Jan	Feb	Mar		
2	D-800	3	98	123		
3	C-590	45	65	98		
4	A-145	3	12	33		
5	A-195	33	13	19		
6	B-201	15	3	6		
7	E-901	0	0	2		
		5	0	1		
		4	3	1		
		5	3	0		

Region3.xls

	A	B	C	D
1	Product ID	Jan	Feb	Mar
2	A-145	21	15	30
3	A-189	14	2	2
4	A-195	0	1	2
5	C-213	2	12	5
6	C-415	5	5	5
7	C-590	34	21	11
8	D-800	9	66	98
9	E-900	5	1	0
10	E-904	3	5	7
11	E-912	0	0	2
12	E-923	1	0	0

Figure 19-7: Three worksheets to be consolidated.

To consolidate this information, start with a new workbook. The source workbooks can be open or not — it doesn't matter.

1. Select the Data⇨Consolidate command. Excel displays its Consolidate dialog box.
2. Select the type of consolidation summary that you want. Use Sum for this example.
3. Enter the reference for the first worksheet to be consolidated. If the workbook is open, you can point to the reference. If it's not open, click on the Browse button to locate the file on disk. The reference must include a range. Use A1:D100. This range is larger than the actual range to be consolidated, but this ensures that the consolidation will still work if new rows are added. When the reference in the Reference box is correct, click on Add to add it to the All References list.
4. Enter the reference for the second worksheet. You can simply edit the existing reference: change Region1 to Region2. Click on Add. This reference will be added to the All References list.
5. Enter the reference for the second worksheet. You can simply edit the existing reference: change Region2 to Region3. Click on Add. This final reference will be added to the All References list.

6. Because the worksheets aren't laid out the same, select the Left Column and Top Row check boxes. This step causes Excel to match the data by using the labels.
7. Select the Create Links to Source Data check box. This causes Excel to create an outline with external references.
8. Click on OK to begin the consolidation.

In seconds, Excel creates the consolidation beginning at the active cell. Figure 19-8 shows the result. Notice that Excel created an outline, which is collapsed to show only the subtotals for each product. If you expand the outline, you can see the details. Examine it further and you'll discover that each detail cell is an external reference formula that uses the appropriate cell in the source file. Therefore, the destination range is updated automatically if any data is changed.

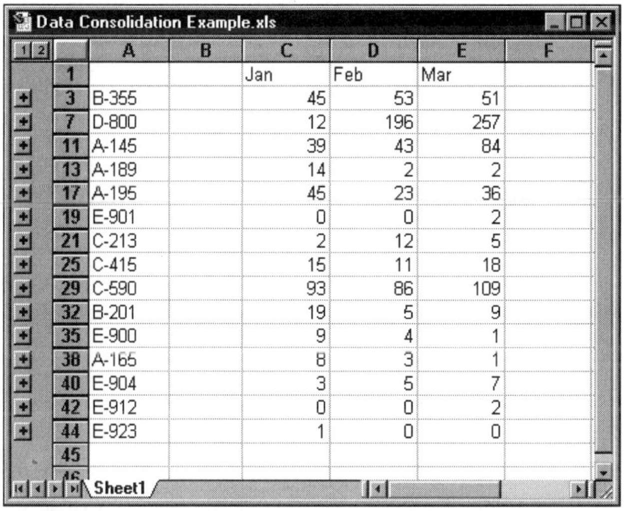
Data Consolidation Example.xls

	A	B	C	D	E	F
1			Jan	Feb	Mar	
3	B-355		45	53	51	
7	D-800		12	196	257	
11	A-145		39	43	84	
13	A-189		14	2	2	
17	A-195		45	23	36	
19	E-901		0	0	2	
21	C-213		2	12	5	
25	C-415		15	11	18	
29	C-590		93	86	109	
32	B-201		19	5	9	
35	E-900		9	4	1	
38	A-165		8	3	1	
40	E-904		3	5	7	
42	E-912		0	0	2	
44	E-923		1	0	0	
45						

Sheet1

Figure 19-8: The result of the consolidation.

More about consolidation

Excel is very flexible when it comes to sources to be consolidated. You can consolidate data from:

- ✦ Workbooks that are open
- ✦ Workbooks that are closed (you'll have to enter the reference manually — but you can use the Browse button to get the filename part of the reference)
- ✦ The same workbook in which you're creating the consolidation

And, of course, you can mix and match any of the preceding in a single consolidation.

Excel remembers the references that you entered in the Consolidate dialog box and saves these with the workbook. Therefore, if you want to refresh a consolidation later, you won't have to reenter the references.

If you perform the consolidation by matching labels, be aware that the matches must be exact. For example, *Jan* does not match *January*. The matching isn't case sensitive, however, so *April* will match *APRIL*. In addition, the labels can be in any order and they need not be in the same order in all of the source ranges.

If you don't choose the Create Links to Source Data check box, Excel won't create formulas. This generates a static consolidation. If the data on any of the source worksheets changes, the consolidation won't update automatically. To update the summary information, you need to select the destination range and repeat the Data⇨Consolidate command.

Tip If you name the destination range `Consolidate_Area`, you don't need to select it before you update the consolidation. `Consolidate_Area` is a name that has special meaning to Excel.

If you choose the Create Links to Source Data check box, Excel creates an outline. This is a standard worksheet outline, and you can manipulate it using the techniques described in Chapter 18.

On the CD-ROM The companion CD-ROM contains an example of data consolidation. The workbook is named CONSOLID.XLS.

Summary

In this chapter, I discuss two important spreadsheet procedures: linking and consolidation. Linking is the process of using references to cells in external workbooks get data for use in your worksheet. Consolidation is the process of combining or summarizing information from two or more worksheets (which can be in multiple workbooks). I cover various methods of linking and consolidation and list potential pitfalls.

✦   ✦   ✦

Creating and Using Array Formulas

In This Chapter

An introduction to the concept of arrays

Advantages and disadvantages of using array formulas

Array formulas that produce a single result versus array formulas that produce results in multiple cells

How to define array constants

Practical examples of array formulas

This chapter introduces a new concept: *array formulas*. Understanding this special type of formula may open a whole new world of analytical capability. Working with arrays (rather than with individual cells) requires a different type of mind-set. Some people never quite get the hang of arrays, and others take to this concept quickly. If you're in the former group, don't despair. Using array formulas can be considered an optional skill.

Introducing Arrays

In this chapter I discuss two concepts:

+ **Array:** A collection of cells or values that is operated on as a group. An array can be stored in cells or be a named constant.

+ **Array Formula:** A formula that uses one or more arrays either directly or as arguments for a function. An array formula can occupy one or more cells.

If you've ever done any computer programming, you've probably been exposed to arrays. An array is a collection of items. Excel's arrays can be one-dimensional or two-dimensional. These dimensions correspond to rows and columns. For example, a one-dimensional array can be a cell range that occupies cells in one row (a horizontal array) or one column (a vertical array). A two-dimensional array occupies cells in one or more rows and columns.

You can perform operations on arrays using array formulas. For example, if you construct an array formula to multiply a five-item vertical array by another five-column vertical array, the result is another five-column vertical array that consists of each element in the first array multiplied by each corresponding element in the second array. Because Excel can fit only one value in a cell, the results of an operation such as this one occupy five cells — and the same array formula is in each of the five cells.

Figure 20-1 illustrates this example. Each cell in the range C1:C5 holds the same formula: {=A1:A5*B1:B5}. The result occupies five cells and contains each element of the first array multiplied by each corresponding element in the second array. The brackets around the formula designate it as an array formula (more about this later).

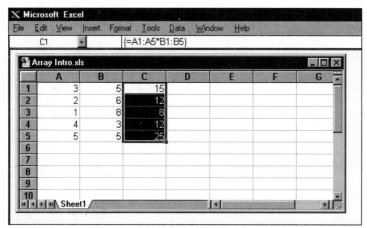

Figure 20-1: A single array formula entered in the range C1:C5 produces results in five cells.

As you'll see, arrays have their pros and cons. At the very least, this feature provides an alternative way of doing some operations and is the only way to perform others.

Advantages of array formulas

Some of the advantages of array formulas (as opposed to single-cell formulas) are as follows:

✦ They can be much more efficient to work with.

✦ They can eliminate the need for intermediary formulas.

✦ They can enable you to do things that would otherwise be difficult or impossible.

✦ They may use less memory.

Disadvantages of array formulas

This list shows a few disadvantages of array formulas:

✦ Some large arrays can slow your spreadsheet recalculation time to a crawl.

✦ They can make your worksheets more difficult for others to understand.

✦ You must remember to enter an array formula with a special key sequence (Ctrl+Shift+Enter). Otherwise, the result won't be what you expect.

Understanding Arrays

In this section, I present several examples to help clarify this concept. As always, you can get more from this chapter if you follow along on your own computer.

Array formulas versus standard formulas

You can often use a single array formula to substitute for a range of copied formulas. Figure 20-2 shows two examples; the upper worksheet uses standard single-result formulas. The formulas use the SQRT function to calculate the square roots of the values in column A. I entered =**SQRT(A3)** into cell B3 and copied it down to the three cells below it. This example uses four different formulas to calculate the results in column B.

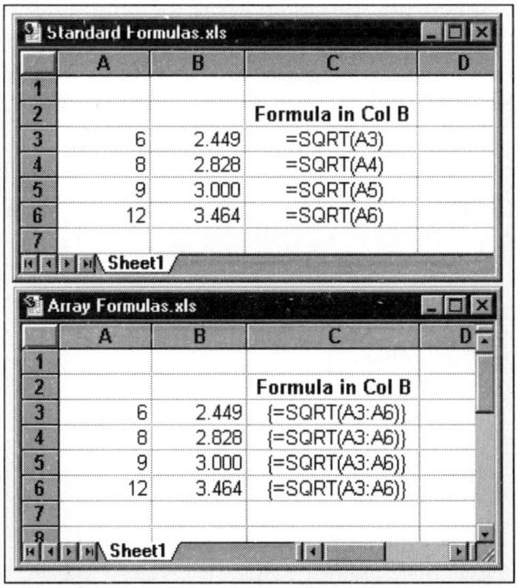

Figure 20-2: These workbooks accomplish the same result, but one uses standard formulas and the other uses an array formula.

The lower workbook uses a single array formula, which is inserted into all four cells. Here are the steps to enter this array formula:

1. Select the range B3:B6.
2. Enter **SQRT(A3:A6)**.
3. Press Ctrl+Shift+Enter to designate the formula as an array formula.

Excel enters the array formula into the three selected cells. It also adds brackets around the formula to indicate that it's an array formula. The key point here is that this example uses only one formula, but the results appear in four different cells because it's operating on a four-cell array.

To further demonstrate that this is in fact one formula, try to edit one of the cells in B3:B6. You'll find that Excel won't let you make any changes. To modify an array formula that uses more than one cell, you must select the entire array before editing the formula.

Note There is virtually no advantage to using an array formula in the preceding example (except perhaps saving the time it takes to copy the formula). The real value of array formulas will become apparent as you work through this chapter.

An array formula in one cell

Figure 20-3 shows another example. The worksheet on the left uses standard formulas to calculate the average change from the pretest to the posttest. The worksheet on the right also calculates the average changes, but it uses an array formula. This array formula resides in only one cell because the result is a single value. This is an example of how an array formula can eliminate the need for intermediary formulas. As you can see, it's not necessary to include an additional column to calculate the change in scores.

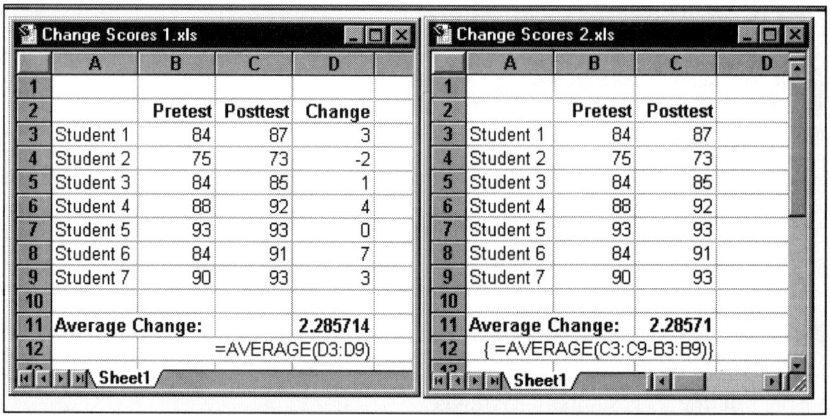

	A	B	C	D		A	B	C	D
1									
2		Pretest	Posttest	Change			Pretest	Posttest	
3	Student 1	84	87	3		Student 1	84	87	
4	Student 2	75	73	-2		Student 2	75	73	
5	Student 3	84	85	1		Student 3	84	85	
6	Student 4	88	92	4		Student 4	88	92	
7	Student 5	93	93	0		Student 5	93	93	
8	Student 6	84	91	7		Student 6	84	91	
9	Student 7	90	93	3		Student 7	90	93	
10									
11	Average Change:			2.285714		Average Change:		2.28571	
12			=AVERAGE(D3:D9)				{ =AVERAGE(C3:C9-B3:B9)}		

Change Scores 1.xls / Sheet1   Change Scores 2.xls / Sheet1

Figure 20-3: Using an array formula to eliminate intermediary formulas.

The formula in cell C11 is as follows:

```
{=AVERAGE(C3:C9-B3:B9)}
```

This array formula operates on two arrays, which are stored in cells. It subtracts each element of B3:B9 from the corresponding element in C3:C9 and produces (in memory) a new seven-element array that holds the result. The AVERAGE function computes the average of the elements in the new array, and the result is displayed in the cell.

Looping with arrays

Excel's array feature lets you perform individual operations on each cell in a range — in much the same way as a program language's looping feature enables you to work with elements of an array. For example, assume that you have a range of cells (named Data) that contain positive and negative values. You need to compute the average of the positive values in the range. Figure 20-4 shows an example.

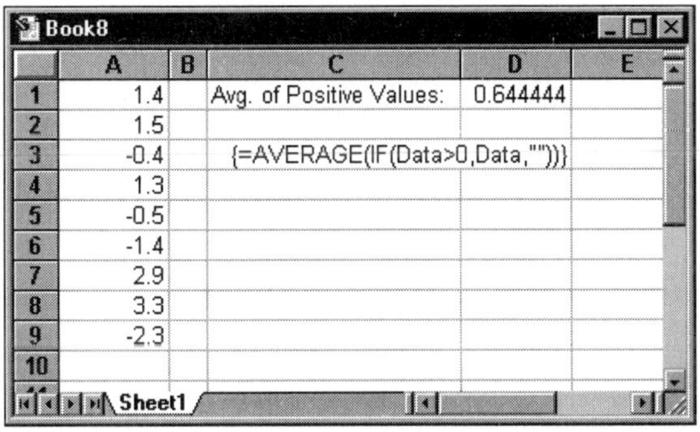

Figure 20-4: You can use an array formula to calculate the average of just the positive values in this range.

One approach is to sort the data and then use the AVERAGE function to calculate the average on just the positive values. A more efficient approach uses the following array formula:

```
={AVERAGE(IF(Data>0,Data,""))}
```

The IF function in this formula checks each element in the input range to see whether it's greater than zero. If so, the IF function returns the value from the input range; otherwise, it returns an empty string. The result is an array that's identical to the input array, except that all nonpositive values are replaced with a null string. The AVERAGE function then computes the average of this new array, and the result is displayed in the cell.

Note The preceding problem also can be solved with the following nonarray formula:

```
=SUMIF(Data,">0",Data)/COUNTIF(Data,">0")
```

Many similar operations cannot be performed with a standard formula, however. For example, if you want to calculate the median of the positive values in a range, an array formula is the only solution.

Later in this chapter I cover more useful examples that use arrays. But now it's time to provide some rules for how to work with arrays and array formulas.

Working with Arrays

This section deals with the mechanics of selecting arrays and entering and editing array formulas. As you'll see, these procedures are a little different from working with ordinary ranges and formulas.

Entering an array formula

When you enter an array formula into a cell or range, you must follow a special procedure so that Excel knows that you want an array formula rather than a normal formula. You enter a normal formula into a cell by pressing Enter. You enter an array formula into one or more cells by pressing Ctrl+Shift+Enter.

You can identify array formulas because they are enclosed in brackets in the formula bar. For example, {=SQRT(A1:A12)} is an array formula.

Note Don't enter the brackets when you create an array formula; Excel inserts them for you. If the result of an array formula consists of more than one value, you must select all the cells before you enter the formula. If you fail to do this, only the first result shows.

Editing an array formula

If an array formula occupies multiple cells, you must edit the entire range as though it were a single cell. The key point to remember is that you can't change just one element of an array formula. If you attempt to do so, Excel pops up the messages shown in Figure 20-5.

The following rules apply to multicell array formulas (if you try to do any of these things, Excel lets you know about it):

   ✦ You can't change the contents of any cell that makes up an array formula.

   ✦ You can't move cells that make up part of an array formula. You can, however, move an entire array formula.

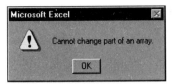

Figure 20-5: Excel's warning message reminds you that you can't edit just one cell of a multicell array.

✦ You can't delete cells that form part of an array formula, but you can delete an entire array.

✦ You can't insert new cells into an array range; this rule includes inserting rows or columns that would add new cells to an array range.

To edit an array formula, select all cells in the array range and activate the formula bar as usual (click on it or press F2). Excel removes the brackets from the formula while you're editing it. Edit the formula and then press Ctrl+Shift+Enter to enter the changes. All the cells in the array now reflect your editing changes.

Formatting arrays

Although you can't change any part of an array formula without changing all parts, you're free to apply formatting to the entire array or just parts of it.

Selecting an array range

You can select an array range manually by using the normal selection procedures. Or, you can use either of the following methods:

✦ Move to any cell in the array range. Issue the Edit⇨Go To command (or press F5), click on the Special button, and then choose the Current Array option. Click on OK to close the dialog box.

✦ Move to any cell in the array range and press Ctrl+/ to select the entire array.

Using Array Constants

So far, the examples in this chapter have used cell ranges for arrays. You also can use constant values as an array. These constants can be entered directly into a formula or defined using the Define Name dialog box. Array constants can be used in array formulas in place of a reference to a range of cells. To use an array constant in an array formula, type the set of values directly into the formula and enclose it in brackets. If you defined a name for the array constant, you can use the name instead.

Array constants can be either one-dimensional or two-dimensional. One-dimensional arrays can be either vertical or horizontal. The elements in a one-dimensional horizontal array are separated by commas. The following example is a one-dimensional horizontal array:

```
{1,2,3,4,5}
```

Because this array constant has five values, it requires five cells (in a row). To enter this array into a range, select a range that consists of one row and five columns. Then enter =**{1,2,3,4,5}** and press Ctrl+Shift+Enter.

Note When you use array constants, you must enter the brackets. Excel won't provide them for you. Here's another horizontal array, this one with seven elements:

```
{"Sun","Mon","Tue","Wed","Thu","Fri","Sat"}
```

Figure 20-6 demonstrates how you would create a named array constant using the Define Name dialog box.

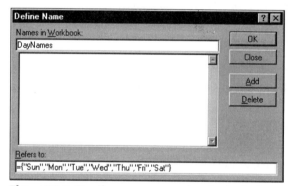

Figure 20-6: Creating an array constant in the Define Name dialog box.

The elements in a one-dimensional vertical array are separated by semicolons. Following is a six-element vertical array:

```
{10;20;30;40;50;60}
```

Here's another example of a vertical array, this one with four elements:

```
{"Widgets";"Sprockets";"Do-Dads";"Thing-A-Majigs"}
```

Two-dimensional arrays also separate the elements in a single row with commas and separate the rows with semicolons. The next example is a 3×4 array (three rows, each of which occupies four columns):

{1,2,3,4;5,6,7,8;9,10,11,12}

Figure 20-7 shows how this array appears in a worksheet. First, I created the array constant and named it MyArray. Then I selected A1:D3 and entered =**MyArray.** I pressed Ctrl+Shift+Enter to enter the array formula into the range.

Figure 20-7: An array constant used in a formula.

Note You can't list cell references, names, or formulas in an array formula in the same way as you list constants. For example, {2*3,3*3,4*3} isn't valid because it lists formulas. {A1,B1,C1} isn't valid either because it lists cell references. Instead, you should use a range reference, such as {A1:C1}.

It's important that you keep an array's dimensions in mind when you're performing operations on it. Consider the following array formula:

={2,3,4}*{10,11}

This formula multiplies a 1×3 array by a 1×2 array. Excel returns an array with three values: 20, 33, and #N/A. Because the second array wasn't large enough, Excel generated #N/A as the third element of the result.

Examples of Using Array Formulas

Perhaps the best way to learn about array formulas is by following examples and adapting them to your own needs. In this section, I present useful examples that give you a good idea of how you can use this feature.

On the CD-ROM All the examples presented in this section can be found in the workbook named ARRAY_FO.XLS on the companion CD-ROM. Each example is presented on a separate worksheet.

Using an array constant

Figure 20-8 shows a practical example of an array constant. I defined the following constant, named SalesRegions:

```
={"S. California";"PacificNW";"SouthWest";"Central";"SouthEast";"NorthEast"}
```

Because the elements are separated by semicolons, this is a vertical array. I selected A4:A9 and entered **=SalesRegions**, followed by Ctrl+Shift+Enter. The worksheet also shows the sales regions displayed horizontally. To do this, I selected A1:F1 and entered the following formula (using Ctrl+Shift+Enter):

```
{=TRANSPOSE(SalesRegions)}
```

The TRANSPOSE function converts a horizontal array to a vertical array (and vice versa).

	A	B	C	D	E	F
1	S. California	Pacific NW	SouthWest	Central	SouthEast	NorthEast
2						
3						
4	S. California					
5	Pacific NW					
6	SouthWest					
7	Central					
8	SouthEast					
9	NorthEast					
10						
11						
12						
13						

Array Formula Examples.xls

ArrayConstants / ValueInList / CountLetters / Ma

Figure 20-8: Using an array constant to enter the names of sales regions.

Note This is just one way to enter a stored list quickly into a range of cells. Perhaps a better approach is to create a custom list in the Custom Lists panel of the Options dialog box.

Identifying a value in a range

If you want to determine whether a particular value is contained in a range, you can use the Edit➪Find command. But you also can do this with an array formula. Figure 20-9 shows a worksheet with a list of names (named `Names`). An array formula in cell E4 checks the name entered into cell B1 (named `TestValue`). If the name exists, it displays the text *Name is in the list*. Otherwise, it displays *Name not found*.

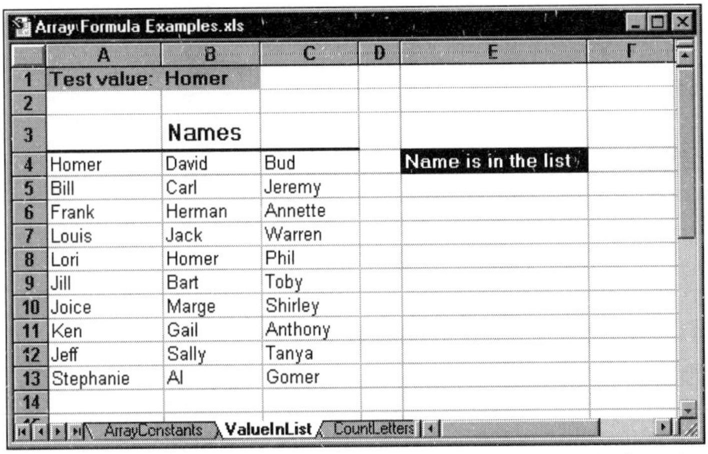

Figure 20-9: Determining whether a range contains a particular value.

The formula in cell E4 is as follows:

```
{=IF(OR(TestValue=Names),"Name is in the list","Name not found")}
```

This formula compares `TestValue` to each cell in the range `Names`. It builds a new array that consists of logical TRUE or FALSE values. The OR function returns TRUE if any of the values in the new array is TRUE. The IF function determines which message to display based on the result.

Counting characters in a range

This example demonstrates how to use nested functions in an array formula to loop through each element in the input range. Figure 20-10 shows a worksheet with text entered in a range named `WordList`. The array formula in cell B1 is as follows:

```
{=SUM(LEN(WordList))}
```

This formula is quite straightforward. It creates an array that consists of the length of each word in the `WordList` range. Then it uses the SUM formula to add the values in this new array. You could accomplish this without an array formula by using an additional column of formulas and then summing the results.

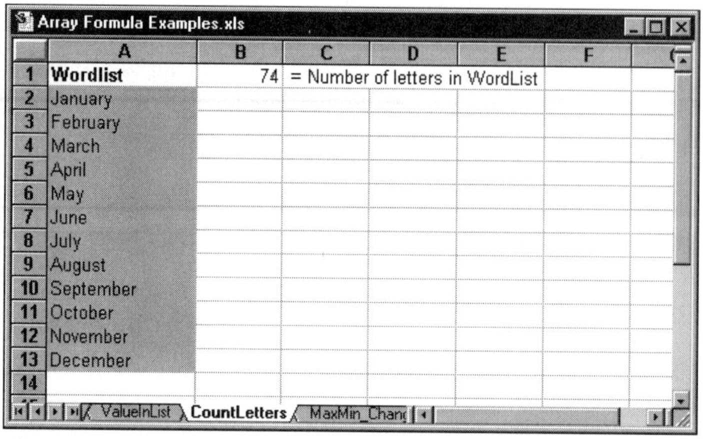
Array Formula Examples.xls

	A	B	C	D	E	F
1	**Wordlist**	74	= Number of letters in WordList			
2	January					
3	February					
4	March					
5	April					
6	May					
7	June					
8	July					
9	August					
10	September					
11	October					
12	November					
13	December					
14						

ValueInList | CountLetters | MaxMin_Chan

Figure 20-10: This array formula counts the number of characters in a range of text.

Computing maximum and minimum changes

Figure 20-11 shows another example of how an array formula can eliminate the need for intermediary formulas. This worksheet shows two test scores for a group of students. Array formulas compare the two tests and calculate the largest decrease and the largest increase. The formulas are as follows:

```
E3:    {=MIN(C3:C11-B3:B11)}
E4:    {=MAX(C3:C11-B3:B11)}
```

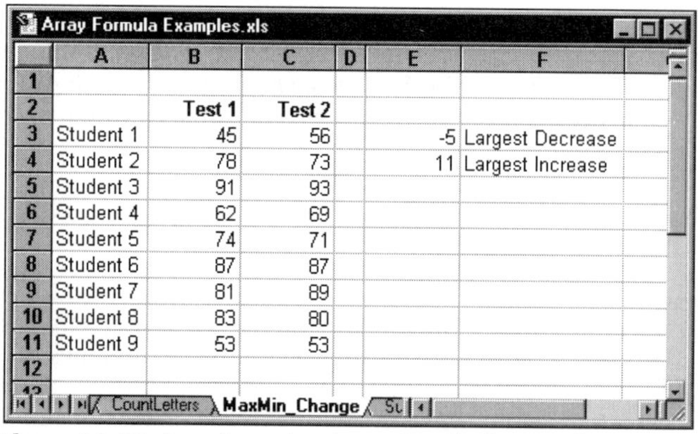
Array Formula Examples.xls

	A	B	C	D	E	F
1						
2		**Test 1**	**Test 2**			
3	Student 1	45	56		-5	Largest Decrease
4	Student 2	78	73		11	Largest Increase
5	Student 3	91	93			
6	Student 4	62	69			
7	Student 5	74	71			
8	Student 6	87	87			
9	Student 7	81	89			
10	Student 8	83	80			
11	Student 9	53	53			
12						

CountLetters | MaxMin_Change | Su

Figure 20-11: Array formulas determine the largest decrease and the largest increase in test scores.

Looping through characters in a cell

The following array formula calculates the sum of the digits in an integer, which is stored in a cell named `Number`:

```
{=SUM(VALUE(MID(Number,ROW($A$1:OFFSET($A$1,LEN(Number)-1,0)),1))))}
```

This is a rather complex formula and makes use of an interesting trick. I'll break the formula down into its parts so that you can see how it works. (Figure 20-12 shows an example.)

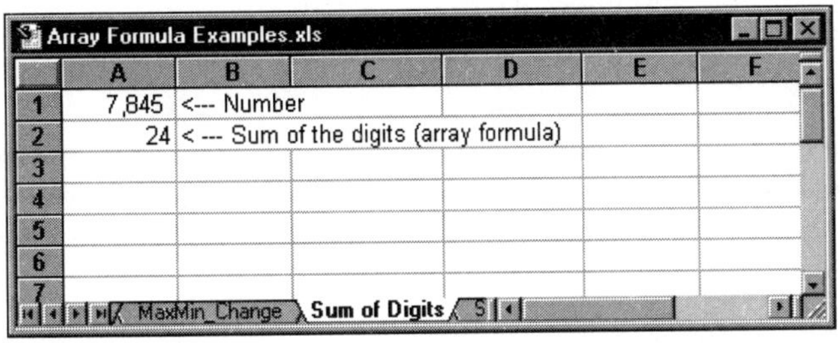

Figure 20-12: An array formula calculates the sum of the digits in a value.

You may be confused by the ROW function (this is the trick). This function is used to generate an array of consecutive integers beginning with 1 and ending with the number of digits in the absolute value of `Number`.

If `Number` is 489, then LEN(Number) is 3. The ROW function can then be simplified as:

```
{=ROW($A$1:OFFSET($A$1,3-1,0))}
```

This formula generates an array with three elements: {1,2,3}. This generated array is used as the second argument for the MID function (the third argument is 1). The MID part of the formula, simplified a bit and expressed as values is:

```
{=MID(489,{1,2,3},1)}
```

This formula generates an array with three elements: {4,8,9}. Simplifying again, and adding the SUM function, we get:

```
{=SUM({4,8,9})}
```

This produces the result of 21.

Following is another version of this formula that also works with negative numbers. I added the ABS function to calculate the absolute value of the function:

```
{=SUM(VALUE(MID(ABS(Number),ROW($A$1:OFFSET($A$1,LEN(ABS(Number))-1,0)),1))))}
```

Summing every *n*th digit in a range

The next example can be quite useful. Suppose that you have a range of values and you want to compute the sum of every third value in the list — the first, the fourth, the seventh, and so on. There's no way to accomplish this with a standard formula. The following array formula does the job, however. It assumes that a cell named Nth determines which values to sum, and the range to sum is named Data.

```
{=IF(Nth=0,0,SUM(IF(MOD(ROW(Data),Nth)=0,Data,0)))}
```

The formula uses the MOD function to determine which values to sum. If the MOD function returns 0, the value is included in the array to sum. Notice that there's a special case for when Nth is 0 (that is, sum every cell in the range). That's because the MOD function returns an error when its second argument is 0.

This formula has a limitation: It works only when Data consists of a single column of values. That's because it uses the ROW function to determine the element in the array.

Figure 20-13 shows an example that uses the preceding array formula plus a series of intermediary formulas to calculate the result without using an array formula.

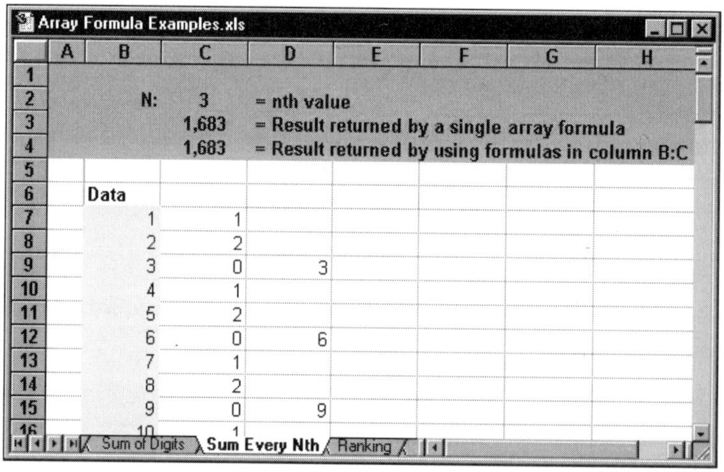

Figure 20-13: You can use an array formula to sum every *n*th element in a range — or use a series of intermediary formulas (a less efficient approach).

An alternate method of ranking

It's often desirable to compute rank orders for a range of data. If you have a worksheet with the annual sales figures for 20 salespeople, for example, you may want to know how each person ranks, from highest to lowest.

If you do this sort of thing, you've probably discovered Excel's RANK function. You may have noticed, however, that the ranks produced by this function don't handle ties the way you might like. For example, if two values are tied for third place, they both receive a rank of 3. Many people prefer to assign each an average (or midpoint) of the ranks — that is, a rank of 3.5 for both values tied for third place.

Figure 20-14 shows a worksheet that uses two methods to rank a column of values (named `Sales`). The first method (column C) uses Excel's RANK function. Column D uses array formulas to compute the ranks. The array formula in cell D2 follows:

```
{=IF((SUM(IF(Sales=B2,1)))=1,(SUM(IF(Sales>=B2,1,0))),(SUM(IF(Sales>=B2,1)))-
    ((SUM(IF(Sales=B2,1)))-1)*0.5)}
```

This formula was entered into cell D2 and then copied to the cells below it.

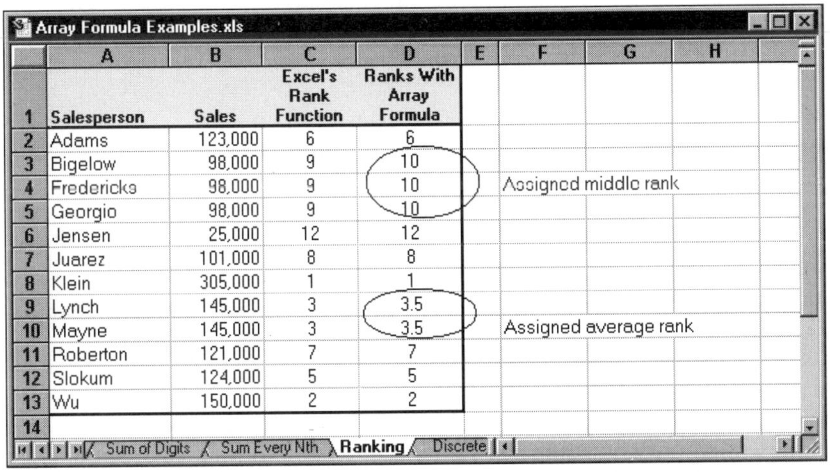

Salesperson	Sales	Excel's Rank Function	Ranks With Array Formula
Adams	123,000	6	6
Bigelow	98,000	9	10
Fredericks	98,000	9	10
Georgio	98,000	9	10
Jensen	25,000	12	12
Juarez	101,000	8	8
Klein	305,000	1	1
Lynch	145,000	3	3.5
Mayne	145,000	3	3.5
Roberton	121,000	7	7
Slokum	124,000	5	5
Wu	150,000	2	2

Figure 20-14: Ranking data with Excel's RANK function and with array formulas.

The formula is rather complex, but breaking it down into parts should help you understand how it works.

Frequency distributions

Before Excel 5, the only way to calculate frequency distributions was to use array formulas. Beginning with Excel 5, however, the COUNTIF function provided a more direct way to generate frequency distributions.

Figure 20-15 shows a worksheet with a series of scores in column A that range from 1 to 4. Column D contains array formulas to calculate the frequency of each score. The formula in D6 is as follows:

```
{=SUM(IF(Scores=C3,1))}
```

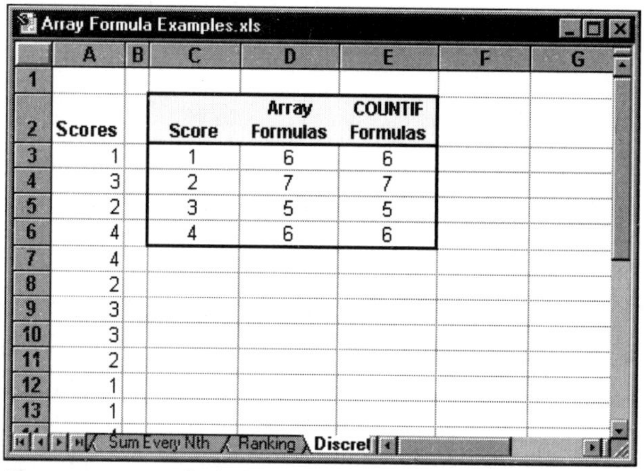

Figure 20-15: Calculating discrete frequency distributions using array formulas and COUNTIF functions.

The corresponding formulas in column E use the COUNTIF function. The formula in E6 is as follows:

```
=COUNTIF(Scores,C3)
```

Both of these methods count specific values. But what if the scores are noninteger values, as in Figure 20-16? Both types of formulas require modification to handle noninteger data. The array formula can be modified as follows:

```
=SUM(IF(Scores>=C3,1))-SUM(IF(Scores>=C4,1))
```

The revised COUNTIF formula follows:

```
=COUNTIF(Scores,">="&C3)-COUNTIF(Scores,">="&C4)
```

Note The array formula requires that you add an additional value in column C so that the last array formula doesn't refer to an empty cell (I added a value of 99).

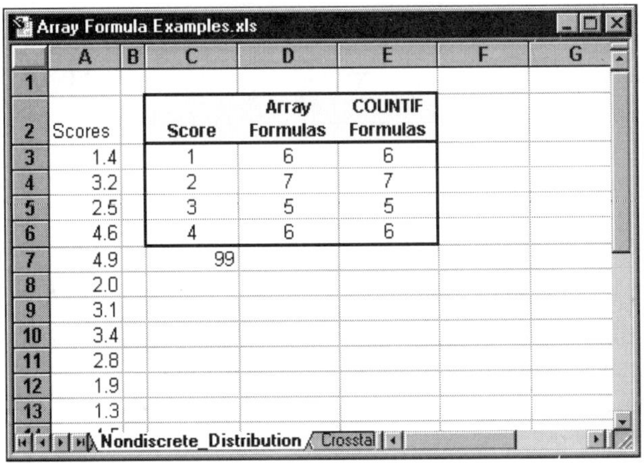

Figure 20-16: Calculating nondiscrete frequency distributions using array formulas and COUNTIF functions.

You also can use the Analysis ToolPak to compute distributions (see Chapter 28). An advantage to using arrays or COUNTIF functions, however, is that these procedures are dynamic and display the correct values if you change the input data.

Dynamic crosstabs

In the preceding section, you see that using COUNTIF is a better alternative than using array formulas for calculating frequency distributions. In this section, I demonstrate how to extend these distributions into another dimension and create crosstabs. In this case, an array formula is the only method that will get the job done. This technique lets you create a dynamic crosstab table that is updated automatically whenever the data is changed.

The worksheet in Figure 20-17 shows a simple expense account listing. Each item consists of the date, the expense category, and the amount spent. Each column of data is a named range, indicated in the first row.

I used array formulas to summarize this information into a handy table that shows the total expenses, by category, for each day. Cell F3 contains the following array formula, which was copied to the remaining 11 cells in the table:

```
{=SUM(IF($E3&F$2=DATES&CATEGORIES,AMOUNTS))}
```

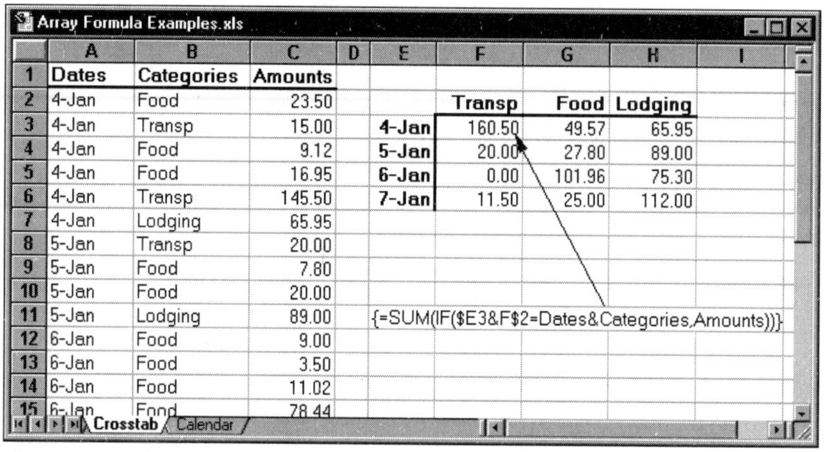

Array Formula Examples.xls

	A	B	C	D	E	F	G	H
1	Dates	Categories	Amounts					
2	4-Jan	Food	23.50			Transp	Food	Lodging
3	4-Jan	Transp	15.00		4-Jan	160.50	49.57	65.95
4	4-Jan	Food	9.12		5-Jan	20.00	27.80	89.00
5	4-Jan	Food	16.95		6-Jan	0.00	101.96	75.30
6	4-Jan	Transp	145.50		7-Jan	11.50	25.00	112.00
7	4-Jan	Lodging	65.95					
8	5-Jan	Transp	20.00					
9	5-Jan	Food	7.80					
10	5-Jan	Food	20.00					
11	5-Jan	Lodging	89.00		{=SUM(IF($E3&F$2=Dates&Categories,Amounts))}			
12	6-Jan	Food	9.00					
13	6-Jan	Food	3.50					
14	6-Jan	Food	11.02					
15	6-Jan	Food	78.44					

Figure 20-17: You can use array formulas to summarize data like this in a dynamic crosstab table.

These array formulas display the totals for each day, by category.

This formula operates similarly to the more simple one that I demonstrate in the preceding section. This one has a few new twists, however. Rather than count the number of entries, the formula adds the appropriate value in the `AMOUNTS` range. It does so, however, only if the row and column name in the summary table matches the corresponding entries in the `DATES` and `CATEGORIES` ranges. It does the comparison by concatenating (using the & operator) the row and column names and comparing the resulting string to the concatenation of the corresponding `DATES` and `CATEGORIES` values. If the two match exactly, the =SUM function kicks in and adds the corresponding value in the `AMOUNTS` range.

This technique can be customized, of course, to hold any number of different categories and any number of dates. You can eliminate the dates, in fact, and substitute people's names, departments, regions, and so on.

Cross-Reference

You also can crosstabulate data by creating a pivot table. But, unlike a pivot table, using the procedure described here is completely dynamic (a pivot table must be updated if the data changes). I discuss pivot tables in Chapter 25.

A single-formula calendar

The final array formula example is perhaps the most impressive. Figure 20-18 shows a monthly calendar that is calculated using a single array formula entered in B6:H11.

This workbook includes a few additional bells and whistles. For example, you can choose the month and year to display by using dialog box controls inserted directly on the worksheet. When you change the month or year, the calendar is updated immediately. The array formula is as follows:

```
{=IF(MONTH(StartDate)<>MONTH(StartDate-StartDOW+Week*7+
     Weekday-1),"",StartDate-StartDOW+Week*7+Weekday-1)}
```

This formula uses a few cell references (StartDate and StartDOW) and two named array constants, defined as follows:

```
Week:     ={0;1;2;3;4;5}
Weekday:  ={1,2,3,4,5,6,7}
```

I leave it up to you to figure out how this works. Suffice it to say that it took more than a few minutes to develop.

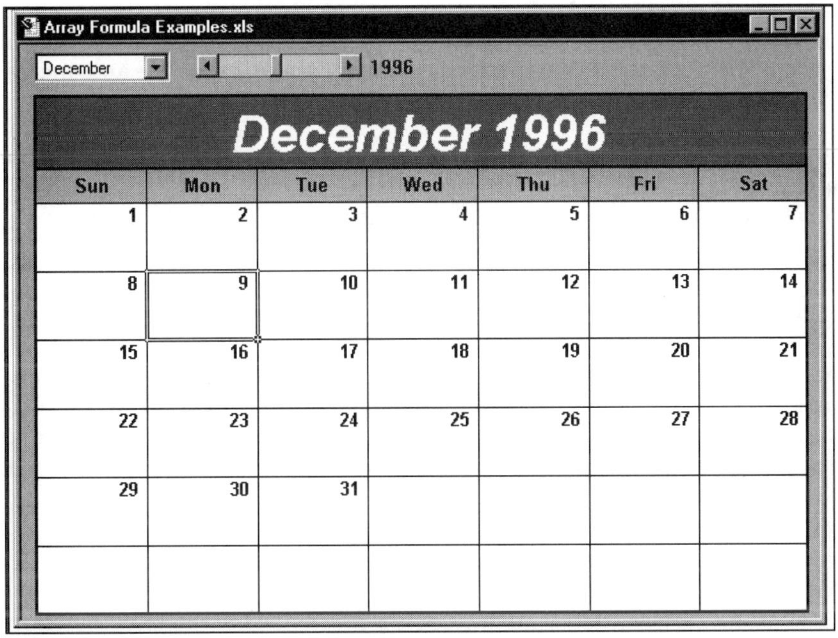

Figure 20-18: This calendar is calculated with a single array formula.

Tips for Array Formulas

If you've followed along in this chapter, you probably understand the advantages of using array formulas. As you gain more experience with arrays, you undoubtedly will discover some disadvantages.

The primary problem with array formulas is that they slow down your worksheet's recalculations, especially if you use large arrays. If speed is of the essence, you probably will want to avoid using large arrays.

Array formulas are one of the least understood features of Excel. Consequently, if you plan to share a worksheet with someone who may need to make modifications, you should probably avoid using array formulas. Encountering an array formula when you don't know what it is can be very confusing.

You may also discover that it's easy to forget to enter an array formula by pressing Ctrl+Shift+Enter. If you edit an existing array, you still must use these keys to complete the edits. Except for logical errors, this problem is probably the most common one that users have with array formulas. If you press Enter by mistake after editing an array formula, just double-click on the cell to get back into Edit mode and then press Ctrl+Shift+Enter.

A limit exists for the number of elements in an array — about 6,500 elements. You probably won't have many occasions when you need arrays of this size. If you do, you can break the array into smaller divisions and use separate array formulas.

Summary

In this chapter, I introduce the concept of array formulas. An array formula is a special type of formula that operates on a group of cells. You can write an array formula by entering a single formula that performs an operation on multiple inputs and produces multiple results –– with each result displayed in a separate cell. I also discuss several practical examples of array formulas.

✦   ✦   ✦

Using Excel in a Workgroup

CHAPTER

◆ ◆ ◆ ◆

In This Chapter

Learning the basics of
computer networks

Understanding how
file reservations work

Using the new shared
list feature

Mailing and routing
workbooks to others

◆ ◆ ◆ ◆

I f you use Excel on a stand-alone computer — a PC that's
not connected to a network — you can skip this chapter
because it applies only to users who run Excel on a network.

Using Excel on a Network

A computer network, often called a *LAN* (Local Area Network),
consists of a group of PCs hooked together. A common type of
network uses a client-server model in which one or more PCs on
the network are essentially dedicated servers (they store files
centrally), and user PCs are clients (they use data in the centrally stored files). Other networks are peer-to-peer networks
that don't have a central server. Users on a network can perform
the following tasks:

+ Access files on other systems.

+ Share files with other users.

+ Share resources such as printers and fax modems.

+ Communicate with each other electronically.

In many offices, LANs now perform functions that formerly
required a mainframe system and dumb terminals. The advantage is that LANs are usually less expensive, easier to expand,
more manageable, and more flexible in terms of software
availability.

This chapter discusses the Excel features that are designed for
network users. Some of these features are new to Excel for
Windows 95.

File Reservations

One of the most useful aspects of a network is that users can access files on other systems. The network has one or more file servers attached. A file server stores files that members of a workgroup need to access. A network's file server may contain, for example, files that store customer lists, price lists, and form letters. Keeping these files on a file server has these two major advantages:

✦ It eliminates the need to have multiple local copies of the files.

✦ It ensures that the file is always up-to-date; for example, you don't want to be working with an obsolete version of your customer list.

Some software applications are *multiuser* applications. Most database software, for example, lets multiple users work on the same database files. One user may be updating customer records in the database while another is extracting records. But what if a user is updating a customer record and another user wants to make a change to that same record? Multiuser database software has *record locking* safeguards built in to ensure that only one user at a time can modify a particular record.

Excel isn't a multiuser application. When you open an Excel file, the entire file is loaded into memory. If the file is accessible to other users, you don't want someone else to be able to open a file that is already open. If the reasons aren't clear, read on.

Note   There is an exception to this that allows multiple users to work on the same work-book. See the next section, "Shared Lists."

Assume that your company keeps its sales information in an Excel file stored on a network server. Albert wants to add this week's data to the file, so he loads it from the server and begins adding new information. A few minutes later, Betty loads the file to correct some errors that she noticed last week. Albert finishes his work and saves the file. A little while later, Betty finishes her corrections and saves the file. Her file writes over the copy Albert saved, and his additions are gone.

This scenario *won't happen* because Excel uses a concept known as *file reservation*. When Albert opens the sales file, he has the reservation for the file. When Betty tries to open the file, Excel informs her that Albert is using the file. If she insists on opening it, the file is opened as *read-only*. In other words, Betty can open the file, but she can't save it under the same name. Figure 21-1 shows the message that Betty receives if she tries to open a file that is in use by someone else.

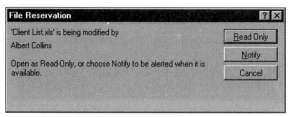

Figure 21-1: The File Reservation dialog box appears if you try to open a file that someone else is using.

Betty has these three choices:

✦ Select Cancel, wait a while, and try again. She may call Albert and ask him when he expects to be finished.

✦ Select Read Only, which lets her open the file but doesn't let her save changes to the same filename.

✦ Select Notify, which opens the file as read-only. Excel pops up a message when Albert is finished using the file.

Figure 21-2 shows the message that Betty receives when the file is available.

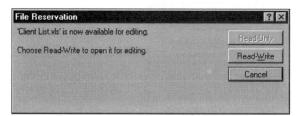

Figure 21-2: The File Reservation dialog box pops up with a new message when the file is available for editing.

Shared Lists

A new feature in Excel for Windows 95 is *shared lists*. This feature allows multiple users to work on the same workbook simultaneously.

Appropriate workbooks for shared lists

Although you can designate any workbook as a shared list, this is really not appropriate for all workbooks. Following are examples of workbooks that work well as shared lists:

✦ **Project tracking.** You may have a workbook that contains status information for projects. If multiple people are involved in the project, they can make changes and updates to the parts that are relevant.

✦ **Customer lists.** With such lists, changes usually occur infrequently, but records are added and deleted.

✦ **Consolidations.** You may create a budget workbook in which each department manager is responsible for his or her department's budget. Usually, each department's budget would be on a separate sheet, with one sheet serving as the consolidation sheet.

Designating a workbook as a shared list

To designate a workbook as a shared list, select the File⇨Shared Lists command. Excel responds with the dialog box shown in Figure 21-3. Select the check box labeled Allow Multi-User Editing and click OK. You'll then be prompted to save the workbook.

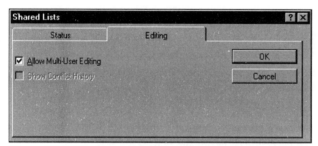

Figure 21-3: The Shared Lists dialog box lets you specify a workbook as a shared list.

When a shared list workbook is open, the window's title bar will display [Shared]. If you no longer want other users to be able to work on the workbook, remove the check mark from the Allow Multi-User Editing check box and save the workbook.

When a shared list workbook is open, Excel monitors the workbook. When you save the workbook, the workbook is updated with any changes made by other users.

Whenever you're working with a shared list, you can find out whether any other users are working on the workbook. Choose the File⇨Shared Lists command and click the Status tab. Excel displays the names of the other users who have the file open (see Figure 21-4).

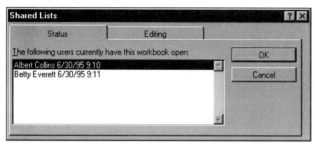

Figure 21-4: The Status tab of the Shared Lists dialog box tells you who else is working on a shared list workbook.

Resolving conflicts

As you may expect, multiple users working on the same file can result in conflicts. For example, if you and someone else make a change to the same cell, this is a conflict. Before saving the file, you must resolve the conflict using the Conflict Resolution dialog box, shown in Figure 21-5. This dialog box appears automatically if Excel discovers a conflict. It describes the conflict and lets you decide which version to use. You also can click one of the buttons at the bottom to set the default for any subsequent changes: use either your changes or the other user's changes.

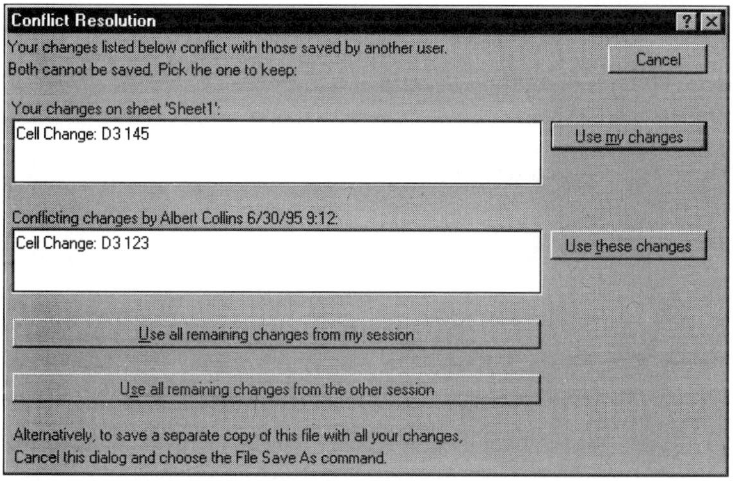

Figure 21-5: The Conflict Resolution dialog box is displayed when two or more users change the same cell in a shared list workbook.

When you select the option labeled Show Conflict History (in the Editing panel of the Shared Lists dialog box), Excel creates a new sheet in your workbook named Conflict History. This is a locked sheet that contains all conflicts for the file, arranged as an autofiltered list (see Chapter 23 for a discussion of autofiltering). Figure 21-6 shows an example of such a list. To remove this list from your workbook, access the Shared Lists dialog box and remove the check mark from the Show Conflict History check box.

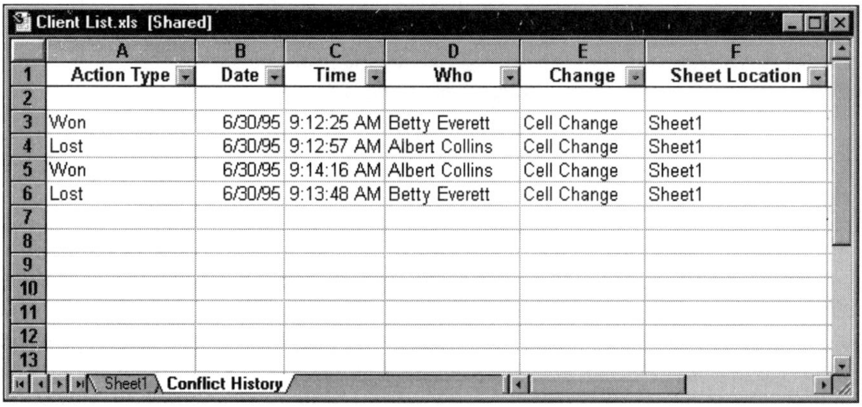

	A	B	C	D	E	F
1	Action Type	Date	Time	Who	Change	Sheet Location
2						
3	Won	6/30/95	9:12:25 AM	Betty Everett	Cell Change	Sheet1
4	Lost	6/30/95	9:12:57 AM	Albert Collins	Cell Change	Sheet1
5	Won	6/30/95	9:14:16 AM	Albert Collins	Cell Change	Sheet1
6	Lost	6/30/95	9:13:48 AM	Betty Everett	Cell Change	Sheet1
7						
8						
9						
10						
11						
12						
13						

Figure 21-6: This list shows a history of all of the conflicts for the shared list workbook.

Limitations of shared lists

When a workbook is being shared, there are limitations as to what you can do with it. These limitations include the following:

✦ You can't add, copy, or modify formulas.

✦ You can't change formatting.

✦ You can't add or delete sheets.

✦ You can't create charts.

✦ You can't create or edit macros.

✦ You can't create or modify names.

✦ You can't hide or unhide sheets.

If you need to perform any of these actions, you must uncheck the Allow Multi-User Editing check box.

Mailing and Routing Workbooks

Excel provides a few additional workgroup features. To use these features, your system must have one of the following installed:

✦ Microsoft Exchange

✦ A mail system compatible with MAPI (Messaging Application Programming Interface)

✦ Lotus cc:Mail

✦ A mail system compatible with VIM (Vendor Independent Messaging)

Note The procedures vary depending on the mail system that you have installed. Because of this, the discussions in following sections are general in nature. For specific questions, consult your network administrator.

Mailing a workbook to others

Electronic mail, or e-mail, has seen enormous growth during the past few years, and its use is expected to skyrocket. Consequently, e-mail has become commonplace in many offices, which is not surprising because it's an efficient means of communication. Unlike a telephone, e-mail doesn't rely on the recipient of the message being available when you want to send the message. Most networks nowadays have electronic-mail software installed.

In addition to sending messages through e-mail, you can send complete files — including Excel workbooks. Like a growing number of software applications, Excel is *mail-enabled,* which means that you don't have to leave Excel to send a worksheet to someone by e-mail.

To send a copy of your workbook to someone on your network, use the File⇨Send command. If you're using Microsoft Exchange, you need to select a profile, and then you see the dialog box shown in Figure 21-7. Enter the recipient (or recipients) and a message, and close the dialog box. This command creates an e-mail message with a copy of your workbook attached. It's important to understand that this command sends a *copy* of the workbook. If the recipient makes changes to the notebook, the changes do not appear in your copy of the workbook.

Tip Another way to send a workbook is to use the Send Mail button on the Workgroup toolbar.

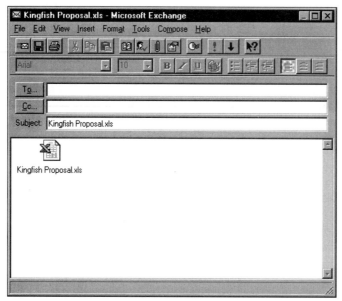

Figure 21-7: Using Microsoft Exchange to send a workbook via e-mail.

Routing a workbook to others

Excel lets you attach a routing slip to a workbook. This feature enables you to send a copy of a workbook to multiple members of a workgroup. For example, if you're responsible for your department's budget, you may need input from others in the department. You can set up the workbook and then route it to the others so that they can make their respective additions. When the routing is finished, the workbook is returned to you, complete with all the input from the others.

Types of routing

When you route a workbook, you have two options: sequential and simultaneous.

Sequential routing enables you to route the workbook sequentially to workgroup members. When the first recipient is finished, the workbook goes to the second recipient. When the second recipient is finished, the workbook goes to the third, and so on. When all recipients have received the workbook, it can be returned to you.

Simultaneous routing enables you to route the workbook to all recipients at once. In this case, you receive a copy of the workbook from each recipient (not just one copy). This type of routing is useful if you want to solicit comments from a group of coworkers, and you want the responses back quickly (you don't want to wait until a single worksheet makes the circuit).

Adding a routing slip

You add a routing slip to a workbook with the File⇨Add Routing Slip command. The Routing Slip dialog box is shown in Figure 21-8.

Click on the Address button to select the workgroup members who will receive the routed workbook. Enter a subject and message text into the appropriate areas and select the type of routing (One After Another or All at Once). Other options let you have the document returned to you and track its status. Click on the Route button to begin the routing.

Figure 21-8: The Routing Slip dialog box.

Tip

A Routing Slip button is on the Workgroup toolbar.

If you prefer, you can create the routing slip but not route the workbook (use the Add Slip button). The routing slip that you create is saved with the workbook. If you want to modify it later, use the File⇨Edit Routing Slip command. Then, to route the workbook, use the File⇨Send Command.

Summary

In this chapter, I present a basic overview of computer networks as they relate to Excel. I explain how the concept of a file reservation prevents two users from modifying a workbook simultaneously. Excel's new shared list feature, however, lets multiple users work on a single workbook at the same time. I conclude the chapter with a discussion of mailing and routing workbooks.

✦   ✦   ✦

Analyzing Data

The chapters in Part IV deal with a key topic for most Excel users: data analysis. I give details on importing data, using worksheet tables and external databases, creating pivot tables, doing what-if analysis and goal seeking, understanding the Solver, and using the Analysis ToolPak add-in.

Importing Data from Other Sources

In This Chapter

Sources for data that
you can use in Excel

Various file formats
that Excel can import

How to copy data
from another
application into Excel
using the Windows
Clipboard

How to import text
files into Excel

When you get right down to it, Excel can be described as a tool that manipulates data — the numbers and text that you use in a worksheet. But before you can manipulate data, it must be present in a worksheet. This chapter describes a variety of data-importing techniques.

An Overview of Importing

There are five basic ways to get data into Excel:

✦ Enter the data manually by typing values and text into cells.

✦ Generate data by using formulas or macros.

✦ Use Query (or a pivot table) to bring in data from an external database.

✦ Copy data from another application, using the Windows Clipboard.

✦ Import data from another (non-Excel) file.

This chapter deals primarily with the last two methods: Clipboard copying and foreign file importing.

Cross-Reference Chapter 29 is somewhat related to this topic. It deals with linking to and from other applications and embedding objects. I discuss querying external databases in Chapter 24 and pivot tables in Chapter 25.

A Few Words about Data

Data is a very broad concept and means different things to different people. Data is basically raw information that can come in any number of forms. For example, data can be numbers, text, or a combination. Most of what you do in Excel involves manipulating data in one way or another.

As computers become more commonplace, data is increasingly available in machine-readable formats (otherwise known as files). Not too long ago, major data suppliers provided printed reports to their clients. Now, it's not uncommon to be offered a choice of formats: paper or disk.

Data stored in files can be in a wide variety of formats. Common file formats for distributing data include Lotus 1-2-3 files (WKS and WK1), dBASE files (DBF), and text files (which come in several varieties). Excel's file format is rather complex and, until this release, it has changed with every version of Excel. Consequently, the Excel file format is not widely used for the general distribution of data.

As an Excel user, it's important that you understand the types of data that you can access either directly or indirectly.

File Formats Supported by Excel

Rarely does a computer user work with only one application or not interact with people using different applications. Suppose that you're developing a spreadsheet model that uses data from last year's budget, which is stored in your company's mainframe. You can request a printout of the data, of course, and manually enter it into Excel. If the amount of data isn't too large, this route may be the most efficient one. But what if you have hundreds of entries to make? Your mainframe probably can't generate an Excel workbook file, but there's an excellent chance that it can send the report to a text file, which you can then import into an Excel worksheet. You can potentially save yourself several hours of work and virtually eliminate data-entry errors.

As you know, Excel's native file format is an XLS file. In addition, Microsoft included the capability to read other file formats directly. For example, you can open a file that was written by several other spreadsheet products such as Lotus 1-2-3. Table 22-1 lists all file formats that Excel can read (excluding its own file types).

To open any of these files, use Excel's File➪Open command and select the file type from the drop-down list labeled Files of type (see Figure 22-1). This causes only the files of the selected type to appear in the file list. If the file is a text file, Excel's Text Import Wizard starts up to help you interpret the file. I discuss the Text Import Wizard later in this chapter.

Table 22-1	
File Formats Supported by Excel	
File Type	**Description**
Text	Space delimited, tab delimited, and comma delimited
Lotus 1-2-3	Spreadsheet files generated by Lotus 1-2-3 for DOS Release 1.*x*, Release 2.*x*, Release 3.*x*, and 1-2-3 for Windows
Quattro Pro/DOS	Files generated by Novell's Quattro Pro for DOS spreadsheet
Microsoft Works 2.0	Files generated by Microsoft Works 2.0
dBASE	Database files in the DBF format
SYLK	Files generated by Microsoft's Multiplan spreadsheet
Data Interchange Format	Files generated by the VisiCalc spreadsheet
Quattro Pro for Windows	Files generated by Novell's Quattro Pro for Windows spreadsheet

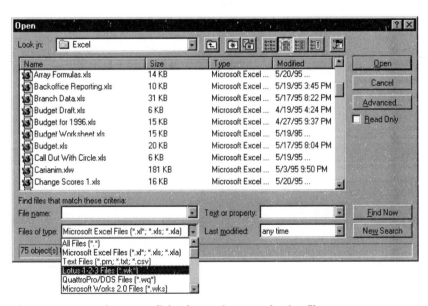

Figure 22-1: Use the Open dialog box to import a foreign file.

It's important to understand, however, that being able to read a file and translating it perfectly are two different matters. In some cases, reading a foreign file into Excel may exhibit one or more of the following problems:

✦ Some formulas aren't translated correctly.

✦ Unsupported functions aren't translated.

✦ Formatting is incorrect.

✦ Column widths are incorrect.

When you open a file that wasn't produced by Excel, examine it carefully to ensure that the data was retrieved correctly.

In the following sections I discuss the various types of files that Excel can read. I discuss these by file type and also list the file extensions that are normally associated with each file type.

Tip If a colleague sends you a file that Excel can't open, don't give up. Simply request that the spreadsheet be saved in a format that Excel *can* read. For example, many applications can save files in 1-2-3 format, and most applications can export to a text file format.

Lotus 1-2-3 spreadsheet files

Lotus spreadsheets come in several flavors:

✦ *WKS files* are single-sheet files used by 1-2-3 Release 1.*x* for DOS. Excel can read and write these files. If you export a workbook to a WKS file, only the active worksheet is saved.

✦ *WK1 files* are single-sheet files used by 1-2-3 Release 2.*x* for DOS. The formatting for these files is stored in ALL files (produced by the Allways add-in) or FM1 files (produced by the Wysiwyg add-in). Excel can read and write all these files. When you save a file to the WK1 format, you can choose which (if any) type of formatting file to generate. If you export a workbook to a WK1 file, only the active worksheet is saved.

✦ *WK3 files* are (potentially) multisheet files generated by 1-2-3 Release 3.*x* for DOS, 1-2-3 Release 4.*x* for DOS, and 1-2-3 Release 1.*x* for Windows. The formatting for these files is stored in FM3 files (produced by the Wysiwyg add-in). Excel can read and write WK3 files with or without the accompanying FM3 file.

✦ *WK4 files* are (potentially) multisheet files generated by 1-2-3 Release 4.*x* for Windows and 1-2-3 Release 5.*x* for Windows (Lotus finally got its act together and eliminated the separate formatting file). Excel can read and write these files.

Note If you'll be importing or exporting 1-2-3 files, I urge you to read the online help for general guidelines and specific types of information that may not be translated.

Tip Excel evaluates some formulas differently from 1-2-3. To be assured of complete compatibility when working with an imported 1-2-3 file, choose Tools⇨Options, select the Transition tab, and check the box labeled Transition Formula Evaluation.

Quattro Pro spreadsheet files

Quattro Pro files exist in several versions:

✦ *WQ1 files* are single-sheet files generated by Quattro Pro for DOS Versions 1, 2, 3, and 4. Excel can read and write these files. If you export a workbook to a WQ1 file, only the active worksheet is saved.

✦ *WQ2 files* are (potentially) multisheet files generated by Quattro Pro for DOS Version 5. Excel can neither read nor write this file format.

✦ *WB1 files* are (potentially) multisheet files generated by Quattro Pro for Windows Versions 1 and 5 (there are no Versions 2 through 4). Excel can read (but not write) this file format.

✦ *WB2 files* are (potentially) multisheet files generated by Quattro Pro for Windows Version 6. Excel can neither read nor write this file format.

Database file formats

DBF files are single-table database files generated by dBASE and several other database programs. Excel can read and write DBF files up to and including dBASE 4.

New! If you have Microsoft Access installed on your system, you can take advantage of a new feature that converts a worksheet list into an Access database file. To use this feature, the Access Links add-in must be installed. Use the Data⇨Convert to Access command.

Excel can't read or write any other database file formats directly. If you install the Query add-in, however, you can use Query to access many other database file formats and then copy or link the data into an Excel worksheet. See Chapter 24 for details.

Text file formats

Text files simply contain data; there's no formatting. Several relatively standard text file formats exist, but there are no standard file extensions.

✦ Each line in *tab-dr limited files* consists of fields separated by tabs. Excel can read these files, converting each line to a row and each field to a column. Excel also can write these files, using txt as the default extension.

✦ Each line in *comma-separated files* consists of fields separated by commas. Sometimes text is in quotation marks. Excel can read these files, converting each line to a row and each field to a column. Excel also can write these files, using csv as the default extension.

✦ Each line in *space-delimited files* consists of fields separated by spaces. Excel can read these files, converting each line to a row and each field to a column. Excel also can write these files, using prn as the default extension.

Tip   If you would like your exported text file to use a different extension, specify the complete file name and extension in quotes. For example, saving a workbook in comma-separated format normally uses the csv extension. If you want your file to be named `output.txt` (with a txt extension), enter **"output.txt"** in the File name box in the Save As dialog box.

When you attempt to load a text file into Excel, the Text Import Wizard kicks in to help you specify how you want the file retrieved. I discuss this in detail later in this chapter.

Other file formats

✦ DIF (Data Interchange Format) file format was used by VisiCalc. Excel can read and write these files.

✦ SYLK (Symbolic Link) file format was used by MultiPlan. Excel can read and write these files.

These files are rarely encountered. I haven't seen a DIF file in ages, and I've never seen a SYLK file.

Using the Clipboard to Get Data

Another method of getting data into your worksheet is to use the Windows Clipboard. The process involves selecting data from another application and copying the data to the Clipboard. Then you reactivate Excel and paste the information to the worksheet. The exact results that you get can vary quite a bit, depending on the type of data that was copied and the Clipboard formats that it supports. Obviously, you must have a copy of the other application installed on your system.

About the Clipboard

As you probably know, whenever Windows is running, you have access to the Windows Clipboard — an area of your computer's memory that acts as a shared holding area for information that has been cut or copied from an application. The Clipboard works behind the scenes, and you usually aren't aware of it. Whenever you select the Edit⇨Copy or Edit⇨Cut commands, the selected data is placed on the Clipboard. Like most other Windows applications, Excel can then access the Clipboard data by way of the Edit⇨Paste command.

Note   Data pasted from the Clipboard remains on the Clipboard after pasting, so you can use it multiple times. But because the Clipboard can hold only one item at a time, when you copy or cut something else, the old Clipboard contents are replaced.

Windows 95 includes an application called *Clipboard Viewer*, which displays the contents of the Clipboard (this application is located in your Windows folder). You can run Clipboard Viewer to look at what (if anything) is currently on the Clipboard. Figure 22-2 shows the Clipboard Viewer displaying information copied from Excel.

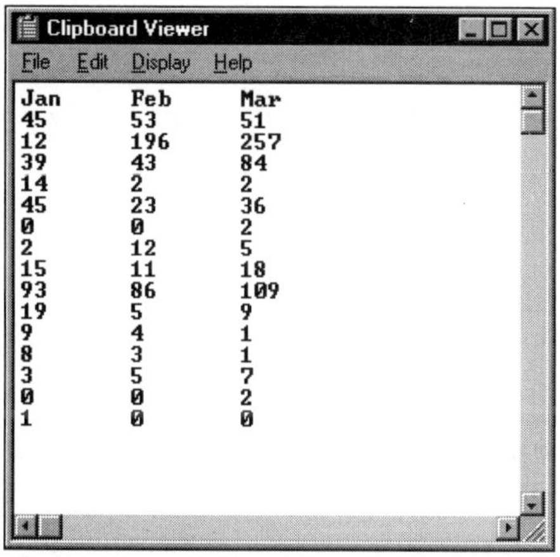

Figure 22-2: The Windows 95 Clipboard Viewer application displays the current contents of the Clipboard.

When you copy or cut data to the Clipboard, the source application places one or more formats along with it. Different applications support different Clipboard formats. When you paste Clipboard data into another application, the destination application determines which format it can handle and typically selects the format that either provides the most information or is appropriate for where it is being pasted. In some cases, you can use the Display command in the Clipboard Viewer application to view the Clipboard data in a different format. If you copy a range of cells to the Clipboard, for example, you can display it as a picture, bitmap, palette (the color palette only), text, OEM text, or a DIB bitmap.

Note The Clipboard format that you select in the Clipboard Viewer doesn't affect how the data is copied. In some cases, however, you can use Excel's Edit⇔Paste Special command to select alternate methods of pasting the data.

Copying data from another Windows application

Copying data from one Windows application to another is quite straightforward. The application you're copying from is considered the *source application,* and the application you're copying to is the *destination application.* Following are the steps to copy data from one application into another:

1. Activate the source document window that contains the information you want to copy.

2. Select the information you want to copy by using the mouse or the keyboard. If Excel is the source application, this information can be a cell, range, chart, or drawing object.

3. Select Edit⇨Copy (or any available shortcut). A copy of the information is sent to the Windows Clipboard.

4. Activate the destination application. If it isn't open, you can start it without affecting the contents of the Clipboard.

5. Move to the appropriate position in the destination application (where you want to paste).

6. Select Edit⇨Paste from the menu in the destination application. If the Clipboard contents aren't appropriate for pasting, the Paste command is grayed out (not available).

Note   In Step 3 in the preceding steps, you also can select Edit⇨Cut from the source application menu. This step erases the selection from the source application after it's placed on the Clipboard.

Tip   Many Windows applications use a common keyboard convention for the Clipboard commands. Generally, this technique is a bit faster than using the menus because these keys are adjacent to each other. The shortcut keys and their equivalents are as follows:

Ctrl+C	Edit⇨Copy
Ctrl+X	Edit⇨Cut
Ctrl+V	Edit⇨Paste

It's important to understand that Windows applications vary in how they respond to data pasted from the Clipboard. If the Edit⇨Paste command isn't available (grayed out on the menu) in the destination application, the application can't accept the information on the Clipboard. If you copy a table from Word for Windows to Excel, the data translates into cells perfectly — complete with formatting. Copying data from other applications may not work as well. For example, you may lose the formatting, or you may end up with all data in a single column rather than in separate columns. As I discuss later, you can use the Convert Text to Columns Wizard to convert this data into columns.

If you plan to do lots of copying and pasting, the best advice is to experiment until you understand how the two applications can handle each others' data.

Copying data from a non-Windows application

You also can use the Windows Clipboard with non-Windows applications running in a DOS window. As you may know, you can run non-Windows programs from Windows. You can do this in a window or in full-screen mode (the application takes over the complete screen).

When you're running a non-Windows application in Windows, you can press Alt+Print Screen to copy the entire screen to the Clipboard. It can then be pasted into a Windows application (including Excel). If you want to copy only part of the screen, you must run the application in a window: just press Alt+Enter to toggle between full-screen mode and windowed mode. You can then click on the Control menu, select Edit⇨Mark, and select text from the window. This window may or may not have a toolbar displayed. If not, right-click on the title bar and select the Toolbar option.

1. Click on the Mark tool and select the text to be copied.

2. Click on the Copy tool to copy the selected text to the Clipboard.

3. Activate Excel.

4. Select the Edit⇨Paste command to copy the Clipboard data into your worksheet.

Figure 22-3 shows Quattro Pro running in a DOS window. Some text is selected.

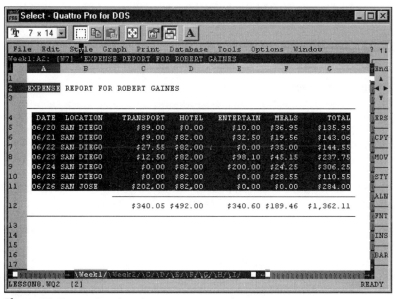

Figure 22-3: Copying data from Quattro Pro for DOS.

If you use this technique and copy to Excel, the information is pasted as text in a single column. In other words, even if the information copied is in the form of neatly formatted columns, it's all pasted into a single column in Excel. But don't fret — you can use Excel's Convert Text to Columns Wizard to convert this data into columns.

Note   You'll find that you're limited to copying one screen of information at a time. In other words, you can't scroll the DOS application while you're selecting text.

Importing Text Files

Text files (sometimes referred to as ASCII files) are usually considered to be the lowest-common-denominator file type. Such files contain only data, with no formatting whatsoever. Consequently, most applications are equipped to read and write text files. So, if all else fails, there's a good chance that you can use a text file to transfer data between two applications that don't support a common file format. Because text files are so commonly used, I devote this entire section to discussing them and explaining how to use Excel's Text Import Wizard.

About text files

It's helpful to think of some text files in terms of a database table. Each line in the text file corresponds to a database record, and each record consists of a number of fields. In Excel, each line (or record) is imported to a separate row and each field goes into a separate column. Text files come in two types:

✦ Delimited text files

✦ Nondelimited text files

Text files consist of plain text and end-of-line markers. Delimited text files use a special character to separate the fields on each line. This character usually is a comma, a space, or a tab (but other delimiters also are used). In addition, text is sometimes (but not always) enclosed in quotation marks.

Nondelimited files don't have a special field separator. Often, however, the fields are a fixed length, which makes it easy to break each line of text into separate columns.

Tip   Depending on the font used, the fields may not appear to line up although they actually do. This is because most fonts are not fixed-width fonts. In other words, each character doesn't use the same amount of horizontal space. For best results, it's a good idea to switch to a fixed-width font when working with text files. Courier New is a good choice; this is the font that Excel uses in its Text Import Wizard dialog box. Figure 22-4 shows the same text displayed in Arial and Courier New fonts.

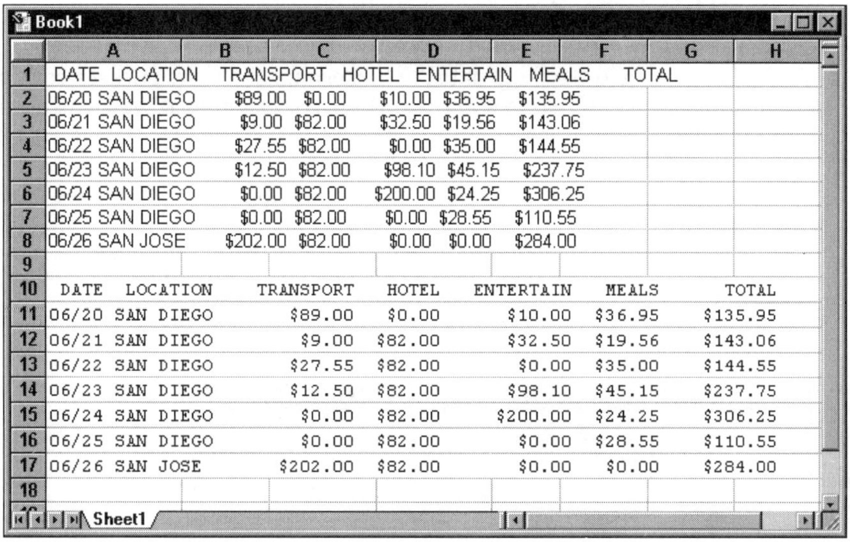
Book1

	A	B	C	D	E	F	G	H
1	DATE LOCATION TRANSPORT HOTEL ENTERTAIN MEALS TOTAL							
2	06/20 SAN DIEGO $89.00 $0.00 $10.00 $36.95 $135.95							
3	06/21 SAN DIEGO $9.00 $82.00 $32.50 $19.56 $143.06							
4	06/22 SAN DIEGO $27.55 $82.00 $0.00 $35.00 $144.55							
5	06/23 SAN DIEGO $12.50 $82.00 $98.10 $45.15 $237.75							
6	06/24 SAN DIEGO $0.00 $82.00 $200.00 $24.25 $306.25							
7	06/25 SAN DIEGO $0.00 $82.00 $0.00 $28.55 $110.55							
8	06/26 SAN JOSE $202.00 $82.00 $0.00 $0.00 $284.00							
9								
10	DATE LOCATION TRANSPORT HOTEL ENTERTAIN MEALS TOTAL							
11	06/20 SAN DIEGO $89.00 $0.00 $10.00 $36.95 $135.95							
12	06/21 SAN DIEGO $9.00 $82.00 $32.50 $19.56 $143.06							
13	06/22 SAN DIEGO $27.55 $82.00 $0.00 $35.00 $144.55							
14	06/23 SAN DIEGO $12.50 $82.00 $98.10 $45.15 $237.75							
15	06/24 SAN DIEGO $0.00 $82.00 $200.00 $24.25 $306.25							
16	06/25 SAN DIEGO $0.00 $82.00 $0.00 $28.55 $110.55							
17	06/26 SAN JOSE $202.00 $82.00 $0.00 $0.00 $284.00							
18								

Sheet1

Figure 22-4: The font used may obscure columns in a text file.

Excel is quite versatile when it comes to importing text files. If each line of the text file is identically laid out, importing is usually problem-free. But if the line contains mixed information, it may require some additional work before the data is usable. For example, some text files are produced by sending a printed report to a disk file rather than the printer. These reports often have extra information such as page headers and footers, titles, summary lines, and so on.

Using the Text Import Wizard

To import a text file into Excel, use the File➪Open command and select Text Files in the drop-down list labeled Files of type. The Open dialog box then displays text files that have an extension of prn, txt, or csv. If the text file that you're importing doesn't have one of these extensions, select the All Files option. Or, you can enter the filename directly in the File name box if you know its name.

Excel examines the file. If the file is a tab-delimited or a comma-separated value file, it often imports it with no further intervention on your part. If the file can be imported in several different ways, however — or if there are no delimiters — Excel displays its Text Import Wizard. This wizard is a series of interactive dialog boxes in which you specify the information needed to break the lines of the text file into columns. You can truly appreciate this time-saving feature only if you have struggled with old data-parsing commands used in other spreadsheet programs (and older versions of Excel).

Tip

To bypass the Text Import Wizard, press Shift when you click on OK in the Open dialog box. Excel then makes its best guess as to how to import the file.

Text Import Wizard: Step 1 of 3

Figure 22-5 shows the first of three Text Import Wizard dialog boxes. In the Original Data Type section, verify the type of data file (Excel almost always guesses correctly). You also can indicate which row to start importing. For example, if the file has a title, you may want to skip the first line.

Notice that the file is previewed at the bottom of the dialog box. You can use the scroll bars to view more of the file. If the characters in the file don't look right, you may need to change the File Origin — which determines which character set to use (in many cases, it won't make any difference). When you're finished with this step, click on the Next button to move to Step 2.

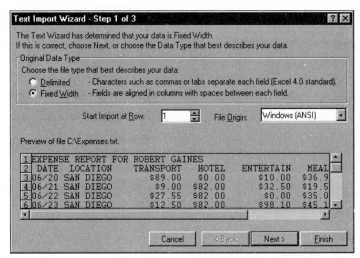

Figure 22-5: Step 1 of the Test Import Wizard.

Text Import Wizard: Step 2 of 3

The dialog box for Step 2 of the Text Import Wizard varies, depending on your choice in the first step. If you selected Delimited, you get the dialog box shown in Figure 22-6. You can specify the type of delimiter, the text qualifier, and whether to treat consecutive delimiters as a single delimiter (this will skip empty columns). The Data Preview section displays vertical lines to indicate how the lines will be broken up. The preview changes as you make choices in the dialog box.

If you selected fixed width, you get the dialog box shown in Figure 22-7. At this point, Excel attempts to identify the column breaks and displays vertical break lines to represent how the lines will break apart into columns. If Excel guesses wrong, you can move the lines, insert new ones, or delete lines that Excel proposes. Instructions are provided in the dialog box.

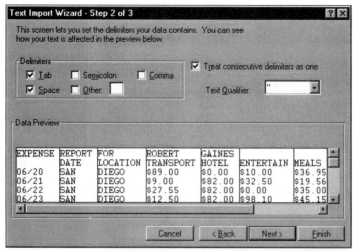

Figure 22-6: Step 2 of the Text Import Wizard (for delimited files).

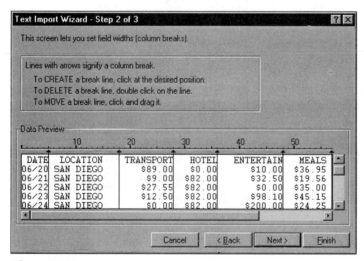

Figure 22-7: Step 2 of the Text Import Wizard (for fixed-width files).

Tip   If you're importing a print image file that includes page headers, you can ignore them when you specify the column indicators. Rather, base the columns on the data. When the file is imported, you can then delete the rows that contain the page headers.

When you're satisfied with how the column breaks look, click on Next to move on to the final step. Or, you can click on Back to return to Step 1 and change the file type.

Text Import Wizard: Step 3 of 3

Figure 22-8 shows the last of the three Text Import Wizard dialog boxes. In this dialog box, you can select individual columns and specify the formatting to apply (General, Text, or Data). You also can specify columns to skip — they won't be imported. When you're satisfied with the results, click on Finish. Excel creates a new workbook (with one sheet) to hold the imported data.

If the results aren't what you expect, close the workbook and try again (text importing often involves trial and error). Don't forget that you can scroll the Data Preview window to make sure that all data will be converted properly. With some files, however, you'll find that it's impossible to import all data properly. In such a case, you may want to import the file as a single column of text and then break lines into columns selectively. The procedure for doing this is discussed in the next section.

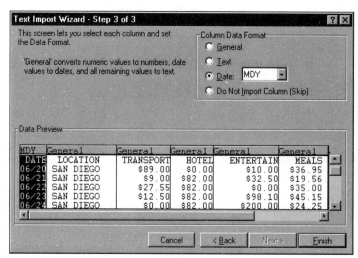

Figure 22-8: Step 3 of the Text Import Wizard.

Using the Text to Columns Wizard

Excel can parse text that is stored in a column. Start by selecting the text (in a single column). Then choose the Data⇨Text to Columns command. Excel displays the first of three Text to Columns Wizard dialog boxes. These dialog boxes are identical to those used for the Text Import Wizard except that the title bar text is different.

Note Unfortunately, you can't use the Data⇨Text to Columns command on a multiple selection, which would be quite handy for parsing imported files with several different layouts. Even worse, you can't use Edit⇨Repeat command to repeat the Text to Columns command.

Summary

In this chapter, I identify the various sources for getting data into Excel: entering data manually, generating data from formulas or macros, using Query or pivot tables, copying data using the Clipboard, and importing foreign files (including text files) into Excel. The chapter focuses on Clipboard operations and file importing.

✦   ✦   ✦

Working with Lists

Research conducted by Microsoft indicates that one of the most frequent uses for Excel is to manage lists, or *worksheet databases*. This chapter covers list management and demonstrates useful techniques that involve lists.

What Is a List?

A list is essentially an organized collection of information. More specifically, a list consists of a row of headers (descriptive text), followed by additional rows of data, which can be values or text. You may recognize this as a database table — which is exactly what it is. Beginning with Excel 5, Microsoft uses the term *list* to refer to a database stored in a worksheet and the term *database* to refer to a table of information stored in an external file. To avoid confusion, I adhere to Microsoft's terminology.

 **Cross-Reference** I cover external databases in Chapter 24.

Figure 23-1 shows an example of a list in a worksheet. This particular list has its headers in row 1 and has 10 rows of data. The list occupies four columns. Notice that the data consists of several different types: text, values, and dates. Column C contains a formula that calculates the monthly salary from the value in column B.

People often refer to the columns in a list as *fields* and to the rows as *records*. Using this terminology, the list shown in the figure has five fields (Name, Annual Salary, Monthly Salary, Location, and Date Hired) and ten records.

	A	B	C	D	E
1	Name	Annual Salary	Monthly Salary	Location	Date Hired
2	James Brackman	42,400	3,533	New York	2/1/93
3	Michael Orenthal	28,900	2,408	Arizona	4/5/94
4	Francis Jenkins	67,800	5,650	New York	10/12/93
5	Peter Yolanda	19,850	1,654	Minnesota	1/4/95
6	Walter Franklin	45,000	3,750	Arizona	2/28/90
7	Louise Victor	52,000	4,333	New York	5/2/94
8	Sally Rice	48,500	4,042	New York	11/21/92
9	Charles K. Barkley	24,500	2,042	Minnesota	6/4/90
10	Melinda Hintquest	56,400	4,700	Arizona	6/1/87
11	Linda Harper	75,000	6,250	Minnesota	8/7/91

Figure 23-1: An example of a list.

Note The size of the lists that you develop in Excel is theoretically limited by the size of a single worksheet. In other words, a list can have no more than 256 fields and can consist of no more than 16,383 records (one row contains the field names). A list of this size would require lots of memory and even then may not be possible. At the other extreme, a list can consist of a single cell — not very useful, but it's still considered a list.

What Can You Do with a List?

Excel provides several tools to help you manage and manipulate lists. Consequently, people use lists for a wide variety of purposes. For some users, a list is simply a method to keep track of information (for example, customer lists); others use lists to store data that will ultimately appear in a report. Following are common list operations:

- ✦ Enter data into the list.
- ✦ Filter the list to display only the rows that meet a certain criteria.
- ✦ Sort the list.
- ✦ Insert formulas to calculate subtotals.
- ✦ Create formulas to calculate results on the list filtered by certain criteria.
- ✦ Create a summary table of the data in the list (this is done using a pivot table; see Chapter 25).

With the exception of the last item, these operations are all covered in this chapter.

Designing a List

Although Excel is quite accommodating when it comes to the information stored in a list, you'll find that it pays off to give some initial thought as to how you want to organize your information. Following are some guidelines to keep in mind when creating lists:

✦ Insert descriptive labels (one for each column) in the first row of the list. This is the header row. If the labels are lengthy, consider using the word-wrap format so that you don't have to widen the columns.

✦ Each column should contain the same type of information. For example, don't mix dates and text in a single column.

✦ You can use formulas that perform calculations on other fields in the same record. If you use formulas that refer to cells outside of the list, make these absolute references; otherwise, you'll get unexpected results when you sort the list.

✦ Don't use any empty rows within the list. For list operations, Excel determines the list boundaries automatically, and an empty row signals the end of the list.

✦ For best results, try to keep the list on a worksheet by itself. If this isn't possible, place other information above or below the list. In other words, don't use the cells to the left or the right of a list.

✦ Use the Window⇨Freeze Panes command to make sure that the headings are visible when the list is scrolled.

✦ You can preformat entire columns to ensure that the data will have the same format. For example, if a column contains dates, format the entire column with the desired date format.

One of the most appealing aspects of spreadsheets is that you can change the layout relatively easily. This, of course, also applies to lists. For example, you may create a list and then decide that it needs another column (field). No problem. Just insert a new column, give it a field name, and your list is expanded. If you've ever used a database management program, you'll appreciate how easy this is.

Entering Data into a List

Entering data into a list can be done in three ways:

✦ Manually, using all standard data entry techniques

✦ Importing it or copying it from another file

✦ Using a dialog box

There's really nothing special about entering data into a list. You just navigate through the worksheet and enter the data into the appropriate cells.

New! Excel for Windows 95 has two new features that assist with repetitive data entry. One feature is known as *AutoComplete*. When you begin to type in a cell, Excel scans up and down the column to see whether it recognizes what you're typing. If it finds a match, Excel fills in the rest of the text automatically. Press Enter to make the entry. The other feature is for mouse users. You also can right-click on a cell and select Pick from list from the shortcut menu (see Figure 23-2). Excel displays a list box that shows all entries in the column. Just click the one that you want; it is entered into the cell (no typing required).

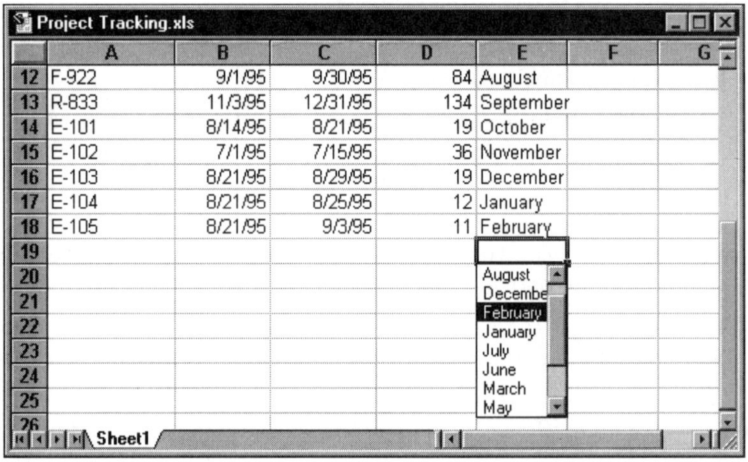
Project Tracking.xls
A
B
C
D
E
F
G
12 F-922 9/1/95 9/30/95 84 August
13 R-833 11/3/95 12/31/95 134 September
14 E-101 8/14/95 8/21/95 19 October
15 E-102 7/1/95 7/15/95 36 November
16 E-103 8/21/95 8/29/95 19 December
17 E-104 8/21/95 8/25/95 12 January
18 E-105 8/21/95 9/3/95 11 February
19
20
21
22
23
24
25
August
Decembe
February
January
July
June
March
May
Sheet1

Figure 23-2: Choosing the Pick from list command on the shortcut menu gives you a list of all items in the current column.

If you prefer to use a dialog box for your data entry, Excel accommodates you. To bring up a data entry dialog box, just move the cell pointer anywhere within the list and choose the Data⇨Form command. Excel determines the extent of your list and displays a dialog box showing each field in the list. Figure 23-3 depicts an example of such a dialog box. Fields that have a formula don't have an edit box.

Note If the number of fields exceeds the limit of your display, the dialog box contains two columns of field names. If your list consists of more than 32 fields, however, the Data⇨Form command won't work. You'll have to forgo this method of data entry and enter the information directly into the cells.

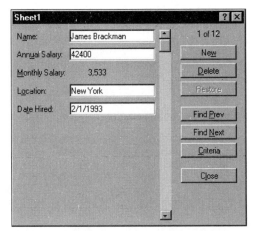

Figure 23-3: The Data➪Form command gives you a handy data entry dialog box.

Entering data with the data entry dialog box

When the data form dialog box appears, the first record in the list is displayed. Notice the indicator in the upper right corner of the dialog box that tells you which record is selected and the total number of records in the list.

To enter a new record, click on the New button to clear the fields. Then you can enter the new information into the appropriate fields. Use Tab or Shift+Tab to move among the fields. When you click on New (or Close), the data that you entered is appended to the bottom of the list. You also can press Enter, which is equivalent to clicking on the New button. If the list contains any formulas, these are also entered into the new record in the list for you automatically.

Tip   If your list is named `Database`, Excel automatically extends the range definition to include the new row(s) that you add to the list using the data form dialog box. Note that this works only if the list has the name `Database`; any other name won't work.

Other uses for the data entry dialog box

You can use the data entry dialog box for more than just data entry. You can edit existing data in the list, view data one record at a time, delete records, and display records that meet certain criteria.

The dialog box contains a number of additional buttons, described as follows:

Delete: Deletes the displayed record.

Restore: Restores any information you edited. You must click on this button before you click on the New button.

Find Prev: Displays the previous record in the list. If you entered a criterion, this button displays the previous record that matches the criteron.

Find Next: Displays the next record in the list. If you entered a criterion, this button displays the next record that matches the criterion.

Criteria: Clears the fields and lets you enter a criterion upon which to search for records. For example, to locate records that have a salary greater than $50,000, enter >**50000** into the Salary field. Then you can use the Find Next and Find Prev buttons to display the qualifying records.

Close: Closes the dialog box (and enters the data that you were entering, if any).

Using Microsoft Access Forms for data entry

New!   If you have Microsoft Access installed on your system, you can use its form creation tools to develop a data entry form for an Excel worksheet. This feature uses the Access Links add-in, which must be loaded. When the add-in is loaded, you have a new command: Data⇨Access Form.

Choosing this command starts Access (if it's not already running) and begins its Form Wizard. Use this tool to create the data entry form. You can then use this form to add data to your Excel worksheet. The worksheet will contain a button with the text View Access Form. Click on this button to use the form. Figure 23-4 shows an Access form being used to enter data into an Excel worksheet.

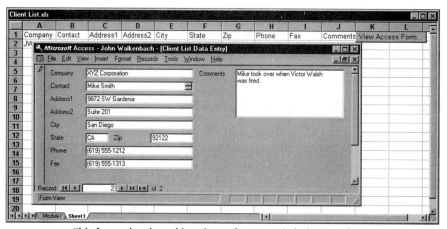

Figure 23-4: This form, developed in Microsoft Access, is being used to enter data into an Excel worksheet.

Filtering a List

Filtering a list is the process of hiding all rows in the list except those that meet some criteria that you specify. For example, if you have a list of customers, you can filter the list to show only those who live in New Jersey. Filtering is a common (and very useful) technique. Excel provides two ways to filter a list:

✦ AutoFilter, for simple filtering criteria

✦ Advance Filter, for more complex filtering

I discuss both of these options in the following sections.

Autofiltering

To autofilter a list, start by moving the cell pointer anywhere within the list. Then choose the Data⇨Filter⇨AutoFilter command. Excel analyzes your list and adds drop-down arrows to the field names in the header row, as shown in Figure 23-5.

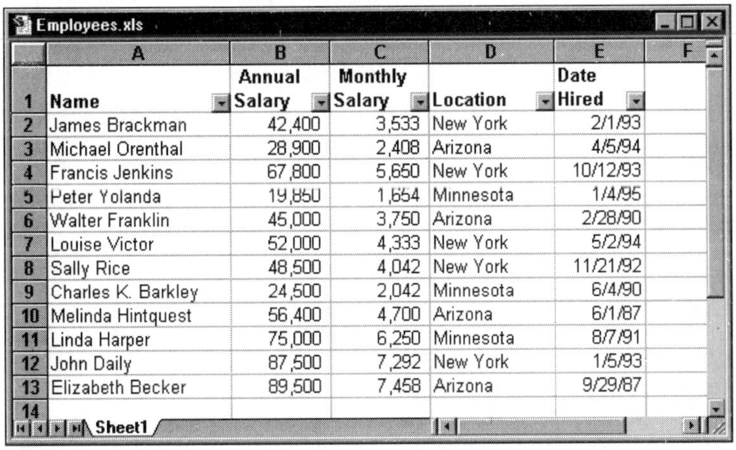

	A	B	C	D	E	F
		Annual	Monthly		Date	
1	Name	Salary	Salary	Location	Hired	
2	James Brackman	42,400	3,533	New York	2/1/93	
3	Michael Orenthal	28,900	2,408	Arizona	4/5/94	
4	Francis Jenkins	67,800	5,650	New York	10/12/93	
5	Peter Yolanda	19,850	1,654	Minnesota	1/4/95	
6	Walter Franklin	45,000	3,750	Arizona	2/28/90	
7	Louise Victor	52,000	4,333	New York	5/2/94	
8	Sally Rice	48,500	4,042	New York	11/21/92	
9	Charles K. Barkley	24,500	2,042	Minnesota	6/4/90	
10	Melinda Hintquest	56,400	4,700	Arizona	6/1/87	
11	Linda Harper	75,000	6,250	Minnesota	8/7/91	
12	John Daily	87,500	7,292	New York	1/5/93	
13	Elizabeth Becker	89,500	7,458	Arizona	9/29/87	
14						

Figure 23-5: The Data⇨Filter⇨AutoFilter command adds drop-down arrows to the field names in the header row.

When you click on the arrow on one of these drop-down lists, the list expands to show the unique items in that column. Select an item and Excel hides all rows except those that include the selected item. In other words, the list is filtered by the item that you selected.

After you filter the list, the status bar displays a message that tells you how many rows qualified. In addition, the drop-down arrow changes color to remind you that the list is filtered by a value in that column.

Note   Autofiltering has a limit. Only the first 250 unique items in the column appear in the drop-down list. If your list exceeds this limit, you can use advanced filtering, described later.

Besides showing every item in the column, the drop-down list includes five other items:

All: Displays all items in the column. Use this to remove filtering for a column.

Top 10: Filters to display the "top 10" items in the list; this is discussed later.

Custom: Lets you filter the list by multiple items; this is discussed later.

Blanks: Filters the list by showing rows that contain blanks in this column.

NonBlanks: Filters the list by showing rows that contain non-blanks in this column.

To display the entire list again, click the arrow and choose All — the first item in the drop-down list. Or, you can select the Data⇨Filter⇨Show All command.

To get out of Autofilter mode and remove the drop-down arrows from the field names, choose the Data⇨Filter⇨AutoFilter command again. This removes the check mark from the AutoFilter menu item and restores the list to its normal state.

Caution   If you have any formulas that refer to data in a filtered list, be aware that the formulas won't adjust to use only the visible cells. For example, if a cell contains a formula that sums values in column C, the formula continues to show the sum for *all* of the values in column C — not just those in the visible rows. The solution to this is to use database functions, which I describe later in this chapter.

Multicolumn autofiltering

Sometimes you may need to filter a list by values in more than one column. Figure 23-6 shows a list comprised of several fields.

Assume that you want to see the records that show modems sold in February. In other words, you want to filter out all records except those in which the Month field is *Feb* and the Product field is *Modem*.

First, get into Autofilter mode. Then click on the drop-down arrow in the Month field and select *Feb*. This filters the list to show only records with *Feb* in the Month field. Then, click on the drop-down arrow in the Product field and select *Modem*. This filters the filtered list — in other words, the list is filtered by values in two columns. Figure 23-7 shows the result.

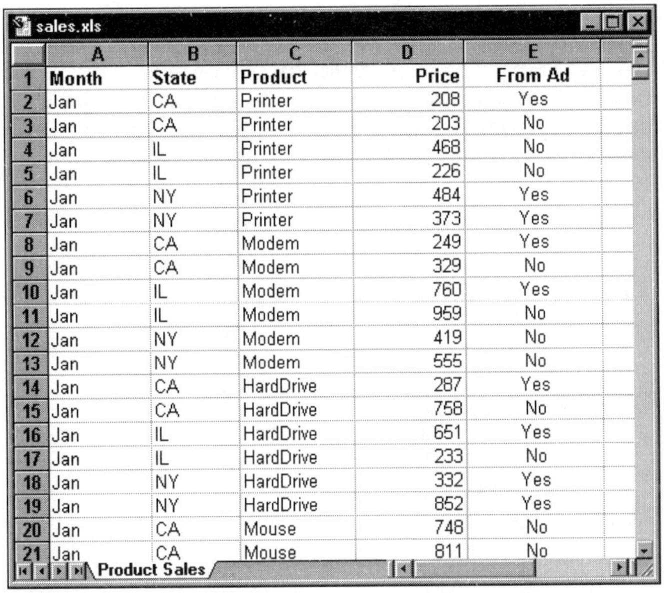

	A	B	C	D	E
1	Month	State	Product	Price	From Ad
2	Jan	CA	Printer	208	Yes
3	Jan	CA	Printer	203	No
4	Jan	IL	Printer	468	No
5	Jan	IL	Printer	226	No
6	Jan	NY	Printer	484	Yes
7	Jan	NY	Printer	373	Yes
8	Jan	CA	Modem	249	Yes
9	Jan	CA	Modem	329	No
10	Jan	IL	Modem	760	Yes
11	Jan	IL	Modem	959	No
12	Jan	NY	Modem	419	No
13	Jan	NY	Modem	555	No
14	Jan	CA	HardDrive	287	Yes
15	Jan	CA	HardDrive	758	No
16	Jan	IL	HardDrive	651	Yes
17	Jan	IL	HardDrive	233	No
18	Jan	NY	HardDrive	332	Yes
19	Jan	NY	HardDrive	852	Yes
20	Jan	CA	Mouse	748	No
21	Jan	CA	Mouse	811	No

Figure 23-6: This list will be filtered by multiple columns.

You can filter a list by any number of columns. The drop-down arrows in the columns that have a filter applied are a different color.

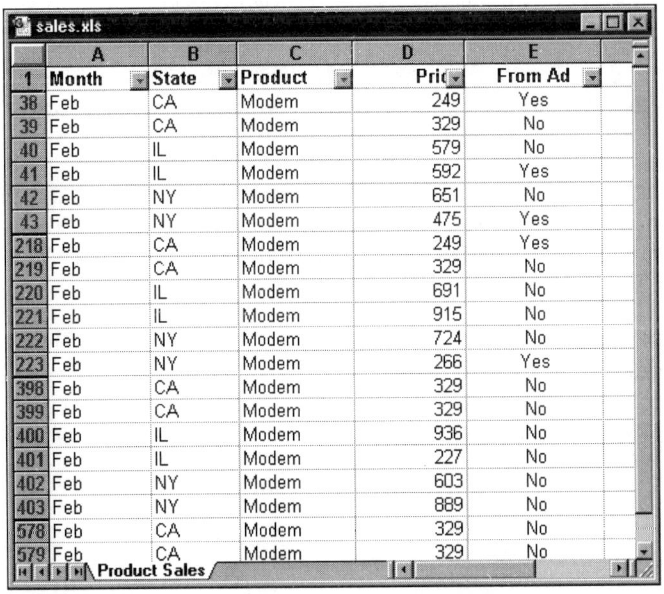

	A	B	C	D	E
1	Month	State	Product	Pric	From Ad
38	Feb	CA	Modem	249	Yes
39	Feb	CA	Modem	329	No
40	Feb	IL	Modem	579	No
41	Feb	IL	Modem	592	Yes
42	Feb	NY	Modem	651	No
43	Feb	NY	Modem	475	Yes
218	Feb	CA	Modem	249	Yes
219	Feb	CA	Modem	329	No
220	Feb	IL	Modem	691	No
221	Feb	IL	Modem	915	No
222	Feb	NY	Modem	724	No
223	Feb	NY	Modem	266	Yes
398	Feb	CA	Modem	329	No
399	Feb	CA	Modem	329	No
400	Feb	IL	Modem	936	No
401	Feb	IL	Modem	227	No
402	Feb	NY	Modem	603	No
403	Feb	NY	Modem	889	No
578	Feb	CA	Modem	329	No
579	Feb	CA	Modem	329	No

Figure 23-7: This list is filtered by values in two columns.

Custom autofiltering

Usually, autofiltering involves selecting a single value for one or more columns. If you choose the Custom option in a drop-down list, you gain a bit more flexibility in filtering the list. Selecting the Custom option displays a dialog box like the one shown in Figure 23-8. The Custom AutoFilter dialog box lets you filter in several ways:

> ✦ **Values above or below a specified value.** For example, sales amounts greater than 10,000.
>
> ✦ **Values within a range.** For example, sales amounts greater than 10,000 AND sales amounts less than 50,000.

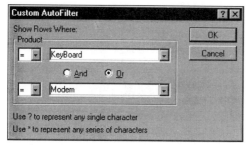

Figure 23-8: The Custom AutoFilter dialog box gives you more filtering options.

> ✦ **Two discrete values.** For example, state equal to *New York* OR state equal to *New Jersey.*
>
> ✦ **Approximate matches.** You can use the * and ? wildcards to filter in a number of other ways. For example, to display only those customers whose last name begins with *B*, use **B*.**

Custom autofiltering can be useful, but it definitely has limitations. For example, if you would like to filter the list to show only three values in a field (such as New York or New Jersey or Connecticut), you can't do it by autofiltering. Such filtering tasks require the advanced filtering feature, which I discuss later in this chapter.

Top 10 autofiltering

New! This feature is new to Excel for Windows 95.

Sometimes you may want to use a filter on numerical fields to show only the highest or lowest values in the list. For example, if you have a list of employees, you may want to identify the 12 employees with the longest tenure. You could use the custom autofilter option, but then you must supply a cutoff date (which you may not know). The solution is to use Top 10 autofiltering.

Top 10 autofiltering is a generic term; it doesn't limit you to the top *10* items. In fact, it doesn't even limit you to the *top* items. When you choose the Top 10 option from a drop-down list, you get the dialog box shown in Figure 23-9.

Figure 23-9: The Top 10 AutoFilter gives you more autofilter options.

You can choose either Top or Bottom and specify any number. For example, if you want to see the 12 employees with the longest tenure, choose Bottom and 12. This filters the list and shows the 12 rows with the smallest values in the Date Hired field. You also can choose Percent or Value in this dialog box. For example, you can filter the list to show the Bottom 5 percent of the records.

Charting filtered list data

You can create some interesting multipurpose charts that use data in a filtered list. The technique is useful because only the visible data appears in the chart. When you change the autofilter criteria, the chart updates itself to show only the visible cells.

Note   In order for this technique to work, make sure that the Plot Visible Cells Only option is enabled in the Options dialog box (Chart panel).

Figure 23-10 shows an example of a chart created with an unfiltered list. It shows sales data for three months for each of four sales regions.

Figure 23-11 shows the same chart, but the list was filtered to show only the North sales region. You can apply other filters, and the chart updates automatically. This technique lets a single chart show several different views of the data.

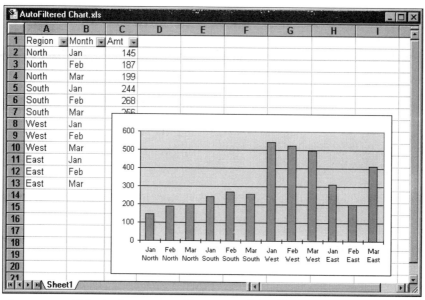

Figure 23-10: This chart was created from an unfiltered list.

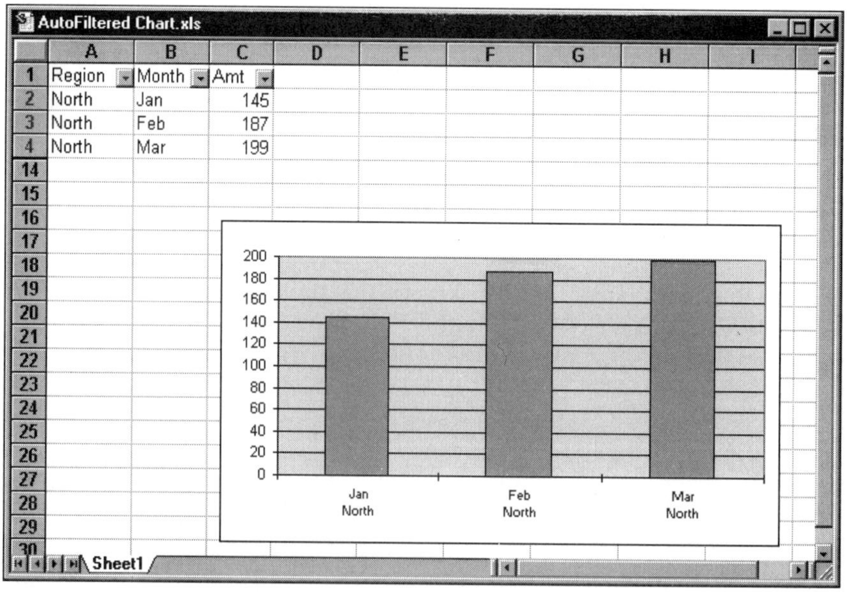

Figure 23-11: The chart from the previous figure, after filtering the list.

On the CD-ROM This workbook, named AUTOFILT.XLS, is available on the companion CD-ROM.

Advanced Filtering

In many cases, you'll find that autofiltering does the job. But if you run up against its limitations, you need to use advanced filtering. Advanced filtering is much more flexible than autofiltering, but it takes a bit of up-front work to use it. Advanced filtering provides you with the following capabilities:

✦ You can specify more complex filtering criteria.

✦ You can specify computed filtering criteria.

✦ You can extract a copy of the rows that meet the criteria to another location.

Setting up a criteria range

Before you can use the advanced filtering feature, you must set up a *criteria range*. A criteria range is a designated range on a worksheet that conforms to certain requirements. The criteria range holds the information that Excel uses to filter the list. It must conform to the following specifications:

✦ It consists of at least two rows, the first row of which must contain some or all field names from the list.

✦ The other rows consist of your filtering criteria.

Caution   Although you can put the criteria range anywhere in the worksheet, it's a good idea not to put it in rows that are used by the list. Because some of these rows are hidden when the list is filtered, you may find that your criteria range is no longer visible after the filtering takes place. Therefore, you should generally place the criteria range above or below the list.

Figure 23-12 shows a criteria range, located in A1:D2, above the list that it uses. Notice that not all field names appear in the criteria range. Fields that aren't used in the selection criteria need not appear in the criteria range.

In this example, the criteria range has only one row of criteria. The fields in each row of the criteria range (except for the header row) are joined with an AND operator. Therefore, the filtered list shows rows in which the Month column equals *January* AND the Type field is *New*. In other words, the list displays only sales to new customers made in January.

To perform the filtering, choose the Data⇨Filter⇨Advanced filter command. Excel displays the dialog box shown in Figure 23-13. Specify the list range and the criteria range, and make sure that the option labeled Filter the List in-place is selected. Click on OK, and the list is filtered by the criteria that you specified.

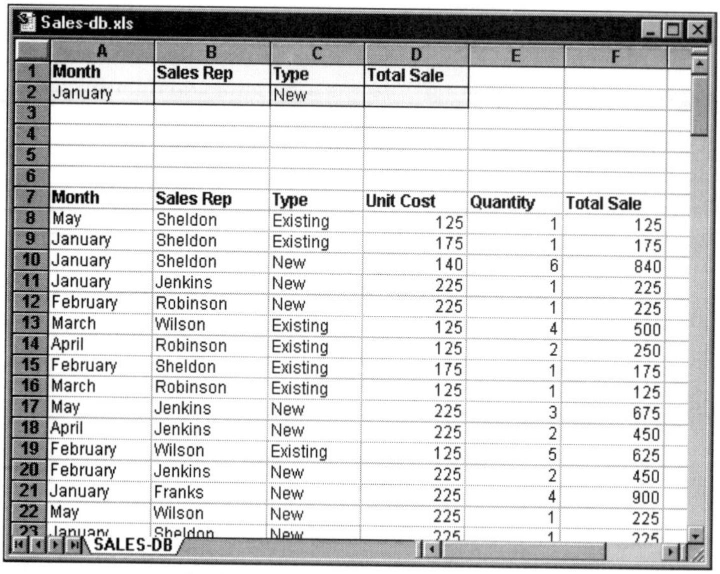

Figure 23-12: A criteria range for a list.

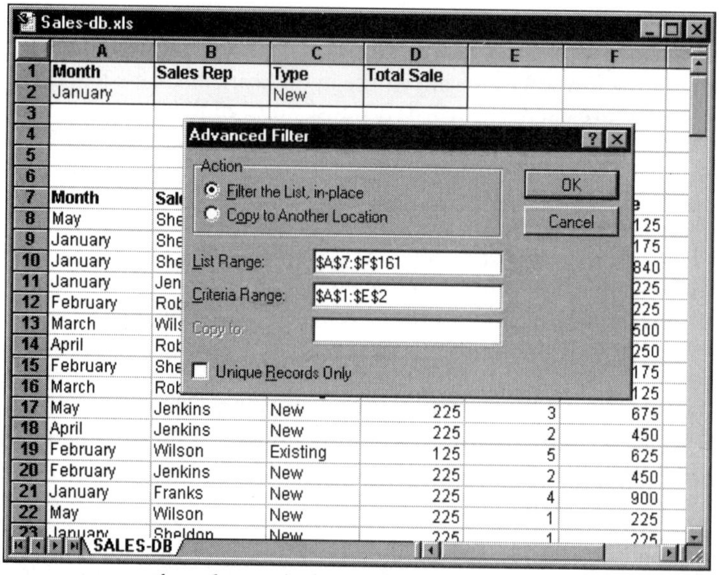

Figure 23-13: The Advanced Filter dialog box.

Multiple criteria

If you use more than one row in the criteria range, the criteria in each row are joined with an OR operator. Figure 23-14 shows a criteria range (A1:D3) with two rows of criteria. In this example, the filtered list shows rows in either of the following:

✦ The Month field is *January* AND the Type field is *New*

✦ The Month field is *February* AND the Total Sale field is greater than 1000

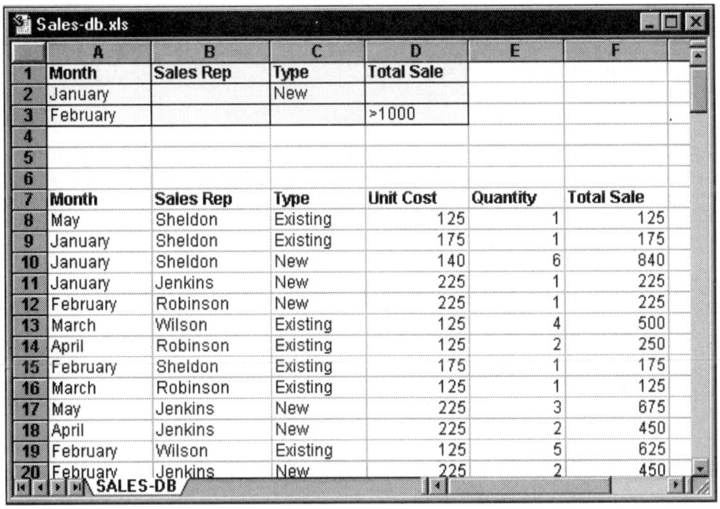

	A	B	C	D	E	F
1	Month	Sales Rep	Type	Total Sale		
2	January		New			
3	February			>1000		
4						
5						
6						
7	Month	Sales Rep	Type	Unit Cost	Quantity	Total Sale
8	May	Sheldon	Existing	125	1	125
9	January	Sheldon	Existing	175	1	175
10	January	Sheldon	New	140	6	840
11	January	Jenkins	New	225	1	225
12	February	Robinson	New	225	1	225
13	March	Wilson	Existing	125	4	500
14	April	Robinson	Existing	125	2	250
15	February	Sheldon	Existing	175	1	175
16	March	Robinson	Existing	125	1	125
17	May	Jenkins	New	225	3	675
18	April	Jenkins	New	225	2	450
19	February	Wilson	Existing	125	5	625
20	February	Jenkins	New	225	2	450

Figure 23-14: This criteria range has two sets of criteria.

This is an example of filtering that could not be done with autofiltering.

A criteria range can have any number of rows, each of which is joined to the others with an OR operator.

Types of criteria

The entries that you make in a criteria range can be either of the following:

✦ **Text or value criteria.** The filtering involves comparisons to a value or string, using operators such as equal (=), greater than (>), not equal to (<>), and so on.

✦ **Computed criteria.** The filtering involves a computation of some sort.

Text or value criteria

Table 23-1 lists the comparison operators that you can use with text or value criteria.

Table 23-1 **Comparison Operators**			
Operator	*Comparison Type*	*Operator*	*Comparison Type*
=	Equal to	<	Less than
>	Greater than	<=	Less than or equal to
]>=	Greater than or equal to	<>	Not equal to

Caution When the comparison involves text, you need to be careful because it may not work the way you think. To filter using an exact match to a string, the string must be entered as a formula. For example, to filter using the string *Existing*, enter =**"Existing"**. If you simply enter **Existing**, it does not produce the desired results.

Table 23-2 shows examples of criteria that use strings.

Table 23-2 **Examples of String Criteria**	
Criteria	*Effect*
>K	Text that begins with *L* through *Z*
<>C	All text, except text that begins with *C*
="January"	Text that matches January
Sm*	Text that begins with *Sm*
s*s	Text that begins with *s* and ends with *s*
s?s	Three-letter text that begins with *s* and ends with *s*

Note The text comparisons are not case sensitive. For example, si* matches *Simpson* as well as *sick*.

Computed criteria

Using computed criteria can make your filtering even more powerful. A computed criteria filters the list based on one or more calculations. Figure 23-15 shows a simple list that consists of project numbers, start dates, end dates, and resources. Above the list, in range A1:A2, is a criteria range. Notice, however, that this criteria range does not use a field header from the list — it uses a new field header. A computed criteria essentially computes a new field for the list. Therefore, you must supply new field names in the first row of the criteria range.

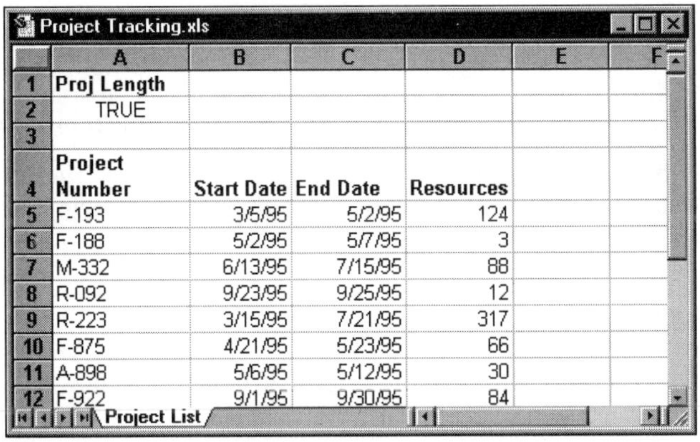

	A	B	C	D	E	F
1	Proj Length					
2	TRUE					
3						
4	Project Number	Start Date	End Date	Resources		
5	F-193	3/5/95	5/2/95	124		
6	F-188	5/2/95	5/7/95	3		
7	M-332	6/13/95	7/15/95	88		
8	R-092	9/23/95	9/25/95	12		
9	R-223	3/15/95	7/21/95	317		
10	F-875	4/21/95	5/23/95	66		
11	A-898	5/6/95	5/12/95	30		
12	F-922	9/1/95	9/30/95	84		

Figure 23-15: This list will be filtered using computed criteria.

Cell A2 contains the following formula:

```
=C5-B5+1>=30
```

This is a logical formula (returns *True* or *False*) that refers to cells in the first row of data in the list; it does *not* refer to the header row. When the list is filtered by this criteria, it shows only rows in which the project length (End Date – Start Date + 1) is greater than or equal to 30 days. In other words, the comparison is based on a computation.

Note You could accomplish the same effect, without using a computed criterion, by adding a new column to the list that contains a formula to calculate the project length. Using a computed criterion, however, eliminates the need to add a new column.

If you would like to filter the list to show only the projects that use above average resources, you could use the following computed criteria formula:

```
=D5>AVERAGE(D:D)
```

This filters the list to show only the rows in which the Resources field is greater than the average of the Resources field.

Following are a few things to keep in mind when using computed criteria:

✦ Don't use a field name in the criteria range that appears in the list. Create a new field name or just leave the cell blank.

✦ You can use any number of computed criteria and mix and match them with noncomputed criteria.

✦ Don't pay any attention to the values returned by formulas in the criteria range. These refer to the first row of the list.

✦ If your computed formula refers to a value outside the list, use an absolute reference rather than a relative reference. For example, use $C$1 rather than C1.

✦ Create your computed criteria formulas using the first row of data in the list (not the field names). Make these references relative, not absolute. For example, use C5 rather than $C$5.

Other advanced filtering operations

The Advanced Filter dialog box gives you two other options, which I discuss in the following paragraphs:

✦ Copy to Another Location

✦ Unique Records Only

Copying qualifying rows

If you choose the Copy to Another Location option in the Advanced Filter dialog box, the qualifying rows are copied to another location in the worksheet or a different worksheet. You specify the location for the copied rows in the Copy to edit box. Note that the list itself is not filtered when you use this option.

Displaying only unique rows

Choosing the option labeled Unique Records Only hides all duplicate rows that meet the criteria you specify. If you don't specify a criteria range, this option hides all duplicate rows in the list.

Using Database Functions with Lists

It's important to understand that Excel's worksheet functions don't ignore hidden cells. Therefore, if you have a SUM formula that calculates the total of the values in a column of a list, the formula returns the same value when the list is filtered.

To create formulas that return results based on filtering criteria, you need to use Excel's database worksheet functions. For example, you can create a formula that calculates the sum of values in a list that meet a certain criteria. Set up a criteria range as described previously. Then enter a formula such as the following:

```
=DSUM(ListRange,FieldName,Criteria)
```

In this case, ListRange refers to the list, FieldName refers to the field name cell of the column that is being summed, and Criteria refers to the criteria range.

Excel's database functions are listed in Table 23-3.

Table 23-3
Excel's Database Worksheet Functions

Function	Description
DAVERAGE	Returns the average of selected database entries
DCOUNT	Counts the cells containing numbers from a specified database and criteria
DCOUNTA	Counts nonblank cells from a specified database and criteria
DGET	Extracts from a database a single record that matches the specified criteria
DMAX	Returns the maximum value from selected database entries
DMIN	Returns the minimum value from selected database entries
DPRODUCT	Multiplies the values in a particular field of records that match the criteria in a database
DSTDEV	Estimates the standard deviation based on a sample of selected database entries
DSTDEVP	Calculates the standard deviation based on the entire population of selected database entries
DSUM	Adds the numbers in the field column of records in the database that match the criteria
DVAR	Estimates variance based on a sample from selected database entries
DVARP	Calculates variance based on the entire population of selected database entries

Cross-Reference Refer to Chapter 10 for general information about using worksheet functions.

Sorting a List

In some cases, the order of the rows in your list doesn't matter. But in other cases, you want the rows to appear in a specific order. For example, in a price list, you may want the rows to appear in alphabetical order by product name. This will make the products easier to locate. Or, if you have a list of accounts receivable information, you may want to sort the list so that the higher amounts appear at the top of the list (descending order).

Rearranging the order of the rows in a list is called *sorting*. Excel is quite flexible when it comes to sorting lists, and you can often accomplish this task with the click of a mouse button.

Simple sorting

To quickly sort a list in ascending order, move the cell pointer to the column upon which you want to sort. Then click the Sort Ascending button on the Standard toolbar. The Sort Descending button works the same way, but it sorts the list in descending order. In both cases, Excel determines the extent of your list and sorts all rows in the list.

Caution   When you sort a filtered list, only the visible rows are sorted. When you remove the filtering from the list, the list is no longer be sorted.

Caution   Be careful if you sort a list that contains formulas. If the formulas refer to cells in the same row, you won't have any problems. But if the formulas refer to cells in other rows in the list, the formulas will not be correct after the sorting. If formulas in your list refer to cells outside the list, make sure that the formulas use an absolute cell reference.

More complex sorting

Sometimes, you may want to sort by two or more columns. This is relevant in order to break ties. A tie occurs when rows with duplicate data remain unsorted. Figure 23-16 shows an example of a list. If this list is sorted by Month, the rows for each month are placed together. But you may also want to show the Sales Reps in ascending order within each month. In this case, you would need to sort by two columns (Month and Sales Rep). Figure 23-17 shows the list after sorting by these two columns.

You can use the Sort Ascending and Sort Descending buttons to do this — but you need to do two sorts. First, sort by the Sales Reps column, and then sort by the Month column. As I explain in the next section, Excel provides a way to accomplish mutlicolumn sorting with a single command.

Excel's sorting rules

Because cells can contain different types of information, you may be curious about how this information is sorted. For an ascending sort, the information appears in the following order:

1. **Values:** Numbers are sorted from smallest negative to largest positive. Dates and times are treated as values. In all cases, the sorting is done using the actual values (not their formatted appearance).

2. **Text:** In alphabetical order, as follows: 0 1 2 3 4 5 6 7 8 9 (space) ! " # $ % & ' ( ) * + , − . / : ; < = > ? @ [\ ] ^ _ ` { | } ~ A B C D E F G H I J K L M N O P Q R S T U V W X Y Z.

By default, sorting is not case sensitive. You can change this, however, in the Sort Options dialog box (described elsewhere in this chapter).

3. **Logical values:** False comes before True.

4. **Error values:** Error values (such as #VALUE! and #NA) appear in their original order and are not sorted by error type.

5. **Blank cells:** Blanks cells always appear last.

Sorting in descending order reverses this sequence — except that blank cells are *still* sorted last.

	A	B	C	D	E	F
7	Month	Sales Rep	Type	Unit Cost	Quantity	Total Sale
8	May	Sheldon	Existing	125	1	125
9	January	Sheldon	Existing	175	1	175
10	January	Sheldon	New	140	6	840
11	January	Jenkins	New	225	1	225
12	February	Robinson	New	225	1	225
13	March	Wilson	Existing	125	4	500
14	April	Robinson	Existing	125	2	250
15	February	Sheldon	Existing	175	1	175
16	March	Robinson	Existing	125	1	125
17	May	Jenkins	New	225	3	675
18	April	Jenkins	New	225	2	450
19	February	Wilson	Existing	125	5	625
20	February	Jenkins	New	225	2	450
21	January	Franks	New	225	4	900
22	May	Wilson	New	225	1	225
23	January	Sheldon	New	225	1	225
24	March	Jenkins	New	225	2	450
25	March	Jenkins	Existing	125	5	625
26	April	Peterson	New	140	2	280
27	February	Franks	Existing	175	2	350
28	May	Robinson	New	140	3	420
29	April	Peterson	Existing	175	6	1050
30	February	Robinson	New	225	3	675

Figure 23-16: This list is unsorted.

Sales-db.xls

	A	B	C	D	E	F
7	Month	Sales Rep	Type	Unit Cost	Quantity	Total Sale
8	January	Franks	New	225	4	900
9	January	Franks	Existing	175	1	175
10	January	Franks	Existing	175	5	875
11	January	Franks	New	225	1	225
12	January	Franks	Existing	175	1	175
13	January	Franks	Existing	125	3	375
14	January	Jenkins	New	225	1	225
15	January	Jenkins	Existing	125	1	125
16	January	Jenkins	New	140	3	420
17	January	Jenkins	Existing	175	2	350
18	January	Jenkins	New	140	1	140
19	January	Peterson	Existing	125	1	125
20	January	Peterson	Existing	125	3	375
21	January	Peterson	New	140	1	140
22	January	Peterson	New	225	1	225
23	January	Robinson	New	140	2	280
24	January	Robinson	Existing	125	5	625
25	January	Robinson	Existing	175	4	700
26	January	Sheldon	Existing	175	1	175
27	January	Sheldon	New	140	6	840
28	January	Sheldon	New	225	1	225
29	January	Sheldon	Existing	125	2	250
30	January	Sheldon	Existing	175	5	875

SALES-DB

Figure 23-17: The list after sorting on two fields.

The Sort dialog box

If you want to sort by more than one field, choose the Data➪Sort command. Excel displays the dialog box shown in Figure 23-18. Simply select the first sort field from the drop-down list labeled Sort By and specify Ascending or Descending order. Then, do the same for the second sort field. If you want to sort by a third field, specify the field in the third section. If the Header Row option is set, the first row (field names) is not affected by the sort. Click on OK and the list's rows rearrange in a flash.

If the sorting didn't occur as you expected, choose the Edit➪Undo command (or press Ctrl+Z) to undo the sorting.

Tip

What if you need to sort your list by more than three fields? It can be done, but it takes an additional step. For example, assume that you want to sort your list by five fields: Field1, Field2, Field3, Field4, and Field5. Start by sorting by Field3, Field4, and Field5. Then, re-sort the list by Field1 and Field2. In other words, sort the three "least important" fields first; they remain in sequence when you do the second sort.

Tip

Often, you want to keep the records in their original order but perform a temporary sort just to see how it looks. The solution is to add an additional column to the list with sequential numbers in it (don't use formulas to generate these numbers). Then, after you sort, you can return to the original order by re-sorting on the field that has the sequential numbers.

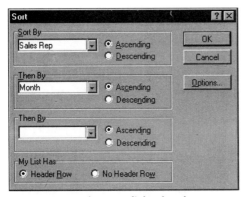

Figure 23-18: The Sort dialog box lets you sort by up to three columns.

How Excel identifies a header row

When you use the Data⇨Sort command, there's no need to select the list before you choose the command. That's because Excel examines the active cell position and then determines the list's boundaries for you. In addition, it makes its best guess as to whether the list contains a header row. If the list has a header row, this row is not included in the sorting.

How does this happen? I'm not sure exactly, but the following seems to be Excel's "thought" process:

1. Select the current region. (You can do this manually: Press F5, click on the Special button, select the Current Region option, and click on OK.)

2. Examine the first row of the selection.

3. Does the first row contain any blanks? If so, this list has no header row.

4. Does the first row contain text? If so, check the other cells. If they also contain text, this list has no header row.

5. Does the first row contain uppercase text and the list itself contain lowercase or proper case text? If so, this list has a header row.

6. Are the cells in the first row formatted differently from the other cells in the list? If so, this list has a header row.

Knowing this information can help you eliminate incorrect sorting. For example, if you want to sort a range that doesn't have header rows, you need to make sure that Excel doesn't sort the data as if it had header rows. The best solution is to use the Sort Ascending and Sort Descending toolbar buttons only when the data you're sorting has headers. If there are no headers, use the Data⇨Sort command and make sure that the No Header Row option is selected.

Sort Options

When you click the Options button in the Sort dialog box, Excel displays the Sort Options dialog, shown in Figure 23-19.

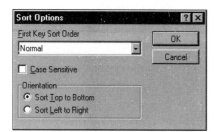

Figure 23-19: The Sort Options dialog gives you some additional sorting options.

These options are described as follows:

First Key Sort Order: Lets you specify a custom sort order for the sort (see the next section).

Case Sensitive: Makes the sorting case sensitive so that uppercase letters appear before lowercase letters in an ascending sort. Normally, sorting ignores the case of letters.

Orientation: Enables you to sort by columns rather than by rows (the default).

Using a custom sort order

Normal sorting is done either numerically or alphabetically, depending on the data being sorted. In some cases, however, you may want to sort your data in other ways. For example, if your data consists of month names, you usually want it to appear in month order rather than alphabetically. In fact, if you sort a list that uses month names, you'll find that this is exactly what happens. Excel, by default, has four "custom lists," and you can define your own. Excel's custom lists are as follows:

Abbreviated days: Sun, Mon, Tue, Wed, Thu, Fri, Sat

Days: Sunday, Monday, Tuesday, Wednesday, Thursday, Friday, Saturday

Abbreviated months: Jan, Feb, Mar, Apr, May, Jun, Jul, Aug, Sep, Oct, Nov, Dec

Months: January, February, March, April, May, June, July, August, September, October, November, December

Note that the abbreviated days and months do not have periods after them. If you use periods for these abbreviations, they are not recognized (and are not sorted correctly).

You may want to create a custom list. For example, your company may have several stores, and you like the stores listed in a particular order (not alphabetical). If you create a custom list, sorting puts the items in the order that you specify in the list. You must use the Data⇨Sort command to sort by a custom list (click on the Options button to specify the custom list).

To create a custom list, use the Custom List panel of the Options dialog box, shown in Figure 23-20. Select the NEW LIST option and make your entries (in order) in the List Entries box. Or, you can import your custom list from a range of cells by using the Import button.

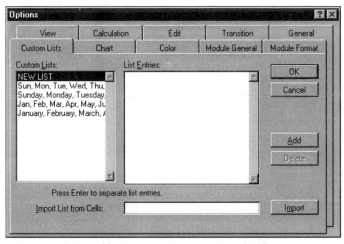

Figure 23-20: Excel lets you create custom sorting lists.

Tip   Custom lists also work with the autofill handle in cells. If you enter the first item of a custom list and then drag the cell's autofill handle, Excel fills in the remaining list items automatically.

Sorting non-lists

You can, of course, sort any range in a worksheet — it doesn't have to be a list. You need to be aware of a few things, however. The Sort Ascending and Sort Descending toolbar buttons may assume (erroneously) that the top row is a header row and not include these cells in the sort (see "How Excel identifies a header row" in this chapter).

Therefore, to avoid potential errors, don't use these toolbar buttons. Rather, select the entire range and use the Data⇨Sort command (making sure that you choose the No Header Row option).

Creating Subtotals

The final topic of this chapter is automatic subtotals — a handy feature that can save you lots of time. To use this feature, your list must be sorted, because the subtotals are inserted whenever the value in a specified field changes. Figure 23-21 shows an example of a list that's appropriate for subtotals. It was sorted on the Month field.

	Month	Sales Rep	Type	Unit Cost	Quantity	Total Sale	G
2	January	Franks	New	225	4	900	
3	January	Franks	Existing	175	5	875	
4	January	Franks	New	225	1	225	
5	January	Franks	Existing	175	1	175	
6	January	Jenkins	New	225	1	225	
7	January	Jenkins	Existing	125	1	125	
8	February	Franks	New	225	4	900	
9	February	Jenkins	New	225	2	450	
10	February	Jenkins	New	225	3	675	
11	February	Jenkins	New	225	3	675	
12	February	Jenkins	New	225	3	675	
13	February	Jenkins	Existing	175	1	175	
14	February	Peterson	New	225	1	225	
15	February	Peterson	New	225	2	450	
16	March	Peterson	Existing	125	2	250	
17	March	Peterson	New	225	2	450	
18	March	Robinson	Existing	125	1	125	
19	March	Robinson	Existing	125	5	625	
20	March	Robinson	New	225	4	900	
21	April	Franks	New	175	4	700	
22	April	Franks	New	175	3	525	
23	April	Jenkins	New	225	2	450	
24	April	Jenkins	New	140	3	420	

Figure 23-21: This list is a good candidate for subtotals, which will be inserted at each change of the month.

To insert subtotal formulas into a list automatically, move the cell pointer anywhere in the list and choose the Data⇨Subtotals command. You see the dialog box shown in Figure 23-22.

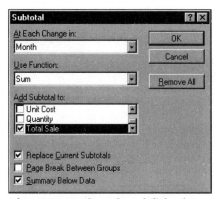

Figure 23-22: The Subtotal dialog box automatically inserts subtotal formulas into a sorted list.

This dialog box offers the following choices:

At Each Change in: This drop-down list displays all fields in your list. The field that you choose must be sorted.

Use Function: This gives you a choice of 11 functions. Usually, you'll want to use Sum (the default).

Add Subtotals to: This list box lists all of the fields in your list. Place a check mark next to the field or fields that you want to subtotal.

Replace Current Subtotal: If this box is checked, any existing subtotal formulas are removed and replaced with the new subtotals.

Page Break Between Groups: If this box is checked, Excel inserts a manual page break after each subtotal.

Summary Below Data: If this box is checked, the subtotals are placed below the data (the default). Otherwise, the subtotal formulas are placed above the totals.

Remove All: This button removes all subtotal formulas in the list.

When you click on OK, Excel analyzes the list and inserts formulas as specified — and also creates an outline for you. The formulas all use the SUBTOTAL worksheet function.

Caution When you add subtotals to a filtered list, the subtotals may no longer be accurate when the filter is removed.

Figure 23-23 shows a worksheet after adding subtotals.

	A	B	C	D	E	F
1	Month	Sales Rep	Type	Unit Cost	Quantity	Total Sale
2	January	Franks	New	225	4	900
3	January	Franks	Existing	175	5	875
4	January	Franks	New	225	1	225
5	January	Franks	Existing	175	1	175
6	January	Jenkins	New	225	1	225
7	January	Jenkins	Existing	125	1	125
8	**January Total**					2525
9	February	Franks	New	225	4	900
10	February	Jenkins	New	225	2	450
11	February	Jenkins	New	225	3	675
12	February	Jenkins	New	225	3	675
13	February	Jenkins	New	225	3	675
14	February	Jenkins	Existing	175	1	175
15	February	Peterson	New	225	1	225
16	February	Peterson	New	225	2	450
17	**February Total**					4225
18	March	Peterson	Existing	125	2	250
19	March	Peterson	New	225	2	450
20	March	Robinson	Existing	125	1	125
21	March	Robinson	Existing	125	5	625
22	March	Robinson	New	225	4	900
23	**March Total**					2350
24	April	Franks	New	175	4	700

Figure 23-23: Excel added the subtotal formulas automatically — and even created an outline.

Summary

In this chapter, I discuss lists. A list is simply a database table stored on a worksheet. The first row of the list (the header row) contains field names and subsequent rows contain data (records). I offer some pointers on data entry and discuss two ways to filter a list to show only rows that meet certain criteria. Autofiltering is adequate for many tasks, but if your filtering needs are more complex, you need to use advanced filtering. I end the chapter with a discussion of sorting and Excel's automatic subtotal feature.

✦   ✦   ✦

Using External Database Files

The preceding chapter described how to work with lists stored in a worksheet. Many users find that worksheet lists are sufficient for their data tracking. Others, however, choose to take advantage of the fact that Excel also can access data stored in external database files. That's the topic of this chapter.

Why Use External Database Files

Accessing external database files from Excel is useful when

✦ The database that you need to work with is very large.

✦ The database is shared with others; that is, other users have access to the database and may need to work with the data at the same time.

✦ You want to work with only a subset of the data that meets certain criteria.

✦ The database is in a format that Excel can't read.

If you need to work with external databases, you may find that you prefer Excel over other database programs. The advantage: After you bring the data into Excel, you can manipulate and format it by using familiar tools.

As you may know, Excel can read some database files directly — specifically, those produced by various versions of dBASE (with a DBF extension). If the database has fewer than 16,384 records and no more than 255 fields, you can load the entire file into a worksheet, memory permitting. Even if you have enough memory to load such a large file, however, Excel's performance likely would be very poor.

In many cases, you may not be interested in all the records or fields in the file. Instead, you may want to bring in just the data that meets certain criteria. In other words, you want to *query* the database and load into your worksheet a subset of the external database. As you'll see, Excel makes this type of operation relatively easy.

To work with an external database file from Excel, you use the MS Query application (which is included with Excel). The general procedure is as follows:

1. Ensure that the MS Query add-in is installed on your system and that the add-in is loaded. (See "No Data⇨Get External Data command?" in this chapter.)

2. Activate a worksheet.

3. Choose the Data⇨Get External Data command. This starts MS Query.

4. In MS Query, you specify the database that you want to use and then create a query — a list of criteria that determines which records you want.

5. Choose Query's File⇨Return Data to Microsoft Excel command. The data that passes your query is copied to the worksheet, where you can do whatever you like with it.

Excel automatically stores information about the query that generated the data. This means that it's a simple matter to modify the query or *refresh* it (update with any changed values). This is particularly useful when the data resides in a shared database that is continually being updated.

Cross-Reference In the next chapter, I discuss pivot tables. As you'll see, you can create a pivot table using data in an external file. You use MS Query to retrieve data.

An Example of Using MS Query

The best way to become familiar with MS Query is to walk through an example.

The database file

On the CD-ROM The file used in this example is named `Budget.dbf` and is located in the Database folder on the companion CD-ROM.

This database file is a dBASE IV database with a single table that consists of 15,840 records. This file contains the following fields:

No Data: External Data command?

MS Query is a separate application, but you can access it directly from Excel. You also can run it as a stand-alone program.

Before you can use MS Query from Excel, make sure that:

✦ The add-in was installed on your system.

✦ The `Msquery.xla` add-in file is loaded.

To determine whether MS Query is ready to use, click on the Data menu. If you see the Get External Data command, you're all set and can skip the rest of this sidebar.

If Excel does not display the Get External Data command on the Data menu, choose the Tools⇨Add-Ins command. If MS Query Add-In appears in the available add-ins list, make sure that this option is checked.

If this option doesn't appear, click on the Browse button and locate the `Msquery.xla` file located in the Excel\Library\Msquery folder. Select the file and click on OK to add this add-in to the list of available add-ins.

If you can't find the `Msquery.xla` file, you need to run Excel's Setup program (or the Microsoft Office Setup program). When Setup starts, choose the Add/Remove button. When Setup finishes, you may have to run through the steps listed in the preceding paragraph to make the Data⇨Get External Data command available.

Sort: A numeric field that holds record sequence numbers.

Division: A text field that specifies the company division (this is either Asia, Europe, N. America, Pacific Rim, S. America).

Department: A text field that specifies the department within the division. Each division is organized into the following departments: Accounting, Advertising, Data Processing, Human Resources, Operations, Public Relations, R&D, Sales, Security, Shipping, and Training.

Category: A text field that specifies the budget category. The four categories are Compensation, Equipment, Facility, and Supplies & Services.

Item: A text field that specifies the budget item. Each budget category has different budget items. For example, the Compensation category includes the following items: Benefits, Bonuses, Commissions, Conferences, Entertainment, Payroll Taxes, Salaries, and Training.

Month: A text field that specifies the month (abbreviated as Jan, Feb, and so on).

Budget: A numeric field that stores the budgeted amount.

Actual: A numeric field that stores the actual amount spent.

Variance: A numeric field that stores the difference between the Budget and Actual.

Some database terminology

People who spend their days working with databases seem to have their own special language. Following are a few terms that can help you hold you own among a group of database mavens.

External database: A collection of data stored in one or more files (not Excel files). Each file of a database holds a single table, and tables are comprised of records and fields.

Field: In a database table, an element of a record that corresponds to a column.

ODBC: An acronym for Open Database Connectivity, a standard developed by Microsoft that uses drivers to access database files in different formats. MS Query comes with drivers for Access, dBASE, FoxPro, Paradox, SQL Server, Excel workbooks, and ASCII text files. ODBC drivers for other databases are available from Microsoft and third-party providers.

Query: To search a database for records that meet specific criteria. This term is also used as a noun; you can write a query, for example.

Record: In a database table, a single element that corresponds to a row.

Refresh: To rerun a query to get the latest data. This is applicable when the database contains information that is subject to change, as in a multiuser environment.

Relational Database: A database that is stored in more than one table or file. The tables are connected by having one or more common fields (sometimes called the *key* field).

Result Set: The data returned by a query, usually a subset of the original database. MS Query returns the result set to your Excel workbook.

SQL: An acronym for Structured Query Language (usually pronounced *sequel*). MS Query uses SQL to query data stored in ODBC databases.

Table: A record- and field-oriented collection of data. A database consists of one or more tables.

The task

The objective of this exercise is to develop a report that shows the first quarter (January through March) actual compensation expenditures of the training department in the North American division. In other words, the query will extract records in which one of the following applies:

✦ The Division is *N. America*, the Department is *Training*, the Category is *Compensation*, and the Month is *Jan*.

✦ The Division is *N. America*, the Department is *Training*, the Category is *Compensation*, and the Month is *Feb*.

✦ The Division is *N. America*, the Department is *Training*, the Category is *Compensation*, and the Month is *Mar*.

Using MS Query to get the data

Note One approach to this task would be to import the entire dBASE file into a worksheet and then use the Data⇨Filter⇨AutoFilter command to filter the data as required. This approach would work because the file has fewer than 16,384 records. This won't always be the case. The advantage of using MS Query is that it imports only the data that's required.

Starting MS Query

Begin with an empty worksheet. Select the Data⇨Get External Data command, which launches and activates MS Query. MS Query is a separate application that is started by Excel. Excel continues to run, and you can switch back and forth between MS Query and Excel if you need to. You'll find, however, that you can't do anything in Excel while it's waiting for data to be returned from MS Query.

Note MS Query resembles Excel in some respects. For example, it has a toolbar that you use to execute some common commands. If you move the mouse pointer over a tool icon, MS Query displays the tool's name and shows a description at the bottom of the screen. Query's toolbar can't be customized, and the tools are displayed in only one size.

Selecting a data source

When MS Query starts, it displays the Select Data Source dialog box, as shown in Figure 24-1. This dialog box lists the data sources known to MS Query — it may or may not be empty, depending on which data sources are defined on your system. If it contains the data source that you need, select it and click on OK.

Click on the Other button to define a new data source. This brings up another dialog box, labeled ODBC Data Sources (see Figure 24-2). This dialog box contains data sources known to the ODBC Manager. To define a new data source, enter a name (use **Budget Database** for this example) and click on the New button.

The next step is to specify the ODBC driver to use. You do this in the Add Data Source dialog box, shown in Figure 24-3. Because the database file in this example is a dBASE file, select the driver named Microsoft dBase Driver (*.dbf) and click on OK.

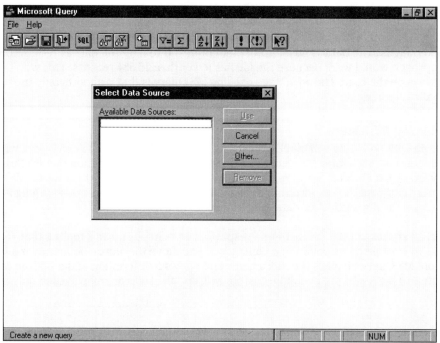

Figure 24-1: The first step is to select a data source.

Figure 24-2: Creating a new data source with the ODBC Data Sources dialog box.

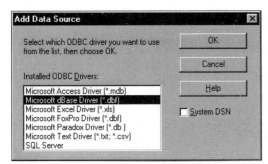

Figure 24-3: In this dialog box, you select the ODBC driver to use for the data source.

When you click OK, you get yet another dialog box, labeled ODBC dBASE Setup. You get a different dialog box for different ODBC drivers. The ODBC dBASE Setup dialog box is shown in Figure 24-4. Follow these steps:

1. Enter **Budget Database** for both the Data Source Name and Description.

2. Select dBase IV from the drop-down list labeled Version.

3. Click on the Select Directory button and specify the drive and folder that contains the file. If you're using the example database on the CD-ROM, this folder is named Database.

Caution | The pre-release version of MS Query that I used generated an error if the directory (folder) name contained a space. This problem may be fixed in the shipping version. If not, make sure that the directory path does not include spaces.

Click on OK twice to close the dialog boxes, and you're back at the original Select Data Source dialog box, which now displays the data source that you just added. Click on the Use button to use the Budget Database source.

Note | You only have to go through these steps once for each data source. The next time that you access MS Query, the Budget Database (and any other database sources that you've defined) appears in the Select Data Source dialog box.

Specifying the database table

After selecting the data source, the next step is to select the table. MS Query displays the Add Tables dialog box, which shows a list of all matching files in the folder that you specified for the data source. Select the `Budget.dbf` file and click on Add. Because this query uses only one database table, click on Close to close the dialog box.

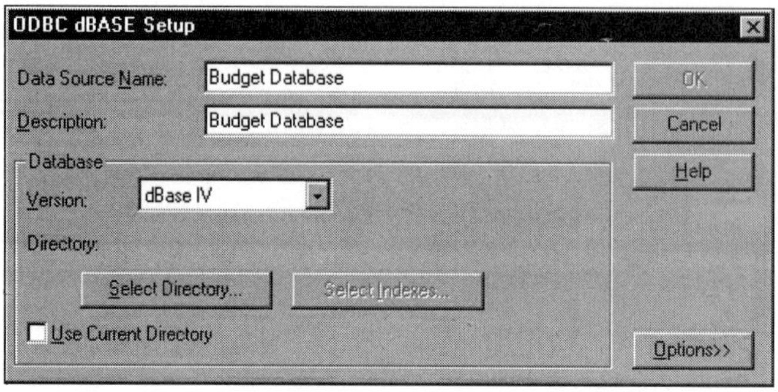

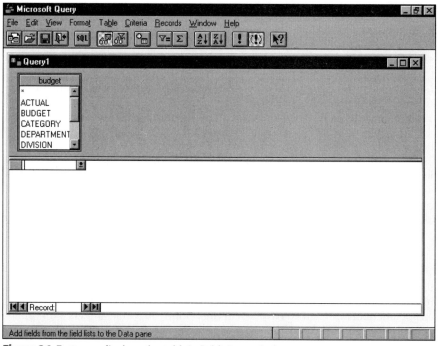

Figure 24-4: The ODBC dBASE Setup dialog box.

At this point, MS Query should appear as in Figure 24-5. The Query1 window is divided into two panes. The upper pane (known as the *table pane*) contains a list of all fields in the database table (known as a *field list*). The lower pane (known as the *data pane*) is blank.

Figure 24-5: Query displays the table's fields in a window.

Selecting the fields

In this step, you add fields to the data pane. This determines which fields from the database are returned to Excel. Recall that the query for this example involves selecting records based on the following fields: Division, Department, Month, Category, and Actual. You also want to add the Item field.

To add the Division field to the data pane, locate it in the field list and double-click on it. This displays the Division field in the data pane, as shown in Figure 24-6.

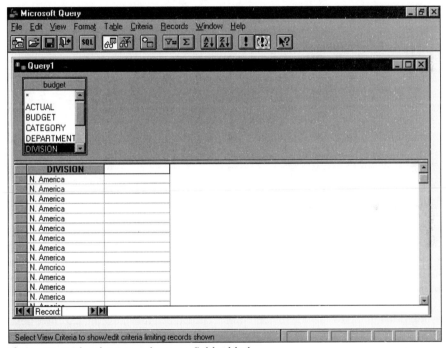

Figure 24-6: The data pane has one field added.

Repeat this for the other fields: Department, Category, Item, Month, and Actual. When you're finished, the Query1 window looks like Figure 24-7.

Tip   To add *all* fields from the field list, you can double-click on the asterisk (*), which appears as the first item in the field list. You also can drag an item from the field list to the data pane.

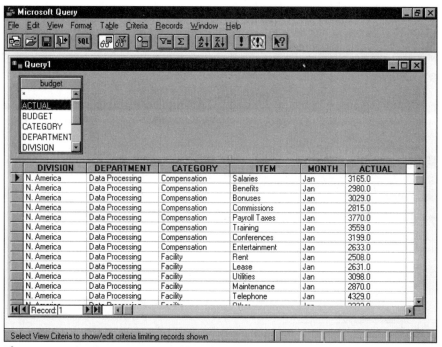

Figure 24-7: The data pane after adding the relevant fields.

The data pane resembles an Excel worksheet — but it's not. For example, you can't enter formulas into the cells. You can, however, change column widths by dragging the border of a field name. To browse through the data, you can use the scrollbars. Or, you can use the navigation buttons (located at the bottom of the window), which enable you to move to the table's beginning or end or to scroll backward or forward by individual records. You also can enter a record number into the text box next to the word *Record* to view a specific record. If you enter 100, for example, the data pane scrolls so that you can view the 100th record in the table.

Note   You can always add other fields to the data pane. Or, you can remove fields that you don't need — just select the field and press Delete.

Specifying record selection criteria

At this point, the data pane displays all the records in the database table. Because you don't want to return all of the records to Excel, you need to specify the record selection criteria. Recall that you're interested only in the records in which one of the following applies:

✦ The Division is *N. America*, the Department is *Training*, the Category is *Compensation*, and the Month is *Jan*.

✦ The Division is *N. America*, the Department is *Training*, the Category is *Compensation*, and the Month is *Feb*.

✦ The Division is *N. America*, the Department is *Training*, the Category is *Compensation*, and the Month is *Mar*.

Before adding the criteria, it's a good idea to make sure that the Automatic Query option is not in effect. Entering the criteria is a multistep process; if the Automatic Query option is on, the process slows significantly because MS Query performs the query after each step. The Auto Query toolbar button has an image of an exclamation point enclosed in parentheses. If this button is highlighted (appears in a lighter color), the Automatic Query option is in effect. To turn the option off, click on the button.

You can add criteria in several ways: choose a command, use the toolbar, or enter them directly. In this example, I use the most straightforward method: entering criteria directly.

You need a place to enter the criteria. Choose the View⇨Criteria command (or click on the Show/Hide Criteria button), and MS Query adds a new pane to the window (the *criteria pane*) between the table pane and the data pane. See Figure 24-8. You can change the size of any pane by dragging a border with your mouse.

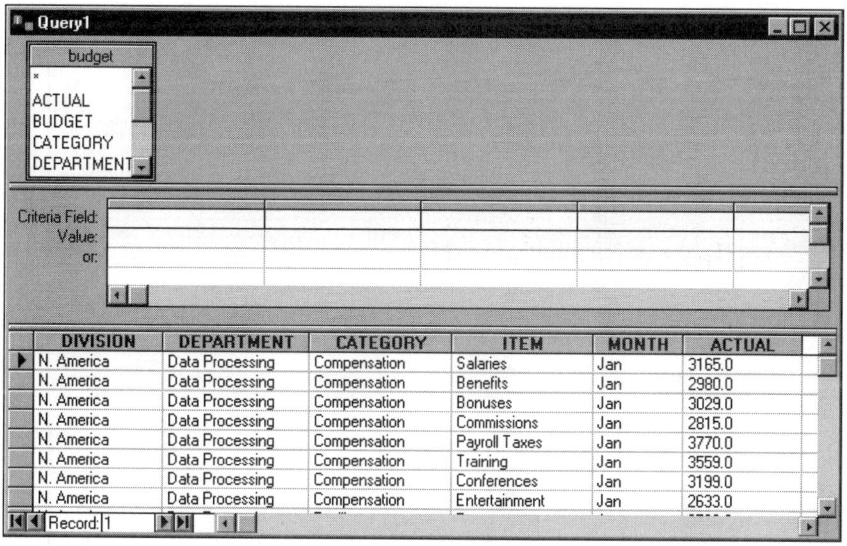

DIVISION	DEPARTMENT	CATEGORY	ITEM	MONTH	ACTUAL
N. America	Data Processing	Compensation	Salaries	Jan	3165.0
N. America	Data Processing	Compensation	Benefits	Jan	2980.0
N. America	Data Processing	Compensation	Bonuses	Jan	3029.0
N. America	Data Processing	Compensation	Commissions	Jan	2815.0
N. America	Data Processing	Compensation	Payroll Taxes	Jan	3770.0
N. America	Data Processing	Compensation	Training	Jan	3559.0
N. America	Data Processing	Compensation	Conferences	Jan	3199.0
N. America	Data Processing	Compensation	Entertainment	Jan	2633.0

Figure 24-8: The criteria pane holds the criteria for the database query.

The criteria pane holds the query criteria. In this example, you have three criteria, so you need to use three rows (plus a row at the top for the field names). With the criteria pane displayed, you now can enter the three-part criteria.

1. Drag the Division field from the field list to the first column of the criteria pane (drag it to the first row, labeled Criteria Field).

2. Enter '**N. America**' in the second row of the first column. Note: The single quotation marks are required if a criterion has a space in it.

3. Drag the Department field from the field list to the second column of the criteria pane.

4. Enter **Training** in the second row of the second column.

5. Drag the Category field from the field list to the third column of the criteria pane.

6. Enter **Compensation** in the second row of the third column.

7. Drag the Month field from the field list to the fourth column of the criteria pane.

8. Enter **Jan** in the second row of the fourth column.

So far, the criteria entered will retrieve the matching records for January. The criteria pane needs two more rows — one for February and one for March. Each row is treated like an OR operator. Continue entering criteria in rows three and four until your screen looks like Figure 24-9.

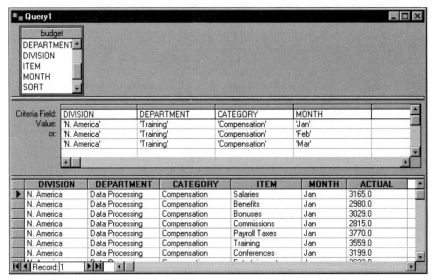

Figure 24-9: The criteria pane holds the three-part criteria.

Note The criteria also can include numbers, expressions, functions, and logical operators. For example, to retrieve records only if the Variance field contains a value greater than zero (that is, the Actual amount exceeds the Budget amount), you enter **Variance** into the Criteria Field line and **>0** in the Value line. MS Query is very flexible in the types of queries that it can handle. The online help system contains detailed information on all your options.

Executing the query

With the criteria entered in the criteria pane, you now can execute the query. Choose the Records⇨Query Now command (or click on the Query Now button on the toolbar — it's the button with the exclamation point). After a few seconds, the data pane displays only the records that match the criteria. (In this example, 24 records qualify).

Note Executing the query while you're in MS Query is optional. When you return the results to Excel (as described in the next section), the query is executed. By examining the results of the query while you're in Query, however, you make sure that the query returns the desired results.

Returning the results to Excel

The final step is to send the results of the query to the Excel worksheet. Choose the File⇨Return Data to Microsoft Excel command. Excel is reactivated, and you see the Get External Data dialog box shown in Figure 24-10.

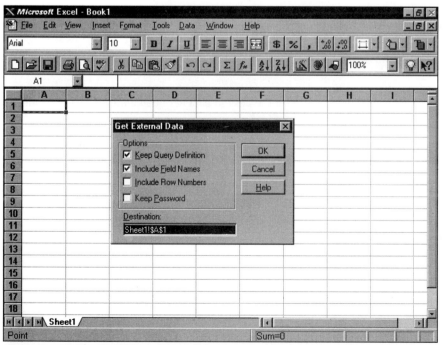

Figure 24-10: The Get External Data dialog box enables you to specify some options for the query results.

For this example, simply accept the default options and choose OK (these options are explained later in the chapter). In a few seconds, the worksheet contains the selected database records (see Figure 24-11). You now can work with this data as you do with any other Excel list. For example, you can insert subtotals or use auto-filtering (as explained in Chapter 23). Query continues to run until you close it manually or exit Excel.

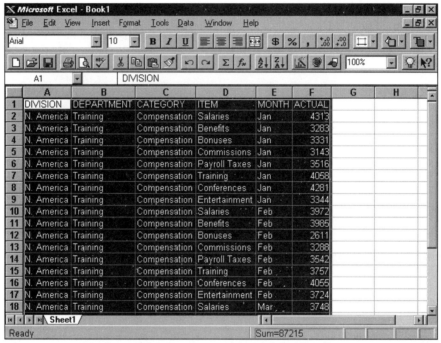

Figure 24-11: The Excel worksheet after the desired data has been retrieved by using Query.

More about MS Query

The preceding example should give you a feel for how MS Query works. In this section, I discuss variations on the basic query and other MS Query techniques.

Refreshing a query

If you load your worksheet file at a later date, it contains the data that you originally retrieved from the external database. The external database may have changed, however, in the interim. Fortunately, you need not go through the entire query definition process again to update your worksheet with the latest values. Excel remembers where the data came from (that is, the query used to retrieve the data). Simply move the cell pointer anywhere within the extracted data table in the worksheet and choose Data➪Refresh Data. Excel launches Query and uses your original query to bring in the current data from the external database.

Note You can use the Data➪Refresh Data command only if you select the Keep Query Definition option in the Get External Data dialog box that's displayed before Query sends the query results to your worksheet.

Changing your query

If you bring the query results into your worksheet and discover that it's not what you want, you can modify the query.

Move the cell pointer anywhere within the query results and choose the Data➪Get External Data command. Excel displays a version of the Get External Data dialog box that has an Edit Query button (see Figure 24-12). Clicking on this button launches Query and loads your original query into the criteria pane. Make your changes to the criteria pane and then choose the File➪Return Data to Microsoft Excel command. Excel is reactivated and you see the Get External Data dialog box. Click on OK and the old query results are replaced by the revised query results.

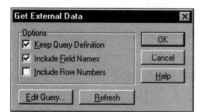

Figure 24-12: Use the Edit Query button to modify an existing query.

Making multiple queries

You can use the Data➪Get External Data command as many times as you need with a single workbook. Each time you issue the command, the results should be stored in a different location — for example, on different worksheets.

Excel automatically keeps track of the query used to produce each query results table. If you want to change or refresh a query, move the active cell pointer to a cell in the table that you want to work with, and then choose Data➪Get External Data (to modify a query) or Data➪Refresh Data (to refresh query results).

The MS Query toolbar

If you work with MS Query a lot, you should become familiar with its toolbar. Unlike Excel, this toolbar is fixed in place and can't be modified in any way.

The accompanying figure shows the MS Query toolbar. The tools, from left to right, are as follows:

New Query: Displays a new (empty) query window in which you create a query. You'll be prompted for the data source.

Open Query: Lets you open a query that has been saved.

Save File: Lets you save the query as a file.

Return Data: Returns the result set to Excel.

View SQL: Displays the query in SQL.

Show/Hide Tables: Toggles the display of the tables pane.

Show/Hide Criteria: Toggles the display of the criteria pane.

Add Table(s): Lets you add one or more additional tables to the table pane.

Criteria Equals: Displays the Add Criteria dialog box.

Cycle Thru Totals: Changes the type of totaling performed in the selected field.

Sort Ascending: Sorts the data in the data pane in ascending order, using the selected field.

Sort Descending: Sorts the data in the data pane in descending order, using the selected field.

Query Now: Executes the query and updates the data pane with the results.

Auto Query: When selected, the query is executed automatically whenever the criteria is changed (this can slow things down dramatically).

Help: Displays help about MS Query commands or toolbar buttons.

Running MS Query by itself

Normally, you run MS Query from Excel. Because MS Query is a stand-alone application, however, you also can run it directly (the executable file is `Msqry32.exe`, and it's located in the Windows\Msapps\Msquery folder).

If you run MS Query by itself, you can't return the data to Excel automatically. You can, however, use the Clipboard to copy data from the data pane to whatever application you want (including Excel).

Using the ODBC Manager

Occasionally, you may need to edit data sources — for example, if you move your database files to a new location. You can do this using the ODBC Manager utility. This program is available in the Windows 95 Control Panel (it's called `32-bit ODBC`). This utility also lets you add new data sources and remove those that you no longer need.

Other Query techniques

In this section, I briefly discuss other capabilities of MS Query. For complete details, refer to the online Help system.

Using the Add Criteria dialog box

In the preceding example, criteria was added to the query by entering text directly into the criteria pane. You also can use the Criteria⇨Add Criteria command to add criteria. This command displays the dialog box shown in Figure 24-13.

The Add Criteria dialog box is quite straightforward. Choose the field from the Field drop-down list. Then select an operator from the Operator drop-down list. The choices are listed and described in Table 24-1. You can click on the Values button to get a list of all unique values in the field. The And and Or option buttons determine where the criteria is placed. If you choose And, the criteria is entered into the current row. If you choose Or, it's entered into a new row. When you click on Add, MS Query translates your request and enters it into the criteria pane.

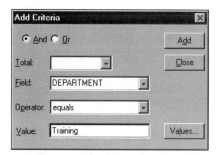

Figure 24-13: The Add Criteria dialog box is another way to add criteria.

Table 24-1 Criteria Operators	
Operator	**What It Does**
equals	Field is identical to value
does not equal	Field is not equal to value
is greater than	Field is greater than value
is greater than or equal to	Field is greater than or equal to value
is less than	Field is less than value
is less than or equal to	Field is less than or equal to value
is one of	Field is in a list of values, separated by commas
is not one of	Field is not in a list of values, separated by commas
is between	Field is between two values, separated by commas
is not between	Field is not between two values, separated by commas
begins with	Field begins with the value
does not begin with	Field does not begin with value
ends with	Field ends with value
does not end with	Field does not end with value
contains	Field contains value
does not contain	Field does not contain value
like	Field is like value (using * and ? wildcard characters)
not like	Field is not like value (using * and ? wildcard characters)
is Null	Field is empty
is not Null	Field is not empty

If you experiment with this dialog box, you'll quickly understand how the requests are translated, and you may be able to save some time by entering more complex queries.

Using multiple database tables

The example in this chapter uses only one database table. Some databases, however, use multiple tables. These databases are known as *relational databases* because the tables are linked by a common field. MS Query lets you use any number of tables in your queries. To see an example of a relational database, load the sample database (called Northwind Traders) that's provided with MS Query. This particular database has six tables.

Reusing queries

If you plan to reuse a query that you defined, you can save it in a file. While MS Query is active, use the File⇨Save Query command and give it a name. You can open a saved query file using the File⇨Open Query command.

Adding and editing records in external database tables

To add, delete, and edit data when using Query, make sure that you choose the Records⇨Allow Editing command. Of course, you can't edit a database file that's set up as read-only. In any case, you need to be careful with this feature because your changes are saved to disk as soon as you move the cell pointer out of the record that you're editing (you do not need to choose File⇨Save command).

Formatting data

If you don't like the data's appearance in the data pane, you can change the font used by selecting Format⇨Font. Be aware that selective formatting isn't allowed (unlike in Excel); changing the font affects all the data in the data pane.

Sorting data

You may find it useful to view the data in the data pane in a different order. To do so, choose Records⇨Sort command (or click on the Sort Ascending or Sort Descending toolbar icon).

Learning More

This chapter isn't intended to cover every aspect of MS Query. Rather, it discusses the basic features that are used most often. MS Query is easy to use, so you can experiment and consult the online Help to learn more. As with anything related to Excel, and best way to master MS Query is to use it — preferably with data that's meaningful to you.

Summary

In this chapter, I introduce MS Query — a stand-alone application that can be executed by Excel. To use this feature, the MS Query add-in must be loaded. MS Query is used to retrieve data from external database files. You can specify the criteria, and MS Query returns the data to your Excel worksheet.

✦   ✦   ✦

Analyzing Data with Pivot Tables

✦   ✦   ✦   ✦

In This Chapter

An introduction to Excel's powerful pivot table feature

How to determine whether your data is appropriate for a pivot table

Steps in creating a pivot table

Modifications that you can make after a pivot table is created

Several pivot table examples

✦   ✦   ✦   ✦

Excel provides many data analysis tools, but the pivot table feature may be the most useful overall. Pivot tables are valuable for summarizing information contained in a database, which can be stored in a worksheet or in an external file.

In this chapter, I demonstrate this innovative feature and suggest how you can use it to view your data in ways you may not have imagined.

What Is a Pivot Table?

A *pivot table* is a dynamic summary of data contained in a database. It lets you create frequency distributions and cross-tabulations of several different data dimensions. In addition, you can display subtotals and any level of detail that you desire. But, as I explain later, a pivot table isn't appropriate for all databases.

The best way to understand the concept of a pivot table is to see one. Start with Figure 25-1, which shows the data that will be used to create the pivot table. This database consists of daily new account information for a three-branch bank. The database tracks the date that each account was opened, the amount, the account type (CD, Checking, Savings, or IRA), who opened the account (a teller or a new accounts representative), the branch at which it was opened, and whether the account was opened by a new customer or an existing customer. The database has 350 records.

On the CD-ROM This workbook, named PVT_BANK.XLS, can be found on the companion CD-ROM and is used in many examples throughout the chapter.

Pivot Table Example.xls

	A	B	C	D	E	F
1	Date	Amount	AcctType	OpenedBy	Branch	Customer
2	9/1/95	340	Checking	New Accts	Central	Existing
3	9/1/95	15,759	CD	Teller	Westside	Existing
4	9/1/95	15,276	CD	New Accts	North County	Existing
5	9/1/95	12,000	CD	New Accts	Westside	Existing
6	9/1/95	5,000	CD	New Accts	North County	Existing
7	9/1/95	7,000	Savings	New Accts	North County	New
8	9/1/95	90,000	CD	New Accts	Central	Existing
9	9/1/95	124	Checking	Teller	Central	Existing
10	9/1/95	400	Checking	Teller	Central	Existing
11	9/1/95	100	Checking	New Accts	Central	Existing
12	9/1/95	14,644	CD	New Accts	Westside	New
13	9/1/95	5,000	Savings	New Accts	Westside	Existing
14	9/1/95	4,623	Savings	New Accts	North County	Existing
15	9/1/95	5,879	Checking	New Accts	Central	Existing
16	9/1/95	3,171	Checking	New Accts	Westside	Existing
17	9/1/95	4,000	Savings	New Accts	Central	Existing
18	9/1/95	5,000	Checking	New Accts	Central	Existing
19	9/1/95	16,000	CD	New Accts	Central	New
20	9/1/95	50,000	Savings	New Accts	Central	Existing
21	9/1/95	13,636	CD	New Accts	North County	Existing

September

Figure 25-1: This database will be used to create a pivot table.

This database contains a lot of information, but it's not all that revealing. In other words, it must be summarized in order to be useful. Summarizing a database is essentially the process of answering questions about the data. Here are a few questions that may be of interest to the bank's management:

- ✦ What is the total deposit amount for each branch, broken down by account type?
- ✦ How many accounts were opened at each branch, broken down by account type?
- ✦ What's the dollar distribution of the different account types?
- ✦ What types of accounts do tellers most often open?
- ✦ How is the Central branch doing compared to the other two branches?
- ✦ Which branch opens the most accounts for new customers?

As you'll see, you can use a pivot table to answer questions like these. It takes only a few seconds and doesn't require a single formula.

Figure 25-2 depicts a pivot table created from the database. It shows the amount of new deposits broken down by branch and account type. This is one of hundreds of different types of summaries that you can produce from this data.

Figure 25-3 shows another pivot table generated from the bank data. This pivot table uses a page field for the Customer item. In this case, the pivot table displays the data only for New customers. Notice that I also changed the orientation of the table (Branches are shown in rows and AcctType is shown in columns).

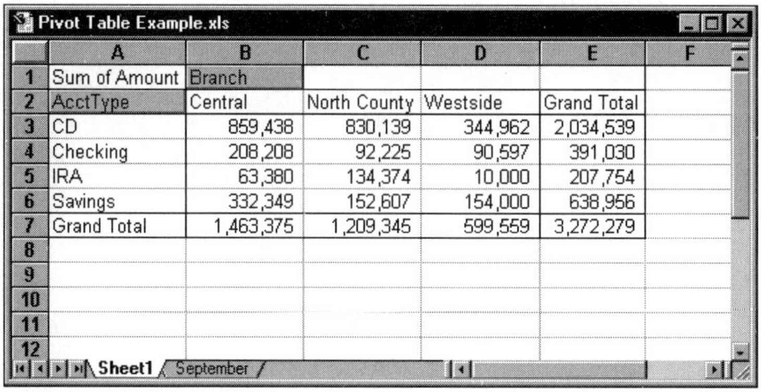

	A	B	C	D	E	F
	Pivot Table Example.xls					_ □ ×
	A	B	C	D	E	F
1	Sum of Amount	Branch				
2	AcctType	Central	North County	Westside	Grand Total	
3	CD	859,438	830,139	344,962	2,034,539	
4	Checking	208,208	92,225	90,597	391,030	
5	IRA	63,380	134,374	10,000	207,754	
6	Savings	332,349	152,607	154,000	638,956	
7	Grand Total	1,463,375	1,209,345	599,559	3,272,279	
8						
9						
10						
11						
12						

Sheet1 / September /

Figure 25-2: A simple pivot table.

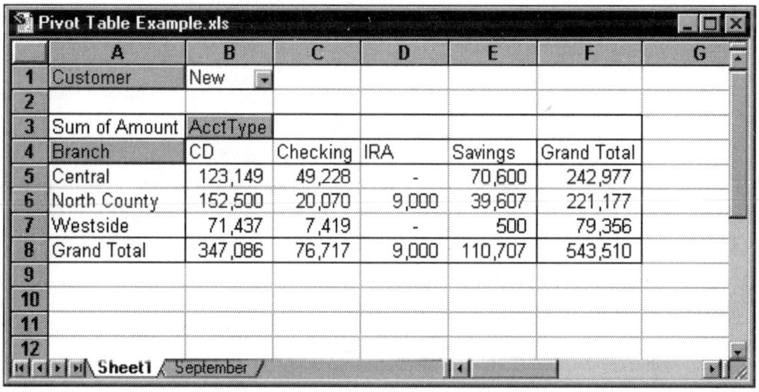

	A	B	C	D	E	F	G
	Pivot Table Example.xls						_ □ ×
	A	B	C	D	E	F	G
1	Customer	New					
2							
3	Sum of Amount	AcctType					
4	Branch	CD	Checking	IRA		Savings	Grand Total
5	Central	123,149	49,228	-		70,600	242,977
6	North County	152,500	20,070	9,000		39,607	221,177
7	Westside	71,437	7,419	-		500	79,356
8	Grand Total	347,086	76,717	9,000		110,707	543,510
9							
10							
11							
12							

Sheet1 / September /

Figure 25-3: A pivot table that uses a page field.

Data Appropriate for a Pivot Table

Before I get into the details of pivot tables, it's important to understand the type of data that's relevant to this feature. The data that you're summarizing must be in the form of a database (although there is an exception to this, which I discuss later). The database can be stored in a worksheet (such a database is sometimes known as a table) or in an external database file. Although Excel can convert any database to a pivot table, not all databases will benefit.

Generally speaking, fields in a database table can be one of two types:

✦ **Data:** Contains a value. In Figure 25-1, the Amount field is a data field.

✦ **Category:** Describes the data. In Figure 25-1, the Date, AcctType, OpenedBy, and Customer fields are category fields because they describe the data in the Amount field.

Pivot table terminology

If you're new to Excel, the concept of a pivot table might be a bit baffling. As far as I know, Microsoft invented the name *pivot table*. It's important to understand the terminology used when working with pivot tables. Refer to the accompanying figure to get your bearings.

Column Field: A field that has a column orientation in the pivot table. Each item in the field occupies a column. In the figure, Product is a column field, and it has two items (Sprockets and Widgets). Column fields can be nested.

Data Area: The cells in a pivot table that contain the summary data. Excel offers several ways to summarize the data (sum, average, count, and so on).

Grand Totals: A row or column that displays totals for all cells in a row or column in a pivot table. You can specify that grand totals be calculated for rows, columns, or both (or neither). The pivot table in the figure has grand totals for rows and columns.

Group: A collection of items that are treated as a single item. You can group items manually or automatically (group dates into months, for example).

Item: An element in a field that appears as a row or column header in a pivot table. In the figure, Sprockets and Widgets are items for the Product field. The Year field has three items (1994, 1995, and 1996), and the State field has two items (California and Oregon).

Page Field: A field that has a page orientation in the pivot table — similar to a slice of a three-dimensional cube. Only one item at a time in a page field can be displayed at one time. In the figure, Region is a page field that's displaying the West item.

Refresh: To recalculate the pivot table after changes to the source data have been made.

Row Field: A field that has a row orientation in the pivot table. Each item in the field occupies a row. Row fields can be nested. In the figure, State and Year are both row fields, and the Year field is nested within the State field.

Source Data: The data that is used to create a pivot table. It can be from a worksheet or an external database.

Subtotals: A row or column that displays subtotals for detail cells in a row or column in a pivot table. In the figure, subtotals are calculated for the State field.

A single database table can have any number of data fields and any number of category fields. When you create a pivot table, you usually want to summarize one or more of the data fields. The values in the category fields, on the other hand, appear in the pivot table as rows, columns, or pages.

Exceptions exist, however, and you may find that Excel's pivot table feature is useful even for databases that don't contain actual numerical data fields. The database in Figure 25-4, for example, doesn't contain numerical data fields. But you can create a useful pivot table that counts fields rather than sums them.

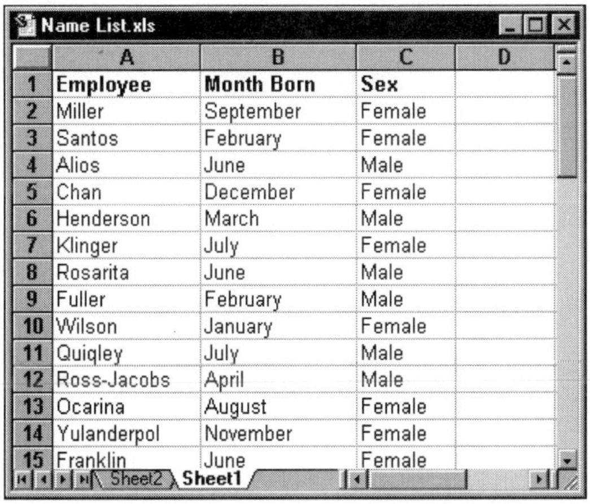

	A	B	C	D
1	Employee	Month Born	Sex	
2	Miller	September	Female	
3	Santos	February	Female	
4	Alios	June	Male	
5	Chan	December	Female	
6	Henderson	March	Male	
7	Klinger	July	Female	
8	Rosarita	June	Male	
9	Fuller	February	Male	
10	Wilson	January	Female	
11	Quigley	July	Male	
12	Ross-Jacobs	April	Male	
13	Ocarina	August	Female	
14	Yulanderpol	November	Female	
15	Franklin	June	Female	

Figure 25-4: This database doesn't have any numerical fields, but it can be used to generate a pivot table.

Figure 25-5 shows a pivot table created from this data. In this case, the table cross-tabulates the Month Born field by the Sex field, and the intersecting cells show the count for each combination of city and sex. (Pivot tables can use other summary methods besides summing).

Creating a Pivot Table

In this section I walk you through the steps to create a pivot table using the PivotTable Wizard — which is the only way that you can create a pivot table. You access the PivotTable Wizard by choosing the Data⇨Pivot Table command.

On the CD-ROM I use the banking account data in the PVT_BANK.XLS workbook on the companion CD-ROM.

Name List.xls				
	A	**B**	**C**	**D**	**E**
1	Count of Employee	Sex			
2	Month Born	Female	Male	Grand Total	
3	January	2	2	4	
4	February	2	2	4	
5	March	0	5	5	
6	April	1	2	3	
7	May	2	0	2	
8	June	3	3	6	
9	July	3	2	5	
10	August	3	2	5	
11	September	4	0	4	
12	October	2	2	4	
13	November	3	1	4	
14	December	2	2	4	
15	Grand Total	27	23	50	

Sheet2 / Sheet1 /

Figure 25-5: This pivot table summarizes non-numeric fields by displaying a count rather than a sum.

Identifying where the data is located

When you issue the Data⇨Pivot Table command, the first of several dialog boxes appears (see Figure 25-6). In this step, you identify the data source. The possible data sources are described in the following sections.

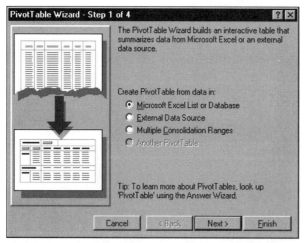

Figure 25-6: The first of four PivotTable Wizard dialog boxes.

Excel list or database

Most of the time, the data that you're analyzing is stored in a worksheet database — which is also known as a list. Databases stored in worksheet are limited to 16,384 records and 256 fields. It's not very efficient to work with a database of this size, however (and memory may not even allow it). The first row in the database should be field names. Other than that, there are no rules. The data can consist of values, text, or formulas.

External data source

If you use the data in an external database for a pivot table, the data is retrieved using Query (a separate application). You can use dBASE files, SQL server data, or other data that your system is set up to access. You'll be prompted for the data source in Step 2 of the PivotTable Wizard.

Cross-Reference I discuss external database access, including Query, in Chapter 24. If you plan to create a pivot table using data in an external database, you should consult Chapter 24 before proceeding.

Multiple consolidation ranges

You also can create a pivot table from multiple tables. This procedure is equivalent to consolidating the information in the tables. But the advantage over other consolidation techniques (discussed in Chapter 19) is that you can work with the consolidated data using all pivot table tools. I present an example of this later in the chapter.

Another pivot table

Excel lets you create a pivot table from an existing pivot table. Actually, this is a bit of a misnomer. The pivot table that you create is based on the *data* that the first pivot table uses (not the pivot table itself). If the active workbook has no pivot tables, this option is grayed out.

Specifying the data

To move on to the next step, click on the Next button. Step 2 of the PivotTable Wizard prompts you for the data. The dialog box varies, depending on your choice in the first dialog box. Figure 25-7 shows the dialog box that appears when you select a worksheet database in Step 1.

Tip If the cell pointer is anywhere within the worksheet database when you issue the Data⇨Pivot Table command, Excel identifies the database range automatically in Step 2 of the PivotTable Wizard.

You can use the Browse button to open a different worksheet and select a range. To move on to Step 3, click on the Next button.

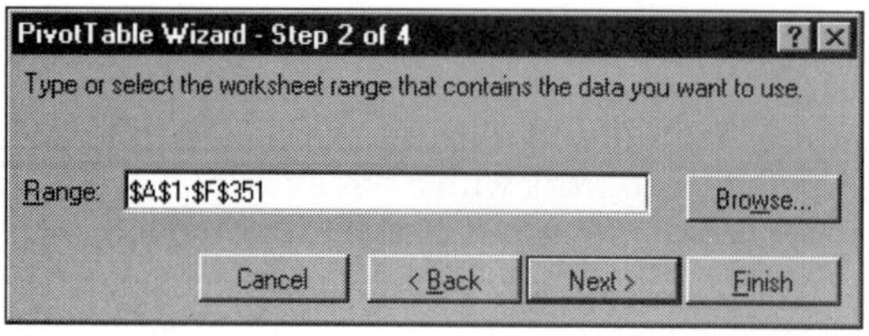

Figure 25-7: In Step 2, you specify the data range.

Setting up the pivot table

The third dialog box of the PivotTable Wizard is shown in Figure 25-8. The fields in the database appear as buttons along the right side of the dialog box. You simply drag the buttons to the appropriate area of the pivot table diagram. The pivot table diagram has four areas:

Row: Values in the field appear as row items in the pivot table.

Column: Values in the field appear as column items in the pivot table.

Data: The field is summarized in the pivot table.

Page: Values in the field appear as page items in the pivot table.

You can drag as many field buttons as you want to any of these locations, and you don't have to use all the fields. Fields that aren't used don't appear in the pivot table.

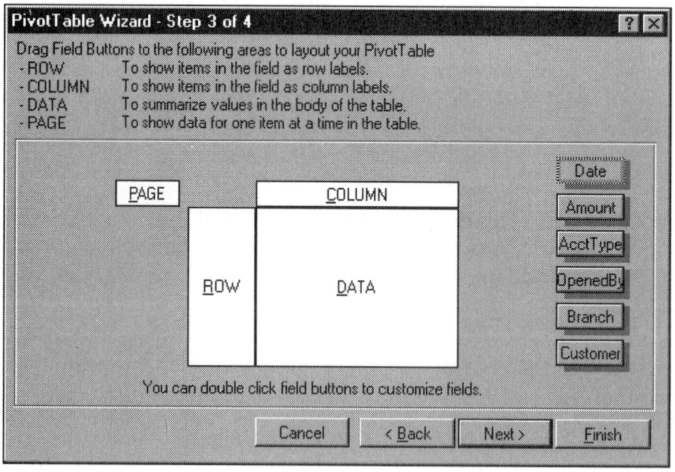

Figure 25-8: In Step 3, you specify the table layout.

When you drag a field button to the Data area, the PivotTable Wizard applies the Sum function if the field has numeric values and the Count function if the field has non-numeric values.

While you're setting up the pivot table in this step, you can double-click on a field button to customize it. You can specify, for example, that a particular field be summarized as a count or other function. You also can specify which items in a field to hide or omit. Be aware, however, that you can customize fields at any time after the pivot table is created.

If you drag a field button to an incorrect location, just drag if off of the table diagram to get rid of it.

Figure 25-9 shows how the dialog looks after I dragged some field buttons to the pivot table diagram. This pivot table will display the sum of the Amount field, broken down by AcctType (as rows) and Customer (as columns). In addition, the Branch field will appear as a page field. Click on the Next button to go on to the next step.

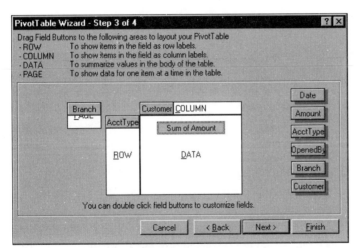

Figure 25-9: The Step 3 PivotTable Wizard dialog box after dragging field buttons to the pivot table diagram.

Pivot table options

The final step of the PivotTable Wizard is shown in Figure 25-10. In this step, you can select some options that determine how the table appears:

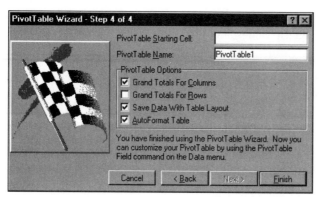

Figure 25-10: In Step 4, you can select some pivot table options.

PivotTable Starting Cell: You can specify a location for the upper-left cell of the pivot table. If you leave this field empty, Excel inserts a new worksheet into the current workbook and locates the pivot table beginning in cell A1.

PivotTable Name: You can provide a name for the pivot table. Excel provides default names in the form of PivotTable1, PivotTable2, and so on.

Grand Totals for Columns: Check this box if you want Excel to calculate grand totals for items displayed in columns.

Grand Totals for Rows: Check this box if you want Excel to calculate grand totals for items displayed in rows.

Save Data With Table Layout: If this option is checked, Excel stores an additional copy of the data (called a pivot table cache) to allow it to recalculate the table more quickly when you change the layout. If memory is an issue, you should keep this option unchecked (updating will be a bit slower).

AutoFormat Table: Check this box if you want Excel to apply one of its AutoFormats to the pivot table. Excel uses the AutoFormat even if you rearrange the table layout.

When you click on the Finish button in this dialog box, Excel creates the Pivot Table. Figure 25-11 shows the result of this example.

Notice that the page field displays as a drop-down box. You can choose which item in the page field to display by choosing it from the list. There's also an item called All, which displays all of the data.

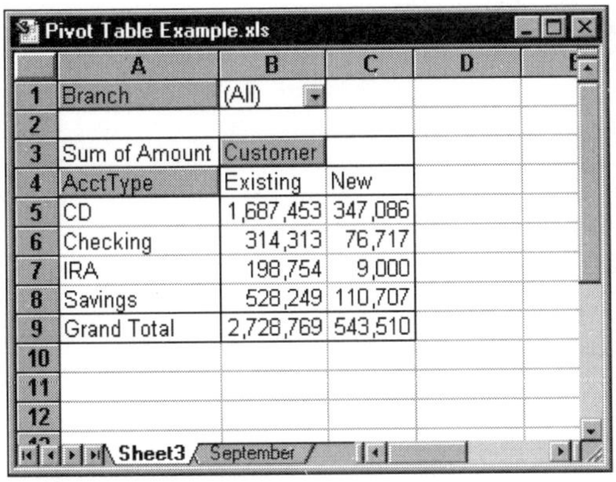

Pivot Table Example.xls

	A	B	C	D
1	Branch	(All)		
2				
3	Sum of Amount	Customer		
4	AcctType	Existing	New	
5	CD	1,687,453	347,086	
6	Checking	314,313	76,717	
7	IRA	198,754	9,000	
8	Savings	528,249	110,707	
9	Grand Total	2,728,769	543,510	
10				
11				
12				

Sheet3 / September

Figure 25-11: The pivot table created by the PivotTable Wizard.

Working with Pivot Tables

Once you've created a pivot table, it's not a static object. You can continue to modify and tweak it until it looks exactly how you want it to look. In this section I discuss modifications that you can make to a pivot table.

Tip

The Query and Pivot toolbar is quite useful when working with pivot tables.

Changing the pivot table's structure

Notice that a pivot table, when displayed in a worksheet, includes the field buttons. You can drag any of the field buttons to a new position in the pivot table (this is known as *pivoting*). For example, you can drag a column field to the row position. Excel immediately redisplays the pivot table to reflect your change. You also can change the order of the row fields or the column fields by dragging the buttons. This step affects how the fields are nested and can have a dramatic effect on how the table looks.

Figure 25-12 shows the pivot table created in the preceding example but after I made a modification to the table's structure. I dragged the page field button (Branch) to the row position. The pivot table now shows details for each item in the AcctType field for each branch.

Describing how to change the layout of a pivot table is more difficult than doing it. I suggest that you create a pivot table and experiment by dragging field buttons around to see what happens.

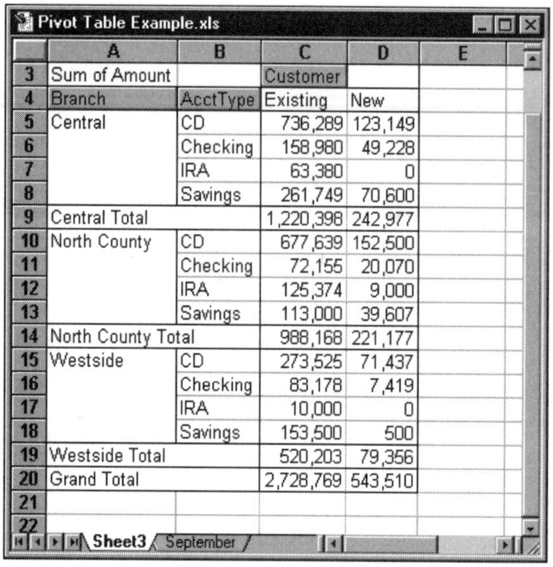

Sum of Amount		Customer	
Branch	AcctType	Existing	New
Central	CD	736,289	123,149
	Checking	158,980	49,228
	IRA	63,380	0
	Savings	261,749	70,600
Central Total		1,220,398	242,977
North County	CD	677,639	152,500
	Checking	72,155	20,070
	IRA	125,374	9,000
	Savings	113,000	39,607
North County Total		988,168	221,177
Westside	CD	273,525	71,437
	Checking	83,178	7,419
	IRA	10,000	0
	Savings	153,500	500
Westside Total		520,203	79,356
Grand Total		2,728,769	543,510

Figure 25-12: This pivot table has two row fields.

Note A pivot table is a special type of range, and (with a few exceptions) you can't make any changes to it. For example, you can't insert or delete rows, edit results, or move cells. If you attempt to do so, Excel displays a message.

Removing a field

To remove a field from a pivot table, just click on the field button and drag it away from the pivot table. The field button changes to a button with an X across it (see Figure 25-13). Release the mouse button, and the table is updated to exclude the field.

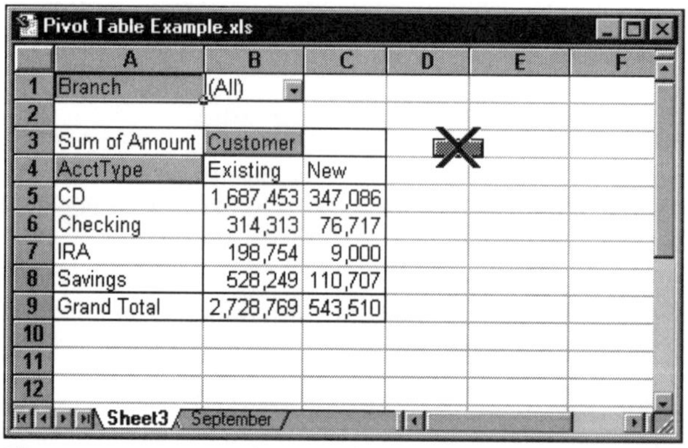

Branch	(All)	
Sum of Amount	Customer	
AcctType	Existing	New
CD	1,687,453	347,086
Checking	314,313	76,717
IRA	198,754	9,000
Savings	528,249	110,707
Grand Total	2,728,769	543,510

Figure 25-13: Removing a pivot table field by dragging it away.

Adding a new field

If you want to add a new field to the pivot table, move the cell pointer anywhere within the pivot table and choose the Data⇨Pivot Table command. Excel displays the third dialog box from the PivotTable Wizard. You can then drag the new field to the desired location in the pivot table diagram. Click on Finish and Excel updates the pivot table with the new field or fields that you added.

Note

You also can remove fields or change the pivot table's structure from this dialog box.

Refreshing a pivot table

Notice that pivot tables don't contain formulas. Rather, Excel recalculates the pivot table every time you make a change to it. If the source database is large, there may be some delay while this recalculation takes place, but for small databases the update is virtually instantaneous.

In some cases, you may change the source data. When this happens, the pivot table doesn't get updated automatically. Rather, you must refresh it manually. To refresh a pivot table, you can use any of the following methods:

✦ Choose the Data⇨Refresh Data command.

✦ Right-click anywhere in the pivot table and select Refresh Data from the shortcut menu.

✦ Click on the Refresh button on the Query and Pivot toolbar.

Customizing a pivot table field

Several options are available for fields within a pivot table. To access these options, simply double-click on a field button (or use the Data⇨Pivot Table Field command). Excel displays a dialog box like the one shown in Figure 25-14.

You can modify any of the following:

Name: Change the name displayed on the field button. You also can do this directly by simply editing the cell that holds the field button.

Orientation: Change how the field's items are displayed. You also can take the more direct approach of dragging the field button to another location, as described previously.

Subtotals: Lets you change the type of subtotaling displayed. Subtotaling is relevant only if you have more than one field displayed as rows or columns. You can make a multiple selection in the list box, which results in more than one line of subtotals. To get rid of subtotals, click on the None option.

Hide Items: Enables you to hide (not display) one or more items from a field. Click on the specific item names that you want to hide.

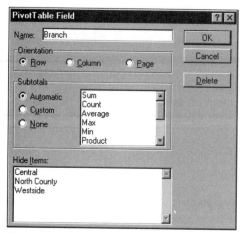

Figure 25-14: Double-clicking on a Pivot-Table field button displays a dialog box like this one.

Formatting a pivot table

When you create a pivot table, you have an option (in Step 4) of applying a table AutoFormat. After the pivot table is created, you can always specify a different AutoFormat. In many cases, the number format used in an AutoFormat is not appropriate for the data. You'll find that if you change the number and then apply an AutoFormat using the option to ignore number formatting, Excel *still* uses the AutoFormat's number format when the pivot table is refreshed.

If you want to use a different number format for the data, you must use the following procedure:

1. Select any cell in the pivot table's data area.

2. Right-click and choose Pivot Table Field from the shortcut menu. Excel displays its Pivot Table Field dialog box.

3. Click on the Number button.

4. Select the number format that you need.

If you use this procedure, the number format sticks even after the pivot table is refreshed.

Grouping pivot table items

A handy feature enables you to group specific items in a field. If one of the fields in your database consists of dates, for example, the pivot table displays a separate row or column for every date. You may find it more useful to group the dates into months or quarters and then hide the details. Fortunately, this is easy to do.

Figure 25-15 shows a pivot table created with the bank database. It shows total balances for each account type (column field) by the Branch (row field). You've been asked to create a report that compares the Central branch to the other two branches combined. The solution is to create a group that consists of the Westside and North County branches.

	A	B	C	D	E	F
	Pivot Table Example.xls					
1	Sum of Amount	AcctType				
2	Branch	CD	Checking	IRA	Savings	Grand Total
3	Central	859,438	208,208	63,380	332,349	1,463,375
4	North County	830,139	92,225	134,374	152,607	1,209,345
5	Westside	344,962	90,597	10,000	154,000	599,559
6	Grand Total	2,034,539	391,030	207,754	638,956	3,272,279
7						
8						
	Pivot Table / September /					

Figure 25-15: The North County and Westside branches will be combined into a group.

To create the group, select the cells to be grouped — in this case A6:A7. Then choose the Data⇨Group and Outline⇨Group command (or you can use the Group button on the Query and Pivot toolbar). Excel creates a new field called Branch2, and this field has two items: Central and Group1 (see Figure 25-16). At this point, you can remove the Original Branch field and change the names of the field and the items. Figure 25-17 shows the pivot table after making these modifications.

	A	B	C	D	E	F
	Pivot Table Example.xls					
1	Sum of Amount		AcctType			
2	Branch2	Branch	CD	Checking	IRA	Savings	G
3	Central	Central	859,438	208,208	63,380	332,349
4	Group1	North County	830,139	92,225	134,374	152,607
5		Westside	344,962	90,597	10,000	154,000
6	Grand Total		2,034,539	391,030	207,754	638,956
7						
8						
	Pivot Table / September /					

Figure 25-16: After grouping the North County and Westside branches.

Figure 25-17: After removing the original Branch field and renaming the new field and items.

Note

The new field name can't be an existing field name. If it is, Excel adds the field to the pivot table. In this example, you can't rename Branch2 to Branch.

Tip

If the items to be grouped are not next to each other, you can make a multiple selection by pressing Ctrl and selecting the items that will make up the group.

If the field items consist of values, dates, or times, you can let Excel do the grouping for you. Figure 25-18 shows part of another pivot table that I generated from the bank database. This time, I used Amount for the row field and AcctType for the column field. The data area shows the count for each combination. This isn't a very useful report because there are so many different items in the Amount field. It can be salvaged, however, by grouping the items into bins.

Figure 25-18: This isn't a very useful pivot table because there are too many different items in the Amount field.

To create groups automatically, select any item in the Amount field. Then choose the Data⇨Group and Outline⇨Group command. Excel displays the Grouping dialog box shown in Figure 25-19. By default, it shows the smallest and largest values — but you can change these to whatever you like. To create groups of $5,000 increments, enter **0** for the Starting at value, **100000** for the Ending at value, and **5000** for the By value (as shown in Figure 25-19). Click on OK, and Excel creates the groups. Figure 25-20 shows the result, which is much more meaningful than the ungrouped data.

Note Excel doesn't do a very good job with the group item names. You'll see that they contain overlapping amounts. For example, does the 0–5000 group include 5000? Or is 5000 included in the 5000–10000 group? I examined the source data and discovered that the problem is with the upper limits in the names. Therefore, you may want to eliminate this ambiguity by manually changing the field names to 0–4999, 5000–9999, and so on.

Figure 25-19: The Grouping dialog box instructs Excel to create groups automatically.

	A	B	C	D	E	F
1	Count of Amount	AcctType				
2	Amount	CD	Checking	IRA	Savings	Grand Total
3	0-5000	3	127	6	36	172
4	5000-10000	4	18	13	31	66
5	10000-15000	56	2	8	1	67
6	15000-20000	19	0	0	2	21
7	20000-25000	0	0	0	1	1
8	25000-30000	1	0	0	1	2
9	30000-35000	0	0	0	2	2
10	35000-40000	2	0	0	0	2
11	40000-45000	0	0	0	1	1
12	45000-50000	1	0	0	0	1
13	50000-55000	4	0	0	1	5
14	65000-70000	0	0	0	2	2
15	75000-80000	5	0	0	0	5
16	90000-95000	3	0	0	0	3
17	Grand Total	98	147	27	78	350

Figure 25-20: After grouping the Amount field items.

Seeing the details

Each cell in the data area of a pivot table represents several records in the source database. You may be interested in seeing exactly which fields contribute to a summary value. Using the banking example, you might want to see a list of the records that make up the total CD accounts in the Central branch. To do so, double-click on the appropriate summary cell in the data area. Excel creates a new worksheet with the records that were used to create the summary. Figure 25-21 shows an example.

Pivot Table Example.xls

	A	B	C	D	E	F	G
1	Date	Amount	AcctType	OpenedBy	Branch	Customer	
2	9/1/95	90000	CD	New Accts	Central	Existing	
3	9/1/95	16000	CD	New Accts	Central	New	
4	9/4/95	13000	CD	New Accts	Central	Existing	
5	9/4/95	13519	CD	New Accts	Central	New	
6	9/4/95	14548	CD	New Accts	Central	Existing	
7	9/4/95	11000	CD	New Accts	Central	New	
8	9/4/95	35000	CD	New Accts	Central	Existing	
9	9/5/95	12000	CD	Teller	Central	Existing	
10	9/6/95	90000	CD	New Accts	Central	Existing	
11	9/6/95	15208	CD	New Accts	Central	Existing	
12	9/7/95	17000	CD	Teller	Central	Existing	
13	9/7/95	14548	CD	New Accts	Central	Existing	
14	9/7/95	11000	CD	New Accts	Central	New	

Pivot Table ⟍ **Sheet3** ⟋ Sheet2 ⟋ Se...

Figure 25-21: Double-clicking on a cell in the data area of a pivot table generates a new worksheet with the underlying data.

Displaying a pivot table on different sheets

If your pivot table is set up to display a field in the Page position, you can see only one slice of the data at a time by using the drop-down list box. Excel has an option, however, that puts each item from a page field on a separate sheet, creating a three-dimensional block of data. When you click on the Show Pages button on the Query and Pivot toolbar, Excel displays the dialog box shown in Figure 25-22. This dialog box lists the page fields in your Pivot Table. Select the fields that you want, and Excel inserts enough new sheets to accommodate each item in that field.

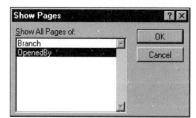

Figure 25-22: The Show Pages dialog box lets you display each page field item on a separate worksheet.

Pivot Table Examples

I firmly believe that the best way to master pivot tables is to work with them — not read about them. The best approach is to use your own data. But if you'd like to work with some prefab pivot tables, I've developed a few for you to use, and they are available on the companion CD-ROM. In this section, I describe additional examples of pivot tables to spark your creativity and help you apply some of these techniques to your own data.

Using a pivot table to consolidate sheets

In Chapter 19, I discuss several ways to consolidate data across different worksheets or workbooks. Excel's pivot table feature gives you yet another consolidation option. Figure 25-23 shows three worksheets, each with monthly sales data for a store in a music store chain. The goal is to consolidate this information into a single pivot table. In this example, the source data is all in a single workbook. This situation may not always be the same, however. The data to be consolidated can be in different workbooks.

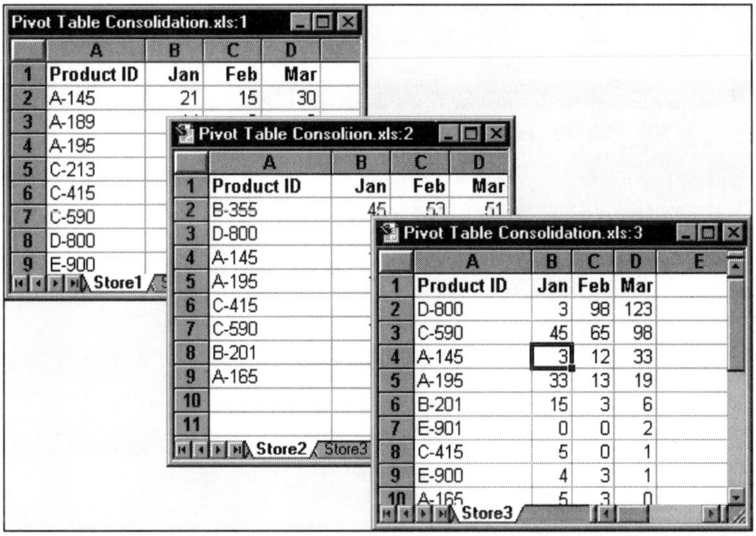

Figure 25-23: These three worksheets will be consolidated with a pivot table.

On the CD-ROM The workbook used in this example can be found on the companion CD-ROM. Its name is PVT_CONS.XLS.

Following are the steps I took to create this pivot table:

1. Start with a new worksheet named Summary.

2. Choose the Data⇨Pivot Table command to display the PivotTable Wizard.

3. Select the Multiple Consolidation Ranges option and click on Next.

4. In Step 2a of the PivotTable Wizard, select the option labeled Create a single page field for me. Click on Next.

5. In Step 2b, specify the ranges to be consolidated. The first range is Store1!$A$1:$D$12 (you can enter this directly, or point to it). Click on Add to add this range to the All Ranges list.

6. Repeat this for the other two ranges (see Figure 25-24). Click on Next to continue to Step 3.

7. The dialog box in Step 3 of the PivotTable Wizard should look familiar. You'll notice, however, that it doesn't include actual field names. Rather, it uses generic names such as Row, Column, and Value. You'll change these names later. Double-click on the button in the data area, and change its function from Sum to Count. Click on Next to continue.

8. Accept all defaults in Step 4 of the PivotTable Wizard, and click on Finish.

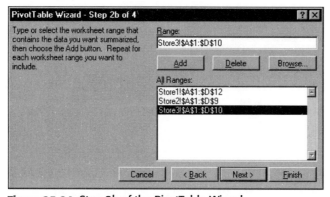

Figure 25-24: Step 2b of the PivotTable Wizard.

Figure 25-25 shows the pivot table. It uses the generic names, which you can change to more meaningful names.

	A	B	C	D	E	
	Pivot Table Consolidation.xls				_ □ ✕	
	A	**B**	**C**	**D**	**E**	
1	Page1	(All)				
2						
3	Sum of Value	Column				
4	Row	Jan	Feb	Mar	Grand Total	
5	A-145	39	43	84	166	
6	A-165	8	3	1	12	
7	A-189	14	2	2	18	
8	A-195	45	23	36	104	
9	B-201	19	5	9	33	
10	B-355	45	53	51	149	
11	C-213	2	12	5	19	
12	C-415	15	11	18	44	
13	C-590	93	86	109	288	
14	D-800	12	196	257	465	
15	E-900	9	4	1	14	
16	E-901	0	0	2	2	
17	E-904	3	5	7	15	
18	E-912	0	0	2	2	
19	E-923	1	0	0	1	
20	Grand Total	305	443	584	1332	

Summary / Store1 / Store2

Figure 25-25: This pivot table uses data from three ranges.

Note In Step 2a of the PivotTable Wizard, you can choose the option labeled I will create the page fields. Doing so lets you provide an item name for each item in the page field (rather than the generic Item1, Item2, and Item3).

Creating charts from a pivot table

Because a pivot table is just a range in a worksheet, you can create a chart from its data. If you set things up right, the chart changes when you change the pivot table's structure. In general, if you follow these rules, you'll be able to produce useful charts from a pivot table:

✦ Don't display subtotals or grand totals. These interrupt the data ranges.

✦ Don't use more than two fields for the row position or the column position.

✦ Select the entire pivot table (but not the page fields) before you create the chart.

Figure 25-26 shows an example of a chart created from a pivot table. This chart is updated whenever I choose a new page field item. Notice that I used a formula for the chart's title, so the chart accurately reflects the data depicted.

On the CD-ROM The workbook used in this example can be found on the companion CD-ROM. Its name is PVT_CHAR.XLS.

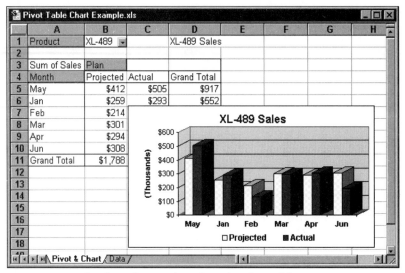

Figure 25-26: The chart changes based on the pivot table.

Analyzing survey data

In this example, I demonstrate how to use a pivot table to analyze survey data obtained via a questionnaire. Figure 25-27 shows part of the raw data typical of that collected from a survey questionnaire. Each record represents the responses for one respondent.

	Name	Sex	Age	State	Item01	Item02	Item03	Item04	Item05	Item06	Iter
1	Name	Sex	Age	State	Item01	Item02	Item03	Item04	Item05	Item06	Iter
2	Subject1	Male	40	Illinois	1	4	4	4	1	1	
3	Subject2	Female	31	Illinois	2	5	1	1	4	2	
4	Subject3	Male	56	New York	1	1	4	2	3	3	
5	Subject4	Male	55	Illinois	2	1	3	5	1	2	
6	Subject5	Female	47	New York	2	2	5	5	4	2	
7	Subject6	Female	51	Illinois	2	4	3	3	1	1	
8	Subject7	Female	48	California	2	4	5	4	5	3	
9	Subject8	Male	39	New York	3	2	1	2	3	4	
10	Subject9	Female	37	California	3	4	4	4	5	1	
11	Subject10	Male	38	New York	2	1	5	5	5	1	
12	Subject11	Male	38	California	4	3	3	2	1	2	
13	Subject12	Female	46	California	2	1	4	5	5	5	
14	Subject13	Female	48	Illinois	4	3	4	3	2	5	
15	Subject14	Female	56	New York	2	3	4	2	1	1	

Averages ⟍ **SurveyData** ⟍ Auto_Create ⟍ Module1

Figure 25-27: This survey data can be tabulated with a pivot table.

On the
CD-ROM The workbook used in this example can be found on the companion CD-ROM. Its
name is PVT_SURV.XLS.

Figure 25-28 show a pivot table that I created to calculate averages for each of the 12
survey items, broken down by sex. Additional page fields make it easy to look at the
results by an age group or by a particular state. Or, for a more complex pivot table,
you can drag one or both of the page fields to a row or column position.

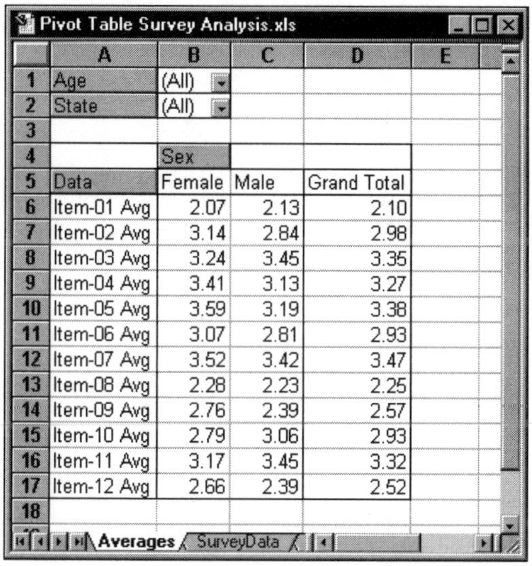

	A	B	C	D	E
	Pivot Table Survey Analysis.xls				
1	Age	(All)			
2	State	(All)			
3					
4		Sex			
5	Data	Female	Male	Grand Total	
6	Item-01 Avg	2.07	2.13	2.10	
7	Item-02 Avg	3.14	2.84	2.98	
8	Item-03 Avg	3.24	3.45	3.35	
9	Item-04 Avg	3.41	3.13	3.27	
10	Item-05 Avg	3.59	3.19	3.38	
11	Item-06 Avg	3.07	2.81	2.93	
12	Item-07 Avg	3.52	3.42	3.47	
13	Item-08 Avg	2.28	2.23	2.25	
14	Item-09 Avg	2.76	2.39	2.57	
15	Item-10 Avg	2.79	3.06	2.93	
16	Item-11 Avg	3.17	3.45	3.32	
17	Item-12 Avg	2.66	2.39	2.52	
18					

Averages / SurveyData /

Figure 25-28: This pivot table calculates
averages for each item.

Figure 25-29 shows another sheet in the workbook. This sheet contains 12 separate
pivot tables, one for each survey item. Each pivot table displays the frequency of
responses and the percentage of responses. Although you could create each table
manually, the workbook includes a macro that creates them all in just a few seconds.

Customer geographic analysis

One of the by-products of creating a pivot table is that you end up with a list of unique
entries in a field. Figure 25-30 shows part of a database that tracks customers. The
field of interest is the State field (which holds the country in the case of non-U.S.
orders). The Type field contains a formula that returns either *Foreign* or *Domestic*,
depending on the length of the entry in the State field. The goal of this example is to
create a map that shows sales by state.

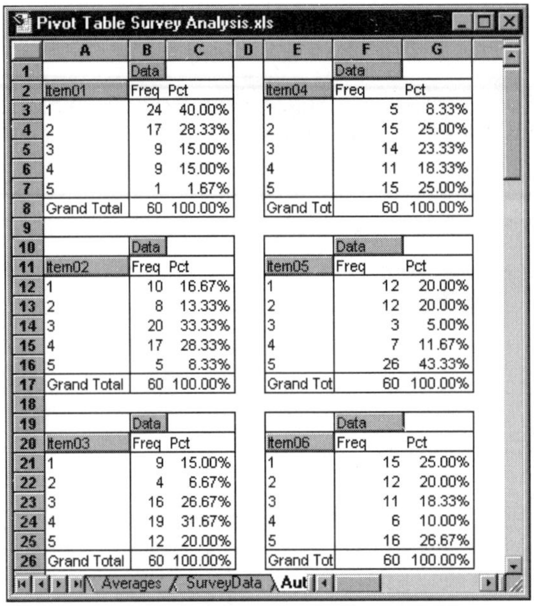

Pivot Table Survey Analysis.xls

	A	B	C	D	E	F	G
1		Data				Data	
2	Item01	Freq	Pct		Item04	Freq	Pct
3	1	24	40.00%		1	5	8.33%
4	2	17	28.33%		2	15	25.00%
5	3	9	15.00%		3	14	23.33%
6	4	9	15.00%		4	11	18.33%
7	5	1	1.67%		5	15	25.00%
8	Grand Total	60	100.00%		Grand Tot	60	100.00%
9							
10		Data				Data	
11	Item02	Freq	Pct		Item05	Freq	Pct
12	1	10	16.67%		1	12	20.00%
13	2	8	13.33%		2	12	20.00%
14	3	20	33.33%		3	3	5.00%
15	4	17	28.33%		4	7	11.67%
16	5	5	8.33%		5	26	43.33%
17	Grand Total	60	100.00%		Grand Tot	60	100.00%
18							
19		Data				Data	
20	Item03	Freq	Pct		Item06	Freq	Pct
21	1	9	15.00%		1	15	25.00%
22	2	4	6.67%		2	12	20.00%
23	3	16	26.67%		3	11	18.33%
24	4	19	31.67%		4	6	10.00%
25	5	12	20.00%		5	16	26.67%
26	Grand Total	60	100.00%		Grand Tot	60	100.00%

Averages / SurveyData / Aut

Figure 25-29: This sheet has 12 pivot tables created by a macro.

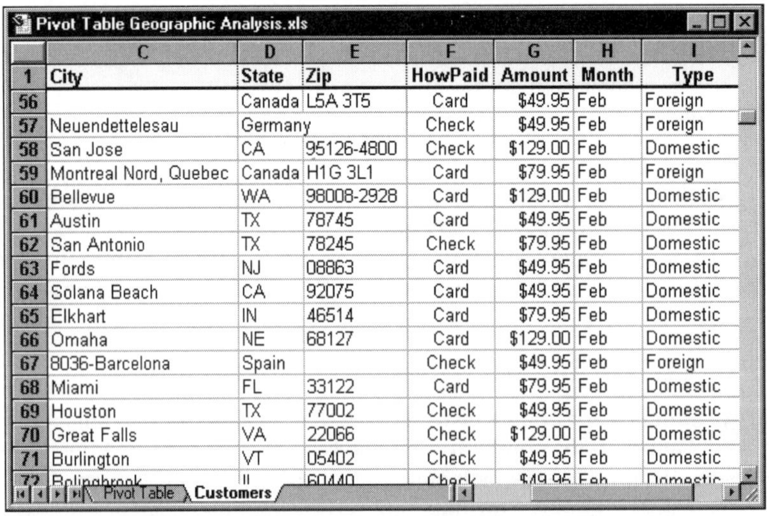

Pivot Table Geographic Analysis.xls

	C	D	E	F	G	H	I
1	City	State	Zip	HowPaid	Amount	Month	Type
56		Canada	L5A 3T5	Card	$49.95	Feb	Foreign
57	Neuendettelesau	Germany		Check	$49.95	Feb	Foreign
58	San Jose	CA	95126-4800	Check	$129.00	Feb	Domestic
59	Montreal Nord, Quebec	Canada	H1G 3L1	Card	$79.95	Feb	Foreign
60	Bellevue	WA	98008-2928	Card	$129.00	Feb	Domestic
61	Austin	TX	78745	Card	$49.95	Feb	Domestic
62	San Antonio	TX	78245	Check	$79.95	Feb	Domestic
63	Fords	NJ	08863	Card	$49.95	Feb	Domestic
64	Solana Beach	CA	92075	Card	$49.95	Feb	Domestic
65	Elkhart	IN	46514	Card	$79.95	Feb	Domestic
66	Omaha	NE	68127	Card	$129.00	Feb	Domestic
67	8036-Barcelona	Spain		Check	$49.95	Feb	Foreign
68	Miami	FL	33122	Card	$79.95	Feb	Domestic
69	Houston	TX	77002	Check	$49.95	Feb	Domestic
70	Great Falls	VA	22066	Check	$129.00	Feb	Domestic
71	Burlington	VT	05402	Check	$49.95	Feb	Domestic
72	Bolingbrook	IL	60440	Check	$49.95	Feb	Domestic

Pivot Table / Customers

Figure 25-30: This customer database would make a good map, but the data is not in the proper format.

The workbook used in this example can be found on the companion CD-ROM. Its name is PVT_GEOG.XLS.

Figure 25-31 shows a pivot table that I created from this data. It displays the data in terms of total amount, plus a count. I used three page fields to filter the data.

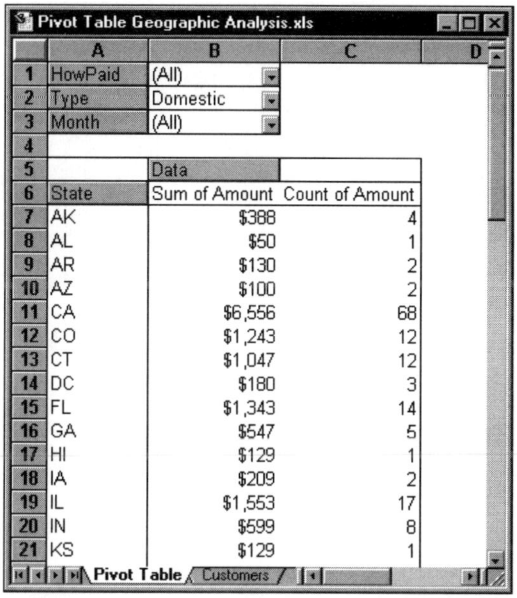

	A	B	C	D
	Pivot Table Geographic Analysis.xls			
1	HowPaid	(All)		
2	Type	Domestic		
3	Month	(All)		
4				
5		Data		
6	State	Sum of Amount	Count of Amount	
7	AK	$388	4	
8	AL	$50	1	
9	AR	$130	2	
10	AZ	$100	2	
11	CA	$6,556	68	
12	CO	$1,243	12	
13	CT	$1,047	12	
14	DC	$180	3	
15	FL	$1,343	14	
16	GA	$547	5	
17	HI	$129	1	
18	IA	$209	2	
19	IL	$1,553	17	
20	IN	$599	8	
21	KS	$129	1	

Figure 25-31: This pivot table is perfect input for an Excel map.

Figure 25-32 shows the map that I created using Excel's mapping feature (described fully in Chapter 17).

Grouping by month and years

The final pivot table example (see Figure 25-33) demonstrates some techniques that involve grouping by dates. The worksheet contains daily pricing data for two years. I created a macro to change the grouping to days, weeks, months, quarters, or years. The macro also changes the range used in the chart.

The workbook used in this example can be found on the companion CD-ROM. Its name is PVT_DATE.XLS.

Figure 25-32: This map was created from the data in the pivot table.

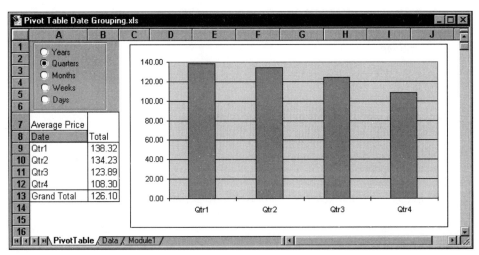

Figure 25-33: Clicking an option button executes a macro that changes the date grouping and updates the chart.

Summary

In this chapter I discuss Excel's pivot table feature. This feature lets you summarize data from a database, which can be stored in a worksheet or in an external file. The examples in this chapter demonstrate some useful techniques. The best way to master this feature, however, is to work with a database with which you're familiar and experiment until you understand how it works.

✦   ✦   ✦

Performing Spreadsheet What-If Analysis

One of the most appealing aspects of spreadsheet programs — including Excel — is that you can use formulas to create dynamic models that instantly recalculate when you change cells to which the formulas refer. When you change values in cells in a systematic manner and observe the effects on specific formula cells, you're performing a type of *what-if* analysis. What-if analysis is the process of asking questions such as, "What if the interest rate on the loan is 8.5 percent rather than 9.0 percent?" or "What if we raise the prices of our products by 5 percent?"

If your spreadsheet is set up properly, answering such questions is a matter of plugging in new values and observing the results of the recalculation. As you'll see, Excel provides useful tools to assist you in your what-if endeavors.

A What-If Example

Figure 26-1 shows a spreadsheet that calculates information pertaining to a mortgage loan. The worksheet is divided into two sections: the input cells and the result cells. Column D shows the formulas in column C. With this worksheet, you can easily answer what-if questions such as the following:

◆ What if I can negotiate a lower purchase price on the property?

◆ What if the lender requires a 20 percent down payment?

◆ What if I can get a 40-year mortgage?

◆ What if the interest rate goes down to 7.5 percent?

You can get the answers by simply plugging in different values in the cells in range C4:C7 and observing the effects in the dependent cells (C10:C13). You can, of course, vary any number of input cells at once.

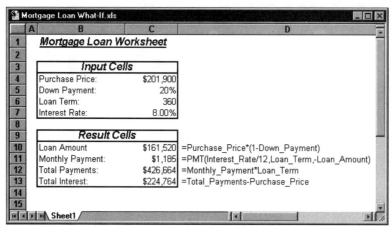

Figure 26-1: This worksheet model uses four input cells to produce the results in the formulas.

Hard code values? No way!

The mortgage calculation example, simple as it is, demonstrates an important point about spreadsheet design: You should always set up your worksheet so that you have maximum flexibility to make changes. Perhaps the most fundamental rule of spreadsheet design is:

> *Do not hard code values in a formula. Rather, store the values in separate cells and use cell references in the formula.*

The term *hard code* refers to the use of actual values, or *constants,* in a formula. In the mortgage loan example, all the formulas use references to cells, not actual values.

You *could* use the value 360, for example, for the loan term argument of the PMT function in cell C11. Using a cell reference has two advantages: First, it makes it perfectly clear what values are being used (they aren't buried in the formula). Second, it makes it easier to change the value.

This may not seem like much of an issue when only one formula is involved, but just imagine what would happen if this value were hard coded into several hundred formulas scattered throughout a worksheet.

Types of What-If Analyses

As you may expect, Excel can handle much more sophisticated models than the preceding example. The remainder of this chapter gets into this topic in more depth. If you need to perform what-if analysis using Excel, you have four basic options:

✦ **Manual what-if analysis:** Plug in new values and observe the effects on formula cells.

✦ **Macro-assisted what-if analysis:** Create macros to plug in variables for you.

✦ **Data tables:** Create a table that displays the results of selected formula cells as one or two input cells are systematically changed.

✦ **Scenario manager:** Create named scenarios and generate reports that use outlines or pivot tables.

I discuss each of these methods in the following sections.

Manual What-If Analysis

There's not a whole lot to say about this method. In fact, the example that opens this chapter is a good one. It's based on the idea that you have one or more input cells that affect one or more key formulas cells. You change the value in the input cells and see what happens to the formula cells. You may want to print the results or save each scenario to a new workbook. The term *scenario* refers to a specific set of values in one or more input cells.

This is how most people perform what-if analysis. There's certainly nothing wrong with it, but you should be aware of some other techniques.

Macro-Assisted What-If Analysis

Using macros is a slightly more sophisticated form of manual what-if analysis. As I discuss in later chapters, a *macro* is a program that performs a number of operations automatically. Rather than change the input cells manually, you create a macro to do it for you. For example, you may have three macros named BestCase, WorstCase, and MostLikely. Running the BestCase macro enters the appropriate values into the input cells. Executing the WorstCase or MostLikely macros enters other values.

If you understand how to create macros, this technique can be simple to set up. You can attach the macros to buttons so that an inexperienced user can see the results of various scenarios that you've predefined.

Figure 26-2 shows a worksheet that's designed for what-if analysis. It's a simple production model with two input cells: the hourly cost of labor and the unit cost for materials. This company produces three products, and each requires a different number of hours and a different amount of materials to produce. The combined total profit is calculated in cell B17. Management is trying to predict the total profit but is uncertain what the hourly labor cost and material costs will be. They've identified three scenarios, as listed in Table 26-1.

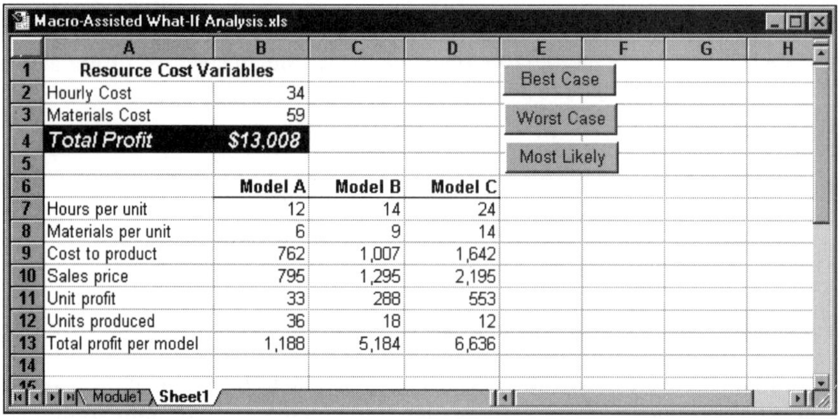

Figure 26-2: This worksheet uses macros to display three different combinations of values for the input cells.

Table 26-1
Three Scenarios for the Production Model

Scenario	Hourly Cost	Materials Cost
Best Case	30	57
Worst Case	38	62
Most Likely Case	34	59

I developed three simple macros and attached one to each of the three buttons on the worksheet. Figure 26-3 shows the VBA macros (also known as subroutines) that are executed when a worksheet button is clicked. These macros simply place values into the named cells on the worksheet. If you would like to change the values used in any of the scenarios, you must edit the macros.

Note If you like the idea of instantly displaying a particular scenario, you'll be interested in learning about Excel's scenario manager, which I describe later in this chapter. The scenario manager does not require macros.

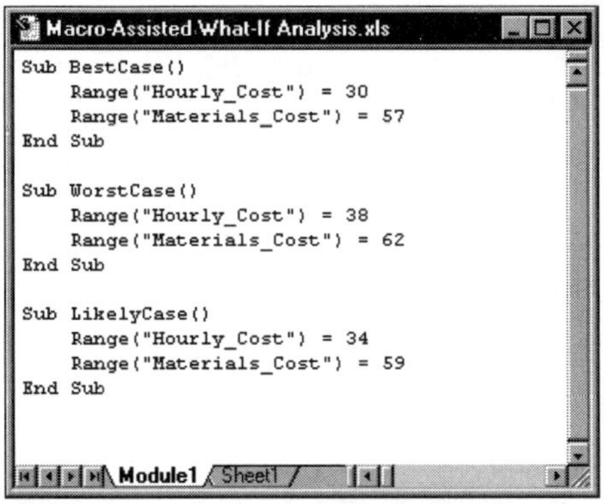

Figure 26-3: These macros simply place different values in the input cells in the worksheet.

Caution The workbook in this example, called WHAT_IF.XLS, is included on the companion CD-ROM.

Creating Data Tables

When you're working with a what-if model, only one scenario at a time can be displayed. But what if you'd like to compare the results of various scenarios? Your choices are as follows:

✦ Print multiple copies of the worksheet, each displaying a different scenario.

✦ Copy the model to other worksheets and set it up so that each worksheet displays a different scenario.

✦ Manually create a table that summarizes key formula cells for each scenario.

✦ Use Excel's Data⇨Table command to create a summary table automatically.

In this section I discuss the last option — the Data⇨Table command. This command lets you create a handy data table that summarizes formula cells for various values of either of the following:

✦ A single input cell

✦ Various combinations of two input cells

For example, in the production model example, you may want to create a table that shows the total profit for various combinations of hourly cost and materials cost. Figure 26-4 shows a two-input data table that I created, which does just that.

	A	B	C	D	E	F	G
	Resource Cost Variables				Best Case		
1							
2	Hourly Cost	30					
3	Materials Cost	57			Worst Case		
4	*Total Profit*	*$17,988*					
5					Most Likely		
6		Model A	Model B	Model C			
7	Hours per unit	12	14	24			
8	Materials per unit	6	9	14			
9	Cost to product	702	933	1,518			
10	Sales price	795	1,295	2,195			
11	Unit profit	93	362	677			
12	Units produced	36	18	12			
13	Total profit per model	3,348	6,516	8,124			
14							
15				**Materials Cost**			
16	$17,988	$54	$55	$56	$57	$58	
17	$30	$19,626	$19,080	$18,534	$17,988	$17,442	
18	$31	$18,654	$18,108	$17,562	$17,016	$16,470	
19	$32	$17,682	$17,136	$16,590	$16,044	$15,498	
20	$33	$16,710	$16,164	$15,618	$15,072	$14,526	
21	$34	$15,738	$15,192	$14,646	$14,100	$13,554	
22	$35	$14,766	$14,220	$13,674	$13,128	$12,582	

Figure 26-4: This data table summarizes the total profit for various combinations of the input values.

Creating a data table is fairly easy, but it has some limitations. The biggest limitation is that it can deal with only one or two input cells at a time. In other words, you can't create a data table that uses a combination of three or more input cells.

Note   The scenario manager, discussed later in this chapter, can produce a report that summarizes any number of input cells and result cells.

Creating a one-input data table

A one-input data table displays the results of one or more result formulas for multiple values of a single input cell. Figure 26-5 shows the general layout for a one-input data table. The table can be located anywhere in the workbook. The left column contains various values for the single input cell. The top row contains formulas or (more often) references to result formulas elsewhere in the worksheet. You can use any number of formula references (including only one). The upper-left cell of the table is not used. Excel calculates the values that result from each level of the input cell and places them under each formula reference.

For this example, I use the mortgage loan worksheet that I refer to earlier in the chapter. It's shown again in Figure 26-6. The goal is to create a table that shows the values of the four formula cells (loan amount, monthly payment, total payments, and total interest) for various interest rates ranging from 7 percent to 9 percent in .25 percent increments.

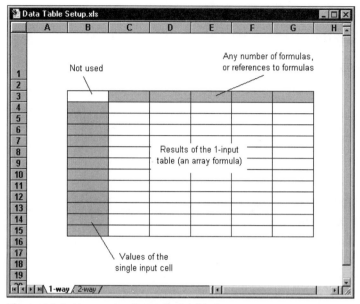

Figure 26-5: How a one-input data table is set up.

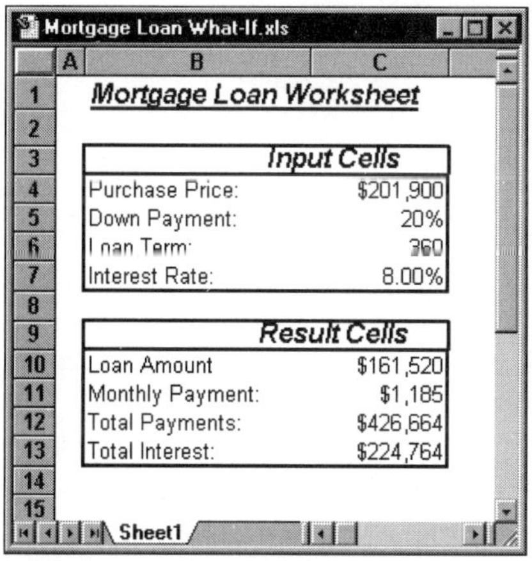

Figure 26-6: This example uses the mortgage
loan worksheet to generate a one-input data table.

Figure 26-7 shows how I set up the data table area. Row 2 consists of references to the
result formulas in the worksheet. For example, cell F3 contains the formula =C10.
Column E has the values of the single-input cell (interest rate) that will be used in the
table. I also add borders to indicate where the calculated values will go.

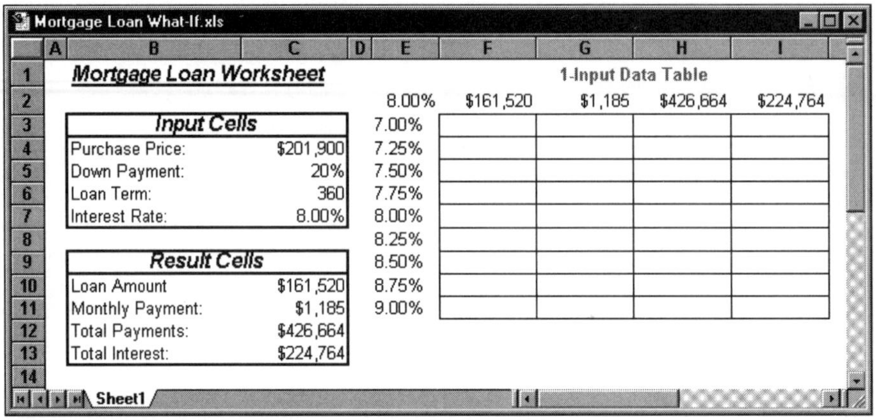

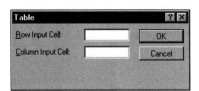

Figure 26-7: Preparing to create a one-input data table.

To create the table, select the range (in this case, E2:I11) and then choose the Data⇨Table command. Excel displays the dialog box shown in Figure 26-8. You have to specify the worksheet cell that you're using as the input value. Because variables for the input cell are located in a column in the data table rather than in a row, you place this cell reference in the text box called Column Input Cell. Enter Interest_Rate (the name for cell C7) or point to the cell in the worksheet. Leave the Row Input Cell field blank. Click on OK and Excel fills in the table with the appropriate results (see Figure 26-9).

Figure 26-8: The Table dialog box.

If you examine the cells that were entered as a result of this command, notice that Excel filled in formulas — more specifically, array formulas that use the TABLE function. As I discuss in Chapter 20, an array formula is a single formula that produces results in multiple cells. Because it uses formulas, the table you produced is updated if you change the cell references in the first row or plug in different interest rate values in the first column.

Note   A one-input table can be arranged vertically (as in this example) or horizontally. If the values of the input cell are placed in a row, you enter the input cell reference in the text box labeled Row Input Cell.

	Mortgage Loan What-If.xls										
	A	B	C	D	E	F	G	H	I	
1	*Mortgage Loan Worksheet*					1-Input Data Table				
2					8.00%	$161,520	$1,185	$426,664	$224,764	
3	*Input Cells*				7.00%	161,520	1,075	386,855	184,955	
4	Purchase Price:		$201,900		7.25%	161,520	1,102	396,666	194,766	
5	Down Payment:		20%		7.50%	161,520	1,129	406,574	204,674	
6	Loan Term:		360		7.75%	161,520	1,157	416,574	214,674	
7	Interest Rate:		8.00%		8.00%	161,520	1,185	426,664	224,764	
8					8.25%	161,520	1,213	436,840	234,940	
9	*Result Cells*				8.50%	161,520	1,242	447,102	245,202	
10	Loan Amount		$161,520		8.75%	161,520	1,271	457,444	255,544	
11	Monthly Payment:		$1,185		9.00%	161,520	1,300	467,866	265,966	
12	Total Payments:		$426,664							
13	Total Interest:		$224,764							
14										

Figure 26-9: The result of the one-input data table.

Creating a two-input data table

As the name implies, a two-input data table lets you vary *two* input cells. The setup for this type of table is shown in Figure 26-10. Although it looks similar to a one-input table, it has one critical difference: a two-input table can show the results of only one formula at a time. With a one-input table, you can place any number of formulas or references to formulas across the top row of the table. In a two-input table, this top row holds the values for the second input cell. The upper-left cell of the table contains a reference to the single result formula.

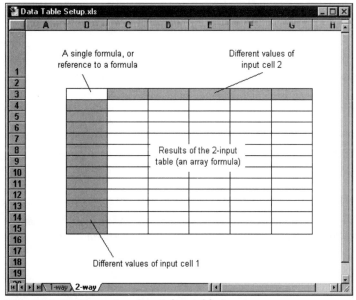

Figure 26-10: How a two-input data table is set up.

In the preceding example, you could create a two-input data table that shows the results of a formula (say, monthly payment) for various combinations of two input cells (such as interest rate and down payment percent). To see the effects on other formulas, you simply create multiple data tables — one for each formula cell that you want to summarize.

I demonstrate a two-input data table with the worksheet shown in Figure 26-11. In this example, a company is interested in conducting a direct-mail promotion to sell its product. The worksheet calculates the net profit from the promotion.

On the CD-ROM

This workbook, named DIR_MAIL.XLS, is available on the companion CD-ROM.

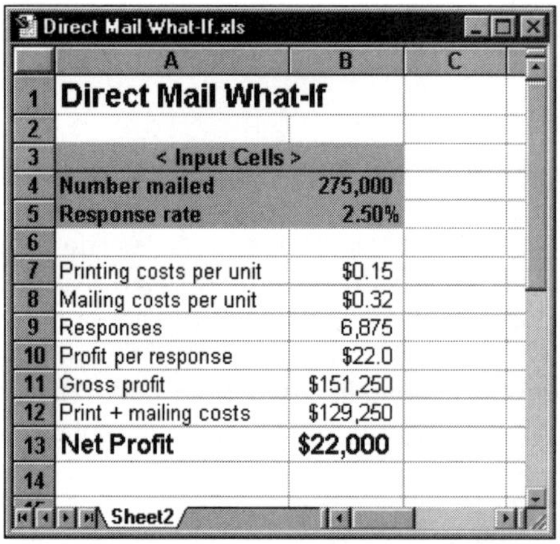

	A	B	C
1	Direct Mail What-If		
2			
3	< Input Cells >		
4	Number mailed	275,000	
5	Response rate	2.50%	
6			
7	Printing costs per unit	$0.15	
8	Mailing costs per unit	$0.32	
9	Responses	6,875	
10	Profit per response	$22.0	
11	Gross profit	$151,250	
12	Print + mailing costs	$129,250	
13	Net Profit	$22,000	
14			

Figure 26-11: This worksheet calculates the net profit from a direct-mail promotion.

This model uses two input cells: the number of promotional pieces mailed and the anticipated response rate. The results area consists of the following:

Printing costs per unit: The cost to print a single mailer. The unit cost varies with the quantity: $.20 each for quantities less than 200,000; $.20 each for quantities of 200,001 through 300,000; and $.15 each for quantities of more than 300,000. I represent this with the following formula:

```
=IF(Number_mailed<200000,0.2,IF(Number_mailed<300000,0.15,0.1))
```

Mailing costs per unit: This is a fixed cost, $.32 per unit mailed.

Responses: This is the number of responses, calculated from the response rate and the number mailed. The formula in this cell is as follows:

```
=Response_rate*Number_mailed
```

Profit per response: This is a fixed value. The company knows that it will realize a profit of $22 per order.

Gross profit: This is a simple formula that multiplies the profit per response by the number of responses:

```
=Profit_per_response*Responses
```

Print + mailing costs: This formula calculates the total cost of the promotion:

```
=Number_mailed*(Printing_costs_per_unit+Mailing_costs_per_unit)
```

Net Profit: This formula calculates the bottom line — the gross profit minus the printing and mailing costs.

If you plug in values for the two input cells, you see that the net profit varies widely — often going negative to produce a net loss.

I create a two-input data table to summarize the net profit at various combinations of quantity and response rate. Figure 26-12 shows how the table is set up in the range A15:I25.

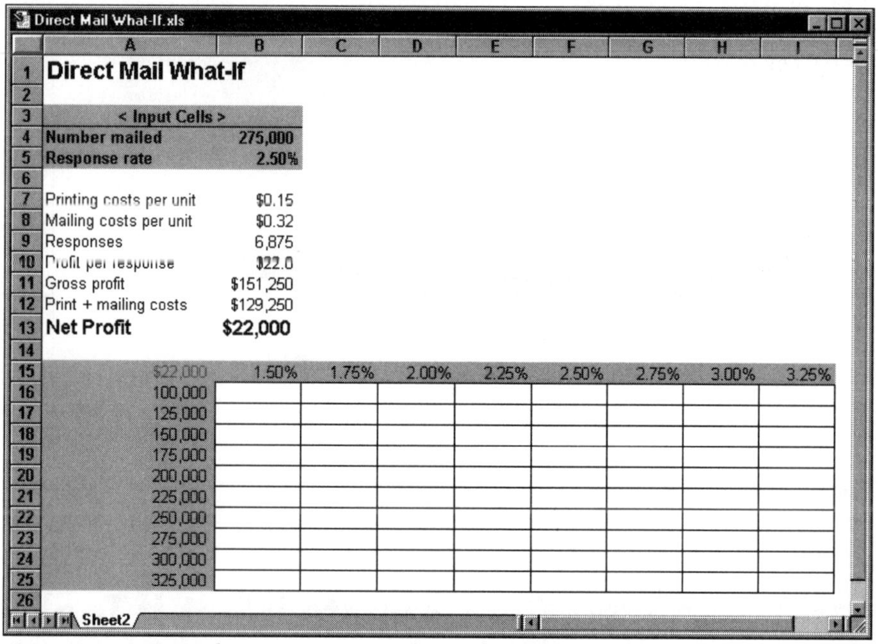

Figure 26-12: Preparing to create a two-input data table.

To create the data table, select the range and issue the Data⇨Table command. The Row Input Cell is `Number_Mailed` (the name for cell B4) and the Column Input Cell is `Response_Rate` (the name for cell B5). Figure 26-13 shows the result of this command.

	A	B	C	D	E	F	G	H	I
14									
15	$22,000	1.50%	1.75%	2.00%	2.25%	2.50%	2.75%	3.00%	3.25%
16	100,000	($24,000)	($18,500)	($13,000)	($7,500)	($2,000)	$3,500	$9,000	$14,500
17	125,000	($30,000)	($23,125)	($16,250)	($9,375)	($2,500)	$4,375	$11,250	$18,125
18	150,000	($36,000)	($27,750)	($19,500)	($11,250)	($3,000)	$5,250	$13,500	$21,750
19	175,000	($42,000)	($32,375)	($22,750)	($13,125)	($3,500)	$6,125	$15,750	$25,375
20	200,000	($28,000)	($17,000)	($6,000)	$5,000	$16,000	$27,000	$38,000	$49,000
21	225,000	($31,500)	($19,125)	($6,750)	$5,625	$18,000	$30,375	$42,750	$55,125
22	250,000	($35,000)	($21,250)	($7,500)	$6,250	$20,000	$33,750	$47,500	$61,250
23	275,000	($38,500)	($23,375)	($8,250)	$6,875	$22,000	$37,125	$52,250	$67,375
24	300,000	($27,000)	($10,500)	$6,000	$22,500	$39,000	$55,500	$72,000	$88,500
25	325,000	($29,250)	($11,375)	$6,500	$24,375	$42,250	$60,125	$78,000	$95,875
26									
27									

Figure 26-13: The result of the two-input data table.

Tip Two-input data tables often make good 3-D charts. An example of such a chart for the direct-mail example is shown in Figure 26-14.

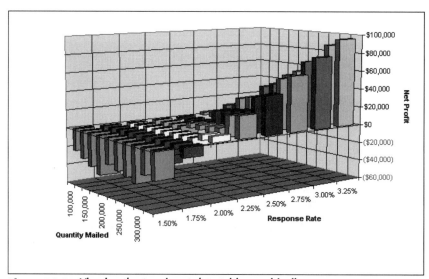

Figure 26-14: Viewing the two-input data table graphically.

Scenario Manager: The Ultimate What-If Tool

Creating data tables is useful, but they have a few limitations:

✦ You can vary only one or two input cells at a time.

✦ The process of setting up a data table is not all that intuitive.

✦ A two-input table shows the results of only one formula cell (although you can create additional tables for more formulas).

✦ More often than not, you're interested in a few select combinations — not an entire table that shows all possible combinations of two input cells.

Excel's scenario manager feature makes it easy to automate your what-if models. You can store different sets of input values (called *changing cells* in the terminology of scenario manager) for any number of variables and give a name to each set. You can then select a set of values by name, and Excel displays the worksheet by using those values. You also can generate a summary report that shows the effect of various combinations of values on any number of result cells. These summary reports can be an outline or a pivot table.

Your sales forecast for the year, for example, may depend on a number of factors. Consequently, you can define three scenarios: best case, worst case, and most likely case. You then can switch to any of these scenarios by selecting the named scenario from a list. Excel substitutes the appropriate input values in your worksheet and recalculates the formulas. This is similar, in some respects, to the macro-assisted what-if technique I describe earlier. You'll find that the scenario manager is easier to use, however.

Defining scenarios

To introduce you to the scenario manager, I start with a simple example: the production model that I use earlier.

On the CD-ROM A different version of the original workbook is available on the companion CD-ROM. This version is named SC_MAN1.XLS.

In this example, I define three scenarios, as depicted in Table 26-2. The Best Case scenario has the lowest hourly cost and materials cost. The Worst Case scenario has high values for both the hourly cost and the materials cost. The third scenario, Most Likely Case, has intermediate values for both of these input cells (this represents the management's best estimate). The managers need to be prepared for the worst case, however — and they are interested in what would happen under the Best Case scenario.

Table 26-2 Three Scenarios for the Production Model		
Scenario	*Hourly Cost*	*Materials Cost*
Best Case	30	57
Worst Case	38	62
Most Likely Case	34	59

Access the scenario manager with the Tools⇨Scenarios command. This command brings up the Scenario Manager dialog box, shown in Figure 26-15.

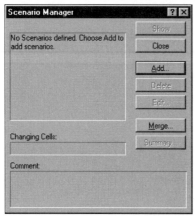

Figure 26-15: The Scenario Manager dialog box lets you assign names to different sets of assumptions.

When you first access this dialog box, it tells you that there are no scenarios defined — which is not too surprising because you're starting out. As you add named scenarios, they appear in this dialog box.

Tip It's excellent practice to create names for the changing cells, plus all result cells that you want to examine. As you'll see, Excel uses these names in the dialog boxes and in the reports that it generates. Using names makes it much easier to keep track of what's going on and makes your reports more readable.

To add a scenario, click on the Add button in the Scenario Manager dialog box. Excel displays its Add Scenario dialog box, which is shown in Figure 26-16. This dialog box consists of four parts:

✦ **Scenario Name:** The name for the scenario. You can give it any name that you like — preferably something meaningful.

✦ **Changing Cells:** The input cells for the scenario. You can enter the cell addresses directly or point to them. Multiple selections are allowed, so the input cells need not be adjacent. Each named scenario can use the same set of changing cells or different changing cells. The number of changing cells for a scenario is limited to 32.

✦ **Comment:** By default, Excel displays who created the scenario and the time it was created. You can change this text, add new text to it, or delete it.

✦ **Protection:** The two options (protecting a scenario and hiding a scenario) are in effect only when the worksheet is protected and the Scenario option is chosen in the Protect Sheet dialog box. Protecting a scenario prevents anyone from modifying it; a hidden scenario doesn't appear in the Scenario Manager dialog box.

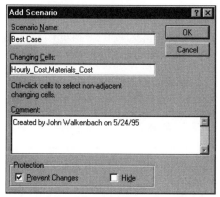

Figure 26-16: The Add Scenario dialog box lets you create a named scenario.

In this example, define the three scenarios listed in the preceding table. The changing cells are Hourly_Cost (B4) and Materials_Cost (B5).

After you fill in the information in the Add Scenario dialog box, click on OK. Excel then displays the Scenario Values dialog box, which is shown in Figure 26-17. This dialog box displays one field for each changing cell that you specified in the previous dialog box. Enter the values for each cell in the scenario. If you click on OK, you return to the Scenario Manager dialog box — which then displays your named scenario in its list. If you have more scenarios to create, click on the Add button to return to the Add Scenario dialog.

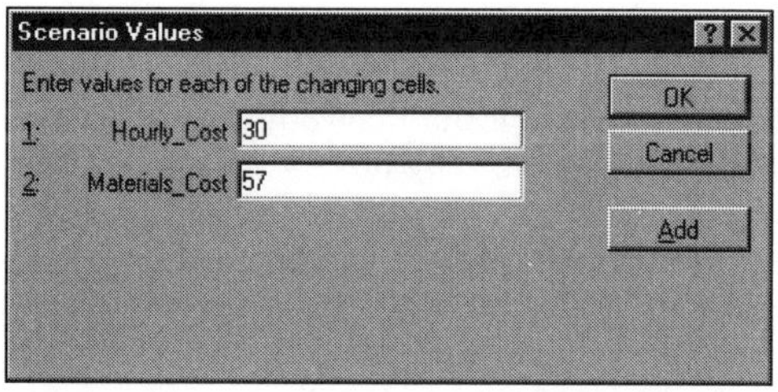

Figure 26-17: You enter the values for the scenario in the Scenario Values dialog box.

Using the Scenarios tool

The Workgroup toolbar includes a tool named Scenarios (that last tool in the accompanying figure). It's a drop-down list box that you can use to create scenarios and display named scenarios. Using this tool may be more efficient than bringing up the Scenario Manager dialog box to create or view a different scenario.

To create a scenario using the Scenarios tool, enter the scenario's values, select the changing cells, and then enter the name for the scenario in the Scenario drop-down box. To view a named scenario, just choose it from the list. Scenarios that you define in this manner also appear in the Scenario Manager dialog box. So, if you want to perform any operations on your scenarios (add comments, edit values, generate reports) you need to use the Tools⇨Scenarios command to bring up the Scenario Manager dialog box.

Displaying scenarios

After you define all scenarios and return to the Scenario Manager dialog box, it displays the names of your defined scenarios. Select one of the scenarios and then click on the Show button. Excel inserts the corresponding values into the changing cells, and the worksheet is calculated to show the results for that scenario.

Modifying scenarios

The Edit button in the Scenario Manager dialog box does what you may expect: It lets you edit a scenario (change one or more of the values for the changing cells). Select the scenario that you want to change, click on the Edit button, choose OK to get to the Scenario Values dialog box, and make your changes. Notice that Excel automatically updates the Comments box with new text that indicates when the scenario was modified.

Merging scenarios

In workgroup situations, you may have several people working on a spreadsheet model, and several people may have defined various scenarios. The marketing department, for example, may have its opinion of what the input cells should be, the finance department may have another opinion, and your CEO may have yet another opinion.

Excel makes it easy to merge these various scenarios into a single workbook by using the Merge button in the Scenario Manager dialog box. Clicking on this button displays the dialog box shown in Figure 26-18.

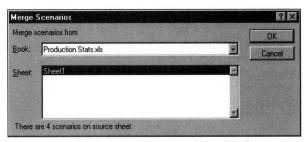

Figure 26-18: The Merge Scenarios dialog box lets you merge scenarios defined by others into your workbook.

Before you merge scenarios, make sure that the workbook from which you're merging is open. Then, click on the Merge button in the Scenario Manager dialog box. Excel displays its Merge Scenarios dialog box. Choose the workbook that you're merging from the Book drop-down list, and then choose the sheet that has the scenarios defined from the Sheet list box (notice that the dialog box displays the number of scenarios in each sheet as you scroll through the Sheet list box). Click on OK and you return to the previous dialog box, which now displays the scenario names merged from the other workbook.

Generating a scenario report

Now it's time to take the scenario manager through its final feat — generating a summary report. When you click on the Summary button in the Scenario Manager dialog box, Excel displays the Scenario Summary dialog box shown in Figure 26-19.

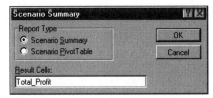

Figure 26-19: The Scenario Summary dialog box lets you to choose a report type and specify the result cells in which you're interested.

You have a choice of report types:

✦ **Scenario Summary:** The summary report is in the form of an outline.

✦ **Scenario PivotTable:** The summary report is in the form of a pivot table (see Chapter 25).

For simple cases of scenario management, a standard Scenario Summary report usually is sufficient. If you have many scenarios defined with multiple result cells, however, you may find that a pivot table provides more flexibility.

The Scenario Summary dialog box also asks you to specify the result cells (the cells that contain the formulas in which you're interested). For this example, select B15:D15 and B17 (a multiple selection). This makes the report show the profit for each product, plus the total profit.

Excel creates a new worksheet to store the summary table. Figure 26-20 shows the Scenario Summary form of the report, and Figure 26-21 shows the Scenario Pivot Table form. If you gave names to the changing cells and result cells, the table uses these names. Otherwise, it lists the cell references.

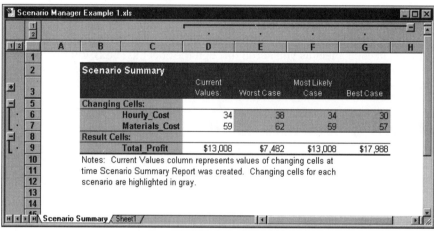

Figure 26-20: A summary report produced by the scenario manager.

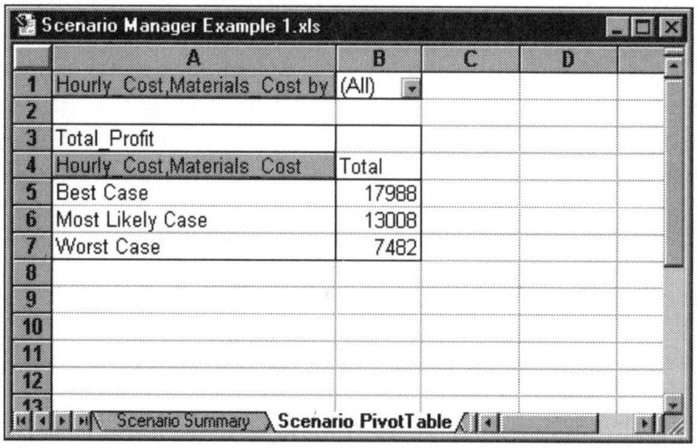

Figure 26-21: A pivot table summary report produced by the scenario manager.

Scenario Manager Limitations

As you work with the scenario manager, you may discover its main limitation: a scenario can use no more than 32 changing cells. If you attempt to use more, you get the message shown in Figure 26-22.

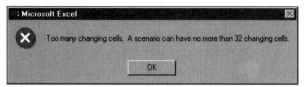

Figure 26-22: The scenario manager is limited to 32 changing cells.

You can get around this limitation by splitting your scenarios into parts. For example, assume that you have a worksheet with monthly sales projects for three years (36 changing cells). You may want to define various scenarios for these projections. But because the number of changing cells exceeds the 32-cell limit, you can break it down into two or three scenarios — each of which uses a different set of changing cells. For example, you can define a scenario for the first 12 months, another for the second 12 months, and yet another for the third 12 months. Then, to display a particular scenario, you must display all three sub-scenarios. Writing simple macros makes this easy. The only down side to using this technique is that the summary reports include superfluous information.

On the CD-ROM The companion CD-ROM contains a file that demonstrates this example (including macros). The workbook is named SC_MAN2.XLS.

Summary

In this chapter, I discuss the concept of spreadsheet what-if analysis. What-if analysis is the process of systematically changing input cells and observing the effects on one or more formula cells. You can perform what-if analysis manually by plugging in different values. You also can use macros to automate this process. Excel's data table feature lets you summarize the result of various values of a single input cell or various combinations of two-input cells. The scenario manager feature makes it easy to create scenarios and generate summary reports.

✦   ✦   ✦

Analyzing Data Using Goal Seeking and Solver

◆ ◆ ◆ ◆

In This Chapter

An introduction to goal seeking, which can be viewed as what-if analysis in reverse

How to perform single-cell goal seeking

How Solver extends the concept of goal seeking

Examples of problems that are appropriate for Solver

◆ ◆ ◆ ◆

In the preceding chapter, I discuss what-if analysis — the process of changing input cells to observe the results on other dependent cells. This chapter looks at that process from the opposite perspective: finding the value of one or more input cells that will produce a desired result in a formula cell.

What-If Analysis — In Reverse

Consider the following what-if question: "What will be the total profit if sales increase by 20 percent?" If your worksheet is set up properly, you can change the value in one cell to see what happens to the profit cell. Goal seeking takes the opposite approach. If you know what a formula result *should* be, Excel can tell you which values of one or more input cells are required to produce that result. In other words, you can ask a question such as, "What sales increase is needed to produce a profit of $1.2 million?" Excel provides two tools that are relevant:

✦ **Goal Seeking:** Determines the value required in a single input cell to produce a result that you want in a dependent (formula) cell.

✦ **Solver:** Determines values required in multiple input cells to produce a result that you want. Moreover, because you can specify certain constraints to the problem, you gain significant problem-solving ability.

I discuss both of these procedures in this chapter.

Single-Cell Goal Seeking

Single-cell goal seeking (also known as backsolving) is a rather simple concept. Excel determines what value in an input cell will produce a desired result in a formula cell. The best way to understand how this works is to walk through an example.

A goal-seeking example

Figure 27-1 shows the mortgage loan worksheet used in the preceding chapter. This worksheet has four input cells and four formula cells. I originally used this worksheet for a what-if analysis example, but now I take the opposite approach. Rather than supply different input cell values to look at the calculated formulas, I let Excel determine one of the input values.

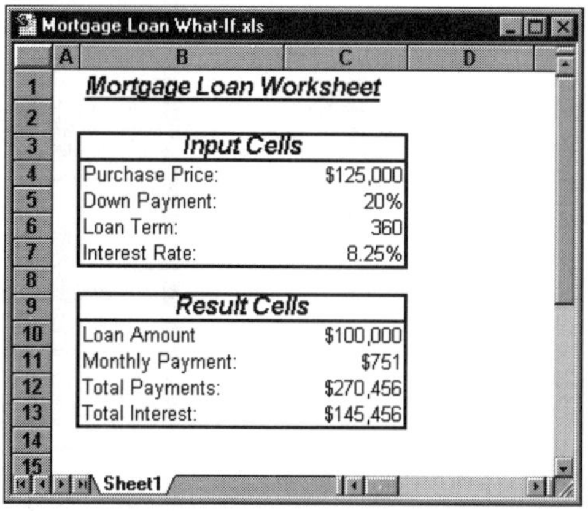

Figure 27-1: This worksheet is a good demonstration of goal seeking.

Assume that you're in the market for a new home and you know that you can afford $1,200 per month in mortgage payments. You also know that a lender will issue a fixed-rate mortgage loan for 8.25 percent, based on an 80 percent loan-to-value (that is, a 20 percent down payment). The question is, "What is the maximum purchase price I can handle?" In other words, what value in cell C4 will cause the formula in cell C11 to result in $1,200? One approach is to plug values into cell C4 until C11 displays $1,200. A more efficient approach is to let Excel determine the answer.

To answer this question, select the Tools⇨Goal Seek command. Excel responds with the dialog box shown in Figure 27-2. Completing this dialog box is similar to forming a sentence. You want to set cell C11 to 1200 by changing cell C4. Enter this information in the dialog box by either typing the cell references or pointing with the mouse. Click on OK to begin the goal-seeking process.

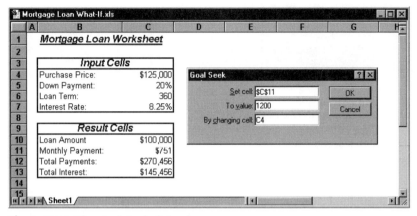

Figure 27-2: The Goal Seek dialog box.

In about a second, Excel announces that it has found the solution and displays the Goal Seek Status box. This box tells you what the target value was and what Excel came up with. In this case, Excel found an exact value. The worksheet now displays the found value in cell C4 ($199,663). As a result of this value, the monthly payment amount is $1,200. At this point, you have two options:

✦ Click on OK to replace the original value with the found value.

✦ Click on Cancel to restore your worksheet to the form it had before you issued the Tools⇨Goal Seek command.

More about goal seeking

If you think about it, you realize that Excel can't always find a value that produces the result you're looking for — sometimes a solution doesn't exist. In such a case, the Goal Seek Status box informs you of that fact (see Figure 27-3). Other times, however, Excel may report that it can't find a solution, but you're pretty sure that one exists. If that's the case, you can try the following:

✦ Change the current value of the changing cell to a value closer to the solution and then reissue the command.

✦ Adjust the Maximum Iterations setting in the Calculation panel of the Options dialog box. Increasing the number of iterations makes Excel try more possible solutions.

✦ Double-check your logic and make sure that the formula cell does indeed depend on the specified changing cell.

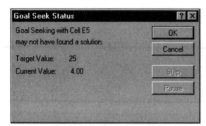

Figure 27-3: When Excel can't find a
solution to your goal-seeking problem,
it tells you so.

Note Like all computer programs, Excel has limited precision. To demonstrate this, enter
=A1^2 into cell A1. Then use the Tools⇨Goal Seek command to find the value in cell
A1 that will make the formula return 16. Excel comes up with a value of 4.00002269 —
which is close to the square root of 16, but certainly not exact. You can adjust the
precision in the Calculation panel of the Options dialog box (make the Maximum
Change value smaller).

Note In some cases, multiple values of the input cell produce the same desired result. For
example, the formula =A1^2 returns 16 if cell A1 contains either −4 or +4. If you use
goal seeking when there are two solutions, Excel gives you the solution that has the
same sign as the current value in the cell.

Perhaps the main limitation of the Tools⇨Goal Seek command is that it can find the
value for only one input cell. For example, it can't tell you what purchase price *and*
what down payment percent will result in a particular monthly payment. If you want
to change more than one variable at a time, use Solver (which I discuss later in this
chapter).

Graphical goal seeking

Excel provides another way to perform goal seeking — by manipulating a graph.
Figure 27-4 shows a worksheet that projects sales for a start-up company. The CFO
knows from experience that companies in this industry can grow exponentially
according to a formula like this one:

```
y*(bX)
```

Table 27-1 lists and describes the variables.

**On the
CD-ROM** The workbook for this example, named GRAPH_GO.XLS, is available on the companion CD-ROM.

Table 27-1		
Variables Used in the Sales Growth Formula		
Variable		**Description**
y		A constant equal to the first year's sales
b		A growth coefficient
x		A variable relating to time

The company managers know that sales during the first year will be $250,000, and they want to increase the company's sales to $10 million by the year 2005. The financial modelers want to know the exact growth coefficient that meets this goal. The worksheet shown in Figure 27-4 uses formulas to forecast the annual sales using the growth coefficient in cell B1. The worksheet has an embedded chart that plots the annual sales.

The initial guess for the growth coefficient is 1.40. As you can see, this number is too low — it results in sales of only $7.231 million for the year 2005. Although you can use the Tools⇨Goal Seek command to arrive at the exact coefficient, there's another way to do it.

Double-click on the chart so that you can edit it and then select the chart series. Now click on the last data column to select only that column in the series (the Name box should display S1P11). Point to the top of the column, and notice that the mouse pointer changes shape. Drag the column up and watch the value change in the Name box. When the value is exactly $10 million, release the mouse button.

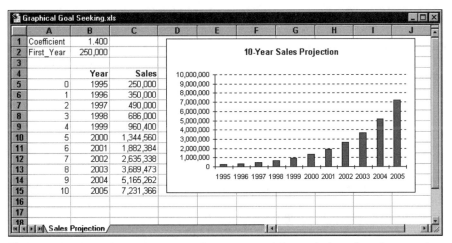

Figure 27-4: This sales projection predicts exponential growth, based on the growth coefficient in cell B1.

Excel responds with the usual Goal Seek dialog box, shown in Figure 27-5. Notice that two fields are filled in for you. Excel just needs to know which cell to use for the input cell. Specify cell B1 or enter **Coefficient** in the edit box. Excel calculates the value of Coefficient necessary to produce the result that you pointed out on the chart. If you want to keep that number (which, by the way, is 1.44612554959157), click on OK. Excel replaces the current value of Coefficient with the new value, and the chart is updated automatically. You can probably appreciate the fact that it would take quite a while to arrive at this number by plugging in successive approximations.

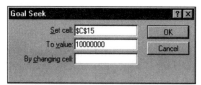

Figure 27-5: The Goal Seek dialog box appears when you directly manipulate a point on a chart that contains a formula.

You won't want to use this graphical method all the time because the normal Tools⇨Goal Seek command is more efficient. But it does demonstrate another way to approach problems, which is helpful for those who are more visually oriented.

As you may expect, goal seeking can get much more impressive when it's used with complex worksheets that have many dependent cells. In any event, it sure beats trial and error.

Introducing Solver

Excel's goal-seeking feature is a useful tool, but it clearly has limitations. It can solve for only one adjustable cell, for example, and it returns only a single solution. Excel's powerful Solver tool extends this concept in the following ways:

✦ You can specify multiple adjustable cells.

✦ You can specify constraints on the values that the adjustable cells can have.

✦ You can generate a solution that maximizes or minimizes a particular worksheet cell.

✦ You can generate multiple solutions to a problem.

Although goal seeking is a relatively simple operation, using Solver can be much more complicated. In fact, Solver is probably one of the most difficult (and potentially frustrating) features in Excel. I'm the first to admit that Solver isn't for everyone. In fact, most Excel users have no use for this feature. But many users find that having this much power is worth spending time to learn about it.

Appropriate problems for Solver

Problems that are appropriate for Solver fall into a relatively narrow range. They typically involve situations that meet the following criteria:

✦ A *target cell* depends on other cells and formulas. Typically, you want to maximize or minimize this target cell or set it equal to some value.

✦ The target cell depends on a group of cells (called *changing cells*) that can be adjusted so that they affect the target cell.

✦ The solution must adhere to certain limitations or *constraints*.

After your worksheet is set up appropriately, you can use Solver to adjust the changing cells and produce the result that you want in your target cell — and simultaneously meet all the constraints that you have defined.

A simple Solver example

I start with a simple example to introduce Solver and then present some increasingly complex examples to demonstrate what it can do.

Figure 27-6 shows a worksheet set up to calculate the profit for three products. Column B shows the number of units of each product, column C shows the profit per unit for each product, and column C contains formulas that calculate the profit for each product by multiplying the units by the profit per unit.

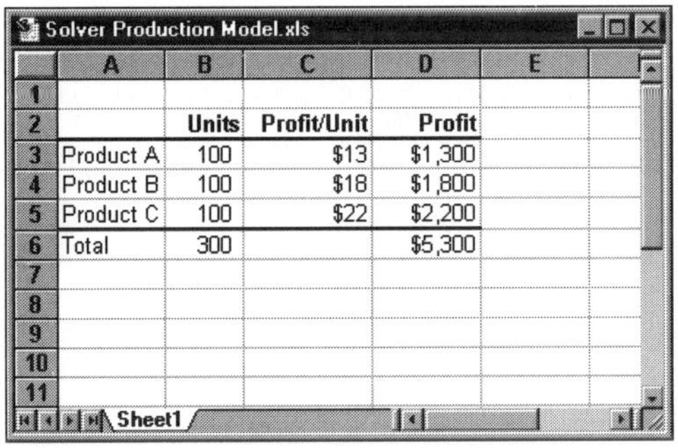

	Units	Profit/Unit	Profit
Product A	100	$13	$1,300
Product B	100	$18	$1,800
Product C	100	$22	$2,200
Total	300		$5,300

Figure 27-6: Use Solver to determine the number of units to maximize the total profit.

It doesn't take an MBA degree to realize that the greatest profit per unit comes from Product C. Therefore, the logical solution is to produce only Product C. If things were really this simple, we wouldn't need tools such as Solver. As in most situations, this company has some constraints to which it must adhere. These constraints are as follows:

No Tools⇨Solver command?

Solver is an add-in, so it's available only when the add-in is installed. If the Tools menu doesn't show a Solver command, you need to install the add-in before you can use it.

Select the Tools⇨Add-Ins command. Excel displays its Add-Ins dialog box. Scroll down the list of add-ins and place a check mark next to the item named Solver Add-In. Click on OK

and Excel installs the add-in and makes the Tools⇨Solver command available.

If Solver Add-In doesn't appear in the list, you need to run Excel's Setup program (or the Setup program for Microsoft Office). Use the Custom option and specify that Solver be installed. Running Setup again takes only a few minutes.

✦ The combined production capacity is 300 total units per day.

✦ The company needs 50 units of Product A to fill an existing order.

✦ The company needs 40 units of Product B to fill an anticipated order.

✦ Because the market for Product C is relatively limited, produce no more than 40 units of this product.

These four constraints make the problem more realistic and challenging. In fact, it's a perfect problem for Solver.

On the CD-ROM   This workbook, named SLV_PROD.XLS, is available on the companion CD-ROM.

The basic procedure for using Solver is as follows:

1. Set up the worksheet with values and formulas.

2. Bring up the Solver dialog box.

3. Specify the target cell.

4. Specify the changing cells.

5. Specify the constraints.

6. Change Solver options if necessary.

7. Let Solver solve the problem.

To start Solver, select the Tools⇨Solver command. Excel displays its Solver Parameters dialog box, as shown in Figure 27-7.

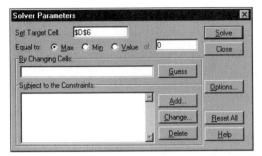

Figure 27-7: The Solver Parameters dialog box.

In this example, the target cell is D6 — the cell that calculates the total profit for three products. Enter (or point to) cell D6 in the Set Target Cell field. Because the objective is to maximize this cell, click on the Max option. Next, specify the changing cells, which is the range B3:B5.

The next step is to specify the constraints on the problem. The constraints are added one at a time and appear in the box labeled Subject to the Constraints. To add a constraint, click on the Add button. Excel displays the Add Constraint dialog box, which is shown in Figure 27-8. This dialog box has three parts: a cell reference, an operator, and a value. The first constraint is that the total production capacity is 300 units. Enter B6 as the cell reference, choose equal (=) from the drop-down list of operators, and enter 300 as the value. Click on Add to add the remaining constraints. Table 27-2 summarizes the constraints for this problem.

When you've entered the last constraint, click on OK to return to the Solver Parameters dialog box — which now lists the four constraints.

At this point, Solver knows everything about the problem. Click on the Solver button to start the solution process. You can watch the progress on-screen, and Excel soon announces that it has found a solution. The Solver Results dialog box is shown in Figure 27-9.

Table 27-2 Constraints Summary	
Constraint	**Expressed As**
Capacity is 300 units	B6=300
At least 50 units of Product A	B3>=50
At least 40 units of Product B	B4>=40
No more than 40 units of Product C	B5<=40

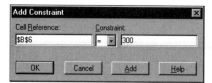

Figure 27-8: The Add Constraint dialog box.

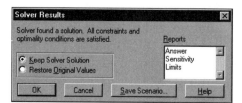

Figure 27-9: Solver displays this dialog box when it finds a solution to the problem.

At this point, you have the following options:

✦ Replace the original changing cell values with the values that Solver found.

✦ Restore the original changing cell values.

✦ Create any or all three reports that describe what Solver did (press Shift to select multiple reports from this list).

✦ Click on the Save Scenario button to save the solution as a scenario so that it can be used by the scenario manager (see Chapter 26).

If you specify any report options, Excel creates each report on a new worksheet, with an appropriate name. Figure 27-10 shows an Answer Report. In the Constraints section of the report, all the constraints except one are *binding,* which means that the constraint was satisfied at its limit, with no more room to change.

This simple example illustrates how Solver works. The fact is, you could probably solve this particular problem manually just as quickly. That, of course, isn't always the case.

More about Solver

Before I present complex examples, I'll discuss the Solver Options dialog box — one of the more feature-packed dialog boxes in Excel. From this dialog box, you control many aspects of the solution process, as well as load and save model specifications in a worksheet range.

Solver Production Model.xls

Microsoft Excel 7.0 Answer Report
Worksheet: [Solver Production Model.xls]Sheet1
Report Created: 12/25/95 9:28

Target Cell (Max)

Cell	Name	Original Value	Final Value
$D$6	Total Profit	$5,310	$5,310

Adjustable Cells

Cell	Name	Original Value	Final Value
$B$3	Product A Units	50	50
$B$4	Product B Units	210	210
$B$5	Product C Units	40	40

Constraints

Cell	Name	Cell Value	Formula	Status	Slack
$B$6	Total Units	300	$B$6=300	Not Binding	0
$B$3	Product A Units	50	$B$3>=50	Binding	-
$B$4	Product B Units	210	$B$4>=40	Not Binding	170
$B$5	Product C Units	40	$B$5<=40	Binding	-

Answer Report 1 / Sheet1

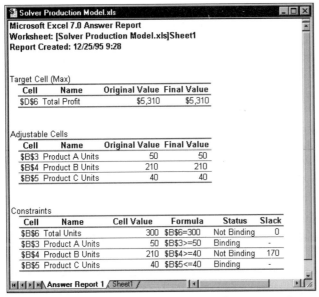

Figure 27-10: One of three reports that Solver can produce.

It's not unusual for Solver to report that it can't find a solution — even when you know that one should exist. Often, you can change one or more of the Solver options and try again. When you choose the Options button in the Solver Parameters dialog box, Excel displays the Solver Options dialog box, as shown in Figure 27-11.

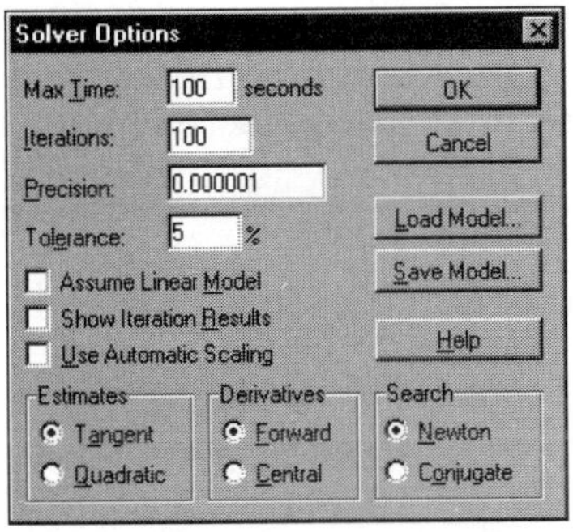

Figure 27-11: You can control many aspects of how Solver solves a problem.

This list describes Solver's options:

Max Time: You can specify the maximum amount of time (in seconds) that you want Solver to spend on a problem. If Solver reports that it exceeded the time, you can increase the time that it spends searching for a solution.

Iterations: Enter the maximum number of trial solutions that you want Solver to perform.

Precision: Specifies how close the Cell Reference and Constraint formulas must be to satisfy a constraint. The problem may be solved more quickly if you specify less precision.

Tolerance: The maximum percentage of error allowed for integer solutions (relevant only if there is an integer constraint).

Assume Linear Model: Can speed up the solution process, but you can use it only if all the relationships in the model are linear. You can't use this option if the adjustable cells are multiplied or divided, or if the problem uses exponents.

Show Iteration Results: If this option is set, Solver pauses and displays the results after each iteration.

Use Automatic Scaling: Turns on automatic scaling. This is useful when the problem involves large differences in magnitude — when you attempt to maximize a percentage, for example, by varying cells that are very large.

Estimates, Derivatives, and Search group boxes: Let you control some technical aspects of the solution. In most cases, you won't need to change these settings.

Save Model: Displays the Save Model dialog box, in which you specify a worksheet reference where the model parameters will be saved.

Load Model: Displays the Load Model dialog box, in which you specify a worksheet reference for the model that you want to load.

Usually, you want to save a model only when you're using more than one set of Solver parameters with your worksheet. This is because the first Solver model is saved automatically with your worksheet (using hidden names). If you save additional models, the information is stored in the form of formulas that correspond to the specification you made (the last cell in the saved range is an array formula that holds the options settings). You can use the Load Model button to save these settings.

Solver Examples

The remainder of this chapter consists of examples of using Solver for various types of problems.

Minimizing shipping costs

This example involves finding alternative options for shipping materials while keeping total shipping costs at a minimum (see Figure 27-12). A company has warehouses in Los Angeles, St. Louis, and Boston. Retail outlets throughout the United States place orders, which then are shipped from one of the warehouses. The object is to meet the product needs of all six retail outlets from available inventory in the warehouses — and keep total shipping charges as low as possible.

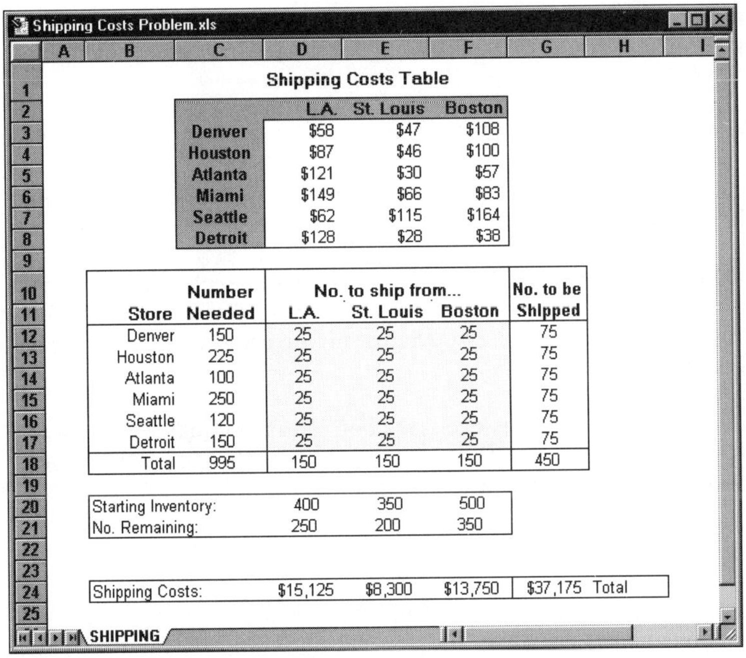

Figure 27-12: This worksheet determines the least expensive way to ship products from warehouses to retail outlets.

On the CD-ROM This workbook, named SHP_CST.XLS, can be found on the companion CD-ROM.

This workbook is rather complicated, so I explain each part:

Shipping Costs Table: This table, at the top of the worksheet, contains per-unit shipping costs from each warehouse to each retail outlet. The cost to ship a unit from Los Angeles to Denver, for example, is $58.

Product needs of each retail store: This information is contained in C12:C17. For example, Denver needs 150 units, Houston needs 225, and so on. C18 holds the total needed.

Number to ship: The shaded range (D12:F17) holds the adjustable cells that Solver will vary (I initialized them all with a value of 25 to give Solver something to start with). Column G contains formulas that total the number of units to be shipped to each retail outlet.

Warehouse inventory: Row 20 contains the amount of inventory at each warehouse, and row 21 contains formulas that subtract the amount shipped (row 18) from the inventory. For example, cell D21 has this formula: =D20 −D18.

Calculated shipping costs: Row 24 contains formulas that calculate the shipping costs. Cell D24 contains the following formula, which was copied to the two cells to the right:

```
=SUMPRODUCT(D3:D8,D12:D17)
```

This formula calculates the total shipping cost from each warehouse. Cell G24 is the bottom line, the total shipping costs for all orders.

Solver fills in values in the range D12:F17 in such a way that each retail outlet gets the desired number of units *and* the total shipping cost is minimized. In other words, the solution minimizes the value in cell C24 by adjusting the cells in D12:F17, subject to the following constraints:

✦ The number of units needed by each retail outlet must equal the number shipped (in other words, all of the orders are filled). These constraints are represented by the following specifications:

```
C12=G12   C14=G14   C16=G16
C13=G13   C15=G15   C17=G17
```

✦ The adjustable cells can't be negative. In other words, shipping a negative number of units makes no sense. These constraints are represented by the following specifications:

```
D12>=0    E12>=0    F12>=0
D13>=0    E13>=0    F13>=0
D14>=0    E14>=0    F14>=0
D15>=0    E15>=0    F15>=0
D16>=0    E16>=0    F16>=0
D17>=0    E17>=0    F17>=0
```

✦ The number of units remaining in each warehouse's inventory must not be negative (that is, they can't ship more than what is available). This is represented by the following constraint specifications:

```
D21>=0    E21>=0    F21>=0
```

Note   Before you solve this problem with Solver, you may try your hand at minimizing the shipping cost manually by entering values in D12:F17. Don't forget to make sure that all the constraints are met. You'll probably find that this is a difficult task — and you'll better appreciate the power behind Solver.

Setting up the problem is the difficult part. For example, you must enter 27 constraints. When you have specified all necessary information, click on the Solve button to set Solver to work. This process takes a while, but eventually Solver displays the solution shown in Figure 27-13.

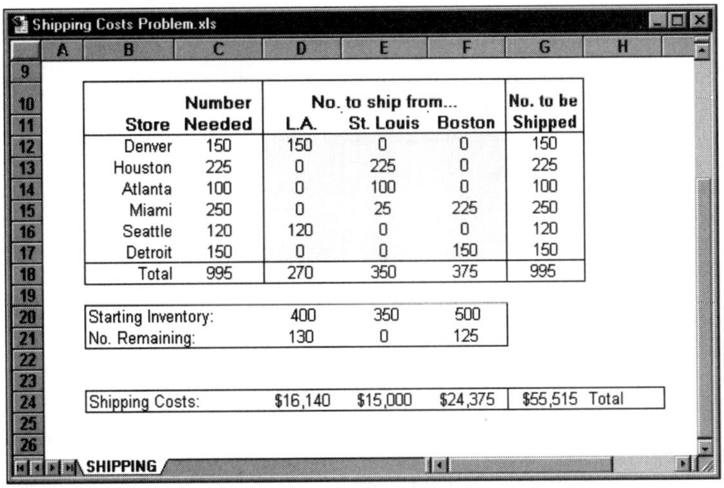

	Number	No. to ship from...			No. to be
Store	Needed	L.A.	St. Louis	Boston	Shipped
Denver	150	150	0	0	150
Houston	225	0	225	0	225
Atlanta	100	0	100	0	100
Miami	250	0	25	225	250
Seattle	120	120	0	0	120
Detroit	150	0	0	150	150
Total	995	270	350	375	995

Starting Inventory:		400	350	500
No. Remaining:		130	0	125

Shipping Costs:		$16,140	$15,000	$24,375	$55,515 Total

Figure 27-13: The solution created by Solver.

The total shipping cost is $55,515, and all the constraints are met. Notice that shipments to Miami come from both St. Louis and Boston.

Scheduling staff

This example deals with staff scheduling. Such problems usually involve determining the minimum number of people that satisfy staffing needs on certain days or times of day. The constraints typically involve such details as the number of consecutive days or hours that a person can work.

Figure 27-14 shows a worksheet set up to analyze a simple staffing problem. The question is, "What is the minimum number of employees required to meet daily staffing needs?" At this company, each person works five consecutive days. As a result, employees begin their five-day workweek on different days of the week.

On the CD-ROM
This workbook, named SLV_STAF.XLS, can be found on the companion CD-ROM. The key to this problem, as with most Solver problems, is figuring out how to set up the worksheet. This example makes it clear that setting up your worksheet properly is critical to working with Solver. This worksheet is laid out as follows:

Day: Column B consists of plain text for the days of the week.

Staff Needed: The values in column C represent the number of employees needed on each day of the week. As you see, staffing needs vary quite a bit by the day of the week.

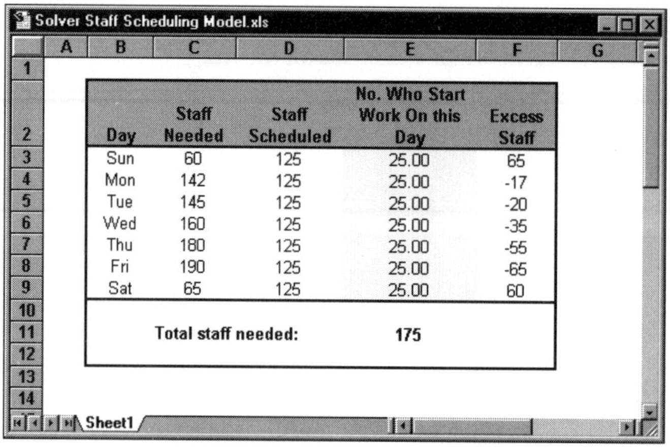

Figure 27-14: This staffing model determines the minimum number of staff members required to meet daily staffing needs.

Staff Schedules: Column D holds formulas that use the values in column E. Each formula adds the number of people who start on that day to the number of people who started on the preceding four days. Because the week wraps around, you can't use a single formula and copy it. Consequently, each formula in column D is different:

```
D3:    =E3+E9+E8+E7+E6
D4:    =E4+E3+E9+E8+E7
D5:    =E5+E4+E10+E9+E8
D6:    =E6+E5+E4+E10+E9
D7:    =E7+E6+E5+E4+E10
D8:    =E8+E7+E6+E5+E4
D9:    =E9+E8+E7+E6+E5
```

Adjustable Cells: Column E holds the adjustable cells — the numbers to be determined by Solver. I initialized these cells with a value of 25 in order to give Solver something to start with. Generally, it's best to initialize the changing cells to values that are as close as possible to the anticipated answer.

Excess Staff: Column F contains formulas that subtract the number of staff members needed from the number of staff members scheduled, to determine excess staff. Cell F3 contains =D3-C3, which was copied to the six cells below it.

Total Staff Needed: Cell E11 is a formula that sums the number of people who start on each day. The formula is =SUM(E3:E9). This is the value that Solver will minimize.

This problem, of course, has constraints. The number of people scheduled each day must be greater than or equal to the number of people required. If each value in column F is greater than or equal to 0, the constraints will be satisfied.

After the worksheet is set up, select Tools⇨Solver and specify that you want to minimize cell E11 by changing cells E3:E9. Next, click on the Add button to begin adding the following constraints:

```
F3>=0
F4>=0
F5>=0
F6>=0
F7>=0
F8>=0
F9>=0
```

Click on Solve to start the process. The solution that Solver finds, shown in Figure 27-15 indicates that a staff of 188 meets the staffing needs and that no excess staffing will exist on any day.

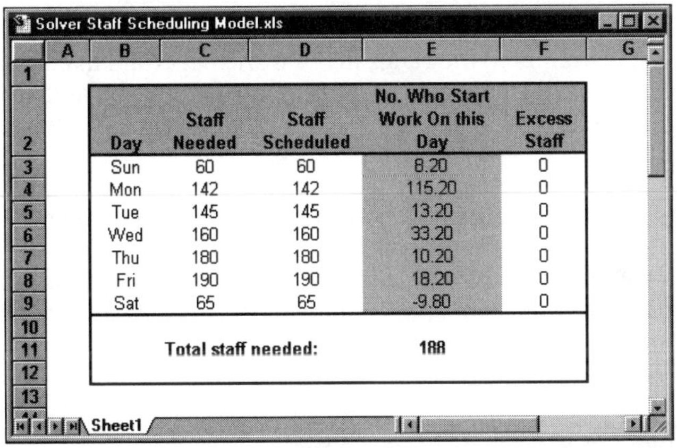

Solver Staff Scheduling Model.xls

Day	Staff Needed	Staff Scheduled	No. Who Start Work On this Day	Excess Staff
Sun	60	60	8.20	0
Mon	142	142	115.20	0
Tue	145	145	13.20	0
Wed	160	160	33.20	0
Thu	180	180	10.20	0
Fri	190	190	18.20	0
Sat	65	65	-9.80	0
Total staff needed:			188	

Figure 27-15: This solution offered by Solver isn't quite right — you have to add more constraints.

But wait! If you examine the results carefully, you notice a few things wrong here:

✦ Solver's solution involves partial people — which are difficult to find. For example, 8.2 people begin their workweek on Sunday.

✦ Second (and more critical) is the suggestion that a negative number of people should begin their workweek on Saturday.

Both of these problems are easy to correct by adding more constraints. Fortunately, Solver enables you to limit the solution to integers by using the integer option in the Add Constraint dialog box. This means that you must add another constraint for each cell in E3:E9. Figure 27-16 shows how you can specify an integer constraint. Avoiding the negative people problem requires seven more constraints of the form E3>=0, one for each cell in E3:E9.

Note These two problems (integer solutions and negative numbers) are quite common when using Solver. They also demonstrate that it's very important to check the results rather than rely on Solver's solution.

Figure 27-16: With many problems, you have to limit the solution to integers. You can do this by selecting the integer option in the Add Constraint dialog box.

Tip If you find that adding these constraints is tedious, save the model to a worksheet range. Then you add new constraints to the range in the worksheet (and make sure that you don't overwrite the last cell in this range). Next, run Solver again and load the modified model from the range that you edited. The example workbook has three Solver ranges stored in it.

After adding these 14 new constraints, run Solver again. This time it arrives at the solution shown in Figure 27-17. Notice that this solution requires 192 people and results in excess staffing on three days of the week. This solution is the best one possible that uses the fewest number of people — and almost certainly is better than what you would arrive at manually.

Day	Staff Needed	Staff Scheduled	No. Who Start Work On this Day	Excess Staff
Sun	60	60	1.00	0
Mon	142	142	118.00	0
Tue	145	145	14.00	0
Wed	160	169	36.00	9
Thu	180	180	11.00	0
Fri	190	191	12.00	1
Sat	65	73	0.00	8
Total staff needed:			**192**	

Figure 27-17: Rerunning Solver after adding more constraints produces a better solution to the staffing model problem.

Allocating resources

The example in this section is a common type of problem that's ideal for Solver. Essentially, problems of this sort involve optimizing the volumes of individual production units that use varying amounts of fixed resources. Figure 27-18 shows an example for a toy company.

On the CD-ROM

This workbook, named SLV_RES.XLS, can be found on the companion CD-ROM.

This company makes five different toys, which use six different materials in varying amounts. For example, Toy A requires 3 units of blue paint, 2 units of white paint, 1 unit of plastic, 3 units of wood, and 1 unit of glue. Column G shows the current inventory of each type of material. Row 10 shows the unit profit for each toy. The number of toys to make are in the range B11:F11 — these are the values that Solver will determine. The goal of this example is to determine how to allocate the resources in order to maximize the total profit (B13). In other words, Solver will determine how many units of each toy to make. The constraints in this example are relatively simple:

✦ Ensure that production doesn't use more resources than are available. This can be accomplished by specifying that each cell in column F is greater than or equal to zero.

✦ Ensure that the quantities produced aren't negative. This can be accomplished by specifying that each cell in row 11 be greater than or equal to zero.

Figure 27-19 shows the results produced by Solver. It shows the product mix that will generate $12,365 in profit. All resources are used in their entirety, except glue.

	A	B	C	D	E	F	G	H	I
1				XYZ Toys Inc.					
2				Materials Needed					
3	Material	Toy A	Toy B	Toy C	Toy D	Toy E	Amt. Avail.	Amt. Used	Amt. Left
4	Red Paint	0	1	0	1	3	625	500	125
5	Blue Paint	3	1	0	1	0	640	500	140
6	White Paint	2	1	2	0	2	1,100	700	400
7	Plastic	1	5	2	2	1	875	1,100	-225
8	Wood	3	0	3	5	5	2,200	1,600	600
9	Glue	1	2	3	2	3	1,500	1,100	400
10	Unit Profit	$15	$30	$20	$25	$25			
11	No. to Make	100	100	100	100	100			
12	Profit	$1,500	$3,000	$2,000	$2,500	$2,500			
13	Total Profit	$11,500							
14									
15									

Figure 27-18: Using Solver to maximize profit when resources are limited.

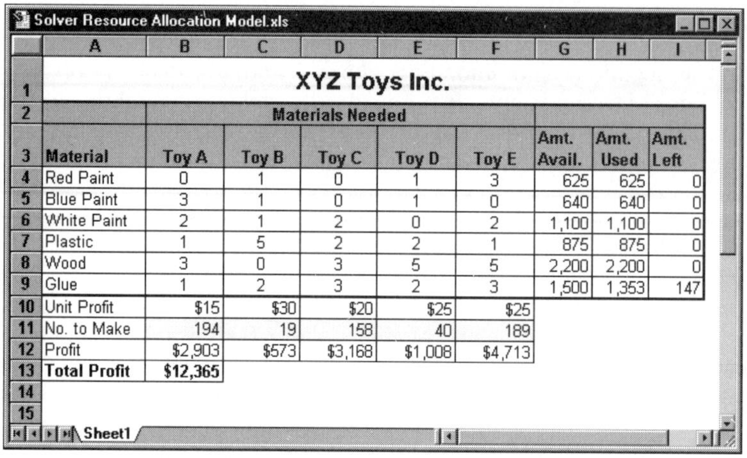

Solver Resource Allocation Model.xls

XYZ Toys Inc.

Material	Toy A	Toy B	Toy C	Toy D	Toy E	Amt. Avail.	Amt. Used	Amt. Left
	Materials Needed							
Red Paint	0	1	0	1	3	625	625	0
Blue Paint	3	1	0	1	0	640	640	0
White Paint	2	1	2	0	2	1,100	1,100	0
Plastic	1	5	2	2	1	875	875	0
Wood	3	0	3	5	5	2,200	2,200	0
Glue	1	2	3	2	3	1,500	1,353	147
Unit Profit	$15	$30	$20	$25	$25			
No. to Make	194	19	158	40	189			
Profit	$2,903	$573	$3,168	$1,008	$4,713			
Total Profit	$12,365							

Sheet1

Figure 27-19: Solver determined how to use the resources in order to maximize the total profit.

Optimizing an investment portfolio

This example demonstrates how to use Solver to help maximize the return on an investment portfolio. Portfolios consist of several investments, each of which has different yields. In addition, you may have some constraints that involve reducing risk and diversification goals. Without such constraints, a portfolio problem becomes a no-brainer: Put all your money in the investment with the highest yield.

This example involves a credit union, a financial institution that takes members' deposits and invests them in loans to other members, bank CDs, and other types of investments. Part of the return on these investments is distributed to the members in the form of dividends, or interest on their deposits. This hypothetical credit union must adhere to some regulations regarding its investments, and the board of directors has imposed some other restrictions. These regulations and restrictions comprise the problem's constraints. Figure 27-20 shows a workbook set up for the problem.

On the CD-ROM

This workbook, named SLV_INVE.XLS, is available on the companion CD-ROM.

The following constraints are the ones to which you must adhere in allocating the $5 million portfolio:

- ✦ The amount invested in new car loans must be at least three times the amount invested in used-car loans (used-car loans are riskier investments). This constraint is represented as C5>=C6*3.
- ✦ Car loans should make up at least 15 percent of the portfolio. This constraint is represented as D14>=.15.

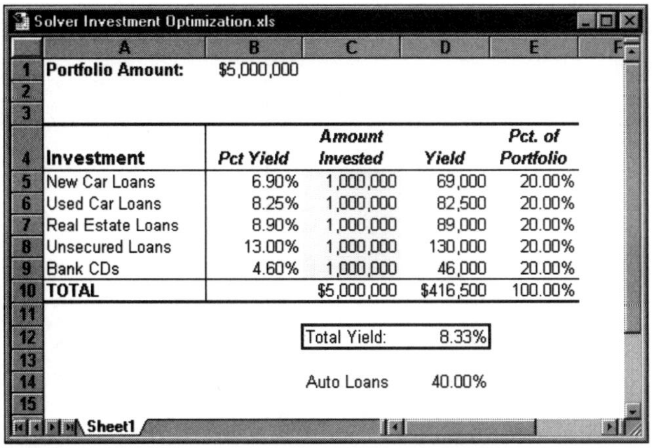

Solver Investment Optimization.xls

	A	B	C	D	E
1	**Portfolio Amount:**	$5,000,000			
2					
3					
4	**Investment**	***Pct Yield***	***Amount Invested***	***Yield***	***Pct. of Portfolio***
5	New Car Loans	6.90%	1,000,000	69,000	20.00%
6	Used Car Loans	8.25%	1,000,000	82,500	20.00%
7	Real Estate Loans	8.90%	1,000,000	89,000	20.00%
8	Unsecured Loans	13.00%	1,000,000	130,000	20.00%
9	Bank CDs	4.60%	1,000,000	46,000	20.00%
10	**TOTAL**		$5,000,000	$416,500	100.00%
11					
12			Total Yield:	8.33%	
13					
14			Auto Loans	40.00%	
15					

Sheet1

Figure 27-20: This worksheet is set up to maximize a credit union's investments, given some constraints.

- ✦ Unsecured loans should make up no more than 25 percent of the portfolio. This constraint is represented as E8<=.25.
- ✦ At least 10 percent of the portfolio should be in bank CDs. This constraint is represented as E9>=.10.
- ✦ All investments should be positive or zero. In other words, the problem requires five additional constraints to ensure that none of the changing cells goes below zero.

The changing cells are C5:C9, and the goal is to maximize the total yield in cell D12. I entered 1,000,000 as starting values in the changing cells. When you run Solver with these parameters, it produces the solution shown in Figure 27-21, which has a total yield of 9.25 percent.

Note

In this example, the starting values of the changing cells are very important. For example, if you use smaller numbers as the starting values (such as 10) and rerun Solver, you'll find that it doesn't do as well. In fact, it produces a total yield of only 8.35 percent. This demonstrates that you can't always trust Solver to arrive at the optimal solution with one try — even when the Solver Results dialog box tells you that *All constraints and optimality conditions are satisfied.* Usually, the best approach is to use starting values that are as close as possible to the final solution.

The best advice? Make sure that you understand Solver well before you entrust it with helping you make major decisions. Try different starting values and adjust options to see whether Solver can do better.

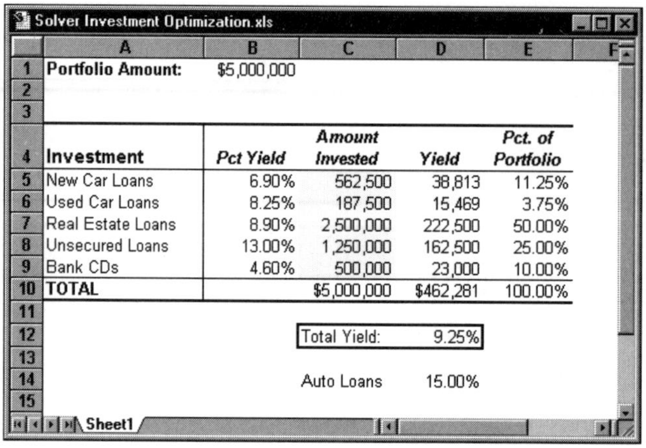
Solver Investment Optimization.xls

	A	B	C	D	E
1	Portfolio Amount:	$5,000,000			
2					
3					
4	Investment	Pct Yield	Amount Invested	Yield	Pct. of Portfolio
5	New Car Loans	6.90%	562,500	38,813	11.25%
6	Used Car Loans	8.25%	187,500	15,469	3.75%
7	Real Estate Loans	8.90%	2,500,000	222,500	50.00%
8	Unsecured Loans	13.00%	1,250,000	162,500	25.00%
9	Bank CDs	4.60%	500,000	23,000	10.00%
10	TOTAL		$5,000,000	$462,281	100.00%
11					
12			Total Yield:	9.25%	
13					
14			Auto Loans	15.00%	
15					

Sheet1

Figure 27-21: The results of the portfolio optimization.

Summary

In this chapter, I discuss two Excel commands: Tools➪Goal Seek and Tools➪Solver. The latter command is available only if the Solver add-in is installed. Goal seeking is used to determine the value in a single input cell that will produce a result you want in a formula cell. Solver determines values in multiple input cells that will produce a result you want, given certain constraints. Using Solver can be challenging because it has many options, and the result it produces isn't always the best one.

✦ ✦ ✦

Analyzing Data with the Analysis ToolPak

◆ ◆ ◆ ◆

In This Chapter

Introduction to the
Analysis ToolPak
add-in

Descriptions and
examples of the 19
tools in the Analysis
ToolPak

Listing of the 93
worksheet functions
that you can use when
the Analysis ToolPak
is installed

◆ ◆ ◆ ◆

Although spreadsheets such as Excel are designed primarily with business users in mind, these products can be found in other disciplines, including education, research, statistics, and engineering. One way that Excel addresses these nonbusiness users is with its Analysis ToolPak add-in. Many of the features and functions in the Analysis ToolPak are valuable for business applications as well.

The Analysis ToolPak: An Overview

The Analysis ToolPak is an add-in that provides analytical capability usually not available. The Analysis ToolPak consists of two parts:

- ✦ 19 analytical procedures
- ✦ 93 built-in worksheet functions

These analysis tools offer many features that may be useful to those in the scientific, engineering, and educational communities — not to mention business users whose needs extend beyond the normal spreadsheet fare.

Making the Analysis ToolPak available

Depending on how Excel was originally installed on your system, you may or may not have access to the Analysis ToolPak. To see whether this add-in is available, select the Tools menu. If the menu displays Data Analysis as an option, you're all set.

If the Tools⇨Data Analysis command is not available on your system, you need to attach the add-in. Select the Tools⇨Add-Ins command, place a check mark next to the Analysis ToolPak add-in, and click on OK. This makes the Analysis ToolPak available whenever you start Excel. If Analysis ToolPak doesn't appear in the list of add-ins, you need to rerun the Setup program for Excel (or Microsoft Office) and choose the Custom option. This lets you copy the files used by the Analysis ToolPak to your hard drive.

When the Analysis ToolPak is available on your system, the following files appear in your Excel\Library\Analysis folder:

```
Analys32.xll
Atpvbaen.xla
Auncres.xla
Arocdb.xla
```

This section provides a quick overview of the types of analyses that you can perform with the Analysis ToolPak. I discuss each tool in detail later in the chapter.

✦ Analysis of variance (three types)

✦ Correlation

✦ Covariance

✦ Descriptive statistics

✦ Exponential smoothing

✦ F-test

✦ Fourier analysis

✦ Histogram

✦ Moving average

✦ Random number generation

✦ Rank and percentile

✦ Regression

✦ Sampling

✦ t-test (three types)

✦ z-test

As you can see, this add-in brings a great deal of new functionality to Excel. These procedures have limitations, however, and in some cases you may prefer to create your own formulas to do some calculations.

Besides the procedures just listed, the Analysis ToolPak provides many additional worksheet functions. These functions cover mathematics, engineering, unit conversions, financial analysis, and dates. These functions are listed at the end of the chapter.

Using the Analysis ToolPak

This section discusses the two components of the Analysis ToolPak: its tools and its functions.

Using the analysis tools

The procedures in the Analysis ToolPak add-in are relatively straightforward. Usually, you select the Tools⇨Data Analysis command, which displays the dialog box shown in Figure 28-1. Then you scroll through the list until you find the analysis tool that you want to use. Click on OK and you get a new dialog box that's specific to the procedure you selected.

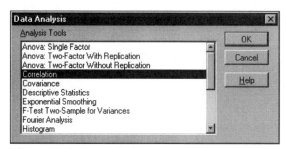

Figure 28-1: The Analysis Tools dialog box lets you select the tool in which you're interested.

Usually, you need to specify one or more input ranges, plus an output range (one cell will do). Alternatively, you can specify that the results are placed on a new worksheet or in a new workbook. The procedures vary in the amount of additional information required. An option that you see in many dialog boxes is whether or not your data range includes labels. If so, you can specify the entire range, including the labels, and indicate to Excel that the first column (or row) contains labels. Excel then uses these labels in the tables it produces. Most tools also provide different output options that you can select, based on your needs.

Note The Analysis ToolPak was developed by a third-party software developer (not Microsoft). Consequently, the dialog boxes contain subtle differences compared to dialog boxes in Excel. For example, if you preselect the input range, the range address is not listed in the dialog box — you need to reselect it.

Caution In some cases, the procedures produce their results using formulas. As a result, you can change your data and the results update automatically. In other procedures, the results are in the form of values, so if you change your data, the results don't reflect your changes. Make sure that you understand what Excel is doing.

Using the Analysis ToolPak functions

Once the Analysis ToolPak is installed, you have access to all additional functions (which are described fully in the online help system). You access these functions just like any other function, and they appear in the Function Wizard dialog box, intermixed with Excel's standard functions.

Note If you'll be sharing worksheets that use these functions, make sure that the user has access to the add-in functions.

The Analysis ToolPak Tools

In this section, I describe each tool and provide an example. Space limitations prevent me from discussing every option available in these procedures. I assume that if you need to use some of these advanced analysis tools, you know what you're doing.

On the CD-ROM Tool examples can be found in the workbook named ATP_EXPL.XLS on the companion CD-ROM.

Analysis of variance

Analysis of variance is a statistical test that determines whether two or more samples were drawn from the same population. The Analysis ToolPak can perform three types of analysis of variance:

✦ **Single-factor:** A one-way analysis of variance, with only one sample for each group of data

✦ **Two-factor with replication:** A two-way analysis of variance with multiple samples (or replications) for each group of data

✦ **Two-factor without replication:** A two-way analysis of variance with a single sample (or replication) for each group of data

Figure 28-2 shows the dialog box for a single-factor ANOVA. Alpha represents the statistical confidence level for the test.

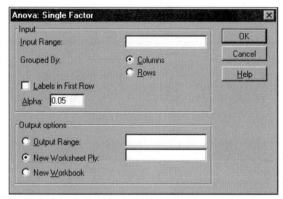

Figure 28-2: Specifying parameters for a single-factor analysis of variance.

The results of an analysis of variance are shown in Figure 28-3. The output for this test consists of the means and variances for each of the four samples, the value of F, the critical value of F, and the significance of F (P-value). Because the probability is greater than the Alpha value, the conclusion is that the samples were drawn from the same population.

Analysis ToolPak Examples.xls

	F	G	H	I	J	K	L
1	Anova: Single Factor						
2							
3	SUMMARY						
4	*Groups*	*Count*	*Sum*	*Average*	*Variance*		
5	Low	8	538	67.25	6680.214		
6	Medium	8	578	72.25	7700.214		
7	High	8	636	79.5	9397.714		
8	Control	8	544	68	6845.714		
9							
10							
11	ANOVA						
12	*Source of Variation*	*SS*	*df*	*MS*	*F*	*P-value*	*F crit*
13	Between Groups	757	3	252.3333	0.032959	0.991785	2.946685
14	Within Groups	214367	28	7655.964			
15							

Read_Me / **Anova** / Correlation / Covariance / Descriptive

Figure 28-3: The results of the analysis of variance.

Correlation

Correlation is a widely used statistic that measures the degree to which two sets of data vary together. For example, if higher values in one data set are typically associated with higher values in the second data set, the two data sets have a positive correlation. The degree of correlation is expressed as a coefficient that ranges from –1.0 (a perfect negative correlation) to +1.0 (a perfect positive correlation). A correlation coefficient of 0 means that the two variables are not correlated.

The Correlation dialog box is shown in Figure 28-4. Specify the input range, which can include any number of variables arranged in rows or columns.

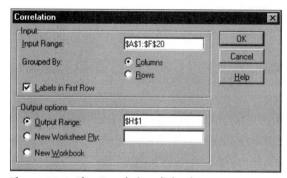

Figure 28-4: The Correlation dialog box.

Figure 28-5 shows the results of a correlation analysis for eight variables. The output consists of a correlation matrix that shows the correlation coefficient for each variable paired with every other variable.

	A	B	C	D	E	F	G	H	I
15									
16		Height	Weight	Sex	Test1	Test2	Test3	Test4	Test5
17	Height	1							
18	Weight	0.84031	1						
19	Sex	0.67077	0.51894	1					
20	Test1	0.09959	0.16347	0.00353	1				
21	Test2	-0.2805	-0.2244	-0.1533	0.83651	1			
22	Test3	-0.4374	-0.3845	-0.0136	-0.445	-0.0203	1		
23	Test4	0.22718	0.00356	-0.2127	0.07838	0.06727	-0.1515	1	
24	Test5	-0.1016	-0.1777	0.04521	0.28937	0.20994	-0.3746	0.01266	1
25									

Read_Me / Anova \ **Correlation** / Covariance / Descriptive

Figure 28-5: The results of a correlation analysis.

Note Notice that the resulting correlation matrix doesn't use formulas to calculate the results. Therefore, if any data changes, the correlation matrix won't be valid. The ATP_EXPL.XLS workbook demonstrates how to create a correlation matrix that uses formulas.

Covariance

The Covariance tool produces a matrix similar to that generated by the Correlation tool. *Covariance* is defined as the average of the product of the deviations of each data point pair from their respective means. Like correlation, this measures the degree to which two variables vary together.

Figure 28-6 shows covariance matrix. Notice that the values along the diagonal (where the variables are the same) are the variances for the variable.

 Note The ATP_EXP.XLS workbook demonstrates how to create a covariance matrix that uses formulas which use the COVAR function. The values generated by the Analysis ToolPak are *not* the same values that you would get if you used the COVAR function.

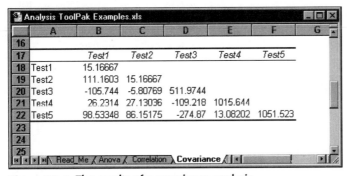

Figure 28-6: The results of a covariance analysis.

Descriptive statistics

This tool produces a table that describes your data with some standard statistics. It uses the dialog box shown in Figure 28-7. The Kth Largest and Kth Smallest option display the data value that corresponds to a rank that you specify. For example, if you check Kth Largest and specify a value of 2, the output shows the second largest value in the input range (the standard output already includes the minimum and maximum values).

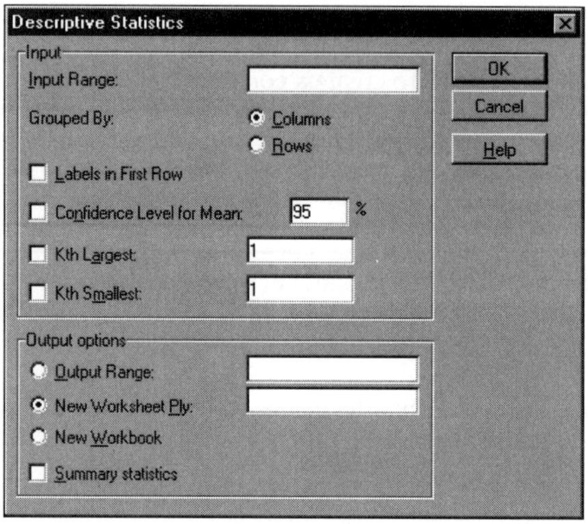

Figure 28-7: The Descriptive Statistics dialog box.

Sample output for the Descriptive Statistics tool is shown in Figure 28-8. This example has three groups. Because the output for this procedure consists of values (not formulas), you should use this procedure only when you're certain that your data won't change; otherwise, you need to reexecute this procedure. The ATP_EXPL.XLS workbook demonstrates how to produce the same results using formulas.

Analysis ToolPak Examples.xls

	E	F	G	H	I	J
1	*W. Coast Sample*		*Midwest Sample*		*E. Coast Sample*	
2						
3	Mean	39.25	Mean	46	Mean	41.35
4	Standard Error	1.84801	Standard Error	2.10763	Standard Error	1.56487
5	Median	37.5	Median	45.5	Median	41.5
6	Mode	37	Mode	52	Mode	37
7	Standard Deviation	8.26454	Standard Deviation	9.42561	Standard Deviation	6.99831
8	Sample Variance	68.3026	Sample Variance	88.8421	Sample Variance	48.9763
9	Kurtosis	1.47266	Kurtosis	-0.47699	Kurtosis	-0.28025
10	Skewness	1.18011	Skewness	0.14121	Skewness	-0.24858
11	Range	32	Range	34	Range	26
12	Minimum	28	Minimum	28	Minimum	28
13	Maximum	60	Maximum	62	Maximum	54
14	Sum	785	Sum	920	Sum	827
15	Count	20	Count	20	Count	20
16	Confidence Level(95.0%)	3.86793	Confidence Level(95.0%)	4.41132	Confidence Level(95.0%)	3.27531

Correlation / Covariance / **Descriptive** / Exponential Smoothing

Figure 28-8: Output from the Descriptive Statistics tool.

Exponential smoothing

Exponential smoothing is a technique for predicting data based on the previous data point and the previously predicted data point. You can specify the *damping factor* (also known as a *smoothing constant*), and it can range from 0 to 1. This determines the relative weighting of the previous data point and the previously predicted data point. You also can request standard errors and a chart.

This procedure generates formulas that use the damping factor that you specified. Therefore, if the data changes, the formulas are updated. Figure 28-9 shows sample output from the exponential smoothing tool.

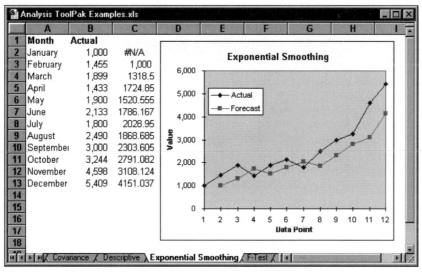

Figure 28-9: Output from the Exponential Smoothing tool.

F-test (two-sample for variance)

The *F-test* is a commonly used statistical test that lets you compare two population variances. The dialog box for this tool is shown in Figure 28-10.

The output for this test consists of the means and variances for each of the two samples, the value of F, the critical value of F, and the significance of F. Sample output is shown in Figure 28-11.

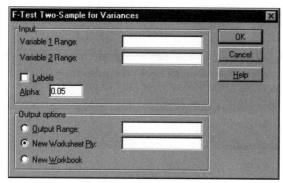

Figure 28-10: The F-test dialog box.

	A	B	C	D	E	F	G
1	Group 1	Group 2		F-Test Two-Sample for Variances			
2	96	39					
3	78	53			Group 1	Group 2	
4	72	51		Mean	75.44444	46.66667	
5	78	48		Variance	109.5278	25	
6	65	51		Observations	9	9	
7	66	42		df	8	8	
8	69	44		F	4.381111		
9	87	42		P(F<=f) one-tail	0.025855		
10	68	50		F Critical one-tail	3.438103		
11							
12							

Covariance / Descriptive / Exponential Smoothing

Figure 28-11: Sample output for the F-test.

Fourier analysis

This tool performs a "fast Fourier" transformation on a range of data. The range is limited to the following sizes: 1, 2, 4, 8, 16, 32, 64, 128, 256, 512, or 1,024 data points. This procedure accepts and generates complex numbers, which are represented as labels.

Histogram

This procedure is useful for producing data distributions and histogram charts. It accepts an input range and a bin range. A *bin* range is a range of values that specify the limits for each column of the histogram. If you omit the bin range, Excel creates ten equal-interval bins for you. The size of each bin is determined by a formula of the following form:

```
=(MAX(input_range)-MIN(input_range))/10
```

The Histogram dialog box is shown in Figure 28-12. As an option, you can specify that the resulting histogram be sorted by frequency of occurrence in each bin.

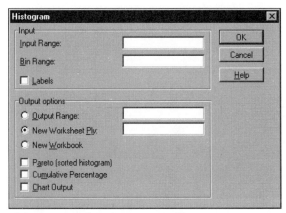

Figure 28-12: The Histogram tool lets you generate distributions and graphical output.

If you specify the sorted histogram option, the bin range must consist of values and can't contain formulas. If formulas appear in the bin range, the sorting done by Excel won't work properly and your worksheet will display error values.

Figure 28-13 shows a chart generated from this procedure. The Histogram tool doesn't use formulas, so if you change any of the input data, you need to repeat the histogram procedure to update the results.

Moving average

The Moving Average tool is useful to smooth out a data series that has a lot of variability. This is best done in conjunction with a chart. Excel does the smoothing by computing a moving average of a specified number of values. In many cases, a moving average lets you spot trends that would otherwise be obscured by the noise in the data.

Figure 28-14 shows the Moving Average dialog box. You can, of course, specify the number of values to be used for each average. An option in this procedure calculates standard errors and places formulas for these calculations next to the moving average formulas. The standard error values indicate the degree of variability between the actual values and the calculated moving averages. When you exit this dialog box, Excel creates formulas that reference the input range that you specify.

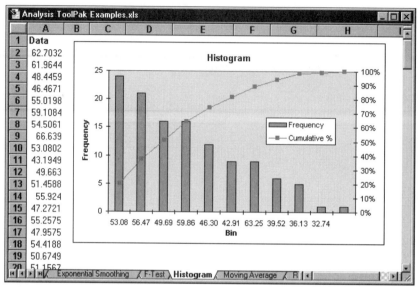

Figure 28-13: Output from the Histogram tool.

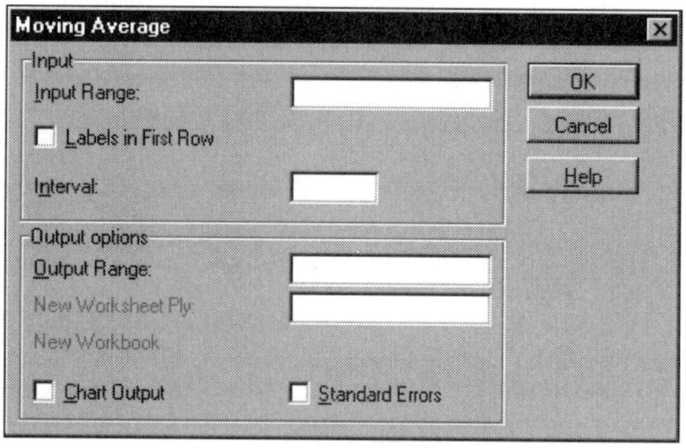

Figure 28-14: The Moving Average dialog box.

Figure 28-15 shows the results of this tool. Notice that the first few cells in the output are #NA. This is because there aren't enough data points to calculate the average for these initial values.

Random number generation

Although Excel has with it a built-in function to calculate random numbers, the Random Number Generation tool is much more flexible because you can specify what type of distribution you want the random numbers to have. Figure 28-16 shows the Random Number Generation dialog box. The Parameters box varies, depending on the type of distribution selected.

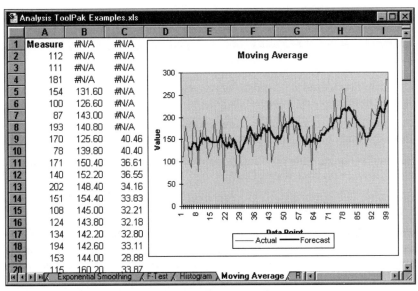

Figure 28-15: Output from the Moving Average tool.

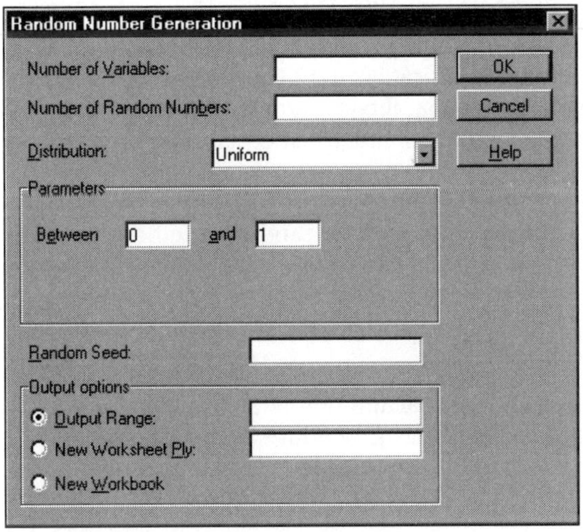

Figure 28-16: This dialog box lets you generate a wide variety of random numbers.

The Number of Variables refers to the number of columns that you want, and the Number of Random Numbers refers to the number of rows that you want. For example, if you want 200 random numbers arranged in 10 columns of 20 rows, you would specify 10 and 20, respectively, in these text boxes.

The Random Seed box lets you specify a starting value that Excel uses in its random-number generating algorithm. Usually, you leave this blank. If you want to generate the same random number sequence, however, you can specify a seed between 1 and 32,767 (integer values only). The distribution options that are available follow:

Uniform: Every random number has an equal chance of being selected. You specify the upper and lower limits.

Normal: The random numbers correspond to a normal distribution. You specify the mean and standard deviation of the distribution.

Bernoulli: The random numbers will be either 0 or 1, determined by the probability of success that you specify.

Binomial: This returns random numbers based on a Bernoulli distribution over a specific number of trials, given a probability of success that you specify.

Poisson: This option generates values in a Poisson distribution. This is characterized by discrete events that occur in an interval, where the probability of a single occurrence is proportional to the size of the interval. The lambda parameter is the expected number of occurrences in an interval. In a Poisson distribution, lambda is equal to the mean, which also is equal to the variance.

Patterned: This option doesn't actually generate random numbers. Rather, it repeats a series of numbers in steps that you specify.

Discrete: This option lets you specify the probability that specific values are chosen. It requires a two-column input range: the first column holds the values and the second column holds the probability of each value being chosen. The sum of the probabilities in the second column must equal 100 percent.

 With previous versions of Excel, I avoided using this procedure because it was extremely slow. With Excel for Windows 95, however, random numbers are generated in the blink of an eye.

Rank and percentile

This tool creates a table that shows the ordinal and percentile ranking for each value in a range. Figure 28-17 shows the results of this procedure. The ATP_EXP.XLS workbook demonstrates how to use formulas to produce the same result.

Regression

The Regression tool calculates a regression analysis from worksheet data. Regression is used to analyze trends, forecast the future, build predictive models, and, often, to make sense out of a series of seemingly unrelated numbers.

Analysis ToolPak Examples.xls

	A	B	C	D	E	F	G
1	**SalesRep**	**Sales**		*Point*	*Sales*	*Rank*	*Percent*
2	Allen	137,676		4	197,107	1	100.00%
3	Brandon	155,449		3	180,414	2	94.40%
4	Campaigne	180,414		17	170,538	3	88.80%
5	Dufenberg	197,107		14	161,750	4	83.30%
6	Fox	130,814		2	155,449	5	77.70%
7	Giles	133,283		11	151,466	6	72.20%
8	Haflich	116,943		19	149,627	7	66.60%
9	Hosaka	107,684		12	145,088	8	61.10%
10	Jenson	128,060		1	137,676	9	55.50%
11	Larson	121,336		18	134,395	10	50.00%
12	Leitch	151,466		6	133,283	11	44.40%
13	Miller	145,088		5	130,814	12	38.80%
14	Peterson	127,995		9	128,060	13	33.30%
15	Richards	161,750		13	127,995	14	27.70%
16	Richardson	117,203		10	121,336	15	22.20%
17	Ryan	102,571		15	117,203	16	16.60%
18	Serrano	170,538		7	116,943	17	11.10%
19	Struyk	134,395		8	107,684	18	5.50%
20	Winfrey	149,627		16	102,571	19	.00%

Moving Average / Random Numbers / **Rank & Percentile**

Figure 28-17: Output from the rank and percentile procedure.

Regression analysis lets you determine the extent to which one range of data (the dependent variable) varies as a function of the values of one or more other ranges of data (the independent variables). This relationship is expressed mathematically, using values that are calculated by Excel. You can use these calculations to create a mathematical model of the data and predict the dependent variable using different values of one or more independent variables. This tool can perform simple and multiple linear regressions and automatically calculate and standardize residuals.

Figure 28-18 shows the Regression dialog box. As you see, it offers many options:

Input Y Range: The range that contains the dependent variable.

Input X Range: One or more ranges that contain independent variables.

Constant is Zero: If checked, this forces the regression to have a constant of zero (which means that the regression line passes through the origin; when the X values are 0, the predicted Y value will be 0).

Confidence Level: The confidence level for the regression.

Residuals: These options specify whether to include residuals in the output. Residuals are the differences between observed and predicted values.

Normal Probability: This generates a chart for normal probability plots.

The results of a regression analysis are shown in Figure 28-19. If you understand regression analysis, the output from this procedure is familiar.

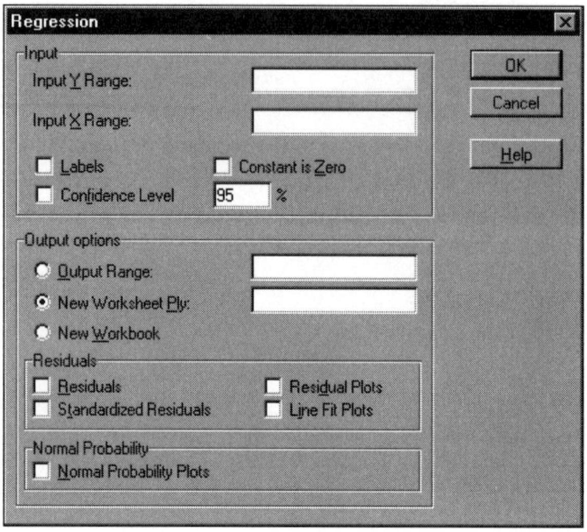

Figure 28-18: The Regression dialog box.

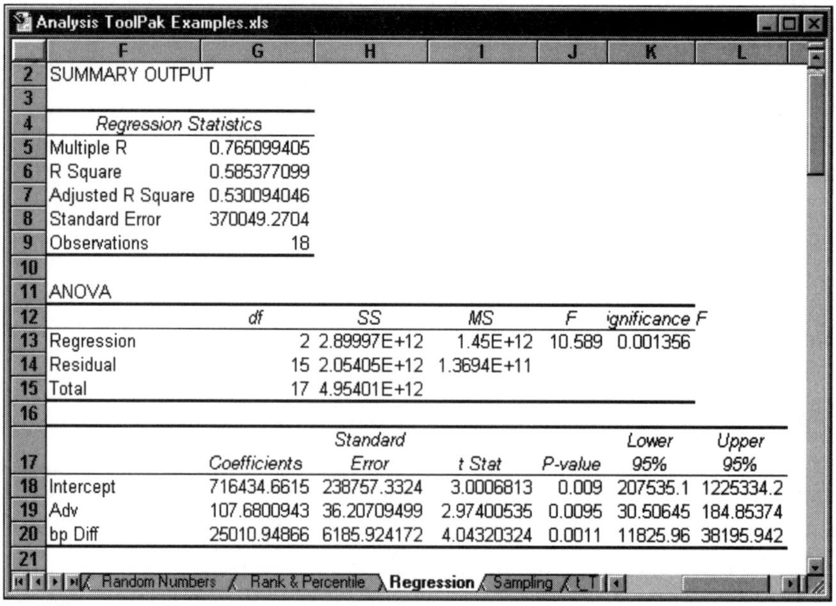

	F	G	H	I	J	K	L
2	SUMMARY OUTPUT						
3							
4	*Regression Statistics*						
5	Multiple R	0.765099405					
6	R Square	0.585377099					
7	Adjusted R Square	0.530094046					
8	Standard Error	370049.2704					
9	Observations	18					
10							
11	ANOVA						
12		*df*	*SS*	*MS*	*F*	*ignificance F*	
13	Regression	2	2.89997E+12	1.45E+12	10.589	0.001356	
14	Residual	15	2.05405E+12	1.3694E+11			
15	Total	17	4.95401E+12				
16							
17		*Coefficients*	*Standard Error*	*t Stat*	*P-value*	*Lower 95%*	*Upper 95%*
18	Intercept	716434.6615	238757.3324	3.0006813	0.009	207535.1	1225334.2
19	Adv	107.6800943	36.20709499	2.97400535	0.0095	30.50645	184.85374
20	bp Diff	25010.94866	6185.924172	4.04320324	0.0011	11825.96	38195.942
21							

Figure 28-19: Sample output from the Regression tool.

Sampling

The Sampling tool generates a random sample from a range of input values. This is useful for working with a subset of a large database. The Sampling dialog box is shown in Figure 28-20. This procedure has two options: periodic and random. A periodic sample selects every *n*th value from the input range, where *n* equals the period that you specify. With a random sample, you simply specify the size of the sample to be selected, and every value has an equal probability of being chosen.

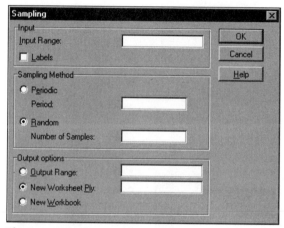

Figure 28-20: The Sampling dialog box is useful for selecting random samples.

t-test

The *t-test* is used to determine whether there is a statistically significant difference between two small samples. The Analysis ToolPak can perform three types of t-tests:

✦ **Paired two-sample for means:** For paired samples, in which you have two observations on each subject (such as a pretest and a posttest). The samples must be the same size.

✦ **Two-sample assuming equal variances:** For independent, rather than paired, samples. It assumes equal variances for the two samples.

✦ **Two-sample assuming unequal variances:** For independent rather than paired samples. It assumes unequal variances for the two samples.

Figure 28-21 shows the dialog box for the paired two-sample t-test. You specify the significance level (alpha) and the hypothesized difference between the two means (that is, the *null hypotheses*).

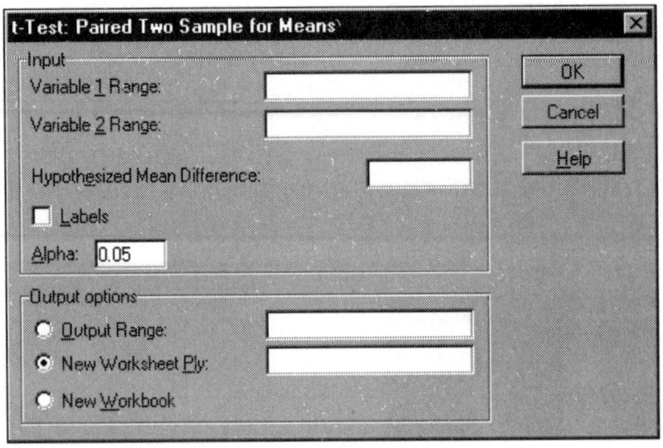

Figure 28-21: The paired t-test dialog box.

Figure 28-22 shows sample output for the paired t-test. Excel calculates *t* for both a one-tailed and two-tailed test.

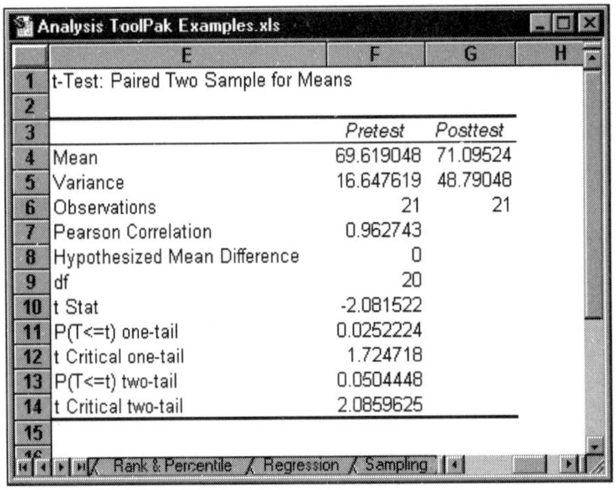

Analysis ToolPak Examples.xls

	E	F	G
1	t-Test: Paired Two Sample for Means		
2			
3		*Pretest*	*Posttest*
4	Mean	69.619048	71.09524
5	Variance	16.647619	48.79048
6	Observations	21	21
7	Pearson Correlation	0.962743	
8	Hypothesized Mean Difference	0	
9	df	20	
10	t Stat	-2.081522	
11	P(T<=t) one-tail	0.0252224	
12	t Critical one-tail	1.724718	
13	P(T<=t) two-tail	0.0504448	
14	t Critical two-tail	2.0859625	
15			

Rank & Percentile / Regression / Sampling

Figure 28-22: Results of a paired t-test.

z-test (two-sample for means)

While t-tests are used for small samples, the z-test is used for larger samples or populations. You must know the variances for both input ranges.

Analysis ToolPak Worksheet Functions

This section lists the worksheet functions available in the Analysis ToolPak. For specific information about the arguments required, click on the Help button in the Function Wizard dialog box.

Remember, the Analysis ToolPak add-in must be installed in order to use these functions in your worksheet. If you use any of these functions in a workbook that you distribute to a colleague, make it clear that the workbook requires the Analysis ToolPak.

These functions appear in the Function Wizard in the following categories:

✦ Date & Time

✦ Engineering (a new category that appears when the Analysis ToolPak is installed)

✦ Financial

✦ Information

✦ Math & Trig

Date & Time category

Table 28-1 lists the Analysis ToolPak worksheet functions in the Date & Time category.

Table 28-1 Date & Time Category Functions	
Function	**Purpose**
EDATE	Returns the serial number of the date that is the indicated number of months before or after the start date
EOMONTH	Returns the serial number of the last day of the month before or after a specified number of months
NETWORKDAYS	Returns the number of whole workdays between two dates
WEEKNUM	Returns the week number in the year
WORKDAY	Returns the serial number of the date before or after a specified number of workdays
YEARFRAC	Returns the year fraction representing the number of whole days between `start_date` and `end_date`

Engineering category

Table 28-2 lists the Analysis ToolPak worksheet functions in the Engineering category. Some of these functions are quite useful for non-engineers as well. For example, the CONVERT function converts a wide variety of measurement units.

Table 28-2	
Engineering Category Functions	
Function	*Purpose*
BESSELI	Returns the modified Bessel function In(x)
BESSELJ	Returns the Bessel function Jn(x)
BESSELK	Returns the modified Bessel function Kn(x)
BESSELY	Returns the Bessel function Yn(x)
BIN2DEC	Converts a binary number to decimal
BIN2HEX	Converts a binary number to hexadecimal
BIN2OCT	Converts a binary number to octal
COMPLEX	Converts real and imaginary coefficients into a complex number
CONVERT	Converts a number from one measurement system to another
DEC2BIN	Converts a decimal number to binary
DEC2HEX	Converts a decimal number to hexadecimal
DEC2OCT	Converts a decimal number to octal
DELTA	Tests whether two numbers are equal
ERF	Returns the error function
ERFC	Returns the complementary error function
FACTDOUBLE	Returns the double factorial of a number
GESTEP	Tests whether a number is greater than a threshold value
HEX2BIN	Converts a hexadecimal number to binary
HEX2DEC	Converts a hexadecimal number to decimal
HEX2OCT	Converts a hexadecimal number to octal
IMABS	Returns the absolute value (modulus) of a complex number
IMAGINARY	Returns the imaginary coefficient of a complex number
IMARGUMENT	Returns the argument q, an angle expressed in radians

Function	Purpose
IMCONJUGATE	Returns the complex conjugate of a complex number
IMCOS	Returns the cosine of a complex number
IMDIV	Returns the quotient of two complex numbers
IMEXP	Returns the exponential of a complex number
IMLN	Returns the natural logarithm of a complex number
IMLOG10	Returns the base-10 logarithm of a complex number
IMLOG2	Returns the base-2 logarithm of a complex number
IMPOWER	Returns a complex number raised to an integer power
IMPRODUCT	Returns the product of two complex numbers
IMREAL	Returns the real coefficient of a complex number
IMSIN	Returns the sine of a complex number
IMSQRT	Returns the square root of a complex number
IMSUB	Returns the difference of two complex numbers
IMSUM	Returns the sum of complex numbers
OCT2BIN	Converts an octal number to binary
OCT2DEC	Converts an octal number to decimal
OCT2HEX	Converts an octal number to hexadecimal

Financial category

Table 28-3 lists the Analysis ToolPak worksheet functions in the Financial category.

Table 28-3 Financial Category Functions	
Function	**Purpose**
ACCRINT	Returns the accrued interest for a security that pays periodic interest
ACCRINTM	Returns the accrued interest for a security that pays interest at maturity
AMORDEGRC	Returns the prorated linear depreciation of an asset for each accounting period
AMORLINC	Returns the prorated linear depreciation of an asset for each accounting period
COUPDAYBS	Returns the number of days from the beginning of the coupon period to the settlement date

(continued)

Table 28-3 *(continued)*

Function	Purpose
COUPDAYS	Returns the number of days in the coupon period that contain the settlement date
COUPDAYSNC	Returns the number of days from the settlement date to the next coupon date
COUPNCD	Returns the next coupon date after the settlement date
COUPNUM	Returns the number of coupons payable between the settlement date and maturity date
COUPPCD	Returns the previous coupon date before the settlement date
CUMIPMT	Returns the cumulative interest paid between two periods
CUMPRINC	Returns the cumulative principal paid on a loan between two periods
DISC	Returns the discount rate for a security
DOLLARDE	Converts a dollar price, expressed as a fraction, into a dollar price, expressed as a decimal number
DOLLARFR	Converts a dollar price, expressed as a decimal number, into a dollar price, expressed as a fraction
DURATION	Returns the annual duration of a security with periodic interest payments
EFFECT	Returns the effective annual interest rate
FVSCHEDULE	Returns the future value of an initial principal after applying a series of compound interest rates
INTRATE	Returns the interest rate for a fully invested security
MDURATION	Returns the Macauley modified duration for a security with an assumed par value of $100
NOMINAL	Returns the annual nominal interest rate
ODDFPRICE	Returns the price per $100 face value of a security with an odd first period
ODDFYIELD	Returns the yield of a security with an odd first period
ODDLPRICE	Returns the price per $100 face value of a security with an odd last period
ODDLYIELD	Returns the yield of a security with an odd last period
PRICE	Returns the price per $100 face value of a security that pays periodic interest

Function	Purpose
PRICEDISC	Returns the price per $100 face value of a discounted security
PRICEMAT	Returns the price per $100 face value of a security that pays interest at maturity
RECEIVED	Returns the amount received at maturity for a fully invested security
TBILLEQ	Returns the bond-equivalent yield for a Treasury bill
TBILLPRICE	Returns the price per $100 face value for a Treasury bill
TBILLYIELD	Returns the yield for a Treasury bill
XIRR	Returns the internal rate of return for a schedule of cash flows
XNPV	Returns the net present value for a schedule of cash flows
YIELD	Returns the yield on a security that pays periodic interest
YIELDDISC	Returns the annual yield for a discounted security (for example, a Treasury bill)
YIELDMAT	Returns the annual yield of a security that pays interest at maturity

Information category

Table 28-4 lists the two Analysis ToolPak worksheet functions in the Information category.

Table 28-4 Information Category Functions	
Function	**Purpose**
ISEVEN	Returns TRUE if the number is even
ISODD	Returns TRUE if the number is odd

Math & Trig category

Table 28-5 lists the Analysis ToolPak worksheet functions in the Math & Trig category.

Table 28-5 Math & Trig Category Functions	
Function	*Purpose*
GCD	Returns the greatest common divisor
LCM	Returns the least common multiple
MROUND	Returns a number rounded to the desired multiple
MULTINOMIAL	Returns the multinomial of a set of numbers
QUOTIENT	Returns the integer portion of a division
RANDBETWEEN	Returns a random number between the numbers that you specify
SERIESSUM	Returns the sum of a power series based on the formula
SQRTPI	Returns the square root of pi

Summary

In this chapter, I discuss the Analysis ToolPak, an add-in that extends the analytical powers of Excel. It includes 19 analytic procedures and 93 new functions. Many of the tools are useful for general business applications, but many are for more specialized uses such as statistical tests.

✦   ✦   ✦

Other Topics

T he three chapters in Part V deal with topics that don't
fit into the other parts. In Chapter 29, I describe how to
share data with other applications by using links. Chapter
30 is devoted to techniques that can make your worksheets
as accurate as possible. Chapter 31 covers the lighter side
of Excel and presents some amusing (and instructive)
games.

P A R T

V

Sharing Data with Other Applications

In This Chapter

Using the Clipboard
to copy data to and
from applications

Creating dynamic
links to other
applications

Embedding objects
from other
applications

Becoming acquainted
with Microsoft Office
binders

Increasingly, Windows applications are designed to work together. The applications in Microsoft Office are a good example. These programs have a common look and feel, and it's quite easy to share data among these applications. In this chapter I explore some ways that you can make use of other applications while working with Excel, along with ways that you can use Excel while working with other applications.

Sharing Data with Other Windows Applications

Besides importing and exporting files, there are essentially three ways to transfer data to and from other Windows applications:

✦ Copy and paste using the Windows Clipboard. This creates a static copy of the data.

✦ Create a link, so changes in the source data are reflected in the destination document.

✦ Embed an entire object from another application into a document.

In the following sections, I discuss these techniques and present an example for each one.

Using the Windows Clipboard

As you probably know, whenever Windows is running, you have access to the Windows Clipboard — an area of your computer's memory that acts as a shared holding area for information that has been cut or copied from an application. The Clipboard works behind the scenes, and you usually aren't aware of it. Whenever you select the Edit⇨Copy or Edit⇨Cut commands, the selected data is placed on the Clipboard. Like most other Windows applications, Excel can then access the Clipboard data by way of the Edit⇨Paste command.

Note   Data pasted from the Clipboard remains on the Clipboard after pasting, so you can use it multiple times. But because the Clipboard can hold only one item at a time, when you copy or cut something else, the old Clipboard contents are replaced.

Copying information from one Windows application to another is quite easy. The application that you're copying from is considered the *source application,* and the application that you're copying to is the *destination application.*

Following are the general steps required to copy from one application to another. This applies both to copying from Excel to another application, and copying from another application to Excel.

1. Activate the source document window that contains the information you want to copy.

2. Select the information by using the mouse or the keyboard. If Excel is the source application, this information can be a cell, range, chart, or drawn object.

3. Select Edit⇨Copy. A copy of the information is sent to the Windows Clipboard.

4. Activate the destination application. If the program isn't running, you can start it without affecting the contents of the Clipboard.

5. Move to the appropriate position in the destination application (where you want to paste it).

6. Select Edit⇨Paste from the menu in the destination application. If the Clipboard contents are not appropriate for pasting, the Paste command is grayed out (not available).

If you're copying a graphics image, you may have to resize or crop it. If you're copying text, you may have to reformat it by using tools available in the destination application. The information that you copied from the source application remains intact, and a copy remains on the Clipboard until you copy something else.

Note   In Step 3 in the preceding steps, you also can select Edit⇨Cut from the source application menu. This step erases the selection from the source application after it is placed on the Clipboard.

Figure 29-1 shows an embedded Excel chart. You can easily insert a copy of this chart into a Word for Windows report. First, select the chart in Excel by clicking on it once. Then copy it to the Clipboard with the Edit⇨Copy command. Next, activate the Word for Windows document into which you want to paste the copy of the chart and move the insertion point to the place where you want the chart placed. When you select Edit⇨Paste from the Word for Windows menu, the chart is pasted from the Clipboard and appears in your document (see Figure 29-2).

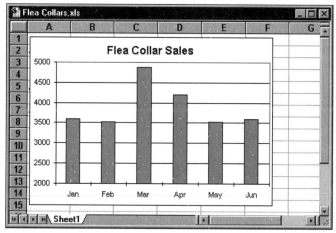

Figure 29-1: An Excel chart ready to be copied into Word for Windows.

Note It's important to understand that Windows applications vary in the way they respond to data pasted from the Clipboard. If the Edit⇨Paste command is not available (grayed out on the menu) in the destination application, the application can't accept the information on the Clipboard. If you copy a range of data from Excel to the Clipboard and paste it into Word for Windows, Word creates a table when the data is pasted. Other applications may respond differently to this data. If you plan to do a great deal of copying and pasting, the best advice is to experiment until you understand how the two applications can handle each other's data.

An important point here is that this copy-and-paste technique is static. In other words, no link exists between what gets copied from the source application and the destination application. If you're copying from Excel to a word processing document, subsequent changes in your Excel worksheet or charts are *not* reflected in the word processing document. Consequently, you have to repeat the copy-and-paste procedure to update the source document with the changes. The next topic presents a way to get around this limitation.

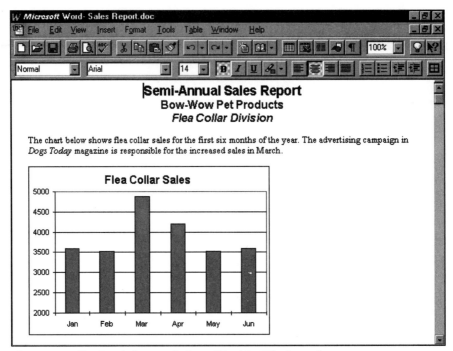

Figure 29-2: The Excel chart copied to a Word for Windows document.

Linking Data

If you want to share data that may change, the static copy and paste procedure described in the preceeding section isn't your best choice. A better solution is to create a dynamic link between data copied from one Windows application to another. So, if the data changes in the source document, these changes are made automatically in the destination document.

When would you want to use this technique? If you generate proposals using a word processor, for example, you may need to refer to pricing information stored in an Excel worksheet. If you set up a link between your word processing document and the Excel worksheet, you can be assured that your proposals always quote the latest prices. Not all Windows applications support dynamic linking, so you must make sure that the application to which you are copying is capable of handling such a link.

Creating links

Setting up a link from one Windows application to another isn't difficult, although the process varies slightly from application to application. Following are the general steps to take:

1. Activate the window in the source application that contains the information that you want to copy.

2. Select the information by using the mouse or the keyboard. If Excel is the server, you can select a cell, range, or entire chart.

3. Select Edit⇨Copy from the source application's menu. A copy of the information is sent to the Windows Clipboard.

4. Activate the destination application. If it isn't open, you can start it without affecting the contents of the Clipboard.

5. Move to the appropriate position in the destination application.

6. Select the appropriate command in the destination application to paste a link. The command varies depending on the application. In Microsoft Office applications, the command is Edit⇨Paste Special.

7. It's likely that a dialog box will appear that lets you specify the type of link to create. The following section provides more details.

More about links

Keep in mind the following when you're using links between two applications:

✦ Not all Windows applications support linking. Furthermore, some programs can be linked *from* but not linked *to*. When in doubt, consult the documentation for the application with which you're dealing.

✦ When you save an Excel file that has a link, the most recent values are saved with the document. When you reopen this document, you are asked whether you want to update the links.

✦ Links can be severed rather easily. If you move the source document to another directory or save it under a different name, for example, the client document is incapable of updating the link. You can usually reestablish the link manually, if you understand how the application manages the links. In Excel, you do this with the Edit⇨Links command, which results in the dialog box shown in Figure 29-3.

✦ You also can use the Edit⇨Links command to break a link.

✦ In Excel, external links are stored in array formulas. If you know what you're doing, you can modify a link by editing the array formula.

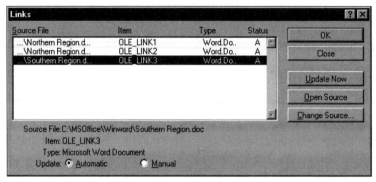

Figure 29-3: The Links dialog box lets you work with links to other applications.

✦ When Excel is running, it responds to link requests from other applications unless you have disabled remote requests. To do this, choose the Tools⮂Options command and select the General tab. Check the Ignore Other Applications check box if you don't want the links to be updated.

Copying Excel Data to Word for Windows

One of the most frequently used software combinations is a spreadsheet and a word processor. In this section, I discuss the types of links that you can create using Microsoft Word for Windows.

Note Most information in this section also applies to other word processors, such as WordPerfect for Windows, and Word Pro. The exact techniques vary, however. I use Word for Windows in the examples because readers who acquired Excel as part of the Microsoft Office have Word installed on their systems. If you don't have a word processor installed on your system, you can use the WordPad application that comes with Windows. The manner in which WordPad handles links is very similar to Word for Windows.

Figure 29-4 shows the Paste Special dialog box from Microsoft Word when a range of data from Excel is on the Clipboard. The result that you get depends on whether the Paste or the Paste Link option is selected and on your choice of the type of item to paste. If you select the Paste Link option, you can choose to have the information pasted as an icon. If so, you can double-click on this icon to activate the source worksheet.

Pasting without a link

Often, you don't need a link when you copy data. For example, if you're preparing a report in your word processor and you simply want to include a range of data from an Excel worksheet, you probably don't need to create a link.

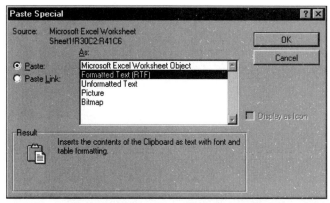

Figure 29-4: The Paste Special dialog box is where you specify the type of link to create.

Table 29-1 describes the effect of choosing the various paste choices when the Paste option is selected — the option that doesn't create a link to the source data.

Table 29-1	
Result of Using the Paste Special Command in Word for Windows (Paste Option)	
Paste Type	**Result**
Microsoft Excel Worksheet Object	An object that includes the Excel formatting. This creates an embedded object, which I describe in the next section of the book.
Formatted Text (RTF)	A Word table, formatted as the original Excel range. There is no link to the source. This produces the same result as using the standard Edit⇨Paste command.
Unformatted Text	Text (not a table) that corresponds to Word's Normal style. Formatting from Excel is not transferred, and there is no link to the source.
Picture	A picture object that retains the formatting from Excel. There is no link to the source. This usually produces better results than the Bitmap option. Double-clicking lets you edit the picture.
Bitmap	A bitmap object that retains the formatting from Excel. There is no link to the source. Double-clicking lets you edit the bitmap.

Figure 29-5 shows how a copied range from Excel appears in Word for Windows using each of the paste special formats.

Note   The pasted data *looks* the same regardless of whether the Paste or Paste Link option is selected.

Note   Some Excel formatting does not transfer when pasted to Word as formatted text. For example, Word doesn't support vertical alignment for table cells (you can use Word's paragraph formatting commands to do this).

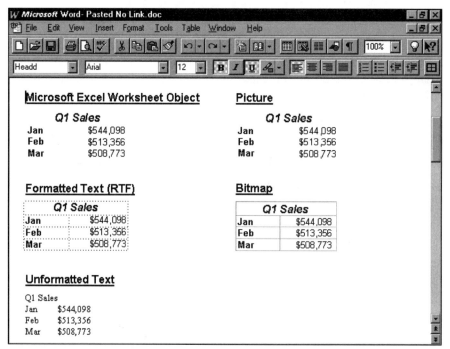

Figure 29-5: Data copied from Excel and pasted using various formats.

Pasting with a link

If the data that you're copying is subject to change, you may want to paste a link. If you paste the data using the Paste Link option in the Paste Special dialog box, you can make changes to the source document and the changes appear in the destination application (a few-seconds delay may occur). The best way to test these changes is to display both applications on-screen, make changes to the source document, and watch for them to appear in the destination document.

Table 29-2 describes the effect of choosing the various paste choices in Word for Windows' Paste Special dialog box when the Paste Link option is selected.

Table 29-2 Result of Using the Paste Special Command in Word for Windows (Paste Link Option)	
Paste Type	*Result*
Microsoft Excel Worksheet Object	A linked object that includes the Excel formatting. Double-click to edit the source data in Excel.
Formatted Text (RTF)	A Word table formatted as the original Excel range. Changes in the source are reflected automatically.
Unformatted Text	Text (not a table) that corresponds to Word's Normal style. Formatting from Excel is not transferred. Changes in the source are reflected automatically.
Picture	A picture object that retains the formatting from Excel. Changes in the source are reflected automatically. This usually produces better results than the Bitmap option. Double-click to edit the source data in Excel.
Bitmap	A bitmap object that retains the formatting from Excel. Changes in the source are reflected automatically. Double-click to edit the source data in Excel.

Embedding Objects

Another method of sharing information between Windows applications is to embed an object in the document. This is known as *Object Linking and Embedding* (OLE). This technique lets you insert an object from another program and use the other program's editing tools to manipulate it whenever you want. The OLE objects can be items such as the ones in this list:

✦ Text documents from other products, such as word processors

✦ Drawings or pictures from other products

✦ Information from special OLE server applications such as Microsoft Word Art and Microsoft Equation

✦ Sound files

✦ Video or animation files

Most of the major Windows applications support OLE. You can embed an object into document in two ways:

✦ Use the Edit⇨Paste Special command and select the "object" choice (if it's available). If you do this, select the Paste option rather than the Paste Link option.

✦ Use the Insert⇨Object command.

Note Some applications, such as those in Microsoft Office, also can embed an object by dragging it from one application to another.

The following sections discuss these two methods and provide a few examples using Excel and Word for Windows.

Embedding an Excel range in a Word document

In this example, the range shown in Figure 29-6 will be embedded in a Word for Windows document.

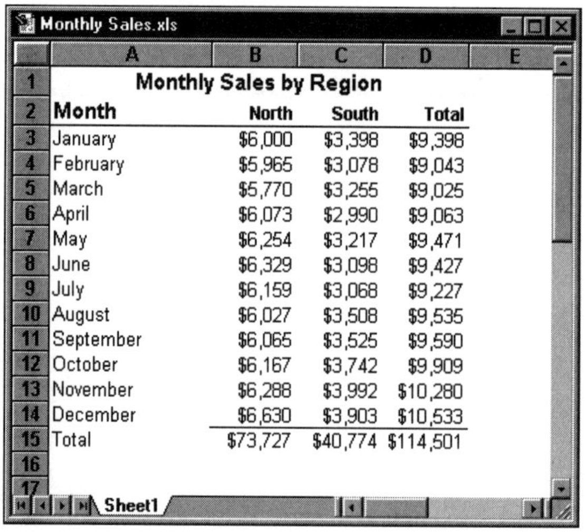

	A	B	C	D	E
1	Monthly Sales by Region				
2	Month	North	South	Total	
3	January	$6,000	$3,398	$9,398	
4	February	$5,965	$3,078	$9,043	
5	March	$5,770	$3,255	$9,025	
6	April	$6,073	$2,990	$9,063	
7	May	$6,254	$3,217	$9,471	
8	June	$6,329	$3,098	$9,427	
9	July	$6,159	$3,068	$9,227	
10	August	$6,027	$3,508	$9,535	
11	September	$6,065	$3,525	$9,590	
12	October	$6,167	$3,742	$9,909	
13	November	$6,288	$3,992	$10,280	
14	December	$6,630	$3,903	$10,533	
15	Total	$73,727	$40,774	$114,501	
16					
17					

Figure 29-6: This range will be embedded in a Word document.

To start, select A1:D15 and copy the range to the Clipboard. Then, activate (or start) Word for Windows. Move the insertion point to the location in the document where you want the table to be. Choose Word's Edit⇨Paste Special command. Select the Paste option (not Paste Link) and choose the Microsoft Excel Worksheet Object format (see Figure 29-7). Click on OK, and the range is pasted to the document.

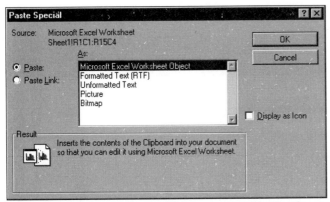

Figure 29-7: This operation embeds an Excel object in a Word document.

The pasted object is not a standard Word for Windows table. For example, you'll find that you can't select or format individual cells in the table. Furthermore, it's not linked to the Excel source range. If you change a value in the Excel worksheet, the change does not appear in the embedded object in the Word document.

If you double-click on the object, however, you'll notice something unusual: Word's menus and toolbars change to those used by Excel. In addition, the embedded object appears with Excel's familiar row and column borders. In other words, you can edit this object *in place* using Excel's commands. Figure 29-8 shows how this looks. To get back to normal, just click anywhere in the Word document.

Note Remember that no link is involved here. If you make changes to the embedded object in Word, these changes are not reflected in the original Excel worksheet. The embedded object is completely independent from the original source.

The advantage to this technique is that you have access to all features in Excel while you are still in Word. Microsoft's ultimate goal is to allow users to focus on their documents — not the application that produces the document.

Tip You can accomplish the embedding as described previously by selecting the range in Excel and then dragging it to your Word document. In fact, you can use the Windows desktop as an intermediary storage location. For example, you can drag a range from Excel to the desktop and create a *scrap*. Then, you can drag this scrap into Word for Windows. The result is an embedded Excel object.

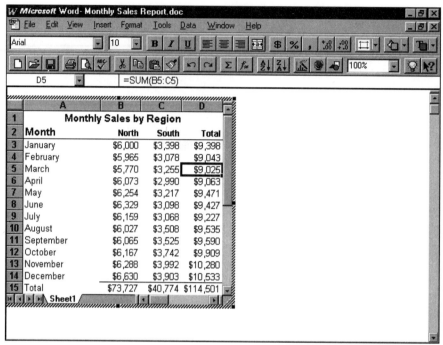

Figure 29-8: Double-clicking on the embedded Excel object lets you edit it in place. Note that Word now displays Excel's menus and toolbars.

Creating a new Excel object in Word

In the preceeding example, a range from an existing Excel worksheet was embedded into a Word document. In this section, I demonstrate how to create a new (empty) Excel object in Word. This may be useful if you're creating a report and need to insert a table of values that doesn't exist in a worksheet. You could insert a normal Word table, but you can take advantage of Excel's formulas and functions to make this task much easier.

To create a new Excel object in a Word document, choose the Insert⇨Object command. Word responds with the dialog box shown in Figure 29-9. The Create New panel lists the types of objects that you can create (this depends on what applications are installed on your system). Choose the Microsoft Excel Worksheet option and click on OK.

Word inserts an empty Excel worksheet object into the document and activates it for you, as shown in Figure 29-10. You have full access to Excel commands, so you can enter whatever you like into the worksheet object. When you're finished, click anywhere in the document. You can, of course, double-click on this object at any time to make changes or additions.

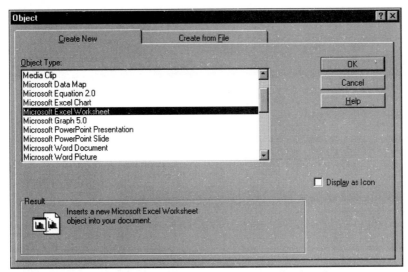

Figure 29-9: Word's Object dialog box lets you create a new object.

Note You can change the size of the object while it's activated by dragging the borders. When the object is not activated, you can crop it to display only cells that contain information. To crop an object in Word, press Shift while you drag a border of the object.

Embedding an existing workbook in Word

Yet another option is to embed an existing workbook into a Word document. Use Word's Insert⇨Object command. In the Object dialog box, click on the tab labeled Create from File (see Figure 29-11). Click on the Browse button and locate the Excel workbook that you want to embed.

A *copy* of the selected workbook is embedded in the Word document. You can double-click on it to make changes, or use it as is. Note that any changes you make to this copy of the document are not reflected in the original workbook.

Embedding objects in an Excel worksheet

The preceding examples involve embedding Excel objects in a Word for Windows document. You'll find that the same procedures can be used for embedding other objects into an Excel worksheet.

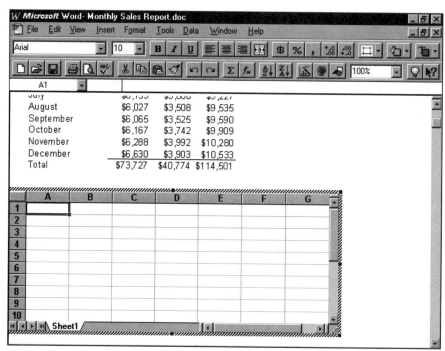

Figure 29-10: Word created an empty Excel worksheet object.

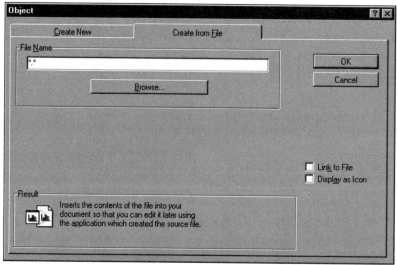

Figure 29-11: This dialog box lets you locate a file to embed in the active document.

For example, if you have an Excel workbook that requires a great amount of explanatory text, you have several choices:

- ✦ You can enter the text into cells. This is tedious and doesn't allow much formatting.

- ✦ You can use a text box. This is a good alternative, but it doesn't offer many formatting features.

- ✦ You can embed a Word document in your worksheet. This gives you full access to all of Word's formatting features.

To embed an empty Word document into an Excel worksheet, choose Excel's Insert⇨Object command. In the Object dialog box, click on the Create New tab and select Microsoft Word Document from the Object Type list.

The result is a blank Word document, activated and ready for you to enter text. Notice that Excel's menus and toolbars are replaced with those from Word. You can resize the document to any size, and the words wrap accordingly. Figure 29-12 shows an example of a Word document embedded in an Excel worksheet.

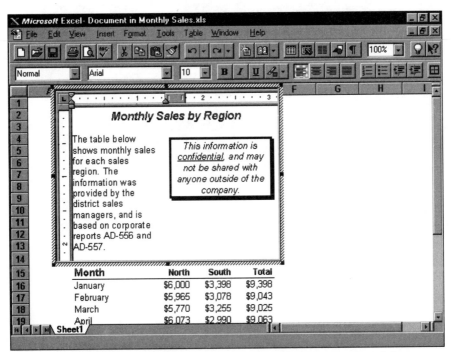

Figure 29-12: A Word for Windows document embedded in an Excel worksheet. The text on the right is contained in a frame (one of Word's formatting features).

You can embed many other types of objects, including audio clips, video clips, MIDI sequences, and even an entire Microsoft PowerPoint presentation.

Note   When you embed a video clip, the actual file is not stored in the Excel document. Rather, a pointer to the original file is used. If, for some reason, you want to embed the complete video clip file, you can use the Object Packager application. Be aware, however, that video clip files are typically quite large, and the time required to open and save the workbook is lengthy.

Microsoft Office includes a few additional applications that you may find useful. These can all be embedded in Excel documents:

✦ **Microsoft Equation:** Lets you create equations (see Figure 29-13 for an example).

✦ **Microsoft Word Art:** Lets you modify text in some interesting ways. Figure 29-14 shows an example.

✦ **MS Organization Chart:** Lets you create attractive organizational charts, as shown in Figure 29-15.

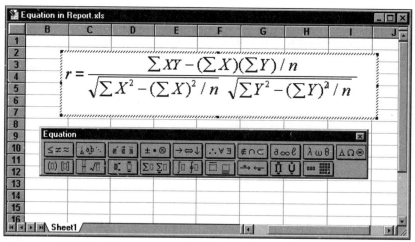

Figure 29-13: This object was created with Microsoft Equation.

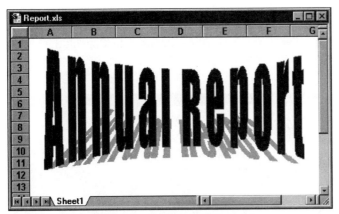

Figure 29-14: An example of Microsoft Word Art.

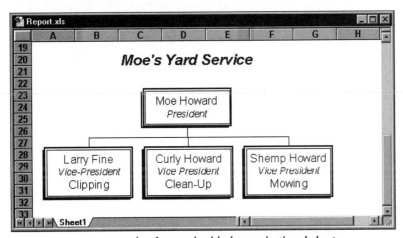

Figure 29-15: An example of an embedded organizational chart.

Using Office Binders

If you have Microsoft Office installed, you may take advantage of a new feature known as *binders*. A binder is a container that can hold documents from different applications: Excel, Word for Windows, and PowerPoint.

You may find that a binder is useful when working on a project that involves documents from different applications. For example, you may be preparing a sales presentation that uses charts and tables from Excel, reports and memos from Word, and slides prepared with PowerPoint. You can store all the information in a single file. Another advantage is that you can print the entire binder, and all pages are numbered successively.

To use a binder, start the Binder application. You get an empty binder. You then can add existing documents or create new documents in the binder. Figure 29-16 shows a binder that contains Word, Excel, and PowerPoint documents. Consult the online help for complete details on using this feature.

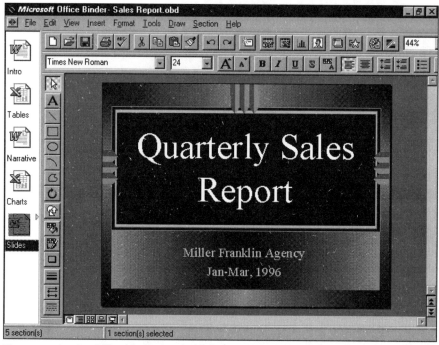

Figure 29-16: An Office binder can hold documents produced by different applications.

Summary

In this chapter, I describe techniques that allow you to use data from other applications. These techniques include standard copy and paste using the Windows Clipboard, dynamic linking between applications, and embedding objects. I also note that Microsoft Office has a new binder feature that lets you work with documents produced by different applications.

✦　　✦　　✦

Making Your Worksheets Error-Free

◆ ◆ ◆ ◆

In This Chapter

An overview of the problems that crop up in spreadsheets

How to trace the relationships between cells in a worksheet

Tools to ensure that your worksheet doesn't contain spelling errors

Techniques that help you understand an unfamiliar workbook

◆ ◆ ◆ ◆

The ultimate goal in developing a spreadsheet solution is to generate accurate results. For simple worksheets, this isn't difficult, and you can usually tell whether the results are correct. But when your worksheets get large or complex, ensuring accuracy becomes more difficult. This chapter provides you with tools and techniques to help you identify and correct errors.

Types of Worksheet Problems

Making a change in a worksheet — even a relatively minor change — may produce a ripple effect that introduces errors in other cells. For example, it's all too easy to accidentally enter a value into a cell that formerly held a formula. This can have a major impact on other formulas, and you may not discover the problem until it's too late. Or you may *never* discover the problem.

An Excel worksheet can have many types of problems. Some problems — such as a formula that returns an error value — are immediately apparent. Other problems are more subtle. For example, if a formula was constructed using faulty logic, it may never return an error value — it simply returns the wrong values. If you're lucky, you'll discover the problem and correct it.

Following are common problems that occur in worksheets:

✦ Incorrect approach to a problem

✦ Faulty logic in a formula

✦ Formulas that return error values

✦ Circular references

✦ Spelling mistakes

✦ Worksheet is new to you, and you can't figure out how it works

Excel provides tools to help you identify and correct some of these problems. In the remaining sections, I discuss these tools along with others that I've developed.

Tracing Cell Relationships

Excel has several useful tools that help you track down errors and logical flaws in your worksheets. In this section, I discuss the following:

✦ Info window

✦ Go To Special dialog box

✦ Excel's built-in auditing tools

These tools are useful for debugging formulas. As you probably realize by now, the formulas in a worksheet can become complicated and refer (directly or indirectly) to hundreds or thousands of other cells. Trying to isolate a problem in a tangled web of formulas can be frustrating.

Before I discuss the features, there are two concepts with which you should be familiar:

✦ **Cell precedents**: This is applicable only to cells that contain a formula. A formula cell's precedents are all cells that contribute to the formula's result. A direct precedent is a cell that is used directly in the formula. An indirect precedent is a cell that is not used directly in the formula but is used by a cell that is referred to in the formula.

✦ **Cell dependents:** Formula cells that depend on a particular cell. Again, the formula cell can be a direct dependent or an indirect dependent.

Often, identifying cell precedents for a formula cell sheds light on why the formula isn't working correctly. On the other hand, it's often helpful to know what formula cells depend on a particular cell.

Using the Info window

Excel offers a useful feature called the *Info window*. My guess is that about 90 percent of Excel users don't know that this feature exists. The Info window is a free-floating window that displays information about the active cell. It's read-only, so you can't make any changes to the information.

To display the Info window, choose the Tools⇨Options command and check the box labeled Info Window in the View panel. Or, you can click on the Show Info Window button on the Auditing toolbar. To close the Info window, click on the Close button in its title bar.

Figure 30-1 shows the Info window on the right side of the screen. As you scroll through the worksheet, the Info window is updated to reflect information for the active cell.

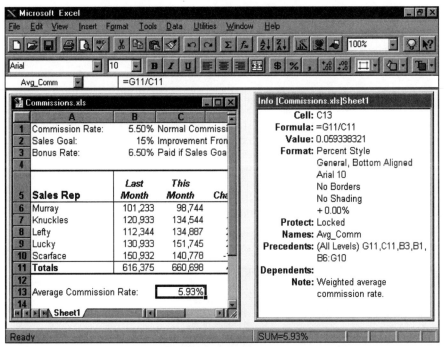

Figure 30-1: The Info window displays key information about the active cell.

By default, the Info window shows only the cell address, the formula, and the cell note. You can determine what types of information are shown in the Info window. When the window is active, a new menu — Info — is available. You can use this menu to select the type of information to display. Your choices are as follows:

Cell: Displays the cell's address.

Formula: Displays the cell's formula, if it has one.

Value: Displays the current value of the cell.

Format: Displays information about the formatting for the cell: its style, number format, alignment, font, border, and pattern.

Protection: Whether the cell is locked, and whether its formula is hidden.

Names: Displays names that use the cell. If the cell is part of a named range, the name appears here.

Precedents: Displays the addresses of the cells on which the cell depends (applicable only if the cell contains a formula). You can choose between direct precedents and all precedents.

Dependents: Displays the addresses of the cells that depend on this cell. You can choose between direct dependents and all dependents.

Note: Displays the cell note, if any.

The options that you select for the Info window aren't saved, so you need to reselect them every time you open the Info window.

The Go To Special dialog box

The Go To Special dialog box can be useful because it lets you specify cells of a certain type that will be selected. To bring up this dialog box, choose the Edit⇨Go To command (or press F5). This displays the Go To dialog box. Click on the Special button, which displays the Go To Special dialog box, shown in Figure 30-2.

If you select a range before issuing the Edit⇨Go To command, the command only looks at the selected cells. If only a single cell is selected, the command operates on the entire worksheet.

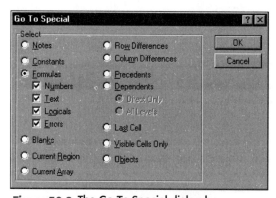

Figure 30-2: The Go To Special dialog box.

You can use this dialog box to select cells of a certain type — which can often be helpful in identifying errors. For example, if you choose the Formulas option, Excel selects all cells that contain a formula. If the worksheet is zoomed out to a small size, this can give you a good idea of how the worksheet is organized (see Figure 30-3). It may also help you spot a common error of a formula overwritten by a value. If you find a cell that's not selected amid a group of selected formula cells, chances are good that the cell formerly contained a formula, but it was replaced by a value.

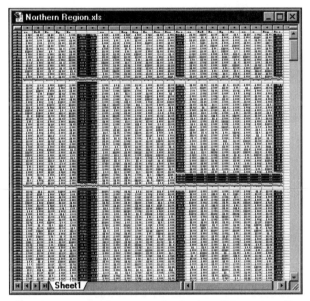

Figure 30-3: Zooming out and selecting all formula cells can give you a good overview of how the worksheet is designed.

You also can use the Go To Special dialog box to identify cell precedents and dependents. In this case, Excel selects all cells that qualify. In either case, you can choose whether to display direct or all levels.

Excel has shortcut keys that you can use to select precedents and dependents. These are listed in Table 30-1.

Table 30-1	
Shortcut Keys to Select Precedents and Dependents	
Key Combination	*What It Selects*
Ctrl+[	Direct precedents
Ctrl+Shift+[	All precedents
Ctrl+]	Direct dependents
Ctrl+Shift+]	All dependents

Tip   You also can select a formula cell's direct dependents by double-clicking on the cell. This technique, however, works only when the Edit Directly in Cell Option is turned off in the Edit panel of the Options dialog box.

Excel's auditing tools

Excel provides a set of interactive auditing tools that you may find helpful. Access these tools by using the Tools⇨Auditing command (which results in a submenu with additional choices), or from the Auditing toolbar, shown in Figure 30-4.

Figure 30-4: The Auditing toolbar.

The tools on the Auditing toolbar, from left to right, are as follows:

✦ **Trace Precedents:** Draws arrows to indicate a formula cell's precedents. Click on this multiple times to see additional levels of precedents.

✦ **Remove Precedent Arrows:** Removes the most recently placed set of precedent arrows.

✦ **Trace Dependents:** Draws arrows to indicate a cell's dependents. Click on this multiple times to see additional levels of dependents.

✦ **Remove Dependent Arrows:** Removes the most recently placed set of dependent arrows.

✦ **Remove All Arrows:** Removes all precedent and dependent arrows from the worksheet.

✦ **Trace Error:** Draws arrows from a cell that contains an error to the cells that may have caused the error.

✦ **Attach Note:** Displays the Cell Note dialog box. This really doesn't have much to do with auditing. It lets you attach a note to a cell.

✦ **Show Info Window:** Displays the Info window (described earlier).

These tools can identify precedents and dependents by drawing arrows (known as cell tracers) on the worksheet. Figure 30-5 shows an example of this. In this case, I selected cell G11 and then clicked on the Trace Precedents toolbar button. Excel drew lines to indicate which cells are used by the formula in G11 (direct precedents).

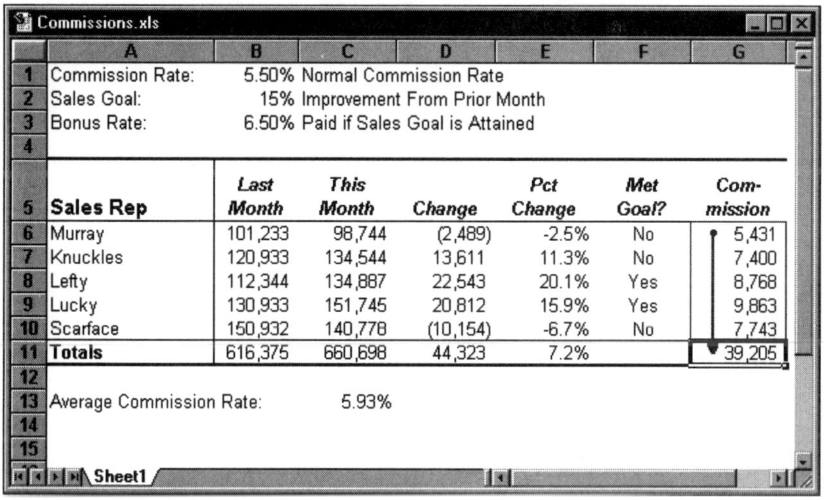

	A	B	C	D	E	F	G
	Commissions.xls						
1	Commission Rate:	5.50%	Normal Commission Rate				
2	Sales Goal:	15%	Improvement From Prior Month				
3	Bonus Rate:	6.50%	Paid if Sales Goal is Attained				
4							
5	**Sales Rep**	*Last Month*	*This Month*	*Change*	*Pct Change*	*Met Goal?*	*Com- mission*
6	Murray	101,233	98,744	(2,489)	-2.5%	No	5,431
7	Knuckles	120,933	134,544	13,611	11.3%	No	7,400
8	Lefty	112,344	134,887	22,543	20.1%	Yes	8,768
9	Lucky	130,933	151,745	20,812	15.9%	Yes	9,863
10	Scarface	150,932	140,778	(10,154)	-6.7%	No	7,743
11	Totals	616,375	660,698	44,323	7.2%		39,205
12							
13	Average Commission Rate:		5.93%				
14							
15							

Sheet1

Figure 30-5: Excel draws line to indicate a cell's precedents.

Figure 30-6 shows what happens when I click on the Trace Precedents button again. This time it adds more lines to show the indirect precedents. The result is a graphical representation of the cells that are used (directly or indirectly) by the formula in cell G11.

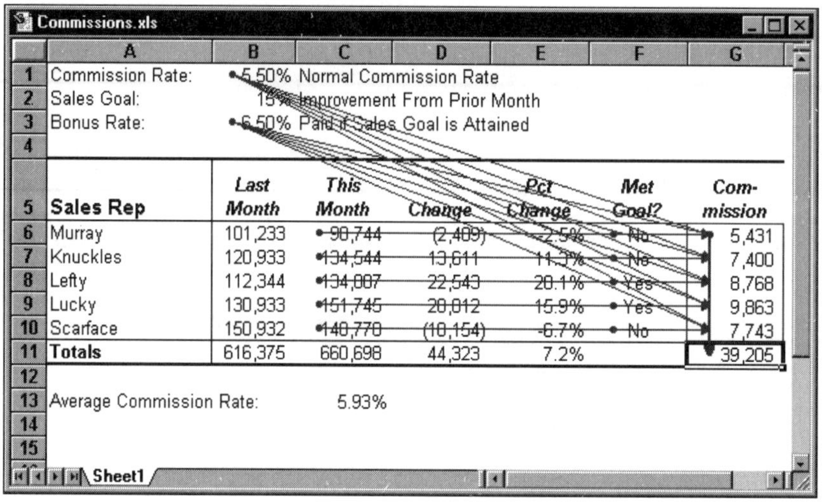

	A	B	C	D	E	F	G
	Commissions.xls						
1	Commission Rate:	5.50%	Normal Commission Rate				
2	Sales Goal:	15%	Improvement From Prior Month				
3	Bonus Rate:	6.50%	Paid if Sales Goal is Attained				
4							
5	**Sales Rep**	*Last Month*	*This Month*	*Change*	*Pct Change*	*Met Goal?*	*Com- mission*
6	Murray	101,233	98,744	(2,489)	-2.5%	No	5,431
7	Knuckles	120,933	134,544	13,611	11.3%	No	7,400
8	Lefty	112,344	134,887	22,543	20.1%	Yes	8,768
9	Lucky	130,933	151,745	20,812	15.9%	Yes	9,863
10	Scarface	150,932	140,778	(10,154)	-6.7%	No	7,743
11	**Totals**	616,375	660,698	44,323	7.2%		39,205
12							
13	Average Commission Rate:		5.93%				
14							
15							

Figure 30-6: Excel draws more lines to indicate the indirect precedents.

Tip This type of interactive tracing is often more revealing when the worksheet is zoomed out to display a larger area.

The best way to learn about these tools is to use them. Start with a worksheet that has formulas and experiment with the various buttons on the Auditing toolbar.

Tracing error values

The Trace Error button on the Auditing toolbar helps you identify the cell that is causing an error value to appear. Often, an error in one cell is the result of an error in a precedent cell. Activate a cell that contains an error and click on the Trace Error button. Excel draws arrows to indicate the error source.

Table 30-2 lists the types of error values that may appear in a cell that has a formula. The Trace Error button works with all these errors.

Table 30-2
Excel Error Values

Error Value	Explanation
#DIV/0!	The formula is trying to divide by zero (an operation that's not allowed on this planet). This also occurs when the formula attempts to divide by a cell that is empty.
#NAME?	The formula uses a name that Excel doesn't recognize. This can happen if you delete a name that's used in the formula or if you have unmatched quotes when using text.
#N/A	The formula refers to an empty cell range.
#NULL!	The formula uses an intersection of two ranges that do not intersect (this concept is described later in the chapter).
#NUM!	There is a problem with a value — for example, you specified a negative number where a positive number is expected.
#REF!	The formula refers to a cell that is not valid. This can happen if the cell has been deleted from the worksheet.
#VALUE!	The formula includes an argument or operand of the wrong type.

Circular references

A circular reference occurs when a formula refers to its own cell — either directly or indirectly. Usually, this is the result of an error (although some circular references are intentional). When a worksheet has a circular reference, Excel displays the cell reference in the status bar. I refer you to the discussion of circular references in Chapter 9.

Other Auditing Tools

The registered version of the Power Utility Pak includes a utility named Auditing Tools. The dialog box for this utility is shown in Figure 30-7. This utility works with the active worksheet and can generate any or all of the following:

✦ **Worksheet map:** A color-coded graphical map of the worksheet that shows the type of contents for each cell — value, text, formula, logical value, or error. See Figure 30-8.

✦ **Formula list:** A list of all formulas in the worksheet, including their current value.

✦ **Summary report:** An informative report that includes details about the worksheet, the workbook that it's in, and a list of all defined names.

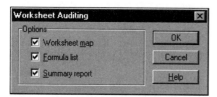

Figure 30-7: The Worksheet Auditing dialog box from the Power Utility Pak.

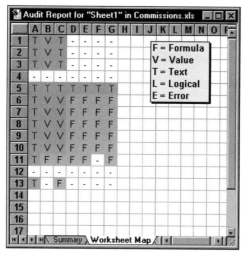

Figure 30-8: This worksheet map was produced by the Auditing Tools utility from the Power Utility Pak.

Spelling and Word-Related Options

Excel includes several handy tools to help you with the non-numeric problems — those related to spelling and words.

Spell checking

If you use a word processing program, you probably run its spelling checker before printing an important document. Spelling mistakes can be just as embarrassing when they appear in a spreadsheet. Fortunately, Microsoft includes a spelling checker with Excel. You can access the spelling checker using any of these methods:

✦ Select the Tools⇨Spelling command.

✦ Click on the Spelling button on the Standard toolbar.

✦ Press F7.

You get the Spelling dialog box shown in Figure 30-9.

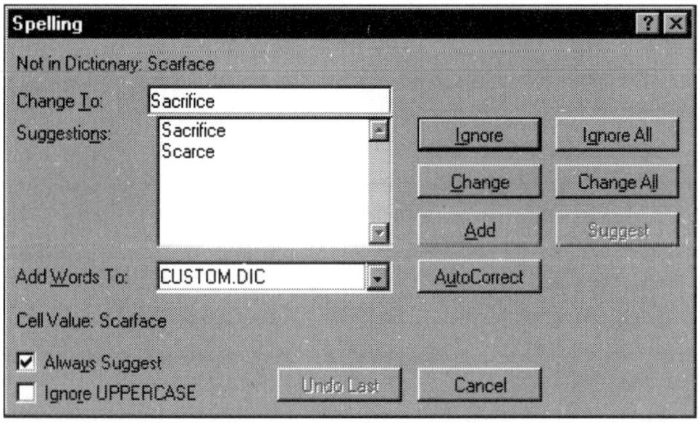

Figure 30-9: The Spelling dialog box.

The extent of the spell checking depends on what was selected when you accessed the dialog box. If a single cell was selected, the entire worksheet is checked; this includes cell contents, notes, text in graphic objects and charts, and page headers and footers. Even the contents of hidden rows and columns are checked. If you select a range of cells, only that range is checked. If you select a group of characters in the formula bar, only those characters are checked.

The Spelling dialog box works similarly to other spelling checkers with which you may be familiar. If Excel encounters a word that isn't in the current dictionary or is misspelled, it offers a list of suggestions. You can respond by clicking on one of the following buttons:

Ignore: Ignores the word and continues the spell check.

Ignore All: Ignores the word and all subsequent occurrences of it.

Change: Changes the word to the selected word in the Change To edit box.

Change All: Changes the word to the selected word in the Change To edit box and changes all subsequent occurrences of it without asking.

Add: Adds the word to the dictionary.

Suggest: Displays a list of replacement words. This button is grayed out if the Always Suggest check box is checked.

AutoCorrect: Adds the misspelled word and its correct spelling to the list of words that are corrected automatically (see the following section). Use this if you frequently misspell a particular word.

Using AutoCorrect

AutoCorrect is a new feature in Excel for Windows 95 and is also available in the other Microsoft Office 95 applications.

AutoCorrect is a handy feature that automatically corrects common typing mistakes. You also can add words to the list that will be corrected automatically. The AutoCorrect dialog box is shown in Figure 30-10. You access this feature with the Tools⇨AutoCorrect command.

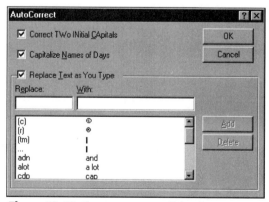

Figure 30-10: The AutoCorrect dialog box.

This dialog has three options:

✦ **Correct Two Initial Capitals:** This option, when enabled, automatically corrects words with two initial uppercase letters. For example, *BUdget* is converted to *Budget*. This is a common mistake among fast typists.

✦ **Capitalize Names of Days:** This option, when enabled, capitalizes the days of the week. If you enter *monday*, Excel converts it to *Monday*.

✦ **Replace Text as You Type**: If this option is selected, AutoCorrect automatically changes words as you type. If this option is not selected, AutoCorrect is turned off.

Excel includes a long list of AutoCorrect entries for commonly misspelled words. In addition, it has AutoCorrect entries for some symbols. For example, *(c)* is replaced with © and *(r)* is replaced with ®. You also can add your own AutoCorrect entries. For example, if you find that you frequently misspell the word *January* as *Janruary*, you can create an AutoCorrect entry so that it's changed automatically. To create a new AutoCorrect entry, enter the misspelled word in the Replace box and the correctly spelled word in the With box. As I note previously, you also can do this in the Spelling dialog box.

Tip　You also can use the AutoCorrect feature to create shortcuts for commonly used words or phrases. For example, if you work for a company named Consolidated Data Processing Corporation, you can create an AutoCorrect entry for an abbreviation, such as cdp. Then, whenever you type *cdp*, Excel automatically changes it to *Consolidated Data Processing Corporation.*

Using AutoComplete

New!　AutoComplete is a new feature in Excel for Windows 95.

AutoComplete automatically finishes a word as soon as it is recognized. In order for the word to be recognized, it must appear elsewhere in the same column. This is most useful when you're entering a list that contains repeated text in a column. For example, assume that you're entering customer data in a list, and one of the fields is City. Whenever you start typing, Excel searches the other entries in the column. If it finds a match, it completes the entry for you. Press Enter to accept it. If Excel guesses incorrectly, keep typing to ignore the suggestion.

Note　If AutoComplete isn't working, select the Tools⇨Options command, click on the Edit tab, and check the box labeled Enable AutoComplete for Cell Values.

You also can display a list of all items in a column by right-clicking on and choosing Pick from list from the shortcut menu. Excel then displays a list box of all entries in the column (see Figure 30-11). Click on the one you want and Excel enters it into the cell for you.

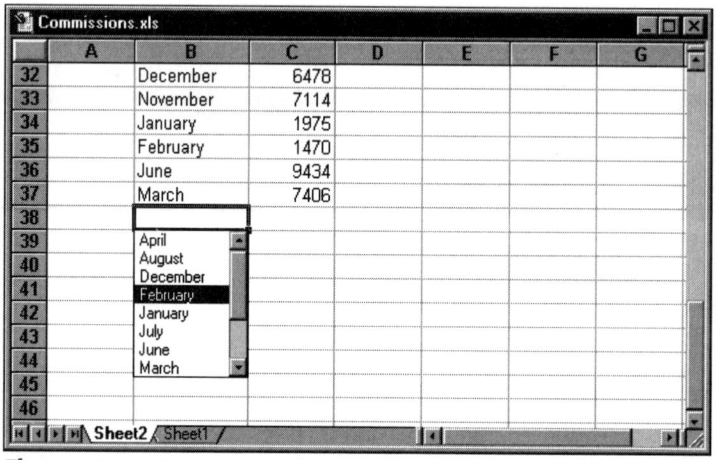

Figure 30-11: Choosing Pick from list from the shortcut menu gives you a list of entries from which to choose.

Learning about an Unfamiliar Spreadsheet

When you develop a workbook yourself, you have a thorough understanding of how it's put together. But if you receive an unfamiliar workbook from someone, it may be difficult to understand how it all fits together — especially if it's large.

Usually, the first step is to identify the bottom line cell or cells. A worksheet typically is designed to produce results in a single cell or in a range of cells. Once you identify this cell or range, you should be able to use the cell-tracing techniques described earlier to determine the cell relationships.

Although every worksheet is different, a few techniques can help you become familiar with an unfamiliar workbook. I discuss these techniques in the following sections.

Zooming out for the big picture

I find that it's often helpful to use Excel's zoom feature to zoom out to get an overview of the worksheet's layout. You can select the View⇨Full Screen command to see even more of the worksheet. When a workbook is zoomed, you can use all of the normal commands. For example, you can use the Edit⇨Go To command to select a name range. Or, you can use the options available in the Go To Special dialog box (explained later) to select formula cells, constants, or other special cell types.

Viewing formulas

Another way to become familiar with an unfamiliar workbook is to display the formulas rather than the results of the formulas. To do this, select the Tools⇨Options command and check the box labeled Formulas in the View panel. You may want to create a new window for the workbook before issuing this command. That way, you can see the formulas in one window and the results in the other.

Figure 30-12 shows an example. The window on the top shows the normal view (formula results). The window on the bottom displays the formulas.

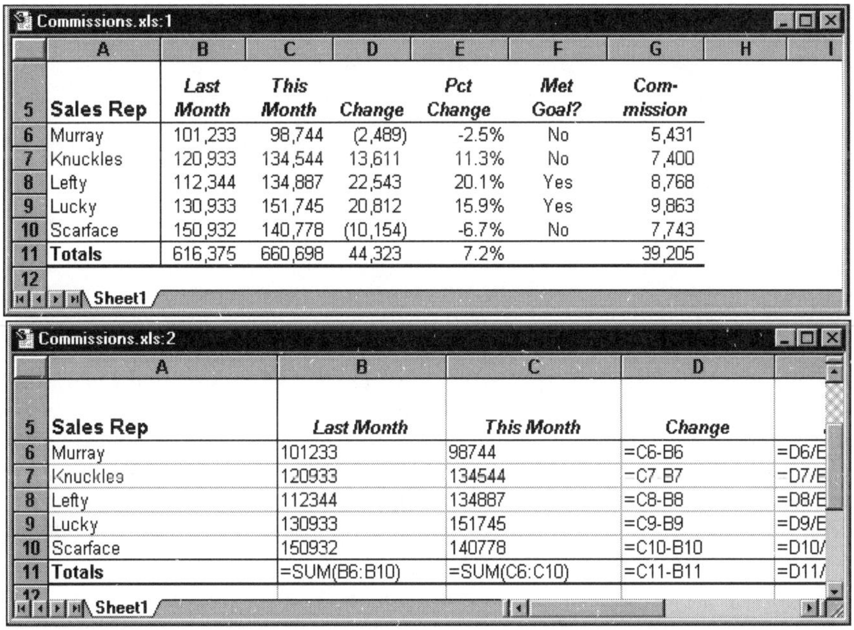

	A	B	C	D	E	F	G	H	I
		Last	This		Pct	Met	Com-		
5	Sales Rep	Month	Month	Change	Change	Goal?	mission		
6	Murray	101,233	98,744	(2,489)	-2.5%	No	5,431		
7	Knuckles	120,933	134,544	13,611	11.3%	No	7,400		
8	Lefty	112,344	134,887	22,543	20.1%	Yes	8,768		
9	Lucky	130,933	151,745	20,812	15.9%	Yes	9,863		
10	Scarface	150,932	140,778	(10,154)	-6.7%	No	7,743		
11	Totals	616,375	660,698	44,323	7.2%		39,205		

Commissions.xls:1

	A	B	C	D	
5	Sales Rep	Last Month	This Month	Change	
6	Murray	101233	98744	=C6-B6	=D6/E
7	Knuckles	120933	134544	=C7-B7	=D7/E
8	Lefty	112344	134887	=C8-B8	=D8/E
9	Lucky	130933	151745	=C9-B9	=D9/E
10	Scarface	150932	140778	=C10-B10	=D10/
11	Totals	=SUM(B6:B10)	=SUM(C6:C10)	=C11-B11	=D11/

Commissions.xls:2

Figure 30-12: The underlying formulas are shown in the window on the right.

Pasting a list of names

If the worksheet uses named ranges (and it should), create a list of the names and their references. To do so, move the cell pointer to an empty area of the worksheet and choose the Insert⇨Name⇨Paste command. Excel responds with its Paste Name dialog box. Click on the Paste List button to paste a list of the names and their references into the workbook. Figure 30-13 shows an example.

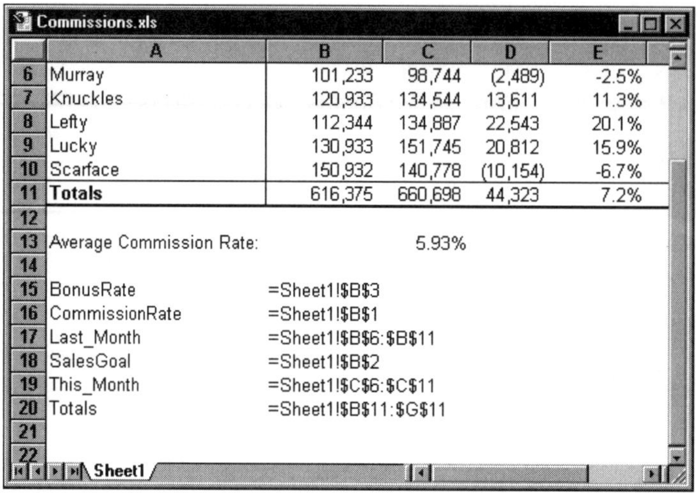

	A	B	C	D	E
6	Murray	101,233	98,744	(2,489)	-2.5%
7	Knuckles	120,933	134,544	13,611	11.3%
8	Lefty	112,344	134,887	22,543	20.1%
9	Lucky	130,933	151,745	20,812	15.9%
10	Scarface	150,932	140,778	(10,154)	-6.7%
11	Totals	616,375	660,698	44,323	7.2%
12					
13	Average Commission Rate:		5.93%		
14					
15	BonusRate	=Sheet1!$B$3			
16	CommissionRate	=Sheet1!$B$1			
17	Last_Month	=Sheet1!$B$6:$B$11			
18	SalesGoal	=Sheet1!$B$2			
19	This_Month	=Sheet1!$C$6:$C$11			
20	Totals	=Sheet1!$B$11:$G$11			
21					
22					

Figure 30-13: Pasting a list of names (in A15:B20) can sometimes help you understand how a worksheet is constructed.

Summary

In this chapter, I discuss tools that can help you make your worksheets error-free. I identify the types of errors that you're likely to encounter. I also cover three tools that Excel provides, which can help you trace the relationships between cells: the Info window, the Go To Special dialog box, and Excel's interactive auditing tools. I go over text-related features, including spell checking and the new AutoCorrect and AutoComplete. I conclude the chapter with general tips that can help you understand how an unfamiliar worksheet is put together.

✦   ✦   ✦

Fun Stuff

Although Excel is used primarily for serious applications, many users discover that this product has a lighter side. This chapter is devoted to the less serious applications of Excel, including games and interesting diversions.

Games

Excel certainly wasn't designed as a platform for games. Nevertheless, I've developed a few games using Excel and have downloaded several others from various online services. I've found that the key ingredient in developing these games is creativity. In almost every case, I had to invent one or more workarounds to compensate for Excel's lack of game-making features. In this section, I show you a few of my own creations. These are either available on the companion CD-ROM or in the registered version of my Power Utility Pak.

Tick-Tack-Toe

Although Tick-Tack-Toe is not the most mentally stimulating game around, everyone knows how to play it. Figure 31-1 shows the Tick-Tack-Toe Game that I developed using Excel. In this implementation, the user plays against the computer. I wrote some formulas and VBA macros to determine the computer's moves, and it plays a reasonably good game — about on par with a three-year-old child. I'm embarrassed to admit that the program has even beaten me a few times (I was distracted).

You can choose who makes the first move (you or the computer) and which marker you want to use (X or O). The winning games and ties are tallied in cells at the bottom of the window.

On the CD-ROM This workbook, named TIC_TOE.XLS, is available on the companion CD-ROM.

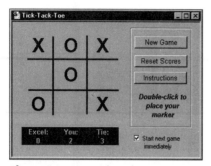

Figure 31-1: My Tick-Tack-Toe Game.

Moving Tile Puzzle

At some time in your life, you've probably played one of those moving tile puzzles. They come in several variations, but the goal is always the same: Rearrange the tiles so that they are in order.

Figure 31-2 shows a version of this game that I wrote in VBA. When you click the tile, it appears to move to the empty position. Actually, no movement is taking place. The program is simply changing the text on the buttons and making the button in the empty position invisible.

Figure 31-2: My Moving Tile Puzzle.

This workbook, called MOVTILES.XLS is available on the companion CD-ROM.

Hangman

Hangman is another game that almost everyone has played. Figure 31-3 shows a version that I developed for Excel. The objective is to identify a word by guessing letters. Correctly guessed letters appear in their proper position. Every incorrectly guessed letter adds a new body part to the person being hanged (and the incorrect letters appear at the top). Ten incorrect guesses and the man is hanged — that is, the game is over.

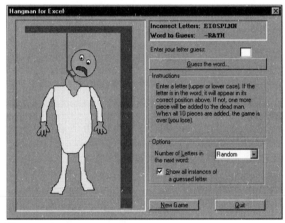

Figure 31-3: My Hangman Game.

The workbook includes 1,400 words, ranging in length from 6 to 12 letters. You can choose how many letters you want in the word or have the number of letters determined randomly. In the unlikely event that you get bored with the 1,400 words supplied, you can easily add new words to the list without having to make any changes to the macros.

The entire game takes place in a dialog box. This dialog box demonstrates some useful techniques. It contains an edit box, which always has the focus. Entering a letter into the edit box executes a macro, which checks the letter and then clears the edit box for the next letter. The result is that you enter letters without having to press Enter or click a button. The hangman graphic that appears in the dialog box is a linked picture. The victim's body parts were created using Excel's drawing tools and are unhidden as incorrect letters are guessed.

On the CD-ROM This workbook, named HANGMAN.XLS, is included on the CD-ROM that accompanies this book.

Trivia Questions

This isn't really a game — it's a workbook that has more than 1,200 trivia questions and answers, categorized into five categories (see Figure 31-4). The workbook provides a way to display the questions and answers. You'll find that this workbook is designed so that it's very easy to modify. For example, you can add new questions and answers and even add new categories — and you'll never need to modify any macros. One of the worksheets in this workbook contains instructions for adding new items or categories.

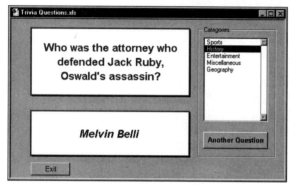

Figure 31-4: This workbook displays random trivia questions from five categories.

On the CD-ROM The workbook named TRIVIA.XLS is included on the CD-ROM that accompanies this book.

Note Most of the questions in this workbook were drawn from a public-domain, DOS-based trivia game that I downloaded several years ago. Consequently, some of the answers (especially in the Sports category) may no longer be correct. Play at your own risk.

Video Poker

Developing my Video Poker Game for Excel (see Figure 31-5) was quite a challenge. I was forced to spend many hours performing research at a local casino in order to perfect this game so that it captures the excitement of a real video poker machine. The only problem is that I haven't figured out a way to dispense the winnings. Oh well, maybe in Version 2.0.

My original intention was to use realistic playing card graphics like those in the Windows Solitaire game. I discovered, however, that Excel insists on storing these graphics as 256-color images — making the size of the file very large. I compromised by developing card images in worksheet cells and using linked pictures. To keep the file size small, I also gave up on my original idea to add sound effects — although this would not be difficult to do.

This version has two games: Joker's Wild (a joker can be used for any card) and Jacks or Better (a pair of jacks or better is required to win). You select which cards to discard by clicking the card face. You can change the game (or the bet) at any time while playing. You also can request a graph that shows your cumulative winnings (or, more typically, your cumulative losses).

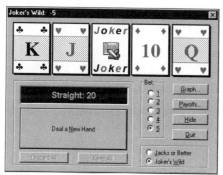

Figure 31-5: My Video Poker Game.

Identifying the various poker hands is done using VBA procedures. The game also has a Hide button that temporarily hides the game. This lets you resume the game when your boss leaves the room.

Note   This game is included with the registered version of the Power Utility Pak. See the coupon in the back of the book for details on how to get your copy.

Dice Game

The goal of the Dice Game is to obtain a high score by assigning dice rolls to various categories. You get to roll the dice three times on each turn, and you can keep or discard the dice before rolling again.

This game takes place on a worksheet, although it looks like a dialog box. Everything is done using VBA and a few formulas. The dice are created in worksheet cells using Wingdings font characters and are linked picture objects. The game even has an Undo button that lets you change your mind after assigning a roll to a category. This game also has a Hide button that lets you return to work and resume the game later on.

Note   This game is included with the registered version of the Power Utility Pak. See the coupon in the back of the book for details on how to get your copy.

Bomb Hunt

Windows comes with a game called Minesweeper. I developed a version of this game for Excel and named it Bomb Hunt (see Figure 31-6). The goal is to discover the hidden bombs in the grid. Double-clicking on a cell reveals a bomb (you lose) or a number that indicates the number of bombs in the surrounding cells. You use logic to determine where the bombs are located. Like Video Poker and the Dice Game, this game includes a Hide button.

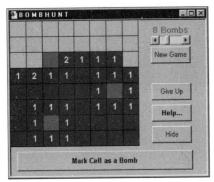

Figure 31-6: My Bomb Hunt Game.

> **Note**   This game is included with the registered version of the Power Utility Pak. See the coupon in the back of the book for details on how to get your copy.

Symmetrical Pattern Drawing

I must admit, this program is rather addictive—especially for doodlers. It lets you create colorful symmetrical patterns by using the arrow keys on the keyboard. Figure 31-7 shows an example. As you draw, the drawing is reproduced as mirror images in the other three quadrants. When you move the cursor to the edge of the drawing area, it wraps around and appears on the other side. This workbook is great for passing the time on the telephone when you're put on hold.

The drawing is all done with VBA macros. I used the OnKey method to trap the following key presses: left, right, up, and down. Each of these keystrokes executes a macro that shades a cell. The cells in the drawing area are very tiny, so the shading appears as lines.

> **On the CD-ROM**   The workbook named PATTERN.XLS is available on the companion CD-ROM.

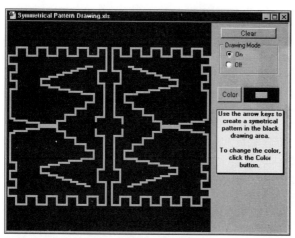

Figure 31-7: My Symmetrical Pattern Drawing worksheet.

For Guitar Players

If you play guitar, check out this workbook. As you see in Figure 31-8, this workbook has a graphic depiction of a guitar's fretboard. It displays the notes (and fret positions) of the selected scale or mode in any key. You can even change the tuning of the guitar, and the formulas recalculate.

Other options include the choice to display half-notes as sharps or flats, pop-up information about the selected scale or mode, and change the color of the guitar neck. This workbook uses formulas to do the calculation, and VBA plays only a minor role. This file was designated a "top pick" on America Online, and I've received positive feedback from fellow pickers all over the world.

On the CD-ROM This workbook, named GUITAR.XLS, is available on the companion CD-ROM.

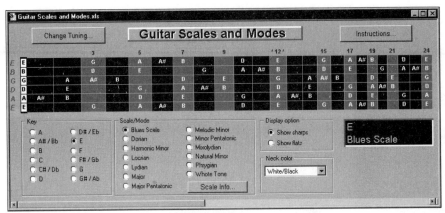

Figure 31-8: My guitar fretboard application.

An April Fools' Prank

Here's a good April Fools' trick to play on an office mate (with luck, one with a sense of humor). Set up his or her copy of Excel so that it automatically loads a workbook with macros that reverse the menus. For example, the Insert⇨Macro⇨Dialog command becomes the Insert⇨Orcam⇨Golaid command. Because the macro that performs this prank is named `Auto_Open`, it will be executed whenever the workbook is opened. If the workbook is saved in the victim's XLStart folder, the workbook opens automatically — and Excel's menus look like they're in a strange language. Figure 31-9 shows how this looks.

> **On the CD-ROM** This workbook, named SHENANIG.XLS, is available on the CD-ROM that accompanies this book. The routine performs its mischief by calling a custom function that reverses the text in the captions (except for the ellipses), converts the new text to proper case, and maintains the original hot keys. The net effect is a worksheet menu system that works exactly like the original (and is even keystroke compatible) but looks very odd.

Before exiting, the macro routine adds an escape route: A new (legible) menu item to the Pleh menu (formerly the Help menu). This new item calls up a macro that returns the menus to normal.

> **Note** Actually, this trick can be rather instructive. For example, I found out that Excel automatically resets some of the menus and menu items. The File menu doesn't get changed, but the Edit menu does. Similarly, the New, Save, and Save As menu items on the File menu appear as they usually do.

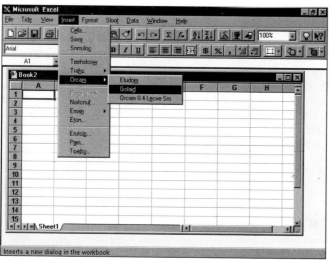

Figure 31-9: Excel with backward menus. The hot keys remain the same.

Typing Tutor

Figure 31-10 shows a dialog box from an application that I developed to help people learn the location of the keys on the keyboard. It was suggested by Colin Anderson, an Internet acquaintance who e-mailed me after reading my *Excel 5 for Windows Power Programming Techniques* (IDG Books, 1994) book. He thought that it would make a good VBA example. I liked the idea so much that I created the Typing Tutor application.

Figure 31-10: My Typing Tutor application.

This application has seven lessons, each of which focuses on a different part of the keyboard. Random letters are displayed, and you simply press the corresponding key. The program calculates the latency between when the letter appears and when the keystroke is made. It also determines whether the *proper* keystroke was made.

I don't make any claims that this actually helps you type better, and I have absolutely no knowledge of typing training. It is likely, however, that you will see some improvement as you work with this program. The results of each lesson (the average latency and the accuracy) are stored in a worksheet database. You can create a chart from this data to plot your progress.

On the CD-ROM
This workbook, named TYPING.XLS, is available on the companion CD-ROM.

Lottery Simulation

Joe Sorrenti downloaded one of my Excel games from CompuServe and sent me one of his in return. This workbook, shown in Figure 31-11, simulates the New York State Pick-6 Lottery — complete with animation and Homer Simpson sound effects.

You can choose your six numbers manually or click the Random Picks button for six random numbers. The balls are placed into the hopper, mixed up, and then chosen one at a time. This is only for amusement, however, because Sorrenti won't pay up if you hit it big.

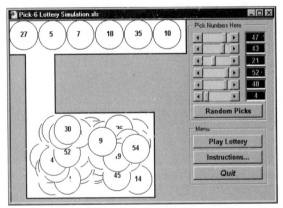

Figure 31-11: Joe Sorrenti's Pick-6 Lottery Simulation.

On the CD-ROM
This workbook, named PICK6.XLS, is available on the companion CD-ROM.

Create Word Search Puzzles

Most daily newspapers feature a word search puzzle. These puzzles contain words hidden in a grid. The words can be vertical, diagonal, horizontal, forwards, or backwards. If you've ever had the urge to create your own word search puzzle, this workbook can make your job a lot easier by doing it for you. You supply the words; the program places them in the grid and fills in the empty squares with random letters. Figure 31-12 shows the puzzle creation sheet plus a sample puzzle created with this application.

This is all done with VBA, and randomness plays a major role. Therefore, you can create multiple puzzles using the same words.

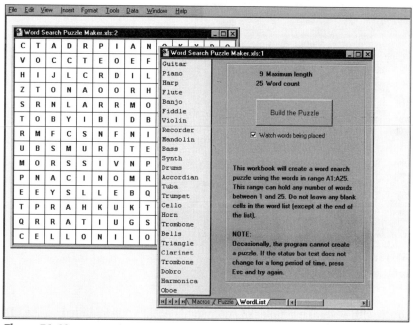

Figure 31-12: My Word Search Puzzle Maker.

This workbook, named WRD_SRCH.XLS is available on the companion CD-ROM.

ASCII Art

If you know where to find it, the Internet has thousands of examples of ASCII art — pictures created using only standard alphanumeric characters. Figure 31-13 shows an example of ASCII art.

By the way, this has absolutely nothing to do with Excel. These files could be displayed just as well in a word processing document. For these pictures to be displayed properly, you must use a fixed-width font, such as Courier New.

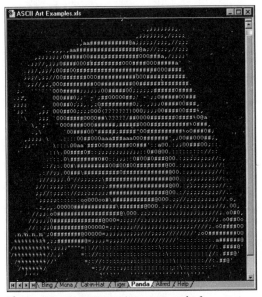

Figure 31-13: ASCII art is composed of alphanumeric characters.

On the CD-ROM A workbook with several examples of anonymous ASCII art is included on the CD-ROM (it's named ASCI_ART.XLS).

Sun Calculations

Several years ago, I downloaded an Excel freeware file that performed some sophisticated calculations regarding the sun. The file included no identifying information, so I don't know who the author is. (If anyone knows, please let me know so that I can give proper credit). I enhanced this file quite a bit, primarily by improving the user interface.

The program calculates various sun-related Items based on a latitude, longitude, and date. It also displays several charts. Figure 31-14 shows an example of this program (the latitude and longitude shown are for San Diego, California). I include a worksheet that has latitudes and longitudes for several other locations — maybe even your hometown.

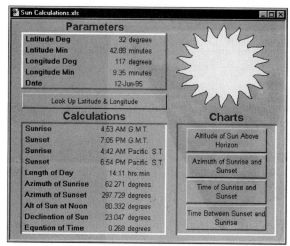

Figure 31-14: This workbook makes sun calculations for any latitude, longitude, and date.

On the CD-ROM

This workbook, named SUN_CALC.XLS, is available on the companion CD-ROM.

Making Noise

If you have a CD-ROM installed on your system, it's likely that you also have a sound card. You can embed WAV sound files in your workbooks to add some sound effects. I put together a few sounds effects for your amusement.

On the CD-ROM The companion CD-ROM contains a workbook named SOUNDFX.XLS, which has some embedded sounds.

Fun with Charts

Excel's charting feature has the potential to be fun. In this section, I provide examples of some non-serious charting applications.

Plotting trigonometric functions

Although I don't know too much about trigonometry, I've always enjoyed plotting various trigonometric functions as XY charts. Sometimes you can come up with attractive images. Figure 31-15 shows an example of a trigonometric plot. Clicking the button changes a random number that makes a new chart.

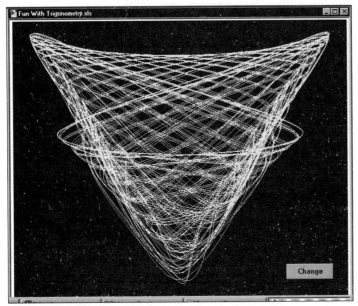

Figure 31-15: This chart plots trigonometric functions.

 This workbook, named FUN_TRIG.XLS, is available on the companion CD-ROM.

Analog clock

Although it's easy to display the time digitally in Excel, displaying the time as an analog clock is a bit more challenging. I'm always up for a challenge, so I created an analog clock, as shown in Figure 31-16.

Actually, this clock is an XY chart with four data series: one for the minute hand, one for the hour hand, one for the second hand, and one for the numbers. I pasted pictures of numbers in place of the markers for one of the data series. The circle is just an oval object pasted on top of the chart. I removed both of the axes from the chart.

The chart is updated every second when the formulas (driven by a NOW function) are updated. Because the updating occurs within a VBA loop, you can't do anything else while the clock is displayed. If you add a few simple macros, you can use this for a screen saver to keep others from looking at your work when you leave your system.

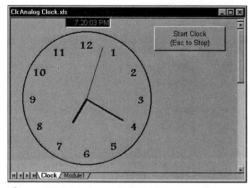

Figure 31-16: My analog clock is actually an XY chart.

On the CD-ROM This workbook, named CLOCK.XLS, is available on the companion CD-ROM.

XY-Sketch

In this workbook, you use the controls to draw an XY chart (see Figure 31-17). Clicking a directional button adds a new X and Y value to the chart's data range, which is then plotted on the chart. You can change the step size, adjust the color, and choose between smooth and normal lines. I include a multilevel Undo button that successively removes data points that you added.

On the CD-ROM This workbook, named XY_SKETC.XLS, is available on the companion CD-ROM.

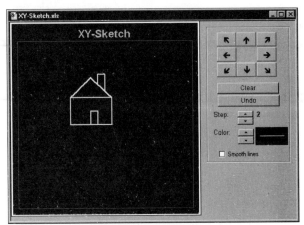

Figure 31-17: My XY-Sketch workbook.

Summary

In this chapter, I present several examples of non-serious applications for Excel. It's likely that some of these examples can be adapted and used in more serious applications (well, maybe not).

✦   ✦   ✦

Customizing Excel

P A R T

◆ ◆ ◆ ◆

In This Part

◆ ◆ ◆ ◆

Most users find that Excel is a fantastic tool right out of the box. But the designers of this product included many additional capabilities that let you customize Excel in a number of ways. In this part, I discuss a variety of topics, including customizing toolbars and menus, creating custom templates, running macros, and creating custom add-ins.

Customizing Toolbars and Menus

◆ ◆ ◆ ◆

In This Chapter

Types of toolbar
customizations that
you can make

How to create custom
toolbars that contain
the buttons you use
most often

How to change the
image displayed on a
toolbar button

How to modify Excel's
menus

◆ ◆ ◆ ◆

You're probably familiar with many of Excel's built-in
toolbars, and it's likely that you've thoroughly explored
the menu system. Excel lets you modify both toolbars and
menus. In this chapter, I explain how to customize the built-in
toolbars, create new toolbars, and change the menus that Excel
displays. Although many of these customizations are most useful
when you create macros (discussed in subsequent chapters),
even nonmacro users may find these techniques helpful.

Customizing Toolbars

Excel comes with more than 200 toolbar buttons and 13 built-in
toolbars. Not all of the available toolbar buttons are on the
prebuilt toolbars. In fact, some of the more useful toolbar
buttons don't appear on any prebuilt toolbar. And many buttons
on the prebuilt toolbars may not be all that useful to you.
Consequently, many users like to create one or more custom
toolbars containing the toolbar buttons that they use most often.

When you start up Excel, it displays the same toolbar configuration that was in effect the last time you used it. Did you ever
wonder how Excel keeps track of this information? When you
exit Excel, it updates a file in your Windows folder. This file
stores your custom toolbars, as well as information about which
toolbars are visible and the on-screen location of each. The
filename is based on your user name, with an XLB extension (for
example, JOHNW.XLB).

If you need to restore the toolbars to their previous configuration, use the File⇨Open command to open this XLB file. This restores your toolbar configuration to the way it was when you started Excel. You can also make a copy of the XLB file and give it a different name. Doing so lets you store multiple toolbar configurations that you can load at any time.

Types of customizations

Following is a summary of the types of customizations that you can make when working with toolbars:

✦ **Remove toolbar buttons from built-in toolbars.** You may want to do this to get rid of toolbar buttons you never use.

✦ **Add toolbar buttons to built-in toolbars.** You can add as many toolbar buttons as you want to any toolbar. The buttons can be custom buttons or buttons from other toolbars, or they can come from the stock of toolbar buttons contained in the 14 categories in the Customize dialog box.

✦ **Create new toolbars.** You can create as many new toolbars as you like, with toolbar buttons from any source.

✦ **Change the functionality of built-in toolbar buttons.** You do this by attaching your own macro to a built-in toolbar button.

✦ **Change the image that appears on any toolbar button.** A rudimentary but functional toolbar button editor is included with Excel. There are also several other techniques that you can use.

Note   Don't be afraid to experiment with toolbars. If you mess up a built-in toolbar, it's very easy to reset it back to its default state. Just select the View⇨Toolbars command, select the toolbar, and click the Reset button.

Hiding and displaying toolbars

As you know, you can display as many toolbars as you like. A toolbar can either be floating or *docked*. A docked toolbar is fixed in place at the top, bottom, left, or right edge of Excel's workspace. Toolbars that contain nonstandard buttons (for example, the Zoom Control) can't be docked on the left or right because the larger control would cause the toolbar to be too wide. Floating toolbars appear in an "always on top" window, and you can change the dimensions of a floating toolbar by dragging a border.

Right-clicking any toolbar or toolbar button displays a shortcut menu that lets you hide or display a toolbar (see Figure 32-1). Not all toolbars appear in this list, however. To get a list of all toolbars, use the Toolbars dialog box. This dialog box lets you hide or display toolbars (among other things). You can access the Toolbars dialog box in two ways:

✦ Select the View➪Toolbars command.

✦ Select Toolbars from the shortcut menu that appears when you right-click on a toolbar.

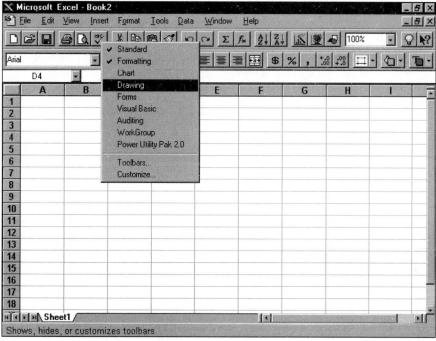

Figure 32-1: Right-clicking on a toolbar or toolbar button displays this shortcut menu.

Either of these methods displays the dialog box shown in Figure 32-2. This dialog box lists all of the available toolbars, including custom toolbars you have created.

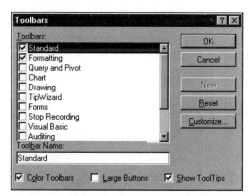

Figure 32-2: The Toolbars dialog box.

The Toolbars dialog box lets you perform the following actions:

✦ **Hide or display any toolbar in the list.** Add a check mark to display a toolbar; remove the check mark to hide it. The changes take effect when you close the dialog box.

✦ **Create a new toolbar.** Enter a name in the Toolbar Name edit box and click on the New button. Excel creates and displays an empty toolbar. You can then add buttons to the new toolbar.

✦ **Reset a built-in toolbar.** Select a built-in toolbar from the list and click on the Reset button. The toolbar is restored to its default state. (This button displays Delete when a custom toolbar is selected.)

✦ **Delete a custom toolbar.** Select a custom toolbar from the list and click on the Delete button. (This button displays Reset when a built-in toolbar is selected.)

✦ **Toggle toolbar button color.** Check or uncheck the Color Toolbars check box.

✦ **Toggle the toolbar button size.** Check or uncheck the Large Buttons check box. If you use a high-resolution video mode, you may find that large toolbar buttons are easier to work with.

✦ **Toggle the tooltips display.** Tooltips are the pop-up messages that display the button names when you pause the mouse pointer over a button. If you find the tooltips distracting, remove the check mark from the Show ToolTips check box. The status bar still displays a description of the button when you move the mouse pointer over it.

In addition, you can make the following changes while the Toolbars dialog box is displayed:

✦ **Move a toolbar button from any displayed toolbar to any other displayed toolbar.** Just click on a button and drag it to its new location.

✦ **Copy a toolbar button from any displayed toolbar to any other displayed toolbar.** Hold down the Ctrl key and click on and drag the button to another location.

✦ **Copy the image on a toolbar button to another button.** Right-click on a button and choose Copy Button Image from the shortcut menu. Right-click on another button and choose Paste Button Image from the shortcut menu.

I describe additional customization options in the next section.

Toolbar autosensing

Normally, Excel displays a particular toolbar automatically when you change contexts; this is called *autosensing*. For example, when you activate a chart, the Chart toolbar appears. You can easily defeat this by hiding the toolbar (click on its Close button or use the View⇨Toolbars command). After you do so, Excel no longer displays that toolbar when you switch to its former context. You can restore this automatic behavior, however, by displaying the appropriate toolbar when you're in the appropriate context. Thereafter, Excel reverts to its normal automatic toolbar display when you switch to that context.

The contexts under which Excel automatically displays toolbars are as follows:

Context	Toolbar Displayed
Activate a chart sheet	Chart
Activate embedded chart	Chart
Activate a VBA module	Visual Basic
Activate a dialog sheet	Forms
Start recording a macro	Stop Recording
Enter full-screen mode	Full Screen
Activate a sheet with a pivot table	Query and Pivot

Using the Customize dialog box

You customize toolbars using the Customize dialog box, shown in Figure 32-3. You can bring up this dialog box in either of two ways:

♦ Select the View⇨Toolbars command and click on the Customize button in the Toolbars dialog box.

♦ Right-click on a toolbar or toolbar button and select Customize from the shortcut menu.

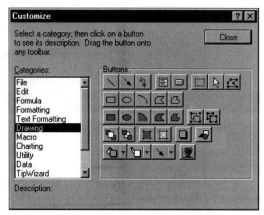

Figure 32-3: The Customize dialog box.

The Customize dialog box contains all of Excel's built-in toolbar buttons, arranged in 14 categories. The last category, Custom, contains 28 additional buttons that don't do anything (you can use these to execute macros). When you select a category, the buttons in that category appear to the right. To find out what a button does, just click on it and then read its description at the bottom of the dialog box. Table 32-1 lists the toolbar button categories.

Table 32-1	
Toolbar Categories	
Category	**Description**
File	Files, sheets, and printing
Edit	Worksheet editing
Formula	Inserts characters in the formula bar
Formatting	Borders, shading, styles
Text Formatting	Fonts and alignment
Drawing	Drawing tools, color, and patterns
Macro	VBA macro tools
Charting	Chart types and customization
Utility	Miscellaneous tools, including workgroup tools

Category	Description
Data	Pivot tables and outlining
TipWizard	TipWizard tools
Auditing	Auditing tools
Forms	Dialog box and worksheet controls
Custom	Button faces that don't do anything (you supply the macro)

Note When the Customize dialog box is displayed, you can copy and move buttons freely among any visible toolbars. To move a button, drag it to its new location. To copy a button, press Ctrl while you drag it. Note that you also can create gaps by moving a toolbar button slightly to the left or right.

Additional toolbar tools

My Power Utility Pak includes a utility called Toolbar Tools. This utility lets you perform toolbar operations that are otherwise impossible. The Toolbar Tools utility lets you perform the following actions:

✦ Hide or display any toolbar interactively (you don't have to close the dialog box).

✦ Rename a custom toolbar (normally impossible).

✦ Copy a custom toolbar (normally impossible).

✦ Change the tooltip for any button (normally requires a macro).

The accompanying figure shows the ToolTip Editor from the Toolbar Tools utility.

The shareware version of the Power Utility Pak is available on the companion CD-ROM.

An example of creating a custom toolbar

In this section, I walk you through the steps to create a custom toolbar. This toolbar will contain buttons to assist you with worksheet formatting. You may want to replace the built-in Formatting toolbar with this new custom toolbar.

On the CD-ROM If you don't want to create this toolbar yourself, you can get it by opening the workbook named TOOLBAR.XLS, which is on the companion CD-ROM.

Following are the steps required to create this new toolbar:

1. Select the View⇨Toolbars command. Excel displays its Toolbars dialog box.

2. Enter **Custom Formatting** (or a name of your choice) in the Toolbar Name edit box and click on the New button. Excel creates an empty (floating) toolbar and displays its Customize dialog box.

3. Click on the Text Formatting category. Excel displays the buttons in this category.

4. Drag the following buttons into the new toolbar: Font, Style, Increase Font Size, Bold, Italic, Underline, Left Align, Right Align, Center Align, Center Across Columns, and Text Color.

5. Click on the Drawing category. Excel displays the buttons in this category.

6. Drag the following buttons into the new toolbar: Color, Pattern.

7. Click on the Formatting category and drag the Border tool and the Decrease Decimal button to the new toolbar.

8. Click on the Forms category and drag the Toggle Gridlines button to the new toolbar.

9. Rearrange the buttons on the new toolbar to your liking. You can leave gaps to group similar buttons. You also can change the width of the Font and Style dropdowns by dragging the right border to the left.

10. When you're satisfied with the custom toolbar, click on Close in the Customize dialog box. You can test the toolbar.

Figure 32-4 shows the completed custom toolbar.

Figure 32-4: A new Custom Formatting toolbar.

Note You'll notice that I seem to have omitted some companion buttons. For example, I added the Increase Font Size button but not the Decrease Font Size button. That's because this button serves double-duty. If you press Shift when you click on the Increase Font Size button, it functions like the Decrease Font Size button. The Decrease Decimal button also works in this matter: Pressing Shift while you click on this button has the same effect as clicking on the Increase Decimal button.

After creating this toolbar, you can always modify it. Or, if you decide you don't want it, use the View⇨Toolbars command, select the custom toolbar, and click the Delete button.

Changing a toolbar button's image

To change the image displayed on a toolbar button, you have several options:

✦ Modify or create the image using Excel's Button Editor dialog box.

✦ Copy an image from another toolbar button.

✦ Using the Clipboard, copy an image from another application.

I discuss each of these methods in the following sections.

Creating images from scratch

Excel's button editor is rather simplistic but is easy to use. To create a new image from scratch, you have to start with something. You might want to use the blank toolbar button in the Custom category of the Customize dialog box. Or maybe you want to make minor changes to an existing button image.

To edit a button image, you must be in toolbar customization mode (either the Toolbars or Customize dialog box must be visible). To begin editing, right-click on the button that you want to edit and then choose Edit Button Image from the shortcut menu. The image appears in the Button Editor dialog box (see Figure 32-5), where you can change individual pixels and shift the entire image up, down, to the left, or to the right. If you've never worked with icons before, you may be surprised at how difficult it is to create attractive images in such a small area.

The Edit Button Image dialog box is straightforward. Just click on a color and then click on a pixel (or drag across pixels). When it looks good, click on OK. Or, if you don't like what you've done, click on Cancel and the button keeps its original image.

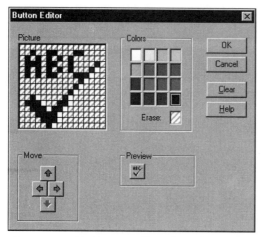

Figure 32-5: The Button Editor dialog box.

How to avoid distorted button images

If you're going to create or modify any toolbar button images, you need to be aware that toolbar buttons can be displayed in regular size or in a larger size. Users with high-resolution video drivers often choose the large button options because the buttons are more legible. Excel's built-in toolbar buttons look good regardless of the button size because each of Excel's built-in toolbar buttons is actually stored as two different bitmaps, one for the normal-sized buttons and one for the large buttons option. Button images that you create are stored as only one bitmap.

If your toolbar button images will be displayed in both sizes, you *must* create them while the toolbar buttons are displayed at regular size.

If you create them in large button mode, you'll be in for a rude awakening when you switch to normal-sized buttons. Excel scales the images to fit the smaller space — but the results are almost always disappointing.

So, the bottom line here is never create or edit your buttons while the large button mode is in effect. Use the regular size button mode exclusively. The normal size of toolbar buttons is 16 pixels wide × 15 pixels high. When you choose the large button size, the buttons are displayed 24 pixels wide × 23 pixels high. This works out to 8 additional pixels. When switching from regular to large buttons, the actual image remains the same size, but Excel pads it with a gray border that's four pixels wide.

Copying and modifying other buttons

Another way to get a button image on a custom toolbar is to copy it from another toolbar button. In toolbar customization mode, right-clicking on a toolbar button displays a shortcut menu that lets you copy a button image to the clipboard or paste the Clipboard contents to the selected button.

On the CD-ROM The CD-ROM that accompanies this book includes BUTTONS.XLS, a workbook that has a custom toolbar with 100 new button images (see Figure 32-6). You can copy any of these images to any other toolbar button. This workbook includes a macro that deletes the custom toolbar from Excel's workspace when the workbook is closed. This prevents the large toolbar from being added to your XLB file — which would increase the size of the file considerably.

Figure 32-6: These toolbar button images are available on the companion CD-ROM.

Copying from the Clipboard

You can copy any image from the Clipboard to a toolbar button. This works best when the copied image is precisely the right size. You can copy an image of any size to a toolbar button, but it is scaled to fit and usually does not look very good.

You can create picture objects in Excel and copy these to toolbar buttons. For optimal results, the dimensions of the picture object should be exactly 11.25×10.50 points, with no border. You can format a cell so that its column width is 1.43 characters wide (11.25 points) and its row height 10.5 points. An image of this size pastes precisely onto a toolbar button face. For large button images, the picture object should be 17.25×16.50 points. This translates to a column width of 2.57 characters and a row height of 16.5 points. Note, however, that images copied to a large-sized button usually don't look good when the buttons are displayed in regular size.

Distributing toolbars

If you would like to distribute a custom toolbar to other users, you can store it in a workbook. To store a toolbar in a workbook file, you must insert a VBA module sheet (unless one already exists). Use the Insert⇨Macro⇨Module command to do this.

Activate a VBA module and choose the Tools⇨Attach Toolbars command. Excel brings up the Attach Toolbars dialog box, shown in Figure 32-7. This dialog box lists all the custom toolbars on your system in the list box on the left. Toolbars already stored in the workbook are listed in the list box on the right. To attach a toolbar, select it and then click on the Copy button. When a toolbar in the right list box is selected, the Copy button says Delete; you can click on it to remove a selected toolbar from a workbook.

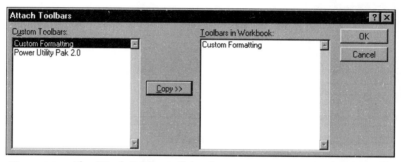

Figure 32-7: The Attach Toolbars dialog box.

A toolbar that's attached to a workbook appears automatically when the workbook is opened, unless the workspace already has a toolbar by the same name.

Note   The toolbar that's stored in the workbook is an exact copy of the toolbar at the time that you attach it. If you modify the toolbar after attaching it, the changed version is not stored in the workbook automatically. You must manually remove the old toolbar and then add the edited toolbar.

Customizing Menus

In this section, I describe how to use Excel's menu editor to modify menus. Modifying menus is most useful when you create macros. For example, you can add a new menu item that executes the macro. I discuss macros in subsequent chapters.

Menu terminology

Menu terminology is often a bit confusing at first because many terms are similar. The following list is official Excel menu terminology, which I use throughout this book.

✦ **Menu Bar:** The row of words that appears directly below the application's title bar. Excel has nine different menu bars that appear automatically, depending on the context. For example, the menu bar displayed when a worksheet is active differs from the menu bar displayed when a chart sheet is active.

✦ **Menu:** A single, top-level element of a menu bar. For example, each of Excel's menu bars has a menu called File.

✦ **Menu Item:** An element that appears in the drop-down list when a menu is selected. For example, the first menu item under the File menu is New. Menu items also appear in submenus and shortcut menus.

✦ **Submenu:** A second-level menu (also known as a *cascading menu*) that is under some menus. For example, the Edit menu has a submenu called Clear.

✦ **Submenu Item:** A menu item that appears in the list when a submenu is selected. For example, the Edit⇨Clear submenu contains the following submenu items: All, Formats, Contents, and Notes.

✦ **Shortcut Menu:** The floating list of menu items that appears when you right-click on a selection or an object. Excel has 25 shortcut menus.

✦ **Enabled:** A menu item that can be used. If a menu item isn't enabled, its text is grayed out and it can't be used.

✦ **Status Bar Text:** Text that appears in Excel's status bar when a menu or menu item is selected. For custom menu items, the status bar text is associated with the macro that is executed by the menu item.

✦ **OnAction:** The macro that is executed when a custom menu item command is executed.

Using the menu editor

The menu editor is a tool that lets you add, remove, or modify elements in Excel's menus. The menu editor is available only when a VBA module is active. You also can use the Menu Editor toolbar button, however (located on the Visual Basic toolbar), which lets you access the menu editor from any type of sheet. The Tools⇨Menu Editor command (or the Menu Editor toolbar button) brings up the dialog box shown in Figure 32-8.

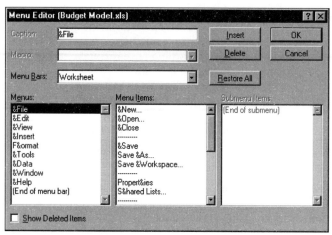

Figure 32-8: Excel's Menu Editor dialog box.

Note The menu editor is for simple modifications only. If you want to do anything fancy, such as change menus on the fly, add check marks to menu items, or disable menu items under certain conditions, you need to write VBA macro code.

The Menu Editor dialog box is divided into several parts. To modify a menu, start by choosing the appropriate menu bar from the Menu Bars drop-down list. The items in this list are described in Table 32-2.

	Table 32-2
	Excel's Menu Bar Items

Menu Bar	Description
Worksheet	The menu bar that appears when a worksheet is active
Chart	The menu bar that appears when a chart sheet is active or when an embedded chart is activated
No Documents Open	The menu bar that appears when no documents are open
Visual Basic Module	The menu bar that appears when a VBA module is active
Shortcut Menus 1	Lets you edit shortcut menus
Shortcut Menus 2	Lets you edit shortcut menus
Shortcut Menus 3	Lets you edit shortcut menus

When you select a menu bar, its menus are displayed in the Menus list box. Select a menu from the Menus list box, and its menu items appear in the Menu Items list box. Select a menu item from the list box and, if there are submenu items, they appear in the Submenu Items list box.

To modify a shortcut menu, choose one of the three Shortcut Menu listings in the Menu Bars drop-down list. The Menu Items list box displays shortcut menus to choose from. As you know, a shortcut menu appears when you right-click on an object or selection. Table 32-3 lists all of Excel's shortcut menus and the context in which they appear.

Table 32-3
Shortcut Menus

Shortcut Menu	Context
Toolbar	A toolbar
Toolbar Button	A toolbar button
Worksheet Cell	A cell or range
Column	An entire worksheet column
Row	An entire worksheet row
Workbook Tab	A workbook tab
Macrosheet Cell	A cell or range on an XLM macro sheet
Title Bar	The title bar of a workbook
Desktop	Excel's background area
Module	A VBA module
Watch Pane	The watch pane in the VBA debug window
Immediate Pane	The immediate pane in the VBA debug window
Debug Code Pane	The debug code pane in the VBA debug window
Drawing Object	A drawing object
Button	A button
Text Box	A text box
Dialog Sheet	A dialog sheet
Chart Series	A data series in a chart

(continued)

Table 32-3 *(continued)*	
Shortcut Menu	*Context*
Chart Text	Text in a chart
Chart Plot Area	The plot area of a chart
Entire Chart	The entire chart
Chart Axis	An axis in a chart
Chart Gridline	A gridline in a chart
Chart Floor	The floor of a 3-D chart
Chart Legend	The legend of a chart

The Insert button lets you insert a new menu, menu item, or submenu item. The item is inserted above the currently selected item. The Delete button removes the selected item (menu, menu item, or submenu item). The Restore All button resets the selected item to its built-in state.

When you insert a new item, you can enter the caption and specify a macro by choosing from a drop-down list of all available macros. To insert a separator bar, just enter a single hyphen as the caption.

You'll find that the menu editor is quite straightforward and easy to use. It has some limitations, however:

✦ You can't use the menu editor to create a new menu bar (but you can do this with VBA).

✦ You can't change the captions for built-in menus or menu items.

✦ The menu editor doesn't recognize any menu changes that you've made using VBA statements. Therefore, the menu structure displayed in the menu editor may not even correspond to the actual menu structure.

✦ If more than one workbook that has a customized menu is open, the actual results of using the menu editor can be unpredictable.

Caution   The menu modifications made with the menu editor are stored in the workbook that is active when you invoke the editor. When the workbook is opened, the customized menus are in effect until the workbook is closed. This can cause some strange things to happen if several workbooks are open, each of which has its own customized menu. For reliable results, it's best to have only one workbook open that has customized menus.

Summary

In this chapter, I discuss how to modify two components of Excel's user interface: toolbars and menus. Users of all levels can benefit from creating custom toolbars. To create new commands that are executed by toolbar buttons, however, you need to write macros. I also discuss how to change the image that appears on a toolbar button. I introduce Excel's menu editor, which is most useful for macro writers.

✦　　✦　　✦

Using and Creating Templates

This chapter covers one of the most potentially useful features in Excel — template files. Templates can be used for a variety of purposes, ranging from custom "fill-in-the-blanks" workbooks to a way to change Excel's defaults for new workbooks or new worksheets.

An Overview of Templates

A *template* is essentially a model that serves as the basis for something else. If you understand this concept, you may save yourself a lot of work in the long run. For example, it could be that you *never* use headers or footers on your printouts. Consequently, every time you print a worksheet, you need to use the File⇨Page Setup command to remove the default headers and footers. The solution is to create a template for new worksheets that already has the default header and footer removed. Then, when you add a new worksheet to a workbook, the worksheet is based on this template and won't print with a header or footer.

Excel supports two types of templates:

   ✦ **Workbook templates:** These are usually ready-to-run workbooks that include formulas. They are usually set up so that a user can simply plug in values and get immediate results. The Spreadsheet Solutions templates are examples of this type of template.

   ✦ **Autotemplates:** These are templates that are the basis for new workbooks or for new sheets inserted into a workbook.

I discuss each template type in the following sections.

Workbook templates

Why use a workbook template? The simple answer is that it saves you from repeating work. Assume that you create a monthly sales report that consists of your company's sales by region, plus several summary calculations and charts. You can create a template file that consists of everything except the input values. Then, when it's time to create your report, you can open a workbook based on the template, fill in the blanks, and you're finished. You could, of course, just use the previous month's workbook and save it with a different name. This is prone to errors, however, because it's easy to forget to use the Save As command and accidentally overwrite the previous month's file.

When you create a workbook based on a template, Excel creates a copy of the template in memory so that the original template remains intact. The default workbook name is the template name with a number appended. For example, if you create a new workbook based on a template named `Sales Report.xlt`, the workbook's default name is `Sales Report1.xls`. The first time you save a workbook that was created from a template, Excel displays its Save As dialog box so that you can give the template a new name if desired.

Excel ships with 10 workbook templates (called *Spreadsheet Solutions* templates), which were developed by Village Software. I discuss these templates, which are useful for personal and business applications, later in this chapter. When you select the File⇨New command, you can select one of these templates from the New dialog box. Click the tab labeled Spreadsheet Solutions to choose a template upon which to base your new workbook (see Figure 33-1).

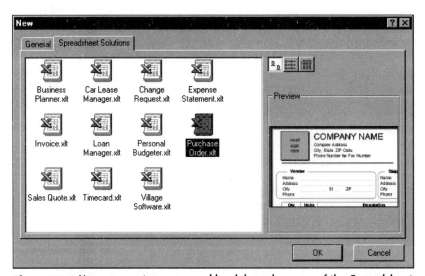

Figure 33-1: You can create a new workbook based on one of the Spreadsheet Solutions templates.

Later in this chapter, I explain how to create custom workbook templates.

Autotemplates

An *autotemplate* is a workbook that is used as the basis for a new workbook, a new worksheet, a new dialog sheet, or a new XLM macro sheet. Autotemplates are stored in your Excel\XLStart folder. An autotemplate workbook can have any of the following names:

Book.xlt: A template for the new default workbook. This template can have any number of sheets, formatted as you like.

Sheet.xlt: A template for a new worksheet added to an existing workbook. This should consist of a single worksheet.

Dialog.xlt: A template for a new dialog sheet added to an existing workbook. This should consist of a single dialog sheet.

Macro.xlt: A template for a new Excel 4.0 macros sheet added to a new workbook (this option is for compatibility purposes and is not very useful). This template should consist of a single XLM macro sheet.

Notice that Excel doesn't support an autotemplate for new VBA modules.

Cross-Reference You may notice that there is no Chart.xlt template file. That's because Excel has a better way to deal with this — chart autoformats. Refer to Chapter 16 to learn how create custom chart autoformats.

If you create a template named Book.xlt and store it in your Excel\XLStart folder, that template is the basis for all new workbooks (unless you specify otherwise by selecting a different template). When you choose the File➪New command, Excel displays its New dialog box. The General panel of this dialog box lists the templates stored in your Excel\XLStart folder, plus the templates stored in your Templates folder (which is a folder in the Excel folder or in the MSOffice folder). If you click on the Workbook icon, the new workbook is based on the Book.xlt template. In other words, if Book.xlt exists, clicking on the Workbook icons uses that template; otherwise, it uses Excel's default workbook.

Note If you click on the New Workbook button on the Standard toolbar, a new workbook is created without a prompt. If you've created a Book.xlt template in your Excel\XLStart folder, the workbook is based on that template. Otherwise, the workbook is a standard workbook with the normal default settings.

If you've created a template named Sheet.xlt and stored it in the Excel\XLStart folder, this template is the basis for new worksheets that you insert into an existing workbook when you choose the Insert➪Worksheet command. For example, you might create a Sheet.xlt file with settings that you prefer (such as modified print settings). Then, worksheets that you insert already have your preferred print settings.

> **Note** When you right-click a sheet tab and choose Insert from the shortcut menu, Excel displays its Insert dialog box (which looks just like the New dialog box). If you've created a template named Sheet.xlt, you can select it by clicking on the icon labeled Worksheet.

If you decide that you'd rather use Excel's default workbook and sheets, just delete the template files (Book.xlt, Sheet.xlt, Dialog.xlt, and Macro.xlt) from the template folder.

Where Templates Are Stored

Template files can be stored anywhere. When you open a template file (with the File⇨Open command), you don't actually open the template. Rather, Excel creates a new workbook based on the template. There are some specific locations, however, that make it easier to access your templates:

✦ Your Excel\XLStart folder. This is where you store autotemplates (Book.xlt, Sheet.xlt, Dialog.xlt, and Macro.xlt). You also can put workbook templates in this folder.

✦ Your Excel\Templates folder (or your MSOffice\Templates folder if you purchased Excel as part of Microsoft Office). Workbook templates stored here appear in the New dialog box.

✦ A folder located inside your Excel\Templates folder (or inside your MSOffice\Templates folder). If you create a new folder within this folder, its name appears as a tab in the New dialog box. Clicking the tab displays the templates stored in that folder. Figure 33-2 shows how the New dialog box looks when there's a new folder (named John's Templates) in the Templates folder.

> **Note** If you've specified an alternate start-up folder (using the General panel of the Options dialog box), templates stored in that location also appear in the New dialog box.

Creating Custom Templates

In this section, I describe how to create workbook templates and autotemplates. As you'll see, it's really quite simple. Because there are two different types, and they can be stored in different locations, I prepared Table 33-1, which summarizes how Excel handles templates.

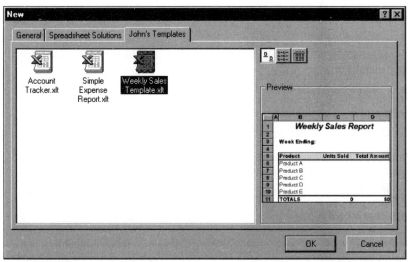

Figure 33-2: The New dialog box displays a new tab, which represents the template files in a folder inside the Templates folder.

Table 33-1
Determining Which Template to Use

If You Want to...	Do This...
Create a custom workbook template	Create the workbook and save it as a template in your Templates folder (or store it in a folder within the Templates folder).
Change characteristics of the default workbook	Create a workbook and save it as Book.xlt in your XLStart folder.
Change characteristics of the default worksheet	Create a single-sheet workbook with the settings that you want and save it as Sheet.xlt in your XLStart folder.
Change characteristics of the default dialog sheet	Create a single-dialog sheet workbook with the settings that you want and save it as Dialog.xlt in your XLStart folder.
Change characteristics of the default VBA module	Can't be done.
Change the characteristics of the default chart	Don't use a template. Use Excel's chart autotemplate feature.
Change characteristics of the default XLM macro sheet	Create a single-XLM macro sheet workbook with the settings that you want and save it as Macro.xlt in your XLStart folder.

Creating a workbook template

A workbook template is essentially a normal workbook, and it can use any of Excel's features such as charts, formulas, and macros. Normally, a template is set up so that the user can enter values and get immediate results.

If the template will be used by novices, you may consider locking all cells except the input cells (use the Protection panel of the Format Cells dialog box for this). Then, protect the worksheet using the Tools⇨Protection⇨Protect Sheet command.

To save the workbook as a template, choose the File⇨Save As command and select Template (*.xlt) from the drop-down list labeled Save as type. Save the template in your Templates folder (or a folder within the Templates folder).

Tip   Before saving the template, you may want to specify that the file be saved with a preview image. Use the File⇨Properties command and check the box labeled Save Preview Picture. That way, the New dialog box displays the preview when the template's icon is selected.

If you later discover that you want to modify the template, you don't open it using the normal methods — this creates a new workbook based on the template. To edit an existing template file, press the Shift key while you select the file in the Open dialog box. This opens the actual xlt template file and does not create a new workbook.

Creating an autotemplate

Creating an autotemplate is equally easy. Just create the template and store it in your XLStart directory. Usually, an autotemplate consists of formatting and settings, but it can include values, text, or formulas. A template named Book.xlt can consist of any number of sheets with any settings that you desire.

Sheet autotemplates usually consist of a single sheet (either a worksheet, a dialog sheet, or an XLM macro sheet). When you insert a new sheet, Excel uses the template for the new sheet (if the template exists). These templates can actually consist of *multiple* sheets, however. For example, if you have a template named Sheet.xlt that has 20 worksheets in it, the Insert⇨Worksheet command inserts 20 new worksheets into your workbook. This is rarely what you want, so it's best to limit autotemplates to a single sheet.

Ideas for Creating Templates

In this section, I list some settings that you may want to change in your Book.xlt or Sheet.xlt autotemplates. In other words, if you don't like Excel's defaults, create a template that uses your own defaults.

Workbook settings

Following is a partial list of the settings that you can adjust and use in a workbook template (Book.xlt). Or you can create several different workbook templates and choose the one you want for each new workbook.

✦ **Number of sheets of each type.** If you're a developer, you may want a template that has a VBA module and a dialog sheet.

✦ **Multiple formatted worksheets.** You can, for example, create a workbook template that has two worksheets: one formatted to print in landscape mode, and one formatted to print in portrait mode.

✦ **Workbook properties.** For example, Excel doesn't store a preview picture of your workbook. Use the File➪Properties command and change the Save Preview Picture option in the Summary panel.

✦ **Several settings in the View panel of the Options dialog box.** For example, you may not like to see sheet tabs, so you can turn this setting off.

✦ **Color palette.** Use the Color panel of the Options dialog box to create a custom color palette for a workbook.

Worksheet settings

Following is a partial list of the settings that you can adjust and use in a worksheet autotemplate:

✦ **Style.** The best approach is to use the Format➪Style and modify the attributes of the Normal style. For example, you can change the font or size, alignment, and so on.

✦ **Custom number formats.** If you create number formats that you use frequently, these can be stored in a worksheet autotemplate.

✦ **Column widths and row heights.** You may prefer that columns be wider or narrower, or you may want the rows to be taller.

✦ **Print settings.** Change these settings in the Page Setup dialog box. You can adjust the page orientation, paper size, margins, header and footer, and several other attributes.

✦ **Sheet settings.** These are options in the Options dialog box. They include gridlines, automatic page break display, and row and column headers. Note that settings that affect the window (for example, scrollbars and sheet tabs) are not stored with sheets.

Using the Template Wizard with Data Tracking

New! The Template Wizard is a new feature in Excel for Windows 95. It doesn't help you create a template. Rather, it helps you set things up so that you can store values in specific cells in a central database. In this section, I describe how to use the Template Wizard to create a system that keeps track of the data entered into workbooks created from a particular template.

Creating the template

This example involves a template that you use to create a weekly sales report. Figure 33-3 shows this template with values filled in. The actual template would not have the data filled in.

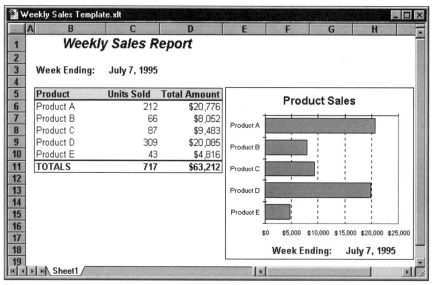

Figure 33-3: A template to produce a weekly sales report.

The template consists of two formulas to calculate the total units and amount, plus a chart that shows the sales by product. In addition, the sheet's page setup was changed to landscape, and the header and footer were removed. The sales manager uses this template to create the weekly report. It's simply a matter of filling in the date, entering the data into the ten cells, and clicking on the Print button on the Standard toolbar.

On the CD-ROM This template is available on the companion CD-ROM. It is named WEEKLY.XLT.

This sales manager also would like to store the weekly sales information in a separate file, however. Keeping all data in a single file would allow trend analysis and make it easier to produce quarterly or annual sales reports.

Calling on the Template Wizard

You can use Excel's Template Wizard to create a link to another file that stores each week's information as a database record. Following is a step-by-step demonstration:

1. Make sure that the Template Wizard add-in is loaded. Use the Tools⇨Add-Ins command and check the box labeled Template Wizard with Data Tracking.

2. Create the workbook that will be used as your template. Erase the data from the input cells and format the workbook as required. This example uses the WEEKLY.XLT workbook.

3. Choose the Data⇨Template Wizard command. Excel displays the dialog box shown in Figure 33-4. Select the workbook and the name and location for the template. Usually, the default settings are fine. Click on Next to move to the next step.

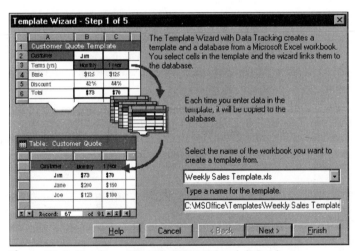

Figure 33-4: The first of five Template Wizard dialog boxes.

4. In the second step of the Template Wizard, select the database format for the file that will store the data tracking information. You can choose from several formats. The default is an Excel workbook, which is a good choice because it lets you easily work with the database. You also can select the location for the database. Click on Next to move on.

5. In the third step, specify the cells that you want to capture to the database. In this example, the cells consist of the week ending date, plus the 10 cells that contain the product sales information. You can use any name for the Field Names. Figure 33-5 shows how this dialog box is filled out for this example. After you enter the information for the 11 cells, click on Next.

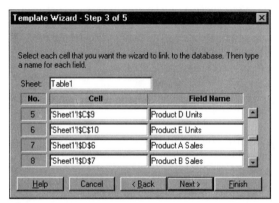

Figure 33-5: In Step 3, you specify the cells that will be captured to the database.

6. In the fourth step, you get the opportunity to add existing data to the database. Because this is a new template, select the option labeled No, skip it. Click on Next to continue.

7. The last step of the Template Wizard, shown in Figure 33-6, summarizes the information that you provided and lets you add a routing slip. This option sends a copy of each workbook created from the template to one or more persons to review. Click on Finish to end the Template Wizard.

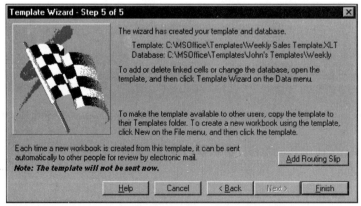

Figure 33-6: In the final step of the Template Wizard, you get an opportunity to add a routing slip to the template.

Using the template

Once you've created your template, you can use it just like any other template. Select the File⇨New command and locate the template file. Excel creates a new workbook from the template. Fill in the data. The formulas calculate the totals, and the product sales are displayed in the chart.

When you save the file, you get the prompt shown in Figure 33-7. Usually, you want to create a new record in the database. You can skip this box if desired. Close the dialog box, and you are prompted for a name for the worksheet.

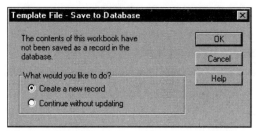

Figure 33-7: Saving the workbook created with the Template Wizard displays this dialog box.

Recall that the Template Wizard lets you choose from several different database file formats. Choosing an Excel workbook format makes it easy to examine the data. You can open the workbook and do whatever you want — create charts, generate new reports, filter the data, and so on.

You also can use this feature in a multiuser environment. For example, other members of your workgroup may use the same template, and their data is transferred to the master database.

Figure 33-8 shows how the database looks after a few weeks of producing sales reports.

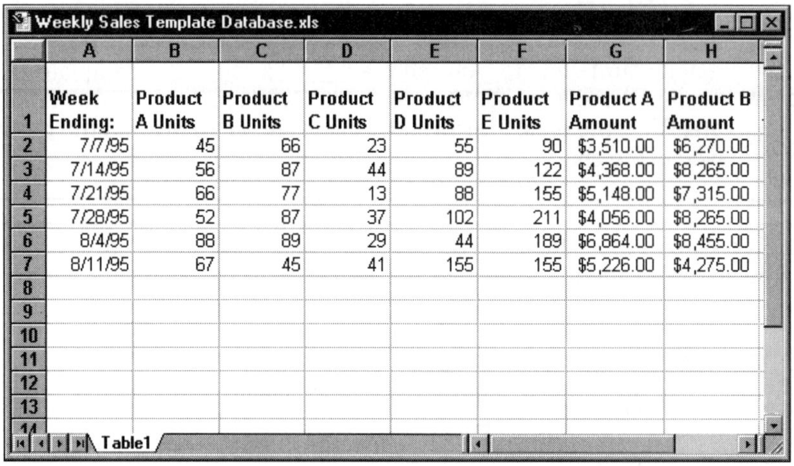

Weekly Sales Template Database.xls

	A	B	C	D	E	F	G	H
1	Week Ending:	Product A Units	Product B Units	Product C Units	Product D Units	Product E Units	Product A Amount	Product B Amount
2	7/7/95	45	66	23	55	90	$3,510.00	$6,270.00
3	7/14/95	56	87	44	89	122	$4,368.00	$8,265.00
4	7/21/95	66	77	13	88	155	$5,148.00	$7,315.00
5	7/28/95	52	87	37	102	211	$4,056.00	$8,265.00
6	8/4/95	88	89	29	44	189	$6,864.00	$8,455.00
7	8/11/95	67	45	41	155	155	$5,226.00	$4,275.00

Figure 33-8: The Template Wizard stores the information in this worksheet database.

Modifying the template

If you need to modify a template that's already been set up to use data tracking, open the template file (press Shift while you choose the template) and choose the Data➪Template Wizard command. The Template Wizard guides you through the steps to change any of the following:

- ✦ The template's name
- ✦ The location of the database
- ✦ The cells that correspond to the database fields
- ✦ The routing slip information

You also can use the Template Wizard to add data from existing workbooks to the database — as long as the data in these workbooks corresponds to the template.

The Template Wizard: How does it work?

You may be interested in knowing that the Template Wizard was created entirely using Excel's VBA macro language and custom dialog box feature. You may also be curious about how it all works. For example, when you create a workbook based on a template, how does Excel know that it should prompt you to store the data in the associated database? And how does it know which database to use?

With a little sleuthing I discovered that templates created by the Template Wizard (and workbooks created from these templates) include two additional sheets, which are "very hidden." In other words, you can't use the Format⇨Sheet⇨Unhide command to make them visible.

You can use VBA to unhide these sheets, however. Insert a new module, enter the code that follows, and choose the Run⇨Start command (or press F5) to execute this macro. The hidden sheets are revealed so that you can examine them.

```
Sub UnhideAll ()
For each Sheet in
           ThisWorkbook.Sheets
Sheet.Visible = True
Next Sheet
End Sub
```

One of the sheets is an XLM macro sheet containing a macro that opens the Template Wizard add-in if it's not already open. The Template Wizard add-in monitors the worksheet and prompts you to store the data when you save the file.

The other hidden sheet is a worksheet that has all of its rows and columns hidden. Unhiding the cells reveals the information needed to store the data: the database format, the folder that holds the database, and the field names.

It's not a good idea to tamper with these hidden sheets. Doing so may cause the template to no longer work properly. It's interesting, however, to take a peek behind the scenes.

Exploring the Spreadsheet Solutions Templates

When you installed Excel, the Setup program copied ten templates to your Excel\Templates folder (or to the MSOffice\Templates folder). These templates provide ready-made solutions for a number of common spreadsheet tasks. The templates provided are as follows:

✦ Business Planner: Helps you create an income statement, balance sheet, and cash flow summary.

✦ Car Lease Manager: Helps you decide how to negotiate a car lease.

✦ Change Request: Helps you track problems and request fixes to products or processes.

✦ Expense Statement: Helps you create expense report forms and a log to track them.

✦ Invoice: Helps you create invoices.

- ✦ Loan Manager: Helps you understand the cost of borrowing money and how to save money doing it.

- ✦ Personal Budgeter: Helps you create a personal budget to track spending and plan savings.

- ✦ Purchase Order: Helps you create purchase orders to send to vendors.

- ✦ Sales Quote: Helps you create sales quotes for prospective customers.

- ✦ Timecard: Helps you create a schedule for managing hourly employees.

If any of these sound as though they might be useful, I urge you to try them. These templates have a common look and feel and are very well done.

Figure 33-9 shows a workbook based on the Car Lease Manager template. The shaded cells contain formulas. Many cells have notes attached that describe what type of input is expected (move the mouse over a cell with a note and the note appears automatically). You can click the Customize button to activate another sheet that lets you customize the workbook. For example, you can add your company logo or name.

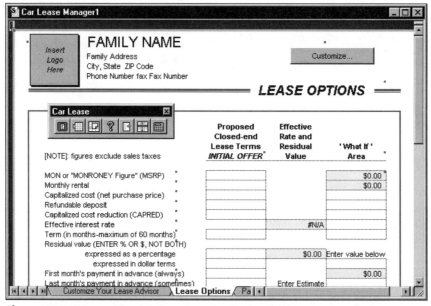

Figure 33-9: This workbook is based on the Car Lease Manager template.

Behind the scenes

The Spreadsheet Solutions templates can be useful, and exploring them might give you ideas for developing your own worksheets. There is more to these templates than meets the eye, however. You may have noticed that these templates are unusually large — all exceed 250K in size. That's because they also include a custom toolbar and several hidden sheets: a VBA macro sheet, a dialog sheet, a worksheet for international conversions, and maybe other sheets. Consequently, every workbook that you create based on one of these templates will be just as large.

Using the common information workbook

Three of the Spreadsheet Solutions templates (`Timecard`, `Sales Quote`, and `Change Request`) can use information stored in a workbook named `Common.xls`, which is stored in your Excel\Library folder. Figure 33-10 shows a workbook based on the `Timecard` template. When you click the Select Employee button, a dialog box appears that lists the entries in the `Common.xls` workbook (see Figure 33-11). When you select an employee, the appropriate fields in the workbook are filled in automatically. You can, of course, modify `Common.xls` to store your actual employee names.

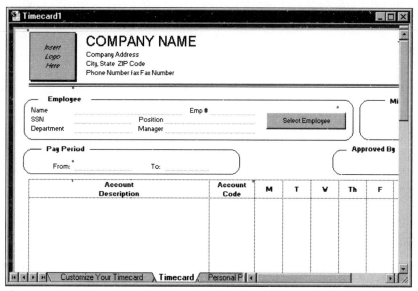

Figure 33-10: This workbook is based on the Timecard template.

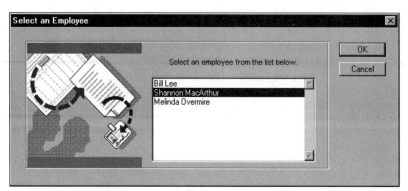

Figure 33-11: This dialog box displays the names stored in the `Common.xls` workbook. Selecting a name transfer the data to the appropriate cells.

Inserting a unique identifier

In some cases, you may want each workbook created from a template to contain a unique number. For example, it's useful to add a unique identification number to each invoice that you generate. You can do this automatically with the Spreadsheet Solutions templates. Click the Add a Number button on the toolbar. The information used to generate unique numbers is stored in the Windows Registry.

Tip   In a multiuser environment, make sure that you select the option labeled Share invoice numbers on network, and select a server that is available to all users. This option is on the Customize sheet. This ensures that the numbers are not duplicated.

Saving data to a database

Some of the Spreadsheet Solutions templates also take advantage of the data-tracking feature that I describe previously. The databases that hold the tracked cells are stored in your Excel\Library folder.

Summary

In this chapter, I introduce the concept of templates. Excel supports two template types: workbook templates and autotemplates. I describe the differences and explain how to create such templates and where to store them. I also discuss the Template Wizard, a new feature in Excel for Windows 95. This tool helps you create templates that can store data in a central database. Finally, I present an overview of the Spreadsheet Solutions templates, which are included with Excel.

✦   ✦   ✦

Using Visual Basic for Applications (VBA)

CHAPTER

34

This chapter is an introduction to the Visual Basic for Applications (VBA) macro language — perhaps the key component for users who want to customize Excel. A complete discussion of VBA would require an entire book. This chapter teaches you how to record macros and create simple macro subroutines. Subsequent chapters expand upon the topics in this chapter.

Introducing VBA Macros

In its broadest sense, a *macro* is a program that automates some aspect of Excel so that you can work more efficiently and with fewer errors. You might create a macro, for example, to format and print your month-end sales report. After the macro is developed and debugged, you can invoke the macro with a single command to perform many time-consuming procedures automatically.

Macros are usually considered one of the advanced features of Excel because you must have a pretty thorough understanding of Excel to put them to good use. The truth is that the majority of Excel users have never created a macro and probably never will. If you want to explore one of the most powerful aspects of Excel, however, you should know about macros. This chapter is designed to acquaint you with VBA, which lets you develop simple macros and execute macros developed by others.

You need not be a power user to use VBA. Casual users can simply turn on Excel's macro recorder: Excel records and then converts your subsequent actions into a VBA macro — which is essentially a program. When you execute this program, Excel performs the actions again. More advanced users, though, can write code that tells Excel to perform tasks that can't be recorded. For example, you can write procedures that display custom dialog boxes, add new commands to Excel's menus, or process data in a series of workbooks.

VBA: One of two macro languages in Excel

VBA was introduced in Excel 5. Prior to that version, Excel used an entirely different macro system known as XLM (or, the Excel 4 macro language). Most users, including me, consider VBA to be a much better option. For compatibility reasons, however, the XLM language is still supported. This means that you can load an older Excel file and still execute the macros stored in it. If you're interested in learning to use macros, I strongly suggest that you focus on VBA.

Cross-Reference I discuss the basic elements of the XLM macro system in Chapter 38.

What you can do with VBA

VBA is an extremely rich programming language with thousands of uses. Here are just a few things that you can do with VBA macros:

✦ **Insert a text string or formula.** If you need to enter your company name into worksheets frequently, you can create a macro to do the typing for you. The AutoCorrect feature also can do this.

✦ **Automate a procedure that you perform frequently.** For example, you may need to prepare a month-end summary. If the task is straightforward, you can develop a macro to do it for you.

✦ **Automate repetitive operations.** If you need to perform some action on 12 different workbooks, you can record a macro while you perform the task once — and then let the macro repeat your action on the other workbooks.

✦ **Create a custom command.** For example, you can combine several of Excel's menu commands so that they are executed from a single keystroke.

✦ **Create a custom toolbar button.** You can customize Excel's toolbars with your own buttons, which execute macros that you write.

✦ **Create a simplified "front end" for users who don't know much about Excel.** For example, you can set up a foolproof data entry template.

✦ **Develop a new worksheet function.** Although Excel includes a wide assortment of built-in functions, you can create custom functions that greatly simplify your formulas.

✦ **Create complete, turnkey, macro-driven applications.** Excel macros can display custom dialog boxes and add new commands to the menu bar.

✦ **Create custom add-ins for Excel.** All the add-ins that are shipped with Excel were created with Excel macros. My Power Utility Pak was developed using VBA exclusively.

VBA module sheets

The VBA code that comprises a macro is stored in an Excel workbook on a special sheet, called a *VBA module sheet*. A workbook can have any number of module sheets, and a single module sheet can store any number of macros.

When you record a VBA macro, Excel inserts an empty module sheet for you directly after the last sheet in your workbook. You also can insert your own module sheets by choosing the Insert⇨Macro⇨Module command (or right-clicking a sheet tab and selecting Insert from the shortcut menu).

Module sheets are quite different from worksheets — in fact, a module sheet is more like a word processing document (see Figure 34-1). When a module sheet is active, the menus are changed to include commands appropriate for modules.

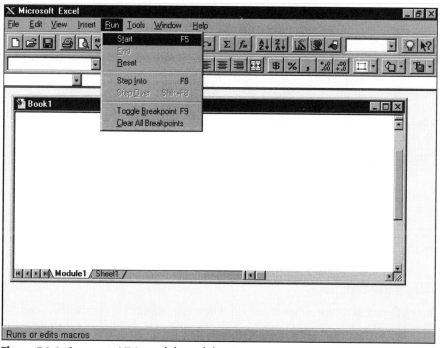

Figure 34-1: An empty VBA module and the Run menu.

Some key definitions

VBA newcomers often are overwhelmed by the terminology used in VBA. I've put together some key definitions to help you keep the terms straight. These terms cover VBA and custom dialog boxes — two important elements used in customizing Excel.

Code: VBA instructions that are produced in a module sheet when you record a macro. You also can enter VBA code manually.

Controls: Objects on a dialog box (or in a worksheet) that you manipulate. Examples include buttons, check boxes, and list boxes.

Custom dialog box: A dialog box that you create in a dialog sheet (I cover this topic in Chapter 36).

Dialog sheet: A sheet in an Excel workbook that holds a custom dialog box.

Function: One of two types of VBA macros that you can create (the other is a subrou-tine). A function returns a single value. You can use VBA functions in other VBA macros or in your worksheets.

Macro: A set of Excel instructions that are performed automatically. Excel macros can be XLM macros or VBA macros. This chapter focuses exclusively on VBA macros. VBA macros are also known as procedures.

Method: An action that is taken on an object. For example, applying the Clear method to a range object erases the contents of the cells.

Module sheet: A sheet in an Excel workbook that holds VBA code.

Object: An element that you manipulate with VBA. Examples include ranges, charts, drawing objects, and so on.

Procedure: Another name for a macro. A VBA procedure can be a subroutine or a function.

Subroutine: One of two types of Visual Basic macros that you can create. The other is a function.

Property: A particular aspect of an object. For example, a range object has properties such as Height, Style, and Name.

Two Types of VBA Macros

A VBA macro (or procedure) can be one of two types: a subroutine or a function. I discuss the difference in the following sections.

VBA subroutines

You can think of a subroutine macro as a new command that can be executed by either the user or by another macro. You can have any number of subroutines on a module sheet.

Figure 34-2 shows a simple VBA subroutine on a module sheet. When this subroutine is executed, VBA inserts the current date into the active cell, formats it, and then adjusts the column width.

Subroutines always start with the keyword *Sub*, the macro's name (every macro must have a unique name), and then a pair of parentheses. (The parentheses are required; they are empty unless the procedure uses one or more arguments.) The End Sub statement signals the end of a subroutine. The lines in between comprise the procedure's code.

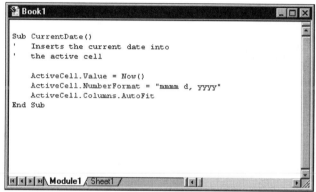

```
Sub CurrentDate()
'    Inserts the current date into
'    the active cell

    ActiveCell.Value = Now()
    ActiveCell.NumberFormat = "mmmm d, yyyy"
    ActiveCell.Columns.AutoFit
End Sub
```

Figure 34-2: This short VBA subroutine adds the current date, formats the cell, and adjusts the column width.

Note The module sheet shown in this figure also includes a comments. Comments are simply notes to yourself and are ignored by VBA. A comment line begins with an apostrophe. You also can put a comment after a statement. In other words, when VBA encounters an apostrophe, it ignores the rest of the text in the line.

You execute a subroutine in any of the following ways:

✦ Choose the Tools⇨Macro command and then select the subroutine's name from the list.

✦ Press its shortcut key combination (if it has one).

✦ Select it from the Tools menu (if it has been assigned to a new command on this menu).

✦ Refer to it in another VBA procedure.

I discuss subroutines in detail later in this chapter.

VBA functions

The second type of VBA procedure is a function. A function always returns a single value (just as a worksheet function always returns a single value). A VBA function can be executed by other VBA procedures or used in worksheet formulas just as you would use Excel's built-in worksheet functions.

Figure 34-3 shows a custom worksheet function defined in a VBA module and in use in a worksheet. This function is named CubeRoot and requires a single argument. CubeRoot calculates the cube root of its argument. A function looks much like a subroutine. Notice, however, that function procedures begin with the keyword *Function* and end with an End Function statement.

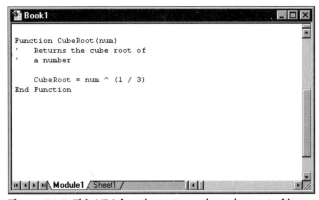

```
Book1

Function CubeRoot(num)
'    Returns the cube root of
'    a number

     CubeRoot = num ^ (1 / 3)
End Function
```

Figure 34-3: This VBA function returns the cube root of its argument.

Creating VBA functions that you use in worksheet formulas can simplify your formulas and let you perform calculations that otherwise might be impossible. I discuss VBA functions in Chapter 35.

Creating VBA Macros

There are two ways to create macros:

✦ Turn on the macro recorder and record your actions.

✦ Enter the code directly into a VBA module.

I discuss both of these methods in this section.

A few words about terminology

With the introduction of VBA in Excel 5, the terminology used to describe Excel's programmable features got a bit muddy. For example, VBA is a programming language, but it also serves as one of Excel's macro languages. So what do you call something written in VBA and executed in Excel? Is it a macro, or is it a program? Excel's online help often refers to VBA code as a macro, so I use that terminology as well.

Recording your actions to create code

Excel's macro recorder translates your actions into VBA code. To start the macro recorder, choose the Tools⇨Record Macro⇨Record New Macro command. Excel displays the Record New Macro dialog box shown in Figure 34-4. When you click the Options button, the dialog box expands and you can change some of the macro options.

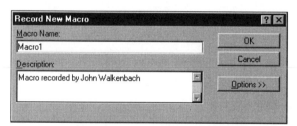

Figure 34-4: The Record New Macro dialog box.

Excel inserts a new module sheet to store the macro. When you're finished recording the macro, choose Tools⇨Record Macro⇨Stop Recording (or click the Stop Macro button on the Stop Recording toolbar).

Note Recording your actions always results in a new subroutine procedure. You can't create a function procedure using the macro recorder.

Entering and editing code

Recording macros is handy, but for more complex macros (or to create a function) you need to enter the code manually into a module sheet. A VBA module sheet works basically like a text editor. You can move through the sheet, select text, insert, copy, cut, paste, and so on.

Notice that the text in a module sheet appears in different colors. Excel color codes the text so that you can easily distinguish the following:

✦ Keywords

✦ Comments

✦ Identifiers

✦ Syntax errors

Tip   You can change the colors used by selecting Tools⇨Options in the Options dialog box, and then select the Module Format tab. You can make other changes in the Module General tab.

When you enter code in a module sheet, you're free to use indenting and blank lines to make the code more readable (in fact, this is an excellent habit). After you enter a line of code, it is evaluated for syntax errors. If none is found, the line of code is reformatted and colors are added to keywords and identifiers. This automatic reformatting adds consistent spaces (before and after an equal sign, for example) and removes extra spaces that aren't needed. If a syntax error is found, you get a pop-up message, and the line is displayed in a different color (red, by default). You need to correct your error before you can execute the macro.

Recording VBA Macros

In this section, I describe the basic steps that you take to record a VBA macro. In most cases, you can record your actions as a macro and then simply play the macro back; you needn't look at the code that's generated. If this is as far as you go with VBA, you won't need to be concerned with the language itself (although a basic understanding of how things work won't do any harm).

Recording

In this example, I record a macro that changes the formatting for the current range selection. The selected range uses Arial 16-point type, boldface, colored red.

1. Enter a value or text into a cell — anything will do. This gives you something to start with.

2. Select the cell that contains the value or text that you entered in the preceding step.

3. Select the Tools⇨Record Macro⇨Record New Macro command. Excel displays the Record New Macro dialog box.

4. Enter a new name for the macro to replace the default Macro1 name. A good name is **FormattingMacro**.

5. Click on the Options button (this expands the dialog box) and make sure that Visual Basic is selected as the Language option.

6. Assign this macro to a new command on the Tools menu by entering **Format Selection** in the edit box labeled Menu Item on Tools Menu.

7. Click on OK. This closes the Record New Macro dialog box. Excel displays a single-button toolbar called Stop Recording. You can click on this button to turn off the macro recorder when you're finished.

8. Select the Format⇨Cells command and click on the Font tab. Choose Arial font, Bold, 16-point type, and make the color red. Click on OK to close the Format Cells dialog box.

9. The macro is finished, so click on the Stop Macro button on the Stop Recording toolbar (or select the Tools⇨Record Macro⇨Stop Recording command).

Examining the macro

The macro was recorded in a new module named Module1. Activate the module and examine the macro. It should consist of the following code:

```
' FormattingMacro Macro
' Macro recorded by John Walkenbach
'
Sub FormattingMacro()
    With Selection.Font
        .Name = "Arial"
        .FontStyle = "Bold"
        .Size = 16
        .Strikethrough = False
        .Superscript = False
        .Subscript = False
        .OutlineFont = False
        .Shadow = False
        .Underline = xlNone
        .ColorIndex = 3
    End With
End Sub
```

The macro recorded is a subroutine (it begins with a Sub statement) named FormattingMacro. The statements tell Excel what to do when the macro is executed.

Notice that Excel inserted comments at the top. This is the information that appeared in the Record New Macro dialog box. These comment lines (which begin with an apostrophe) aren't really necessary, and deleting them has no effect on how the macro runs.

You may notice that the macro recorded some actions that you didn't take. For example, it sets the Strikethrough, Superscript, and Subscript properties to False. This is just a by-product of the method Excel uses to translate actions into code. Excel sets the properties for every option in the Font tab of the Format Cells dialog box.

Testing the macro

Before you recorded this macro, you set an option that assigned the macro to a new command on the Tools menu. To test the macro, activate a worksheet (it can be the worksheet that contains the VBA module, or any other worksheet). Select a cell or range and choose the Tools⇨Format Selection command. The macro immediately changes the formatting of the selected cell(s).

Continue testing the macro with other selections. The macro always applies exactly the same formatting.

Editing the macro

Once you record a macro, you can change it (although you must know what you're doing). Assume that you discover that you really wanted to make the text 14 point rather than 16 point. You could rerecord the macro. But this is a simple modification, so editing the code is more efficient. Just activate Module1, locate the statement that sets the font size, and change 16 to 14. You also can remove the following lines:

```
.Strikethrough = False
.Superscript = False
.Subscript = False
.OutlineFont = False
.Shadow = False
.Underline = xlNone
```

Removing these lines causes the macro to ignore the properties referred to in the statements. For example, if the cell has underlining, the underlining won't be affected by the macro.

The edited macro is as follows:

```
Sub FormattingMacro()
    With Selection.Font
        .Name = "Arial"
        .FontStyle = "Bold"
        .Size = 14
        .ColorIndex = 3
    End With
End Sub
```

Test this new macro and you'll see that it performs as it should. Also, notice that it doesn't remove a cell's underlining, which occurred in the original version of the macro.

Another example

In this example, I show how to record a slightly more complicated VBA macro that converts formulas into values. This action is usually a two-step process: copy the range to the Clipboard and then choose Edit➪Paste Special (with the Values option selected) to paste the values over the formulas. This macro combines these steps into a single command.

Furthermore, you want to be able to access this command by pressing a shortcut key combination (Ctrl+F) or choosing a new command from the menu (Tools➪Convert Formulas to Values).

Here are the steps required to create this macro:

1. Enter some formulas into a range (=RAND() is a good formula for this example).

2. Select the range.

3. Choose Tools➪Record Macro➪Record New Macro. Excel displays the Record Macro dialog box.

4. Click on the Options button to expand the dialog box.

5. Complete the dialog box so that it looks like Figure 34-5. This assigns the macro the name FormulaConvert. It also assigns the macro to a new menu item on the Tools menu and gives it a Ctrl+F shortcut key. Using an ampersand (&) makes the letter *F* underlined in the command. Click on OK to begin recording.

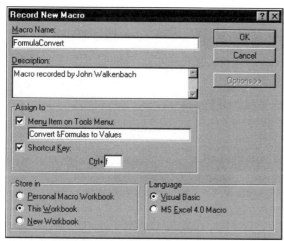

Figure 34-5: How the Record New Macro dialog box should look when recording the sample macro.

6. With the range still selected, choose the Edit⇨Copy command to copy the range to the Clipboard.

7. Select the Edit⇨Paste Special command, click on the Values option, and then click on OK to close the dialog box.

8. Press Esc to cancel paste mode. (Excel removes the moving border around the selected range.)

9. Click the Stop Macro button (or choose the Tools⇨Record Macro⇨Stop Recording command).

To test the macro, activate a worksheet, enter some formulas, and select the formulas. You can execute the macro in any of three ways:

✦ Press Ctrl+F.

✦ Choose the new Tools⇨Convert Formulas to Values command.

✦ Choose Tools⇨Macro and double-click the macro name (FormulaConvert).

Excel converts the formulas in the selected range to their values — in a single step instead of two.

Caution   Be careful, because you can't undo the conversion of formulas to values. Actually, it's possible to edit the macro so that its results can be undone, but the procedure is beyond the scope of this discussion.

The new command on the Tools menu (Convert Formulas to Values) goes away when you close the workbook but reappears when you reopen it. In other words, the command appears only when the macro that it executes is available.

Tip   You also can assign a macro to drawing objects (such as a button) or custom buttons on a toolbar. To assign a macro to a drawing object, right-click the object, choose Assign Macro from the shortcut menu, select the macro, and click on OK. To assign a macro to a custom icon, use the View⇨Toolbars command and click on the Customize button. In the Categories list box, select Custom and drag any button to the toolbar that you're customizing. The Assign Macro dialog box pops up so that you can select the macro.

The recorded macro follows:

```
' FormulaConvert Macro
' Macro recorded by John Walkenbach
'
' Keyboard Shortcut: Ctrl+f
'
Sub ConvertFormulas()
    Selection.Copy
    Selection.PasteSpecial Paste:=xlValues, Operation:=xlNone, _
        SkipBlanks:=False, Transpose:=False
    Application.CutCopyMode = False
End Sub
```

Excel added some comment lines that describe the macro. The actual macro begins
with the Sub statement. The subroutine has three statements. The first simply copies
the selected range. The second statement, which is displayed on two lines (the
underscore character means that the statement continues on the next line), pastes
the Clipboard contents to the current selection. The second statement has several
arguments, representing the options in the Paste Special dialog box. The third
statement cancels the moving border around the selected range (I generated the
statement by pressing Esc after the paste operation).

Note If you prefer, you can delete the underscore character in the second statement and
combine the two lines into one (a VBA statement can be any length). This action may
make the macro easier to read.

More about recording VB macros

If you followed along with the preceding examples, you should have a better feel for
how to record macros. If you find the VBA code confusing, don't worry — you don't
really have to be concerned with it as long as the macro you record works correctly. If
the macro doesn't work, it's often easier to rerecord it rather than edit the code.

A good way to learn about what gets recorded is to set up your screen so that you can
see the code being generated while you're in macro record mode. To do so, use the
Window⇨New command to create a new window to your worksheet, and then display the
module sheet in one window and the worksheet in the other. Figure 34-6 shows an example.

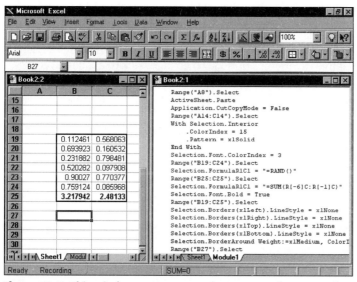

Figure 34-6: This windows arrangement lets you see the VBA code
as you record your actions.

Absolute versus relative recording

If you're going to work with macros, it's important that you understand the concept of *relative* versus *absolute recording*. Normally, when you record a macro, Excel stores exact references to the cells that you select (that is, it performs absolute recording). If you select the range B1:B10 while you're recording a macro, for example, Excel records this selection as

```
Range("B1:B10").Select
```

This means exactly what it says: "Select the cells in the range B1:B10." When you invoke this macro, the same cells are always selected regardless of where the active cell is located.

You may have noticed that the Tools⇨Record Macro cascading menu has an option labeled Use Relative References. When you select this command, Excel changes its recording mode from absolute to relative. Selecting a range of cells will be translated differently, depending on where the active cell is. For example, if cell A1 is active when you record a macro to select the range B1:B10, the following statement is recorded:

```
ActiveCell.Offset(0, 1).Range("A1:A10").Select
```

This statement can be translated as: "From the active cell, move 0 rows and 1 column, and then treat this new cell as if it were cell A1. Now select what would be A1:A10." In other words, a macro recorded in relative mode starts out using the active cell as its base and then stores relative references to this cell. As a result, you get different results depending on the location of the active cell. When you play back this macro, the cells that are selected depend on the active cell. It selects a 10-row-by-1-column range that is offset from the active cell by 0 rows and 1 column.

Note When Excel is recording in relative mode, the cascading menu displays a check mark next to the Use Relative References option. To change back to absolute recording, just select the command again to remove the check mark.

The recording mode — either absolute or relative — can make a *major* difference in how your macro performs. Therefore, it's important that you understand the distinction.

Caution When you record macros, be careful when you use commands such as Shift+Ctrl+right arrow or Shift+Ctrl+down arrow (commands that extend the selection to the end of a block of cells). Excel doesn't record this type of command as you might expect. Rather, it records the actual cells that you made in the selection (either in an absolute or relative manner, depending on the mode). When you play back the macro with a different size range, the selection may not be correct (and you may not even realize it).

Recording at a specific location

When you begin recording a macro, Excel normally creates a new subroutine to hold the recorded statements. Sometimes you may want to record new actions to be added to an existing macro. You have two choices:

✦ Record the macro and then copy and paste the code to the other subroutine.

✦ Instruct Excel to begin recording at a specific location in a VBA module.

To begin recording at a specific location, activate the VBA module and move the cursor to the location where you want the recorded code to be inserted. Select the Tools⇨Record Macro⇨Mark Position for Recording Command. Then, to start recording at the marked position, choose the Tools⇨Record Macro⇨Record at Mark command.

Storing macros in the Personal Macro Workbook

If you record a macro that is useful in many different worksheets, you may want to store it in your Personal Macro Workbook so that it's always available. Otherwise, you need to open this particular worksheet whenever you want to use this macro. To record the macro into your Personal Macro Workbook, choose that option in the Record Macro dialog box before you start recording.

Most macros created by users are designed for a specific workbook. But you may want to use some macros in all your work. You can store these general-purpose macros in the Personal Macro Workbook so that they are always available to you. The Personal Macro Workbook is loaded whenever you start Excel; the file, `Personal.xls`, is stored in the XlStart folder, which is in your Excel folder.

The Personal Macro Workbook is normally in a hidden window (to keep it out of the way). If you record a macro to this workbook, you need to unhide the window (choose the Window⇨Unhide command) before you can edit or view the macro.

If you store macros on the Personal Macro Workbook, you don't have to remember to open the Personal Macro Workbook when you load a workbook that uses macros. If you unhide the Personal Macro Workbook, though, make sure that you hide it before you exit Excel or it won't be hidden the next time you start Excel.

When you want to exit Excel, Excel asks whether you want to save changes to the Personal Macro Workbook.

Writing VB Code

As demonstrated in the preceding sections, the easiest way to create a simple macro is to record your actions. To develop more complex macros, however, you have to enter the VBA code manually — in other words, write a program. To save time, you can often combine recording with manual entry.

Before you can begin writing VBA code, you must have a good understanding of topics such as objects, properties, and methods — and it doesn't hurt to be familiar with common programming constructs such as looping and If-Then statements.

This section is an introduction to VBA programming, which is essential if you want to write (rather than record) VBA macros. This is not intended to be a complete instructional guide. My *Excel For Windows 95 Power Programming Techniques, 2nd Edition* (scheduled for publication by IDG Books Worldwide in early 1996), covers all aspects of VBA and advanced spreadsheet application development.

A quick tour of VBA

VBA is a complex feature, and it's easy to get overwhelmed. To set the stage for the details of VBA, I've prepared a concise summary of how VBA works.

✦ You perform actions in VBA by writing (or recording) code in a VBA module sheet and then executing the macro in any of a number of ways. VBA modules are stored in an Excel workbook, and a workbook can hold any number of VBA modules.

✦ A VBA module consists of subroutine procedures. A subroutine procedure is basically computer code that performs some action on or with objects. Here's an example of a simple subroutine called ShowSum (it adds 1 + 1 and displays the result):

```
Sub ShowSum()
    Sum = 1 + 1
    MsgBox "The answer is " & Sum
End Sub
```

✦ A VBA module also can store function procedures. A function procedure returns a single value. A function can be called from another VBA procedure or even used in a worksheet formula. Here's an example of a function named AddTwo (it adds two values, which are supplied as arguments):

```
Function AddTwo(arg1, arg2)
    AddTwo = arg1 + arg2
End Function
```

✦ VBA manipulates objects. Excel provides you with more than 100 objects that you can manipulate. Examples of objects include a workbook, a worksheet, a range on a worksheet, a chart, and a drawn rectangle.

✦ Objects are arranged in a hierarchy. Objects can act as containers for other objects. For example, Excel itself is an object called Application, and it contains other objects such as Workbook objects and Toolbar objects. The Workbook object can contain other objects such as Worksheet objects and Chart objects. A Worksheet object can contain objects such as Range objects, PivotTable objects, and so on. The arrangement of these objects is referred to as an object model. Excel's object model is depicted in the online help system (see Figure 34-7).

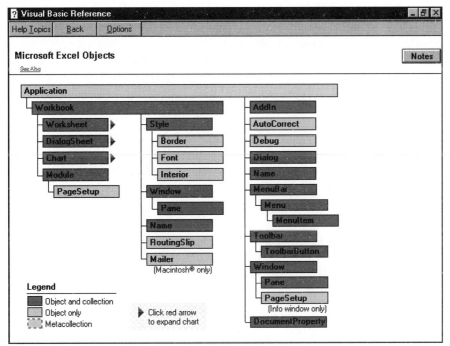

Figure 34-7: A depiction of part of Excel's object model.

✦ Like objects form a collection. For example, the Worksheets collection consists of all worksheets in a particular workbook. The Toolbars collection consists of all Toolbar objects. Collections are objects in themselves.

✦ You refer to an object by specifying its position in the object hierarchy, using a period as a separator.

For example, you can refer to a workbook named `Book1.xls` as

```
Application.Workbooks("Book1")
```

This refers to the `Book1.xls` workbook in the Workbooks collection. The Workbooks collection is contained in the Application object (that is, Excel). Extending this to another level, you can refer to Sheet1 in `Book1` as follows:

```
Application.Workbooks("Book1").Worksheets("Sheet1")
```

You can take it to still another level and refer to a specific cell as follows:

```
Application.Workbooks("Book1").Worksheets("Sheet1").Range("A1")
```

✦ If you omit specific references, Excel uses the *active* objects. If `Book1` is the active workbook, the preceding reference can be simplified as follows:

```
Worksheets("Sheet1").Range("A1")
```

If you know that Sheet1 is the active sheet, you can simplify the reference even more:

```
Range("A1")
```

✦ Objects have properties. A property can be thought of as a *setting* for an object. For example, a Range object has properties such as *Value* and *Name*. A Chart object has properties such as *HasTitle* and *Type*. You can use VBA to determine object properties and also to change them.

✦ You refer to properties by combining the object with the property, separated by a period. For example, you can refer to the value in cell A1 on Sheet1 as follows:

```
Worksheets("Sheet1").Range("A1").Value
```

✦ You can assign values to variables. To assign the value in cell A1 on Sheet1 to a variable called *Interest*, use the following VBA statement:

```
Interest = Worksheets("Sheet1").Range("A1").Value
```

✦ Objects have methods. A method is an action that is performed with the object. For example, one of the methods for a Range object is ClearContents. This method clears the contents of the range.

✦ You specify methods by combining the object with the method, separated by a period. For example, to clear the contents of cell A1, use:

```
Worksheets("Sheet1").Range("A1:C12").ClearContents
```

✦ VBA also includes all the constructs of modern programming languages, including arrays, looping, and so on.

Believe it or not, this all describes VBA in a nutshell. Now you just have to learn the details, some of which I cover in the rest of this chapter.

Objects and collections

VBA is an object-oriented language. This means that it manipulates *objects*, such as ranges, charts, drawing objects, and so on. These objects are arranged in a hierarchy. The Application object (which is Excel) contains other objects. For example, the Application object contains these objects:

✦ Addin

✦ Debug

✦ Dialog

✦ Menubar

✦ Toolbar

✦ Window

✦ Workbook

Each of these objects can contain other objects. For example, a Workbook object can contain the following objects:

✦ Chart

✦ DialogSheet

✦ Mailer

✦ Module

✦ Name

✦ RoutingSlip

✦ Style

✦ Window

✦ Worksheet

Each of these objects, in turn, can contain other objects. A Worksheet object, for example, can contain the following objects:

✦ DrawingObject

✦ Outline

✦ PageSetup

✦ PivotTable

✦ Range

✦ Scenario

A collection consists of all like objects. For example, the collection of all Workbook objects is known as the Workbooks collection. You can refer to an individual object in a collection by using an index number, or a reference. For example, if a workbook has three worksheets (named Sheet1, Sheet2, and Sheet3), you can refer to the first object in the Worksheets collection in either of these ways:

```
Worksheets(1)
Worksheets("Sheet1")
```

Properties

The objects that you work with have *properties*, which you can think of as attributes. For example, a range object has properties such as Column, Row, Width, and Value. A chart object has properties such as Legend, ChartTitle, and so on. ChartTitle also is an object, with properties such as Font, Orientation, and Text. Excel has many objects, and each has its own set of properties. In a VB module, you can:

✦ Examine an object's current property setting and take some action based on it.

✦ Change an object's property setting.

You refer to a property by placing a period and the property name after the object's name. For example, the following VB statement sets the Value property of a range named `frequency` to 15 (that is, it causes the number 15 to appear in the range's cells):

```
Range("frequency").Value = 15
```

Some properties are *read-only*, which means that you can examine but can't change the property. For a single-cell range object, the Row and Column properties are read-only properties: you can determine where a cell is (in which row and column), but you can't change the cell's location by changing these properties.

A range object also has a Formula property, which is not read-only; that is, you can insert a formula into a cell by changing its Formula property. The following statement inserts a formula into a cell named `total` by changing the cell's Formula property:

```
Range("total").Formula = "=SUM(A1:A10)"
```

Note   Contrary to what you may think, a cell in a worksheet is not an object. When you want to manipulate a single cell, you use the Range object (with only one cell in it).

An object of which you need to be aware is the Application object, which is actually Excel, the program. The Application object has several useful properties, such as the following:

✦ **Application.ActiveWorkbook:** Returns the active workbook (a workbook object) in Excel.

✦ **Application.ActiveSheet:** Returns the active sheet (a sheet object) of the active workbook.

✦ **Application.ActiveCell:** Returns the active cell (a range object) object of the active window.

✦ **Application.Selection:** Returns the object currently selected in the active window of the Application object.

It's important to understand that properties can return objects. In fact, that's exactly what the preceding examples do. The result of Application.ActiveCell, for example, is a range object. Therefore, you can access properties by using a statement such as the following:

```
Application.ActiveCell.Font.Size=15
```

In this case, Application.ActiveCell.Font is an object and Size is a property. The preceding statement sets the Size property to 15; that is, it causes the font in the currently selected cell to have a size of 15 points.

Because Application properties are so commonly used, you can omit the object qualifier (Application). For example, to get the row of the active cell, you can use a statement such as the following:

```
ActiveCell.Row
```

There can be many different ways to refer to the same object. Assume that you have a workbook named `Sales` and it's the only workbook open. Further assume that this workbook has one worksheet named Summary. You can refer to the Summary sheet in any of the following ways:

```
Workbooks("Sales.xls").Worksheets("Summary")
Workbooks(1).Worksheets(1)
Workbooks(1).Sheets(1)
Application.ActiveWorkbook.ActiveSheet
ActiveWorkbook.ActiveSheet
ActiveSheet
```

The method that you use is determined by how much you know about the workspace. For example, if there is more than one workbook open, the second or third method is not reliable. If you want to work with the active sheet (whatever it may be), either of the last three methods would work. To be absolutely sure that you're referring to a specific sheet on a specific workbook, the first method is your best choice.

Methods

Objects also have *methods*. You can think of a method as an action taken with an object. For example, range objects have a Clear method. The following VBA statement clears the range named `total`, an action equivalent to selecting the range and then choosing the Edit⇨Clear⇨All command:

```
Range("total").Clear
```

In VBA code, methods look like properties, but they are very different.

Variables

Like all programming languages, VBA enables you to work with variables. In VBA (unlike in some languages), you don't need to declare variables explicitly before you use them in your code (although it's definitely a good practice).

In the following example, the value in cell A1 on Sheet1 is assigned to a variable named *rate*:

```
Rate = Worksheets("Sheet1").Range("A1").Value
```

You then can work with the variable *rate* in other parts of your VBA code. Note that the variable *rate* is not a named range. This means that you can't use it as such in a worksheet formula.

Controlling execution

VBA uses many constructs that are found in most other programming languages. These constructs are used to control the flow of execution. In this section, I introduce a few of the more common programming constructs.

The If-Then construct

One of the most important control structures in VBA is the If-Then construct. This common command gives your applications decision-making capability. The basic syntax of the If...Then structure is

```
If condition Then statements [Else elsestatements]
```

Following is an example (which doesn't use the option Else clause). This subroutine checks the active cell. If it contains a negative value, the cell's color is changed to red. Otherwise, nothing happens.

```
Sub CheckCell()
    If ActiveCell.Value < 0 Then ActiveCell.Font.ColorIndex = 3
End Sub
```

A VBA analogy

If you like analogies, here's one for you. It may help you understand the relationships between objects, properties, and methods in VBA. In this analogy, I compare Excel with a fast-food restaurant chain. Ready?

The basic unit of Excel is a workbook object. In a fast-food chain, the basic unit is an individual restaurant. With Excel, you can add workbooks and close workbooks, and all of the open workbooks are known as Workbooks (a collection of Workbook objects). Similarly, the management of a fast-food chain can add restaurants and close restaurants; all of the restaurants in the chain can be viewed as a collection of Restaurant objects.

An Excel workbook is an object, but it also contains other objects such as worksheets, charts, VBA modules, and so on. Furthermore, each object in a workbook can contain its own objects. For example, a Worksheet can contain Range objects, PivotTable objects, Drawing objects, and so on.

Continuing with the analogy, a fast-food restaurant (such as a workbook) contains objects such as the Kitchen, DiningArea, and ParkingLot. Furthermore, management can add or remove objects from the Restaurant object. For example, they may add a DriveupWindow object. Each of these objects can contain other objects. For example, the Kitchen object has a Stove object, VentilationFan object, Chef object, Sink object, and so on.

Excel's objects have properties. For example, a Range object has properties such as Value and Name, and a Rectangle object has properties such as Width, Height, and so on. Not surprisingly, objects in a fast-food restaurant also have properties. The Stove object, for example, has properties such as Temperature and NumberofBurners. The VentilationFan has its own set of properties (TurnedOn, RPM, and so on).

Besides properties, Excel's objects also have methods, which perform an operation on an object. For example, the ClearContents method erases the contents of a Range object. An object in a fast-food restaurant also has methods. You can easily envision a ChangeThermostat method for a Stove object, or a SwitchOn method for a VentilationFan object.

With Excel, methods sometimes change an object's properties. The ClearContents method for a Range changes the Range's Value property. Similarly, the ChangeThermostat method on a Stove object affects its Temperature property.

With VBA, you can write subroutine procedures to manipulate Excel's objects. In a fast-food restaurant, the management can give orders to manipulate the objects in the restaurants ("Turn the stove on and switch the ventilation fan to high."). Now is it clear?

For-Next loops

For example, you can use a For-Next loop to process a series of items. Its syntax is as follows:

```
For counter = start To end [Step stepval]
        [statements]
        [Exit For]
        [statements]
Next [counter]
```

Here's an example of a For-Next loop:

```
Sub SumSquared()
    Total = 0
    For Num = 1 To 10
        Total = Total + (Num ^ 2)
    Next Num
    MsgBox Total
End Sub
```

This example has one statement between the For statement and the Next statement. This single statement is executed 10 times. The variable Num takes on successive values of 1, 2, 3, and so on up to 10. The variable Total stores the sum of Num squared, added to the previous value of Total. The result is a value that represents the sum of the first ten integers squared. This result is displayed in a message box.

The With-End With construct

Another construct that you'll encounter if you record macros is the With-End With construct. This is a shortcut way of dealing with several properties or methods of the same object. Here's an example:

```
Sub AlignCells()
    With Selection
        .HorizontalAlignment = xlCenter
        .VerticalAlignment = xlCenter
        .WrapText = False
        .Orientation = xlHorizontal
    End With
End Sub
```

The following subroutine performs exactly the same operations but doesn't use the With-End With construct:

```
Sub AlignCells()
    Selection.HorizontalAlignment = xlCenter
    Selection.VerticalAlignment = xlCenter
    Selection.WrapText = False
    Selection.Orientation = xlHorizontal
End Sub
```

The Select Case construct

The Select Case construct is useful for choosing among two or more options. The syntax for the Select Case structure is as follows:

```
Select Case testexpression
    [Case expressionlist-n
        [statements-n]] . . .
    [Case Else
        [elsestatements]]
End Select
```

The following example demonstrates the use of a Select Case construct. In this example, the active cell is checked. If its value is less than 0, it's colored red. If it's equal to zero, it's colored blue. If the value is greater than zero, it's colored black.

```
Sub CheckCell()
    Select Case ActiveCell.Value
        Case Is < 0
            ActiveCell.Font.ColorIndex = 3 'Red
        Case 0
            ActiveCell.Font.ColorIndex = 5 'Blue
        Case Is > 0
            ActiveCell.Font.ColorIndex = 1 'Black
    End Select
End Sub
```

Any number of statements can go below each Case statement, and they all get executed if the case is true. If you use only one statement, as in the preceding example, you may want to put the statement on the same line as the Case statement.

A macro that can't be recorded

Following is a VBA macro that can't be recorded because it uses an If-Then structure. This macro enables you to quickly identify cells that exceed a certain value. When you run this macro, it prompts the user for a value. Then it evaluates every cell in the selection. If the cell's value is greater than the value entered by the user, the macro makes the cell bold and red.

```
Sub SelectiveFormat()
'This procedure selectively shades cells greater than
'a specified target value
'Get target value from user
    Message = "Change attributes of values greater than or equal to..."
    Target = InputBox(Message)
    Target=Val(Target)

'Evaluate each cell in the selection
    For Each Item In Selection
        If IsNumeric(Item) Then
            If Item.Value >= Target Then
                With Item
                    .Font.Bold = True
                    .Font.ColorIndex = 3 'Red
                End With
            End If
        End If
    Next Item
End Sub
```

On the CD-ROM This macro is available on the companion disc in the workbook named VBA_SUB.XLS.

Although this macro may look complicated, it's actually simple when you break it down.

First, the macro assigns text to a variable named Message. It then uses the InputBox function to solicit a value from the user. The InputBox function has a single argument (which is the Message variable), and returns a string. I use the Val function to convert this string to a value and then assign it to a variable called Target.

The For-Next loop checks every cell in the selected range. The first statement within the loop uses the IsNumeric function to determine whether the cell can be evaluated as a number. This is important because a cell without a value will generate an error when we access the Value property in the next statement. If the cell is numeric, it is checked against the target value. If it's greater than or equal to the target value, the Bold and ColorIndex properties are changed. Otherwise, nothing happens and the loop is incremented.

After entering this macro, named SelectiveFormat, into a module sheet, you can use the Tools⇨Macro command (with the Options button) to assign it a shortcut key combination, such as Ctrl+S. You also can use the Macro Options dialog box to add this macro to the Tools menu (see Figure 34-8).

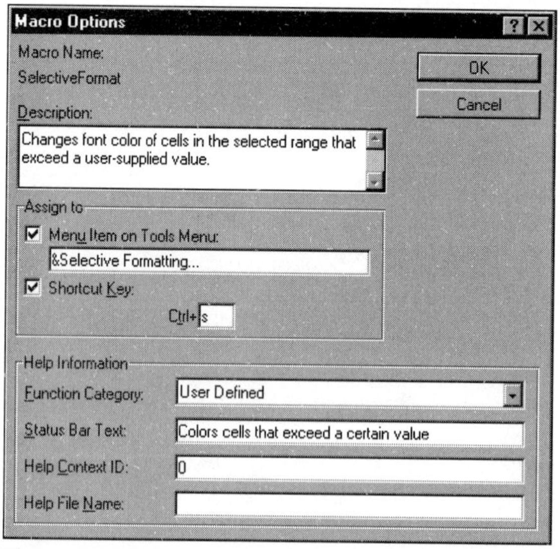

Figure 34-8: You can execute this macro by pressing Ctrl+S or choosing a new command from the Tools menu.

Figure 34-9 shows the macro in action. Note that you must select the range before you execute the macro.

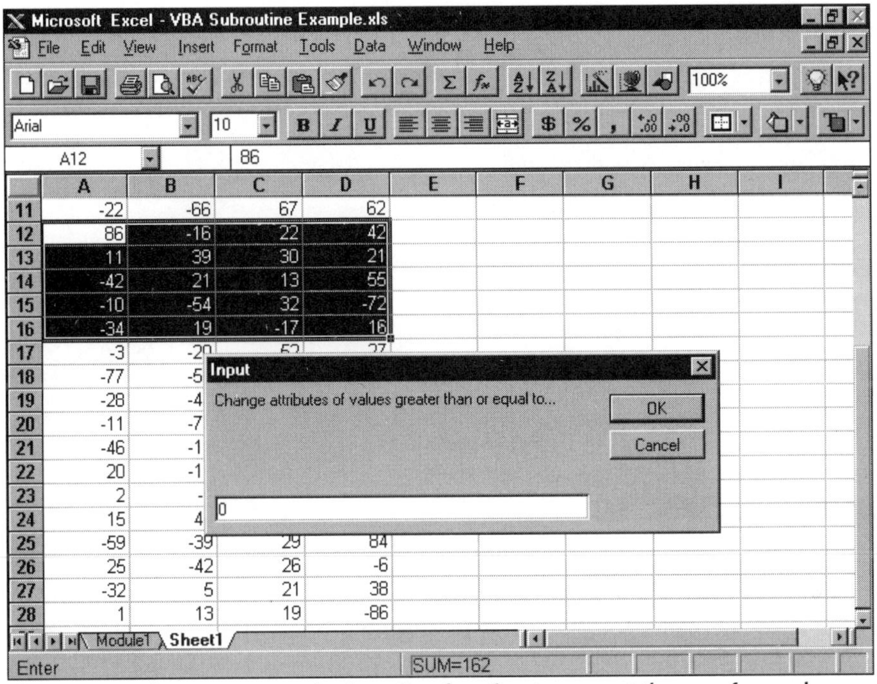

Figure 34-9: The macro uses the InputBox function to prompt the user for a value.

As macros go, this example is not very good. It's not very flexible and it doesn't include any error handling. For example, if a non-range object (such as a graphic object) is selected, the macro halts and displays an error message. To avoid this error message and abort the macro if anything except a range is selected, you can insert the following statement as the first statement in the procedure (directly below the Sub statement):

```
If TypeName(Selection) <> "Range" Then Exit Sub
```

This causes the macro to halt if the selection is not a Range object.

You'll also notice that the macro is executed even if you click Cancel in the input box. To avoid this problem, enter the following statement directly above the Target=Val(Target) statement:

```
If Target = "" then Exit Sub
```

This aborts the subroutine if Target is empty.

**On the
CD-ROM** A much more versatile version of this utility is part of the Power Utility Pak (see Figure 34-10). The shareware version is available on the companion CD-ROM.

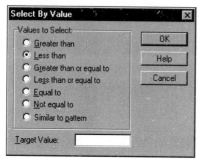

Figure 34-10: The Select By Value utility in the Power Utility Pak is a more versatile version of this macro.

Learning More

This chapter barely scratches the surface of what you can do with VBA. If this is your first exposure to VBA, you're probably a bit overwhelmed by objects, properties, and methods. I don't blame you. If you try to access a property that an object doesn't have, you get a runtime error and your VBA code grinds to a screeching halt until you correct the problem. Fortunately, there are several good ways to learn about objects, properties, and methods.

Read the rest of the book

This book has three more chapters devoted to VBA. Chapter 35 covers VBA functions, Chapter 36 describes custom dialog boxes, and Chapter 37 consists of useful (and informative) VBA examples.

Record your actions

The absolute best way — without question — to become familiar with VBA is to turn on the macro recorder and record actions that you make in Excel. It's even better if the VBA module in which the code is being recorded is visible while you're recording.

Use the online help system

The main source of detailed information about Excel's objects, methods, and procedures is in the online help system. Help is very thorough and easy to access. When you're in a VBA module, just move the cursor to a property or method and press F1. You get help that describes the word under the cursor.

Use the Object Browser

The Object Browser is a handy tool that lists every property and method for every object available. You can bring up the Object Browser in any of the following three ways, but you must be working in a VBA module:

✦ Choose the View➪Object Browser command from the menu.

✦ Click on the Object Browser tool on the Visual Basic toolbar.

✦ Press F2.

The Object Browser is shown in Figure 34-11.

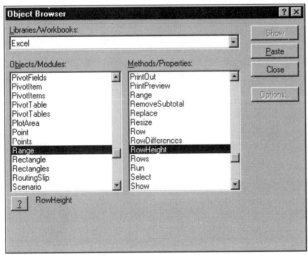

Figure 34-11: The Object Browser is a good reference source for learning about objects, properties, and methods.

The pull-down list labeled Libraries/Workbooks includes a list of all open workbooks, plus at least two additional type library entries: Excel and VBA. Your selection in this list determines what is displayed in the Objects/Modules portion of the dialog box. Also, your selection in the Objects/Modules list determines what is displayed in the Methods/Properties section.

Choosing the VBA type library at the top lets you view VBA's built-in functions and constants. Choosing the Excel type library displays a list of Excel's objects and constants on the left and the properties and methods for the selected object on the right. The Question-mark button is a direct link to online help; clicking on it brings up the help topic for the selected object or property.

If you select a workbook in the Libraries/Workbooks list, the Object Browser displays a list of all modules in the Objects/Modules portion of the dialog box. When you select a module, the Methods/Properties section displays the procedures and functions in the module.

Experiment with the Immediate pane

VBA has some useful debugging tools built in. One of these is the Immediate pane of the Debug window. To display this window, activate a VBA module and choose the View⇨Debug Window command (or press Ctrl+G). You get a window like the one shown in Figure 34-12.

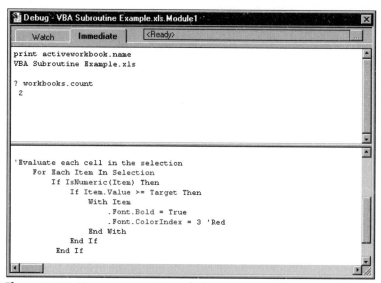

Figure 34-12: You can enter VBA code into the Immediate pane of the Debug window and see the results instantly.

The top part of this window has two tabs, Watch and Immediate. Make sure that you click the Immediate tab to display the Immediate pane. You can enter VBA statements into the Immediate pane and display results. For example, you can enter the following statement:

```
Print ActiveWorkbook.Name
```

VBA evaluates the statement and enters the result in the line below. Although the Debug window is most useful for debugging VBA code, you also can use it to experiment with VBA and immediately see the results. You'll almost always want to use the Print command to see the results of what you type. A shortcut for Print is a question mark (?). For example, if you enter the following line:

```
? Application.Name
```

VBA evaluates this expression and displays the result in the next line: Microsoft Excel.

Buy another book

OK, I promise. This is the last plug for my other book, *Excel For Windows 95 Power Programming Techniques, 2nd Edition,* due from IDG Books Worldwide in early 1996. I've received feedback from hundreds of first-edition users who claim it's the best Excel/VBA book available. You be the judge.

Summary

Chapter 34 introduces VBA, one of two macro languages included with Excel. If you want to learn macro programming, VBA is the language to use. In this chapter, you learn that a VBA module can contain subroutine procedures and function procedures and that VBA is based on objects, properties, and methods. You also learn how to use the macro recorder to translate your actions into VBA code and write simple code directly in a VBA module. Three other chapters in this book provide additional information about VBA.

✦   ✦   ✦

Creating Custom Worksheet Functions

◆ ◆ ◆ ◆

In This Chapter

An introduction to
custom VBA function
procedures

How to use custom
functions in work-
sheets and in other
VBA procedures

A discussion of
function arguments,
with examples

Special considerations
when debugging
custom functions

Using the Function
Wizard with custom
functions

◆ ◆ ◆ ◆

As I mention in the preceding chapter, VBA lets you create two types of procedures: subroutines and functions. This chapter focuses on functions.

Overview of VBA Functions

Function procedures that you write in VBA are quite versatile and can be used in two situations:

+ As part of an expression in a different VBA procedure
+ In formulas that you create in a worksheet

In fact, you can use a function procedure anywhere that you can use an Excel worksheet function or a VBA built-in function. Custom functions also appear in the Function Wizard, so they appear to be part of Excel.

Excel contains hundreds of predefined worksheet functions. With so many from which to choose, you may be curious as to why anyone would need to develop additional functions. The main reason is that creating a custom function can greatly simplify your formulas by making them shorter — and shorter formulas are more readable and easier to work with. For example, you can often replace a complex formula with a single function. Another reason is that you can write functions to perform operations that would otherwise be impossible.

An Introductory Example

The process of creating custom functions is relatively easy once you understand VBA. Without further ado, here's an example of a VBA function procedure.

A custom function

This example function, named *NumSign*, uses one argument. It returns a text string *Positive* if its argument is greater than zero, *Negative* if the argument is less than zero, and *Zero* if the argument is equal to zero. The function is shown in Figure 35-1.

```
Custom Function Examples.xls                        _ □ ×

Function NumSign(InVal)
    Select Case InVal
        Case Is < 0: NumSign = "Negative"
        Case 0:      NumSign = "Zero"
        Case Is > 0: NumSign = "Positive"
    End Select
End Function


│◄│◄│►│►│\ Module1 / Sheet1 /          │◄│
```

Figure 35-1: A custom function.

You could, of course, accomplish the same effect with the following worksheet formula, which uses a nested IF function:

```
=IF(A1=0,"Zero",IF(A1>0,"Positive","Negative"))
```

Most would agree that the custom function solution is easier to understand and to edit.

 On the CD-ROM The NumSign function is available in the FUNCTION.XLS workbook on the companion CD-ROM.

Using the function in a worksheet

When you enter a formula that uses the NumSign function, Excel executes the function to get the result (see Figure 35-2). This function works just like any built-in worksheet function. You can insert it in a formula by using the Function Wizard (custom functions are located in the User Defined category). You also can nest custom functions and combine them with other elements in your formulas.

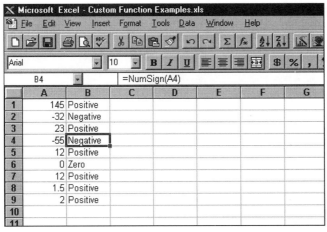

Figure 35-2: Using a custom function in a worksheet formula.

Using the function in a VBA subroutine

The following VBA subroutine procedure, which is defined in the same module as the custom NumSign function, uses the built-in MsgBox function to display the result of the NumSign function.

```
Sub ShowSign()
    CellValue = Sheets("Sheet1").Range("A1").Value
    MsgBox NumSign(CellValue)
End Sub
```

In this example, the variable CellValue contains the value in cell A1 on Sheet1 (this variable could contain any value, not necessarily obtained from a cell). CellValue is then passed to the function as its argument. Figure 35-3 shows the result of executing the NumSign subroutine.

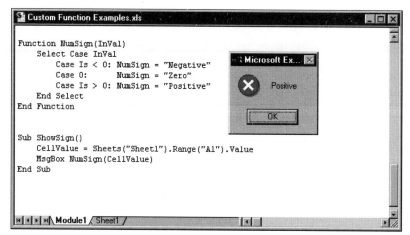

Figure 35-3: Using a custom function in a VBA subroutine.

Analyzing the custom function

In this section, I describe the NumSign function. Here again is the code:

```
Function NumSign(InVal)
    Select Case InVal
        Case Is < 0: NumSign = "Negative"
        Case 0:      NumSign = "Zero"
        Case Is > 0: NumSign = "Positive"
    End Select
End Function
```

Notice that the procedure starts with the keyword *Function* rather than *Sub*, followed by the name of the function (*NumSign*). This custom function uses one argument (*InVal*); the argument's name is enclosed in parentheses. *InVal* is the cell or variable that will be processed. When the function is used in a worksheet, the argument can be a cell reference (such as A1) or a literal value (such as –123). When it's used in another procedure, the argument can be a numeric variable, a literal number, or a value obtained from a cell. The second line is simply a comment that describes what the function does.

The function uses the Select Case construct (described in Chapter 34) to take a different action, depending on the value of InVal. If InVal is less than zero, NumSign is assigned the text *Negative*. If InVal is equal to zero, NumSign is *Zero*. If InVal is greater than zero, NumSign is *Positive*. The value returned by a function is always assigned to the function's name.

The procedure ends with an End Function statement.

About Function Procedures

A custom function procedure has a lot in common with a subroutine procedure, which I cover in the preceding chapter. Function procedures have some important differences, however, which I discuss in this section.

Declaring a function

The syntax for declaring a function is as follows:

```
[Public | Private][Static] Function name [(arglist)][As type]
      [statements]
      [name = expression]
      [Exit Function]
      [statements]
      [name = expression]
End Function
```

Public indicates that the function is accessible to all other procedures in all other modules in the workbook. (Optional.)

Private indicates that the function is accessible only to other procedures in the same module. (Optional.) Private functions can't be used in worksheet formulas and do not appear in the Function Wizard.

Static indicates that the values of variables declared in the function are preserved between calls, rather than being reset. (Optional.)

Function is a keyword that indicates the beginning of a function procedure. (Required.)

name can be any valid variable name. When the function finishes, the single-value result is assigned to the function's name. (Required.)

arglist is a list (one or more) of variables that represent arguments passed to the function. The arguments are enclosed in parentheses. Use a comma to separate arguments. (Optional.)

type is the data type returned by the function. (Optional.)

statements are valid VBA statements. (Optional.)

Exit Function is a statement that causes an immediate exit from the function. (Optional.)

End Function is a keyword that indicates the end of the function. (Required.)

Note   Keep in mind that a value is assigned to the function's name when a function is finished executing.

To create a custom function, start by inserting a VBA module (or you can use an existing module). Enter the keyword *Function* followed by the function's name and a list of the arguments (if any) in parentheses. Insert the VBA code that performs the work — and make sure that the variable corresponding to the function's name has the appropriate value (this is the value that the function returns). End the function with an End Function statement.

Function names must adhere to the same rules for variable names, and you can't use a name that looks like a worksheet cell (for example, a function named J21 won't be accepted).

What a function can't do

When you develop a function, you must realize that a function can't perform certain types of actions. For example, you can't develop a function that changes the formatting of a cell (this is something that nearly everyone tries to do — with no luck). In other words, functions are basically passive procedures that return a value. If you attempt to perform an action that is not allowed, the function returns an error.

Executing function procedures

Although there are many ways to execute a subroutine procedure, you can execute a function procedure in just two ways:

✦ Call it from another procedure.

✦ Use it in a worksheet formula.

From a procedure

You can call custom functions from a procedure just as you call built-in VBA functions. For example, after you define a function called CalcTax, you can enter a statement like the following:

```
Tax = CalcTax(Amount, Rate)
```

This statement executes the CalcTax custom function with Amount and Rate as its arguments. The function's result is assigned to the Tax variable.

In a worksheet formula

Using custom function in a worksheet formula is like using built-in functions. You must ensure that Excel can locate the function procedure, however. If the function procedure is in the same workbook, you don't have to do anything special. If the function is defined in a different workbook, you may have to tell Excel where to find it in one of three ways:

✦ **Precede the function's name with a file reference**. For example, if you want to use a function called CountNames that's defined in a workbook named MyFunctions, you can use a reference such as the following:

```
=MyFunctions.xls!CountNames(A1:A1000)
```

If you insert the function with the Function Wizard, the workbook reference is inserted automatically.

✦ **Set up a reference to the workbook.** You do this with the Tools➪References command (which is available only when a VBA module is active). If the function is defined in a referenced workbook, you don't need to precede the function name with the workbook name.

✦ **Create an add-in.** When you create an add-in from a workbook that has function procedures, you don't need to use the file reference when you use one of the functions in a formula; the add-in must be installed, however. I discuss add-ins in Chapter 40.

Notice that your function procedures don't appear in the Macros dialog box when you issue the Tools➪Macro command. This is because you can't execute a function directly. As a result, you need to do extra, up-front work to test your functions as you're developing them. One approach is to set up a simple subroutine that calls the function. If the function is designed to be used in worksheet formulas, you can enter a simple formula to test it as you're developing the function.

Function Arguments

Keep in mind the following about function procedure arguments:

✦ Arguments can be variables (including arrays), constants, literals, or expressions.

✦ Some functions do not have arguments.

✦ Some functions have a fixed number of required arguments (from 1 to 60).

✦ Some functions have a combination of required and optional arguments.

In the following section, I present a series of examples that demonstrate how to use arguments effectively with functions. Coverage of optional arguments is beyond the scope of this book.

Example: A function with no argument

Like subroutines, functions need not have arguments. Excel, for example, has a few built-in worksheet functions that don't use arguments. These include RAND, TODAY, and NOW.

Here's a simple example of a function that has no arguments. The following function returns the UserName property of the Application object. This is the name that appears in the Options dialog box (General tab). This is a simple example, but it can be useful because there is no other way to get the user's name to appear in a worksheet formula.

```
Function User()
'    Returns the name of the current user
     User = Application.UserName
End Function
```

When you enter the following formula into a worksheet cell, the cell displays the name of the current user:

```
=User()
```

Note   As with Excel's built-in functions, when you use a function with no arguments, you must include a set of empty parentheses.

The following example is a simple subroutine that uses the User custom function as an argument for the MsgBox function. The concatenation operator (&) joins the literal string with the result of the User function.

```
Sub ShowUser()
    MsgBox ("The user is " & User())
End Sub
```

Example: A function with one argument

This section contains a more complex function designed for a sales manager who needs to calculate the commissions earned by the sales force. The commission rate is based on the amount sold — those who sell more earn a higher commission rate. The function returns the commission amount, based on the sales made (which is the function's only argument — a required argument). The calculations in this example are based on the following table:

Monthly Sales	Commission Rate
0 – $9,999	8.0%
$10,000 – $19,999	10.5%
$20,000 – $39,999	12.0%
$40,000+	14.0%

There are several ways to calculate commissions for various sales amounts entered into a worksheet. You could write a formula such as the following:

```
=IF(AND(A1>=0,A1<=9999.99),A1*0.08,IF(AND(A1>=10000,A1<=19999.99), A1*0.105
    ,IF(AND(A1>=20000,A1<=39999.99),A1*0.12,IF(A1>=40000,A1*0.14,0))))
```

This is a bad approach for a couple reasons. First, the formula is overly complex. Second, the values are hard coded into the formula, making the formula difficult to modify if the commission structure changes.

A better approach is to use a lookup table function to compute the commissions. For example:

```
=VLOOKUP(A1,Table,2)*A1
```

An even better approach is to create a custom function such as the following:

```
Function Commission(Sales)
'    Calculates sales commissions
    Tier1 = 0.08
    Tier2 = 0.105
    Tier3 = 0.12
    Tier4 = 0.14
    Select Case Sales
        Case 0 To 9999.99: Commission = Sales * Tier1
        Case 1000 To 19999.99: Commission = Sales * Tier2
        Case 20000 To 39999.99: Commission = Sales * Tier3
        Case Is >= 40000: Commission = Sales * Tier4
    End Select
End Function
```

After you define this function in a VBA module, you can use it in a worksheet formula or call the function from other VBA procedures.

Entering the following formula into a cell produces a result of 3,000 (the amount, 25,000, qualifies for a commission rate of 12 percent):

```
=Commission(25000)
```

Even if you don't need custom functions in a worksheet, creating function procedures can make your VBA coding much simpler. If your VBA procedure calculates sales commissions, for example, you can use the exact same function and call it from a VBA subroutine. Here's a tiny subroutine that asks the user for a sales amount and then uses the Commission function to calculate the commission due and to display it:

```
Sub CalcComm()
    Sales = InputBox("Enter Sales:")
    MsgBox "The commission is " & Commission(Sales)
End Sub
```

The subroutine starts by displaying an input box that asks for the sales amount. Then the procedure displays a message box with the calculated sales commission for that amount. The Commission function must be available in the active workbook; otherwise, Excel displays a message saying that the function is not defined.

Example: A function with two arguments

This example builds upon the previous one. Imagine that the sales manager implements a new policy: the total commission paid is increased by 1 percent for every year that the salesperson has been with the company. I modified the custom Commission function (defined in the preceding section) so that it takes two arguments — both of which are required arguments. Call this new function *Commission2*:

```
Function Commission2(Sales, Years)
'    Calculates sales commissions based on years in service
    Tier1 = 0.08
    Tier2 = 0.105
    Tier3 = 0.12
    Tier4 = 0.14
    Select Case Sales
        Case 0 To 9999.99: Commission2 = Sales * Tier1
        Case 1000 To 19999.99: Commission2 = Sales * Tier2
        Case 20000 To 39999.99: Commission2 = Sales * Tier3
        Case Is >= 40000: Commission2 = Sales * Tier4
    End Select
    Commission2 = Commission2 + (Commission2 * Years / 100)
End Function
```

The modification was quite simple. I just added the second argument (Years) to the Function statement and included an additional computation that adjusts the commission before exiting the function.

Here's an example of how you write a formula by using this function (it assumes that the sales amount is in cell A1, whereas the number of years the salesperson has worked is in cell B1):

```
=Commission2(A1,B1)
```

On the
CD-ROM Both versions of the Commission function are available in FUNCTION.XLS on the companion CD-ROM.

Example: A function with a range argument

This example demonstrates how to use a worksheet range as an argument. Actually, it's not at all tricky; Excel takes care of the details behind the scenes.

Assume that you want to calculate the average of the five largest values in a range named Data. Excel doesn't have a function that can do this, so you would probably write a formula such as:

```
=(LARGE(Data,1)+LARGE(Data,2)+LARGE(Data,3)+LARGE(Data,4)+LARGE(Data,5))/5
```

This formula uses Excel's LARGE function, which returns the nth largest value in a range. The preceding formula adds the five largest values in the range named Data and then divides the result by 5. The formula works fine, but it's rather unwieldy. And what if you decide that you needed to compute the average of the top *six* values? You would need to rewrite the formula — and make sure that all copies of the formula also get updated.

Wouldn't it be easier if Excel had a function named TopAvg? For example, you could use the following (nonexistent) function to compute the average:

```
=TopAvg(Data,5)
```

This is an example of when a custom function can make things much easier for you. Following is a custom VBA function, named *TopAvg*. It returns the average of the top n values in a range.

```
Function TopAvg(InRange, Num)
'    Returns the average of the highest Num values in InRange
    Sum = 0
    For i = 1 To Num
        Sum = Sum + Application.Large(InRange, i)
    Next i
    TopAvg = Sum / Num
End Function
```

This function takes two arguments: InRange (which is a worksheet range) and Num (the number of values to average). It starts by initializing the Sum variable to 0. It then uses a For-Next loop to calculate the sum of the nth largest values in the range. Note that I used Excel's LARGE function within the loop. Because the function is part of the Application object, I had to precede it with Application. Finally, TopAvg is assigned the value of Sum divided by Num.

Note You can use all of Excel's worksheet functions in your VBA procedures *except* those that have equivalents in VBA. For example, VBA has a Rand function that returns a random number. Therefore, you can't use Excel's RND function in a VBA procedure.

On the CD-ROM The TopAvg function is available in FUNCTION.XLS on the companion CD-ROM.

Debugging Custom Functions

Debugging a function procedure can be a bit more challenging than debugging a subroutine procedure. If you develop a function that will be used in worksheet formulas, you'll find that an error in the function procedure simply results in an error display in the formula cell (usually #VALUE!). In other words, you won't receive the normal runtime error message that helps you locate the offending statement. Following are three methods that you may want to use:

✦ **Place MsgBox functions at strategic locations to monitor the value of specific variables.** Fortunately, message boxes in function procedures do pop up when the procedure is executed. But make sure that you only have one formula in the worksheet that uses your function, or the message boxes appear for each formula that's evaluated.

✦ **Test the procedure by calling it from a subroutine procedure.** Runtime errors display as normal, and you can either fix the problem (if you know it) or jump right into the debugger.

✦ **Set a breakpoint in the function and then use Excel's debugger to step through the function.** You then can access all the normal debugging tools.

Dealing with the Function Wizard

Excel's Function Wizard is a handy tool that lets you choose a worksheet function; you even can choose one of your custom worksheet functions. The Function Wizard also prompts you for the function's arguments.

Note Function procedures defined with the Private keyword do not appear in the Function Wizard. You also can display a description of your custom function in the Function Wizard. You add a description in the Description field in the Macro Options dialog box, shown in Figure 35-4. To display this dialog box, move the cursor anywhere within the custom function procedure and press F2. This displays the Object Browser dialog box. Click on the Options button to display the Macro Options dialog box.

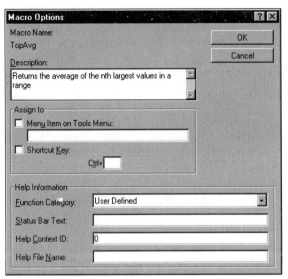

Figure 35-4: Entering a description for a custom function.
This description will appear in the Function Wizard dialog box.

Custom functions are listed under the User Defined category, and there is no straight-forward way to create a new function category for your custom functions.

Figure 35-5 shows the first Function Wizard dialog box, listing the custom functions in the User Defined category. In the second Function Wizard dialog box, the user is prompted to enter arguments for a custom function — just as in using a built-in worksheet function.

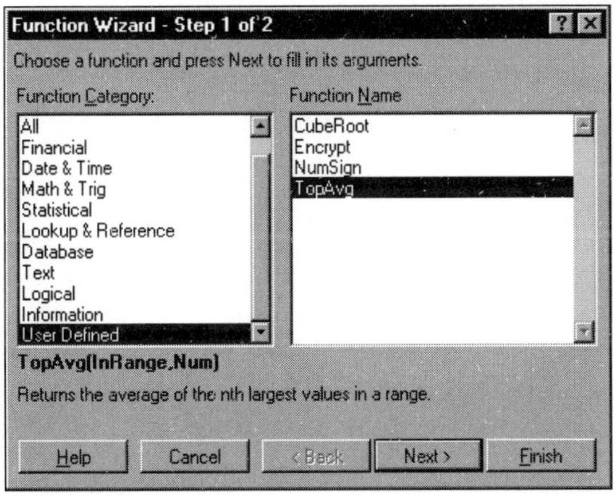

Figure 35-5: The Function Wizard also can insert custom functions.

Note   When you access a built-in function from the Function Wizard, the second dialog box displays a description of each argument. Unfortunately, you can't provide such descriptions for custom functions.

Learning More

The information in this chapter scratches the surface when it comes to creating custom functions. It should be enough to get you started, however, if you're interested in this topic. Refer to Chapter 37 for more examples of useful VBA functions. You may be able to use the examples directly or adapt them for your needs.

Summary

In this chapter, you read how to create and use custom VBA functions. These functions can be used in worksheet formulas and in other VBA procedures. I provide several examples, and you can refer to Chapter 37 for more examples.

✦   ✦   ✦

Creating Custom Dialog Boxes

In This Chapter

Why you may need to create a custom dialog box for your macro

A description of two simple alternatives to custom dialog boxes

How to create a custom dialog box

Linking dialog box controls to worksheet ranges

Several examples of custom dialog boxes

Y ou can't use Excel very long without being exposed to dialog boxes. Excel, like most Windows programs, uses dialog boxes to obtain information, clarify commands, and display messages. If you develop VBA macros, you can create your own dialog boxes that work just like those built into Excel. This chapter introduces you to custom dialog boxes.

Why Create Custom Dialog Boxes?

Some macros that you create behave exactly the same every time you execute them. For example, you may develop a macro that enters a list of your employees. This macro always produces the same result and requires no additional user input. You may develop other macros, however, that you would like to behave differently under different circumstances, or that offer some options for the user. In such cases, the macro may benefit from a custom dialog box.

Here's an example of a simple macro that makes each cell in the selection uppercase. It uses VBA's built-in UCase function.

```
Sub ChangeCase()
    For Each cell In Selection
        cell.Value = UCase(cell.Value)
    Next cell
End Sub
```

This macro is useful, but it could be even more useful. For example, it would be nice if the macro could also change the cells to lowercase or proper case. This modification is not difficult to make. But if you make this change to the macro, you need some method of asking the user what type of change to make to the cells. The solution is to present a dialog box like the one shown in Figure 36-1. This dialog box was created on a dialog sheet in the workbook and displayed by a VBA macro.

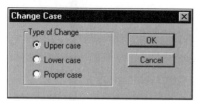

Figure 36-1: A custom dialog box that asks the user for an option.

Another solution would be to develop three macros — one for each type of text case change. Combining these three operations into a single macro and using a dialog box is a more efficient approach, however. I discuss this example, including how to create the dialog box, later in the chapter.

Custom Dialog Box Alternatives

Although it's not difficult to develop custom dialog boxes, sometimes it's easier to use the tools built into VBA. For example, VBA includes two functions (MsgBox and InputBox) that let you display simple dialog boxes without creating a dialog sheet. These dialog boxes can be customized in some ways, but they certainly don't offer the options available in a custom dialog box.

The InputBox function

The InputBox function is useful for obtaining a single input from the user. A simplified version of the function's syntax is as follows:

```
InputBox(prompt[,title][,default])
```

prompt is text that is displayed in the input box.

title is the text that appears in the input box's title bar. (Optional)

default is the default value. (Optional)

Here's an example of how you can use the InputBox function:

```
Rate = InputBox("Current commission rate?","Commission Worksheet")
```

When this VBA statement is executed, Excel displays the dialog box shown in Figure 36-2. Notice that this example uses only the first two arguments and does not supply a default value. When the user enters a value and clicks OK, the value is assigned to the variable *Rate*.

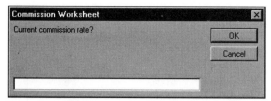

Figure 36-2: This dialog box is displayed by the InputBox function.

VBA's InputBox function always returns a string, so it may be necessary to convert the results to a value. You can use the Val function to convert a string to a value, as follows:

```
Rate = Val(InputBox("Current commission rate?","Commission Worksheet"))
```

The MsgBox function

VBA's MsgBox function is a very handy way to display information and to solicit simple input from users. I use VBA's MsgBox function in many of this book's examples to display a variable's value. A simplified version of the MsgBox syntax is as follows:

```
MsgBox(prompt[,buttons][,title])
```

prompt is text that is displayed in the message box.

buttons is the code for the buttons that will appear in the message box. (Optional)

title is the text that appears in the message box's title bar. (Optional)

You can use the MsgBox function by itself or assign its result to a variable. If you use it by itself, don't include parentheses around the arguments. The following example displays a message and does not return a result:

```
Sub MsgBoxDemo()
    MsgBox "Click OK to continue"
End Sub
```

Figure 36-3 shows how this message box appears.

Figure 36-3: A
simple message box.

To get a response from a message box, you can assign the result of the MsgBox function to a variable. In the following code, I use some built-in constants (described later) to make it easier to work with the values returned by MsgBox:

```
Sub GetAnswer()
    Ans = MsgBox("Continue?", vbYesNo)
    Select Case Ans
        Case vbYes
'           ...[code if Ans is Yes]...
        Case vbNo
'           ...[code if Ans is No]...
    End Select
End Sub
```

When this procedure is executed, the *Ans* variable will contain a value that corresponds to vbYes or vbNo. The Select Case statement determines the action to take based on the value of Ans.

You can easily customize your message boxes because of the flexibility of the buttons argument. Table 36-1 lists the built-in constants that you can use for the button argument. You can specify which buttons to display, whether an icon appears, and which button is the default.

Table 36-1
Constants Used in the MsgBox Function

Constant	Value	Description
vbOKOnly	0	Display OK button only
vbOKCancel	1	Display OK and Cancel buttons
vbAbortRetryIgnore	2	Display Abort, Retry, and Ignore buttons
vbYesNoCancel	3	Display Yes, No, and Cancel buttons
vbYesNo	4	Display Yes and No buttons
vbRetryCancel	5	Display Retry and Cancel buttons
vbCritical	16	Display Critical Message icon

Constant	Value	Description
vbQuestion	32	Display Warning Query icon
vbExclamation	48	Display Warning Message icon
vbInformation	64	Display Information Message icon
vbDefaultButton1	0	First button is default
vbDefaultButton2	256	Second button is default
vbDefaultButton3	512	Third button is default
vbSystemModal	4096	System modal; all applications are suspended until the user responds to the message box

The following example uses a combination of constants to display a message box with a Yes button and a No button (vbYesNo), and a question mark icon (vbQuestion); the second button is designated as the default button (vbDefaultButton2) — which is the button that is executed if the user presses Enter. For simplicity, I assigned these constants to the *Config* variable and then used *Config* as the second argument in the MsgBox function.

```
Sub GetAnswer()
    Config = vbYesNo + vbQuestion + vbDefaultButton2
    Ans = MsgBox("Process the monthly report?", Config)
    If Ans = vbYes Then RunReport
    If Ans = vbNo Then End
End Sub
```

Figure 36-4 shows how this message box appears when the GetAnswer subroutine is executed. If the user clicks the Yes button (or presses Enter), the routine executes the procedure named RunReport (which is not shown). If the user clicks the No button,

Figure 36-4: The buttons argument of the MsgBox function determines what appears in the message box.

the routine is ended with no action. Because the title argument was omitted in the MsgBox function, Excel uses the default title ("Microsoft Excel").

The routine that follows is another example of using the MsgBox function.

```
Sub GetAnswer2()
    Msg = "Do you want to process the monthly report?"
    Msg = Msg & Chr(10) & Chr(10)
    Msg = Msg & "Processing the monthly report will take approximately "
    Msg = Msg & "15 minutes. It will generate a 30-page report for all "
    Msg = Msg & "sales offices for the current month."
    Title = "XYZ Marketing Company"
    Config = vbYesNo + vbQuestion
    Ans = MsgBox(Msg, Config, Title)
    If Ans = vbYes Then RunReport
    If Ans = vbNo Then End
End Sub
```

This example demonstrates an efficient way to specify a longer message in a message box. I used a variable (Msg) and used the concatenation operator (&) to build the message in a series of statements. The Chr(10) function inserts a character that starts a new line. I also used the title argument to display a different title in the message box. Figure 36-5 shows how this message box appears when the procedure is executed.

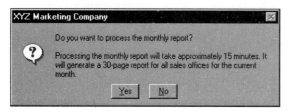

Figure 36-5: A message box with a longer message and a title.

Creating Custom Dialog Boxes

The InputBox and MsgBox functions will do just fine for many cases, but if you need to obtain more information, then you need to create a custom dialog box.

Following is a list of the general steps that you'll typically take:

1. Determine exactly how the dialog box will be used and where it will fit into your VBA macro.

2. Insert a new dialog sheet and add the appropriate controls to it.

3. Link the controls to worksheet cells (if appropriate). In some cases, you might want to attach a macro to a control.

4. Modify your macro so that it displays the dialog box.

5. Modify your macro code so that it obtains the information from the dialog box and uses it.

I discuss more details in the following sections.

The author's OptionsBox function

I like the idea of using functions (such as InputBox and MsgBox) to display dialog boxes, so I wrote my own. My OptionsBox function creates and displays a dialog box that consists of a series of option buttons. The selected option button is returned by the function.

The OptionsBox function's syntax is as follows:

```
OptionsBox(array,[title])
```

The array argument is an array of strings that will be used for the option buttons. The title argument is a title that's displayed in the dialog box. For example, you can use the following code to generate and display a dialog box with three options:

```
Sub OB_Test()
    Dim States(3) as String
    States(1) = "Montana"
    States(2) = "Oregon"
    States(3) = "Idaho"
    Title = "Select a Place to
Live"
    Ans =OptionsBox(States,Title)
End Sub
```

The accompanying figure shows the dialog box that is generated.

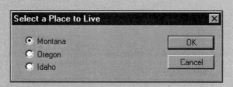

The OptionsBox function is written in VBA (of course). The function inserts a new dialog sheet, adds the option buttons, sizes the dialog box accordingly, and then displays the dialog box. The user's choice is assigned to the function. When the user clicks OK (or Cancel) the dialog sheet is deleted. You might think that this would be rather slow because a new dialog box is created "on the fly." Actually, it all happens amazingly fast — so fast that you probably wouldn't guess that you weren't using a built-in function.

The OptionsBox function can be found in the OPTIONS.XLS workbook on the companion CD-ROM.

Working with dialog sheets

Excel stores custom dialog boxes on dialog sheets (one dialog box per sheet). When you insert a dialog sheet, Excel displays a worksheet with a nearly empty dialog box (see Figure 36-6); the dialog box includes only an OK button and a Cancel button, which are used in most dialog boxes.

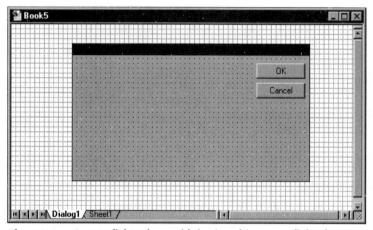

Figure 36-6: A new dialog sheet with its (nearly) empty dialog box.

When you activate a dialog sheet, Excel displays the Forms toolbar, which makes it easy to add controls to the dialog box. The Forms toolbar is shown in Figure 36-7.

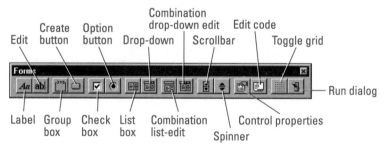

Figure 36-7: The Forms toolbar appears when you activate a dialog sheet.

Tip   You also can insert some of the dialog box controls directly on to an Excel worksheet. The controls that work on both dialog sheets and worksheets are the following: Label, Group Box, Create Button, Check Box, Option Button, List Box, Drop-Down, Scrollbar, and Spinner.

You use the tools on the Forms toolbar to add controls to the dialog box. After you add a control, you can move and resize it by using standard techniques.

Linking controls

You can link some of the dialog box controls to a worksheet cell or range. For example, you may want to link a check box control to a cell. When the check box is checked, the cell contains True; when it's not checked, the cell contains False. A drop-down list box control can be linked to a single-column vertical range of cells. In this case, each cell in the range contains one of the choices in the drop-down list box. In addition, another cell can be linked to hold the choice selected by the user.

Note   Linking a control to a cell is not the only way to obtain the information from the dialog box. Another way is to write VBA code to read the control's value directly — avoiding a worksheet link. I discuss this method later.

To link a dialog box control to a cell, right-click the control and choose Format Object from the shortcut menu. Select the Control tab from the Format Object dialog box and create the links.

Figure 36-8 shows the Format Object dialog box for a drop-down list box control (the dialog box varies with each type of control). In this case, the list that's displayed is the range A1:A12 on Sheet1, and the user's selection appears in cell B16 of Sheet1. You also can control the number of lines that drop down when the control is selected (in this example, eight).

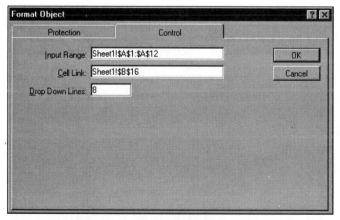

Figure 36-8: This Format Object dialog box enables you to link a drop-down list box to cells in a worksheet.

Displaying custom dialog boxes

The only way to display a custom dialog box is by using the Show method in a VBA macro. The following procedure displays the dialog box located on the Dialog1 sheet:

```
Sub ShowDialog()
    DialogSheets("Dialog1").Show
'    ... [other statements]
End Sub
```

When the dialog box is displayed, the macro is halted until the dialog box is closed. Then the remaining statements in the procedure are executed.

The Show method also generates a value. If the dialog box is closed normally (by clicking the OK button), the Show method generates the value True. If the dialog box is canceled (by clicking the Cancel button) the Show method generates the value False.

In most cases, you won't want to continue if the user clicks the Cancel button. Therefore, you need to test for this in your macro. The example that follows demonstrates how to do this. I assigned the dialog box result to a variable (*DBoxOK*). When the dialog box is closed, VBA executes the next statement, which checks the value of *DBoxOK*. If *DBoxOK* is False, the subroutine is exited with no further action. If *DBoxOK* is True, the subroutine continues.

```
Sub ShowDialog()
    DBoxOK = DialogSheets("Dialog1").Show
    If Not DBoxOK Then Exit Sub
'    ... [other statements]
End Sub
```

The routine below demonstrates another way to accomplish this without using a variable. All of the statements that will be executed if the user clicks OK are placed between the If-Then and End If statements. If the user clicks Cancel, none of these statements are executed.

```
Sub ShowDialog2()
    If DialogSheets("Dialog1").Show Then
'        ... [other statements]
    End If
End Sub
```

Using information from custom dialog boxes

The purpose of a dialog box is to get information from the user. When the user responds to a dialog box, your macro needs to obtain the information and use it. There are two ways to do this:

✦ If the control is linked to a cell, you can read the result from the cell.

✦ Read the result directly from the dialog box control.

Dialog box controls are objects, and you can access their properties using VBA. For example, to determine whether an option button (named *Option1*) on dialog sheet Dialog1 is selected, you can check its Value property by using a statement such as the following:

```
Selected = DialogSheets("Dialog1").OptionButtons("Option1").Value
```

If the variable *Selected* is equal to the built-in constant xlOn, then the option button is selected. If *Selected* is equal to the built-in constant xlOff, the option button is not selected. I present an example in the next section.

A Custom Dialog Box Example

In this section, I demonstrate how to develop a custom dialog box. The example is an enhanced version of the ChangeCase example that I presented at the beginning of the chapter. Recall that the original version of this macro changes the text in the selected cells to uppercase. This modified version asks the user what type of case change to make: uppercase, lowercase, or proper case.

Creating the dialog box

This dialog box needs to obtain one piece of information from the user: the type of change to make to the text. Because only one option can be selected, option buttons controls are appropriate. Following are the steps required to create the custom dialog box. Start with an empty workbook.

1. Insert a new dialog sheet with the Insert⇨Macro⇨Dialog command. The new sheet contains a dialog box with two controls: an OK button and a Cancel button.

2. Make sure that the Forms toolbar is displayed. If it isn't, choose View⇨Toolbars and select Forms from the list of toolbars.

3. Click on the Option Button tool and drag in the dialog box. The option button has a default name (*Option Button 4*), and the name appears as text.

4. Change the name of this option button by using the Name box. Make the name *Upper*.

5. Change the text displayed in this option button by double-clicking it and entering the new text. Make the text **Upper case**.

6. Add two more option buttons to the dialog box.

7. Name the second option button *Lower*, and change its text to **Lower case**.

8. Name the third option button *Proper*, and change its text to **Proper case**.

9. Click on the Group Box tool and drag so that it encloses the three option buttons.

Note Make sure that the option buttons are completely enclosed by the group box. You may need to make the option buttons narrower so that they fit. Or you can increase the width of the group box. If the option buttons are not completely enclosed, the dialog box may not work properly.

10. Change the dialog box's title bar text to **Change Case**.

11. Adjust the dialog box's size so that it looks something like Figure 36-9. To do so, just select the dialog box and drag its borders.

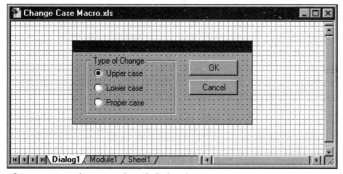

Figure 36-9: The completed dialog box.

Modifying the macro

The modified macro follows:

```
Sub ChangeCase()
'    Exit if a range is not selected
     If TypeName(Selection) <> "Range" Then Exit Sub

'    Show the dialog box
     DBoxOK = DialogSheets("Dialog1").Show
'    Exit if dialog is canceled
     If Not DBoxOK Then Exit Sub
'    Upper case
     If DialogSheets("Dialog1").OptionButtons("Upper").Value = xlOn Then
         For Each cell In Selection
             cell.Value = UCase(cell.Value)
         Next cell
     End If
```

```
'    Lower case
     If DialogSheets("Dialog1").OptionButtons("Lower").Value = xlOn Then
         For Each cell In Selection
             cell.Value = LCase(cell.Value)
         Next cell
     End If
'    Proper case
     If DialogSheets("Dialog1").OptionButtons("Proper").Value = xlOn Then
         For Each cell In Selection
             cell.Value = Application.Proper(cell.Value)
         Next cell
     End If
End Sub
```

The macro starts by checking the type of the selection. If it's not a range, the procedure ends. Next, it displays the dialog box and assigns the result to the *DBoxOK* variable. If the dialog is cancelled, the subroutine is exited. Otherwise the macro continues. Notice that the macro consists of three separate blocks. Only one block is executed, determined by which option button is selected. In this example, I read the value directly from the dialog box (instead of using a cell link).

Note Notice that VBA has a UCase and a LCase function, but not a function to convert text to proper case. Therefore, I used Excel's PROPER worksheet function (preceded by Application) to do the conversion.

When the macro is executed, the controls retain their previous settings. In this case, the selected option button will be the last one selected. If you like, you can initialize the dialog box controls before you show the dialog box. For example, if you wanted the dialog box to default to the uppercase option, you could insert the following statement before the statement that shows the dialog:

```
DialogSheets("Dialog1").OptionButtons("Upper").Value = xlOn
```

Making the macro available

At this point, everything should be working properly. There's really no easy way to execute the macro, however. A good way to execute this macro would be from a new command on the Tools menu.

Activate the VBA module and choose the Tools⇨Macro command. Make sure that ChangeCase is listed in the Macro Name/Reference box, and click the Options button. Excel displays its Macro Options dialog box, as shown in Figure 36-10.

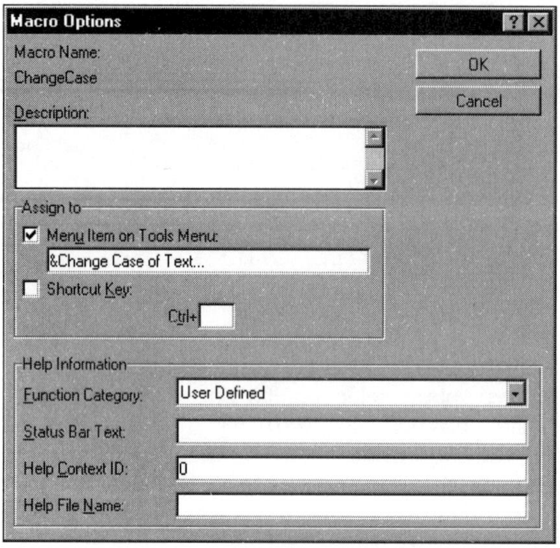

Figure 36-10: The Macro Options dialog box.

Enter the following in the box labeled Menu Item on Tools Menu, and click OK:

```
&Change Case of Text...
```

After performing this operation, the Tools menu will have a new command: Change Case of Text. Using an ampersand (&) before the first letter causes that letter to be underlined in the menu.

Testing the macro

The final step is to test the macro and dialog box to make sure that they work properly. Activate a worksheet and select some cells that contain text. Choose the Tools⇨Change Case of Text command, and the custom dialog box appears. Make your choice and click OK. If everything was done correctly, the text in the cells should be changed appropriately.

Because this is a general-purpose macro, you'll want to be able to execute it from any workbook. There is a problem with the macro, however. If you attempt to execute the macro while a workbook that does not contain the macro is active, you get the error message shown in Figure 36-11.

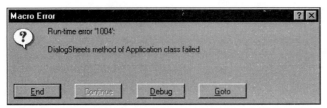

Figure 36-11: This error occurs if you attempt to execute the macro from a different workbook.

What's the problem? Excel looks for the Dialog1 sheet in the active workbook. If it can't be found, the error occurs. This macro needs to be corrected so that it can be executed from any workbook.

Correcting the macro

There are a few ways to correct the problem. One way is to precede the reference to the dialog sheet with a workbook qualifier. Here's an example:

```
DBoxOK = Workbooks("Dialog Example").DialogSheets("Dialog1").Show
```

This is not a good solution because it would cause the macro to fail if the workbook is renamed. A better solution is to use the ThisWorkbook property of the Application object. ThisWorkbook returns the workbook where the macro is stored — and it works regardless of the workbook's name. Here's an example of how this would be used:

```
DBoxOK = ThisWorkbook.DialogSheets("Dialog1").Show
```

You have to make this change in every statement that refers to the dialog sheet.

Yet another approach is to create an object variable that refers to the dialog sheet. An object variable lets you refer to an object by a simpler name — and also speeds up execution. Use the keyword *Set* to create an object variable. For example, to create an object variable (*Dialog*) that refers to the dialog sheet named Dialog1, insert the following statement at the top of the subroutine:

```
Set Dialog = ThisWorkbook.DialogSheets("Dialog1")
```

Once the object variable is defined, you can replace every instance of ThisWorkbook.DialogSheets("Dialog1") with Dialog.

Following is the finalized macro, which uses an object variable.

```
Sub ChangeCase()
'    Create object variable
     Set Dialog = ThisWorkbook.DialogSheets("Dialog1")
'    Exit if a range is not selected
     If TypeName(Selection) <> "Range" Then Exit Sub

'    Show the dialog box
     DBoxOK = Dialog.Show
'    Exit if dialog is cancelled
     If Not DBoxOK Then Exit Sub
'    Upper case
     If Dialog.OptionButtons("Upper").Value = xlOn Then
         For Each cell In Selection
             cell.Value = UCase(cell.Value)
         Next cell
     End If
'    Lower case
     If Dialog.OptionButtons("Lower").Value = xlOn Then
         For Each cell In Selection
             cell.Value = LCase(cell.Value)
         Next cell
     End If
'    Proper case
     If Dialog.OptionButtons("Proper").Value = xlOn Then
         For Each cell In Selection
             cell.Value = Application.Proper(cell.Value)
         Next cell
     End If
End Sub
```

On the CD-ROM The workbook that contains this macro is on the companion disk. The file is named CHG_CASE.XLS.

Another Custom Dialog Box Example

This example is a simple application that uses a dialog box to add data to a worksheet database. The dialog box asks the user for a person's name (using an edit box), his or her sex (using option buttons), and the month of birth (using a list box). It then transfers this information to the next empty row in the worksheet. The procedure repeats until the Cancel button is clicked.

Initial setup

The first step is to prepare the workbook. Start with a new workbook with four sheets, named as follows:

✦ A worksheet named Database

✦ A worksheet named Values

✦ A VBA module named Macros

✦ A dialog sheet named Dialog1

On the Database worksheet, enter titles for the database, as shown in Figure 36-12.

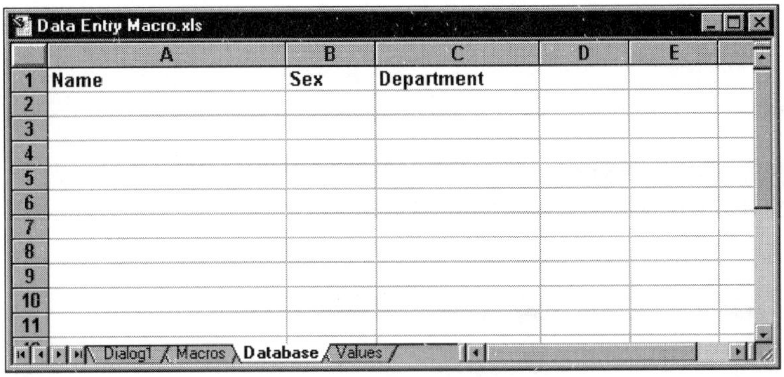

Figure 36-12: The data will be stored on this worksheet.

On the Values worksheet, enter the 12 month names in A1:A12, as shown in Figure 36-13. Name this range `MonthNames`. These are the items that will appear in the list box. In addition, give the name SelectedMonthIndex to cell A14 (this will store the index number of the month that's selected from the list box). Name cell A15 SelectedMonthName and enter the following formula:

```
=INDEX(MonthNames,SelectedMonthIndex)
```

This formula extracts the correct month name from the list. For example, if the user selects February, the SelectedMonthIndex cell contains 2 and the formula returns February.

Designing the dialog box

The next step is to create the dialog box. Figure 36-14 shows the end result.

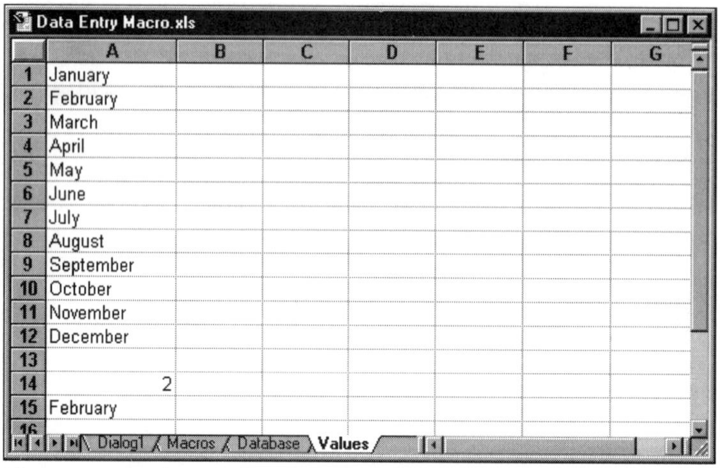

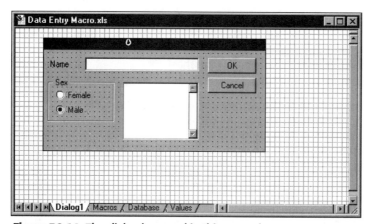

Figure 36-13: These items will be used in the list box.

Figure 36-14: The dialog box used in this example.

To create this dialog box, activate the Dialog1 sheet and make sure that the Forms toolbar is displayed. Then follow these steps:

1. Click on the Label button and drag in the dialog box to create a label. Double-click the default text of the label and change the text to **Name**.

2. Add an edit box control to the dialog box. Use the Name box to change its name to *EditName*.

3. Add two option buttons and change their text to display **Male** and **Female**. Name one of the option buttons *OptionMale* and the other *OptionFemale*.

4. Add a group box control to surround the two option buttons, and enter **Sex** as its title. Make sure that the option buttons are completely enclosed by the group box (you may have to change the width of the option buttons).

5. Add a list box control to the dialog box (list box displays the month names).

6. Double-click the dialog's title bar and change the title bar caption to **Data Entry**.

7. Move and size the controls and dialog box frame so that the dialog box resembles Figure 36-14.

Linking the list box to the worksheet

The list box control is empty and needs to be filled with the month names listed on the Values worksheet. Right-click the list box and choose Format Object from the shortcut menu. Click the Control tab of the Format Object dialog box and fill in the fields so that it looks like Figure 36-15. The Input Range is the range that holds the items for the list box. The Cell Link is the cell that contains the index number of the selected item. These names were defined earlier.

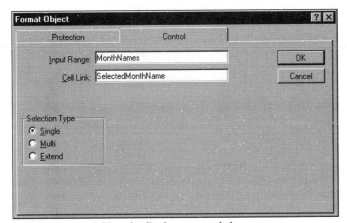

Figure 36-15: Linking the list box to worksheet ranges.

At this point, you can test the dialog box by clicking the Run Dialog tool on the Forms toolbar (or by choosing the Tools⇨Run Dialog command). This displays the dialog box so that you can see how it looks in action, also allowing you to test the controls.

Creating the VBA macro

The macro that I created for this project follows. It starts by creating an object variable to simplify the references to the dialog box. The second statement is a label that's used later in the routine. The text box is cleared and the dialog box is displayed.

If the user clicks Cancel, the routine ends with no further action. Otherwise, the data is retrieved from the dialog box and stored in three variables: *TheName*, *TheSex*, and *TheMonth*. I used Excel's COUNTA function to count the number of cells in column C that contain information. This value is incremented by one — which is the row number of the next empty row. The data is entered into the Database worksheet and then the GoTo Start statement causes the macro execution to jump back to the Start label. The macro continues in this loop until the user clicks Cancel in the dialog box.

```
Sub EnterData()
    Set Dialog = DialogSheets("Dialog1")
Start:
'    Clear the name box
    Dialog.EditBoxes("EditName").Text = ""

'    Show the dialog box
    DboxOK = Dialog.Show

'    Exit if Cancelled
    If Not DboxOK Then Exit Sub

'    Get the data from the dialog sheet
    TheName = Dialog.EditBoxes("EditName").Text

    If Dialog.OptionButtons("OptionFemale").Value = xlOn Then _
        TheSex = "Female" Else TheSex = "Male"

    TheMonth = Worksheets("Values").Range("SelectedMonthName")

'    Determine the next empty row
    Row = Application.CountA(Sheets("Database").Range("C:C")) + 1
'    Put the data in the database
    Worksheets("Database").Cells(Row, 1) = TheName
    Worksheets("Database").Cells(Row, 2) = TheSex
    Worksheets("Database").Cells(Row, 3) = TheMonth
'    Repeat until cancelled
    GoTo Start
End Sub
```

Testing it

To test the project, simply execute the EnterData macro. You could add a command to the Tools menu, but this application is designed to run only from the workbook that contains the macro. Therefore, a better way to start the macro is by clicking a button. Add a button (from the Drawing toolbar) to the Database worksheet and assign the EnterData macro to the button.

When you click the button, the macro is executed and the dialog box is displayed. If it doesn't work properly, retrace the steps described earlier.

Potential modifications

The application works, but it could use a few improvements. For example, the dialog box doesn't have any accelerator keys associated with the controls (which makes it difficult to use the dialog box without a mouse). In addition, the order of the controls needs some adjustment. I discuss these modification in the next section.

On the CD-ROM
This workbook, named DATA_ENT.XLS, is available on the companion CD-ROM.

More on Creating Custom Dialog Boxes

Creating custom dialog boxes can make your macros much more versatile. You can create custom commands that display dialog boxes that look exactly like those Excel uses. This section contains some additional information to help you develop custom dialog boxes that work like those built into Excel.

Adding accelerator keys

Dialog boxes should not discriminate against those who want to use the keyboard rather than a mouse. All of Excel's dialog boxes work equally well with a mouse and a keyboard because each control has an associated accelerator key. The user can press Alt plus the accelerator key to work with a specific dialog box control.

It's a good idea to add accelerator keys to your custom dialog boxes. You do this in the Format Object dialog box (click on the Control tab). Figure 36-16 shows the Format Object dialog box for an option button object. To make the accelerator key for this button *F* (and cause it to be underlined), select the object, right-click, and choose Format Object from the shortcut menu. Then enter **F** in the edit box next to Accelerator Key. Click on OK to close the dialog box. When this dialog box is running, pressing Alt+F will have the same effect as clicking the option button.

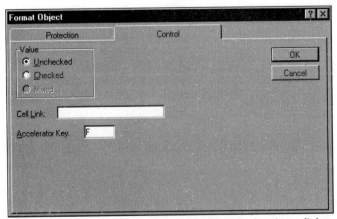

Figure 36-16: You can designate an accelerator key for a dialog box control using the Format Object dialog box.

Obviously, the letter you enter as the accelerator key must be a letter contained in the text of the object. It can be any letter in the text (not necessarily the first letter). You should ensure that an accelerator key is not duplicated in a dialog box. If you have duplicate accelerator keys, the accelerator key acts on the first control in the "tab order" of the dialog box (explained shortly).

Note   The underlined letter does not appear when you're editing the dialog box. The accelerator key is underlined when you execute the dialog box, however. The easy way to check the results of assigning a hot key is to click on the Run Dialog tool on the Forms toolbar.

Edit box objects don't display any text, but you can assign an accelerator key to a label that describes the edit box. Pressing the accelerator key then activates the next control in the tab order (which should be the edit box).

Controlling tab order

In an earlier section, I refer to a dialog box's tab order. When you're working with a dialog box, pressing Tab and Shift+Tab cycles through the dialog box's controls. When you create a custom dialog box, you should make sure that the tab order is correct. Usually, this means that tabbing should move to the controls in a logical sequence.

To view or change the tab order in a custom dialog box, right-click anywhere on the dialog sheet (except on a control) and choose Tab Order from the shortcut menu. Excel displays the Tab Order dialog box, shown in Figure 36-17.

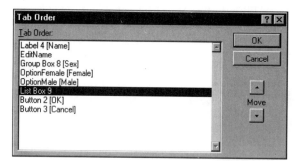

Figure 36-17: The Tab Order dialog box lets you adjust the order in which the controls are activated when the user presses Tab.

This dialog box displays the name of each control in the dialog box in a list. The list corresponds to the tab order of the controls. The first control on the list is the control that is activated when the dialog box first appears. The activated control in a dialog box has the *focus* — it's the control that the user is currently manipulating.

To change the tab order, select a control in the Tab Order dialog box and then click one of the Move buttons to move the control up or down in the list. Adjusting the tab order is important when you use edit box controls. Each edit box control should have a label next to it (with an accelerator key defined). Make sure that the edit box follows the label in the tab order. When the user presses the accelerator key assigned to the label, the edit box is activated. This happens because a label can't be selected, so Excel activates the *next* control in the tab order.

Learning More

On the CD-ROM

Mastering custom dialog boxes takes practice. It's a good idea to closely examine the dialog boxes that Excel uses; these are examples of well-designed dialog boxes. You can duplicate most (but not all) of the dialog boxes that Excel uses. The exceptions are tabbed dialog boxes (such as the Options dialog box) and dialog boxes that use check marks in a list box (such as the Add-Ins dialog box). Also, custom dialog boxes do not display the question mark icon (for help) in their title bar.

Many users find that it's helpful to study examples that others have developed. Therefore, I developed several dialog box examples and included them on the companion CD-ROM (they are named DIALOG.XLS). The examples are described briefly in the following sections. If you are interested in using any of these techniques, I urge you to study the dialog boxes and their associated VBA code.

Get a password

This dialog box, shown in Figure 36-18, demonstrates how to use the Password Edit property of an edit box (this property is set in the Format Object dialog box). When the user enters text in the dialog box, it appears as a series of asterisks.

Figure 36-18: When the Password Edit property of an edit box is set, text entered appears as asterisks.

New! The Password property is new to Excel for Windows 95. Be aware that if you use this feature in a dialog box, the dialog box will not work properly if the workbook is opened by Excel 5.

Zap selection

This dialog box, shown in Figure 36-19, demonstrates that dialog boxes don't have to be dull and unexciting. It uses clip art pasted to the dialog sheet. The large text was created in a cell and copied as a picture, then pasted to the dialog box.

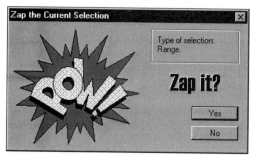

Figure 36-19: Using clip art in a dialog box.

Dialog boxes that change sizes

The dialog box in this example changes sizes when the user clicks on the Options button. This is shown in Figures 36-20 and 36-21. The macro adjusts the Height property of the DialogFrame object.

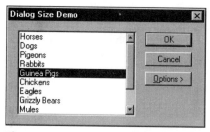

Figure 36-20: A custom dialog box.

Figure 36-21: A custom dialog box expanded in size after clicking the Options button.

Selecting a range

This dialog box (shown in Figure 36-22) demonstrates how to select a range in an edit box. The edit box's Edit Validation setting is set to References. This allows the user to activate the edit box and then select a range by dragging in the worksheet.

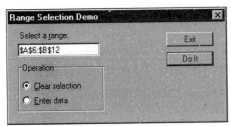

Figure 36-22: This edit box accepts a range.

Linked pictures in a dialog box

The final example, shown in Figure 36-23, demonstrates how to use linked picture objects in a dialog box. The dice are actually pictures of cells formatted with the Wingdings font.

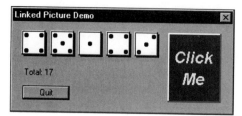

Figure 36-23: These dice are linked picture objects.

Summary

In this chapter, I describe how to create dialog boxes and use them with your VBA macros. I also cover two VBA functions — InputBox and MsgBox — which can sometimes take the place of a custom dialog box. The chapter includes several useful examples to help you understand how to use this feature.

✦   ✦   ✦

VBA Programming Examples

✦ ✦ ✦ ✦

In This Chapter

Practical examples of
using VBA for
common operations

Using VBA to
manipulate graphic
objects

Tips on making your
VBA routines faster

✦ ✦ ✦ ✦

My philosophy about learning to write Excel macros
places heavy emphasis on examples. I've found that a
well-thought-out example often communicates a concept much
better than a lengthy description of the underlying theory. In this
book, I chose to avoid a painstaking description of every nuance
of VBA. I take this approach for two reasons. First, space limitations prohibit such a discussion. But more to the point, the VBA
language is described very well in Excel's online help system.

This chapter consists of several examples that demonstrate
common VBA techniques. You may be able to use some of the
examples directly. But in most cases, you'll need to adapt them
to your own needs. I organize these examples into the following
categories:

- ✦ Working with ranges
- ✦ Changing Excel's settings
- ✦ Working with graphic objects
- ✦ Working with charts
- ✦ Learning ways to speed up your VBA code

On the CD-ROM All subroutines and functions in this chapter can be found in the
VBA.XLS workbook on the companion CD-ROM. This workbook
has a separate VBA module for each category.

Working with Ranges

Most of what you do in VBA will probably involve worksheet ranges. When you work with range objects, keep the following points in mind:

✦ You don't need to select a range to work with it.

✦ If you do select a range, its worksheet must be active.

✦ The macro recorder doesn't always generate the most efficient code. Often, you can use the recorder to create your macro and then edit the code to make it more efficient.

✦ It's a good idea to use named ranges in your VBA code. For example, `Range("Total")` is better than `Range("D45")`. In the latter case, you would need to modify the macro if you added a row above row 45.

✦ The macro recorder doesn't record keystrokes used to select a range. For example, if you record Ctrl+Shift+right arrow to select to the end of a row, you find that Excel records the actual range selected.

✦ If you create a macro that works on the current range selection, be aware that the user can select entire columns or rows. In most cases, you don't want to loop through every cell in the selection. You need to create a subset of the selection that consists only of nonblank cells.

✦ Be aware that Excel allows multiple selections. For example, you can select a range, press Ctrl, and select another range. You can test for this in your macro and take appropriate actions.

The examples in the following sections demonstrate these points.

Copying a range

Copying a range is a frequent activity in macros. When you turn on the macro recorder and copy a range from A1:A5 to B1:B5, you get a VBA macro like this:

```
Sub CopyRange()
    Range("A1:A5").Select
    Selection.Copy
    Range("B1").Select
    ActiveSheet.Paste
    Application.CutCopyMode = False
End Sub
```

This macro works, but it's not the most efficient way to copy a range. You can accomplish exactly the same result with the following one-line macro:

```
Sub CopyRange2()
    Range("A1:A5").Copy (Range("B1"))
End Sub
```

This takes advantage of the fact that the Copy method can use an argument that specifies the destination. Information such as this is available in the online help system.

The example demonstrates that the macro recorder doesn't always generate the most efficient code.

Note As you see, it's not necessary to select an object in order to work with it. Note that Macro2 doesn't select a range; therefore, the active cell doesn't change when this macro is executed.

Copying a variable size range

Often, you want to copy a range of cells in which the exact row and column dimensions are unknown.

Figure 37-1 shows a range on a worksheet. This range consists of a number of rows, and the number of rows can change from day to day. Because the exact range address is unknown at any given time, writing a macro to copy the range can be challenging.

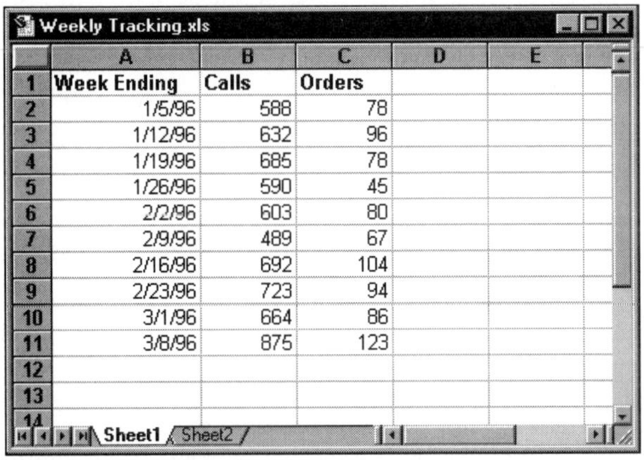

Figure 37-1: This range can consist of any number of rows.

The macro that follows demonstrates how to copy this range from Sheet1 to Sheet2 (beginning at cell A1). It uses the CurrentRegion property, which returns a range object that corresponds to the active block of cells. This is equivalent to choosing the Edit⇨Go To command, clicking on the Special button, and selecting the Current Region option.

```
Sub CopyCurrentRegion()
    Range("A1").CurrentRegion.Copy
    Sheets("Sheet2").Select
    Range("A1").Select
    ActiveSheet.Paste
    Sheets("Sheet1").Select
    Application.CutCopyMode = False
End Sub
```

Selecting to the end of a row or column

You've probably gotten into the habit of using key combinations such as Ctrl+Shift+right arrow and Ctrl+Shift+down arrow to select from the active cell to the end of a row or column. You may be surprised to discover that these types of keystroke combinations do not get recorded by the macro recorder. Rather, the address of the actual range selected is what gets recorded. As I describe in the preceding section, you can use the CurrentRegion property to select an entire block. But suppose you want to select one column from a block of cells?

Fortunately, VBA can accommodate this type of action. The following VBA subroutine selects the range beginning at the active cell and extending down to the last cell in the column. When the range is selected, you can do whatever you want with it — copy it, move it, format it, and so on.

```
Sub SelectDown()
    Range(ActiveCell, ActiveCell.End(xlDown)).Select
End Sub
```

This example uses the End method of the Range object, which returns a Range object. The End method takes one argument, which can be any of the following constants: xlUp, xlDown, xlToLeft, xlToRight.

Selecting a row or column

The macro that follows demonstrates how to select the column of the active cell. It uses the EntireColumn property, which returns a range that consists of a column.

```
Sub SelectColumn()
    ActiveCell.EntireColumn.Select
End Sub
```

As you may suspect, there's also an EntireRow property that returns a range that consists of a row.

Moving a range

Moving a range consists of cutting it to the Clipboard and then pasting it to another area. If you record your actions while performing a move operation, the macro recorder generates code like the following:

```
Sub MoveRange()
    Range("A1:C6").Select
    Selection.Cut
    Range("A10").Select
    ActiveSheet.Paste
End Sub
```

As I demonstrate with copying earlier in this chapter, this is not the most efficient way to move a range of cells. In fact, you can do it with a single VBA statement, as follows:

```
Sub MoveRange2()
    Range("A1:C6").Cut (Range("A10"))
End Sub
```

This takes advantage of the fact that the Cut method can use an argument that specifies the destination.

Looping through a range efficiently

Many macros perform an operation on each cell in a range, or they may perform selective actions based on the content of each cell. These operations usually involve a For-Next loop that processes each cell in the range.

The following example demonstrates how to loop through a range. In this case, the range is the current selection. In this example, *Cell* is a variable name that refers to the cell being processed. Within the For-Next loop, the single statement evaluates the cell and changes its interior color if the cell value is positive.

```
Sub ProcessCells()
    For Each Cell In Selection
        If Cell.Value > 0 Then Cell.Interior.ColorIndex = 6
    Next Cell
End Sub
```

The preceding example works, but what if the selection consists of an entire column or an entire range? This is not uncommon because Excel lets you perform operations on entire columns or rows. But in this case, the macro seems to take forever because it loops through each cell — even those that are blank. What's needed is a way to process only the nonblank cells.

This can be accomplished using the SelectSpecial method. In the following example, the SelectSpecial method is used to create two new objects: the subset of the selection that consists of cells with constants, and the subset of the selection that consists of cells with formulas. Each of these subsets is processed, with the net effect of skipping all blank cells.

```
Sub SkipBlanks()
'    Ignore errors
    On Error Resume Next

'    Process the constants
    Set ConstantCells = Selection.SpecialCells(xlConstants, 23)
    For Each cell In ConstantCells
        If cell.Value > 0 Then cell.Interior.ColorIndex = 6
    Next cell

'    Process the formulas
    Set FormulaCells = Selection.SpecialCells(xlFormulas, 23)
    For Each cell In FormulaCells
        If cell.Value > 0 Then cell.Interior.ColorIndex = 6
    Next cell
End Sub
```

The SkipBlanks subroutine works equally fast, regardless of what is selected. For example, you can select the range, select all columns in the range, select all rows in the range, or even select the entire worksheet. In all these cases, only the cells that contain constants or values are processed. It's a vast improvement over the ProcessCells subroutine presented earlier.

Notice that I used the following statement in the subroutine:

```
On Error Resume Next
```

This statement causes Excel to ignore any errors that occur and simply process the next statement. This is necessary because the SpecialCells method produces an error if no cells qualify. To tell Excel to return to normal error-checking mode, use the following statement:

```
On Error GoTo 0
```

Prompting for a cell value

As I discuss in Chapter 36, you can take advantage of VBA's InputBox function to solicit a value from the user. Figure 37-2 shows an example.

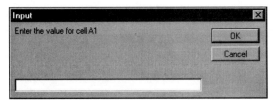

Figure 37-2: Using VBA's InputBox function to get a value from the user.

You can assign this value to a variable and use it in your subroutine. Often, however, you want to place the value into a cell. The following subroutine demonstrates how to ask the user for a value and place it into cell A1 of the active worksheet, using only one statement:

```
Sub GetValue()
    Range("A1").Value = InputBox("Enter the value for cell A1")
End Sub
```

Determining the type of selection

If your macro is designed to work with a range selection, it's important that you be able to determine that a range is actually selected. Otherwise, the macro will probably fail. The following subroutine identifies the type of object that is currently selected:

```
Sub SelectionType()
    MsgBox TypeName(Selection)
End Sub
```

If a Range object is selected, the MsgBox displays *Range*. If your macro is designed to work only with ranges, you can use an If statement to ensure that a range is actually selected. Here's an example that beeps, displays a message, and exits the subroutine if the current selection is not a Range object:

```
Sub CheckSelection()
    If TypeName(Selection) <> "Range" Then
        Beep
        MsgBox "Select a range."
        Exit Sub
    End If
'    ... [Other statements go here]
End Sub
```

Another way to approach this is to define a custom function that returns True if the selection is a Range object, False otherwise. Here's a function that does just that:

```
Function IsRange(sel) As Boolean
    IsRange = False
    If TypeName(sel) = "Range" Then IsRange = True
End Function
```

Identifying a multiple selection

As you know, Excel allows you to make a multiple selection by pressing Ctrl while you select objects or ranges. This can cause problems with some macros; for example, you can't copy a multiple selection that consists of nonadjacent ranges. The following macro demonstrates how to determine whether the user has made a multiple selection:

```
Sub MultipleSelection()
    If Selection.Areas.Count > 1 Then
        MsgBox "Multiple selections not allowed."
        Exit Sub
    End If
'   ... [Other statements go here]
End Sub
```

This example uses the Areas method, which returns a collection of all objects in the selection. The Count property returns the number of objects in the collection.

Following is a function that returns True if the selection is a multiple selection.

```
Function IsMultiple(sel) As Boolean
    IsMultiple = False
    If Selection.Areas.Count > 1 Then IsMultiple = True
End Function
```

Changing Excel's Settings

Some of the most useful macros are simple subroutines that change one or more of Excel's settings. For example, it takes quite a few actions to simply change the Recalculation mode from automatic to manual.

This section contains two examples that demonstrate how to change settings in Excel. These examples can be generalized to other operations.

Boolean settings

A Boolean setting is one that is either on or off. For example, you may want to create a macro that turns the row and column headings on and off. If you record your actions while you access the Options dialog box, you find that Excel generates the following code if the headings are turned on:

```
ActiveWindow.DisplayHeadings = False
```

It generates the following code if the headings are turned off:

```
ActiveWindow.DisplayHeadings = True
```

This may lead you to suspect that the heading display requires two macros: one to turn the headings on and one to turn them off. Actually, this isn't true. The following subroutine uses the Not operator to effectively toggle the heading display from True to False and from False to True.

```
Sub ToggleHeadings()
    If TypeName(ActiveSheet) <> "Worksheet" Then Exit Sub
    ActiveWindow.DisplayHeadings = Not ActiveWindow.DisplayHeadings

End Sub
```

The first statement ensures that the active sheet is a worksheet; otherwise, an error occurs. This technique can be used with any other settings that take on Boolean (True or False) values.

Non-Boolean settings

For non-Boolean settings, you can use the following Select Case structure. This example toggles the Calculation mode and also displays a message indicating the current mode:

```
Sub ToggleCalcMode()
    Select Case Application.Calculation
        Case xlManual
            Application.Calculation = xlAutomatic
            MsgBox "Automatic Calculation Mode"
        Case xlAutomatic
            Application.Calculation = xlManual
            MsgBox "Manual Calculation Mode"
    End Select
End Sub
```

Working with Graphic Objects

As you know, VBA subroutines can work with any type of Excel object, including graphic objects embedded on a worksheet's draw layer. This section provides a few examples of using VBA to manipulate graphic objects.

Adding a reminder note

Excel lets you attach a note to any cell using the Insert⇨Note command. In some cases, however, you may prefer to create a note to yourself that's always visible.

The following example adds a text box directly to the right of the active cell and formats it to look like an electronic equivalent of one of those ubiquitous yellow sticky notes. It then inserts the active cell address into the text box (see Figure 37-3).

```
Sub AddReminderNote()
'    Get coordinates based on activecell
     TBLeft = ActiveCell.Left + ActiveCell.Width
     TBTop = ActiveCell.Top
     TBWidth = 93
     TBHeight = 62
'    Create a text box
     ActiveSheet.TextBoxes.Add(TBLeft, TBTop, TBWidth, TBHeight).Select

'    Format text box
     With Selection
        .Interior.ColorIndex = 6
        .Shadow = True
        .Placement = xlMove
        .PrintObject = False
        .Text = Activecell.Address
     End With
End Sub
```

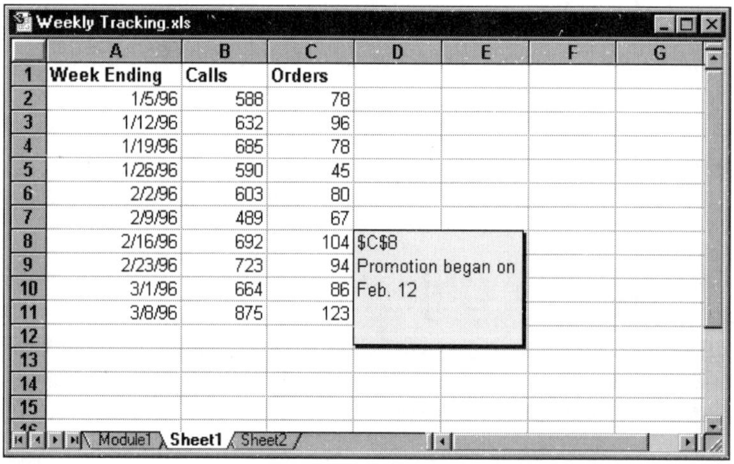

Figure 37-3: A macro to add a reminder note to a worksheet.

If object protection is enabled on the worksheet, this macro fails. Therefore, it's a good idea to have the macro check for a protected sheet before trying to add a text box. You can insert the following block of code at the beginning of the subroutine. If the worksheet is protected, the code displays a message and exits the routine.

```
'    Check for protected sheet
     If ActiveSheet.ProtectDrawingObjects Then
         MsgBox "Worksheet is protected."
         Exit Sub
     End If
```

Hiding and unhiding a text box

The macro in this example demonstrates how to hide and unhide a text box object. This can be useful for providing instructions. For example, you can create a text box that describes how to use a particular worksheet. But you don't want to display the text box all of the time, because it takes up valuable screen space. Therefore, you can develop a macro that toggles the Visible property of the text box. Then you can attach the macro to a button or toolbar button.

This example assumes that the text box is named Instructions. It uses the Not operator to toggle the Visible property.

```
Sub ToggleInstructions()
    ActiveSheet.DrawingObjects("Instructions").Visible = _
        Not ActiveSheet.DrawingObjects("Instructions").Visible
End Sub
```

Figure 37-4 shows a worksheet with a button that executed the ToggleInstructions macro. In this figure, the text box is visible.

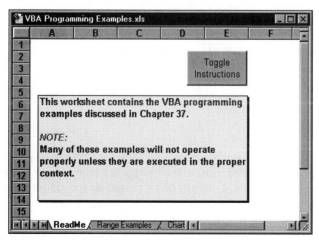

Figure 37-4: The visibility of this text box can be toggled by clicking on the button.

Creating a text box to match a range

The following example creates a text box that is positioned precisely over the selected range of cells. This is useful if you want to make a text box that covers up a range of data.

```
Sub CreateTextBox()
    If TypeName(Selection) <> "Range" Then Exit Sub
'   Get coordinates of range selection
    TBLeft = Selection.Left
    TBTop = Selection.Top
    TBWidth = Selection.Width
    TBHeight = Selection.Height
'   Create a text box
    ActiveSheet.TextBoxes.Add(TBLeft, TBTop, TBWidth, TBHeight).Select
End Sub
```

The macro first checks to make sure that a range is selected. If not, the subroutine is exited with no further action. If a range is selected, the coordinates (Left, Top, Width, and Height) are assigned to four variables. These variables then are used as the arguments for the Add method of the TextBoxes collection.

Following is a more sophisticated version of this macro that works with a multiple selection of cells. It creates a text box for each area in the multiple selection. It uses a For-Next loop to cycle through each area in the range selection. If the range has only one area (not a multiple selection), the For-Next loop is activated only one time.

```
Sub CreateTextBox2()
    If TypeName(Selection) <> "Range" Then Exit Sub
    For Each part In Selection.Areas
'     Get coordinates of selection
      TBLeft = part.Left
      TBTop = part.Top
      TBWidth = part.Width
      TBHeight = part.Height
'     Create a text box
      ActiveSheet.TextBoxes.Add(TBLeft, TBTop, TBWidth, TBHeight).Select
    Next part
End Sub
```

Working with Charts

Manipulating charts with VBA can be confusing, mainly because of the large number of objects involved. To get a feel for this, turn on the macro recorder, create a chart, and perform some routine chart editing. You may be surprised by the amount of code that's generated.

Once you understand the objects in a chart, however, you can create some useful macros. This section presents a few macros that deal with charts. When writing macros that manipulate charts, it's important to understand some terminology. An embedded chart on a worksheet is a ChartObject object. Before you can do anything to a ChartObject, you must activate it. The following statement activates the ChartObject named Chart 1.

```
ActiveSheet.ChartObjects("Chart 1").Activate
```

Once activated, you can refer to the chart in your VBA code as the ActiveChart. If the chart is on a separate chart sheet, it becomes the active chart as soon as the chart sheet is activated.

Modifying the chart type

The first example here changes the chart type of every embedded chart on the active sheet. It makes each chart an area chart by adjusting the Type property of the ActiveChart object. A built-in constant, xlArea, represents an area chart.

```
Sub ChartType()
    For Each cht In ActiveSheet.ChartObjects
        cht.Activate
        ActiveChart.Type = xlArea
    Next cht
End Sub
```

The example uses a For-Next loop to cycle through all of the ChartObject objects on the active sheet. Within the loop, the chart is activated and then the chart type is assigned a new value.

The following macro performs the same function but works on all chart sheets in the active workbook:

```
Sub ChartType2()
    For Each cht In ThisWorkbook.Charts
        cht.Activate
        ActiveChart.Type = xlArea
    Next cht
End Sub
```

Modifying properties

The following example changes the legend font for all charts on the active sheet. It uses a For-Next loop to process all ChartObject objects.

```
Sub LegendMod()
    For Each cht In ActiveSheet.ChartObjects
        cht.Activate
        With ActiveChart.Legend.Font
            .Name = "Arial"
            .FontStyle = "Bold"
            .Size = 12
        End With
    Next cht
End Sub
```

Applying chart formatting

This example applies several different formatting types to the active chart. A chart must be activated before executing this macro. You activate an embedded chart by selecting it. Activate a chart on a chart sheet by activating the chart sheet.

```
Sub ChartMods()
    ActiveChart.Type = xlArea
    ActiveChart.ChartArea.Font.Name = "Arial"
    ActiveChart.ChartArea.Font.FontStyle = "Regular"
    ActiveChart.ChartArea.Font.Size = 9
    ActiveChart.PlotArea.Interior.ColorIndex = xlNone
    ActiveChart.Axes(xlValue).TickLabels.Font.Bold = True
    ActiveChart.Axes(xlCategory).TickLabels.Font.Bold = True
    ActiveChart.Legend.Position = xlBottom
End Sub
```

I created this macro by recording my actions as I formatted a chart. Then I cleaned up the recorded code by removing irrelevant lines.

VBA Speed Tips

VBA is fast, but it's often not fast enough. This section presents some programming examples that you can use to help speed up your macros.

Turning off screen updating

You've probably noticed that, when you execute a macro, you can watch everything that occurs in the macro. Sometimes this is instructive, but once you get the macro working properly, it can be annoying and slow things down considerably.

Fortunately, there's a way to disable the normal screen updating that occurs when you execute a macro. Insert the following statement to turn screen updating off:

```
Application.ScreenUpdating = False
```

If, at any point during the macro, you want the user to see the results of the macro, use the following statement to turn screen updating back on:

```
Application.ScreenUpdating = True
```

Preventing alert messages

One of the benefits of using a macro is that you can perform a series of actions automatically. You can start a macro and then get a cup of coffee while Excel does its thing. Some operations cause Excel to display messages that must be attended to, however. For example, if your macro deletes a sheet, you see the message shown in the dialog box in Figure 37-5. These types of messages mean that you can't execute your macro unattended.

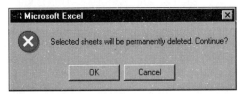

Figure 37-5: You can instruct Excel not to display these types of alerts while a macro is running.

To avoid these alert messages, insert the following VBA statement:

```
Application.DisplayAlerts = False
```

When the subroutine ends, the DisplayAlerts property is automatically reset to True (its normal state).

Simplifying object references

As you probably have discovered, references to objects can get very lengthy. For example, a fully qualified reference to a Range object may look like this:

```
Workbooks("MyBook").Worksheets("Sheet1").Range("InterestRate")
```

If your macro uses this range frequently, you may want to create an object variable by using the Set command. For example, to assign this Range object to an object variable named *Rate*, use the following statement:

```
Set Rate = Workbooks("MyBook").Worksheets("Sheet1").Range("InterestRate")
```

After this variable is defined, you can use the variable *Rate* instead of the lengthy reference.

Besides simplifying your coding, you'll find that using object variables also speeds up your macros quite a bit. I've seen some macros execute twice as fast after creating object variables.

Declaring variable types

Usually, you don't have to worry about the type of data that's assigned to a variable. Excel handles all these details behind the scenes. For example, if you have a variable named *MyVar*, you can assign a number or any type to it. You can even assign a text string to it later in the procedure.

But if you want your procedures to execute as fast as possible, you should tell Excel in advance what type of data will be assigned to each of your variables. This is known as declaring a variables type.

Table 37-1 lists all data types supported by VBA. This table also lists the number of bytes that each type uses, the range of possible values, and the number of significant digits.

Table 37-1
Data Types

Data Type	Bytes Used	Range of Values	Significant Digits
Boolean	2	True or False	1
Integer	2	−32,768 to 32,767	5
Long	4	−2,147,483,648 to 2,147,483,647	10
Single	4	−3.402823E38 to 1.401298E45	7
Double (negative)	8	−1.79769313486232E308 to −4.94065645841247E−324	15
Double (positive)	8	4.94065645841247E−324 to 1.79769313486232E308	15
Currency	8	−922,337,203,685,477.5808 to 922,337,203,685,477.5807	19
Date	8	1/1/100 to 12/31/9999	NA
String	1/char	Varies	NA
Object	16 + 1/char	Any defined object	NA
Variant	Varies	Any data type	NA
User-defined	Varies	Varies	NA

If you don't declare a variable, Excel uses the Variant data type. In general, it's best to use the data type that uses the smallest number of bytes yet still can handle all the data assigned to it. When VBA works with data, execution speed is a function of the number of bytes that VBA has at its disposal. In other words, the fewer bytes used by data, the faster VBA can access and manipulate the data.

To declare a variable, use the Dim statement before you use the variable for the first time. For example, to declare the variable *Units* as an integer, use the following statement:

```
Dim Units as Integer
```

To declare the variable *UserName* as a string, use the following:

```
Dim UserName as String
```

If you know that *UserName* will never exceed 20 characters, you can declare it as a fixed-length string, as follows:

```
Dim UserName as String * 20
```

If you declare a variable within a procedure, the declaration is valid only within that procedure. If you declare a variable outside of any procedures (but before the first procedure), the variable will be valid in all procedures in the module.

If you use an object variable (as described previously), you can declare the variable as an object data type. Here's an example:

```
Dim Rate as Object
Set Rate = Workbooks("MyBook").Worksheets("Sheet1").Range("InterestRate")
```

To force yourself to declare all variables that you use, insert the following statement at the top of your module:

```
Option Explicit
```

If you use this statement, Excel displays an error message if it encounters a variable that hasn't been declared.

Summary

In this chapter, I present several examples of VBA code that work with ranges, Excel's settings, graphic objects, and charts. In addition, I discuss techniques that you can use to make your VBA macros run faster.

✦   ✦   ✦

Running XLM Macros

◆ ◆ ◆ ◆

In This Chapter

An overview of
Excel's XLM macro
system

Why Excel has two
macro languages

What you need to
know to execute XLM
macros

Simple XLM
troubleshooting tips

◆ ◆ ◆ ◆

This is a rather unusual chapter because it describes a
feature whose use I don't recommend. I include this chapter
for those who may inherit an Excel workbook that contains XLM
macros (that is, macros developed using the Excel 4 macro
language). Therefore, this chapter focuses on what you need to
know to *execute* XLM macros. It doesn't tell you how to *write*
such macros. If you're interested in learning to write macros in
Excel, you should learn the VBA macro language, which I discuss
in other chapters in this part.

An Overview of XLM Macros

In this section, I introduce you to XLM macros and provide a
brief comparison to VBA.

Why two macro languages?

Excel for Windows 95 supports two entirely different macro
languages. XLM macros have been available in all versions of
Excel, but Excel 5 introduced a new language called Visual Basic
for Applications (VBA). For compatibility reasons, however, the
XLM language is still supported. This means that you can load an
older Excel file and still execute the XLM macros stored in it.

Note Although the XLM macro language supports all features in Excel
for Windows 95, Microsoft doesn't guarantee that the XLM
language will continue to be expanded to support features in
future versions of Excel. This is sufficient reason to use VBA for
your macro development.

You may wonder why Microsoft created an entirely new macro language for Excel (VBA) when it already included a macro language (XLM). The answer is that Microsoft didn't develop VBA for Excel — it developed VBA for its complete line of Office products. Eventually, all Microsoft Office products will include the VBA macro language.

What is an XLM macro?

An XLM macro, like a VBA macro, is used to automate operations. XLM macros are stored on XLM macro sheets (XLM macros don't work if you create them on a normal worksheet). An XLM macro consists of a series of functions that are evaluated on command. These functions can be either normal worksheet functions or special macro functions. Although a worksheet function typically performs a *calculation*, a macro function usually specifies an *action* to be performed. XLM includes hundreds of special-purpose macro functions.

XLM versus VBA

Almost everyone who has taken the time to learn both of Excel's macro languages agrees that VBA is superior to XLM. Figures 38-1 and 38-2 show a simple procedure coded in XLM and VBA respectively. This macro works on the selected cells and changes the text color to blue and the cell background color to yellow, and makes the text bold. Most agree that the VBA code is much easier to read. More importantly, however, the VBA code is easier to modify when the need arises.

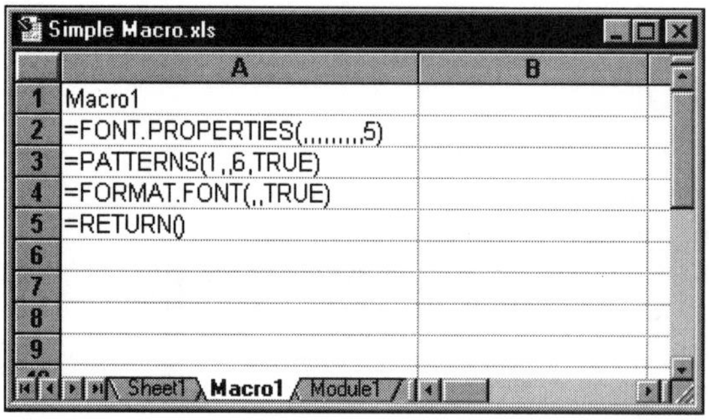

Figure 38-1: A simple macro coded in Excel's XLM language.

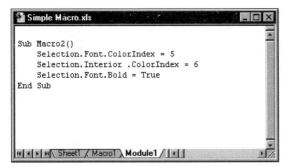

```
Simple Macro.xls                          _ □ ×

Sub Macro2()
    Selection.Font.ColorIndex = 5
    Selection.Interior .ColorIndex = 6
    Selection.Font.Bold = True
End Sub




|◄|◄|►|►|\ Sheet1 / Macro1 \ Module1 / |◄| |
```

Figure 38-2: A simple macro coded in Excel's VBA language.

Following are key areas in which VBA and XLM differ.

✦ **Basic structural differences.** XLM commands are actually functions, which are evaluated and return a value. VBA commands are more in line with traditional programming languages and use concepts such as subroutines and functions. Compared to VBA, XLM macros are *very* difficult to read and modify.

✦ **Portability.** The XLM language is found only in Excel. VBA, on the other hand, will eventually be part of all Microsoft Office applications — making it much more general-purpose.

✦ **Different sheet types.** XLM macros reside on a special XLM macro sheet (described later). VBA code is stored in a VBA module.

✦ **Variables.** VBA lets you use variables that aren't associated with a worksheet value. Any variable used in XLM must reside in a cell.

✦ **Data typing.** With VBA, you can declare the data type for each variable used. This lets you conserve memory and increase speed.

✦ **Strings.** In XLM, text strings are limited to 255 characters. VBA doesn't have this limit (unless you want to insert the text into a cell).

✦ **Compatibility.** XLM macros work in all versions of Excel (assuming that you don't perform actions not available in previous versions). VBA macros work only with Excel 5 and later versions.

Moving up from XLM

If you're an experienced XLM user and created lots of XLM macros, you're probably wondering whether there's a utility that can automatically translate your XLM macros to VBA. You're out of luck; no such utility exists and it is unlikely that one will be developed.

Because Excel for Windows 95 still supports the XLM language, you don't really need to convert your XLM macros. But if you *really* want to convert your macros — or you simply

want to find the VBA equivalent for an XLM function, use the online help system. Access the Answer Wizard and enter **VBA equivalents**. It lists several topics. Choose the topic named Visual Basic Equivalents for Macro Functions and Commands. You get a screen that contains each XLM macro function or command in alpha-betical order. The adjacent column in the help window contains the equivalent Visual Basic command.

XLM macro sheets

As I mention earlier, XLM macros are stored on macro sheets, which are officially known as MS Excel 4.0 macro sheets. Figure 38-3 shows an empty XLM macro sheet — which looks remarkably like an empty worksheet. By default, XLM macro sheets are named Macro1, Macro2, and so on.

Note   You may encounter some files with an XLM extension rather than the normal XLS extension. An XLM extension indicates a file that was generated with a version of Excel prior to version 5.0 — which was the first version to support multisheet files. A file with an XLM extension consists of a single sheet (an XLM macro sheet).

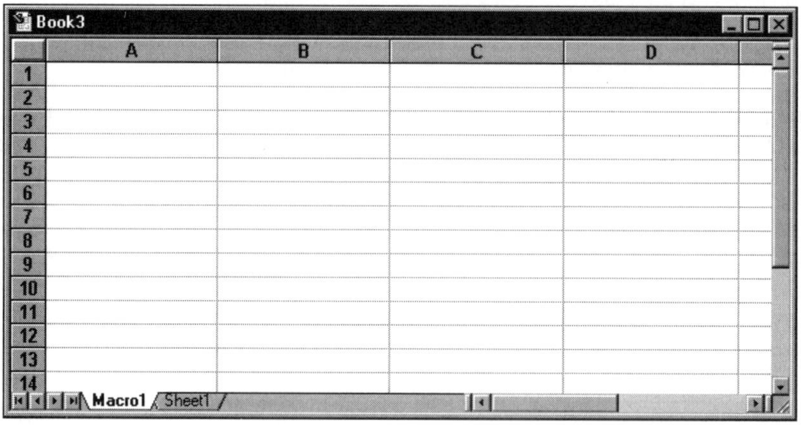

Figure 38-3: An empty XLM macro sheet.

An XLM macro sheet is similar to a worksheet, with a few major differences:

✦ The default view shows formulas rather than the values they produce. When you enter a formula into a cell in an XLM macro sheet, the result is not usually visible. Rather, you see the formula in the cell. You can display the values in an XLM macro sheet by selecting the Tools⇨Options command and unchecking the Formula option in the View panel.

✦ The default column width in an XLM macro sheet is wider than in a worksheet, which makes it handy for viewing formulas. As with a worksheet, you can widen the columns. This is often helpful because displayed formulas don't spill over to adjacent cells.

✦ When a macro sheet is the active document, the Function Wizard (invoked by the Insert⇨Function command or the Function Wizard tool) lists XLM macro functions as well as worksheet functions.

✦ Formulas on an XLM macro sheet are calculated only when the macro is executed. In other words, Excel handles recalculation in XLM macro sheets differently than in worksheets.

Two types of macros

Like VBA, Excel's XLM macro system supports two types of macros: command macros and function macros.

✦ **Command macros:** Think of command macros as new commands that can be executed by the user or by another macro. A command macro can combine several Excel commands into one command or automatically perform a series of operations. You can execute a command macro by using the Tools⇨Macro command or by typing its Ctrl+key shortcut (if it has one).

✦ **Function macros:** The second type of macro is a custom function that jumps into action only when necessary. Unlike command macros, function macros can be used in worksheet formulas, just like normal Excel functions.

Macro names

Although it's not required, most XLM macros have a name. When you choose the Insert⇨Name⇨Define command while an XLM macro sheet is active, the Define Name dialog box is slightly different than normal (see Figure 38-4). It includes a section labeled Macro that specifies what type of macro you're naming (either a function macro or a command macro). You also can assign a shortcut keystroke combination to execute the macro (command macros only). You can use this dialog box to determine whether an XLM macro is a command macro or a function macro. Notice also that you can assign function macros to a Function Wizard category. You can even create a custom category, which is not possible using VBA.

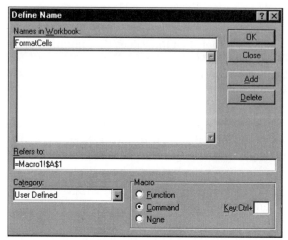

Figure 38-4: The Define Name dialog box while an XLM sheet is active.

Interpreting XLM Macros

By any standard, XLM macros are cryptic and often difficult to interpret. In this section I briefly describe how XLM macros are structured so that (if the need arises) you can at least partially understand what's going on.

Figure 38-5 shows an XLM macro that increases each value in the selected range by a specified percentage. Notice that the macro is made up of a series of functions in a single column. The first statement is just a label to identify the macro (this is optional). Usually, the macro has a name, which is often the same as the label in its first cell. The macro ends with the =RETURN() function.

	A
1	**IncreaseByPercent_XLM**
2	=INPUT("Percent Increase:",1)
3	=ECHO(FALSE)
4	=SET.NAME("OriginalSelection",SELECTION())
5	=ERROR(FALSE)
6	=SELECT.SPECIAL(2,1)
7	=ERROR(TRUE)
8	=FOR.CELL("CurrentCell",SELECTION(),TRUE)
9	=FORMULA(CurrentCell*(1+A2),CurrentCell)
10	=NEXT()
11	=SELECT(OriginalSelection)
12	=RETURN()
13	

XLM and VBA Macros.xls — Sheet1 / Module1 \ **Macro1**

Figure 38-5: This XLM macro increases each cell in the selection by a specified percentage.

XLM uses hundreds of special functions to perform actions. I describe each function in this macro so that you can get a feel for how this system works.

```
=INPUT("Percent Increase:",1)
```

The preceding function displays an input box that asks the user for a percentage value. When the user enters a value, the function returns that value and it is stored in the macro cell.

```
=ECHO(FALSE)
```

This function turns off screen updating, which speeds up the macro.

```
=SET.NAME("OriginalSelection",SELECTION())
```

The original selection is saved to an object variable named OriginalSelection. This is because the macro will work with a subset of the selection that consists only of constant values — no text or formulas.

```
=ERROR(FALSE)
```

This function turns off error checking. This is necessary because the next function causes an error if no cells qualify.

```
=SELECT.SPECIAL(2,1)
```

This function selects the cells in the original selection that are values and constants. This function takes two arguments. The "2" represents constants, and the "1" represents values. These arguments are described in the online Help file.

```
=ERROR(TRUE)
```

This function turns error checking back on.

```
=FOR.CELL("CurrentCell",SELECTION(),TRUE)
```

This function is the beginning of a For-Next loop. This loop goes through each cell in the selection (which is now a subset of the original selection). The name "CurrentCell" is used to refer to the current cell in the loop.

```
=FORMULA(CurrentCell*(1+A2),CurrentCell)
```

This function multiplies the value of the current cell by 1 plus the value in A2 — which is the value that the user inputs.

```
=NEXT()
```

This function is the end of the For-Next loop. The preceding function is executed once for each cell in the selection.

```
=SELECT(OriginalSelection)
```

This statement selects the original selection. It's not a good practice for a macro to change the user's selection.

```
=RETURN()
```

This function signals the end of the macro.

To help you compare XLM and VBA macros, I wrote the same macro using VBA. It's listed in Figure 38-6.

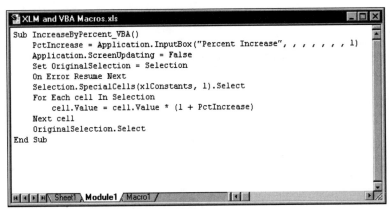

Figure 38-6: This VBA macro increases each cell in the selection by a specified percentage.

The XLM macro took me approximately five times longer to develop — although it really isn't a fair comparison because my XLM skills have become a bit rusty since VBA arrived.

Here are a few key points to keep in mind about XLM macros:

✦ Each macro function is evaluated in order, beginning with the first cell, although the flow of statements can change.

✦ XLM macros can execute other XLM macros — similar in concept to executing a subroutine. When the called macro is completed, the next statement in the calling macro is executed.

✦ When a macro function is evaluated, it returns a value in its cell. You can use these returned values in other macro functions.

On the CD-ROM
Both the XLM and VBA versions of the macro just described are available on the companion CD-ROM. The workbook name is XLM_VBA.XLS.

Methods of Executing XLM Macros

In this section, I discuss the various ways to execute an XLM macro. These are the same methods that you can use to execute a VBA macro.

Function macros

Custom functions created with the XLM language can be used in worksheet formulas. You can enter the function directly or use the Function Wizard. Other macros also can use custom XLM functions.

Command macros

XLM command macros can be executed in a number of ways:

✦ **Using the Tools⇨Macro command.** When you issue this command, all available macros (XLM and VBA) are listed in the dialog box. To execute the macro, just select it and click on the Run button.

✦ **Using a shortcut key.** If the macro is assigned a shortcut key, you can press the assigned key combination to execute the macro.

✦ **From a command on the Tools menu.** You have the option of assigning the macro to a command that appears on Excel's Tool menu. This is done in the Macro Options dialog box. Choose the Tools⇨Macro command, select the macro command that you want to add, and then click on Options. You can then assign the macro to the Tools menu. You also can use this method to remove a command from the Tools menu.

✦ **From a custom toolbar button.** An XLM macro can be assigned to a tool on a toolbar.

✦ **From a button or other graphic object.** An XLM macro can be assigned to a button or any other drawing object.

✦ **Automatically.** Some XLM macros are executed automatically when certain events occur. You can identify these macros because they use one of several special names. These special macro names are as follows:

   Auto_Open: Executes whenever the file is opened

   Auto_Close: Executes whenever the file is closed

   Auto_Activate: Executes whenever the document window is activated (but not when the document is opened)

   Auto_Deactivate: Executes whenever the document window is deactivated (but not when the document is closed)

✦ **Run a macro from a macro.** XLM macros can execute other macros. This capability is analogous to calling a subroutine from a programming language.

✦ **From a custom menu.** As I discuss in Chapter 32, Excel lets you create new menus. This capability makes it possible to create new commands that execute macros.

Troubleshooting XLM Macros

If you encounter an XLM macro that doesn't seem to be working correctly, you can try a few things to figure out the problem. Usually, the best approach is to contact the developer for assistance — especially if you're not familiar with XLM macros. But that's not always possible. Following are a few ideas for troubleshooting XLM macros:

✦ **Make sure that you are executing the macro in the proper context.** For example, the macro may be written so that it executes only when a certain worksheet is active.

✦ **Identify the name used.** Use the Insert⇨Name⇨Define command to see a list of the names used. This list includes worksheet names as well as XLM sheet names.

✦ **Try "stepping through" the macro.** When an error occurs in an XLM macro, Excel displays the Macro Error dialog box shown in Figure 38-7. You can click on Halt to stop the macro, Step to step through it line by line, or Continue to ignore the error. Often, stepping through a macro helps you become familiar with it.

Figure 38-7: The Macro Error dialog box lets you step through a macro one line at a time.

Summary

In this chapter, I present a cursory overview of the XLM macro system. If you want to learn macro programming, you should learn the VBA language. I compare the XLM language with VBA, describe how to execute XLM macros, and present a few simple troubleshooting tips.

✦   ✦   ✦

Creating User-Oriented Applications

◆ ◆ ◆ ◆

In This Chapter

An overview of user-oriented spreadsheet applications

Features that make Excel an ideal environment for creating user-oriented applications

A detailed description of a sample application that demonstrates many useful techniques

◆ ◆ ◆ ◆

This chapter ties together some of the topics presented in the previous chapters. More specifically, I discuss the concept of a user-oriented application. Then I put this information to practical use by describing a relatively complex application that I developed. This application includes features that are common to a wide variety of spreadsheet applications.

What Is a User-Oriented Application?

If you have come this far, I assume that you're at least a moderately experienced spreadsheet user and that you probably have developed several Excel spreadsheets. The time you spent working on each project depended on how you were going to use it. For some spreadsheets, you probably didn't care how they looked. You wanted to get a quick answer to a question. Other spreadsheet projects — particularly those that others would use — demanded more attention to detail.

Because this chapter is about spreadsheet applications, it's only fair that I provide a working definition. A *spreadsheet application* is a spreadsheet file (or group of files) designed so that someone other than the developer can perform useful work without extensive training.

Most of your spreadsheet work is probably done for yourself. Sure, you may print reports and charts for others to see, but it's a safe bet that the majority of your workbook files aren't shared with others. This chapter takes spreadsheet development to the next level and provides some pointers on how to create spreadsheet applications for use by others — those who haven't had the benefit of toiling for hours with formulas, creating and debugging macros, and designing the perfect dialog box.

Although I don't cover all the intricacies, this chapter should provide a good jumping-off place for your own explorations.

One of the most appealing aspects of computers and software is that they *automate* various tasks. For example, you don't have to understand your computer's boot-up process — it happens automatically. Similarly, you don't have to know how Excel calculates its PMT function; all you have to know is what the arguments are.

The following list gives a few examples of why you may want (or need) to create worksheets for others:

✦ You need to enter lots of data — and your time is worth more than a clerk's. You can set up the worksheet so that it's relatively foolproof and provides the clerk with simple instructions.

✦ Your coworkers want to do some numerical analysis and what-if projections, but they are only vaguely familiar with Excel. You can set up the worksheet and create custom dialog boxes so that your coworkers get the results they need with minimal effort (and knowledge of Excel).

✦ Your administrative assistant is in charge of tracking your budget expenditures, but he's not very well trained in Excel. You can set up a menu-driven budget tracking sheet to enter the data and automatically generate reports.

✦ The field salespeople have to generate price quotes on the spot. All of them carry laptops, but they don't understand Excel. You can create a customized quote-generation worksheet that prompts the user for relevant information and then displays or prints the results.

✦ Your boss wants to access some important data that's accessible on the LAN. Because she's not too good with computers, you can set up a spreadsheet application that automatically loads the data that she wants and displays charts — all with push-button ease.

This list could go on for many pages. You probably can think of a dozen examples that fit your situation. If you can't, perhaps this chapter will be relevant to you in the future.

Excel Features for Developers

Spreadsheet-based application development will become increasingly important during the next few years. Thanks to VBA and custom dialog box features, Excel is a highly programmable product — arguably the best choice for developing spreadsheet-based applications. The following list describes the key Excel features that make it a good choice for application development:

✦ **File structure:** The multisheet workbook orientation makes it easy to organize elements of an application.

✦ **MS Query:** You can access important data directly from the spreadsheet environment.

✦ **VBA language:** You can create structured programs and macros directly in Excel.

✦ **Dialog controls on worksheets:** Excel makes it easy to add controls, such as buttons, list boxes, and option lists, to a worksheet — often with little or no macro programming required.

✦ **Custom dialog boxes:** It's relatively easy to create professional-looking dialog boxes to interact with the user.

✦ **Customizable menus:** You can change elements of the menus, add to existing menus, or create entirely new menus.

✦ **Customizable toolbars:** You can create new toolbars consisting of existing buttons or custom buttons that execute your macros.

✦ **Extensive protection options:** You can keep your applications confidential and protected from changes.

✦ **Capability to create "compiled" add-ins:** You can create uneditable XLA files with a single command. Because these files attach seamlessly to Excel, it appears as though the program has new commands. I discuss this feature in Chapter 40.

✦ **Custom worksheet functions:** With VBA, you create custom worksheet functions to simplify formulas and calculations.

Developing an Application

The remainder of this chapter focuses on developing a user-oriented spreadsheet application. A few readers may be able to use this application without modification; it's designed to be general in nature. The point, however, is to demonstrate common principles. Most readers will probably learn quite a bit by working through this chapter and examining the end product. It demonstrates useful techniques that are appropriate for other types of projects. At the very least, this chapter may spark your imagination and give you new insights to Excel. The project incorporates the following elements:

✦ A worksheet database

✦ A pivot table

✦ Complex (but clever) formulas

✦ VBA macros

✦ A custom toolbar

✦ A custom menu

✦ Custom dialog boxes

On the
CD-ROM   This application, named DATABASE.XLS, is available on the companion CD-ROM. I
recommend that you open this workbook as you read through this chapter.

Project goals

The sample application is designed for a small mail-order company. The company
receives orders for its products and then ships the products to the customers.
The application is designed to meet the following goals:

✦ It should be easy to use.

✦ It should be relatively foolproof — that is, it should be able to catch common
errors.

✦ The application must allow the company to track the following information for
each order: order date, customer name and address, customer phone number,
product(s) ordered and quantity of each, how payment was made (check or
credit card), and total amount due (including sales tax and shipping and
handling charges).

✦ The application needs to generate a packing list for each order received. The
packing list should list the products ordered and compute the total purchase
amount.

✦ The application must be flexible in how it handles products, because the
company is continually adding new products and removing others.

✦ The company needs to generate reports that show sales by product and by
month.

The approach

The first question to ask is how the data will be stored. Because the company is
relatively small, a worksheet database (rather than an external database file) will be
appropriate. To satisfy the ease-of-use requirement, you need a method to enter data
(simply entering it into the cells is considered too difficult). You also need a way to
keep track of the current product offerings. Another worksheet database will be
appropriate. I start by opening a new workbook and setting up the two databases.

Getting acquainted with the customer database application

Before you begin exploring the Customer Database Application described in this chapter, you should take some time to become familiar with how it works from the end-user's perspective.

When you open the workbook, you'll see a new menu (Customer Data), plus a custom toolbar named Customer Data toolbar.

To enter data: Choose the Data Entry command on the Customer Data menu. This displays a custom dialog box. Enter some customer information, select a product, and specify a quantity. Click on the Copy to Database button to transfer the information to the database. If required data is missing, you get a message to that effect. If the customer ordered more products, specify the product and quantity, and click on the Copy to Database button again. To enter data for a new customer, clear the fields by clicking on the Clear Fields button.

To create packing lists: Activate the Customers worksheet and select the rows that correspond to the customers for which you want to create packing lists. You don't need to select the entire row — cells in a single column will do. Because a customer's order can consist of multiple records, make sure that your selection includes all records for each customer (the program warns you if don't select all records for a customer). Choose the Print Packing Lists command from the Customer Data menu. You get a dialog box to confirm your selection (you can modify the selection while this dialog box is displayed). You also can choose to print the packing lists automatically or be prompted before printing each one.

To view the pivot table: The workbook contains a pivot table that summarizes the sales by product and by month. To view this pivot table, choose the View Pivot Table command from the Customer Data menu. This refreshes the pivot table to include all customer records. Then activate the PivotTable sheet.

To view the product list: The list of products, unit prices, and shipping and handling charges is stored on the Products worksheet. Because price changing is not normally an end-user function, there isn't a menu command to view this list. Click on the Products tab to activate the worksheet. In this sheet, you can add products, change product names, change prices, and so on. All of your changes are reflected in other parts of the application.

To change company information: The worksheet named "Globals" contains information about the company. You can activate this sheet and make changes, which are reflected in other parts of the application.

Workbook contents

The DATABASE.XLS consists of nine sheets:

> **Read Me:** A worksheet with some descriptive information. This sheet is not essential to the application and can be deleted.

> **Customers:** A worksheet that holds the Customer database. This database consists of records for each product purchased. It is described in the next section.

PackList: A worksheet that holds a single-page packing list. Data from the Customer database is transferred to this sheet before printing.

PivotTable: A worksheet that holds a pivot table that summarizes the product sales by product and by month.

Products: A worksheet that holds the Products database. This database is a list of products, unit prices, and shipping and handling charts. It is described in a later section.

Globals: A worksheet that holds general information such as company name and address, sales tax rate, and so on. It is described in a later section.

DataDlg: A dialog sheet that holds the custom data entry dialog box.

PackListDlg: A dialog sheet that holds the custom dialog box that confirms the user's choice of records to create packing lists.

Macros: The VBA subroutines used in the application.

The Customer database

It's helpful to start developing an application by designing the structure of the database, which will be the central element of this application. Following are the fields for the customer database:

Date Ordered: The date that the order was entered into the database. This can be determined automatically.

Name: The customer's name. For this application, there's no need to use separate fields for the first and last name.

Address1: The first of two fields for the customer's address.

Address2: The second of two fields for the customer's address.

City: The customer's city.

State: The customer's state (using standard two-letter state abbreviations).

Zip: The customer's zip code.

Phone: The customer's phone number.

Product: The product ordered. Note that if the customer orders more than one product, each product has a separate record in the database. The customer information is repeated for each subsequent product ordered.

Quantity: The quantity of the product ordered.

HowPaid: How payment was made (either credit card or check).

Subtotal: A calculated field — the Quantity multiplied by the product's price. Because the unit price is not a field in the database, the price will have to be retrieved from the Product database.

S&H: The shipping and handling charge for the product, multiplied by the Quantity. Again, the shipping and handling charge will be retrieved from the Product database.

Tax Collected: The sales tax. This tax is charged only if the customer's State is the same as the company's state.

Total: A calculated field: the sum of the Subtotal, S&H, and Tax Collected fields.

I entered these field names in the first row of the Customers worksheet.

The Product database

As I note previously, this application requires a second database to keep track of the current product offerings. This database will consist of three fields:

Product Name: The product's name.

Price: The unit price for the product.

S&H: The shipping and handling charge per unit of the product sold.

I entered these field names in a worksheet named Products. I also entered hypothetical product names, prices, and shipping and handling charges (see Figure 39-1).

	A	B	C	D	E
	Product Name	**Price**	**S&H**		
1	Product Name	Price	S&H		
2	Book: Chord Finder	11.49	3.00		
3	Book: Finger-Picking Classics	19.95	3.00		
4	Book: Flat-Picking Classics	19.95	3.00		
5	Electronic Tuner	99.95	4.00		
6	Glass Slide	9.95	2.00		
7	Guitar Earrings	15.95	3.00		
8	Guitar Necktie	29.95	4.00		
9	Guitar Polish	7.95	2.00		
10	Headphone Amp	59.95	3.00		
11	Pick-Pak	4.95	1.00		
12	Stainless Steel Slide	11.95	2.00		
13	Stay-On Guitar Strap	15.95	3.00		
14	Strings: Acoustic Heavy	7.95	1.50		
15	Strings: Acoustic Light	7.95	1.50		
16	Strings: Acoustic Medium	7.95	1.50		
17	Strings: Electric Heavy	8.95	1.50		
18	Strings: Electric Light	8.95	1.50		
19	Strings: Electric Medium	8.95	1.50		
20	Sure-Stay Capo	13.95	3.00		

Customer Database Application.xls

PivotTable ╲ **Products** ╱ Globals

Figure 39-1: This simple database keeps track of the company's current product line.

Global data

This workbook has an additional worksheet named Globals (see Figure 39-2). This sheet has settings that are used throughout the workbook. You can change the information in column B and everything in the workbook adjusts automatically. For example, if you want to use the workbook for your own company, you can change the information on the Globals sheet, which eliminates the need to search the entire workbook to make the changes.

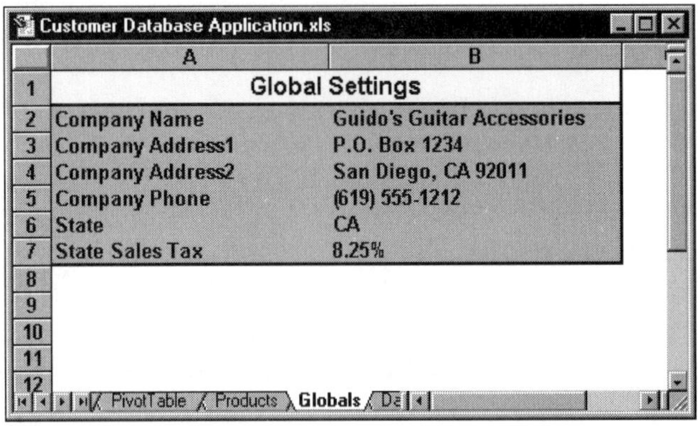

Figure 39-2: This worksheet stores global information used in the application.

Creating the data entry dialog box

Once the databases were defined, I set out to design a custom dialog box for data entry. This dialog box went through several incarnations, and the final result is shown in Figure 39-3. The dialog sheet name is DataDlg.

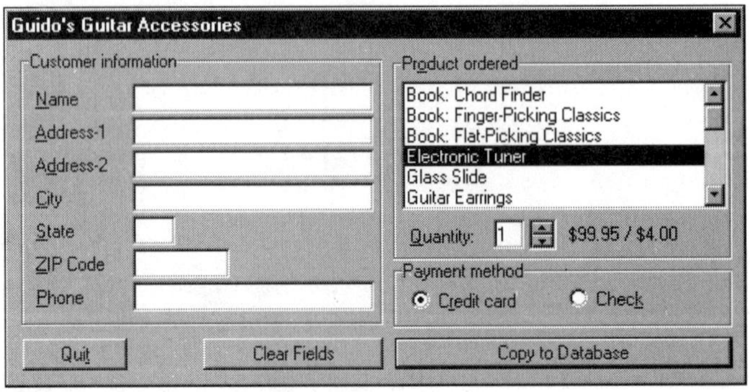

Figure 39-3: The data entry dialog box.

The dialog box displays four sections:

✦ **Customer information:** This section consists of labels and edit boxes.

✦ **Product ordered:** This section contains a list box with all products, an edit box for the quantity, and a spinner to change the quantity. A label displays the price and shipping and handling charge for the selected product and quantity.

✦ **Payment method:** Two option buttons appear in this section.

✦ **Buttons:** Buttons here close the dialog box (Quit), clear the data (Clear Fields), and copy the data to a new record in the customer database (Copy to Database).

Following is a discussion of dialog box sections.

Customer information

This section is straightforward. It's a series of labels and edit boxes. Each label has an accelerator key that activates the corresponding edit box. I also adjusted the tab order of the dialog box so that the Tab key moves through the edit boxes in the proper sequence.

Most of these fields are required — the data will not be transferred to the database if the data is missing. The optional fields are Address-2 and Phone.

Product ordered

The list box notes all products in the Products database. Because the number of products can vary, I chose not to link the box to the Products data. Rather, I wrote the following VBA code to transfer the product names to the list box:

```
Set ProductBox = DialogSheets("DataDlg").ListBoxes("ProductBox")
ProductBox.RemoveAllItems
For i = 1 To Application.CountA(Range("ProductList")) - 1
    ProductBox.AddItem Text:=Sheets("Products").Range("A1").Offset(i,0)
Next I
```

I created an object variable called *ProductBox* to make it easier to refer to the list box. Then I used the RemoveAllItems procedure to empty the list box of its previous contents. I used a For-Next loop to add the product names one by one. Notice that I used Excel's COUNTA worksheet function to determine the number of products in the database.

The quantity ordered is indicated in the edit box. I didn't need to use a spinner control here, but it's a nice touch. The problem, however, is to keep the text in the edit box in sync with the Value property of the spinner control. To solve this problem, I created two more VBA subroutines. One (QuantityChange) was assigned to the edit box, and the other (SpinnerClick) was assigned to the spinner. These subroutines follow:

```
Sub QuantityChange()
'    Executed when the spinner edit box in the data entry dialog is changed
'    This ensures that the spinner is in synch with the edit box
     DataDlg.Spinners("Spin1").Value = Val(DataDlg.EditBoxes("ebProd1").Text)
End Sub
Sub SpinnerClick()
'    Executed when the spinner in the data entry dialog is clicked
'    This ensures that the spinner is in synch with the edit box
     DataDlg.EditBoxes("ebProd1").Text = DataDlg.Spinners("Spin1").Value
End Sub
```

These two subroutines are similar. When the edit box text is changed, the subroutine sets the spinner's value to the value in the edit box. And when the spinner is clicked on, the SpinnerClick subroutine transfers the spinner's value to the edit box. Obviously, both pieces of information (the product and the quantity) are required. The data won't be transferred to the database if no product is selected or the quantity is zero.

The dialog contains a label named *Price*. This label is updated with the price and shipping and handling charges whenever the product or quantity is changed in the dialog box.

Payment method

To make it easy to specify the payment method, I used two option buttons — one for Credit card and one for Check.

Buttons

A key consideration here was that I didn't want the user to invoke the dialog box for each record entered. In other words, to speed up data entry, I chose to keep the dialog box displayed until the user clicks on the Quit button. Therefore, I arranged it so that the Copy to Database button executes a macro (named DumpData) but doesn't close the dialog box (its Dismiss property is set to False).

Clicking on the Clear Fields button executes a macro that clears the edit boxes. When the data is copied to the database, the edit boxes are not cleared. This is to facilitate multiple products (remember, each database record is one product, and a customer can order multiple products).

The Quit button closes the dialog box. When the dialog box is closed, a subroutine named RedefineDatabase is executed. This subroutine changes the definition of the range named CustomerData to include the newly entered rows. This range name is used by the pivot table (described later).

The customer database application macros

This application uses quite a few VBA macros — 16, to be exact. To help you get your bearings, I've prepared a summary that lists each macro, briefly describes what it does, and indicates how it is called. The macros in the Macros module appear in alphabetical order.

Auto_Close: Hides the custom toolbar and reminds the user to back up the workbook. Executed automatically when the application is closed.

Auto_Open: Displays the custom toolbar and activates the Customers sheet. Executed automatically when the application is opened.

CalculatePricing: Computes and inserts the pricing fields for customer records. If the argument is missing, the current selection is used. Executed by the DumpData subroutine. Also can be executed using the Customer Data menu or the custom toolbar.

DisplayPricing: Updates a label control in the DataDlg dialog box with the price and shipping and handling fees for the selected product. Executed when the list box is changed. Also executed when the quantity edit box or spinner is changed.

DumpData: Transfers data from the DataDlg dialog box. Executed when the Copy to Database button is clicked.

EnterData: Displays the DataDlg dialog box. Executed using the Customer Data menu or the custom toolbar.

GotoCustomers: Activates the Customers worksheet. Executed by several subroutines and also can be executed using the Customer Data menu or the custom toolbar.

GotoPackingList: Activates the PackList worksheet. Executed by several subroutines

and also can be executed using the Customer Data menu or the custom toolbar.

InitializeDataEntry: Clears the fields in the DataDlg dialog box. Executed by the EnterData subroutine and when the Clear Fields button in the DataDlg dialog box is clicked.

MakePackingList: Creates packing list(s) for the selected records in the customer database. Executed using the Customer Data menu or the custom toolbar.

PrintSheet: Prompts the user to print the active sheet. Executed using the Customer Data menu or the custom toolbar.

QuantityChange: Transfers the value of the quantity edit box in the DataDlg dialog box to the spinner. This is executed whenever the user changes the value in the edit box and ensures that the spinner's value corresponds to the edit box text.

RedefineDatabase: Updates the Customer Data range name to include all records on the Customers worksheet. Executed by the EnterData and RefreshPivot subroutines and also can be executed using the Customer Data menu or the custom toolbar.

RefreshPivot: Redefines the CustomerData range and refreshes the pivot table. Executed using the Customer Data menu or the custom toolbar.

SpinnerClick: Transfers the value of the spinner control in the DataDlg dialog box to the edit box. This is executed whenever the user changes the spinner control and ensures that the edit box's text corresponds to the spinner's value.

ToggleHelpText: Changes the visible property of a text box named HelpText on the active sheet. Executed using the Customer Data menu or the custom toolbar.

Transferring the dialog box data to the database

When the Copy to Data button in the dialog is clicked, the DumpData macro is executed. This macro performs the following actions:

✦ Verifies that a product was selected in the list box and that the quantity is greater than zero

✦ Verifies that the required customer information fields in the edit boxes are not empty

✦ Determines the next available row in the Customer database to copy the data to

✦ Copies the data

✦ Executes another subroutine (named CalculatePricing) that calculates the price fields (Subtotal, S&H, Tax Collected, and Total)

You may be wondering why I didn't use worksheet formulas to calculate the pricing information. Although this would be possible (and perhaps easier), I avoided using formulas for two reasons. First, recalculating the formulas would slow down the application. More important, if a change is made to a product's price, all records in the database would be affected. Clearly this is not desirable. As it stands, a pricing change affects only products ordered after the price change takes effect.

Note   The CalculatePricing subroutine also can be executed manually. For example, if you choose to enter the data directly into the cells, you can then select the rows that you entered and execute the CalculatePricing subroutine to fill in the pricing fields.

Creating packing lists

This application also was designed to create and print packing lists that accompany each order. Because a single customer's order can consist of multiple records in the Customer database, this was a bit tricky.

I created a macro (MakePackingList) to work with the rows in the user's selection. I created a custom dialog box on the PackListDlg sheet that lets the user verify the selection and change it if necessary. The selection can consist of a single customer's records or records for a group of customers. This dialog box, shown in Figure 39-4, also has a check box. When checked, the user is prompted before each packing list is printed. If it's not checked, the packing lists are printed without user intervention.

Figure 39-4: The user can change the records to be processed in this dialog box.

When the dialog box is closed, the macro assigns some variables. It creates an object variable (*WorkRange*) that consists of the range specified in the edit box. It also creates variables that hold the number of records in the selection (*NumRecords*) and the row number of the first record (*FirstRecord*) and last record (*LastRecord*) in the selection. This code follows:

```
    '    Get details about the selected records
         Set WorkRange = Range(PackListDlg.EditBoxes("Records").Text)
         NumRecords = WorkRange.Rows.Count
         FirstRecord = WorkRange.Rows(1).Row
         LastRecord = WorkRange.Rows(NumRecords).Row
```

I also built in error checking to ensure that all records for a customer are included. For example, a customer may have ordered three products. If the selection does not include all three records, the packing list will be incorrect.

I did this checking by comparing the name in the first row of the selection with the name in the record directly above the first row of the selection. The macro also compares the name in the last row of the selection with the name in the record directly below the last row of the selection. If either of these comparisons is true, it means that not all records for the customer were selected. The code that performs this checking is as follows:

```
'   Warn if there is the same name above or below selected records
    ExtraName = False
    If Customers.Cells(FirstRecord - 1, NAME_COL) = _
        Customers.Cells(FirstRecord, NAME_COL) Then ExtraName = True
    If Customers.Cells(LastRecord + 1, NAME_COL) = _
        Customers.Cells(LastRecord, NAME_COL) Then ExtraName = True
    If ExtraName Then
        Msg = "A matching name was found directly "
        Msg = Msg & "above or below the selected range."
        Msg = Msg & Chr(10) & Chr(10)
        Msg = Msg & "Continue with this selection?"
        Ans = MsgBox(Msg, vbCritical + vbYesNo + vbDefaultButton2, APPNAME)
    If Ans <> vbYes Then Exit Sub
    End If
```

If the program determines that not all records for the customer were selected, it displays the message box shown in Figure 39-5. If the user clicks on the No button, the routine is halted.

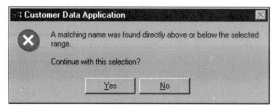

Figure 39-5: This message box ensures that all records for a customer are included in the packing list.

The remainder of the macro processes each record in the selection and transfers the data to the appropriate cells in the PackList sheet. The VBA code checks the name in the next record to determine whether the packing list is finished. If the name is the same, it means that the customer has another record in the database. If the name is different, it means that the packing list for the current customer is finished.

The PackList worksheet is shown in Figure 39-6. The company name, address, and phone number use references to the Globals worksheet.

Notice that the PackList worksheet contains formulas. Some of the formulas are straightforward. For example, unit prices are determined using a VLOOKUP function that uses the information in the Products worksheet.

Some of the other formulas may seem rather unusual, however. When the macro is transferring the data to the PackList sheet, it enters the row number into cell A1 (which is named PackListRecord). Several of the formulas on the PackList worksheet use this cell to create a reference to the data on the Customers sheet. For example, the cell that displays the date ordered contains the following formula:

```
=INDIRECT("Customers!A" & PackListRecord)
```

This formula uses the INDIRECT function to create a cell reference. For example, if PackListRecord is 25 (which means that the current record is in row 25 of the Customers sheet), the formula would be equivalent to the following:

```
=INDIRECT(Customers!A25)
```

This formula returns the date in cell A25 on the Customers worksheet.

I use the same technique to bring in the customer's name and address. The lengthy formula that follows (in cell C9) displays the information from columns B through E. I broke the formula into lines to make it more legible.

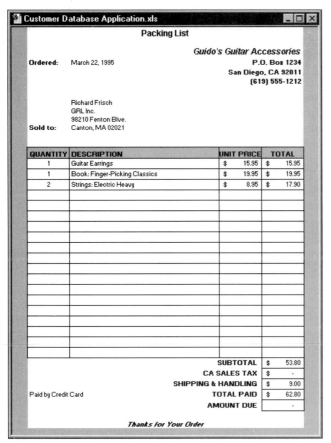

Figure 39-6: This worksheet is the packing list form.

```
=INDIRECT("Customers!B"&PackListRecord)
&CHAR(10)
&INDIRECT("Customers!C"
&PackListRecord)
&CHAR(10)
&INDIRECT("Customers!D"&PackListRecord)
&IF(INDIRECT("Customers!D"&PackListRecord)=0,"",CHAR(10))
&INDIRECT("Customers!E"&PackListRecord)&", "
        &INDIRECT("Customers!F"&PackListRecord)&" "
        &INDIRECT("Customers!G"&PackListRecord)
```

Note that this formula uses the CHAR function to insert a line-break character (the cell's word-wrap property is set). The IF function is used to handle cases in which the Address2 field of the record is empty. Using this indirect referencing simplifies the process of transferring the database information to the packing list.

The pivot table

The workbook has a sheet named PivotTable, which contains the pivot table shown in Figure 39-7. This pivot table summarizes the product sales by month. Additional page fields are included to filter the summary by how the order was paid, or by state.

The pivot table is based on the range named `CustomerData`. This range name is updated whenever the data entry dialog box is closed. You also can execute the RedefineDatabase subroutine to update this range name.

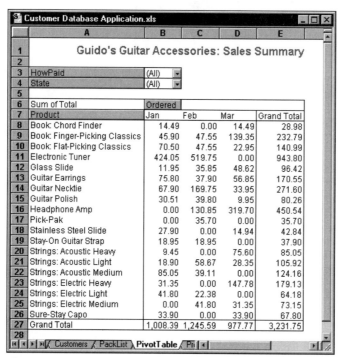

Figure 39-7: This pivot table summarizes sales by product and month.

The RedefineDatabase subroutine follows:

```
Sub RedefineDatabase()
'    Redefines the database to include all records

    Dim Customers As Object
    Dim LastRow As Integer, Ans As Integer
    Dim TheRange As String
    Set Customers = ThisWorkbook.Worksheets("Customers")
    Customers.Activate
```

```
        LastRow = Application.CountA(Customers.Range("A:A"))
        Customers.Cells(LastRow, 1).Select
        Selection.CurrentRegion.Select
        TheRange = Selection.Address(ReferenceStyle:=xlR1C1)
        ActiveWorkbook.Names.Add Name:="CustomerData", _
            RefersToR1C1:="=Customers!" & TheRange
        Customers.Cells(LastRow, 1).Select
    End Sub
```

After the CustomerData range is redefined, the pivot table is refreshed and the PivotTable sheet is activated. I used the following code:

```
With Sheets("PivotTable")
    .PivotTables("PivotTable1").RefreshTable
    .Activate
End With
```

User help

The application also has a simple help system built in. Help information is provided in text boxes (one on each worksheet). Each text box is named HelpText. A macro (ToggleHelpText) toggles the Visible property of the text box. This macro is as follows:

```
Sub ToggleHelpText()
    On Error Resume Next
    Application.ScreenUpdating = False
    With ActiveSheet.DrawingObjects("HelpText")
        .Visible = Not ActiveSheet.DrawingObjects("HelpText").Visible
        .Top = ActiveWindow.Panes(1).VisibleRange.Top + 10
        .Left = 20
    End With
End Sub
```

I used the On Error Resume Next statement to eliminate the error message that would appear if the sheet doesn't have a text box named HelpText. The macro changes the Top property of the text box to correspond to the visible area of the worksheet. This ensures that the text box is placed in a position that is currently visible. Figure 39-8 shows an example of a text box.

Note Each text box also has the ToggleHelpText macro assigned to it. Therefore, the text box also can be hidden by clicking on it.

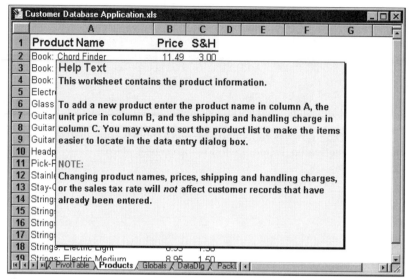

Figure 39-8: This application uses text boxes to provide user help.

The custom menu

I used the Tools⇨Menu Editor command to create the Customer Data menu (see Figure 39-9). Each menu item executes a macro. The menu items and their macros are listed in Table 39-1.

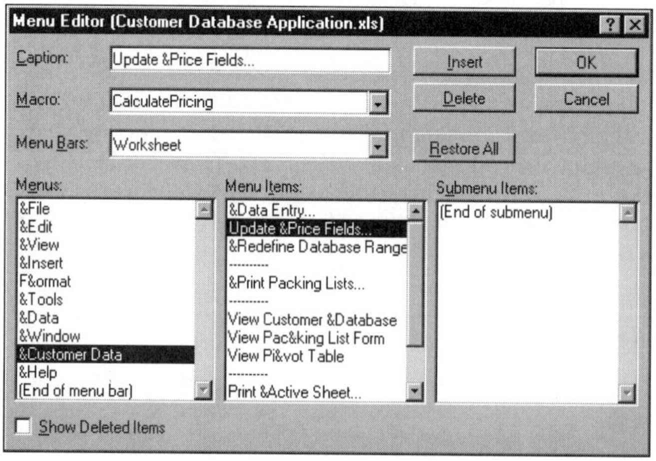

Figure 39-9: The Menu Editor.

Table 39-1
Menu Items Used in the Customer Database Application

Menu Item	Macro
&Data Entry...	EnterData
Update &Price Fields...	CalculatePricing
&Redefine Database Range	ReDefineDatabase
-	(None, item separator)
&Print Packing Lists...	MakePackingList
-	(None, item separator)
View Customer &Database	GotoCustomers
View Pac&king List Form	GotoPackingList
View Pi&vot Table	RefreshPivot
-	(None, item separator)
Print &Active Sheet...	PrintSheet
-	(None, item separator)
Toggle &Help	ToggleHelpText

The Customer Data menu that results is shown in Figure 39-10. Notice that items consisting of a single hyphen (-) result in item separators on the menu. I used the ampersand (&) to specify the hot keys for each menu item. Menu items that display a dialog box have ellipses (...), which is the standard Windows style.

Notice that when a menu item is selected, the status bar displays a description of the command. These descriptions are associated with the macro that is executed. For example, to enter status bar text for the CalculatePricing macro, I chose the Tools⇨Macro command, selected CalculatePricing from the macro list, and then clicked on the Options button. This displayed the Macro Options dialog box. I then entered the description in the field labeled Status Bar Text (see Figure 39-11).

	I	J	K				O	
1	**Product**	**Quantity**	**HowPaid**				**Total**	
95	Strings: Electric Heavy	1	Credit Card				10.45	
96	Book: Finger-Picking Classics	1	Credit Card				24.60	
97	Book: Finger-Picking Classics	1	Check				22.95	
98	Strings: Electric Heavy	2	Check				20.90	
99	Strings: Electric Heavy	2	Check				20.90	
100	Book: Chord Finder	1	Credit Card				14.49	
101	Book: Finger-Picking Classics	1	Credit Card				22.95	
102	Guitar Earrings	1	Check	15.95	3.00	0.00	18.95	
103	Strings: Electric Heavy	2	Check	17.90	3.00	0.00	20.90	
104	Guitar Earrings	1	Credit Card	15.95	3.00	0.00	18.95	
105	Book: Finger-Picking Classics	1	Credit Card	19.95	3.00	0.00	22.95	
106	Strings: Electric Heavy	2	Credit Card	17.90	3.00	0.00	20.90	
107	Strings: Electric Medium	3	Credit Card	26.85	4.50	0.00	31.35	
108	Sure-Stay Capo	2	Check	27.90	6.00	0.00	33.90	
109	Strings: Acoustic Light	1	Check	7.95	1.50	0.00	9.45	
110	Strings: Acoustic Light	2	Credit Card	15.90	3.00	0.00	18.90	
111	Stainless Steel Slide	1	Credit Card	11.95	2.00	0.99	14.94	
112	Strings: Electric Heavy	2	Credit Card	17.90	3.00	1.48	22.38	
113								

Customer Data menu items:
- Data Entry...
- Update Price Fields...
- Redefine Database Range
- Print Packing Lists...
- View Customer Database
- View Packing List Form
- View Pivot Table
- Print Active Sheet...
- Toggle Help

Sheet tabs: Customers / PackList / PivotTable / Products / Globals

Create packing list(s) from selected records and (optionally) print the packing lists

Figure 39-10: The Customer Data menu.

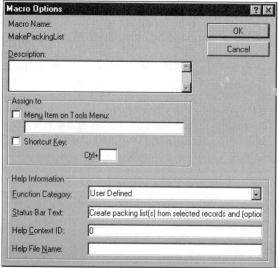

Figure 39-11: Use the Macro Options dialog box to enter
text that appears in the status bar when a menu item is selected.

The custom toolbar

The custom toolbar is named Customer Data Toolbar. This toolbar, as shown in Figure 39-12, consists of nine buttons. These functions are all available on the Customer Data menu. I created the toolbar to give the user another way of performing common operations.

Figure 39-12: The Customer Data Toolbar.

I created most of the toolbar images using Excel's Button Editor dialog box. Other images were borrowed from other Excel toolbar buttons. Table 39-2 lists the toolbar buttons and the macro that each button executes.

Table 39-2 Custom Toolbar Buttons and Macros	
Button Name	*Macro*
Enter customer data	EnterData
Create packing lists for the selected records	MakePackingList
Print the active sheet	PrintSheet
Redefine the database to include all records	RedefineDatabase
CalculatePricing	Calculate pricing information for the selected records
Activate the customer database sheet	GotoCustomers
Activate the packing list sheet	GotoPackingList
View the pivot table	RefreshPivot
Toggle help text	ToggleHelpText

Note   I used the Toolbar Tools utility in the Power Utility Pak to create the tooltips for these toolbar buttons. The only other way to insert custom tooltips is to create a macro.

Summary

In this chapter, I present an overview of the concept of a user-oriented application and explain why Excel is an ideal choice for such an application. I then discuss the details of such an application named DATABASE.XLS, which is available on the companion CD-ROM.

✦   ✦   ✦

Creating Custom Excel Add-Ins

For developers, one of the most useful features in Excel is the capability to create add-ins. In this chapter, I discuss this concept and provide a practical example of creating an add-in.

What Is an Add-In?

Generally speaking, a spreadsheet *add-in* is something that's added to the spreadsheet to give it additional functionality. For example, many add-ins are available for 1-2-3 for DOS that give new features to the program. These new features can be industry-specific features (for example, third-party financial forecasting add-ins) or general features such as on-screen formatting (for example, the Wysiwyg add-in that's included with 1-2-3). Some add-ins provide new worksheet functions that can be used in formulas. Usually, the new features blend in well with the original interface, so they appear to be part of the program. Lotus originated the concept of spreadsheet add-ins, and dozens of third-party developers market add-in products for 1-2-3.

Excel's approach to add-ins is a bit different, because any knowledgeable Excel user can create add-ins from XLS workbooks. An Excel add-in is basically a different form of an XLS workbook file. Any XLS file can be converted into an add-in. Add-ins are always hidden, however, so you can't display worksheets or chart sheets that are contained in an add-in. But you can access its VBA subroutines and functions and display dialog boxes contained on dialog sheets.

Following are some typical uses for Excel add-ins:

   ♦ **To store one or more custom worksheet functions.** When the add-in is loaded, the functions can be used like any built-in worksheet function.

✦ **To store Excel utilities.** VBA is ideal for creating general-purpose utilities that extend the power of Excel. My Power Utility Pak is an example of this.

✦ **To store proprietary macros.** If you don't want end users seeing (or modifying) your macros, store the macros in an add-in. The macros can be used, but they can't be viewed or changed.

Excel ships with several useful add-ins (see "Add-ins included with Excel"), and you can acquire other add-ins from third-party vendors or online services. In addition, Excel includes the tools to let you create your own add-ins. I explain how to do this later in the chapter, but first I need to cover some background.

Working with Add-Ins

The best way to work with add-ins is to use Excel's add-in manager, which you access with the Tools⇨Add-Ins command. This command displays the dialog box shown in Figure 40-1. The list box contains all add-ins that Excel knows about. Those that are checked are currently open. You can open and close add-ins from this dialog box by checking or unchecking the check boxes.

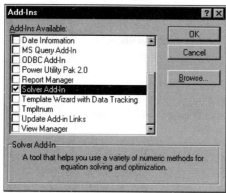

Figure 40-1: The Add-Ins dialog box.

Caution Most add-in files also can be opened by using the File⇨Open command. You'll find that once an add-in is opened, however, you can't use the File⇨Close command to close it. The only way to remove the add-in is to exit and restart Excel or write a macro to close the add-in.

When an add-in is opened, you may or may not notice anything different. In nearly every case, however, some change is made to the menu — either a new menu or one or more new menu items on an existing menu. For example, when you open the Analysis ToolPak add-in, this add-in gives you a new menu item on the Tools menu: Data Analysis. When you open my Power Utility Pak add-in, you get a new Utilities menu, located between the Data and Window menus.

It's important to understand that an add-in may look like it's part of Excel — but it may not always act like it. For example, you'll notice some subtle differences in how the dialog boxes work in the Analysis ToolPak.

Add-ins included with Excel

Following are the add-ins included with Excel. Depending on how Excel was installed, you may not have access to all these add-ins. To install missing add-ins, rerun Excel's Setup program (or the Microsoft Office Setup program).

Access Links Add-In: Lets you use Micro-soft Access forms and reports with Excel worksheets (Access must be installed on your system).

Analysis ToolPak: Statistical and engineering tools, plus new worksheet functions.

Analysis ToolPak — VBA: VBA functions for Analysis ToolPak.

AutoSave: Automatically saves your workbook at a time interval that you specify.

MS Query Add-In: Works with Microsoft Query to bring external data into a worksheet.

ODBC Add-In: Lets you use ODBC functions to connect to external data sources directly.

Report Manager: Prints reports that consist of a set sequence of views and scenarios.

Solver Add-In: A tool that helps you use a variety of numeric methods for equation solving and optimization.

Template Utilities: Utilities used by the Spreadsheet Solutions templates. This is loaded automatically when you use one of these templates.

Template Wizard with Data Tracking: Helps you create custom templates.

Update Add-in Links: Updates links to MS Excel 4.0 add-ins to directly access the new built-in functionality.

View Manager: Creates, stores, and displays different views of a worksheet.

Why Create Add-Ins?

Most Excel users have no need to create add-ins. But if you develop spreadsheets for others — or if you simply want to get the most out of Excel — you may be interested in pursuing this topic further.

There are several reasons why you may want to convert your XLS application to an add-in. Among them are the following:

✦ **To prevent access to your code.** When you distribute an application as an add-in, the end users can't view the sheets in the workbook. If you use proprietary techniques in your VBA code, this can prevent it from being copied (or at least make it more difficult).

✦ **To avoid confusion.** If an end user loads your application as an add-in, the file is not visible — and is therefore less likely to confuse novice users or get in the way. Unlike a hidden XLS workbook, an add-in can't be unhidden.

✦ **To simplify access to worksheet functions.** Custom worksheet functions that are stored in an add-in don't require the workbook name qualifier. For example, if you have a custom function named MOVAVG stored in a workbook named `Newfuncs.xls`, you would have to use a syntax like the following to use this function in a different workbook:

```
=NEWFUNC.XLS!MOVAVG(A1:A50)
```

But if this function is stored in an add-in file that's open, the syntax is much simpler because you don't need to include the file reference:

```
=MOVAVG(A1:A50)
```

✦ **Easier access.** Once you identify the location of your add-in, it appears in the Add-Ins dialog box, with a friendly name and a description of what it does.

✦ **Better control over loading.** Add-ins can be opened automatically when Excel starts, regardless of the directory in which they are stored.

✦ **No prompts when unloading.** When an add-in is closed, the user never sees the *Save change in...?* prompt.

Creating an Add-In

Although any workbook can be converted to an add-in, not all workbooks benefit by this. In fact, workbooks that consist only of worksheets become unusable because add-ins are hidden.

In fact, the only types of workbooks that benefit from conversion to an add-in are those with macros. For example, you may have a workbook that consists of general-purpose macros (subroutines and functions). This makes an ideal add-in.

Creating an add-in is quite simple. This section describes how to create an add-in from a normal workbook file.

1. **Develop your application and make sure that everything works properly.** Don't forget to include a method to execute the macro or macros. You may want to add a new menu item to the Tools menu.

2. **Test the application by executing it when a *different* workbook is active.** This simulates its behavior when it's an add-in, because an add-in is never the active workbook. You may find that some references no longer work. For example, the following statement works fine when the code resides in the active workbook but fails when a different workbook is active:

   ```
   Dialogsheets("MyDialog").Show
   ```

   You could qualify the reference with the name of the workbook object, like this:

   ```
   Workbooks("MYBOOK.XLS").Dialogsheets("MyDialog").Show
   ```

   This method is not recommended, because the name of the workbook changes when it's converted to an add-in. The solution is to use the ThisWorkbook qualifier, as follows:

   ```
   ThisWorkbook.Dialogsheets("MyDialog").Show
   ```

3. **Select the File⇨Summary Info command and enter a brief descriptive title in the Title field and a longer description in the Comments field.** This step is not required, but it makes it easier to use the add-in.

4. **Activate any VBA module or any dialog sheet in the workbook and select the Tools⇨Make Add-In command.** Excel responds with the dialog box that suggests the current workbook name, with an XLA extension. Click on OK and the add-in is created.

Note It's important to understand that once an add-in is created, it can't be modified. Think of the original XLS version of the file as the source file and the XLA version as the compiled file. If you need to make any changes to your add-in, make them in the XLS version and then create a new add-in.

An Add-In Example

In this section, I discuss the steps in creating a useful add-in. This add-in is designed to work with dates. When the active cell contains a date, the add-in displays a dialog box with useful information about the date.

On the CD-ROM Both the XLS and XLA version of this file are on the companion CD-ROM. The workbook's name is DATEINFO.XLS (and DATEINFO.XLA for the XLA version).

Setting up the workbook

This workbook consists of three sheets: a worksheet (named DateSheet), a dialog sheet (named DateDlg), and a VBA module (named DateMod).

The macro, ShowDateInfo, follows:

```
Sub ShowDateInfo()
'    Displays information about the date in the active cell

'    Exit if the active cell does not contain a date
    If Not IsDate(ActiveCell.Value) Then
        MsgBox "The active cell does not contain a date."
        Exit Sub
    End If

'    Transfer the date to the DateSheet
    ThisWorkbook.Sheets("DateSheet").Range("A1").Value = ActiveCell.Value

'    Display the dialog box
    ThisWorkbook.DialogSheets("DateDlg").Show
End Sub
```

This macro is rather simple (all calculations occur on the DateSheet worksheet). I set it up so that this macro can be executed by pressing Ctrl+D or by choosing the Tools⇨Date Information command.

The macro first checks the active cell. If it doesn't contain a date, it displays a message box and the subroutine ends with no further action. If the active cell contains a date, the date is transferred to cell A1 on the DateSheet. Formulas calculate various information about the date. Figure 40-2 shows the DateSheet.

Note Two of the formulas use custom functions, which are defined in the DateMod module. The DAYSINMONTH function returns the number of days in the month. The WEEKDAYNUM determines how many days of the same weekday have occurred in the year (for example, January 9, 1996, is the second Tuesday of the year).

The dialog box (shown in Figure 40-3) contains a linked picture object. I created this object by copying the range from DateSheet to the Clipboard. Then I activated the dialog sheet, pressed Shift, and selected the Edit⇨Paste Picture Link command (this command is available only when the Shift key is pressed).

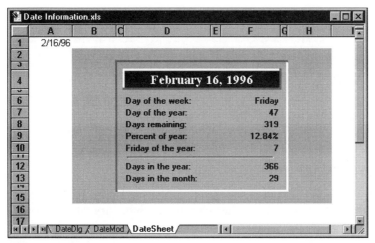

Figure 40-2: This worksheet has formulas that calculate nformation about the date in cell A1.

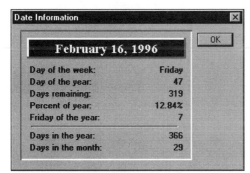

Figure 40-3: This dialog box has a picture that is linked to the worksheet range.

Testing it

Before converting this workbook to an add-in, it's necessary to test it. Testing should be done when a different workbook is active to simulate what will happen when the workbook is an add-in. Remember, an add-in is never the active sheet.

Open a new workbook and insert a date into a cell. Activate the cell and execute the ShowDateInfo macro by pressing Ctrl+D or by choosing the Tools⇨Date Information command. The dialog box should appear with information about the date in the active cell.

Note Notice that the following statements in the ShowDateInfo module use references to ThisWorkbook:

```
ThisWorkbook.Sheets("DateSheet").Range("A1").Value = ActiveCell.Value

ThisWorkbook.DialogSheets("DateDlg").Show
```

The ThisWorkbook property returns the workbook in which the current macro code is running. This makes it possible to execute the macro while any workbook is active.

Adding descriptive information

This step is recommended but not necessary. Choose the File➪Properties command to bring up the Properties dialog box. Then click on the Summary tab, as shown in Figure 40-4.

Enter a title for the add-in in the Title field. This is the text that will appear in the Add-Ins dialog box. In the Comments field, enter a description. This information will appear at the bottom of the Add-Ins dialog box when the add-in is selected.

Date Information.xls Properties

General | Summary | Statistics | Contents | Custom

Title: Date Information

Subject:

Author: John Walkenbach

Manager:

Company:

Category:

Keywords:

Comments: Add-in that displays useful information about the date in the active cell.

Template:

☐ Save Preview Picture

OK   Cancel

Figure 40-4: Use the Properties dialog box to enter descriptive information about your add-in.

Creating the add-in

Before creating the add-in, save the workbook. To create the add-in, activate either the DateMod or the DateDlg sheet and choose the Tools⇨Make Add-In command. You get the Make Add-In dialog box shown in Figure 40-5. Select a location and name for the add-in file. Usually, you want to keep the add-in's name the same as the XLS version's name. Click on the Save button to create the add-in.

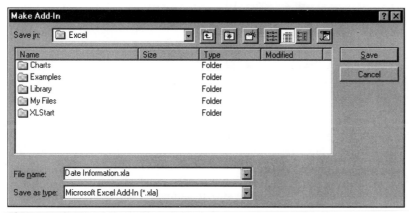

Figure 40-5: The Make-Add-In dialog box.

Opening the add-in

To avoid confusion, close the XLS workbook before opening the add-in created from it. Then select the Tools⇨Add-Ins command. Excel displays its Add-Ins dialog box. Click on the Browse button and locate the add-in that you just created. After you do so, the Add-Ins dialog box displays the add-in in its list. Notice that the information you provided in the Properties dialog box appears here (see Figure 40-6). Click on OK to close the dialog box and open the add-in.

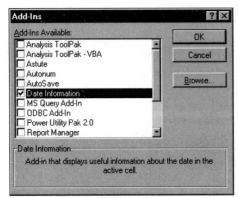

Figure 40-6: The Add-Ins dialog box, with the new add-in selected.

When the add-in is open, the Tools menu displays a new menu item (Date Information) that executes the ShowDateInfo macro in the add-in. The Ctrl+D key combination also executes that macro. Also notice that the two custom functions (DAYSINMONTH and WEEKDAYNUM) appear in the Function Wizard. These functions can be used in your worksheet formulas as long as the add-in is open.

Note If you want to make modifications to the add-in, you must do so in the XLS version of the file. Then, use the Tools⇨Make Add-In command again to re-create the add-in. Use the same name to replace the old copy with the updated version.

Summary

In this chapter, I discuss the concept of add-ins — files that add new capabilities to Excel. I explain how to work with add-ins and why you may want to create custom add-ins. I close the chapter with an example of an add-in that displays information about a specific date in the active cell.

✦   ✦   ✦

Appendixes

Installing Excel for Windows 95

This appendix describes how to install Excel for Windows 95 and provides instructions for adding options that may not have been included in the original installation.

First-Time Installation

Excel for Windows 95 may already be installed on your system. If not, you need to run the Setup.exe program. The exact procedures vary somewhat, depending on whether you purchased Excel separately or as part of Microsoft Office 95 (which includes other applications in addition to Excel). In the examples that follow, I assume that you're installing Office 95.

To start Setup, insert the CD-ROM. Then click on the Start button on the Windows taskbar. Select Run and enter **setup** preceded by the CD-ROM device and a colon. For example, if your CD-ROM drive is drive D, type **d:setup** and press Enter.

If you're installing from floppy disks, precede **setup** with the floppy disk drive letter (probably **A**) and a colon.

The Setup program asks for some initial information and then displays the dialog box shown in Figure A-1. For optimal control over what gets installed, choose the Custom option. If your hard drive space is limited (as on a laptop system), you may want to choose the Compact option.

Figure A-1: Installing Excel using the Microsoft Office for Windows 95 Setup program.

Selecting Custom shows a list of Excel components that you can choose. If you're installing Office 95, select Excel and click on the Change Option button. In either case, you get a dialog box like the one shown in Figure A-2.

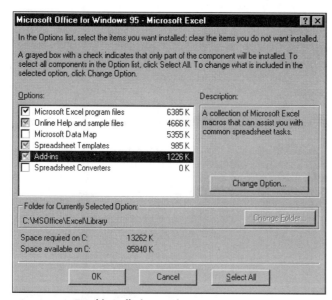

Figure A-2: Excel installation options.

The options are as follows:

◆ Microsoft Excel program files

◆ Online Help and sample files

◆ Microsoft Data Map

◆ Spreadsheet Templates

◆ Add-ins

◆ Spreadsheet Converters

Most of these options include suboptions, which you select by clicking on the Change Option button. For example, the Add-ins option has seven suboptions, shown in Figure A-3.

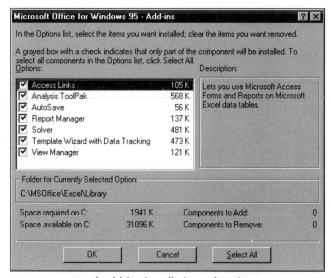

Figure A-3: Excel Add-ins installation suboptions.

Note It's a good idea to examine all the options to make sure that the features you need get installed. You can always add options that you omit during the original installation, however.

After you select all the options, click on OK and continue the installation. You now can start Excel from the Start button in the taskbar.

Rerunning Setup

Several of Excel's features are optional and may not have been placed on your system when Excel was originally installed. To use any of these features, you need to rerun the original Setup program (either Excel's Setup program or the Office 95 Setup program). Don't worry — this won't take nearly as long as the original process. Before running Setup, make sure that Excel is not running.

Caution   When installing options, do *not* uncheck options that are already installed. If you do, they will be removed.

Using Online Help: A Primer

Excel's online help system has always been good. But the help available with Excel for Windows 95 is better than ever. However, the online help system can be a bit intimidating for beginners, because you can get help in many ways. This appendix assists you in getting the most out of this valuable resource.

Why Online Help?

In the early days of personal computing, software programs usually came bundled with bulky manuals that described how to use the product. Some products included rudimentary help that could be accessed online. Over the years, that situation gradually changed. Now, online help is usually the *primary* source of documentation, which may be augmented by a written manual.

Once you become accustomed to it, you'll find that online help (if it's done well) offers many advantages over written manuals:

+ There's no need to lug around a manual — especially important for laptop users who do their work on the road.

+ You don't have to thumb through a separate book, which often has a confusing index.

+ You can search for specific words and then select a topic that's appropriate to your question.

+ In some cases (for example, writing VBA code), you can copy examples from the Help window and paste them into your application.

+ Help sometimes includes embedded buttons that you can click on to go directly to the command that you need.

Types of Help

Excel offers several types of online help:

✦ **Tooltips.** Move the mouse pointer over a toolbar button and the button's name appears.

✦ **TipWizard.** Excel monitors your actions while you work. If there is a more efficient way of performing an operation, the TipWizard button on the Standard toolbar changes color. Click on this button to read Excel's tip.

✦ **Status bar descriptions.** The status bar at the bottom of the screen displays a description of the selected menu command or toolbar button.

✦ **Dialog box help.** When a dialog box is displayed, click on the Help button in the title bar (it has a question mark on it) and then click on any part of the dialog box. Excel pops up a description of the selected control. Figure B-1 shows an example.

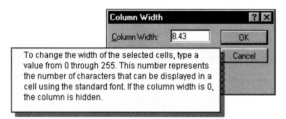

Figure B-1: Getting a description of a dialog box control.

✦ **1-2-3 help.** The Help⇨Lotus 1-2-3 Help command provides help designed for those who are familiar with 1-2-3's commands.

✦ **Detailed help.** This is what's usually considered online help. As you'll see, there are several ways to locate a particular help topic.

Accessing Help

When working with Excel for Windows 95, you can access the online help system by pressing F1 or by choosing the Help⇨Microsoft Excel Help Topics command. Either method displays a tabbed dialog box with four panels. I discuss each of these panels in the sections that follow.

Contents

Figure B-2 shows the Contents panel of the Help Topics dialog box. This panel is useful for getting general information about a topic.

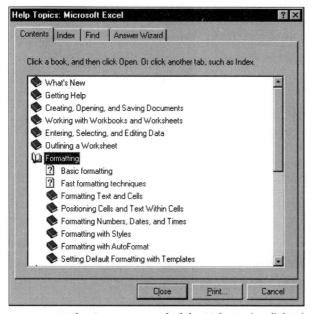

Figure B-2: The Contents panel of the Help Topics dialog box.

This panel is arranged as an outline and lets you access general information. When you double-click on a book icon, it expands to show subtopics (each with a Question-Mark icon). Double-click on it again and the subtopics are collapsed. Double-click on a Question-mark icon, and you get a new window that describes the topic. Figure B-3 shows one such window. In this case, the Help window has buttons that lead to other topics.

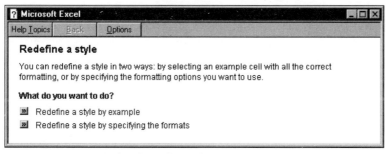

Figure B-3: An example of a Help Topic.

Note To return to the original Help Topics dialog box, click on the Help Topics button. Or, click on the Back button (if it's available) to go back to the previous Help Topics window.

Index

Figure B-4 shows the Index panel of the Help Topics dialog box. The topics are arranged alphabetically, much like an index for a book. You can enter the first few letters in the box at the top to quickly scroll to an index entry.

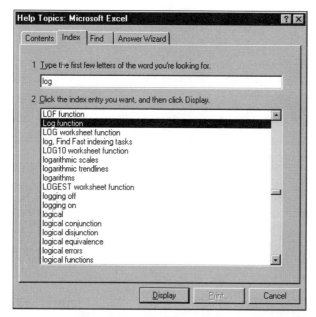

Figure B-4: The Index panel of the Help Topics dialog box.

When you double-click on an index entry, Excel displays a list of all applicable topics in a dialog box. Double-click on a topic to get to the Help Topics window.

Find

 The Find panel represents a new feature in Excel for Windows 95 — the capability to find all topics that contain a particular word or words. The first time that you access this feature, there will be a slight delay as the index file is created.

Figure B-5 shows the Find panel of the Help Topics dialog box.

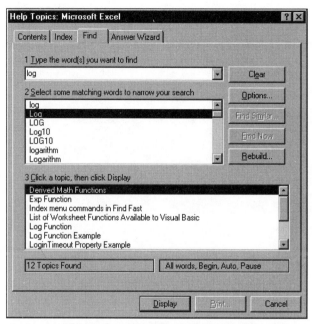

Figure B-5: The Find panel of the Help Topics dialog box.

To help you narrow down your search, you can control several options by clicking on the Options button. This displays the Find Options dialog box shown in Figure B-6. These choices are self-explanatory.

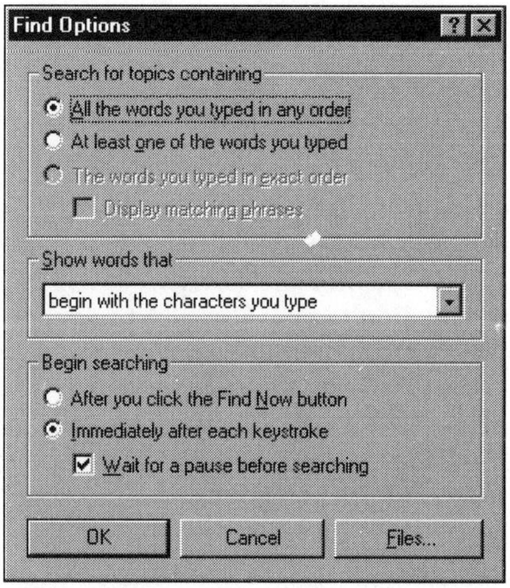

Figure B-6: Use the Find Options dialog box to set options.

Answer Wizard

New! The Answer Wizard is another new feature. This lets you enter a question and get a list of Help Topics that may answer your question. Figure B-7 shows the Answer Wizard panel of the Help Topics dialog box.

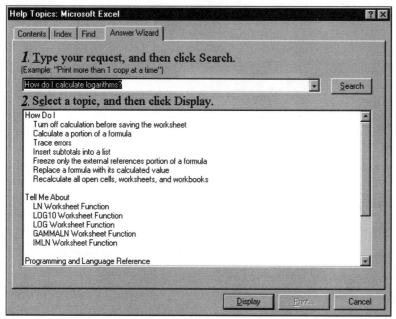

Figure B-7: The Answer Wizard panel of the Help Topics dialog box.

Mastering Help

The information provided in this appendix gets you started using online help. Everyone develops his or her own style for accessing this help, and I urge you to explore this resource. Even if you think you understand a topic in Excel fairly well, you can often discover one or two subtle features that you didn't know about. A thorough understanding of how to use the online help system will definitely make you a more productive Excel user.

✦   ✦   ✦

What's New in Excel for Windows 95?

This appendix contains a complete listing and brief description of all new features in Excel for Windows 95. If you've used Excel 5, this provides a quick overview of the differences you can expect to find.

General Features

32-bit application

Excel for Windows 95 is a 32-bit application. This means that it requires a 32-bit operating environment such as Windows 95 or Windows NT. To the typical user, this means faster response time, fewer memory restrictions, and fewer problems with system resources. It also means that Excel for Windows 95 will not run on Windows 3.x.

Faster

According to Microsoft, Excel for Windows 95 has been fine-tuned for speed. These speed enhancements range from 20 percent to 600 percent, or approximately 50 percent faster than Excel 5 overall.

Uses long filenames

You are no longer limited to eight-character filenames. Files can now use up to 255 characters, including spaces and some punctuation symbols.

Supports scraps

You can select a range and drag it to the desktop to create a *scrap*. You then can drag it back to another worksheet or to another application. This feature, in essence, uses the desktop as a temporary storage location.

Spreadsheet Solutions templates

Excel for Windows 95 comes with ten templates for common spreadsheet applications such as invoices, purchase orders, mortgage calculations, and so on.

Cross-Reference See Chapter 33 for information about templates.

Template Wizard with data tracking

A new Template Wizard lets you turn an existing Excel workbook into a template. You also can set up a system to copy specified cells to a separate database automatically.

Cross-Reference Refer to Chapter 33 for more information about this feature.

Support of Office binders

If you purchased Excel as part of Microsoft Office, you can create *binders* that consist of one or more documents from other Office applications. This provides an easy way to store multiapplication projects — and even print them with consecutive page numbers.

Cross-Reference See Chapter 29 for more information on Office binders.

Different Look

Many parts of Excel for Windows 95 look different because of the operating environment. Other differences are due to changes in Excel itself.

Animation

Excel now performs animation for certain actions. For example, when you change the width of a column, you can see the column's width change in an animated fashion. Animation also occurs when you insert or delete rows and columns. If you don't like this feature, turn it off in the Edit panel of the Options dialog box.

Scrollbars

Workbook scrollbars automatically adjust to the length and width of the data in the worksheet, preventing users from scrolling past the active area of a worksheet. Scrollbars also display "scroll tips" that tell you which row or column you will see when you release the scrollbar.

Cell tips

Excel for Windows 95 still supports cell notes, but this version displays them automatically when you move the mouse cursor over a cell that has a cell note (similar to what happens when you move the mouse pointer over a toolbar button).

Improved dialog boxes

Several of Excel's dialog boxes have been significantly improved.

Number format dialog box

The numeric formatting dialog box is rearranged to make it easier to use. It also shows an example of how your number looks as you apply various number formats.

File Open dialog box

The File Open dialog box is significantly enhanced. You can select how to view the files and perform common file functions (delete, copy, rename, and so on) directly from the dialog box. The new *Favorites* feature lets you quickly change to a different folder without traversing directory trees. The *FindFast* feature lets you quickly locate files by name, date, location, and even contents.

Print dialog box

This dialog box is better organized and has more options.

Help Features

Excel uses the new Windows 95 Help style, which makes online help easier to access. In many cases, the online help is more thorough than in the previous version.

Cross-Reference Refer to Appendix B for complete details on using the online help system.

Answer Wizard

You can locate information by typing your request in the form of a question, such as, "How do I turn off these gridlines?" Excel's help system displays a list of topics that are relevant.

Quick tips in dialog boxes

Excel's dialog boxes all have a question-mark icon next to the Close button. You can click on this button and then click on any part of the dialog box for a quick explanation of what that part does.

Interactive answers

The online help now features buttons that take you directly to the command or setting to accomplish the task that you're seeking help with.

Data Entry Features

Excel for Windows 95 has several new features that assist in entering data.

AutoCorrect

Excel monitors your typing and corrects common errors on the fly. You also can customize the AutoCorrect list to create your own shorthand codes that expand into words or phrases automatically.

AutoComplete

When you start typing, Excel scans the current column. If it recognizes a word or phrase, it finishes it for you. Press Enter to complete the entry. If you don't like this feature, turn it off in the Edit panel of the Options dialog box.

Improved drag and drop

Excel now lets you use drag and drop to copy or move cells between worksheets and workbooks. You also can drag a range to another application without having to tile the windows.

Access forms

You can now use forms developed in Microsoft Access as data-entry forms for your worksheets.

Data Analysis Features

Excel for Windows 95 has a several new features related to data-analysis.

Top 10 autofilter

The autofilter feature has been enhanced. You can filter a list in terms of the top (or bottom) *n* values or percents.

Cross-Reference I discuss autofiltering in Chapter 23.

AutoCalculate display

When you select a range of cells, Excel displays the sum of the selected cells in the status bar. You can right-click on the status bar display to show other information: average, count, count of the number cells, minimum, or maximum.

Faster pivot tables

The pivot table feature is now much faster and uses less memory than in Excel 5.

Cross-Reference I discuss pivot tables in Chapter 25.

Data Map

You can create maps from worksheet data. Excel for Windows 95 ships with a copy of Data Map, an OLE server application that you can access from Excel.

Cross-Reference Chapter 17 is devoted to map-making.

Access reports

You can create complex Microsoft Access reports or mailing labels from a worksheet list or external database.

Workgroup Features

Excel for Windows 95 has several new features designed to make it easier to share work with others.

 I discuss workgroup features in Chapter 21.

Shared lists

Multiple users can now work on the same workbook at the same time. Excel will prompt you if multiple users enter conflicting information.

Support for Microsoft Exchange

You can "publish" a workbook file to a Microsoft Exchange public folder to give other users access to the file.

Automated network drive mapping

You can open or link to files on a network without having to map the drive first.

File Filters

Excel for Windows 95 now supports the following file formats:

✦ Lotus 1-2-3 for Windows (WK4)

✦ Novell Quattro Pro for Windows (WB2)

✦ Microsoft Access (export only)

Macros

Excel for Windows 95 supports both the XLM and VBA macro languages. XLM hasn't changed since the previous version, but VBA has a few improvements.

Improved VBA help

The online help for VBA is much better organized and more thorough. It also includes more code samples, which you can copy and paste to your modules.

Data Access Objects

Macro programmers can use the Microsoft Access database engine to access data in external databases.

New protection options

A new option lets macros modify protected worksheets without having to disable protection.

Modeless Debug window

The Debug window is now modeless, which means that you don't have to close the window in order to activate another window.

Support for passwords in edit box

The Edit Box control now has an option that displays the user's entry as a series of asterisks. This is designed for dialog boxes in which the user enters a password.

Support for mouse pointer shapes

You can now change the shape of the mouse pointer without resorting to API calls.

Worksheet Function Reference

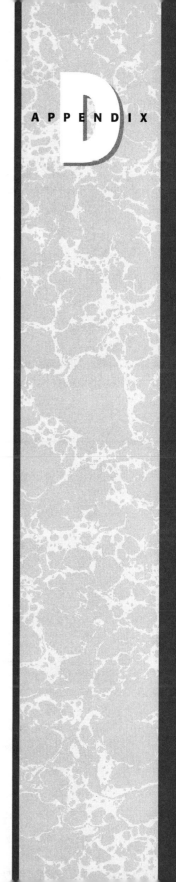

This appendix contains a complete listing of Excel's worksheet functions. The functions are arranged alphabetically, by categories used by the Function Wizard. Some of these functions (indicated in the lists that follow) are available only when a particular add-in is attached.

For more information about a particular function, including its arguments, select the function in the Function Wizard and click on the Help button.

Table D-1
Database Category Functions

Function	What It Does
DAVERAGE	Returns the average of selected database entries
DCOUNT	Counts the cells containing numbers from a specified database and criteria
DCOUNTA	Counts nonblank cells from a specified database and criteria
DGET	Extracts from a database a single record that matches the specified criteria
DMAX	Returns the maximum value from selected database entries
DMIN	Returns the minimum value from selected database entries
DPRODUCT	Multiplies the values in a particular field of records that match the criteria in a database
DSTDEV	Estimates the standard deviation based on a sample of selected database entries
DSTDEVP	Calculates the standard deviation based on the entire population of selected database entries
DSUM	Adds the numbers in the field column of records in the database that match the criteria
DVAR	Estimates variance based on a sample from selected database entries
DVARP	Calculates variance based on the entire population of selected database entries
SQL.OPEN**	Makes a connection to a data source via ODBC
SQL.EXEC.QUERY**	Executes an SQL statement on an SQL.OPEN connection
SQL.BIND**	Specifies where to place SQL.EXEC.QUERY results
SQL.RETRIEVE**	Retrieves SQL.EXEC.QUERY results
SQL.RETRIEVE.TO.FILE**	Retrieves SQL.EXEC.QUERY results to a file
SQL.CLOSE**	Terminates an SQL.OPEN connection
SQL.GET.SCHEMA**	Returns information on an SQL.OPEN connection
SQL.ERROR**	Returns error information on SQL* functions
SQL.REQUEST**	Requests a connection and executes an SQL query
QUERYGETDATA***	Gets external data using Microsoft Query
QUERYGETDATADIALOG***	Displays a dialog box to get data using Microsoft Query
QUERYREFRESH***	Updates a data range using Microsoft Query

* Available only when the Analysis ToolPak add-in is attached

** Available only when the ODBC add-in is attached

*** Available only when the MS Query add-in is attached

Table D-2
Date & Time Category Functions

Function	What It Does
DATE	Returns the serial number of a particular date
DATEVALUE	Converts a date in the form of text to a serial number
DAY	Converts a serial number to a day of the month
DAYS360	Calculates the number of days between two dates based on a 360-day year
EDATE*	Returns the serial number of the date that is the indicated number of months before or after the start date
EOMONTH*	Returns the serial number of the last day of the month before or after a specified number of months
HOUR	Converts a serial number to an hour
MINUTE	Converts a serial number to a minute
MONTH	Converts a serial number to a month
NETWORKDAYS*	Returns the number of whole workdays between two dates
NOW	Returns the serial number of the current date and time
SECOND	Converts a serial number to a second
TIME	Returns the serial number of a particular time
TIMEVALUE	Converts a time in the form of text to a serial number
TODAY	Returns the serial number of today's date
WEEKDAY	Converts a serial number to a day of the week
WEEKNUM*	Returns the week number in the year
WORKDAY*	Returns the serial number of the date before or after a specified number of workdays
YEAR	Converts a serial number to a year
YEARFRAC*	Returns the year fraction representing the number of whole days between start_date and end_date

* Available only when the Analysis ToolPak add-in is attached

Table D-3
Engineering Catagory Functions

Function	What It Does
BESSELI*	Returns the modified Bessel function In(x)
BESSELJ*	Returns the Bessel function Jn(x)
BESSELK*	Returns the modified Bessel function Kn(x)
BESSELY*	Returns the Bessel function Yn(x)
BIN2DEC*	Converts a binary number to decimal
BIN2HEX*	Converts a binary number to hexadecimal
BIN2OCT*	Converts a binary number to octal
COMPLEX*	Converts real and imaginary coefficients into a complex number
CONVERT*	Converts a number from one measurement system to another
DEC2BIN*	Converts a decimal number to binary
DEC2HEX*	Converts a decimal number to hexadecimal
DEC2OCT*	Converts a decimal number to octal
DELTA*	Tests whether two values are equal
ERF*	Returns the error function
ERFC*	Returns the complementary error function
GESTEP*	Tests whether a number is greater than a threshold value
HEX2BIN*	Converts a hexadecimal number to binary
HEX2DEC*	Converts a hexadecimal number to decimal
HEX2OCT*	Converts a hexadecimal number to octal
IMABS*	Returns the absolute value (modulus) of a complex number
IMAGINARY*	Returns the imaginary coefficient of a complex number
IMARGUMENT*	Returns the argument theta, an angle expressed in radians
IMCONJUGATE*	Returns the complex conjugate of a complex number
IMCOS*	Returns the cosine of a complex number
IMDIV*	Returns the quotient of two complex numbers
IMEXP*	Returns the exponential of a complex number
IMLN*	Returns the natural logarithm of a complex number

Function	What It Does
IMLOG10*	Returns the base-10 logarithm of a complex number
IMLOG2*	Returns the base-2 logarithm of a complex number
IMPOWER*	Returns a complex number raised to an integer power
IMPRODUCT*	Returns the product of two complex numbers
IMREAL*	Returns the real coefficient of a complex number
IMSIN*	Returns the sine of a complex number
IMSQRT*	Returns the square root of a complex number
IMSUB*	Returns the difference of two complex numbers
IMSUM*	Returns the sum of complex numbers
OCT2BIN*	Converts an octal number to binary
OCT2DEC*	Converts an octal number to decimal
OCT2HEX*	Converts an octal number to hexadecimal

* Available only when the Analysis ToolPak add-in is attached

Table D-4
Financial Category Functions

Function	What It Does
ACCRINT*	Returns the accrued interest for a security that pays periodic interest
ACCRINTM*	Returns the accrued interest for a security that pays interest at maturity
AMORDEGRC*	Returns the depreciation for each accounting period
AMORLINC*	Returns the depreciation for each accounting period
COUPDAYBS*	Returns the number of days from the beginning of the coupon period to the settlement date
COUPDAYS*	Returns the number of days in the coupon period that contains the settlement date
COUPDAYSNC*	Returns the number of days from the settlement date to the next coupon date
COUPNCD*	Returns the next coupon date after the settlement date
COUPNUM*	Returns the number of coupons payable between the settlement date and maturity date

(continued)

Table D-4 *(continued)*

Function	What It Does
COUPPCD*	Returns the previous coupon date before the settlement date
CUMIPMT*	Returns the cumulative interest paid between two periods
CUMPRINC*	Returns the cumulative principal paid on a loan between two periods
DB	Returns the depreciation of an asset for a specified period using the fixed-declining balance method
DDB	Returns the depreciation of an asset for a specified period using the double-declining balance method or some other method that you specify
DISC*	Returns the discount rate for a security
DOLLARDE*	Converts a dollar price, expressed as a fraction, into a dollar price, expressed as a decimal number
DOLLARFR*	Converts a dollar price, expressed as a decimal number, into a dollar price, expressed as a fraction
DURATION*	Returns the annual duration of a security with periodic interest payments
EFFECT*	Returns the effective annual interest rate
FV	Returns the future value of an investment
FVSCHEDULE*	Returns the future value of an initial principal after applying a series of compound interest rates
INTRATE*	Returns the interest rate for a fully invested security
IPMT	Returns the interest payment for an investment for a given period
IRR	Returns the internal rate of return for a series of cash flows
MDURATION*	Returns the Macauley modified duration for a security with an assumed par value of $100
MIRR	Returns the internal rate of return where positive and negative cash flows are financed at different rates
NOMINAL*	Returns the annual nominal interest rate
NPER	Returns the number of periods for an investment
NPV	Returns the net present value of an investment based on a series of periodic cash flows and a discount rate
ODDFPRICE*	Returns the price per $100 face value of a security with an odd first period
ODDFYIELD*	Returns the yield of a security with an odd first period
ODDLPRICE*	Returns the price per $100 face value of a security with an odd last period

Function	What It Does
ODDLYIELD*	Returns the yield of a security with an odd last period
PMT	Returns the periodic payment for an annuity
PPMT	Returns the payment on the principal for an investment for a given period
PRICE*	Returns the price per $100 face value of a security that pays periodic interest
PRICEDISC*	Returns the price per $100 face value of a discounted security
PRICEMAT*	Returns the price per $100 face value of a security that pays interest at maturity
PV	Returns the present value of an investment
RATE	Returns the interest rate per period of an annuity
RECEIVED*	Returns the amount received at maturity for a fully invested security
SLN	Returns the straight-line depreciation of an asset for one period
SYD	Returns the sum-of-years' digits depreciation of an asset for a specified period
TBILLEQ*	Returns the bond-equivalent yield for a Treasury bill
TBILLPRICE*	Returns the price per $100 face value for a Treasury bill
TBILLYIELD*	Returns the yield for a Treasury bill
VDB	Returns the depreciation of an asset for a specified or partial period using a declining balance method
XIRR*	Returns the internal rate of return for a schedule of cash flows that is not necessarily periodic
XNPV*	Returns the net present value for a schedule of cash flows that is not necessarily periodic
YIELD*	Returns the yield on a security that pays periodic interest
YIELDDISC*	Returns the annual yield for a discounted security. For example, a Treasury bill
YIELDMAT*	Returns the annual yield of a security that pays interest at maturity

* Available only when the Analysis ToolPak add-in is attached

Table D-5
Information Category Functions

Function	What It Does
CELL	Returns information about the formatting, location, or contents of a cell
COUNTBLANK	Counts the number of blank cells within a range
ERROR.TYPE	Returns a number corresponding to an error type
INFO	Returns information about the current operating environment
ISBLANK	Returns TRUE if the value is blank
ISERR	Returns TRUE if the value is any error value except #N/A
ISERROR	Returns TRUE if the value is any error value
ISEVEN*	Returns TRUE if the number is even
ISLOGICAL	Returns TRUE if the value is a logical value
ISNA	Returns TRUE if the value is the #N/A error value
ISNONTEXT	Returns TRUE if the value is not text
ISNUMBER	Returns TRUE if the value is a number
ISODD*	Returns TRUE if the number is odd
ISREF	Returns TRUE if the value is a reference
ISTEXT	Returns TRUE if the value is text
N	Returns a value converted to a number
NA	Returns the error value #N/A
TYPE	Returns a number indicating the data type of a value

* Available only when the Analysis ToolPak add-in is attached

Table D-6
Logical Category Functions

Function	What It Does
AND	Returns TRUE if all its arguments are TRUE
FALSE	Returns the logical value FALSE
IF	Specifies a logical test to perform
NOT	Reverses the logic of its argument
OR	Returns TRUE if any argument is TRUE
TRUE	Returns the logical value TRUE

Table D-7
Lookup & Reference Category Functions

Function	What It Does
ADDRESS	Returns a reference as text to a single cell in a worksheet
AREAS	Returns the number of areas in a reference
CHOOSE	Chooses a value from a list of values
COLUMN	Returns the column number of a reference
COLUMNS	Returns the number of columns in a reference
HLOOKUP	Looks in the top row of an array and returns the value of the indicated cell
INDEX	Uses an index to choose a value from a reference or array
INDIRECT	Returns a reference indicated by a text value
LOOKUP	Looks up values in a vector or array
MATCH	Looks up values in a reference or array
OFFSET	Returns a reference offset from a given reference
ROW	Returns the row number of a reference
ROWS	Returns the number of rows in a reference
TRANSPOSE	Returns the transpose of an array
VLOOKUP	Looks in the first column of an array and moves across the row to return the value of a cell

Table D-8
Math & Trig Category Functions

Function	What It Does
ABS	Returns the absolute value of a number
ACOS	Returns the arccosine of a number
ACOSH	Returns the inverse hyperbolic cosine of a number

(continued)

Table D-8 *(continued)*

Function	What It Does
ASIN	Returns the arcsine of a number
ASINH	Returns the inverse hyperbolic sine of a number
ATAN	Returns the arctangent of a number
ATAN2	Returns the arctangent from x and y coordinates
ATANH	Returns the inverse hyperbolic tangent of a number
CEILING	Rounds a number to the nearest integer or to the nearest multiple of significance
COMBIN	Returns the number of combinations for a given number of objects
COS	Returns the cosine of a number
COSH	Returns the hyperbolic cosine of a number
COUNTIF	Counts the number of nonblank cells within a range which meets the given criteria
DEGREES	Converts radians to degrees
EVEN	Rounds a number up to the nearest even integer
EXP	Returns e raised to the power of a given number
FACT	Returns the factorial of a number
FACTDOUBLE	Returns the double factorial of a number
FLOOR	Rounds a number down, toward 0
GCD*	Returns the greatest common divisor
INT	Rounds a number down to the nearest integer
LCM*	Returns the least common multiple
LN	Returns the natural logarithm of a number
LOG	Returns the logarithm of a number to a specified base
LOG10	Returns the base-10 logarithm of a number
MDETERM	Returns the matrix determinant of an array
MINVERSE	Returns the matrix inverse of an array
MMULT	Returns the matrix product of two arrays
MOD	Returns the remainder from division
MROUND*	Returns a number rounded to the desired multiple

Function	What It Does
MULTINOMIAL*	Returns the multinomial of a set of numbers
ODD	Rounds a number up to the nearest odd integer
PI	Returns the value of pi
POWER	Returns the result of a number raised to a power
PRODUCT	Multiplies its arguments
QUOTIENT*	Returns the integer portion of a division
RADIANS	Converts degrees to radians
RAND	Returns a random number between 0 and 1
RANDBETWEEN*	Returns a random number between the numbers you specify
ROMAN	Converts an Arabic numeral to Roman, as text
ROUND	Rounds a number to a specified number of digits
ROUNDDOWN	Rounds a number down, toward 0
ROUNDUP	Rounds a number up, away from 0
SERIESSUM*	Returns the sum of a power series based on the formula
SIGN	Returns the sign of a number
SIN	Returns the sine of the given angle
SINH	Returns the hyperbolic sine of a number
SQRT	Returns a positive square root
SQRTPI*	Returns the square root of (number * pi)
SUBTOTAL	Returns a subtotal in a list or database
SUM	Adds its arguments
SUMIF	Adds the cells specified by a given criteria
SUMPRODUCT	Returns the sum of the products of corresponding array components
SUMSQ	Returns the sum of the squares of the arguments
SUMX2MY2	Returns the sum of the difference of squares of corresponding values in two arrays
SUMX2PY2	Returns the sum of the sum of squares of corresponding values in two arrays
SUMXMY2	Returns the sum of squares of differences of corresponding values in two arrays
TAN	Returns the tangent of a number
TANH	Returns the hyperbolic tangent of a number
TRUNC	Truncates a number to an integer

* Available only when the Analysis ToolPak add-in is attached

Table D-9
Statistical Category Functions

Function	What It Does
AVEDEV	Returns the average of the absolute deviations of data points from their mean
AVERAGE	Returns the average of its arguments
BETADIST	Returns the cumulative beta probability density function
BETAINV	Returns the inverse of the cumulative beta probability density function
BINOMDIST	Returns the individual term binomial distribution probability
CHIDIST	Returns the one-tailed probability of the chi-squared distribution
CHIINV	Returns the inverse of the one-tailed probability of the chi-squared distribution
CHITEST	Returns the test for independence
CONFIDENCE	Returns the confidence interval for a population mean
CORREL	Returns the correlation coefficient between two data sets
COUNT	Counts how many numbers are in the list of arguments
COUNTA	Counts how many values are in the list of arguments
COVAR	Returns covariance, the average of the products of paired deviations
CRITBINOM	Returns the smallest value for which the cumulative binomial distribution is less than or equal to a criterion value
DEVSQ	Returns the sum of squares of deviations
EXPONDIST	Returns the exponential distribution
FDIST	Returns the F probability distribution
FINV	Returns the inverse of the F probability distribution
FISHER	Returns the Fisher transformation
FISHERINV	Returns the inverse of the Fisher transformation
FORECAST	Returns a value along a linear trend
FREQUENCY	Returns a frequency distribution as a vertical array
FTEST	Returns the result of an F-test

Function	What It Does
GAMMADIST	Returns the gamma distribution
GAMMAINV	Returns the inverse of the gamma cumulative distribution
GAMMALN	Returns the natural logarithm of the gamma function, G(x)
GEOMEAN	Returns the geometric mean
GROWTH	Returns values along an exponential trend
HARMEAN	Returns the harmonic mean
HYPGEOMDIST	Returns the hypergeometric distribution
INTERCEPT	Returns the intercept of the linear regression line
KURT	Returns the kurtosis of a data set
LARGE	Returns the k-th largest value in a data set
LINEST	Returns the parameters of a linear trend
LOGEST	Returns the parameters of an exponential trend
LOGINV	Returns the inverse of the lognormal distribution
LOGNORMDIST	Returns the cumulative lognormal distribution
MAX	Returns the maximum value in a list of arguments
MEDIAN	Returns the median of the given numbers
MIN	Returns the minimum value in a list of arguments
MODE	Returns the most common value in a data set
NEGBINOMDIST	Returns the negative binomial distribution
NORMDIST	Returns the normal cumulative distribution
NORMINV	Returns the inverse of the normal cumulative distribution
NORMSDIST	Returns the standard normal cumulative distribution
NORMSINV	Returns the inverse of the standard normal cumulative distribution
PEARSON	Returns the Pearson product moment correlation coefficient
PERCENTILE	Returns the k-th percentile of values in a range
PERCENTRANK	Returns the percentage rank of a value in a data set
PERMUT	Returns the number of permutations for a given number of objects
POISSON	Returns the Poisson distribution
PROB	Returns the probability that values in a range are between two limits

(Continued)

Table D-9 *(continued)*

Function	What It Does
QUARTILE	Returns the quartile of a data set
RANK	Returns the rank of a number in a list of numbers
RSQ	Returns the square of the Pearson product moment correlation coefficient
SKEW	Returns the skewness of a distribution
SLOPE	Returns the slope of the linear regression line
SMALL	Returns the k-th smallest value in a data set
STANDARDIZE	Returns a normalized value
STDEV	Estimates standard deviation based on a sample
STDEVP	Calculates standard deviation based on the entire population
STEYX	Returns the standard error of the predicted y-value for each x in the regression
TDIST	Returns the student's t-distribution
TINV	Returns the inverse of the student's t-distribution
TREND	Returns values along a linear trend
TRIMMEAN	Returns the mean of the interior of a data set
TTEST	Returns the probability associated with a student's t-Test
VAR	Estimates variance based on a sample
VARP	Calculates variance based on the entire population
WEIBULL	Returns the Weibull distribution
ZTEST	Returns the two-tailed P-value of a z-test

Table D-10
Text Category Functions

Function	What It Does
CHAR	Returns the character specified by the code number
CLEAN	Removes all nonprintable characters from text
CODE	Returns a numeric code for the first character in a text string

Function	What It Does
CONCATENATE	Joins several text items into one text item
DOLLAR	Converts a number to text, using currency format
EXACT	Checks to see if two text values are identical
FIND	Finds one text value within another (case-sensitive)
FIXED	Formats a number as text with a fixed number of decimals
LEFT	Returns the leftmost characters from a text value
LEN	Returns the number of characters in a text string
LOWER	Converts text to lowercase
MID	Returns a specific number of characters from a text string starting at the position that you specify
PROPER	Capitalizes the first letter in each word of a text value
REPLACE	Replaces characters within text
REPT	Repeats text a given number of times
RIGHT	Returns the rightmost characters from a text value
SEARCH	Finds one text value within another (not case sensitive)
SUBSTITUTE	Substitutes new text for old text in a text string
T	Converts its arguments to text
TEXT	Formats a number and converts it to text
TRIM	Removes spaces from text
UPPER	Converts text to uppercase
VALUE	Converts a text argument to a number

Excel's Shortcut Keys

This appendix is a complete listing of the shortcut keys available in Excel. The shortcuts are arranged by context.

Note The keys listed assume that you are not using the Transition Navigation Keys, which are designed to emulate Lotus 1-2-3. You can select this option in the Transition tab of the Options dialog box.

Table E-1
Moving through a Worksheet

Key(s)	What It Does
Arrow keys	Move left, right, up, or down one cell
Home	Moves to the beginning of the row
PgUp	Moves up one screenful
Ctrl+PgUp	Moves to the previous sheet
PgDn	Moves down one screenful
Ctrl+PgDn	Moves to the next sheet
Ctrl+Home	Moves to the first cell in the worksheet (A1)
Ctrl+End	Moves to the last active cell of the worksheet
Ctrl+arrow key	Moves to the edge of a data block. If the cell is blank, moves to the first nonblank cell
F5	Prompts for a cell address to go to
Ctrl+Tab	Moves to the next window
Ctrl+Shift+Tab	Moves to the previous window

Table E-2
Selecting Cells in the Worksheet

Key(s)	What It Does
Shift+arrow key	Expands the selection in the direction indicated
Shift+spacebar	Selects the entire row
Ctrl+spacebar	Selects the entire column
Ctrl+Shift+spacebar	Selects the entire worksheet
Shift+Home	Expands the selection to the beginning of the current row
Ctrl+*	Selects the block of data surrounding the active cell
F8	Extends the selection as you use navigation keys
Shift+F8	Adds other nonadjacent cells or ranges to the selection; Shift+F8 again ends Add mode
F5	Prompts for a range or range name to select
Ctrl+G	Prompts for a range or range name to select
Ctrl+A	Select All

Table E-3
Moving within a Range Selection

Key(s)	What It Does
Enter	Moves the cell pointer to the next cell down in the selection
Shift+Enter	Moves the cell pointer to the previous cell up in the selection
Tab	Moves the cell pointer to the next cell to the right in the selection
Shift+Tab	Moves the cell pointer to the previous cell to the left in the selection
Ctrl+period (.)	Moves to the next corner of the current cell range
Ctrl+Tab	Moves to the next cell range in a nonadjacent selection
Ctrl+Shift+Tab	Moves to the previous cell range in a nonadjacent selection
Shift+Backspace	Collapses the cell selection to just the active cell

Table E-4
Editing Keys in the Formula Bar

Key(s)	What It Does
F2	Begins editing the active cell
Arrow keys	Moves the cursor one character in the direction of the arrow
Home	Moves the cursor to the beginning of the line
End	Moves the cursor to the end of the line
Ctrl+right arrow	Moves the cursor one word to the right
Ctrl+left arrow	Moves the cursor one word to the left
Del	Deletes the character to the right of the cursor
Ctrl+Del	Deletes all characters from the cursor to the end of the line
Backspace	Deletes the character to the left of the cursor

	Table E-5 **Formatting Keys**	
Key(s)	**What It Does**	
Ctrl+1	Format⇨[Selected Object]	
Ctrl+B	Sets or removes boldface	
Ctrl+I	Sets or removes italic	
Ctrl+U	Sets or removes underlining	
Ctrl+5	Sets or removes strikethrough	
Ctrl+Shift+~	Applies the general number format	
Ctrl+Shift+!	Applies the comma format with two decimal places	
Ctrl+Shift+#	Applies the date format (day, month, year)	
Ctrl+Shift+@	Applies the time format (hour, minute, AM/PM)	
Ctrl+Shift+$	Applies the currency format with two decimal places	
Ctrl+Shift+%	Applies the percent format with no decimal places	
Ctrl+Shift+&	Applies border to outline	
Ctrl+Shift+_	Remove all borders	
Alt+'	Format⇨Style command	

Table E-6 Other Shortcut Keys	
Key(s)	**What It Does**
Ctrl+9	Hides rows
Ctrl+Shift+(	Unhides rows
Ctrl+0 (zero)	Hides columns
Ctrl+Shift+)	Unhides columns
Ctrl+A	After typing a valid function name in a formula, displays Step 2 of the Function Wizard
Ctrl+Shift+A	After typing a valid function name in a formula, inserts the argument names and parentheses for the function
Alt+=	Inserts the AutoSum formula
Ctrl+;	Enters the current date
Ctrl+Shift+:	Enters the current time
Ctrl+X	Edit⇨Cut command
Ctrl+Delete	Edit⇨Cut command
Ctrl+C	Edit⇨Copy command
Ctrl+Insert	Edit⇨Copy command
Ctrl+V	Edit⇨Paste command
Shift+Insert	Edit⇨Paste command
Ctrl+Z	Edit⇨Undo command
Alt+Backspace	Edit⇨Undo command
Ctrl+R	Edit⇨Fill Right command
Ctrl+D	Edit⇨Fill Left command
Ctrl+N	File⇨New command
Ctrl+O	File⇨Open command
Ctrl+S	File⇨Save command
Ctrl+P	File⇨Print command
Ctrl+F	Edit⇨Find command
Ctrl+H	Edit⇨Replace command
Delete	Edit⇨Clear command

Table E-7
Function Keys

Key(s)	What It Does
F1	Help➪Contents command
Shift+F1	Context-sensitive help
F2	Edits the active cell
W/Shift+F2	Insert➪Note command
Ctrl+F2	Displays the Info window
F3	Insert➪Name➪Paste command
Shift+F3	Insert➪Function command
Ctrl+F3	Insert➪Name➪Define command
Chtr+Shift+F3	Insert➪Name➪Create command
F4	Changes cell reference while editing a formula
Ctrl+F4	File➪Close command
Alt+F4	File➪Exit command
F5	Edit➪Go To command
Shift+F5	Edit➪Find command
Ctrl+F5	Restores a minimized workbook window to its previous size
F6	Moves to the next pane in a split window
Shift+F6	Moves to the previous pane in a split window
Ctrl+F6	Activates the next open window
Ctrl+Shift+F6	Activates the previous open window
F7	Tools➪Spelling command
Ctrl+F7	Allows moving the current window with the arrow keys
F8	Toggles selection Extend mode on and off
Shift+F8	Toggles selection Add mode on and off
Ctrl+F8	Allows resizing of the current window with the arrow keys
F9	Recalculates all open worksheets

Key(s)	What It Does
Shift+F9	Recalculates the current worksheet
Ctrl+F9	Minimizes the current window
F10	Activates the menu bar
Shift+F10	Activates the shortcut menu (simulates right-clicking)
Ctrl+F10	Maximizes the current window
F11	Insert⇨Chart⇨As New Sheet command
Shift+F11	Insert⇨Worksheet command
Ctrl+F11	Insert⇨Macro⇨MS Excel 4.0 Macro command
F12	File⇨Save As command
Shift+F12	File⇨Save command
Ctrl+F12	File⇨Open command
Ctrl+Shift+F12	File⇨Print command

What's on the Companion CD-ROM?

The CD-ROM that comes with this book contains many useful files. The information on the CD-ROM is arranged as a series of nested folders. I describe what's in these folders in the following sections.

Introduction

This CD-ROM takes advantage of a new feature in Windows 95: AutoRun. When you insert the CD-ROM into your CD-ROM drive, it automatically executes a program called `Autorun.exe` (see Figure F-1), which is stored in the Intro folder. This program lets you view a short video introduction by yours truly, read an introductory message, or click on a button to browse the CD-ROM.

Figure F-1: When you insert the CD-ROM, you can choose from these options.

Tip To prevent AutoRun from executing, press Shift while inserting the CD-ROM.

Chapter Examples

The Chapters folder contains several other folders — one for each chapter that includes one or more sample files.

On the CD-ROM If you're reading a chapter and see the icon pictured to the left, you can locate that file by opening the appropriate folder. If you're reading Chapter 25, for example, you'll find the sample files referenced in that chapter in the folder named Ch25.

You can open the example workbooks directly from the CD-ROM — there's no need to copy them to your hard drive. If you make any changes to a file, you must save it to your hard drive (CD-ROM is read-only). Use Excel's File⊃Save As command to do this.

Database

This folder contains a large dBASE file (`Budget.dbf`) that is used in some of the examples in the book. The file has 15,840 records.

This file contains the following fields:

   Sort: A numeric field that holds record sequence numbers

   Division: A text field that specifies the company division

Department: A text field that specifies the department within the division

Category: A text field that specifies the budget category

Item: A text field that specifies the budget item

Month: A text field that specifies the month

Budget: A numeric field that stores the budgeted amount

Actual: A numeric field that stores the actual amount spent

Variance: A numeric field that stores the difference between the Budget and Actual

Excel Software

The XL_SW folder contains a variety of shareware and freeware files.

Power Utility Pak

The Power Utility Pak was developed by me. The shareware version of the Power Utility Pak contains most (but not all) of the functionality of the full registered version. The version on the CD-ROM is a special 32-bit version (2.0a) and will not work with Excel 5 (a separate version for Excel 5 is also available).

Description
The Power Utility Pak is a comprehensive package that adds new features to Excel and can make you more productive. The package includes

- ✦ 21 general-purpose spreadsheet utilities
- ✦ 22 new worksheet functions
- ✦ Enhanced shortcut menus
- ✦ A new Utilities menu to access the utilities
- ✦ A custom toolbar to access the utilities (optional)
- ✦ Detailed, context-sensitive, online help for the utilities and functions

Note The complete source code for the Power Utility Pak also is available. This well-documented VBA code contains a wealth of information and dozens of useful techniques that will help users master Visual Basic for Applications. The complete source files are available to registered users for an additional $20.

These utilities add new features to Excel and can improve productivity by performing multiple operations with a single command — or by doing things that are otherwise impossible in Excel. Following is a brief description of the utilities included with the Power Utility Pak.

Text Tools: Manipulates text in cells in a number of ways. Text can be changed to uppercase, lowercase, or proper case. This utility can also add specific text to the beginning or end of each cell — or delete a fixed number of characters from each cell. The Stats button displays the number of words and characters in the selected text. This utility also works with cells that contain values.

Select by Value: Selects a group of cells based on its value or text content. For example, this utility can be used to flag all cells in a range that have a negative value. The Select by Value utility selects these cells automatically, and you can then apply formatting to make the values stand out. This utility also works with dates and text.

Interactive Zooming: Magnifies or reduces a worksheet or chart interactively. A handy scroller and preview button let you see the results before you commit to them.

Reminder Note: Adds a reminder note to a worksheet, chart, or dialog sheet. You can choose the color and text style and determine whether it will print. Other options hide, display, or delete all reminder notes.

Object Align, Size and Space: A fast, easy, and reliable way to align and resize drawn objects on a worksheet, chart, or in a custom dialog box. Another option adjusts the objects so that they are evenly spaced. (See Figure F-2.)

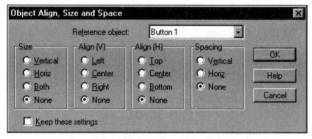

Figure F-2: The Object Align, Size and Space utility lets you adjust drawn objects quickly and reliably.

Calculator: Displays a handy mousable calculator (which also accepts input from the keyboard). The result of the calculation can be pasted into a cell.

3D Cell Shading: Adds an attractive 3-D background to a cell or range. You can choose either a raised look or a depressed look, choose the color, and specify the line thickness.

Insert 3D Text: Converts the text in a cell or range to an attractive graphic object with a 3-D look.

Date and Time: Runs the Windows 95 Date/Time utility, which displays the current date, time, and day of the week. You also can also adjust the system time and date.

Insert-a-Date: Inserts a formatted date into a cell. You choose the date from a calendar display and can select from a variety of date formats. As an option, the column width can be automatically adjusted to accommodate the pasted date.

Perpetual Calendar: Displays a handy and attractive pop-up calendar for any month in the years between 1900 and 2078 (see Figure F-3). The calendar picture can even be pasted into a worksheet or chart. Another option creates a new workbook nicely formatted as a calendar — perfect for scheduling.

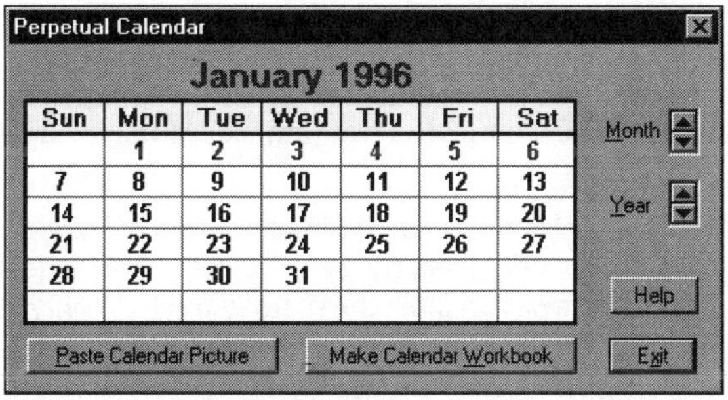

Figure F-3: The Perpetual Calendar utility displays a calendar for any month.

Reminder Alarm: Displays a reminder message at a specified time. After setting the alarm, Excel's title bar displays the time for which the alarm is set. The reminder message is accompanied by three beeps, so the reminder will be effective even if you're not working in Excel.

Time Tracker: Keeps track of the amount of time spent working on various projects (and the projects need not be Excel projects). You can track time spent on up to four projects and customize the project or client names used.

Object Properties: Displays the dimensions and positions of graphic objects. You can enter new dimensions or reposition the object by specifying coordinates, or use the "nudge" buttons to move or resize in 1-pixel increments. This utility also lets you hide and unhide objects (something that normally requires a macro). See Figure F-4.

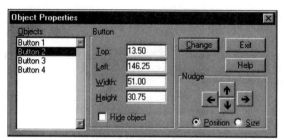

Figure F-4: The Object Properties utility makes it easy to move or resize graphic objects.

Super Go To: Allows easy navigation through multiple workbooks and worksheets. You can select the workbook, sheet, or range to activate. A handy preview mode displays the selection (even if it's in a hidden or minimized workbook). The dialog box can be used in two sizes (smaller, if range names aren't used).

Workbook Table of Contents: Displays a handy table of contents that lists all sheets in the active workbook. It also displays the type of sheet (worksheet, macro sheet, chart, and so on), and you can filter the display to show only sheets of a certain type. Double-clicking quickly activates the selected sheet.

Save With Backup: Saves the active workbook with a backup copy. Normally, saving a workbook to a floppy disk to make a backup is a cumbersome procedure, because Excel "remembers" the floppy drive as the workbook's location. When the file is saved again, it will be saved to the floppy disk — unless you remember to use the File⇨Save As command to redirect the save back to the hard drive. This utility saves a workbook to the selected floppy disk (or another directory) and then saves it back to the hard drive — all in one step.

Batch Printing: Prints a group of workbooks unattended. The user can choose any number of files to print. The user can choose exactly what gets printed — worksheets, chart sheets, VBA modules, or dialog sheets.

Auditing Tools: Creates a new workbook with information about the active worksheet, a graphical map, and a list of formulas.

Bubble Chart Wizard: Converts an X-Y chart into an attractive bubble chart — a chart type that Excel does not directly support.

Toolbar Tools: Lets the user change the tooltips associated with any toolbar button. Also supports copying and renaming toolbars (operations that most users would say is impossible).

The Power Utility Pak also includes 22 functions that can be used in worksheets. These functions work exactly like Excel's built-in functions and even appear in the Function Wizard (see Figure F-5). The functions are described next.

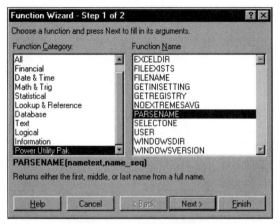

Figure F-5: The Power Utility Pak worksheet functions can be used just like Excel's built-in functions.

Contains(text1,text2,casesensitive): Returns TRUE if text1 is contained in text2.

CountAVisible(value1,value2...): Similar to Excel's COUNTA function, but it returns the count of just the visible cells — perfect for use with Excel's autofilter and outline features.

DaysinMonth(date): Returns the number of days in the month for a date.

ExcelDir(): Displays the full path for the folder in which Excel is installed.

FileExists(Filename): Returns TRUE if a specified file exists.

FileName(): Displays the full path and filename of the workbook.

GetINISetting(INIfile,Section,Entry): Returns the setting for a particular entry in an INI file.

InsertString(instring,origstring,pos): Inserts a string at a specified position in another string.

IsLike(text,pattern): Returns TRUE if text is "like" pattern. Pattern is a string that uses * and ? wildcard characters. For example, =IsLike("Johnson","John*") returns TRUE.

MonthWeek(date): Returns the calendar week in the month for any date. Perfect for applications such as payroll.

NoExtremesAvg(range): Returns the average of a range of values, but excludes the highest and lowest values — a common procedure to eliminate the effects of extreme values or outliers.

ParseName(string,name): Splits a name into its component parts: first name, last name, middle name. It even handles common titles (Mr., Ms., Dr.) and knows what to do when a name is followed by "Jr."

ReadRegistry(key,valuename): Returns an entry from the Windows 95 Registry database.

RemoveSpaces(text): Removes all of the spaces from a string.

Scramble(text,recalc): Accepts text or a value and returns it — scrambled randomly.

SelectOne(range,recalc): Returns a single value chosen at random from a range.

StaticRand( ): Returns a random number that doesn't change when the worksheet is recalculated.

SumVisible(number1,number2...): Similar to Excel's SUM function, but it returns the sum of just the visible cells — perfect for use with Excel's autofilter and outline features.

User( ): Returns the name of the current user.

WhichDay(weekdaynum,DOW,themonth,theyear): Returns a date that corresponds to a request such as "the first Friday in November," or the "last Monday in June."

WindowsDir(): Displays the full path of the Windows folder.

WindowsVersion(): Returns the version number of the version of Windows that is currently running.

Installation instructions

Note Running the Power Utility Pak directly from the CD-ROM is not recommended.

To install the Power Utility Pak, follow these instructions:

1. Create a new folder on your hard drive. I recommend that you create a folder named Power inside your Excel\Library folder.

2. Copy all of the Power Utility Pak files to this new folder.

3. Start Excel.

4. Select the Tools⇨Add-Ins command. Excel will display its Add-Ins dialog box.

5. Click on the Browse button in the Add-Ins dialog box.

6. Locate the folder where you copied the files, and select the Power.xla file.

7. Close the Add-Ins dialog box.

8. The Power Utility Pak add-in will be installed. You will also get a new custom toolbar, plus a new menu command: Utilities.

Complete online help is provided for all of the utilities and worksheet functions.

How to register

As a special offer for readers of this book, you can register the Power Utility Pak for only $9.95 (a savings of $30.00). To do so, you must use the coupon located in the back of this book. You can contact me at the following address:

JWalk and Associates
P.O. Box 12861
La Jolla, CA 92039-2861

e-mail: 70363.3014@compuserve.com

Amortization Schedules

This application, from Ohio Star Software, generates fixed-rate and variable-rate loan schedules.

Description

`Gener8.xlm` is an Excel macro that runs automatically when the workbook is opened. `Gener8.xlm` also can be restarted during the same Excel session by pressing Ctrl+Shift+A. When you open `Gener8.xlm`, you'll see an introductory screen. Select "Generate a Schedule" to go on to the input screen. The input screen is used to provide basic information about the loan (term, rate, and so on). Please note that you can't enter any data into the variable-rate-related fields unless you select the variable-rate option. When all fields have been completed, click on OK. The macro will generate a loan schedule and a chart based on the information provided.

Figure F-6 shows the dialog box into which you enter the loan parameters.

`Gener8.xlm` supports variable interest rates and extra principal payments. For variable-rate loans, it can project a worst-case interest rate change based on the loan's maximum rate and maximum increase per adjustment period. It allows all components of the monthly payment (insurance, taxes, and so on) to be changed at any point in the loan. The amortization schedules show annual totals for interest and principal paid and show graphically how the interest and principal vary over the life of the loan.

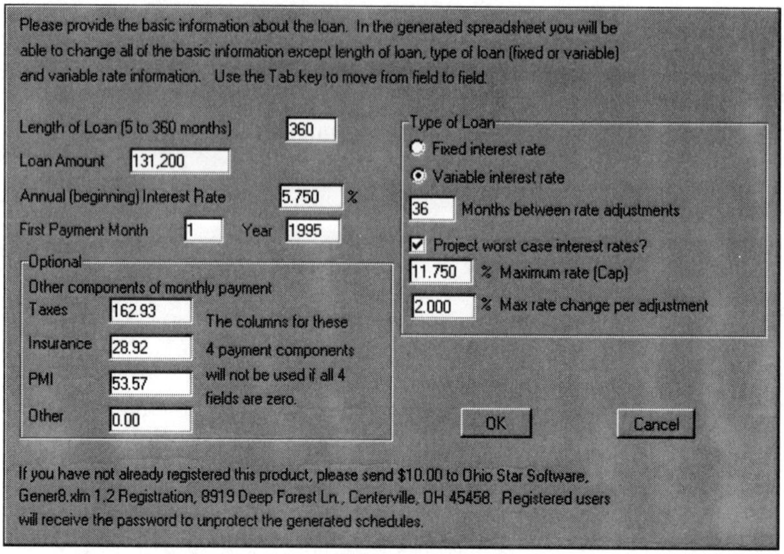

Please provide the basic information about the loan. In the generated spreadsheet you will be able to change all of the basic information except length of loan, type of loan (fixed or variable) and variable rate information. Use the Tab key to move from field to field.

Length of Loan (5 to 360 months)	360
Loan Amount	131,200
Annual (beginning) Interest Rate	5.750 %
First Payment Month 1 Year 1995	

Optional
Other components of monthly payment

Taxes	162.93	The columns for these
Insurance	28.92	4 payment components
PMI	53.57	will not be used if all 4
Other	0.00	fields are zero.

Type of Loan
- ○ Fixed interest rate
- ⦿ Variable interest rate

36 Months between rate adjustments

☑ Project worst case interest rates?

11.750 % Maximum rate (Cap)

2.000 % Max rate change per adjustment

[OK]   [Cancel]

If you have not already registered this product, please send $10.00 to Ohio Star Software, Gener8.xlm 1.2 Registration, 8919 Deep Forest Ln., Centerville, OH 45458. Registered users will receive the password to unprotect the generated schedules.

Figure F-6: The input dialog box from `Gener8.xlm`.

Installation instructions
This workbook can be opened directly from the CD-ROM.

How to register
The registration fee is $10. Registration instructions are provided on the CD-ROM. You can contact Dave Grimmer at the following address:

Ohio Star Software
8919 Deep Forest Lane
Centerville, OH 45458

e-mail: 70412.2455@compuserve.com.

Depreciation Schedules

This application, also developed by Ohio Star Software, generates depreciation schedules for tax and book purposes.

Description

`Deprec8.xlm` is an Excel macro that runs automatically when the file is opened. The macro also can be restarted during the same session by pressing Ctrl+Shift+A (for the input screen) or Ctrl+Shift+Z (for the introductory screen).

When you open Deprec8.xlm, you'll see an introductory screen. Select "Generate a Depreciation Schedule" to go on to the input screen. The input screen is used to provide basic information about the asset (value, description, and so on). When all fields are completed, click on OK to generate a depreciation schedule based on the information provided.

This macro uses the IRS-defined Modified Accelerated Cost Recovery System (MACRS) to calculate annual depreciation amounts. For tax purposes, most tangible, depreciable property placed in service after 1986 must be depreciated under MACRS. This macro gives you the option of using the MACRS half-year or midquarter convention for property being depreciated over 3, 5, 7, 10, 15, or 20 years. Schedules for 27.5 and 39 years use the IRS-defined MACRS midmonth convention. For book purposes, Deprec8.xlm generates schedules of any duration, with either straight-line, double-declining balance, or the sum of the years digits method. This macro handles fiscal years that don't follow the calendar year, as well as salvage values for book purposes.

Additional documentation is provided in the file.

Note   Deprec8.xlm can't eliminate the need for consulting advice from an accountant. Ohio Star Software is not responsible for any problems caused by the improper use of this software, the improper application of accounting principles, or the violation of tax laws.

Installation instructions
This workbook can be opened directly from the CD-ROM.

How to register
The registration fee is $10, and registration instructions are provided on the CD-ROM. You can contact Dave Grimmer at the following address:

Ohio Star Software
8919 Deep Forest Lane
Centerville, OH 45458

e-mail: 70412.2455@compuserve.com.

Holidays

Holidays.xla is an Excel add-in from Spreadsheet Solutions that lets you find the dates for more than 130 holidays.

Installation instructions

To use this add-in, follow these instructions:

1. Copy the files in the folder to your hard drive (the Excel\Library folder is a good location).

2. Start Excel.

3. Select the Tools⇨Add-Ins command. Excel will display its Add-Ins dialog box.

4. Click on the Browse button in the Add-Ins dialog box.

5. Locate the folder where you copied the files, and select Holidays.xla.

6. Close the Add-Ins dialog box.

7. The add-in will be installed. You can access the new worksheet functions by using the Function Wizard.

How to register

The registration fee is $10. Write to the following address:

Spreadsheet Solutions
P.O. Box 11047
Shorewood, WI 53211

e-mail: 74002.2373@compuserve.com

Periodic Table

Periodic.xla is an Excel add-in that contains functions that return information about the periodic table. It is also from Spreadsheet Solutions.

Installation instructions

To use this add-in, follow these instructions:

1. Copy the files in the folder to your hard drive (the Excel\Library folder is a good location).

2. Start Excel.

3. Select the Tools⇨Add-Ins command. Excel will display its Add-Ins dialog box.

4. Click on the Browse button in the Add-Ins dialog box.

5. Locate the folder where you copied the files, and select Periodic.xla.

6. Close the Add-Ins dialog box.

7. The add-in will be installed. You can access the new worksheet functions by using the Function Wizard.

How to register
The registration fee is $10. Write to the following address:

Spreadsheet Solutions

P.O. Box 11047
Shorewood, WI 53211

e-mail: 74002.2373@compuserve.com

Which Day of the Week

WhichDOW.xla is an Excel add-in that contains 36 functions that determine any logical day of the month — for example, the third Friday in November. This add-in is from Spreadsheet Solutions.

Installation instructions
To use this add-in, follow these instructions:

1. Copy the files in the folder to your hard drive (the Excel\Library folder is a good location).

2. Start Excel.

3. Select the Tools⇨Add-Ins command. Excel will display its Add-Ins dialog box.

4. Click-on the Browse button in the Add-Ins dialog box.

5. Locate the folder where you copied the files, and select WhichDOW.xla.

6. Close the Add-Ins dialog box.

7. The add-in will be installed. You can access the new worksheet functions by using the Function Wizard.

How to register
The registration fee is $10. Contact the following address:

Spreadsheet Solutions
P.O. Box 11047
Shorewood, WI 53211

e-mail: 74002.2373@compuserve.com

Checkbook for Excel

Checkbook for Excel, from Daniel Ireland, provides a user-friendly but powerful spreadsheet/database for managing your checking account. A simple yet powerful interface provides all the necessary features for managing your account without all the excess baggage and overhead associated with the popular personal finance packages such as Quicken and Microsoft Money. This makes Checkbook for Excel faster and less complicated. Why burden yourself and your computer with expense-tracking and budgeting features that you'll never use? Checkbook for Excel provides exactly what you need: a simple, easy way to maintain and balance your checking account.

Installation instructions

To use Checkbook, copy the `Chkxl10.xlw` workbook to the directory of your choice. Documentation is provided in `Chkxl10.wri`. The application is in the Excel 4 file format. If you're using Excel 5 or later, you can continue to save it in that format or you can save it in the current version.

Figure F-7 shows a screen from Checkbook.

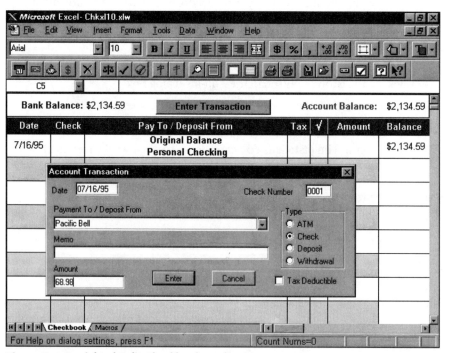

Figure F-7: Daniel Ireland's Checkbook application.

Registration information

Daniel doesn't require payment for use of this add-in, but he would appreciate it if you would register with him. Contact Daniel at the following address:

Daniel J. Ireland
5806 Irishtown Rd.
Bethel Park, PA 15102

Reminder

Reminder, also from Daniel Ireland, is a simple yet powerful add-in for Microsoft Excel 4.0 or higher that does what its name implies. It allows you to schedule events that Excel then remembers. When the set time for the event arrives, Excel reminds you with an alarm and a message and also opens a preappointed file, if you desire. It functions much like the scheduling software that comes with many Windows front ends (Norton Desktop and so on), but it's more powerful and easier to use; it uses only a fraction of the memory and works exclusively in Excel.

Installation instructions

To use Reminder, simply put the `Reminder.xla` file in your Excel startup directory, usually \Excel\Xlstart. Or, use Excel's Add-In Manager to add it to the startup list. Select the Tools⇨Add-Ins command, choose Browse and then select the `Reminder.xla` file. When you start Excel, there will be an additional command added to the bottom of the Tools menu called Reminder. Selecting the Tools⇨ Reminder command displays the Reminder dialog box, shown in Figure F-8.

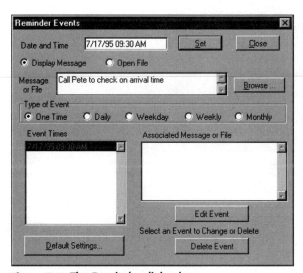

Figure F-8: The Reminder dialog box.

This add-in is documented in the Reminder.wri file.

Registration information
Daniel doesn't require payment for use of this add-in, but he would appreciate it if you would register with him. Contact Daniel at the following address:

Daniel J. Ireland
5806 Irishtown Rd.
Bethel Park, PA 15102

Super Hide

Super Hide is an add-in developed by Christopher Bourdon. This add-in simplifies the process of hiding and unhiding sheets in a workbook.

Using the add-in
When you select the Tools⇨Super Hide/Unhide command, you'll see the dialog box shown in Figure F-9. The list box on the left shows the hidden sheets, and the list box on the right shows the visible sheets. You can transfer sheets from one list box to the other by using the buttons. Click on the Execute button to hide or unhide the sheets.

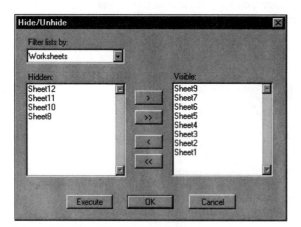

Figure F-9: The Hide/Unhide dialog box.

Installation instructions
For best results, copy the Superhde.xla file to your Excel\Library folder. Then select the Tools⇨Add-Ins command, click on the Browse button, and locate Superhde.xla. When the add-in is loaded, the Tools menu will have a new command: Super Hide/Unhide.

Registration information

This is freeware, and registration is not required. In addition, the author made the original source file available. You can contact Christopher Bourdon by e-mail at cbourdon@interramp.com.

Toolbar Configuration Utility

Steve James, who lives in the U.K., contributed a useful add-in utility that lets you configure Excel toolbars.

Description

The Toolbar list box contains the names of the currently defined toolbars in Excel. To work with a particular toolbar, click on it in the list box. The name of the toolbar you are manipulating is displayed in the Name edit box. The Properties box indicates whether the toolbar is a built-in Excel bar, and whether it is visible on the screen at the moment. The Coordinates box gives information about the position of the toolbar on the screen. The Position box indicates where the toolbar is docked or if it is floating.

The Reset button removes any custom buttons from the toolbar and also removes any macros attached to standard buttons. This button essentially returns the toolbar to its "out-of-the-box" state. This button is only enabled for built-in toolbars.

Choose the Buttons button to manipulate the buttons on the toolbar. This displays a new dialog box. The Button list box contains the names of all buttons on the current toolbar. The word *<gap>* indicates a separating gap on the toolbar. The ID box indicates the internal button ID of built-in buttons. You cannot edit this value. The ToolTip box shows the tooltip for the button that pops up when the mouse pointer is over the button. To change the tooltip (for built-in or custom buttons), type the new tooltip and choose the Update button.

The macro edit box shows the name of the macro associated with the button. To change the macro, type a new macro name and choose the Update button. The Properties box indicates whether the button is built-in, enabled, already pushed (for example, the Bold button on the Formatting toolbar is pushed when the active cell is formatted as bold), or whether a gap exists between buttons. The Built-In face check box indicates whether or not you have changed the default face on the button. To restore the built-in face if it has been changed, choose the Reset Face button.

Installation instructions

To use this add-in, follow these instructions:

1. Copy the files in the folder to your hard drive (the Excel\Library folder is a good location).

2. Start Excel.

3. Select the <u>T</u>ools⇨Add-<u>I</u>ns command. Excel will display its Add-Ins dialog box.

4. Click on the Browse button in the Add-Ins dialog box.

5 Locate the folder where you copied the files, and select `Toolbar.xla`.

6. Close the Add-Ins dialog box.

7. The add-in will be installed. You can access it using the <u>T</u>ools⇨Toolbar <u>C</u>onfiguration command.

Registration information

You can contact Steve by e-mail at Steve_XL@stevej.demon.co.uk.

Windows 95 Software

PolyView

Polybytes' PolyView is a multithreaded, 32-bit application for Windows NT and Windows 95. It provides viewing and image manipulation support for GIF, JPEG, TIFF, photo-CD, and Windows, as well as OS/2 8-and 24-bit BMP files.

Figure F-10 shows an example of PolyView.

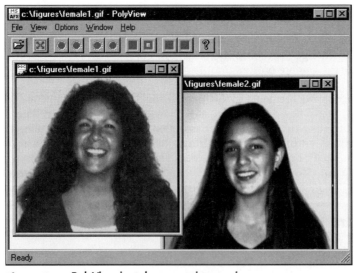

Figure F-10: PolyView is a shareware image viewer.

Description

PolyView is handy for viewing graphic files and performing some basic image manipulation. To view a file, you can drag it to the PolyView window, or use the File⇨Open command to select a file. You also can display a slide show of graphic image files.

PolyView is completely described in the online Help file.

Tip   Use the Options⇨Register File Types command to create associations for specific file formats. Then, you can double-click on a file and start PolyView automatically with the graphic file loaded.

Installation instructions

Create a new folder and copy all of the files to the new folder. You can then add PolyView to your Start menu, if desired.

How to register

PolyView is distributed as shareware. Registered users will receive product update notifications and problem assistance. To register your copy, send $20 to the following address:

Polybytes
3427 Bever Avenue S.E.
Cedar Rapids, Iowa 52403

e-mail: PolyView@aol.com.

Time Logger

Responsive Software's Responsive Time Logger is a Windows application that helps you keep track of your time. Figure F-11 shows Time Logger in action.

Description

Time Logger performs the following:

1. It lets you easily record information about what you did and when you did it.

2. It lets you analyze and document the time that you've spent on different projects and tasks.

3. It automatically prints time reports and invoices and helps you keep track of the payment of those invoices.

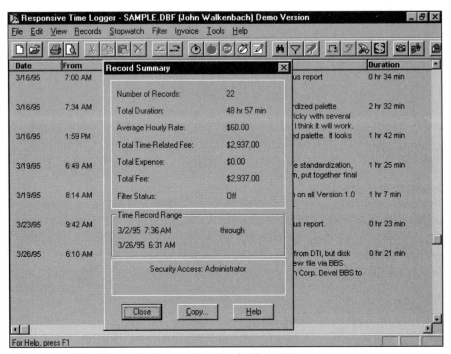

Figure F-11: Time Logger helps you keep track of your time.

In addition, Time Logger is a true "component application" in that it can share the workload with your existing applications. Here's an example: Time Logger stores all of the time record and accounts receivable data in standard dBASE-format files. Thus, you have the option of analyzing the data with any application that can read these files (and that includes most database applications as well as Excel). Although Time Logger produces great time reports all by itself, you may have a sophisticated database and report-writing application that can do a better job. If so, you can use that application for analysis and reporting of the data that Time Logger collects.

The shareware version works exactly like the full-featured version, except that the number of time records allowed is limited, and you can't print time reports (although print preview is available).

Installation instructions

To install Time Logger, execute the `Tldemo32.exe` program and follow the instructions on-screen.

How to order

The full version of Time Logger is $79. You can contact Responsive Software at the following address:

Responsive Software
1901 Tunnel Rd.
Berkeley, CA 94705

800-669-4611 or 510-843-1034

e-mail: 76367.3673@compuserve.com

Flo'

Flo', developed by the VALIS Group, is an interesting graphics program.

Description

According to the developer, Flo' is the most advanced image-warping software
on any platform. It has the capability to perform global and local rubberlike distortions without digital artifacts. You can scale, translate, rotate, skew, or perform
arbitrary transformations on any part of an image while the rest of the image remains
unchanged. The result is as if the image were stretched on a piece of rubber canvas.
You can animate these changes over time, and Flo' supports any number of
keyframes. Flo' automatically generates the in-between frames for you.

Note Make sure that you check out the two sample animation files provided with Flo'.

Flo's features include the following:

- ✦ Hierarchical unlimited undo/redo; every operation is saved and is editable
- ✦ Any number of keyframes.
- ✦ Outputs AVI or FLIC animations as well as still images.
- ✦ Imports and exports more than a dozen file formats (TIFF, TARGA, JPG, GIF, BMP, and so on).
- ✦ Alpha channel support — alpha channel is automatically distorted with image.
- ✦ Subpixel sampling rendering engine.
- ✦ Distortion/warping engine based on fluid mechanics.
- ✦ Quality of distortions is far superior to what morphing programs produce with no edge or tearing artifacts.
- ✦ Freeform Plasticity technology — realtime geometric distortion.
- ✦ Resolution-independent Region of Change technology — Flo's curved region-creation tools make Bezier curves and spline-style controls obsolete.
- ✦ Flo' is a 32-bit application that works with Windows 95.

Figure F-12 shows an image that was warped with Flo'.

Installation instructions

To install Flo', execute the `Install.exe` program and follow the instructions.

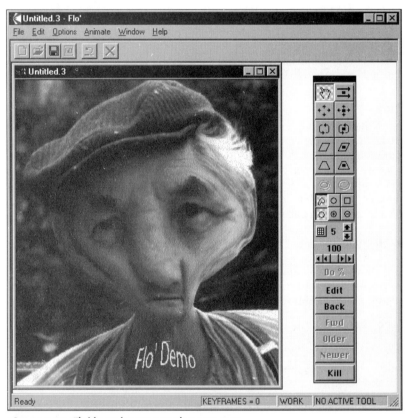

Figure F-12: Flo' is an image-warping program.

Additional information

VALIS also offers another version of Flo' without animation capabilities: Flo' Lite.
Contact the VALIS Group at the following address:

The VALIS Group
2346 Mar East St.
Tiburon, CA 94920

415-435-5404 or 800-VALIS04

email: valisgroup@aol.com

OsoSoft shareware

The CD-ROM includes seven shareware products from OsoSoft, headed by George Campbell. You can test these products directly from the CD-ROM.

Note These products are not written specifically for Windows 95 (for example, they don't support long filenames). However, George is currently updating them all for full Windows 95 support.

Contact:
OsoSoft
1472 Sixth Street
Los Osos, CA 93402

Voice: 805-528-1759
FAX: 805-528-3074
BBS: 805-528-3753

CompuServe: 74774,442

On CompuServe: GO OSOSOFT

Filer

Filer is a file-finding utility for Windows that can search across all the drives on your PC, including CD-ROM and Network drives for any file, based on standard DOS wildcard specs. Filer is a multimedia file viewer as well, letting you show AVI, MOV, and FLI movies; hear WAV, MID, and RMI sound files; and view dozens of graphics formats. You can even preview uninstalled TrueType fonts.

You can also search for and find duplicate filenames on your hard disks, something that can save megabytes of hard disk space.

Further, you can manage files from within Filer. Copy, move, delete, rename, or wipe files in one easy step. You can launch programs or data files using either standard Windows associations or up to 36 custom associations that you set up.

Registration fee: $25

Prompter

Public speaking is a chore, at best. Prompter is designed to make that chore as light as possible. Like a professional TelePrompTer, the program offers automatic scrolling of your speech at any rate you choose. Font sizes are completely changeable. An elapsed time counter helps you keep on track, too.

Prompter includes a complete speech editor, with a capacity of one hour's worth of text. A single command lets the speechwriter determine the exact time the speech will take to deliver at any stage. Speeches can also be printed in any font and font size, and printouts offer automatic header lines. Prompter learns your speech pacing and saves that information for you on command.

While using Prompter on the lectern as a prompting device, pressing any key instantly pauses scrolling. Press another key and scrolling begins again. Scroll rate is adjustable with a press of the plus or minus keys during speech delivery.

The latest version also includes reversed, mirror-image text for mirror applications. Also new: a pronunciation character inserter and highlighted scrolling mode.

Price: $25 shareware registration

AdMaker

If you ever need to design small display ads for your business or for others, you know what a pain the job can be. Using a program not specifically designed for the job means complicated setups, time-wasting extra tasks, and worse.

AdMaker 3.5 is designed to create these ads. That's all it does. Using a WYSIWYG display window and an easy-to-use interface, you can create ads up to 7.5×9.5 inches in size, complete with up to four PCX or BMP clip art images. Use any TrueType or ATM font, either plain or reversed, or even rotated up to 90 degrees in either direction.

Here's a list of some of AdMaker's powerful features:

- ✦ Easy interface, familiar to Rockford! and MultiLabel users
- ✦ Layouts up to 7.5×9.5 inches
- ✦ 100 percent and 200 percent size printouts
- ✦ Automatic crop marks
- ✦ Save dimension templates for future use
- ✦ Up to four scalable PCX or BMP images
- ✦ Layout grid display
- ✦ Zoom command for large ads
- ✦ Position text with a mouse click
- ✦ Rotate text
- ✦ Insert special characters
- ✦ Right-click on any command for help

✦ Create filled boxes

✦ Print text over graphics

✦ Use formatted serial numbers

✦ Save and load template files for custom labels

✦ Enter dimensions in any measurement system

✦ Print out customized text and customer approval lines

Price: $30 shareware registration

Fonter

Fonter lets you view and print Windows TrueType and Adobe Type Manager fonts in several ways. On-screen, you can view any font, complete with a font sample window showing text in that font. A full-screen view allows zooms on three levels and displays the entire character set. You can also view an on-screen ANSI grid and a keyboard simulation for any font. Both of these displays can be printed with a mouse click. Another feature allows users to create BMP clip art files for any character in 72-point size. This is especially useful for creating clip art images of dingbat and symbolic characters.

Printing features include font lists, with samples for all or selected fonts. Users can also print full-page font samples, showing multiple sizes and so on. A full-page ANSI chart is another printing option. For convenience, users may automatically print complete font books for all fonts installed on their system.

Price: $20 shareware registration

Figure 13 shows an example of Fonter.

MultiLabel

MultiLabel lets users create customized labels, complete with clip art, any TrueType or ATM font, text alignment, and line drawings by using Windows 3.1 and any graphics-capable printer fully supported by Windows. Labels can also include automatic serialization on duplicate labels, character formats inserted in lines of text, and automatic bullets. Users can insert up to two PCX or BMP clip art images, with full scaling and positioning control. Custom text alignments and a grid overlay allow precise placement of text and graphics. Built-in line, circle, and box-drawing tools add flexibility. A WYSIWYG display of the label is always visible. The program automatically supports all Avery Laser Label formats or users can create customized label sizes.

There's even an Address Book module that holds up to 750, five-line entries in each data file. Field codes inserted in the label allow full merge capabilities. Full search tools aid in record selection. Users can print all or selected addresses or any other data stored in the Address Book on the labels, along with other text. The program supports all Windows-compatible printers, including PostScript and dot-matrix devices.

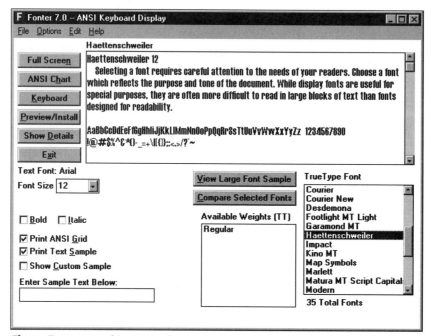

Figure F-13: OsoSoft's Fonter shareware product.

MultiLabel introduces many new features in this latest version. You can now

- ✦ Print text and graphics in color
- ✦ Position text with a mouse click
- ✦ Rotate text
- ✦ Insert special characters
- ✦ Right-click on any command for help
- ✦ Create filled boxes
- ✦ Print text over graphics
- ✦ Use formatted serial numbers
- ✦ Save and load template files for custom labels
- ✦ Enter dimensions in any measurement system
- ✦ Import comma-delimited files from other programs
- ✦ Print entire sheets of labels from one Address Book entry

✦ Use AutoFit to make long Address Book fields fit on the label

✦ Create large labels and zoom the display

✦ Create postcards, name tags, Rolodex cards

✦ Use any Avery label type

Price: $20 shareware registration

Rockford

Rockford is the premiere business card design and printing program for Windows. Users can design and print professional-quality business cards, complete with clip art, all TrueType and ATM fonts and text alignments, and line drawings created with the internal drawing tools. Four border styles are also available. Users can insert up to two BMP or PCX clip art images, with full scaling and positioning. A WYSIWYG display of the card is always visible. Users can print 200 percent layout sheets or four-up layouts to take to print shops, or print sheets of ready-to-cut cards on card stock paper. Rockford also supports all styles of precut card stock available from several sources for ready-to-use cards. Fine adjustments in printing allow compensation for printer variations.

You also get full support for both PCX and BMP files, support for all Windows-compatible printers, including dot-matrix and PostScript devices, and an on-screen layout grid plus precise positioning of text and graphics. There's even a link to Windows PaintBrush for easy editing of clip art images.

Rockford introduces many new features in this latest version. You can now

✦ Print text and graphics in color

✦ Position text with a mouse click

✦ Rotate text

✦ Adjust left and top margins to match preprinted card stock

✦ Insert special characters

✦ Right-click on any command for help

✦ Create filled boxes

✦ Print text over graphics

✦ Use formatted serial numbers

✦ Enter dimensions in any measurement system

✦ Print vertical or horizontal cards on prescored stock

Price: $20 shareware registration

NOTE: Rockford Professional, available for $30, includes additional clip art, plus customer sign-off areas and user advertising messages on layout sheets.

WinClip

WinClip is the ideal Windows 3.1 clip art cataloging program. With it, users can preview BMP and PCX images in 1-, 4-, 8-, and 24-bit formats on any display adapter. Full scrolling and zoom features make previewing images easy. Printing options include printing of individual images, selected images, or entire directories of images. All printouts have a binding margin and include file and directory names. Zoom percentages allow printing at any scale. Additionally, double-click on an image or filename to load the image into a bitmap editor of your choice.

You can view BMP, PCX, and GIF files, get support for all graphics-capable Windows printers (including dot-matrix, COLOR, and PostScript devices), and obtain powerful management tools. File management is one of the key features. Users can copy, move, or delete single files or selected files. This lets you manage clip art files by moving and copying them into selected directories for easy access. It offers CD-ROM support, too.

WinClip supports WMF, TGA, RLE, DIB, and ICO files, plus conversions from many formats to BMP. Choose between four fixed-sized thumbnail printouts, from .5 to 1.5 inches. Up to 150+ images per page. There are user-settable margins, too.

Figure F-14 shows an example of WinClip.

Price: $20 shareware registration

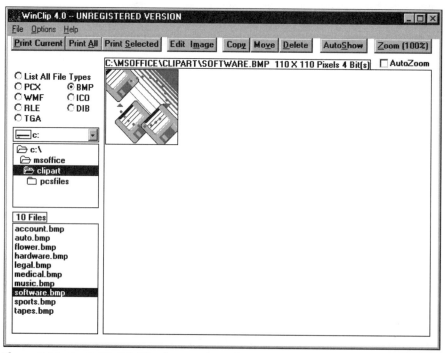

Figure F-14: OsoSoft's WinClip shareware product.

Index

B

C

(Continued)

F

H

Q

T

(Continued)

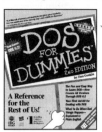

Title	Author	ISBN	Price
			12/20/94

INTERNET / COMMUNICATIONS / NETWORKING

Title	Author	ISBN	Price
CompuServe For Dummies™	by Wallace Wang	1-56884-181-7	$19.95 USA/$26.95 Canada
Modems For Dummies™, 2nd Edition	by Tina Rathbone	1-56884-223-6	$19.99 USA/$26.99 Canada
Modems For Dummies™	by Tina Rathbone	1-56884-001-2	$19.95 USA/$26.95 Canada
MORE Internet For Dummies™	by John R. Levine & Margaret Levine Young	1-56884-164-7	$19.95 USA/$26.95 Canada
NetWare For Dummies™	by Ed Tittel & Deni Connor	1-56884-003-9	$19.95 USA/$26.95 Canada
Networking For Dummies™	by Doug Lowe	1-56884-079-9	$19.95 USA/$26.95 Canada
ProComm Plus 2 For Windows For Dummies™	by Wallace Wang	1-56884-219-8	$19.99 USA/$26.99 Canada
The Internet For Dummies™, 2nd Edition	by John R. Levine & Carol Baroudi	1-56884-222-8	$19.99 USA/$26.99 Canada
The Internet For Macs For Dummies™	by Charles Seiter	1-56884-184-1	$19.95 USA/$26.95 Canada

MACINTOSH

Title	Author	ISBN	Price
Macs For Dummies®	by David Pogue	1-56884-173-6	$19.95 USA/$26.95 Canada
Macintosh System 7.5 For Dummies™	by Bob LeVitus	1-56884-197-3	$19.95 USA/$26.95 Canada
MORE Macs For Dummies™	by David Pogue	1-56884-087-X	$19.95 USA/$26.95 Canada
PageMaker 5 For Macs For Dummies™	by Galen Gruman	1-56884-178-7	$19.95 USA/$26.95 Canada
QuarkXPress 3.3 For Dummies™	by Galen Gruman & Barbara Assadi	1-56884-217-1	$19.99 USA/$26.99 Canada
Upgrading and Fixing Macs For Dummies™	by Kearney Rietmann & Frank Higgins	1-56884-189-2	$19.95 USA/$26.95 Canada

MULTIMEDIA

Title	Author	ISBN	Price
Multimedia & CD-ROMs For Dummies™, Interactive Multimedia Value Pack	by Andy Rathbone	1-56884-225-2	$29.95 USA/$39.95 Canada
Multimedia & CD-ROMs For Dummies™	by Andy Rathbone	1-56884-089-6	$19.95 USA/$26.95 Canada

OPERATING SYSTEMS / DOS

Title	Author	ISBN	Price
MORE DOS For Dummies™	by Dan Gookin	1-56884-046-2	$19.95 USA/$26.95 Canada
S.O.S. For DOS™	by Katherine Murray	1-56884-043-8	$12.95 USA/$16.95 Canada
OS/2 For Dummies™	by Andy Rathbone	1-878058-76-2	$19.95 USA/$26.95 Canada

UNIX

Title	Author	ISBN	Price
UNIX For Dummies™	by John R. Levine & Margaret Levine Young	1-878058-58-4	$19.95 USA/$26.95 Canada

WINDOWS

Title	Author	ISBN	Price
S.O.S. For Windows™	by Katherine Murray	1-56884-045-4	$12.95 USA/$16.95 Canada
MORE Windows 3.1 For Dummies™, 3rd Edition	by Andy Rathbone	1-56884-240-6	$19.99 USA/$26.99 Canada

PCs / HARDWARE

Title	Author	ISBN	Price
Illustrated Computer Dictionary For Dummies™	by Dan Gookin, Wally Wang, & Chris Van Buren	1-56884-004-7	$12.95 USA/$16.95 Canada
Upgrading and Fixing PCs For Dummies™	by Andy Rathbone	1-56884-002-0	$19.95 USA/$26.95 Canada

PRESENTATION / AUTOCAD

Title	Author	ISBN	Price
AutoCAD For Dummies™	by Bud Smith	1-56884-191-4	$19.95 USA/$26.95 Canada
PowerPoint 4 For Windows For Dummies™	by Doug Lowe	1-56884-161-2	$16.95 USA/$22.95 Canada

PROGRAMMING

Title	Author	ISBN	Price
Borland C++ For Dummies™	by Michael Hyman	1-56884-162-0	$19.95 USA/$26.95 Canada
"Borland's New Language Product" For Dummies™	by Neil Rubenking	1-56884-200-7	$19.95 USA/$26.95 Canada
C For Dummies™	by Dan Gookin	1-878058-78-9	$19.95 USA/$26.95 Canada
C++ For Dummies™	by Stephen R. Davis	1-56884-163-9	$19.95 USA/$26.95 Canada
Mac Programming For Dummies™	by Dan Parks Sydow	1-56884-173-6	$19.95 USA/$26.95 Canada
QBasic Programming For Dummies™	by Douglas Hergert	1-56884-093-4	$19.95 USA/$26.95 Canada
Visual Basic "X" For Dummies™, 2nd Edition	by Wallace Wang	1-56884-230-9	$19.99 USA/$26.99 Canada
Visual Basic 3 For Dummies™	by Wallace Wang	1-56884-076-4	$19.95 USA/$26.95 Canada

SPREADSHEET

Title	Author	ISBN	Price
1-2-3 For Dummies™	by Greg Harvey	1-878058-60-6	$16.95 USA/$21.95 Canada
1-2-3 For Windows 5 For Dummies™, 2nd Edition	by John Walkenbach	1-56884-216-3	$16.95 USA/$21.95 Canada
1-2-3 For Windows For Dummies™	by John Walkenbach	1-56884-052-7	$16.95 USA/$21.95 Canada
Excel 5 For Macs For Dummies™	by Greg Harvey	1-56884-186-8	$19.95 USA/$26.95 Canada
Excel For Dummies™, 2nd Edition	by Greg Harvey	1-56884-050-0	$16.95 USA/$21.95 Canada
MORE Excel 5 For Windows For Dummies™	by Greg Harvey	1-56884-207-4	$19.95 USA/$26.95 Canada
Quattro Pro 6 For Windows For Dummies™	by John Walkenbach	1-56884-174-4	$19.95 USA/$26.95 Canada
Quattro Pro For DOS For Dummies™	by John Walkenbach	1-56884-023-3	$16.95 USA/$21.95 Canada

UTILITIES / VCRs & CAMCORDERS

Title	Author	ISBN	Price
Norton Utilities 8 For Dummies™	by Beth Slick	1-56884-166-3	$19.95 USA/$26.95 Canada
VCRs & Camcorders For Dummies™	by Andy Rathbone & Gordon McComb	1-56884-229-5	$14.99 USA/$20.99 Canada

WORD PROCESSING

Title	Author	ISBN	Price
Ami Pro For Dummies™	by Jim Meade	1-56884-049-7	$19.95 USA/$26.95 Canada
MORE Word For Windows 6 For Dummies™	by Doug Lowe	1-56884-165-5	$19.95 USA/$26.95 Canada
MORE WordPerfect 6 For Windows For Dummies™	by Margaret Levine Young & David C. Kay	1-56884-206-6	$19.95 USA/$26.95 Canada
MORE WordPerfect 6 For DOS For Dummies™	by Wallace Wang, edited by Dan Gookin	1-56884-047-0	$19.95 USA/$26.95 Canada
S.O.S. For WordPerfect™	by Katherine Murray	1-56884-053-5	$12.95 USA/$16.95 Canada
Word 6 For Macs For Dummies™	by Dan Gookin	1-56884-190-6	$19.95 USA/$26.95 Canada
Word For Windows 6 For Dummies™	by Dan Gookin	1-56884-075-6	$16.95 USA/$21.95 Canada
Word For Windows For Dummies™	by Dan Gookin	1-878058-86-X	$16.95 USA/$21.95 Canada
WordPerfect 6 For Dummies™	by Dan Gookin	1-878058-77-0	$16.95 USA/$21.95 Canada
WordPerfect For Dummies™	by Dan Gookin	1-878058-52-5	$16.95 USA/$21.95 Canada
WordPerfect For Windows For Dummies™	by Margaret Levine Young & David C. Kay	1-56884-032-2	$16.95 USA/$21.95 Canada

DUMMIES QUICK REFERENCES

1/26/95

Fun, Fast, & Cheap!

CorelDRAW! 5 For Dummies™ Quick Reference
by Raymond E. Werner

ISBN: 1-56884-952-4
$9.99 USA/$12.99 Canada

Windows "X" For Dummies™ Quick Reference, 3rd Edition
by Greg Harvey

ISBN: 1-56884-964-8
$9.99 USA/$12.99 Canada

Word For Windows 6 For Dummies™ Quick Reference
by George Lynch

ISBN: 1-56884-095-0
$8.95 USA/$12.95 Canada

WordPerfect For DOS For Dummies™ Quick Reference
by Greg Harvey

ISBN: 1-56884-009-8
$8.95 USA/$11.95 Canada

Title	Author	ISBN	Price
DATABASE			
Access 2 For Dummies™ Quick Reference	by Stuart A. Stuple	1-56884-167-1	$8.95 USA/$11.95 Canada
dBASE 5 For DOS For Dummies™ Quick Reference	by Barry Sosinsky	1-56884-954-0	$9.99 USA/$12.99 Canada
dBASE 5 For Windows For Dummies™ Quick Reference	by Stuart J. Stuple	1-56884-953-2	$9.99 USA/$12.99 Canada
Paradox 5 For Windows For Dummies™ Quick Reference	by Scott Palmer	1-56884-960-5	$9.99 USA/$12.99 Canada
DESKTOP PUBLISHING / ILLUSTRATION/GRAPHICS			
Harvard Graphics 3 For Windows For Dummies™ Quick Reference	by Raymond E. Werner	1-56884-962-1	$9.99 USA/$12.99 Canada
FINANCE / PERSONAL FINANCE			
Quicken 4 For Windows For Dummies™ Quick Reference	by Stephen L. Nelson	1-56884-950-8	$9.95 USA/$12.95 Canada
GROUPWARE / INTEGRATED			
Microsoft Office 4 For Windows For Dummies™ Quick Reference	by Doug Lowe	1-56884-958-3	$9.99 USA/$12.99 Canada
Microsoft Works For Windows 3 For Dummies™ Quick Reference	by Michael Partington	1-56884-959-1	$9.99 USA/$12.99 Canada
INTERNET / COMMUNICATIONS / NETWORKING			
The Internet For Dummies™ Quick Reference	by John R. Levine	1-56884-168-X	$8.95 USA/$11.95 Canada
MACINTOSH			
Macintosh System 7.5 For Dummies™ Quick Reference	by Stuart J. Stuple	1-56884-956-7	$9.99 USA/$12.99 Canada
OPERATING SYSTEMS / DOS			
DOS For Dummies® Quick Reference	by Greg Harvey	1-56884-007-1	$8.95 USA/$11.95 Canada
UNIX			
UNIX For Dummies™ Quick Reference	by Margaret Levine Young & John R. Levine	1-56884-094-2	$8.95 USA/$11.95 Canada
WINDOWS			
Windows 3.1 For Dummies™ Quick Reference, 2nd Edition	by Greg Harvey	1-56884-951-6	$8.95 USA/$11.95 Canada
PRESENTATION / AUTOCAD			
AutoCAD For Dummies™ Quick Reference	by Ellen Finkelstein	1-56884-198-1	$9.95 USA/$12.95 Canada
SPREADSHEET			
1-2-3 For Dummies™ Quick Reference	by John Walkenbach	1-56884-027-6	$8.95 USA/$11.95 Canada
1-2-3 For Windows 5 For Dummies™ Quick Reference	by John Walkenbach	1-56884-957-5	$9.95 USA/$12.95 Canada
Excel For Windows For Dummies™ Quick Reference, 2nd Edition	by John Walkenbach	1-56884-096-9	$8.95 USA/$11.95 Canada
Quattro Pro 6 For Windows For Dummies™ Quick Reference	by Stuart A. Stuple	1-56884-172-8	$9.95 USA/$12.95 Canada
WORD PROCESSING			
Word For Windows 6 For Dummies™ Quick Reference	by George Lynch	1-56884-095-0	$8.95 USA/$11.95 Canada
WordPerfect For Windows For Dummies™ Quick Reference	by Greg Harvey	1-56884-039-X	$8.95 USA/$11.95 Canada

Order Center: **(800) 762-2974** *(8 a.m.–6 p.m., EST, weekdays)*

12/20/94

Quantity	ISBN	Title	Price	Total

Shipping & Handling Charges

	Description	First book	Each additional book	Total
Domestic	Normal	$4.50	$1.50	$
	Two Day Air	$8.50	$2.50	$
	Overnight	$18.00	$3.00	$
International	Surface	$8.00	$8.00	$
	Airmail	$16.00	$16.00	$
	DHL Air	$17.00	$17.00	$

*For large quantities call for shipping & handling charges.
**Prices are subject to change without notice.

Ship to:

Name _____

Company _____

Address _____

City/State/Zip _____

Daytime Phone _____

Payment: ☐ Check to IDG Books (US Funds Only)

☐ VISA   ☐ MasterCard   ☐ American Express

Card # _____ Expires _____

Signature _____

Subtotal _____

CA residents add
applicable sales tax _____

IN, MA, and MD
residents add
5% sales tax _____

IL residents add
6.25% sales tax _____

RI residents add
7% sales tax _____

TX residents add
8.25% sales tax _____

Shipping _____

Total _____

Please send this order form to:

IDG Books Worldwide
7260 Shadeland Station, Suite 100
Indianapolis, IN 46256

Allow up to 3 weeks for delivery.
Thank you!

IDG BOOKS WORLDWIDE LICENSE AGREEMENT

Important — read carefully before opening the software packet. This is a legal agreement between you (either an individual or an entity) and IDG Books Worldwide, Inc. (IDG). By opening the accompanying sealed packet containing the software disc, you acknowledge that you have read and accept the following IDG License Agreement. If you do not agree and do not want to be bound by the terms of this Agreement, promptly return the book and the unopened software packet to the place you obtained them for a full refund.

1. License. This License Agreement (Agreement) permits you to use one copy of the enclosed Software program(s) on a single computer. The Software is in "use" on a computer when it is loaded into temporary memory (i.e., RAM) or installed into permanent memory (e.g., hard disk, CD-ROM, or other storage device) of that computer.

2. Copyright. The entire contents of this disc and the compilation of the Software are copyrighted and protected by both United States copyright laws and international treaty provisions. You may only (a) make one copy of the Software for backup or archival purposes, or (b) transfer the Software to a single hard disk, provided that you keep the original for backup or archival purposes. The individual programs on the disc are copyrighted by the authors of each program respectively. Each program has its own use permissions and limitations. To use each program, you must follow the individual requirements and restrictions detailed for each in Appendix F of this Book. Do not use a program if you do not want to follow its Licensing Agreement. None of the material on this disc or listed in this Book may ever be distributed, in original or modified form, for commercial purposes.

3. Other Restrictions. You may not rent or lease the Software. You may transfer the Software and user documentation on a permanent basis provided you retain no copies and the recipient agrees to the terms of this Agreement. You may not reverse engineer, decompile, or disassemble the Software except to the extent that the foregoing restriction is expressly prohibited by applicable law. If the Software is an update or has been updated, any transfer must include the most recent update and all prior versions. Each shareware program has its own use permissions and limitations. These limitations are contained in the individual license agreements that are on the software discs. The restrictions include a requirement that after using the program for a period of time specified in its text, the user must pay a registration fee or discontinue use. By opening the package which contains the software disc, you will be agreeing to abide by the licenses and restrictions for these programs. Do not open the software package unless you agree to be bound by the license agreements.

IDG BOOKS WORLDWIDE REGISTRATION CARD

RETURN THIS REGISTRATION CARD FOR FREE CATALOG

Title of this book: Excel For Windows 95 Bible

My overall rating of this book: ❑ Very good [1] ❑ Good [2] ❑ Satisfactory [3] ❑ Fair [4] ❑ Poor [5]

How I first heard about this book:

❑ Found in bookstore; name: [6] _____

❑ Advertisement: [8]

❑ Word of mouth; heard about book from friend, co-worker, etc.: [10]

❑ Book review: [7]

❑ Catalog: [9]

❑ Other: [11]

What I liked most about this book:

_____

_____

What I would change, add, delete, etc., in future editions of this book:

_____

_____

Other comments:

_____

Number of computer books I purchase in a year: ❑ 1 [12] ❑ 2-5 [13] ❑ 6-10 [14] ❑ More than 10 [15]

I would characterize my computer skills as: ❑ Beginner [16] ❑ Intermediate [17] ❑ Advanced [18] ❑ Professional [19]

I use ❑ DOS [20] ❑ Windows [21] ❑ OS/2 [22] ❑ Unix [23] ❑ Macintosh [24] ❑ Other: [25]_____

(please specify)

I would be interested in new books on the following subjects:
(please check all that apply, and use the spaces provided to identify specific software)

❑ Word processing: [26]

❑ Data bases: [28]

❑ File Utilities: [30]

❑ Networking: [32]

❑ Other: [34]

❑ Spreadsheets: [27]

❑ Desktop publishing: [29]

❑ Money management: [31]

❑ Programming languages: [33]

I use a PC at (please check all that apply): ❑ home [35] ❑ work [36] ❑ school [37] ❑ other: [38] _____

The disks I prefer to use are ❑ 5.25 [39] ❑ 3.5 [40] ❑ other: [41]_____

I have a CD ROM: ❑ yes [42] ❑ no [43]

I plan to buy or upgrade computer hardware this year: ❑ yes [44] ❑ no [45]

I plan to buy or upgrade computer software this year: ❑ yes [46] ❑ no [47]

Name: _____   Business title: [48] _____   Type of Business: [49] _____

Address (❑ home [50] ❑ work [51]/Company name: _____)

Street/Suite# _____

City [52]/State [53]/Zipcode [54]: _____   Country [55] _____

❑ **I liked this book!** You may quote me by name in future
IDG Books Worldwide promotional materials.

My daytime phone number is _____

IDG BOOKS

THE WORLD OF
COMPUTER
KNOWLEDGE

Author's e-mail address
70363.3014@compuserve.com
John Walkenbach

□ **YES!**

Please keep me informed about IDG's World of Computer Knowledge.
Send me the latest IDG Books catalog.